THE HISTORY AND TECHNIQUE

OF THE COUNTER–TENOR

THE HISTORY AND TECHNIQUE

OF

THE COUNTER–TENOR

A STUDY OF

THE MALE HIGH VOICE

FAMILY

Peter Giles

SCOLAR PRESS

Published by
SCOLAR PRESS
Gower House
Croft Road
Aldershot
Hants GU11 3HR
England

Ashgate Publishing Company
Old Post Road
Brookfield
Vermont 05036
USA

British Library Cataloguing–in–Publication Data:

Giles, Peter
  History and Technique of the Counter–Tenor – History
  I. Title
  783.8609

Library of Congress Cataloguing–in–Publication Data:

Giles, Peter.
  The history and technique of the counter–tenor / Peter Giles.
        p.   cm.
  Includes bibliographical references and indexes.
  Contents: v. 1. History – v. 2. Technique.
    1. Countertenors. 2. Vocal music–history and criticism.
  3. Singing–history. 4. Singing methods. I. Title.
  ML1460.G56 1993
  783.8'6–dc20   93–24937 CIP MN

ISBN 0 85967 931 4

Printed in Great Britain by the University Press, Cambridge

Alfred Deller

atque

John Whitworth

a quibus tota res
in Anglia iterum incepta est

Contents

Foreword

James Bowman

I really feel that this book should be sub-titled 'Everything you ever wanted to know about counter-tenors, but were afraid to ask'. Those incessant but perfectly justified questions like 'How did you discover that you were a counter-tenor?' or 'What IS the difference between a male alto and a counter-tenor?' now have their answer, backed up by an impressive amount of historical and musicological information.

Although we counter-tenors are now hopefully an integral part of the musical scene, there was still a great need for a sensible, factual study which didn't read as an apology or as an excuse. The fact that we sing at a higher pitch than the other adult male voices does not instantly make us a peculiar breed – distant relatives of the castrati. There is no 'mystique'. We are just singers who, for one reason or another, have preferred to develop the upper reaches of our voices, and this has become a natural means of vocal expression.

It is only right that this book should be dedicated to the late Alfred Deller. We are all in his debt.

London, March 1981
& Redhill, June 1992

x

List of Illustrations

xii

Preview

The following comments were received from Graham F. Welch, Michael Howard, Charles Cleall, Harry Christophers, Michael Chance, W. John Hough, Alan Ardouin and John Whitworth on reading the manuscript of the complete work:

Peter Giles is not only a writer but a performer, teacher, graphic artist and an experienced exponent of the counter–tenor voice. Above all, he is a singer and has rewarded us with this second treatise on the rise of the counter–tenor voice through many centuries.

In many ways, the counter–tenor/male alto/haute–contre, or whatever we care to name this phenomenon, is having a revival, mainly in the world of opera, thanks (in England and the U.S.A.) to Benjamin Britten's *Midsummer Night's Dream* and *Death in Venice*. Only last year, Sir Harrison Birtwistle's *Gawain* (commissioned by the Royal Opera House) produced a fascinating rôle for Kevin Smith as Bishop Baldwin, and Philip Glass and Leonard Bernstein have explored the hidden magic of the counter–tenor voice.

There is now a need for knowledge and understanding about what this name – counter–tenor or male alto or haute–contre, and so on – is, how it works, where it comes from, and how it was used. Peter Giles's comprehensive research succeeds magnificently in finding answers to all these questions.

This work provides the interested reader with a rare opportunity to engage in one of the abiding controversies of the musical world. It traces the development of the male falsetto voice across the millenium, and demonstrates its problematic nature. The evidence that Peter Giles has gathered gives a fascinating insight into the dissent over nomenclature and even over the physiological basis of singing that persists to the present day, particularly with regard to its subject.

It is a book not merely for singers and instrumentalists who happen to be musicians, nor just for musicologists, nor for those who promote performances in concert halls, opera houses, or theatres, but also for artists, architects, writers, clerics, politicians and for many others.

It is a book which will reward every thoughtful reader with a sense of responsibility by giving him a survey of artistic evolution, a work of compelling, comprehensive and documentary value which will give pause to everyone with courage enough to consider what is happening to Western civilization as we approach the second millenium.

Justly hailed by W. John Hough as 'remarkably erudite' and a 'magnum opus', it perpetually refreshes the reader by delving into byways so rare and delightful as to keep one's nose in the book long after one may have intended to put the work down. Its contents are infinitely thoughtful, and so continually verified by references that we soon accept it as a text of exceptional academic worth.

Students of social history will find much that is thought−provoking and challenging. The reader is not expected always to agree with the author's thesis, but to be stimulated. For example, the author's views on popular music and trends in current musical education (such as the increase in mixed choirs) should provide a rich source for debate.

Peter Giles's narrative draws on a wide range of sources, and other inferential evidence. His conclusions are thoughtful and pointed. A particular strength of the book lies in its extensive bibliography, and the many related extracts woven into the text.

Perhaps its major significance lies in the assembly and organization of historical data, reflecting many hours of careful research. As with all stimulating texts, reconstruction of the past provides some answers, and simultaneously raises important questions.

This book informs the debate concerning the authenticity of the counter−tenor voice in the performance of much old music, and makes a worthwhile contribution to our knowledge and understanding.

Until recently, singers had little knowledge of how they sang. They knew when it felt right, and their audiences knew when it sounded wrong; but when it feels or sounds wrong it is helpful if technique can be analysed and faults corrected. The basic physiology of voice production should be understood by all singers, whether they perform or teach.

Peter Giles enthusiastically ensured that first he understood the science of voice production and then translated that science into an art−form, so that singers can relate to it. Though physics and medicine impinge strongly upon singing, these esoteric matters must be far from the singer's mind during performance. Paradoxically, this book and Mr Giles's associated *Method*[1] will help them to do so.

The author has unearthed information about important singers long forgotten, whose recordings make them worth remembering, hearing and studying; the whole gamut of his study helps to fill an enormous gap in the lore of singers and singing.

It may be recommended not only to singers of the standard repertoire but also to the aspiring pop−singer.

Are we on the verge of a revival of singing for pleasure? It needs but a few dedicated young musicians to explore the possibilities of the voice to rekindle public interest and enthusiasm for this innate but subtle and evocative human activity.

[1] *A Basic Counter−Tenor Method*, Thames Publishing, 1988

Acknowledgements

First, I thank my wife Elizabeth, for the truly countless hours she has spent assisting me to put this work together, and for perceptive editorial assistance throughout.

I am also extremely grateful for the invaluable help of friends and colleagues: Charles Cleall, for his unique help and for editing and assembling the preview and providing the glossary; Alan Ardouin, F.R.C.S., D.L.O., for his overseeing of the strictly physiological section and for helpful prefatorial comments, and Frederic Hodgson for his unfailing support and assistance.

I am indebted to, and thank, James Bowman for his Foreword; also John Whitworth, Harry Christophers, Graham F. Welch, Michael Chance and Michael Howard for their warm contributions towards pages xv–xvi.

For invaluable help, advice, and/or special contributions, large or small (some including their published material), I am also indebted to W. John Hough, Elsa Scammell, Frances Killingley, the late Colin Scull, Patrick Johns, Séan Osborne, the late Frank Ll. Harrison, Rebecca Stewart, Susan Butt, John Jeffreys, Joan Rimmer, Ian Harwood, Graham F. Welch, Brian Crosby, Wil and Dymmy Barten, Simon R. Hill, David Baldwin, Roderick Williams, John Purchese, Antony Hopkins, Niven Miller, Grayston Burgess, Mark Lawson, Lawrence Watts, Donald Burrows, Dorothy Owen, Anthony Burton, David Mallinder, Jon Williams, Christopher Norton–Welsh, Raimund Gilvan, Christopher Page, Richard Turbet, Ann Savours, Richard Hill, Raymond Leang, Robert White, Ian Thompson, Bruce Wood, Marjorie M. Gleed, Maxine Handy and 'Mr Bennett' (to whom apologies: I mislaid his letter, and therefore his initials).

I acknowledge and thank the following for their kindness in giving permission to reproduce illustrations or photographs: Her Majesty the Queen, the Dean and Chapter of Canterbury Cathedral, Peggy Deller, James Bowman, John Whitworth, Paul Esswood, Russell Oberlin, Owen Wynne, Susan Butt, Grayston Burgess, Jochem Kowalski, Catherine Ashmore, Michael Chance, Lois Lang–Sims, Christine Breeds, John Wheeler, Raymond Leang, The Guildhall Library, The Kent Messenger Group, The Warden and Fellows of All Souls' College Oxford and Bowers & Brittain.

Similarly, I acknowledge and thank those who generously allowed substantial quotations from music or other copyright material:

A.P. Watt:	*A History of British Music*, Percy M. Young
BBC Enterprises Ltd:	*Oh Yes It Is!*, Gerald Frow
Chappell Music Ltd:	*On the Art of Singing*, Sims Reeves
David Higham Associates:	*Music in Medieval Britain*, Frank Ll. Harrison
Dent Ltd:	*Tudor Music*, David Wulstan
Dobson Books Ltd:	*Bel Canto*, Elster Kay

xviii

Duckworth Ltd:	*The Grand Tradition*, J. B. Steane
Gardiner, Julian:	*A Guide to Good Singing and Speech*
Grindle, W. H:	*Irish Cathedral Music*
Mollie Hardwick:	*Alfred Deller: A Singularity of Voice*
HarperCollins Ltd:	*Collins Encyclopaedia of Music*
Joseph Patelson Music House:	*The Free Voice*, Cornelius L. Reid
Lewer, David:	*A Spiritual Song* (Templars Union)
Methuen London (incorporating Eyre & Spottiswoode):	*English Cathedral Music*, E. H. Fellowes
Novello & Co Ltd:	Extracts from sheet music
Opera Magazine Ltd:	'Wexford Festival Review', Rodney Milnes
Orpheus Publications:	Extracts from *The Musical Times*
Oxford University Press:	*English Madrigal Composers*, E. H. Fellowes and various musical excerpts from *Medieval Music*, by Marroco and Sandon
	The Church Anthem Book and sheet music extracts
Penguin Books Ltd:	*The Raw Materials of Music*, Brian Trowell
	The Pelican History of Music
Peters Editions Ltd:	Schubert's *Nachthelle*
	A King's Musician for the Lute and Voice: John Abell, George Farmer
Robert Hale Ltd:	*The Voice of the Mind*, E. Herbert–Caesari
Stainer & Bell Ltd:	*Observations on the Florid Song*, Francesco Tosi (Galliard)
	A Manual of Voice Training, E. Davidson Palmer
Stainer & Bell with Musica Britannica Trust:	Extracts from *Musica Britannica*
Tatnell, Roland:	Quotations from 'Falsetto Practice: A Brief Survey', (*The Consort*, 1965)
The Macdonald Group:	*The Organ*, W. L. Sumner
The Royal School of Church Music:	*English Church Music, 1965*
Wulstan, David:	Extracts from *Vocal Colour in English Sixteenth–century Polyphony*

Apologies are due to the following, whom I have failed to trace: the Executors of the late A. K. Holland; Anthony Frisell and Messrs Bruce Humphries of Boston, USA (several letters to whom were returned marked unknown).

Acknowledgements are due to: The National Portrait Gallery, The National Gallery, The Victoria and Albert Museum, W.W. Norton & Co. Inc. and Faber & Faber, Ltd, for the use of illustrations and/or musical examples.

It is inevitable that some names may accidentally have slipped through the mesh. To any who have helped in this huge but intricate task, but may have been omitted, inadvertently (though no less hurtfully) from this list, I offer my apologies and thanks. Any such omissions or inaccuracies of acknowledgement will be put right in any later edition.

Introduction

It is reasonable to suggest that anyone who might write about an historic voice, its characteristics and its background might be one or more of these:

A musical historian
A musicologist
A distinguished or well–known solo singer
A celebrated teacher of the voice
An experienced teacher of the voice
An experienced working singer
A writer on the artistic process and aesthetics

The present author is, perhaps, a combination of the last three. This work covers a broader width than that with which most musicologists would attempt to deal. This volume forms an artist's book, and is likely to demonstrate associated characteristics. 'The artist can often reach where reason fails or falters'. I hope that the reader will sympathise with this perception. Certainly, the complete work can and should be seen as both an individual journey and a basis for reflection.

The subject with which we are concerned is complex. Despite this, it is not very extensively covered. There have been a number of useful and searching if relatively brief articles (mostly academic) or letters to journals. It has been discussed to only a small extent in wider–ranging works on early music and monographs of modest size which deal with certain aspects of the subject. There have been a number of broadcast talks. Yet, other than my own books, *The Counter–Tenor*, 1982, and *A Basic Counter–Tenor Method*, 1988, there has been no attempt at a fully comprehensive work. *The Counter–Tenor* should be seen, now, as no more than the sketch made before the full–scale mural.

Another source of information are singers' biographies. *A Singularity of Voice*, Alfred Deller's biography, Frederic Hodgson's autobiography *Choirs and Cloisters* and H. Munro Davison's *Random Recollections* are all recommended. William Windsor's unpublished *Journal* is also of great interest (see page 113). There may well be more unpublished personal accounts and the author would welcome any information about these.

My own introduction to the virtuoso counter–tenor voice occurred as follows:[2]

> I encountered a record of Alfred Deller when I was in early adolescence. I still remember the impact. As time passed, I knew that I myself must sing counter–tenor one day, if my voice continued the way it seemed to be heading. Indeed, my vocal change occurred ambiguously. I was singing in a full range 'treble', progressively more powerful, until, aged sixteen and a half, I moved into the back stalls to sing alto. The very top notes faded quickly. I acquired a new, stronger, lower range. Eagerly, I began to consult every possible encyclopedia of music, ancient and modern, to see how each defined alto and counter–tenor. I searched works on voice–production by the cognoscenti of past and present.
>
> In the mid 1950s, as a young enthusiast in middle teenage years, I could find very few articles of length on the counter–tenor/alto question. The most useful seemed to be the famous paper by W. John Hough, 'The Historical Significance of the Counter–Tenor' (nineteen and a half pages), given to the Royal Musical Association in 1937. It was a good springboard for the student.
>
> Hardly any writers suggested that the solo counter–tenor still existed, despite the living proof of Alfred Deller and, slightly later, John Whitworth. I could not understand why so few writers on matters vocal seemed to notice them. These writers perpetuated a viewpoint which could be summed up as follows: 'Falsetto singing, that peculiarly English cathedral choir aberration, is weak, unnatural and unmanly. No singer worth the name indulges in it. Before the 18th century, much music was written for a legendary male alto called counter–tenor. That voice is now extinct. Cathedral altos are at best a feeble, hooty bunch, useless for solo work'.
>
> I began to wonder, if so few appreciated the counter–tenor, or even admitted his modern existence, how likely he was to take his rightful place permanently.

It might appear that worries have proved groundless. All seems well, but is it? We shall see.

There can be few, if any, aspects of our theme that are not mentioned in the present work. Many complex questions are raised and aired, and most are given an answer. The following 'collage' of viewpoints attempts to introduce the complexity of the subject.

To begin with, there are those who associate counter–tenor or alto historically only with England. Others argue that it was a European voice–range. Others still say that it, or its use, was known anciently world–wide, though without any formal name. There is even a claim that the counter–tenor began only in the years following the Restoration in England in 1660.

Some argue that contratenor or counter–tenor was merely a part, a musical device in the harmony: that originally it was never a human voice–type as such. 'Counter–tenor', they explain, was an anglicised version of 'contratenor' and acquired a meaning as a human voice

---

[2] Peter Giles, *The Counter–Tenor* (Muller, 1982), pp. xi–xii

only by a widening of English terminology. Yet others argue that the <u>term</u> counter–tenor, not the voice, originated in Europe and came later to England only in the fifteenth century.

In the present century, it is often claimed that the 'counter–tenor' voice is audibly different from that of the 'alto'; the difference being discerned easily. Some would find the word 'alto' problematical without the prefix 'male'. Others are totally against the prefix, arguing that 'male' is self–evident, historically and philologically. Furthermore, it is claimed that counter–tenor and alto are one and the same: merely different abbreviations of the original term 'contratenor altus' and therefore interchangeable. Modestly–gifted altos often see the counter–tenor as an alto with a greater range and ring and tenors of moderate ability often see him similarly as a sort of super–tenor.

There are those who maintain that great range was indeed expected of the counter–tenor, judging from manuscripts which include the title 'counter–tenor' or 'alto', but they often add that terminology is unimportant and often unclear. Some people argue that there must have been at least two types of counter–tenor: one high (falsetto), one lower (tenor voice). Others say that 'high' and 'low' denote specialisms, and that the working range of counter–tenor or alto was always restricted to about a twelfth. Another opinion is that a counter–tenor could or should have been able to sing whatever the work in question demanded.

Equally strong and differing views are held on <u>timbre</u>. Some say that, despite the tenor–sounding name, the tonal quality of the counter–tenor sounds, and should sound, androgynous: a mixture of male tenor and female contralto. Others point out that, because 'tenor' itself means merely <u>tenere</u> (to hold), to ascribe a tonal quality to it is inaccurate and misleading. The same argument can be applied to the word 'alto', which means 'high'.

Others argue that the counter–tenor, an extremely rare voice, should sound like a tenor but higher and smaller–toned. Another argument is that the counter–tenor is a normal, modern tenor, lyric or otherwise, who can sing very high without strain and with normal tenor quality and volume throughout his whole vocal range.

Another argument involves the 'break' between basic voice and head voice. If there is none, it is said, the singer is a genuine counter–tenor. If a break exists, he is not one, but merely a 'falsetto–alto'. Another reasoning is that if a 'tenor' moves into falsetto – pure head–voice – he is not a genuine counter–tenor. The awkward fact that most tenors do have to negotiate register changes in normal practice is not usually mentioned in this context.

There is more argument over what is head–voice and what is not. There is disagreement over what constitutes falsetto and what does not. There are differences of opinion about the ancient term falsettist. One school of thought claims that the falsettist is any singer who uses falsetto in the higher part of his voice. Others claim that a falsettist is one who stays <u>exclusively</u> in falsetto.

Yet again, there is what could be called the religious/secular division, particularly in England, though there are some parallels in a few other European countries where, it is often claimed, falsettists only ever sang in churches. It is based on the concept that alto and counter–tenor were always different voices. One claim is that alto has always been a cathedral or church voice, but that the counter–tenor was secular, with a more powerful sound quality suited to the stage, and that over the centuries there have been only rare instances in which some singers have sung in both places. Vocal titles in this religious/secular argument have even been reversed. A middle view is that counter–tenors, of both titles, were employed in most vocal areas, like other singers.

There is further disagreement about nomenclature: counter–tenor, alto, contraltino, contralto–tenor, tenorino, tenor–altino, haute–contre. The viewpoint exists that the French haute–contre voice is the same instrument as the English counter–tenor (which in itself could mean two different things). Another view insists that the haute–contre was a high, light tenor, while the English counter–tenor was exclusively a falsettist (with no qualification of this term). The Italian contraltino, some argue, might have been the equivalent of haute–contre and that type of English counter–tenor who uses both chest voice and developed falsetto. Seemingly endless shades of opinion include the contention that a contraltino was or might have been the same as a tenorino, or tenor–altino.

Even referring to counter–tenor is disagreed upon, and these terms are still used: Counter Tenor, Counter-Tenor, counter tenor, Counter tenor, Countertenor or countertenor. Similar arguments concern *contra–tenor* and *haute–contre*.

We come now to inevitable disagreement over the effects of historical pitch on vocal types and their employment. At one end of the spectrum, there is even a view that the more we learn about early pitches, the less likely it is that the counter–tenor (falsettist, or part–falsettist, as seen and heard today) was used at all! At the other end, people argue that early pitches made no important difference to the properly trained counter–tenor voice. Pointing to the many pitch variations before the advent of what we now call standard pitch (where A4 = 440Hz), they argue that hypotheses and controversies about pitch are probably doomed to remain so, in perpetuity.

Though few people now muddle castrato with counter–tenor, one more informed opinion maintains that confusion is indeed possible because some falsettists could sing as high as some castrati. Certainly, in the eighteenth century, some operatic or oratorio rôles were sung by both types of voice on different occasions, just as women deputized for both and were substituted, in their turn, by counter–tenors and castrati. There was, and is, even (an apparently groundless) suspicion that certain English high counter–tenors were secretly castrati.

Modern preoccupation with feminism has led to stirrings of a further potential complication. Attention has been drawn to occasional loose terminology in original eighteenth– and early nineteenth–century programmes in order to provide a reason to call women singers counter–tenors when today they again substitute for them in the concert repertoire.

There can be few subjects, then, which might be argued over so diversely. This volume attempts to address these complexities and much more; therefore I make no apology for the anthological nature of certain sections of this work.

It is impossible, and probably fatal in this science–obsessed age, to discuss the voice without using scientific or physiological support, yet I align myself with pre–Garcia and pre–medical pedagogic methods.

John Hough's invaluable paper, 'The Historical Significance of the Counter-Tenor' (1937) was brief, but influential. His citations and other sources, notably those for René Jacobs's excellent nineteen–page article, 'The Controversy Concerning the Timbre of the Countertenor' (1983), which appeared in English a year after *The Counter–Tenor*, have proved invaluable in stimulating me to further investigation and deliberation. Other articles are acknowledged in the text.

Before *c*1890 and the beginning of sound recording, we have only written accounts of voices and personalities of the past. Such description, though valuable, is subjective. Fortunately there are other sources of information. Writing, painting, sculpture, musical instruments, architecture, artefacts, design and dress variously contain the quintessence of each historical period. Things seen, touched and experienced, are tangible, less open to ambiguity;

though it must be admitted that everyone reacts differently to almost everything. Nevertheless, intuitive perception helped by experience of these cultural adjuncts can yield valuable insights. In turn, something of the ambience of the crucible from which the counter-tenor came can be experienced. Some further discussion of this matter follows, but an awareness of it runs like an undercurrent throughout the work. In fact, though the approach employed is conventional to begin with (that is, historical and evolutionary in style), it widens to become more lateral in approach. To some, this may smack of idiosyncracy. Others may see it differently. I am aware, of course, that idiosyncracy is not 'politically or academically correct' in a work of this type.

Though there are obvious notable disadvantages, one of the gains in working outside the established, academic milieu is that a writer does not move exclusively along the acceptable, well-trodden path or is directed to consult only 'correct' or approved works of reference, in the 'right' library. He does not always imbibe, however unconsciously, only the currently fashionable cup, or even parade the accepted 'alternative view' of the moment. Instead, even the questions might be different – perhaps more diverse.

Indeed, the difference between the two approaches should be seen as an example of the contrast between 'convergence' and 'divergence'. Liam Hudson wrote perceptively on these in the 1960s.[3]

I hope that these volumes will prove helpful to fellow counter-tenors, music students, the musically interested public and music directors and even as a stimulant or source of ideas to the musicologist. Many people are wearied by the eternal question: 'What is the difference, if any, between alto and counter-tenor?' Amid endless argument, one has often been tempted to cry, 'Let altos be called altos and tenors remain tenors. Forget you ever heard the term counter-tenor'! Yet to do this is no real answer.

I therefore present the fruits of one counter-tenor's long investigation and experience in solo, ensemble, lecturing, recording and broadcast work in Britain, United States, Canada and continental Europe: the many years as boy and man in church and cathedral music.

Two even more personal notes are necessary before this preamble is complete. The first is an apology to a noted early twentieth-century counter-tenor. I intended only a passing reference to him in 1982 – wrongly, because now I know of his importance – and compounded the 'first error' with a second mistake which arose because the elderly singer who first acquainted me with Clarke's full name dropped a crucial aspirate in the process. Only after publication of *The Counter-Tenor* did I find to my chagrin that 'Atherley Clarke' should have been 'Hatherley Clarke'! I hope that this time I have done him full justice.

The second is not an apology but a recognition of a seemingly supernatural presence. Here in Canterbury, where the counter-tenor's modern renaissance started, I am always aware of the illustrious Alfred Deller looking over my shoulder as I sing and as I write. Indeed, it feels particularly fitting that, on my resignation from the choir of Canterbury Cathedral after twenty-seven years, Deller's grandson, Jeremy, should have been appointed in my place.

---

[3] Liam Hudson, *Contrary Imaginations* (Methuen, 1966)

xxiv

'Mr Pate'

In my study there is a chunky brown, custom–made wooden box, with brass handle and hinges. It contains a minutely dissected human skull: an excellent specimen, showing the cranial cavities in highly revealing and significant detail. It is kept assembled by clips and springs.

This skull was used by Ernest George White to help formulate his theories on Sinus Tone Production in the early years of this century. A notable *disjecta membra*, it occupies a significant place, not only in The Ernest George White Society, but also in the history of vocal teaching.

The identity and exact date of the (probably) male skull are unknown, but it is now wrapped in an Oxford University rowing scarf: blue with the University crest.

Unless he were a pathologist, the convergent–thinking scientist would normally consider the skull's identity unimportant. Its primary function, both originally for White and for others since, is to present the 'shell' of the human head to help to demonstrate certain theories, and to be used, when appropriate, as a teaching aid. However, the more imaginative mind cannot leave it there. The labyrinthine skull is the mysterious temple from which, in life, comes the voice. Contemplating this wonder leads one to divergent or lateral thinking: a mind–process of a different order to that of all but the greatest scientists.

While it amused White, with complete objectivity, to call the skull 'Charlie', I have imagined a very different *persona* for him: 'Mr Pate.' The punning name is nicely apt, for John Pate, a noted counter–tenor in Purcell's day, sang the part of Mopsa in the well–known duet from the opera *The Fairy Queen*, and because the present work is concerned primarily with what is termed the male 'head–voice'.

In truth, this volume discusses much more, but its most important aspect relates not only to the real Mr Pate, but also to the 'Mr Pate' who is a corporeal representative of the counter–tenor, his method of voice production and his place in musical history.

Peter Giles

Bridge, near Canterbury, November 1993

The pitch–system used throughout this work is as follows:

B^2 C^3 D^3 E^3 F^3 G^3 A^3 B^3 C^4 D^4 E^4 F^4 G^4 A^4 B^4 C^5 D^5 E^5 F^5 G^5

Part One

HISTORY

The past is a foreign country:
they do things differently there

wrote L.P. Hartley at the start of
his novel *The Go–Between*

but do they, always?

Hartley's often–quoted phrase is in
danger of becoming an undeserved cliché,
but his lines seem particularly apt
at the opening of a work such as this.

1 The Status Quo

Soprano, Contralto, Tenor and Bass form the 'cast' of Mendelssohn's *Elijah* and are the 'oratorio big four'. Nineteenth-century operatic convention is responsible for a 'received' scheme also of four voices that has been 'traditional' for about a century and three-quarters:

Heroine: Soprano
Heroine's friend, queen, or mother-earth figure: Contralto
Hero, or light relief: Tenor
Villain, trusty old friend, or father: Bass

Earlier opera, oratorio, Passion and cantata 'cast/soloist lists' looked very different; as the counter-tenor voice has its roots in pre-Mendelssohn music, it is all too often left out of popular reckoning as a 'normal' vocal type: it fits neither of the received 'standard' oratorio or opera categories. To dismiss the voice as suitable only for the cathedral choir or for 'early music' is a failure to accord it historical and musical justice.

Eighteenth-century castrati, and their unrivalled voices and incredible technique, earned them idolatory and followings like those of present-day pop stars. High voices have always fascinated people. A music critic wrote in 1960:[1]

> The long-held top notes of an Italian soprano are sometimes hardly distinguishable from a scream, and are therefore at once repellent and delightful. Heroic parts are always given to tenors only. Verdi admitted baritones to respectability. The angelic choirboy is admired for his high notes. Folk-singers regularly pitch their songs as high as their voices can manage. The eighteenth century liked the loud, strong, and high sounds of the castrato .... So does taste dictate to nature. Perhaps it is this very versatility of the larynx that assures its permanent pre-eminence among instruments of music.

While examining the male high voice, this book confines itself mostly to European culture. Nevertheless, there must be a sideways glance at other rich traditions – Negro, Aboriginal and Asian – which relate to our subject. Certainly, western Caucasians are not the only males to make use of what we call 'falsetto' or 'head-voice'.

We should consider briefly the instinctive use by early man of voice in its two main modes: 'fundamental' and 'falsetto'. An anthropologist might explain matters differently, but

---

[1] 'The Voice and its Vagaries' in *The Times*, 24 June 1960

the following is an attempt to form an account of the possible origins of human phonation.

Animals possess, to varying degree, elements which can be recognised as crude parallels to human vocal equipment. Chimpanzees can be heard using both fundamental and falsetto modes and mention is made in Part Two of the gibbon. Initial utterances of primitive man must have been in grunted or shouted raw basic voice, but it could not have been long before more sophisticated vocal development began, encouraged by various factors.

Other than outwardly audible phenomena, the primitive human being could hardly fail to be aware of its closest source of sound. The body itself possesses the ability, unfortunate propensity, or need, to produce sound–effects other than vocal. Examples include whistling, tapping the teeth or side of the cheek while varying the shape of the mouth; others are the result of action, over–action or even malfunction of the digestive system: the rumble of the stomach, the belch or flatus. In addition, there is what we know colloquially as the 'raspberry': air expelled forcefully through closed lips, or against the hand. (There are even some rudimentary effects of basic and falsetto modes obtainable by varying the position and action of the lips against the hand.) Air can be squeaked out through the palms of the hands, or by placing the hand under the armpit and using a pumping action by the arm interesting resonances can be produced, with effects much beloved of still–primitive schoolboys. All have potential pitch variation; in some cases, exploitable purposely (if desired) with practice, especially by those blessed with a rare gift, like 'Le Petomane': Joseph Pujol (1857–1945). Potentially, the body is a veritable orchestra. Nothing is unnatural, though some phenomena, like those demonstrated by Pujol, are extremely rare.

Shouted attempts at communication and expression are likely to have occasioned demands for increasing levels of vocal sophistication and to have created awareness of their specific functions. Physical effort of some kind – lifting, for example – might well have produced a sudden falsetto note, as might a scream of fear, or vocal experiments in an echoing cave or gorge.

The first attempts at any activity other than hunting, fighting, eating, mating and sleeping were probably linked early on with specific vocal expressions of, or reactions to, further demands for these basic needs. Imitation of things seen, heard or experienced appear to have played a major part in the origins of creativity; to this testify the amazing Lascaux cave paintings. Animal calls and sounds, heard initially during hunting, must have been among the first subjects for vocal imitation or parody. (This interest was to re–surface much later in sixteenth– and seventeenth–century madrigals and similar vocal forms which imitated animal sounds.) Many types of animal seem to move easily and frequently into falsetto mode.

Very soon, the limitations of the basic human male voice would have been reached; crude, enjoyable power changed to strain. Delight and exhilaration at escaping the discomfort of forced, highly–pitched notes, may have originated in attempts to mimic women's or children's voices, to imitate animals with high calls, or even in a reaction to birds and insects soaring enjoyably into their unlimited, unphysical world. Man's longing to fly is as old as man. The earthbound yearns to rise, weightless.

A combination of all these could have encouraged that first falsetto cry.

Whatever the case, in addition to chance, imitation, and vocal experiment, it seems that in the millennia following the emergence of 'voice', especially falsetto mode, mankind discovered a powerful inherent and instinctive sense of magic and the supernatural. So were created the spiritual or religious senses: those essentially extra–ordinary, not merely 'out–of–body' but supra–body and supra–normal experiences inherent in the human condition.

Certainly, falsetto, with its eerie, asexual, ambiguous and disembodied quality, is part of mankind's mystic, primaeval psyche. It evokes enchantment and has long been associated with religious ceremony and other rituals. Both culturally sophisticated and primitive peoples across the world still use falsetto variously for these purposes.

The yodel might be thought of as a folk–instrument, one developed from the need to communicate in mountainous terrain, and it is not unique to the Swiss. We all share the urge to produce echoes in promising places – take a small child into a huge cathedral, and await results! Thus the descendants of primitive man still explore the acoustic potential of a resonant cave....

Falsetto was certainly developed to a highly sophisticated degree in the East. Traditional Chinese music–drama employed it. In the Chinese philosophy, *yang* represents the light, bright and masculine, and *yin* represents the dark, mysterious, and feminine. In these ideas we may discern a perceptive reference – not necessarily an unintentional one – to vocal tonal quality (though this is not to suggest that a bright–toned soprano voice is somehow a 'masculine' one!) – because *yang* and *yin* seems to suggest contrasting timbres in male and female voices of comparable, perhaps alto, pitch.

As we will see, there is considerable evidence to suggest that falsettists' art formed many of the main tonal colourings of early Medieval music in Europe. It is likely that the travels of Crusaders, and near–Eastern influence upon them, were partly responsible. Similar influences are discernible in Medieval European art. Falsetto singing was practised and admired in the near East by the eighth century at the latest; by very early Medieval times European singers seem to have adopted much the same nasal or semi–nasal falsetto and vocal style.

Some Arabic music employs falsetto. T. E. Lawrence referred to it in *The Seven Pillars of Wisdom*:[2]

> Each evening round the fires, they had music; not the monotonous open–throated roaring of the tribes, nor the exciting harmony of the Ageyl, but the falsetto quarter–tones and trills of urban Syria.

Koranic recitation, with its tonal subtleties and significant degrees of nasality, demonstrates well something of the influential qualities encountered by the Crusaders. Some of its characteristics are likely to have been in place in Western voice production already.

The Moorish invasion of Spain in the eighth century resulted in the art of falsetto voice production's passing into Spanish culture. When the Moslems crossed the Pyrenées in 720, they encountered the Frankish kingdom ruled by Charles Martel, grandfather of Charlemagne. Martel's defeat of the Moslim at Poitiers in 732 is unlikely to have eradicated all Eastern cultural influence in what is now Western France and which was later to become strongly linked with England.

The effects of the Moorish invasion, including the advent of 'Spanish falsetto', were not confined to the Iberian Peninsula. Travelling singers, the troubadours of southern France, the trouvères of northern France, the aristocratic German minnesingers or poet–singers, the golliards who roamed France, Germany and Britain, and the jongleurs (or gleemen), all seem to have had their origins in, or to have been connected with, the Moorish invasion of Europe.

Troubadours sang of the idealization of womanhood. There were strong religious overtones

---

[2] T. E. Lawrence, *The Seven Pillars of Wisdom* (Cape, 1926, repr. 1935), p. 232

in their songs, which were linked with the rise of the cult of the Blessed Virgin Mary. It is easy to connect this with the use of falsetto by these male singers. It is thought that a few women singers, called 'trebairitz' and perhaps disguised as men, may have been among the troubadours and trouvères. If so, their presence may have encouraged rather than discouraged male singers to use falsetto. Two contrasted 'voices' employed by one singer would be an advantage for characterization or other musical effect.

As the wandering singers moved freely round France and Italy, falsetto art was taken through Europe, with obvious results. It was in France that the vocal style of troubadours seems to have entered the formal world of the church; probably as early as the eleventh century.

It might be suggested that, other than as a manifestation of one aspect of vocal instinct, modern 'pop' use of falsettists on the Afro-American pattern is merely another example of outside creative influence on European music and thus a healthy cross-fertilization. It could be argued that Moorish falsetto techniques were exactly this, especially in the tenth and eleventh centuries and later. Yet, when it is not a genuine inheritance from jazz and blues (which were originally both black art forms and a cultural catharsis: a freeing from perceived restriction), the adoption of falsetto by the 'pop' industry often seems contrived and, like the industry itself, crudely commercial in aim. Of course, before the coming of the Moors to Spain in early Medieval times, there was no rich commonwealth of music in Europe. No sumptuous, thousand-year tradition existed in which had been created probably the greatest musical works of art ever likely to be conceived by man. There is, however, genuine cross-cultural influence today; there are valuable studies of this and various absorbing aspects of ethnomusicology.

It should be seen, then, that the vocal mode usually termed 'head-voice' or 'falsetto' is instinctive and ancient in origin.

The sophistication of the nineteenth-century oratorio 'big four' and the 'operatic status quo' seems to be worlds away from the vocal instincts of primaeval man and the gradual development of the art of falsetto singing. 'Big four' and 'status quo' represent not the summit nor even a plateau on the way to a zenith of vocal art, but merely an aspect of a range of musical hills and mountains.

It is ironic that Mendelssohn finished *Elijah* in 1847, while Darwin was writing *The Origin of Species* (which was published, after some trepidation and delay, in 1853), the first attempt to explain scientifically the anthropological basis of the human race. For *Elijah* became part of a culture which sought to stifle or disguise the earthy and basic side of the human condition. Mendelssohn's oratorio came to epitomise the culture which strongly influenced the rest of the century and beyond; the age of *Elijah* was one of unyielding order and straight-laced establishment, challenged (as by Darwin) only at great risk. Even its subject matter, the rebellion but eventual return of the people of God to Him and His true way, seems particularly fitting to Victorian 'morality' which sought to sweep from view the public scandals and improprieties typical of the eighteenth century. There was tremendous confidence in the way forward; the tenor soloist seems to voice nineteenth-century hopes and ideals when he sings in the sumptuous key of A flat major: 'Then shall the righteous shine forth as the sun in their heav'nly Father's realm'. At the height of its long popularity, Mendelssohn's oratorio rivalled the pre-eminent place which Handel's *Messiah* held, and still holds, in England; but *Elijah* coloured and to some extent still distorts the popular perception of all that preceded it.

Our vocal perception of older music is still affected not only by the 'big four' idea, but also by nineteenth-century enthusiasm for grand gestures. Large choral societies with two or three hundred singers still roar out *Messiah* in the 'Victorian' manner. Such performances might still be mounted for fun or for special occasions or perhaps purposely to recreate nine-teenth-century performances, and these can be thrilling – yet Handel intended the work for a small band with a male chorus of perhaps thirty-five singers.

Imagine a Christmas performance in the local town hall given by a local choral society joined by the town's operatic society and amateur orchestra. Even in the 1990s, organizers rarely seem to consider engaging a solo counter-tenor as well as a contralto. Both voices sang in the first performances of *Messiah*, and until the middle of the nineteenth century performances employed either. How often do we hear Handel's numerous alternative versions of various arias?[3]

Another nineteenth-century legacy has been that many Baroque and Classical works are still regularly performed a semitone or more too high because modern instruments which 'evolved' during that century are therefore not designed to be played at the likely original pitches of earlier music. Until recently, many works have thus been left just outside comfortable range of many, though certainly not all, counter-tenors. Thankfully, particularly in London, but increasingly in the provinces, the 'early music' movement is now encouraging ensembles and orchestras to refurnish themselves with 'period' instruments. Early music has now become a mainstream alternative, helped greatly by excellent and perceptive recordings.[4]

Writing in the early 1950s, Thurston Dart opined:[5]

> ...Bach's *Mass in B Minor* ought properly to be performed in B flat minor or even A minor; the opening movement of *Messiah* should be in D sharp minor; Beethoven's *Ninth Symphony* should be in D flat minor or even in C (which would make the solo and chorus parts much less of a strain to sing). Obviously, transpositions of this kind will sometimes be quite impossible to carry out, since they make certain passages quite unplayable on instruments using today's standard tuning.

Dart seems to have been thinking in late nineteenth-century or early twentieth-century terms, in which semitonal instrumental transposition was the only means available to approach an earlier pitch. At least in print, he allowed himself the confusion of pitch and key. Some of his estimates of the difference between early and modern pitches are now thought slightly excessive by some authorities. Opinion in these matters shifts continually and fashionably, but is still too much conditioned by the practicalities or otherwise of semitonal keyboard transposition.

Despite the apparently growing number of counter-tenors, the widening awareness of this voice and now the serious interest in the voice abroad, it is possible in the United Kingdom to sense a feeling of 'thus far and no further'. Except in opera and cathedral music, is there almost a counter-tenor recession? Contraltos (called 'altos') and high tenors using modern vocal techniques, though with little or no vibrato, have begun to reappear in specialist early music in place of counter-tenors. Though musicological experiment and theorizing are no doubt partly responsible, to avoid using the historic male high voice in music clearly written originally for it often seems wanton and contrived. Such a practice is based, apparently, on

[3] see Richard Luckett, *Handel's Messiah: A Celebration* (Gollancz, 1992), especially pp. 240–1
[4] a useful account of the present state of the 'early music' movement is to be found in 'It's the Real Thing – or is it?' in BBC Music Magazine, March 1993
[5] Thurston Dart, *The Interpretation of Music* (Hutchinson, 1954), p. 56

considerations not always genuinely concerned with authentic musical and historical procedure, but would appear to be a matter of fashionable expediency.

Falsetto seems to be a phenomenon instinctively present in the male psyche. In some cultures it lies nearer to the surface than in ours. Today, the markedly falsetto 'whoop' of approval or joy, currently fashionable amongst the young of both sexes, emanates from the United States. It would appear to have its origins in Afro-American culture, hence its automatic appearance on the European youth scene, but now begins to be heard across a wider age range as an appreciative reaction to artistic or sporting performances or personal experiences. Despite the ever increasing influence of 'pop' culture on the taste of the public, it would still seem possible to make this claim: that the majority of older adults retain the notion that the serious singing voice must express gender in the most obvious way of all, by its pitch. Is it prejudice or custom that a woman's singing voice is thought to sound higher than a man's, merely because speaking voices usually do?

Whatever their origins, 'automatic' viewpoints such as these can stand, but have not always stood, in the way of art. We have only to recall the Italian operatic castrati of the eighteenth century, and the monumental back-lash which built up against them during the nineteenth century. Hypocrisy is a charge levelled with some justification against the Victorians and their dark varnished paintings, false propriety, frilled table-leg covers, coverings-up, tonings-down, and their censored Bibles, Shakespeare and folk-songs.

Jonathan Miller, writing in 1980, described beautifully what has happened to early and classical opera:[6]

> Opera is encrusted with barnacles and seaweed and the accumulated mess of virtually one hundred years of often very thoughtless productions. I think it's often necessary to scrape that off in order to get back to the clean lines of its original artificiality.

'Thoughtless' is perhaps slightly misleading, as no doubt some changes were obviously made deliberately. We surely may assume that included in the 'scraping-off' operation is careful examination of vocal allocation in pre-nineteenth-century operas and the opening up, in new works, of a cliché-ed vocal system. The rediscovery and re-employment of the secular solo counter-tenor is part of this.

Male falsetto singing is therefore not unique to Western art, music or modern 'pop' culture, neither is it merely a quirky English manifestation. This high, natural male voice, some semblance at least of which almost every man possesses, is utterly normal.

As we begin to explore the origins of the counter-tenor in detail, the reader should note that in the text (and often in quotations) the terms 'counter-tenor' and 'alto' are used interchangeably in general references to the high male voice as it is understood popularly today. When discussion must be more detailed and any possible differences between alto and counter-tenor voices are discussed, generality is suspended.

Admittedly, the subject is viewed from a generally English standpoint. The traditional counter-tenor seems so very English, yet this tradition was and is again much wider. There appear to be grounds for claiming that European high voice types diverged slightly, in some periods, from vocal practices in the British Isles. However, as we shall see, the nature of that

---

[6] Dr Jonathan Miller, *Radio Times*, 1980

divergence, when it occurred, may be found to be surprising. In Renaissance music especially, as Rebecca Stewart has described in detail in her paper,[7] parts of mainland Europe seem to have developed and used a wider variety of high male voices. England, characteristically conservative in artistic matters, was less interested (it would seem) in classifying, pigeon–holing or exploiting specialist vocal types. Perhaps English suspicion of absolutism, system or excess, was a reason for this.

At first, the result appears to have been a straightforward and versatile English high voice type, termed a counter–tenor. Further investigation qualifies this slightly, but the survival of the counter–tenor was also due to innate English conservatism, which (luckily) was marginally more powerful than the frosty winds of ignorance, neglect and prejudice.

In order to study the counter–tenor, we need to trace his part in the development of harmony itself:[8]

> Looking back over the previous 1,600 years or so, it is clear that up to this point the history of music is predominantly the history of vocal music, and for two obvious reasons; the first is that the voice is the most natural of all instruments, and the second that during most of this period the church was the main centre of artistic activity and sacred music must obviously be vocal. Even if we leave out sacred music, the predominance of vocal over instrumental music is still overwhelming...

Though the following account of the development of the voice and of harmony may be too simplified for the specialist, the beginnings of European harmony are most convenient for our purpose.

---

[7] Rebecca Stewart, 'A Physiological and Linguistic Study of Male Vocal Types, Timbres and Techniques in the Music of Josquin des Prez', *Proceedings of the Josquin Symposium, 1984* in *Tijdschrift van de Vereniging voor Nederlaandse Muziekgeschiedenis* (deel XXXV – 1/2, 1985)

[8] Alec Harman & Anthony Milner, 'Late Renaissance and Early Baroque Music' in *Man and His Music* (Barrie & Rockcliff, 1959, repr. Barrie & Jenkins Ltd., 1988), p. 388

2 The Crucible

The nomenclature of voices was centuries in settling. Except in rare instances, specific vocal labels began to be applied only from the latter part of the sixteenth century, and remained ambiguous for some time beyond this. Until the sixteenth century, therefore, reference to an individual singer's voice was broadly adjectival.

Early biographers frequently note details of a man's singing voice and musicianship. St Dunstan (*c*909–988) was thus described:[1]

> *Habebat ... vocis/pulchritudinem ... suavitatem ... et altitudinem.* (He had ... loveliness of voice ... sweetness [of voice] ... and height [of voice].)

Our interest in this lies not only in his 'high-pitched voice' (the usual meaning), but also in the word 'altitudinis' which suggests both 'height' and 'depth' [sic] and even 'sublimity'. Thus his voice could have been of enormous range. There is no mention of a vocal type.

However, the word 'tenor' occurs early, its meaning taken from *tenere*, to hold. In fact, it describes the nature of the part – a strong tune against which other parts could play. Ignore its modern meaning as a medium-to-high or high male voice; it started, as all terms started, as a part to be sung or played. Tinctoris, the Flemish theorist and composer, wrote in 1487:[2]

> In loud music, a tenor part is played on a bombard; a low contratenor (and, indeed, often any contratenor), on a trombone.

To take a later example, Anthony Wood of Oxford, speaking of the year 1657, said that:[3]

> Gentlemen in private meeting played three, four and five parts with viols – as treble viol, tenor, counter-tenor and bass...

We still talk in a similar way concerning instrumental parts, or in harmony paperwork, on occasion, but the human voice seems to have been the basis for the development of harmony and it is the sung parts which form that harmony; and like the development of titles for other voice-types, eventually led to the term 'counter-tenor'.

---

[1] *Vita* (The early life of St Dunstan), p. 417

[2] Tinctoris, *De Inventione et Usu Musicae, c*1436–1511, G.S.S. 1950, Grove's *Dictionary*, 5th edn, pp. 537–9

[3] Anthony Wood, quoted by Cummings in *Henry Purcell* (Sampson Low, 1881), p. 91

Though harmony existed in various forms and cultures for centuries before Gregorian chant, we must first turn to unison plainsong, the basis of modern Western harmony. (The relationship of plainsong and folk–melody, with implications for the beginnings of rudimentary harmony, are touched on later.) The following historical sequence is, of course, much simplified.

As primitive harmony and counterpoint began their slow development, the original plainsong remained the main tune. This was termed 'vox principalis' or 'tenor'. It was not consistent in range. Sometimes it was pitched high, as if for a modern tenor voice and sometimes it was more baritone in character; at other times, the pitch was as high as a modern counter–tenor line. This 'tenor' was added to, first by one part then another, over many years of experiment.

We are so accustomed to regard developments in any art as logical creative progression that we often forget that steps forward can come as a result of observed accident. In music, it is possible that organum (which is considered to be the first known Western harmony) probably happened because a tone–deaf monk, or dozing cleric, droned unknowingly above or below his brethren. Perhaps it may have occurred through the serendipity of someone's failing to reach a unison too high or low for his voice to attain. On the other hand, it and the term 'organum' itself, may have developed as a result of hearing primitive organs.

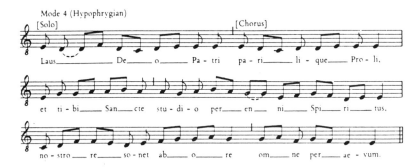

Example 1. Antiphon, 'Laus Deo Patri'

The first exposition of the nature of strict organum occurs as early as the ninth century in Musica Enchiriadis.[4] The added part ('vox organalis', later 'descant') was at first beneath then either above or below the plainsong tenor, or both above and below, and was doubled in octaves, note for note. The result is known as parallel organum. (Depending on the set pitch of the tenor, this could produce, alternately or simultaneously, an accidental temporary bass or an accidental temporary alto. The latter could well have been sung by a falsetto.)

If boys were present in the architectural Quire, they would be likely to sing discant – almost certainly with only their low chest register at first – when it was within their range to join in the higher notes sung by the men. David Wulstan, discussing the possible use of boys in early choirs, argues convincingly for their presence and musical employment.[5]

At this point, today's enquirer will perhaps be wondering how women's voices were

---

[4] See Grove's *Dictionary*, 6th edn, p. 800–802

[5] David Wulstan, 'Birdus tantum natus decorare magistrum', *Byrd Studies*, ed. Brown and Turbet (Cambridge University Press, 1992), pp. 80–81

employed. After all, there were many communities of nuns. St Gilbert of Sempringham, *c*1085–1189, founded the only specifically English religious order: the Gilbertians. First, he established a community of nuns. Concerned with vocal procedure there, and presumably with the spread of 'improper' music in other convents, he wrote:[6]

> We do not permit our nuns to sing. We absolutely forbid it, preferring with the Blessed Virgin to hymn indirectly in a spirit of humility, rather than with Herod's notorious daughter to pervert the minds of the weak with lascivious strains.

By 'lascivious strains', he surely meant the supposed sinful voluptuousness of harmony. Gilbert followed in the footsteps of St Paul, who wrote:[7]

> Let the woman learn in silence, with all subjection. But I suffer not a woman to teach, nor to usurp authority over the man, but to be in silence.

Presumably, this could hardly be appropriate in a convent, except in relation to visiting priests, or Gilbert's parallel establishments of canon–chaplains; but, while smiling at, regretting, or concurring with what some would term St Paul's male chauvinism, we should remember that, because the early church took his instruction literally, mixed choirs were never even a remote possibility. This fact, more than almost anything else, was responsible for the development of high male voices in formal music.

Despite Gilbert, nuns must have sung plainsong, and other women must have performed music, but the latter activity was probably confined to essentially informal domestic or rural leisure–time music–making, including pilgrimage journeys.

From about 1100, 'vox organalis' began to be placed only above 'vox principalis'. This important move created what came to be the standard relationship between a plainsong and one additional voice.

Example 2. Parallel organum (9th–10th century) sequence Rex caeli Domine

---

[6] Gilbert of Sempringham, *Institutiones ad Moriales Ordinis Pertinentes*, in Dugdale's *Monasticon* (London, 1817–1830), volume 6. See also R. Graham, *St. Gilbert of Sempringham and the Gilbertians* (London, 1901)

[7] First Epistle of Paul to Timothy, chapter 2, vv. 11 & 12 (A.V.)

By the middle of the twelfth century, free organum had been developed. It was no longer note–for–note, and often moved in contrary motion. In the following example, the plainsong tenor is interrupted by 'tropes', two basic freely–composed non–plainsong parts. Ordinary, unison plainsong continued as 'bread–and–butter' chanting throughout the development of organum. Harmonized passages did not displace unison plainchant but were added to it and were mostly sung either by soloists or perhaps by a smaller group. Notice that, in the example, the trope–voices are equal and pitched at about our modern tenor range, crossing each other freely. The harmonic intervals are octaves, fifths, fourths and unisons – consonances – and a few thirds, regarded at this date as dissonances.

Older, note–for–note organum became known as 'discantus'–style (it remained very popular) and the newer free organum was simply termed 'organum'–style.

Example 3. Free organum (12th century): trope 'Agnus Dei'

In the twelfth and thirteenth centuries, melismatic organum continued to develop into independent counterpoint. The plainsong tenor moves slowly in the example given, while the upper organum part moves freely and independently of the lower part.

The great Parisian school at Notre Dame produced the important composers Léonin (c1170), and Pérotin (c1200) from whom the previous example of organum comes. It is in mixed form. Plainsong tenor is now combined with two upper parts, which dance freely across each other in dotted rhythms and in phrases of differing lengths. We may assume that these parts were sung by voices resembling our modern counter–tenor or tenor.

Example 4. Melismatic organum (12th century): School of St. Martial:
'Benedicamus Domino'

In the late twelfth and early thirteenth centuries, the terms vox principalis and vox organalis had begun to be superseded by the terms tenor (usually with a Latin text) and duplum, the second part, sometimes labelled motetus (surprisingly, with a secular or at least a differing text), and triplum, the third part. Pérotin sometimes even added quadruplum, a fourth part. These parts were, of course, sung by any voices able to sustain them; the human voice was not yet labelled at all.

The development of early and primitive polyphony is bound up with the increasing exploitation of various ranges of the male voice. Its higher reaches and dramatic possibilities had not been much liked by St Bernard of Clairvaux (1090–1153):[8]

> The words of the Holy Spirit should not be sung in soft, broken voices in a somewhat womanish manner, but uttered with manly sounds and feelings. Yes indeed, it is seemly for men to sing in manly voices, and not to ape, as it were, the wantonness of actors with shrill or false voices used in an effeminate manner.

This passage not only expresses the saint's fears regarding the integrity of sung worship, and anxieties about sexual ambiguities, but provokes interesting speculation about the style and techniques employed by twelfth–century actor/singers.

Once polyphonic music began to develop in earnest, difficulties inevitably arose from musical experiments. Another important churchman, Aelred of Rievaulx (*c*1109–1166), issued a commination against what he disliked in the church music he experienced. In this, too, are more implications than Aelred probably intended: first, its description of the nature of the sound made; second, in our terms, the sometimes ambiguous use of language (for instance, he speaks of an adult male 'treble') and third, a reminder that voices were seldom unaccompanied, but coloured with various instruments. We should, though, remember that the seventeenth–century translator, Prynne,[9] used Stuart technical terms:

> Whence hath the Church so many organs and musicall instruments? To what purpose, I pray you, is that terrible blowing of belloes, expressing rather the crashes of thunder than the sweetnesse of a voyce? To what purpose serves that contraction and inflection of the voyce? This man sings a base, that a small meane, another a treble, a fourth divides, and cuts asunder, as it were, certain middle notes: one while the voyce is strained, anon it is remitted, now it is dashed and then again it is enlarged with a lowder sound. Sometimes, which is a shame so to speake, it is enforced into a horse's neighing: sometimes the masculine vigour being laid aside it is sharpened with the shrillnesse of a woman's voyce: now and then it is writhed and retorted into a certaine artificial circumvolution. Sometimes thou may'st see a man with an open mouth, not to sing, but to breathe out his last gaspe by shutting in his breath, and by a certain ridiculous interception of his voyce as it were to threaten silence, and now again to imitate the agonies of a dying man, or the

---

[8] Latin original quoted by Hough, 'The Historical Significance of the Counter-Tenor', PMMA, 1937, p. 2. This translation by David Stone, 1989
[9] Aelred of Rievaulx, *Speculum Charitatis* (1123), part–quoted by Hough, p. 2

ecstasies of such as suffer. In the meantime the common people standing by, trembling and astonished, admire the sound of the organ, the noyse of the cymballs and musicall instruments, the harmony of the pipes and cornets.

We should remember that conscious or unconscious imitation of animal and bird cries (which involve constant and inevitable repetition) would surely have been influential. An example is the cockerel's morning crow, echoed by others: a sound which, in part, incorporates a falsetto–like effect. Pérotin, for instance, might well have been influenced by animal calls:

Example 5. Pérotin (12th century) organum 'Alleluya' (Nativitas)

Aelred mentions particular vocal effects like nasal tremolando and vibrato. Most scholars seem to agree that these were a particular characteristic of the Notre Dame school. It appears that Aelred was used to four–part singing, which was to become quite common by the start of the thirteenth century. John of Salisbury (d. 1180), friend and secretary of Thomas Becket, was one of the most illustrious Bishops of Chartres. He also was worried by much of what he had heard:[10]

> The very service of the Church is defiled, in that before the face of the Lord, in the very sanctuary of sanctuaries, they, showing off as it were, strive with the effeminate dalliance of wanton tones and musical phrasing to astound, enervate, and dwarf simple souls. When one hears the excessively caressing melodies of voices beginning, chiming in, carrying the air, dying away, rising again, and dominating, he may well believe that it is the song of the Sirens and not the sound of men's voices; he may marvel at the flexibility of tone which neither the nightingale, the parrot, or any bird with greater range than

---

[10] *Frivolities of Courtiers and Footprints of Philosophers*, a translation of *Policraticus* by John of Salisbury, ed. Pike (1938), p. 32

these can rival. Such indeed is the ease of running up or down the scale, such the dividing or doubling of the notes and the repetitions of the phrases and their incorporation one by one; the high and the very high notes are so tempered with the low or somewhat low that one's very ears lose the ability to discriminate, and the mind, soothed by such sweetness, no longer has power to pass judgement upon what it hears. When this type of music is carried to the extreme it is more likely to stir lascivious sensations in the loins than devotion in the heart. But if it is kept within reasonable limits it frees the mind from care, banishes worry about things temporal, and by imparting joy and peace and by inspiring a deep love for God, draws souls to association with the angels.

During the twelfth century, in France, non–plainsong tenors began to appear and were called conductus; these were free melodies, similar in all parts, which were later harmonized like plainsong tenors but in simpler rhythmic structures. A medieval German theorist, describing the procedure for composing conductus, gives us a valuable account of his method:[11]

First, choose the loveliest melody you can think of, then write a descant to it in the manner shown. If you wish to add a third part, look carefully at the melody and the descant, so that the third part will not be discordant with them both together.

It seems that 'discant' or 'descant' had several definitions, and that one of these allowed for a descant to be added below or above existing plainsong. Later, composers rather lost interest in conductus form and concentrated instead on the development of the motet.

During the late thirteenth century, another device evolved: a contratenor (or contra–tenor) part, sometimes called concordans. It was termed contra–tenor because it was against the tenor, i.e., it straddled or crossed it freely, much as the trope–voices of free organum did with each other. Contra–tenor sometimes achieved intervals strange for the time – even, occasionally, a major seventh. The indication 'contra–tenor', however, was rare in English usage before the time of the Old Hall Manuscript, a collection of Mass sections and motets by named English composers c1370–1420. The English adoption of the term contra–tenor is, as Frank Ll. Harrison observed, part of a process of proximation, which eventually became mutual, of French and English styles.[12]

It would seem that the term 'contra–tenor' was used in England from about 1400 to the time of the Eton Choirbook, c1500. We should look at MS. 139 of the Old Hall collection, which Harrison considered to be c1405. In this piece, there occurs a 'contra–tenor de cantu feriali' added to an Agnus Dei setting in regular homo–rhythmic style. Harrison pointed out that there are the indications 'contra–tenor de virgo Sancta Katerina' and 'contra–tenor de vos quid admiramini' beside French compositions in the leaves of Durham Cathedral library MSC 1.20. He dated this 1358–1360, and thought its provenance Durham or Oxford.[13] See also p. 27 regarding the 'Newgat cowntur–tenur'.

---

[11] *Pelican History of Music*, Vol. I, p. 226

[12] Frank Ll. Harrison, in a private letter to the author, 1 October 1987

[13] Frank Ll. Harrison, loc. cit.

Example 6. Isorhythmic motet, anonymous English early 14th century, pre-Old Hall MS.

Guillaume de Machaut (*c*1300–1377) is a brilliant figure, and was the leader of Ars Nova, the New Art. He composed the first fully polyphonic Mass; at least, his *Messe de Notre Dame* seems to be the earliest complete polyphonic setting extant. The next example demonstrates not only how low the contra–tenor part could be, in that it fulfilled the duties of both modern bass and (in this case) modern tenor, but also that because it lacks text it was probably an instrumental part in this instance.

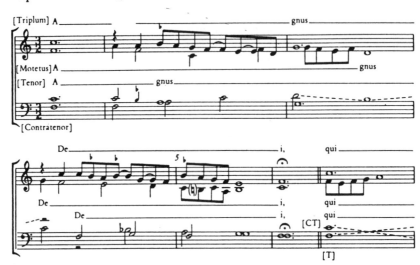

Example 7. Guillaume de Machaut (c1300–c1377) Agnus Dei (i) from Mass VIII

Interestingly, motetus here corresponds to our modern alto part in range, as does triplum.[14] We are still far from a settled nomenclature.

In England, fa–burden was to take development of harmony a big step forward with its amazing thirds and sixths. Fa–burden could be defined as originally an improvised three–part polyphonic elaboration of plainchant recitation in the fifteenth century. The three parts were almost certainly formed by the singing of thirds or fifths below the plainsong, which was itself transposed up a fifth and sung by the mean(e), or middle, part. A high part moved in parallel fourths above the mean(e). Later composers sometimes used the lowest part as a cantus firmus in preference to the actual plainsong.

In the written form of the originally improvisatory technique eventually known as English discant, or descant, a plainsong was added to by a single additional voice, largely in contrary motion, in note–by–note fashion. Pure discant remained a favourite device. Later, the term seems to have been extended, less strictly, to refer to the top voice part of three. There is an almost peculiarly English fondness for 'descants', in the modern sense of an added melody high above a hymn or song, and an instance of this fondness for a high–flying part, and an apparent reference to falsetto singing, occurs in Chaucer's *The Canterbury Tales*, 1388. The notorious 'Miller's Tale', lines 145–146, has:

> And playen songes on a small rubible [a small harp, or citerne?]
> Therto he song somtyme a loud quynyble [five–fold; i.e., a fifth part, or a part
> an octave above the treble]

And in *The Image of Ypocrisy*, (iii. line 78) by John Skelton (1460–1529), we find:

> They finger ther fidles,
> And cry in quinibles.

There are several points of interest here. *New Grove* (the 6th edition) gives 'quinible' as a voice or part pitched an octave above the treble, i.e., a fourth above quatreble. (During the fifteenth century, the part normally sung by boys was termed quatreble; it was this word that was later contracted to treble.) *New Grove* goes on to say that English usage seems to be

---

[14] Compare the edition by Frank Ll. Harrison. PMFC XV, p. 32 (O.U.P.). Triplum becomes duplum; O.U.P.'s Motetus is Triplum. The former has one note lower in range than the latter, and ends a fourth below it.

loosely confined to the general sense of a high–pitched song or voice. Nevill Coghill's translation of the Chaucer tales has:[15]

> He played a two–stringed fiddle, did it proud;
> And sang a high falsetto rather loud.

The instrument possesses a pungent, nasal, soprano tone–quality. If we take the small two–stringed rubible as being near the range of the three–stringed instrument which has strings sounding D5, G4, C5, Absalon must have been singing high, and, as Coghill suggests, using a high, loud falsetto. Another point is that bowing two strings simultaneously, and adding a voice, would produce three musical parts. It seems significant that, in both examples, disparately dated, the chosen instrument to which quinible is added is the fiddle (a rubible, or rebec, is an early fiddle). The falsetto quinible seems therefore to have been a well–established device. Grove tells us that, even by the fifteenth century, English treatises do not mention it. Therefore, Skelton must be referring to an old–fashioned, well–loved or well–worked musical effect, with a hint of mockery. In Chaucer, there is more than a hint.

Dunstable treated the top part increasingly like a harmonized tune in the modern manner, except that his discant is not necessarily always the high–flying part above the treble that we are used to hearing today. Example 8 is part of an antiphon in fa–burden style: an 'Ave Regina Coelorum', with a top part called 'discant'. The Marian plainsong tune (developed with additions) is mostly in the top part; the fa–burden part proper is the second line down (contra–tenor). It is this part which supplies the characteristic sweetness of the English style. (The main harmonies are all 6/3 and 5/8 chords, disregarding the ornamental additions). What is nicely called 'migrant cantus firmus' – the occasional placing of plainsong in another part for the odd phrase – is an English invention. (It is interesting to note, in examples 8 and 9, that the discant part seems to be our modern high or first (alto) counter–tenor part. Example 8 has contra–tenor as either low counter–tenor or modern tenor; the tenor part as modern second tenor or baritone.)

Example 9, by Leonel Power (c1370–1445), demonstrates the English manner of the harmonised tune. Note that the lowest voice is labelled 'counter'. This is not an early Anglicising of contra–tenor. Harrison wrote:[16]

> In an anonymous treatise it is said of 'counter': 'the whech sight was contrived out of the syght of the mene degre of descant turnyd upsodoun'. I have not met 'counter' (distinguished in this treatise clearly from 'countertenor') in a music–manuscript. For descant teaching purposes, it was what we would call a bass, below the given 'playnson'. The countertenor, here and in music–manuscripts, has intervals both above and below the given part. As he [the original writer] says, just before: 'For whan the tenor is hye, the countertenor may be low and whan the tenor is low than the countertenor may be the mene'. 'Gymel', in this treatise in the form 'countergemel', in music–manuscripts signals an additional part in the same range as one already there, as it were a splitting of a part.

---

[15] (Penguin, 1951), p. 108
[16] Lit. cit., 1 October 1987

Power wrote a treatise on discant, but it dealt only with quatreble and treble sights (or parts). Harrison continued:[17]

> Discanting for other singers using the sights of mean, countertenor, and counter (the latter in a pitch–range below the plainsong) was treated in other handbooks. Neither logically, nor in historical terms, therefore, may English discant be used of three–part composition. [That is, that the term 'English discant' should not be used to describe three–part composition as a form. The title 'discant' is there applicable to a part.] It may suitably be replaced by the modern term 'homorhythmic'. With a plainsong, or plainsong–derived voice, as the middle one of three, the usage of the treatises suggests treble, plainsong, or tenor, and counter. Outside the special context of church music, the everyday terms for three part music would have been treble, mean, and tenor, or burden.

Example 8. Antiphon 'Ave Regina Coelorum', John Dunstable (d. 1435)
for (top to bottom) Descant, Contratenor and Tenor

---

[17] Ibid.

Example 9. Votive antiphon in English discant style, Leonel Power (c1370–1445)

The early fifteenth–century Wakefield Mystery plays include the following lines:[18]

1st Shepherd:	Let me sing the tenory
2nd Shepherd:	And I the treble so high
3rd Shepherd:	Then the mean falls to me
	Let's see how ye chant
	[They sing]

The three shepherds, singing and cross–talking, are a light–hearted build–up to the Nativity scene. First, we note that the third man offers to sing a treble and not a counter–tenor, as the high part. Other than a loose allusion to a high–pitched voice, this supports Harrison's point about the later adoption of the term in England. Second, we are made aware of the English instinct or love for three voices (Three Man's Song), with the high–voice top line. Third, we

---

[18] Wakefield Cycle, c1420, *The second Shepherd's Play*, ed. and adapted Kenneth Pickering, 1986

might argue that the three sung ranges mentioned, in order of listing in modern parlance, are baritone, alto (or counter–tenor), and tenor.

Shakespeare provides another example:[19]

> ...three–man song–men all, and very good ones; but they are most of them meanes and bases...

Medieval drama began in church, and developed out of the liturgy. Actors, singers and musicians were therefore all male – though some scholars think that nuns may have taken part occasionally. When the plays were transferred outside the church (partly because the buildings were proving too small for the increasingly large audiences), townsfolk themselves took part. The Guilds – which were all–male – continued to undertake to put on one play each within the cycle.

Whether women, other than nuns, took part seems to be a point of disagreement. Until recently, it was confidently thought that they did not, and many scholars and historians still believe this. Our interest lies mainly as follows: if women took part, does this change our understanding of the willingness and enthusiasm of men to use falsetto singing and speaking voices in medieval drama? If women were performers, would it alter our conception of the need for use of falsetto in such drama? No; we may be sure that falsetto or head–voice singing was used freely. Boys, too, were used in plays staged inside and outside the church. Their voices were used more and more as the choir and harmony developed.

In parts of continental Europe, from the time of the Renaissance onwards, women were increasingly appearing on the professional stage, and presumably sang when called upon to do so by the demands of the plot. In England their first appearances however followed an ordinance of Charles II in 1662 which forbade male actors to take female rôles.

An illustration of the use of falsetto in court drama and spectacle is provided by Olivier de la Marche, organiser of stupendous scenic effects at the Banquet of the Oath of the Pheasant in 1454. After astonishing dramatic displays and tableaux, '...It transpires that the lady (who was actually played by Olivier de la Marche himself) represented Mother Church at the mercy of the Infidel (the elephant), as the lament she sang (in falsetto) was designed to move the hearts of the assembled company before they took their vows.'[20]

The serious establishment of the male singing voice as a solo or choral instrument was the foundation of our European vocal system. Choral range spread both upwards and downwards. Eventually, contra–tenor became permanently split into two distinct parts: at first labelled contra–tenor and contra–tenor secundus and then contra–tenor altus and contra–tenor bassus. When they lost their intrinsic involvement with the tenor, they thenafter remain each side of it, except for special effects. These two separate parts eventually discarded their contra–tenor prefix, first the lower, then the higher; but it would seem that the latter (altus) always kept contra–tenor (or more usually, counter–tenor) as its alternative title, in England at least.

There was continued indecision as to what the lower part should be called. Though the simple term bassus triumphed eventually, manuscripts contain a variety of names for the new bass part, such as subcontra, baritonans, baricanor, baripsaltes, basis, basistenor, or theumatenor.

---

[19] *The Winter's Tale*, act 4, sc. iii, l.
[20] Christopher Hogwood, *Music in Court* (The Folio Society, London, 1977), p. 24

The contra–tenor split occurred in the middle of the fifteenth century. Two composers associated with the establishment of what eventually became the modern four–part choir are Johannes Ockeghem (1425–95) and Jacob Obrecht (1430–1505). Previously tightly knit medieval voice parts have now become carefully–spaced strata in which the four voices had definite territory (see example 10). The tenor now tended to remain a slightly higher part in the texture, as a result of the new bassus's being permanently below it. Contra–tenor altus had risen correspondingly. Example 11, part of an English mass, demonstrates this well. Four parts had subdivided rapidly into five, six, or more.

Example 10. Johannes Ockeghem (c1425–1495), Sanctus *(first section)*
from the 'Missa Prolationum' for (top to bottom) Contra–tenor altus, Tenor and Bassus

The range of early mean parts suggests that counter–tenors might well have sung them either alone, or with boys using their chest register. Later, the mean range became a higher part and, it is argued, was sung exclusively by boys. Yet this is by no means certain, when one remembers the tradition and power of the high falsettist. Illness or weakness of choristers might well have demanded that men sang the part: a situation not unknown today.

These early male choirs were both the product of, and catalyst for, development of European harmony. Thus, all European formal choral music has the monastic or collegiate choir as its ancestor. (Nuns may have sung some organum, but when one recalls Gilbert of Sempringham and the social facts of medieval life it seems unlikely that they could have been influential innovators. On the other hand, mention should be made of Hildegard of Bingen (1098?–1179) the German abbess, composer and poet, who wrote a cycle of vocal settings of seventy–seven poems arranged according to the liturgical calendar. She is now recognised as an important composer in her own right. Others may yet be discovered.)

Because the male choir benefitted from a full range of voices, lowest to highest, all the important vocal developments took place in, and were the result of, these choirs and foundations. Nevertheless it has been suggested that though motets, both sacred and very secular, originated in this milieu, they would have spread outside for lively impromptu mixed–voice performance in market square and convivial places of wine and song.

Induction to the tradition began early. Boy trebles in a monastic or collegiate choir were educated at a school run by the foundation either expressly to supply boy choristers, or because the education of the young was a function of most abbeys or minsters of any size. No doubt, one suspects, it was a shrewd mixture of both.

The next example is a 'Sanctus' by the fifteenth–century English composer, Cousin, a near contemporary of Ockeghem. It not only illustrates the split in the contra–tenor part, but also gives a glimpse of English choir usage at this time, and in it is prefigured the birth of the future cathedral choir's repertory.

Example 11. Sanctus *from cyclic mass, Cousin (mid–15th century)*

As Harrison wrote:[21]

> The size and balance of the choirs of collegiate churches and colleges in the later Middle Ages, as well as what the statutes reveal about the qualifications and training of their members, show that the performance of polyphonic music was an essential part of their function. In their establishment of similar choirs, monasteries followed in the footsteps of secular institutions, and at the same time took advantage of the presence of a qualified master for their stipendiary singers to employ him for some of their own services. The institution and development of balanced groups of singers was the most significant feature of the musical history of the later Middle Ages, and was comparable in importance to the rise of the orchestra in the eighteenth and nineteenth centuries. It was closely related to the original and growth of choral polyphony, as distinct from the polyphony of soloists practised in the larger secular and monastic choirs in earlier centuries.

Such an important situation requires a closer look. Percy M. Young explains that, at least in England, cathedral and collegiate foundations were likely to be ahead of monastic choirs in the use of boys' voices. We know that, in the last years of Edward I's reign (1272–1307), the Chapel Royal was brought into line with secular cathedrals by the apparently new employment of boy choristers. Yet there is evidence of boys in the Chapel Royal of Sigbert, king of the East Angles, at Dunwich, in A.D. 635.[22]

Whether or not boys were used by the immediately post–Conquest Chapel Royal is unclear, but in 1303 there is the first detailed mention of boys as members of the Royal Foundation. The Calendar of Patent Rolls for 1303 states that 'Richard of Nottingham and Thomas Duns, choirboys of the Chapel Royal, were sent to Oxford' when their voices broke.[23] In 1316, other boys were sent to Cambridge.

In 1421–2, the last year of Henry V's reign, there were sixteen Children (the official name

---

[21] Frank Ll. Harrison, *Music in Medieval Britain* (repr. Knuf, 1980), pp. 44–45
[22] David Baldwin, *The Chapel Royal, Ancient and Modern* (Duckworth, 1990), p. 313
[23] Loc. cit.

for the Chapel Royal boys), but numbers had dwindled to just six by the following year. They increased and decreased variously over subsequent centuries.[24]

Unlike monastic and secular cathedral musical foundations, which existed (and still exist) primarily to perform the *opus Dei* to perfection without the need to gratify or serve royal or aristocratic patrons (or even a congregation), the Chapel Royal is the body of priests and singers appointed to minister to the spiritual and temporal needs of the Sovereign and the Royal Household wherever they might be. As such, 'It is a collection of people, not a building, although it has become identified since the rise of the great Tudor palaces with certain buildings in which it regularly conducts divine service.'[25]

Originally the comprehensive daily schedule of the Chapel Royal seems to have resembled that of other choral foundations. It was certainly so by the late fifteenth century, but there were additionally–prescribed duties connected with the choir's attendance upon the Sovereign.

Percy M. Young, in describing the Sarum Customary (1210) gave us a useful picture of early choral foundations and their arrangements:[26]

> Under the general direction of the Precentor of a cathedral, vicars–choral and singing–boys performed the music of the Liturgy. The boys were housed in clergy residences, and prepared for junior church appointments or for a higher education, leading to eventual promotion to the superior ranks of the clergy. The vicars–choral gradually formed themselves into separate corporations, and throughout the Middle Ages occupied a position of some independence of and considerable importance in the development of church music. Subordinate to the vicars–choral, there were in due course professional singing–men of lower ecclesiastical rank than that of deacon. These were the lay–clerks. In monastic foundations, the whole community formed the choir which, as in a secular cathedral, was directed by the Precentor, to whom the Succentor acted as assistant. Instruction in plainsong was part of the education of every novice. That monks were sometimes inclined to protest against the imposition on them of a musical education is demonstrated by two monks, of the reign of Henry II, possibly from Norwich, who complained of the difficulties of learning church music in the poem 'Un–comly in Cloystre'. It was not until the fourteenth century that singing–boys were employed in the performance of liturgical music in monastic foundations; and only then outside the monks' choir. Until the fifteenth century, larger groups of singers in church were concerned only with unison plainsong. Polyphony, as it developed, was for solo singers and players.

This could suggest that extensive, higher counter–tenor singing might well have developed earlier in monastic choirs than in those of secular foundations which used boys to supply the top musical line.

Though it might all be a matter of unevenly surviving documentary evidence, it seems that on the continent boys were employed much earlier, on a widespread and regular basis, to sing

[24] Op. cit., p. 315 and *passim*
[25] Op. cit. (dust jacket)
[26] Percy M. Young, *A History of British Music* (Ernest Benn, 1973), pp. 20–21

liturgical music in monasteries. (This may have established an early continental preference for a more chest-based and chest-conscious boys' tone.) Odo of Saint-Maur, who studied at Cluny, wrote a musical handbook in the eleventh century which set out a method of teaching boys to attain perfect sight-reading in less than a week. The choirboys' lot was not easy:[27]

> At Nocturns, if the boys commit any fault in the psalmody or other singing, either by sleeping or such like transgressions, let there be no sort of delay, but let them be stripped forthwith of frock and cowl and beaten in their shirts only, with pliant and smooth osier rods provided for that special purpose.

In the Cluniac Monastery of St-Benigne at Dijon (later the cathedral), Guido of Arezzo (*c*995–*c*1050) wrote:[28]

> Should anyone doubt that I'm telling the truth, let him come, make a trial, and hear what small boys can do under our direction; boys who have until now been beaten for their gross ignorance of the psalms.

So boys clearly were used for the upper part at least in some monasteries. Despite the shortage of evidence, it would be surprising if English monastic practice differed very much. Some foundations seem to have to employed boys' voices separately from those of the monks, but if boys were present in monastic schools (as they certainly were at Canterbury, for example), they might surely have sung the treble line in the monks' quire on occasion, before the fourteenth century.

The problem is that even late medieval manuscripts do not include details of specific voices or instruments to be used; it is thought that the voices and instruments were often interchanged. Our chief interest lies in this question: if boys did not sing the high parts when such parts were needed, who did? They must have been supplied by what we might generically term falsettists, unless instruments were employed.

Monastic, cathedral and collegiate foundations varied in size; some communities at full muster were enormous at the height of the monastic period, and they filled a large quire like that at Canterbury. However, choirs – in the modern meaning of specialist singers – were not large. We are all familiar with the small choral group in medieval art, standing round a single lectern, singing from one large choir-book. The maximum size of group, or semi-chorus, depicted numbers about ten – not that the artist would have normally been concerned to show the exact number of singers, as some writers have suggested. A larger choir would have sung from at least two choir part-books, one per side, a custom which began in about the middle of the fifteenth century, according to contemporary illustrations.

Irrespective of the size of the whole singing community – the surrounding, unison plainsong choir – semi-choruses singing in harmony continued to be modest in size, and comparable with English cathedral and collegiate choirs today, which now average sixteen boys and eight men. By the later fifteenth century, both sides of the choir sang harmonised music, and specialist singers were divided in the midst of the community. This 'decani' and 'cantoris' system survives today: the singers are so described as being on the Dean's side and

---

[27] Odo of Saint-Maur (879?–942), the reputed author of *Dialogus de Musica*
[28] Grove's *Dictionary*, 4th edn

Precentor's side respectively.

There are many written details of the sizes of the various establishments.[29] Our chief interest here is the implied presence and proportional numbers of high male voices. Mention of specific voice–range or type is, of course, rare. At least one–third of the singers (increasingly skilled as music became more sophisticated with more vocal parts and more diverse), could be described, it would seem, as 'alti' – high counter–tenors.

What appears to be the first mention, in English sources, of a counter–tenor singer, had occurred in 1388:[30]

> Perauenture on ware *post sumptum temporis plausus*. A cowntur–tenur at Newgat *cantabit carcere clausus*.

The exact meaning of this is unclear but a modern paraphrase and translation, ignoring the obviously intended partial rhyming and scanning, might be: 'Perhaps, unaware, he accepts applause when time is gone. A counter–tenor in Newgate will give song imprisoned in a cell'.[31]

The first–named counter–tenor, described it would seem with an idiomatic brevity that recalls 'Joe "Mr Piano" Henderson', is to be found in the Manuscript Chantilly in the Musée Condé. The manuscript has a collection of motets by various composers, including one by 'J. de alto bosco'. 'Alto' could merely mean high voice, but equally he might have been a falsettist, possibly the J. de Bosco known to have been a singer at the Papal Chapel in Avignon in 1394. More prosaically, he might have come from a high wood; one hopes not!

By and large, however, the personnel of early choirs is tantalizingly anonymous.

We can divine something of the skills required by each man both from the music and from written descriptions. In York Minster, by 1507, the vicars had to undertake to study polyphonic singing before proper admission.[32] Each new vicar was required to take an oath to learn pricksong and fa–burden if he had a tenor voice, or descant, pricksong and fa–burden if his voice was not tenor. This suggests that all non–tenors were expected to be able to supply both the highest and lowest parts. Non–tenors, it would seem, were a collection of contra–tenori, some bassus and some altus. The implication is that the tenor stood apart as a vocal type. All this implies an increased tendency towards vocal classification.

At Leconfield (or Leckingfield) Castle near Beverley in the East Riding of Yorkshire, there existed before the Reformation a private choral establishment which rivalled the Chapel Royal. In addition to Dean, Sub–Dean and a number of priests, there was a musical body of listed, specific voices. This list, a rare occurrence at this date, indicates several points for our purposes: among them the numbers of singers per part, and how nomenclature had settled in normal parlance. The lists are in the *Household Book* of Henry Algernon Percy, the 5th Earl of Northumberland:[33]

---

[29] Harrison, op. cit., pp. 19–20

[30] *Pol Poems* (1859), I 277, quoted O.E.D., 1971 edn

[31] Translation by Ian Thompson, 1992

[32] Harrison, op. cit., p. 181

[33] Henry Algernon Percy, *Household Book*, 1770, quoted by Hawkins in his *History of the Science of Music*, London 1776. See also Wulstan, *Tudor Music* (Dent, 1985), pp. 234–7 and Donald Burrows, *Handel and the English Chapel Royal*, vol. 2 (Open University Ph. D. dissertation), a valuable insight into the choirs of such foundations and their constituent voices.

GENTYLLMEN *and* CHILDERYN *of the* CHAPELL.

ITEM Gentyllmen and Childryn of the Chapell xiij
Viz.Gentillmen of the Chapell viij Viz.ij Bassys – ij Tenors – and
iiij Countertenors – Yoman or Grome of the Vestry j – Childeryn
of the Chapell v Viz. ij Tribills and iij Meanys – xiiij.
Gentillmen of the Chapell – ix Viz. The maister of the Childre j –
Tenors ij – Countertenors iiij – The Pistoler j – and oone for the
Organys Childer of the Chapell – vj.
    ' The gentlemen ande childrin of my lordis chapell whiche be
' not appointid to uttend at no tyme, but oonely in exercifing of
' Goddis fervice in the chappell daily at Mattins, Lady-Mafs,
' Highe-Mafs, Even-fonge, and Complynge.

        ' Gentlemen of my lordis chappell.
' Furft.   A bafs.
' Item.   A feconde bafs.
' Item.   The thirde bafs.
' Item.   A maifter of the childer, a countertenor.
' Item.   A feconde countertenour.
' Item.   A thirde countertenour.
' Item.   A iiijth countertenour.
' Item.   A ftanding tenour.
' Item.   A feconde ftanding tenour.
' Item.   A iijd ftandyng tenour.
' Item.   A fourth ftanding tenour.

        ' Childrin of my lordis chappell.
' Item.   The fyrft child a trible.
' Item.   The ijd child a trible.

' Item.   The iijd child a trible.
' Item.   The iiijth child a fecond trible.
' Item.   The vth child a fecond trible.
' Item.   The vjth child a fecond trible.
'The noumbre of thois parfons as childrin of my lordis chap-
' pel vj.'

' The orderynge of my lordes chapell in the queare at
' mattyngis, mafs, and evynfonge. To ftonde in ordure as
' hereafter followeth, fyde for fyde daily.
    ' The deane fide.   ' The feconde fide.
    ' The Deane.   ' The Lady-maffe prieft.
    ' The fubdeane.   ' The gofpeller.
    ' A baffe.   ' A baffe.
    ' A tenor.   ' A countertenor.
    ' A countertenor.   ' A countertenor.
    ' A countertenor.   ' A tenor.
    ' A countertenor.   ' A countertenor.
                              ' A tenor.

' The ordurynge of my lordes chappell for the keapinge of our
    ' Ladyes maſſe thorowte the weike.

' Sonday.   ' Monday.

' Maſter of the Childer a coun-   Maſter of the Childer a Coun-
    ' tertenor.   ' tertenor.
    ' A tenor.   ' A countertenour.
    ' A tenour.   ' A counter-tenor.
    ' A baſſe.   ' A tenor.

'Twiſday.   ' Wedynſday.

'Maſter of the childer a coun-   ' Maſter of the childer a coun-
    ' tertenour.   ' tertenor.
    ' A countertenour.   ' A countertenour.
    ' A countertenour.   ' A tenour.
    ' A tenour.   ' A baſſe.

' Thurſdaie   ' Fryday.

' Maſter of the childer a coun-   ' Maſter of the childer a coun-
    ' tertenor.   ' tertenor.
    ' A countertenoure.   ' A countertenour.
    ' A countertenoure.   ' A countertenour.
    ' A tenoure.   ' A baſſe.

' Satturday.   ' Fryday.

' Maſter of the childer a coun-   ' And upon the ſaide Friday
    ' tertenor.   ' th'ool chapell, and evry day
    ' A countertenor.   ' in the weike when my lord
    ' A countertenour.   ' ſhall be preſent at the ſaide
    ' A tenour.   ' maſſe.

' The orduringe for keapinge weikly of the orgayns one after an
    ' outher as the namys of them hereafter followith weikly.

' The maiſter of the childer, yf he be a player, the firſt weke.
' A countertenor that is a player the ijde weke.
' A tenor that is a player the thirde weke.
' A baſſe that is a player the iiijth weke.
' And every man that is a player to keep his cours weikly.'

The choir at Leconfield (Leckingfield) Castle, Yorkshire, in the early 16th century

Note that, in the more formal list of voice parts, counter–tenors are placed next to basses. May this be their order of prestige or because of the shared origin of the two parts? That this is nothing more significant than the alphabetical order of Bass, Counter–tenor and Tenor seems unlikely at this date. Note also the stated number of counter–tenors. The voice's range and type has assumed great importance.

    Another possible, parallel, interpretation is that because, except in its upper reaches the individual counter–tenor voice was not as loud as those of the tenor and bass, the choir needed more counter-tenors. They may well have had the light tonal quality we know today with pure head voices in the majority. This would be at odds with musicologists who think of early counter-tenors as our modern tenor (with modern technique) and early tenors as if they were baritones. Only three basses seem to be listed. Perhaps one or two of the six counter-tenors would be expected to 'straddle' the tenor part, in historical manner, by singing on occasion what we would call baritone range. If so, this would reinforce our historical understanding; and many counter-tenors since have instinctively used their chest voices too.

The word 'standing' before tenor is of interest. Possibly it is an allusion to the traditional but by that date largely obsolescent rôle of the tenor 'to hold' or to provide the cantus firmus or vox principalis. There are four tenors, presumably to allow for maintenance of this historic rôle.

Notice that the first counter-tenor is the Master of the Children. This underlines what should be obvious: that the highest male voice is most suited to teach the boys their part. The appointment looks permanent; if it were not, surely his voice type would have been listed first, followed by the incidental post of Master? This dual rôle also suggests that the origin of the saying that 'all choir-masters and organists sing alto' is an ancient one. But, as was customary at this date, the chapel singing men took equal turns to play and/or maintain the organ. (Later references to and discussion of the constitution of Sainte-Chapelle, Paris, and the choir of the Chapel Royal in London, will be seen to be germane to this.)

A personal description occurs in a letter from the Venetian Ambassador to the Signory of Venice. In 1515, he had wined and dined with Henry VIII and then heard mass sung by the Chapel Royal Choir in Richmond Palace:[34]

> ... and after a grand procession had been made, high mass was sung by the
> King's choristers whose voices are more divine than human; non cantavano
> ma giubilavano; and as to the counter-bass voices, they probably have not
> their equal in the world.

He was, of course, speaking of an event in a foreign country, but in using the term 'counter bass', he may have showed an erudite awareness of the traditional bass/alto relationship. However, it is perhaps likelier that he referred not to alti but bassi (from contra tenor bassus), using the then normal Italian term contrabassi.

In a sixteenth-century poem, there is a description of the counter-tenor voice, or voice part, which describes its function beautifully:[35]

> The bass and treble are extremes,
> the tenor standeth sturdily,
> the counter rangyth then me seems.

Perhaps the loveliest early reference to the counter-tenor voice, rather than part, dates from 1502:[36]

---

[34] Calendar of State Papers, Venetian, vol. 2, p. 247

[35] Grove's *Dictionary*, 5th edn, p. 482

[36] 1502 *Ord Christen Men* (W. de W., 1506), v. iv 393, quoted in O.E.D., 1971 edn

> I understande by ... counter tenouer (of the gloryous melodye of paradyse) the
> loye [ioye=joy?] and the gladnes of the blessyd men and women of paradyse.

In addition to this apt description of the ethereal quality of male pure head-voice, it is interesting to note the early mention of its androgynous character.

In fact, at this period, other than the lists at Leckingfield Castle, it would seem that factual mention of the voice range in question is rarer than poetic description. This is not surprising: the familiar is commonplace, and needs no reference. Often, of course, in more general descriptions, the presence of counter-tenors may be inferred. At Chichester Cathedral in 1530, there was added to the existing foundation of vicars choral, using a title unusual for what has been known, post-Reformation, as a cathedral of the Old Foundation, a 'foundation of four lay clerks'. We may surely assume that one, probably two, were to be counter-tenors, because these four were to be singers of polyphonic music, and we are told that their voices were to blend well together, and that one at least should be a good natural bass. Their combined voices were to have a range of fifteen or sixteen notes.[37] By Weelkes's time, at the end of the century, these four had doubled to eight.

It seems that by the early sixteenth century a traditional penchant for three-part harmony was still favoured highly in England, though it was not unique to this country. Richard Cromwell, in Rome with an embassy, seems to have taken singers with him (possibly some of the Gentlemen of the Chapel Royal?), and to have arranged for three-part songs to be performed for the Pope. This may have been to display English musical techniques, and to impress him with his singers' vocal skill. ('Three Men's Song', the male voice trio – or, more properly, terzet – was to survive centuries and various changes of musical styles in England, as we shall see. There is mention, for example, of 'two merry three-men's-songs' in Dekker's *The Shoemaker's Holiday*, 1600.) We may assume that the top part was sung by what we would now call a counter-tenor, high or low.

It was still required of an early sixteenth-century singer in England that he could discant on a plainsong, or 'counter' a popular tune, *extempore*. Musica Britannica's *Music at the Court of Henry VIII* gives a very good idea of the results that might be expected.[38]

It seems that, at this date, counter-tenor altus and bassus were still thought compatible, vocally. Yet the Chichester stipulation seems to suggest that specialist singers, such as a natural bass, were required, as well as those implied to be baritones with an extension into head voice. Most singers, that is, those not specialist tenors or specialist basses, were therefore required to be versatile 'enough to sing either in a true or falsetto voice', according to John Stevens.[39] We may dislike his conception of 'true or falsetto', and this is discussed more fully later in connection with the feigned voice. John Stevens continues:

> The idea is sometimes put forward that English men have a prerogative of
> natural, straightforward singing, and that this singing displaced the old falsetto
> singing. Neither the music itself or the acid comments of the Reformers, nor
> the general tone of courtly life (with its tendency to garnish everything)

---

[37] Bishop of Sherborne, Donations, 1531–4, copy two; Sussex County Library, Chichester, f. 18

[38] *Musica Britannica, Volume XVIII, Music at the Court of Henry VIII* (R. M. A., Stainer & Bell, 1962)

[39] John Stevens, *Music and Poetry in the Early Tudor Court* (Cambridge University Press, 1979), p. 312

supports the idea. The popularity of the counter-tenor (presumably using a falsetto when necessary) has already been suggested. At one time Northumberland's Chapel had six counter-tenors to two tenors and two basses.

An examination of the Leckingfield lists would suggest a discrepancy in Stevens's arithmetic, but his point is made.

A letter about the appointment of John Taverner (*c*1495–1545) as Master of the Choir at Cardinal College, Oxford (Wolsey's foundation, later to become Christ Church), specified that he must have 'both his breste att will', plus the handling of an instrument.[40] 'Breste' was a term used for the voice, so the passage might indicate the use of the chest voice and falsetto.

We might take stock at this date: research shows that the counter-tenor voice range, or ranges, by whatever name, seems to have been cultivated just as strongly in most continental countries as in Britain.

It is at this point that the first questions regarding any possible differences between alto and counter tenor might begin to arise. We consider these matters more fully later, but we might now introduce briefly, en route, some of the main facets. It should be stressed that, in late Renaissance Europe and, for reasons which will become clearer, particularly in Josquin de Prez (1440–1521), we have a seed-bed for vocal practice until the early nineteenth century.

It is suggested by some, including Rebecca Stewart, that the alto and contra-tenor voices of Josquin's date were (in the Low Countries at least) closely related, but distinct. As mentioned already, there are those who argue that contra-tenor was never a voice as such: that it, and the English counter-tenor, were not exact equivalents. However, the term contra-tenor does seem to have been employed to refer to the human voice, as well as to a musical part. Much later, 'contratenor' was still being used in England by Barnard and Boyce in their collections of cathedral music in 1641 and 1760–1778 respectively. Throughout her paper,[41] Rebecca Stewart equates head-voice with falsetto; the reader should study her valuable but apparently sometimes contradictory paper in its entirety.

Contra-tenors in Josquin's choirs and in their continental contemporary establishments, seem to have been French or Franco-Flemish. At another slight but relevant tangent, again looking ahead, the predominant cultural influence in Purcell's time would still be French, but always on a traditional English foundation, itself with past and contemporary Italian influence. Rebecca Stewart reminds us:[42]

> Even in the modern [twentieth-century] French 'school' of singing, 'the falsetto' sometimes comprises the entire upper range of the tenor voice, and a considerable portion of the upper range of the light baritone, as well.

Her researches confirm what others have argued, that the contra-tenor (or eventually, counter-tenor), had its origins in a two-register vocal range and use, of versatile quality and character:[43]

---

[40] Ibid., p. 309
[41] Rebecca Stewart, 'Male Vocal Types in the Music of Josquin des Prez'
[42] Ibid, p. 103
[43] Loc. cit.

> The contra-tenor is clearly a two-register singer .... Josquin's ... conscious use of ... the contra-tenor as a mixture of tenor and alto registers ...

Rebecca Stewart adds firmly that by the fifteenth century and the time of Josquin:

> ... The higher contra-tenor range is beginning to show possibilities of being appropriated by the typical Italian [male] contralto (low alto vocal-type of the later 16th century).

But she still argues that alto and contra-tenor were distinct and different voices. We will return to this later.

Because the church was still the principal centre of artistic activity, all male voice-types and ranges, including Josquin's contra-tenors, were primarily affected by sacred music and choirs, even though secular vocal ensembles thrived as well.

The traditional sound of boys' and men's voices together, and indeed the use of all voices, may alter slightly over centuries. Cultural and musical demands twist and turn. However, we must not forget that it is from this physiological, psychological and ecclesiastical choral background that the sophisticated European male high voice first came. The importance of this will recur in other sections of the present work.

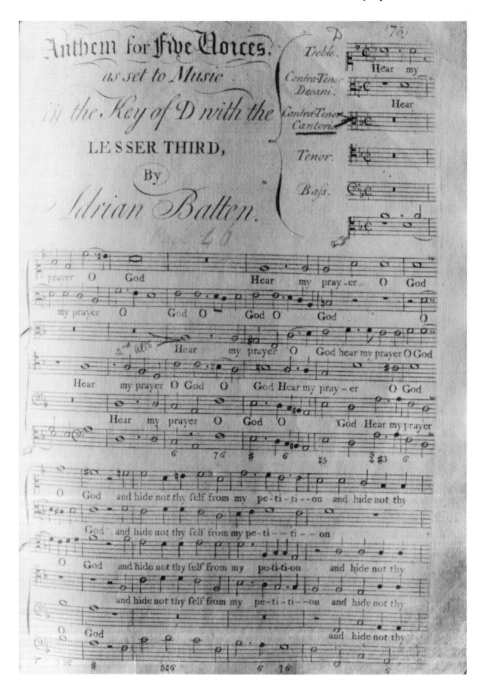

Example 12. 'Hear my Prayer', Adrian Batten (c1591–1637)
as printed in Boyce's 'Cathedral Music'
in the second half of the eighteenth century

3 Developments

Let us review the European choral situation in the early sixteenth century. In England and in other European countries, something very like our modern English cathedral or traditional male collegiate choir was in place.

Before subdivision, the standard English pre–Reformation polyphonic choir consisted of high treble, mean(e), contra–tenor or counter–tenor, tenor and bassus. Boys sang the high treble, and boys or possibly high falsettists (though not described as such) sang the mean – perhaps together? Adult means were long established. The contra–tenor altus was sung mainly in falsetto/head–voices; that is, by singers who employ pure head–voice for much of or all their range. The choir was divided antiphonally and harmony was sung by both sides.

The standard immediately post–Reformation choir comprised: mean (a medium–high compromise between the old high treble and lower mean voice parts), altus (counter–tenor), tenor and bass. Boys sang the new higher mean and men sang the other parts. Peter le Huray[1] tabulated in detail the various choral foundations and their sizes, though not their voice parts.

Post–Reformation religious demands were the main reason for the adoption, for a time, of a simple homophonic style of composition with syllabic word setting. First Lutheran and then increasing Calvinist influences influenced a powerful low–church faction who required that the new English texts could be heard clearly. Intricate polyphonic effects were obviously not appropriate to this end.

Despite this, vocal sub–divisions, especially with two alto parts (M.A.A.T.B.), were gradually re–introduced during the following decades, but the choir remained basically a four–part one. There was something of a distinction between music written specifically for the new services and the wistful, often wonderful, compositions of men like Byrd who clearly yearned for a return to former glories. Their motets and masses could never be sung in public.

The Roman church itself was not unaffected by the fashion for textual clarity in church music. Pope Marcellus II summoned the singers of the Capella Sistina on Good Friday, 1555. After criticizing their flippant behaviour during services, he instructed them to change their attitude; in future they should sing 'with properly modulated voices, and so that everything could be both heard and understood properly'.[2] This command was two–pronged: part of it concerns music of polyphonic complexity which made words unintelligible, but an equally important aspect of it seems to refer to excessive vocal ornamentation.

---

[1] Peter le Huray, *Music and the Reformation in England, 1549–1660* (Cambridge University Press, repr. 1988, pp. 14–17. See also Peter Philips, *English Sacred Music, 1549–1649* (Gimell, Oxford, 1991), *passim*, and David Wulstan, *Tudor Music* (Dent, 1985)

[2] H. Coates, *Palestrina* (Dent, 1938), p. 41

Nevertheless, during the latter half of the sixteenth century, the severity of 'for every syllable a note' became largely disregarded. Despite puritanical influences, sub-divisions, including high-flying treble parts, had re-established themselves, though not permanently. It may seem surprising, but English composers seem to have produced less of the normal four-part polyphony usual in most other European countries. The English high treble and lower mean boys' voice parts which had developed in the fifteenth century, and which were still popular in the early sixteenth, were partly responsible for the additional complexity of English music.

For various reasons, by the close of the sixteenth century in England the four basic parts still varied somewhat in terminology. In liturgical music, boys sang the highest part, which was usually labelled Mean(e) though, (it is reiterated) as in later centuries and to the present day, there may have been occasions when the male high voice was employed instead. Certainly, high-voiced men sang the next part down, the altus. Those with highish-to-medium voices occupied the next part down, the tenor, a part now rather higher-ranged than originally. Low voices were gathered on the bottom part, the bassus.

In secular or non-liturgical music, most frequently the parts had come to be labelled cantus (or superius or medius), altus or contratenor, tenor, bassus, quintus and sextus, and music written for non-liturgical use was often scored for unusual combinations of voices. Some variation from country to country existed, but particularly outside Italy the leading music publishers (including those of ayres by such composers as Dowland) remind us of what was usual: cantus, altus, tenor, and bassus. The parts, particularly those for madrigals, often appear on the same double-spread with music and text facing four different directions for the quartet of singers round a table.

In England, there was the option of the term counter-tenor (thus Anglicised) for altus. Florio (1598)[3] defines the term alto as appertaining to 'a counter-tenor treble in musicke'. This delightful mix of terms suggests that he may have viewed the high alto as counter to the treble, in the same way that the original counter to the tenor had been counter-tenor, though it is more likely a reference to 'high counter-tenor'.

We should remember that altus denoted a high part sung by a high voice. That many of the altus parts appear only medium, or even low, in tessitura can mislead. Quite apart from questions of pitch (discussed later), however low the altus part, it was still higher, overall, than the tenor by the early sixteenth century. A man singing it must mostly be in the higher reaches of his voice.

The importance attached to counter-tenors generally is reflected in the continued high proportion of them in the English Chapel Royal at the turn of the sixteenth century, where there were eight boys, eight counter-tenors, four tenors and four basses.

In sixteenth-century France, the haute-contre (alto) tradition flourished in parallel fashion. In about 1585, 'Nicholas Mauregan, Anglois' was engaged by the French royal chapel (Sainte-Chapelle in Paris) 'pour chanter sa partie de haute-contre au coeur et à l'aigle'. Hough thought Morgan was the singer of the same name who was a Gentleman of the English Chapel Royal (sworn in 1566), but there is an intriguing mystery about him.[4]

---

[3] Grove's *Dictionary*, 6th edn, p. 655

[4] See Appendix One, 'The Nicholas Morgan Mystery'. Also: Michel Brenet, *Les Musiciens de la Sainte-Chapelle du Paris*, (1910; facsimile edn, Minkoff, 1973), *The Musical Antiquary*, 1912-13, vol. iv, pp. 59-60, and David Baldwin, *The Chapel Royal, Ancient and Modern*, Duckworth, 1991

In France, until the Revolution, the musical directors of maîtrises (the choir schools of major churches and cathedrals) and the Chapelles Royales were, as in England, influential and notable in the maintainance and development of national musical culture. Of these, La Sainte–Chapelle Royale du Palais and La Chapelle Royale, Versailles, were probably the most important, musically and historically. They were the equivalents of the London–based Chapel Royal. All three establishments possessed an élite choral foundation of Gentlemen and boys. Places in these choirs were eagerly sought, competed for and, once attained, jealously prized by singers.

Michel Brenet's book about the Chapelle Royale in Paris reveals a number of fascinating points concerning the nomenclature of the singers there from the thirteenth to the eighteenth centuries. It is the equivalent of a combination of the Cheque or Check Book and official records of the English Chapel Royal. There are lists and minute detail of singers and musicians. As would be expected, during the thirteenth and fourteenth centuries there are no obvious ascriptions as to voice part or type. From the fifteenth century onwards, increasing mention is made of the voice part of each singer. Sometimes, there are lists of the full choir, with a breakdown of the voice names.

The boy choristers (*les enfants de choeur*) are referred to frequently. Sometimes, an haute–contre (high–contra, a term occasionally used in post–Restoration England) is mentioned as Maître des Les Enfants [sic] – a position, as we have seen, often historically filled by a male high voice singer, with obvious musical advantages. One such was M[aît]re Artus Auscousteaux who was listed as 'clerc haute contre' 12 December 1635, and at other dates around this time, as master of the children of the choir and master of the music. (Further biographical facts about him are to be found in Grove's *Dictionary*, 3rd edition.)

Brenet's book includes details not only of the terms used for or about the various voice parts (tenoriste, contre tenore, haute–contre, [voix de] teneur, dessus, contre, basse contre, basse, voix de taille, basse taille, (haute) taille, bas–superius), but also of the frequency or paucity of their employment between the fifteenth and eighteenth centuries. There is no mention of alto, or counter–tenor, as such, throughout this period, and only one example of 'contretenor', and this is during the fifteenth century. 'Haute–contre' appears to have been the equivalent of alto or counter–tenor. The term tenoriste is used a number of times during the fifteenth century, and the term occurs similarly in the sixteenth century, but it is never used later. The first mention of contre, used alone, occurs in the fifteenth century and it is used from then onwards until the middle of the seventeenth century. Voix de teneur occurs only in the early sixteenth century on a number of occasions, and then disappears. Basse taille, haute taille, or just taille occur from the middle of the seventeenth century until 1789.

By far the largest number of references throughout are to haute–contre, from the beginning of the sixteenth century onwards, and to 'basse contre', from 1519 onwards. Both terms survive until the suppression of the Royal foundation during the French Revolution. The last months of the foundation make poignant reading: the final entries are inventories of furniture and fittings and a list of foundation–members who were victims of the revolutionary tribunal and guillotine.

The large number of references to the haute–contre suggest a number of possibilities. One is that, from the start of the sixteenth century, singers of the tenor line were considered to be the norm and therefore unremarkable, so that though they were unmentioned by voice–part, they were represented by the individual singer's name alone. Another possibility is that the ranks of the haute–contre or basse–contre provided singers to the tenor line. (Some might argue very strongly that the disappearance of voix de teneur indicated that the high tenors were all considered to be haute–contres. Tenor technique almost certainly involved falsetto – especially with the consistently high tessituras of French tenor parts, including those written by Berlioz and Poulenc!)

What are we to make of the following, dated 1665? Voices who were to sing on a special occasion in Sainte–Chapelle were listed[5] as:

> ... Trois superius et deux bas–superius, trois haute–contres, trois tailles, un concordant, quat[r]e basse–contres et deux enfants de choeur ...

Unless 'superius' refers to male sopranos, first and second (which would seem possible, because only two boys were to sing on the same occasion), we seem to have 'superius' as equivalent of first and second altos, haute–contres as very high tenor, tailles as tenor, and basse–contres as basses. Another possibility is that the 'superius' singers, who were high and medium–high falsettists, sang with the boys, and that the alto part was taken by haute–contres – these, variously, being the equivalent of the medium/high and low counter–tenors with which we are familiar today. Finally, it is possible that the 'superius' singers included Blaise Berthod (c1610–1677), the only known French castrato singer, who was employed at the Chapelle Royale from 1634 to 1677. It is necessary to study good urtext editions of the music of Du Mont (1610–1684) and Lully (1632–1687) to understand what these points imply in actual musical practice; the whole subject is complex, and certainly not well understood, even in France.

Bearing this information in mind, together with that from various other researchers – for example, that of Rebecca Stewart and others on the music and voices of Josquin's time – there seems no reason to suppose that the French needed to lure male high voices like Morgan from England purely for lack of their own. The voice was European.

As we have seen, at least until the eighteenth century, except for the cultivation of castrati, the high male–voice tradition on the continent of Europe seems to have been similar to that which obtained in England. For many years, the notable school of Spanish falsettists had sent singers throughout the continent, particularly into France and Italy, and especially into the Sistine Chapel Choir. From 1503, when Ferdinand of Spain captured Naples, to 1700, almost all Italy came under Spanish influence. The only notable exception was Venice.

It is thought possible that the famous boys' choir at Montserrat in Spain may owe much of its past reputation and tonal quality to links with the Spanish falsetto school. Some of these very high falsettists may have come to England in 1660 to help with post–Restoration musical regeneration – one might have been a certain Damascene whom we discuss later.

Despite the usually–acknowledged musical and cultural interaction between European countries throughout the centuries, particularly those adjacent geographically, there can be surprising ignorance – a mistaken tendency to think that a tradition is unique to one country. A good example is the Frenchman, A. E. Charon, who wrote about the haute–contre in France in his *Manuel Complet de Musique*, 1836–9. He did not much like this voice:

> Charon seems to have been unaware of the English alto, for he regarded it (haute–contre or alto singing) as a uniquely French aberration.[6]

---

[5] Brenet, op. cit., p. 216
[6] Frances Killingley, *The Musical Times*, March 1974, p. 217

Yet falsettists, head–voice singers, had been commonplace in several European countries for centuries.

Why did high falsettists join and even usurp the boys in many continental choirs? Was the kind of high vocal tone which had come to be admired fiercer and stronger than could easily be obtained from boys? It may have been so, yet the following description seems to suggest otherwise. Dr Burney quotes in his *History* from a seventeenth–century writer on the subject:[7]

> Du Cange (1610–1688) in his *Glossarium ad scriptores mediae et infimae latinitatis*, derives the word 'falset' from 'Fausetum', a term used, during the middle–ages in the same sense; and this, he supposes, from 'faucibus' whence the high tones of voice proceed. 'Pipeth' was sometimes used in a similar sense to express 'piping', or such high singing as imitated the sound of pipes or small flutes. These 'feigned voices', as we should call them, seem to have been much in request for the treble parts of vocal compositions, at the beginning of the last century, when women were not allowed to sing: as appears from a letter written by the celebrated traveller Pietro della Valle to Bapt. Doni, of which more notice will be taken hereafter .... Lodovico 'Falsetto', Gio. Luca 'Falsetto', Guiseppe 'Tenore', and Melchior 'Basso', singers mentioned in this letter, had their cognomens from their species of voice. Singing in 'falset' had very early admission in the Church, during times of 'Discant'.

In the earlier sixteenth century, the highest or superius parts of most masses and motets were written for falsettists or for boys, or for both. The altus part was probably sung by what in England would be called low counter–tenors; either falsetto–tenors or exclusively head–voice singers with powerful, low tones.

Sistine Chapel choirboys from the Orphanotropia or Scholae Cantorum seem first to have been augmented and then to have been displaced by the more powerful high falsettists. They, in turn, were augmented and then displaced by castrati. We may note Du Cange's description of falsettists' 'piping tone'. 'Piping', though possibly attractive, does not seem to be exciting or necessarily fiercer than the boys' tone.

At first, it appears, falsettists were required to blend with the boys' voices, but this was neither a long–lasting situation nor the complete story. The expert falsettist's voice was (and is, with training) suited to virtuoso diminutions (improvised ornamentation) in motets, for which moderate volume is suited. However, the tone employed is unlikely to have been 'piping' on every occasion. Many tonal colours would have been available and, indeed, necessary. The vocal impact on the falsettists of the first castrato to be engaged must have been considerable, and it proved influential. We are accustomed, today, to consider the Sistine Choir's tone as appropriately full–blooded and Latin in character. Some semblance of this style must always have existed in Spain and Italy. So the explanation of Du Canges's insipid description of the Spanish falsettists may lie with the date of him who wrote it, several decades after the death in 1625 of the last Sistine high falsettist. Du Cange never heard him, or them.

---

[7] Charles Burney, *A General History of Music* (London, 1776–1789, repr. Dover 1935, ed. Mercer), p. 240

Spanish falsetto technique was a carefully kept secret. Though castrati, like most singers, employed falsetto techniques, it is generally accepted that the Spanish falsettists were not castrated; the very term suggests a quite different variety of singer. We have some of the names of Spanish falsettists and composers in the papal choir: Cristobal Morales (1500–1553), Tomas Luis da Victoria (c1548–1612), Bartolomeo Escobedo and Francisco Soto de Langa (1539–1619). This last-named is known to have preserved his voice until the age of eighty.[8]

Ludovico Viadana (1564–1645) advises employment of falsettists in his works, according to the famous set of rules he placed before his *Cento Concerti* of 1602. He claims that the said voices give an improved effect. Boys, he says, 'sing carelessly and with little grace'.[9]

The higher vocal parts of Italian madrigals were probably sung by falsettists, too (though not exclusively, because women took part increasingly in chamber ensembles), for reasons similar to those regarding their employment in sacred music.

Rimbault quotes Strype's record of the singing by what seem to have been Spanish falsettists in England:[10]

> On October 18th, 1554, Philip, King of Spain, came down on horseback from Westminster unto Paul's with many Lords, being received under a Canopy at the West End. And the Lord Vincent Montague bare the sword before the king. There he heard Mass sung by Spaniards, a Spanish Bishop celebrating, and after Mass he went back to Westminster to dinner.

Hough suggested that Byrd, as a St Paul's Cathedral chorister, might well have heard, met, and later been influenced by the Spaniards in the writing of his *Mass for Three Voices*, but surely he would not have needed outside influence to write for falsettists, however we might interpret the term? He was firmly in a tradition which already possessed them, even if the term itself does not appear to have been used in England. The English tradition generally, by the time of the publication of Byrd's Masses in the early 1590s, does not seem to have expected or employed the extremely high falsetto tessitura associated with Spanish and Italian choirs. Like other, earlier examples (by Leonel Power for instance), Byrd's *Mass for Three Voices* appears to be intended for, and most suited to, A.T.B. voices; though boy 'means' could have taken the top part had Byrd's illegal masses been available to them.

Sir Francis Drake (c1545–1596) is thought[11] to have sung counter-tenor. His father, Edmund Drake, moved with his large family from the west country to live near Chatham Dockyard, Kent, where he was a 'reader of prayers to the navy'. At the accession of Elizabeth to the English throne, Drake senior, an outspoken Protestant, became Vicar of Upchurch, near Chatham. Francis Drake, too, was a fervent Protestant. It seems more than possible that his counter-tenor label originated from his singing in church, or emanated from his later career on board ship: perhaps both. (See Appendix Eight for more about Drake, and about falsetto in English ships.) Did he ever hear Spanish falsettists? Did he, for that matter, hear English

[8] Grove's *Dictionary*, 4th edn, under 'Sistine Choir', pp. 473–6, and Hough, op. cit., p. 3, quoting Adami (1663–1743), *Observatione per Ben Regolare il Coro dei Cantori Della Cappella Pontificia* (Rome, 1711)
[9] Ludovico Viadana, *Cento Concerti Ecclesiastici* (1602), quoted by Arnold in his *Thorough Bass*
[10] *Eccles. Mem.*, vol. iii, p. 201; quoted Hough, pp. 3–4
[11] Roger Fiske, *English Theatre Music in the Eighteenth Century* (O.U.P., 2nd edn, 1987), p. 55

castrati? There was a rumour at Queen Elizabeth's court, reported by Drake, that a certain fellow Devonian, Richard Champernowne, who had a choir at Modbury Castle, near Plymouth, was 'a gelder of boys' to preserve their voices. Champernowne denied this strenuously. Apparently, Robert Cecil wanted one of his boys with a fine voice for his chapel choir at Burghley House, Lincolnshire. It might have been a court joke that got out of hand, but, if true, such a rumour has implications for the high counter–tenor tradition in England. Were some such counter–tenors really castrati in disguise? If so, the whole matter of discreet operations on boys achieved a degree of secrecy unmatched in Italy.[12]

The English lutenist composer, John Dowland (1563–1626), has been thought by some to have sung counter–tenor, though no evidence has appeared so far that seems to support this. There is even argument as to whether he was a singer at all. Most of his songs lie either rather high for counter–tenor, or low, depending on the octave used. (Though anybody who has heard, for example, Alfred Deller's early recording of *In Darkness Let Me Dwell* could surely never doubt the appropriateness of the voice–type and its vocal quality, or that Dowland would have approved.)

Shakespeare could well have had a counter–tenor in mind when, in the Clown's song 'O Mistress Mine', from *Twelfth Night*, he wrote: 'O stay and hear your true love's coming, that can sing both high and low'. Such a voice would seem apposite to the ambiguous character of the Clown, but in the absence of clearer vocal direction in the text this suggestion may be thought too fanciful.

Stage songs are usually frustratingly unclear regarding vocal designation and pitch. Despite the absence of women from the Elizabethan stage, songs for boy or young counter–tenor actors have not always been easily identifiable. However, about forty early Elizabethan viol–consort songs have been discovered; most of these are for boys or voices of similar range to sing, and many can be directly connected with choirboy actors and plays. 'Come Tread the Path', from the tragedy *Tancred and Gismunda*, seems a good example of the genre. Another is 'Sellie Poore Joas'. Both were probably written by Byrd.[13] Their vocal ranges are eminently suited to the counter–tenor; indeed, judging from their apparent pitch, they appear more suitable for him than a boy, particularly in a noisy theatre. Because, in the first song, the rôle of the singer seems ambiguous and indeed, judging by the text, could be a female (though taken by a young male), we must assume that an older or more mature counter–tenor would not be appropriate in the part. The second song is one of the popular 'lullaby' type, in this case sung by a 'nurse', which could allow for a boy, or a counter–tenor of any age. It is in the alto clef. Both songs, taken on their own, commend themselves to the counter–tenor.

John Jeffreys has provided us with useful references; he wrote:[14]

> Last week I reaquainted myself with Dekker's *Shoemaker's Holiday* [1600], and noted in Act 2, scene 3, a directive, at the end of the beer–song verse, 'Close with the tenor boy' and wondered if this could possibly refer to a counter–tenor. As it baldly stands, it is enigmatic and a paradox. In all my Elizabethan probings I never again came across a 'tenor boy'.

[12] A. L. Rowse, *The Elizabethan Renaissance: the Cultural Achievement* (Macmillan, 1972), p. 110
[13] see Peter le Huray, op. cit., pp. 219–220 and 236 (note), for further mention of choirboy plays; also John Jeffreys, *The Life and Works of Philip Rosseter* (Roberton Publications, Aylesbury, 1990), ch. II, *passim*
[14] John Jeffreys, private letter to the author, 1 December 1992

In this case, the association with a drinking song suggests a youth or young man rather than a child. The term 'boy' is probably used here, as elsewhere, generically. Theatrical usage and custom today still employs the phrase 'boys and girls' for the company in some types of production. The youth–tenor would have been light–voiced and at least partly head–voiced, perhaps a tenor–altino by later definition, though nothing was so specific in the Tudor theatre. On the other hand, if by reason of plot the above directive for 'tenor boy' referred to an older boy with unmutated voice, he might well have been using chest voice – what we today would call a boy–alto.

Earlier references to Clown and clowning bring us to Henry Chettle. He provides us with an early example of the counter–tenor in humorous vein, and a reference to the traditional mimicry of women by men:

> And now sir, to you that was wont like a Sob–sister in a gown of rugge rent on the left shoulder, to sit singing the Counter–tenor by the Cage in South- warke: me thinks ye should not looke so coyly on olde Cuckoe. What man, it is not your signe of the Ape and the Urinall can carry away our olde acquaintance?[15]

Unless 'like a Sob–Sister' refers only to the 'gown of rugge', this humorous passage could be claimed as a useful indication of an androgynous quality in the sixteenth–century counter- tenor – a quality found, indeed, in many since that time. It is the falsetto aspect of the range which possesses a bi–sexual or even a sexless character. Pitch, perhaps, is not the attribute of first significance, and we will return to this matter.

We may assume that, in street performance, the style of vocalists was often a parody or caricature of serious singers of the time. There is a theory that in medieval times, and later, musicians were employed only either inside the house or hall, or just as outside players, and that they played different types of instruments. It is thought that street singers, too, would not have been considered suitable for indoor music-making because of their vocal style, appearance and behaviour.

It would seem that falsetto, in all its varieties, was commonplace in the cries of street traders in London and other cities:

> The other cry, which was much more musical, was that of two persons, father and son, who sold lines. The father, in a strong, clear tenor, would begin the strain in the major key, and when he had finished, his son, who followed at a short distance behind him, in a shrill falsetto, would repeat it in the minor ...[16]

In thronged streets, plangent falsetto tone would have penetrated myriad street cries and noise. The yodelling milkman of only a few decades ago was a survival of the practice. In the evenings and at night, sleep would have been rendered difficult or impossible in those closely populated neighbourhoods by men and women singing, even shrieking, popular ditties of the

---

[15] Henry Chettle, *Kind–Hartes Dream*, 1592, in the chapter headed 'William Cucoe to all close juglers wisheth the discovery of their crafts, and punishments for their knaveries'

[16] Percy Scholes, *Oxford Companion to Music* (O.U.P., repr. 1961), p. 992

day. Beggars, entertainers and buskers were as much in evidence then as now.

Falsetto buskers, like street or London Underground (subway) performers today, would merely have been using the popular instrument. Now it is usually the strained voice, or sometimes folk–falsetto; or the guitar, ghetto–blaster or saxophone. It might well have been similar then: high head–voice for penetration – there being no resonant Underground passages – with optional instrumental accompaniment. Was the 'Cage at Southwarke' under a bridge arch?

Mayhew gives us vivid descriptions of street conditions in 1851; conditions which had remained comparable with those of the eighteenth, seventeenth and earlier centuries. Mayhew's reports should be studied. A coster told him: 'We are fond of music. Nigger music was very much liked among us, but it's stale now ...'[17] We note the reference to black music – an influence then, as today. Consider the falsetto nature of much of it. In Mayhew, there is also much mention of 'cat–calling' as a general description of raucous phonation. Altos have often been accused, usually in jest, of sounding like cats! (One modern canzonet for three altos is based on cat–calls.)

The London streets known by Charles Dickens rang not only with traders' cries and (genuine) negro serenaders, but also probably with crude representatives of glee singers. Here, as in other cases, ballad singers were influenced by the concert rooms and music halls. Certainly, the sexual–dialogue character of many street ballads throughout the centuries made the use of falsetto useful and appropriate.

Sebastian Westcote, the Almoner of St Paul's Cathedral, London, and the possible teacher of the composer Peter Philips, made a will dated 8 April 1582. It includes:[18]

> I give to the pettycanons of the said cathedral, to bring my body to the church
> 5 li, and to the vicars [i.e. vicars choral] of the said church 4 li.
> To the ten choirasters there 5 li ...
> ... to the poor prisoners in the Fleet, Marshallsea, King's Bench, White Lyon
> in Southwark, the two Counters, Newgate ... 6s 8d.

All these places were prisons, or used as such, but the phrase 'the two Counters' is intriguing. If it had been a former hostelry or public house, like the White Lyon in Southwark, it would seem likely to have been written 'The Two Counters'. On the other hand, the 'Counter in the Poultry' was a makeshift prison establishment, consisting of 'some four houses west of the parish church of St Mildred's in Bread Street', according to Stow.[19] Father Garnet reported that it was 'a very evil prison without comfort'.[20]

The original reference invites further contemplation. Were the two counters poor buskers, well–known in the London streets, similar to him who sang 'Counter–tenor by the Cage?' Or were they in prison? Or were they even counter–tenor vicars–choral, somehow become misplaced in the will list? Perhaps they were an intriguing combination of these? We have already noted 'the cowntur tenor at Newgat' (see page 27). There seems to have been some

[17] Henry Mayhew, *The Street Trader's Lot – London 1851* (Readers' Union Edition, p.11)

[18] *The Musical Antiquary* (O.U.P., 1912–13), p. 187

[19] John Stow, *Survey of London* (1589), ed. Thoms, pp. 99 and 131

[20] John Gerard, *The Autobiography of an Elizabethan*, trans. from Latin by Philip Carman (Longmans Green & Co., 1956), p. 234

association of this voice, or title, with prisons and prison–life. Why? Perhaps counter–tenor or high falsetto, spoken, monotoned or chanted, was a means of easier communication between cells, or to the outside world? Or was 'counter' a reference to he who counts time away? Certainly, there was recognised word–play on the term 'cownter' or 'counter' in connection with prison life.[21]

Street crier: 'Ha' ye any rats or mice to kill?' (Gibbons's 'Cries of London')

Well–known street cries, together with some gibberish, and incorporating some dance, were used in Italian villota before the end of the sixteenth century. In England, Orlando Gibbons's setting of *The Cries of London* is an 'In Nomine', a form of Fancy which has a cantus firmus of plainsong, in this case 'Gloria tibi Trinatis'. Onto this academic instrumental framework Gibbons placed a witty barrage of popular cries: those of tinkers, watchmakers and beggars – all who plied their wares in the narrow streets of early seventeenth–century London. Near the end, in the first alto part, is the plea: 'Bread and meat for the poor pris'ners of the Marshalsea, for Christ Jesus' sake, bread and meat'. It seems no coincidence that the characteristic tone of the counter–tenor voice was chosen for this sudden ecclesiastical note. The pitch and narrow range (F4 to A4) and the plainsong–like phrase, together with the straight head–voice tone so obviously intended, create a sudden pious poignancy amongst the overtly secular cries round it, perhaps to characterise lament (or contrition) and pity. There can be no doubt that its hearers would have instantly recognised a familiar effect.

Weelkes and Dering also composed settings of the cries. In that of Weelkes, the piece ends with: 'Now let us sing, and so we make an end with Alleluia'. For a useful account of street music in England and abroad, see Scholes.[22] There are also links between London cries and farce jigs.[23]

There is a valuable account by Thomas Coryate (1577–1617), the traveller and writer, of a solemn feast at Venice and an unknown counter–tenor:[24]

Of the singers there were three or four so excellent that I think few or none in Christendome do excell them, especially one, who had such a pureness and (as I may in a manner say) such a super–naturall voice for sweetnesse that I think there was never a better singer in all the world, insomuch that he did not only give the most pleasant contentment that could be imagined, to all the hearers but also did as it were astonish and amaze them. I alwaies thought that he was an Eunuch, which if he had beene, it had taken away some part

[21] See 1971 *Oxford English Dictionary*

[22] *The Oxford Companion to Music*, 1955, pp. 991–4

[23] C. R. Baskervill, *The Elizabethan Jig* (University of Chicago Press, 1929 and Dover, 1965), pp. 163, 287, 289, 290, 291 and 293

[24] Thomas Coryate (or Coryat), *Coryat's Crudities, 1611* (modern edn, MacLehose, Glasgow, 1905)

of my admiration, because they do most commonly sing passing well, but he was not: so therefore it was much more admirable. Againe it was the more worthy of admiration because he was a middle aged man of about forty years old. For nature doth more commonly bestow such a singularity of voice upon boyes and striplings, than upon men of such years. Besides it was farre more excellent because it was nothing forced, strained or affected, but came from him with the greatest facilitie that I ever heard. Truly I think that had a Nightingale beene in the same roome and contended with him for the superioritie, something perhaps he might excell him because God hath granted that little birde such a priviledge for the sweetnesse of his voice, as to none other: but I think he could not much. To conclude, I attribute so much to this rare fellow for his singing, that I think the country where he was borne, may be as proude for breeding so singular a person as Smyrna was of her flower ...

Although in previous centuries in England the solo high falsettist seems to have been commonly available, by the sixteenth and the first half of the seventeenth century, his use in English choirs appears to have become rarer. Secular solo work would have continued. Vocal needs at the Restoration, however, were to make his voice–range invaluable.

High falsettists continued unchallenged abroad, in the Sistine Choir and elsewhere, but what appeared at first to be only a small threat was destined to push them from their exalted position. The first mention of a castrato in Rome is by Luigi Dentini, a member of St Philip Neri's Congregation of the Oratory.[25] On 20 April 1558, the castrato soprano Ferdinando Bustamente was admitted to the Capella Sistina. (The date is variously reported: Haböck gives 1562.)[26] The first unequivocal reference to the admittance of castrati in the Sistina Diary is the entry for 22 April, 1599. Two Oratorian priests, each of them described as 'eunuchus', were made members of the Sistina.[27] By the end of the century, two castrati were there. Apparently, Lassus had six in his choir at the Ducal Chapel, Munich, in 1560.[28]

Whether or not the Munich alto Massimo Troiano was a castrato is not absolutely clear. His Italian name suggests either that he was a castrato or a 'Spanish' falsettist. He was a member of the Munich Cappella, and from 1567 to 1570 was becoming known as a composer of villanelle. He wrote an important account of an aristocratic wedding at the Munich Court[29] in which there is a chapter dealing with the organization and personnel of the Cappella. The singers performed Mass every morning in the Court Chapel. They were joined by wind instruments on Sundays and Feast Days.

Castrati were singing in St Mark's, Venice, by 1570. However, Elsa Scammell writes:[30]

There is a great deal of difficulty in assigning the entry of the *first* [present author's emphasis] castrato to the Sistine. The early lists give no dates of

[25] Luigi Dentini, *Dialoghi della Musica* (Romen, 1553)

[26] Franz Haböck, *Die Kastraten und Ihre Gesanskunst* (Stuttgart, 1927), p. 165

[27] Anthony Milner, 'The Sacred Capons', *The Musical Times* (February 1973), p. 250

[28] Peter Stadlen, 'Glories of the Disembodied Voice' in *The Daily Telegraph*, April 1967, reviewing Henry Pleasants, *The Great Singers* (Gollancz, 1967)

[29] There were two editions of this account, entitled *Discorsi* (Munich, 1568) and *Dialoghi* (Venice, 1569)

[30] Elsa Scammell, letter to the author, 30 August ?1984

birth, nor age at entry, often no type of voice or place of origin. – (Celari – long sections of I Cantori Della Capella Sistina, taken from the Farnasi MSS.) I do not agree with Haböck, but the subject is a very tricky one.

Fuller discussion of the castrato is to be found in Appendix Nine, but suffice to say now that with the increase of these brilliant artificial voices, the high falsettists relatively declined on the continent. The last Sistine Chapel high falsettist, Giovanni di Sanctos (or Sanctis); another Spaniard, died in 1625. By then, the Sistine Choir was overflowing with castrati.[31]

Fashion had changed in Italy. This can be learned from 'Discorso di Pietro della Valle', which was published in Doni's *De Praestantia Musicae II* of 1640. Pietro della Valle includes mention of some of the better falsettists of the late sixteenth century, such as Lodovico, who it seems possessed a lovely cantabile technique, but whose coloratura was mediocre; and Giovanni Luca, a 'gran cantore di gorge e di passaggi' with a very high range ('alto alle stelle'); and Orazietto, a falsettist who also sang tenor.[32] The seventeenth century saw the decline, but not necessarily the extinction, of the high falsettist in Italy.

In England, choir life seems to have gone on much as before. We have a useful picture of the Chapel Royal men in 1633. Besides eight trumpeters, seven basses, four tenors, two organists, eight Children, a serjeant of the vestry, two grooms and two servants, there are the following counter–tenors:[33]

Thomas Day	
Tho: Pier	
Henry Lawes	Contraten[s]
Rich[d] Sandy	
Tho: Laughton	
Nath: Pownell	

A description of the five voices, treble, mean, counter–tenor, tenor and bass, as employed in England, appears in Charles Butler's *Principles of Musick*, published in 1636:[34]

> De [the] Countertenor or *Contra tenor*, is so called, becaus it answereth de [the] Tenor, though commonly in higher keyz: and therefore is fittest for a man of a sweet shril voice. Which Part though it hav little Melodi by itself; (as consisting much of monotoni's) yet in Harmoni it hath the greatest grac': specially when it is sung with a right voice which is too rar'.

(In order to make it more clear, the original spelling has been partially modernized.)

The phrase 'right voice' might intrigue some. The term, 'right whale' – the harpooner's

---

[31] Sistine Chapel records

[32] Quoted by René Jacobs, 'The Controversy Concerning the Timbre of the Countertenor', *Alte Musik Praxis und Reflexion* (Amadeus Verlag, 1983), p. 302

[33] Andrew Ashbee, *Records of English Court Music, Vol. III (1625–1649)* (Ashbee/Scolar Press, 1988), p. 71. Dr Ashbee's edition of these important Records (which already extends to seven volumes) is a rewarding collection of information, and the reader is directed to it.

[34] Charles Butler, *The Principles of Musick in Singing and Setting* (1636), pp. 41–2

commonest quarry; that is, the standard entity – is a good parallel. It surely suggests a cultivated, natural–sounding high voice, as opposed to a demonstrably unsophisticated and unblending one. Some modern writers, however, are attracted to the idea that it refers to what they call natural tenor production, as opposed to falsetto. Others might claim that it refers to use of chest– plus head–voice technique, probably parallel to (then) contemporary Italian usage. But this technique was surely already known and used in England. A possible paraphrase of Butler might go as follows:

> The counter–tenor or contra–tenor is so called because it is in opposition or contrast to the tenor, though usually it occupies a territory higher in the scale (i.e., further up the keyboard); and therefore is most appropriate for a man of sweet high voice. Though in ensemble the counter–tenor voice has little melody in itself (as [in church music] it tends to be of one vocal colour), in the harmony it has the highest possible gracefulness – being subtle and willing to submerge its personality – especially when sung with a natural–sounding voice.

An alternative interpretation of the last sentence might read:

> Though the counter–tenor part has little melody (as its vocal progressions are often of little interest to sing), in harmony its quality and effect are such as to imbue the ensemble with maximum grace ...

Butler was enthusiastic about verse anthems and the place of solo counter–tenors in them. For him, no music was preferred above a solemn anthem 'wherein a sweet Melodious Treble or Counter Tenor singe single, and de [the] ful Qir answereth ...'[35] In Anglican choir terminology, verse–singing is the generic term for any passage sung by solo voices in any number of parts as opposed to the full choir. The term is a play on words: usually whole verses from the psalms or canticles are sung this way, and the soloists alternate, or take 'turns' (the Latin for 'I turn' or 'change' being *verso*) with verses sung by the full choir.

There is an intriguing glimpse into the singing at Lichfield and Hereford cathedrals in 1634, which includes mentions of counter–tenors. It is reported in a *Short Survey of Twenty Six Counties* ... that:[36]

> Lichfield. And no sooner were we lighted, but the Cathedral knell call'd us away to prayers: there we entered a stately, neat fabricke; the organs and voyces were deep and sweet, their anthems we were much delighted with, and of the voyces, 2 trebles, 2 counter–tennors, and 2 bases, that equally on each side of the quire most melodiously acted and performed their parts. [Michael East, or Este, was organist here in 1634.]
> Hereford. There we heard a most sweet organ, and voyces of all parts, tenor, counter–tenor, treble, and base; and amongst that orderly, snowy crew of quiristers, our landlord guide did act his part in a deep and sweet diapason.

---

[35] Butler, op. cit., p. 41
[36] Quoted by William Sumner, *The Organ...* (Macdonald, 1952), pp. 127–8

The Lichfield counter-tenor reference would appear to be much concerned with its part in verse-singing, with two of the trebles and two basses, but that at Hereford seems to describe the full choir of four parts. We might note that the authors of the Survey were military officers from Norwich, not musicians; they appear also to have been organ enthusiasts.

Example 13. 'Plead thou my Cause', Thomas Weelkes (c1575–1623)

An altogether different sort of reference to altos may be found at the Chapel Royal at this date:[37] 'Two layclerks [presumably Gentlemen of the Chapel], both altos, were criticized for slackness and incompetence ...'

During his Episcopal visitation of that same year of 1634, Archbishop Laud asked the Dean and Chapter of Salisbury if they took care to elect men of 'skill and good voices' into the choir, 'so that there be not more of tenors therein, which is an ordinary voice, than there be of basses and counter-tenors, which do best furnish the choir'.[38] In 1636, he wrote to the Dean and Chapter of Wells and urged them to elect either a bass or a counter-tenor to fill the current vacancy. The election of the tenor, he said, would be a great mistake in such a small choir as theirs.[39]

---

[37] Quoted Peter le Huray, op. cit., p. 71

[38] Quoted Peter le Huray from the 'Fourth Report' of the *Historical Manuscripts Commission*, in his op. cit., p. 120

[39] Ibid.

The Chapel Royal provides, for perhaps the first but certainly not the last time, a vivid link of a counter–tenor singer with scandal, or trouble, bad temper, violence, violent death, and yet again, by implication, with prison:[40]

> 1638. Thomas Loughton a counter–tenor [appointed 1627] in his fury slinging a payre of sizers at his wife strake her in the head whereof she dyed within 3 dayes after vz the last of December, 1638, for which he was deprived of his place in ye Chappell'.

On the European continent, both higher and lower–range falsettists, counter–tenors, or haute–contre singers, seem to have continued in choirs and as soloists outside them, despite the brilliance of the castrati. A glance at the works of Scarlatti, Buxtehude, Viadana, Marcello, and other continental composers reveals music clearly written for the counter–tenor range, both in solo and ensemble. It seems surprising that some argue that these were intended exclusively for castrato–contralto; the tessitura is mostly so comfortable and right for the counter–tenor range that this is doubtful. Study, for instance, these solo cantatas for alto: *Infirmata Vulnerata*, by Alessandro Scarlatti; and *Jubilate Domino*, by Buxtehude, to see what is meant. Of course, much of this music could have been written with either voice in mind, in the customary manner.

Following the positive lead from Italy, from the beginning of the seventeenth century, the Age of the Castrato, or Evirato, was destined to last for nearly two centuries. It would dominate church music, opera, and what today would be called the concert platform. Counter–tenors, high and low, flourished in England; this country, according to Westrup,[41] was to wait until 1668 for a castrato to appear anywhere in the kingdom:

> The Frenchman, Italian–trained, who sang in the revival of Fletcher's *The Faithful Shepherdess* in 1668, attracted great attention.

The following short summary of his areas of activity, followed by the wider survey, should vivify the foregoing accounts of the counter–tenor in England after the accession of James I in 1603.

The early seventeenth century offered great opportunities for the counter–tenor range. Cathedral and Chapel Royal demanded its almost constant use for solos or in duet, trio, or semi–chorus combinations. The secular equivalents of these, court music, odes, welcome songs, and the like, demonstrated the same interest. There were consort songs 'to the viols', or in 'broken' consorts, sacred and secular. It might seem that there were fewer songs to lute accompaniment, but the question of variable pitch affects these; the parallel use of at least two main instrumental pitches in the sixteenth and seventeenth centuries is relevant to both solo and choral singing.

So far in this book, little has been said of the organ – the instrument which until this point in the narrative has nearly always accompanied singers in cathedral or church, and sometimes also in secular music. Quite clearly, the tonal quality and character of that instrument affects singers and is itself affected by them, particularly in England; this will be discussed later.

---

[40] *Bodleian Register*, quoted D. Baldwin in private letter to author, 29 September 1992
[41] J. A. Westrup, *Purcell* (Dent, 1937), p. 96

We will conclude this chapter at the Civil War and the Commonwealth which followed it, but at this point it seems useful to look more widely at the decades before 1649. (The reader in search of a more complete account should start by referring to Christopher Hill's *The Century of Revolution 1603–1714*[42] and Eric Blom's *Music in England*.[43]) The place and function of the singer, in particular the counter–tenor, our special interest here, may be visualized through the following account. Indeed, it is arguable that the first crisis and threat to the continuation of the counter–tenor tradition in England occurred during the mid-seventeenth century.

Though usually regarded something of an anticlimax after the glories of the reign of Elizabeth I, the arts in England in the first decades of the seventeenth century were far from being in decline. Nevertheless, the traditional divide between court and city drama had deepened; this and the complex politics of the time and its intense religious conflicts were reflected in the other arts. Political polarisation worsened during the reign of Charles I (1625–1649), who possessed a 'high' and expensive enthusiasm for, and knowledge of, the fine arts. His taste extended also to lavish Court entertainments. It is easy to see how, in a period increasingly influenced by Puritan thinking, so–called élitist artistic activity would first irritate and then incense those prevented from participation in it, or those who were against it on principled religious or moral grounds.

The 'new music' inaugurated in Italy at the close of the sixteenth century by Caccini and Monteverdi and their school to varying degrees influenced English composers, including the brothers William and Henry Lawes, John Hilton the Younger, Martin Peerson, William Child, John Jenkins, Benjamin Rogers, Christopher Gibbons, Matthew Locke and Nicholas Lanier (Master of the King's Music to Charles I and eventually to Charles II; composer, painter and singer – possibly a counter–tenor).[44]

Henry Lawes (1596–1662), from a 1642 portrait by an unknown artist

Of special interest to us is Henry Lawes (1596–1662). He was a counter–tenor and a Gentleman of the Chapel Royal where he was employed as both singer and lutenist. He wrote the music for Milton's masque *Comus*, for the famous performance at Ludlow Castle on Michaelmas Night 1634, and he performed the rôle of the Attendant Spirit. He composed over four hundred songs. Secular solo vocal music seems to have become the most important area of musical activity during the first decades of the seventeenth century – a development which accelerated in the reign of Charles I. It is ironic that, despite this, Barnard's important collection, *The First Book of Selected Church Musick*, was published at so late a date as 1641.

---

[42] Nelson, 1961

[43] Pelican Books, 1942, repr. 1945

[44] See Michael I. Wilson, *Nicholas Lanier, Master of the King's Musick* (Scolar Press, 1994)

The early seventeenth–century theatre was chiefly concerned with the writing and performing of masques and these included music as a major part of the production. Occasionally, they were mere adaptations of or interpolations into plays, after the model of the Masque in *The Tempest*, but more frequently they were new, self-contained theatre pieces. The traditions of Elizabethan drama lingered on, but following the first decade of the reign of James I, social conflicts increased, official censorship tightened, and Puritanism extended its influence. As a result, the popular theatre began to decline.

Poets and writers of various viewpoints were also affected by censorship (which was in the hands of the bishops) and other influences or pressures emanating from politicians and Puritans. Important names, of which there are many, include those of George Herbert, John Donne, Ben Jonson, John Milton, George Wither and Henry Vaughan.

In architecture, Inigo Jones, originally a stage–set designer for masques, was the bringer of Renaissance Classicism to England when he created the Banqueting House in Whitehall, with its painted ceilings by Rubens, and the Queen's House at Greenwich. He also made the designs to transform the medieval St Paul's Cathedral into an outwardly Renaissance building. Archbishop William Laud's ill–timed or ill–advised attempts to re–catholicize the very protestant Church of England of that time promised new opportunities for the arts and craftsmanship in the church and, though few new churches were built in this period, church vestments, refurbishing and refitting reflected Laudian influences and preparation for increased ritual. Screens, altar coverings and altar–rails, carved woodwork, organs, and painted ceilings were erected under Laud's influence in direct opposition to Puritan and Low–Church ideas.

Under the patronage of Charles I, Dutch influence was powerful in painting, sometimes at the expense of native artists. Anthony van Dyck, Peter Paul Rubens, Daniel Mystens and Peter Lely were nevertheless followed promisingly by William Dobson (1610–1646), whose early death robbed England of a major painter.

The struggle for power between King and Parliament went on for about twenty years, between 1629 and 1649. The events leading to the Civil War which could be attributed directly to King Charles's autocratic attitude, and to the closely related political and religious attitudes of the time, brought eventual Nemesis in the persons of Oliver Cromwell and the Ironsides. Despite the determination and ill–advised optimism of its High Church opponents, Puritanism had long been an influence which threatened to engulf church and country, but only after the King was finally defeated at Naseby in 1645, and parliamentary rule became a reality, was the full impact of Puritan zealotry felt.

Even then, it would be a mistake to suppose that although the Monarchy, the Court, all episcopalian, sacramental aspects of the Church of England and cathedral and sophisticated church music were abolished; and, although most theatres were closed and public merry-making was officially suppressed, that consort music, secular singing and the performing arts generally also faded away. As Christopher Hill wrote in 1961,[45]

> Historians are now beginning to realize that the Interregnum [The Commonwealth] was no artistic wilderness.

In many ways the arts found different and sometimes unexpected means of expression. Despite sporadic desecration of churches and cathedrals, the vandalism of many organs and the

---

[45] Op. cit., p. 185

occasional burning of church music books, not all puritans were totally iconoclastic. Cromwell, lover and patron of music and portrait painting, himself enjoyed the Latin motets of Richard Dering when they were played on the organ, provided they were performed domestically and certainly not in church as part of Divine Service. Except that his father, John Milton the elder, was a musician and composer, it might at first seem extraordinary that the Puritan poet John Milton could write:[46]

> But let my due feet never fail,
> To walk the studious Cloysters pale,
> And love the high embowed Roof,
> With antick Pillars massy proof,
> And storied Windows richly dight,
> Casting a dimm religious light,
> There let the pealing Organ blow,
> To the full voic'd Quire below,
> In Service high, and Anthem cleer,
> As may with sweetnes, through mine ear,
> Dissolve me into extasies,
> And bring all Heav'n before mine eyes.

It is a vision which could not be farther from the conventional view of Puritanical theology and the reformed ethos of worship; its duality epitomizes the period.

Composers, now actually prevented from writing anthems and other service music, turned necessarily and (at least officially) exclusively to songs and instrumental pieces. Music publishing actually increased during the Commonwealth period. For example, despite the Puritan climate, John Playford's collection of folk tunes, *The English Dancing Master*, first appeared in 1651. *A Musicall Banquet*, his miscellany of rounds, catches and pieces for viols, was also published in 1651. However,[47]

> Numerous... as these works are and valuable as is the evidence they afford of
> the widely spread practice of music under the Puritan regime, artistically they
> came to very little; the taste of English composers had sadly degenerated in
> fifty years.

Though the standard of composition may have declined, there was plenty of work for musicians, including many former lay–clerk singers, among whom were counter–tenors. Some of this employment was decidedly risky. For example, though theatre buildings were closed, theatrical activity went underground:[48]

> In 1642, as part of the programme of moral reform instigated by Parliament,
> the theatres were closed. What had been a vigorous part of life in London was

---

[46] *Il Penseroso*, lines 155–166

[47] Ernest Walker, *A History of Music in England* (Oxford University Press, 1907; rev. edn 1952), p. 154

[48] Taylor Downing and Maggie Millman, *Civil War* (Collins and Brown, 1991), p. 103

taken away. Yet theatrical productions continued, in clandestine and private ways; like many aspects of life under the Commonwealth, wider tolerance was given than is commonly supposed. Soldiers would raid premises occasionally, clearing out the audience, arresting actors and confiscating costumes, but frequently they turned a blind eye until complaints were made or abuses became too flagrant.

Pre-eminent among the clandestine London theatres was the Red Bull, in the Clerkenwell district just north of the City. It had been a theatre before the wars, and came to specialize in the presentation of 'drolls', comic plays frequently with a lewd content, many written by its leading actors who always managed to stay one jump ahead of the soldiers. What the masses could enjoy the aristocrats also continued to patronize. In the private surroundings of nearby Rutland House, in the late 1650s, some of the earliest English operas like the 'Siege of Rhodes' were being performed, building upon the tradition of the Court masque which had flourished as part of the exclusive culture around Charles I. The Restoration theatre with its style quite distinct from that of pre-1642 did not appear after twenty years of total prohibition; rather it was the result of development.

Paradoxically, perhaps because the strictest aspects of the Commonwealth régime had relaxed somewhat, the first performances of opera in English and the first appearance of women on the English public stage, date from the late sixteen-fifties. For example, D'Avenant's *The Cruelty of the Spaniards in Peru*, the music for which has been lost, was performed at the Cockpit, Drury Lane, London, every afternoon for some time in 1658.

It is surprising but true that some traditionally-designed churches were built during the Commonwealth period. Sir Robert Shirley's church of 1653 at Staunton Harold, Leicestershire, is a fine and well-known example. Others less-known include small churches in the West Riding of Yorkshire and in Westmorland, built and repaired on her estates by Lady Anne Clifford, who had High Anglican and Royalist sympathies. (She also was connected with Knole House in Kent, where the private chapel is still furnished in the Laudian manner.) It seems likely that secret Anglican services were held in these and more concealed venues, after the brave example of Roman Catholic recusant worship a century before. The now-prohibited anthems and Anglican service music may well have been sung, perhaps together with some Latin motets on the basis that one 'might as well be hanged for a sheep as for a lamb'.

Singing as an activity or pastime, therefore, not only survived but probably flourished even in what has often been mistakenly regarded as an artistically barren period of nearly twenty years. No doubt many ex-choristers, displaced as boys just like the lay-clerks from choirs throughout the country, continued to sing when they grew into men. In normal circumstances, a reasonable proportion would have become counter-tenors, but the question needs to be asked: 'What impact is Puritanical thinking and policy likely to have had on singing-style?' In answer, a useful parallel may perhaps be drawn between attitudes to singing and sermon styles during the Commonwealth.

Bishop Lancelot Andrewes and his school preferred an elaborate, scholastic, learned, and highly ornate style; the Puritans demanded plain sermons, addressed to the understanding not of scholars but of ordinary men. The object of the Puritan preachers was not to impress but to convince.[49]

To the Puritan mind, partisan theology and hearty religious fervour permeated all aspects of everyday life. However, as Eric Blom wrote:[50]

> We must remember that the Cromwellian conception of the Commonwealth was not communistic or proletarian. He had no notion that a "gentleman's" accomplishments could possibly be incompatible with it, and he encouraged such accomplishments...

All sophisticated singing, and ornate styles of music, notably when paraded on stage or in church, were in danger of being associated with frippery, High Church practices, and with a politically and religiously unacceptable anti–Puritan, anti–revolutionary public affirmation. If so, the high counter–tenor may well have been considered a particularly brazen manifestation of artificiality, of degenerate cavalier–flourish and Royalist–flavoured ostentation. His performance, even in secular music, is likely to have smacked not only of the ritual practices of Laud, but worse still, hinted at those of Popery, and dare it be whispered, castration. The sound and style of the high counter–tenor was perhaps as far from down–to–earth honest singing by 'the honest man in search of his personal God' as it was possible to be.

More detailed discussion of the technical aspects of voice production is to be found in Part Two; but suffice to say here that the traditional use of head–voice is likely to have continued in normal practice as an accepted and appropriate extension to the basic male voice. But the specialist male high head–voice, of which the Elizabethans, Jacobeans and to a lesser extent the Carolinians, were so fond, probably lost favour under the restrictions of the Commonwealth, and so faded from popularity – except perhaps in the underground theatre.

Perhaps here we may discern something of the basis for the mistaken view (discussed in the next chapter) that the counter–tenor voice began only at Charles II's Restoration. Rather, while the low counter–tenor continued to be cultivated to some extent, it was the high counter–tenor voice which was not to be born but re–launched in England in 1660.

'Swash' from Barnard's 'The First Book of Selected Church Musick', 1641

---

[49] Hill, op. cit., p. 183
[50] Blom, op. cit., p. 70

4 Halcyon Days

In the event, the years following the English Restoration in 1660 were to prove especially beneficial for counter–tenor singers, in both their secular and ecclesiastical areas of operation. It is likely that those who had been lay–clerks had become more involved in secular music (and perhaps surreptitiously also in church music) and had been able to keep their voices in trim, hoping for a speedy end to the régime.

Some died waiting. We know of two in the Chapel Royal: Richard Sandy, who had been paid his stipend in 1646 and 1647 by the Committee of the Revenue, because Charles I and his court were on the run. He died 9 May 1653, and was buried in St Margaret's Church, Westminster. Thomas Day, who died 10 April 1653, was buried in Westminster Abbey. Four French musicians returned to France.[1]

Some retired. Others taught or composed music. No doubt many went through difficult financial straits: it was to be a twenty years' wait for settled times. In rare cases, such as that at King's College, Cambridge, lay–clerks and organist (Henry Loosemore) were retained by the foundation.[2]

The boy is father to the man. Lose the boys, and within a generation or two there are few men singers. Whereas, before 1640, each cathedral and collegiate foundation no doubt boasted many superb boy singers, the twenty–year gap meant that at the Restoration in 1660 there were no boys whatsoever, and so no trained treble line. This could have meant the end of the English male choir tradition (though perhaps not of counter–tenors) for ever, but the Chapel Royal gave a vital lead in the revival of the choral tradition. The Chapel, cornetts, counter–tenors and conservatism saved the situation. Counter–tenors were not, perhaps, employed principally to bolster the trebles (though some cornetts may have done so) but to provide a vocal alternative until the boys were trained to their former sophistication for solo and verse work. Male high voices naturally continued to take major rôles as soloists and chorus altos, once skilled boy singers were available again.

After a few years, choirs were re–stocked with excellent boys in full numbers. We are used to being told that before the eighteenth century the ratio of boys to men was almost exactly the reverse of what we know today. This may have been true of some choirs, like that of the Chapel Royal (though not all the Gentlemen sang at every service), but quite another arrangement was in existence at Magdalen College, Oxford, about 1680,[3] where the choir

---

[1] Andrew Ashbee, *R.E.C.M.*, vol. III, (Ashbee/Scolar Press, 1988), p. 129

[2] John B. Lott, Preface to Loosemore's *Litany* (Novello, 1902)

[3] Francis Knights, 'A Restoration Version of Gibbons' Short Service', *Organists' Review*, June 1990, p. 271

consisted of sixteen choristers and eight lay clerks. This proportion may be contrasted with those in Weelkes's choir at Chichester Cathedral in 1602 (see page 31), and at Winchester College in 1598 when there were sixteen choristers and six men. All three foundations were the average size of similar choirs today.

Yet it would seem that for a time the re-establishment of the male choir tradition was not always so successful in the provinces. Roger North (1653–1734) was an enthusiastic supporter of church music. (He was also against theatricality in ecclesiastical performance, which suggests that he would not have liked some developments at the Chapel Royal.) He recorded that, other than at the Chapel Royal, St Paul's Cathedral, and similar foundations, standards were low, that it was hard to get voices, and that teaching and training were poor. He mentioned press-gangs which obtained boys – these methods were not new: they had been employed during the reign of Queen Elizabeth I and before. Some choirs were so obviously low in standard, perhaps because they were poorly trained, that North wrote in 1728:[4]

> One might, without a desperate solecism, maintain that, if female choristers [women] were taken into choirs, it would be vast improvement of choral music, because they come to a judgement, as well as voice, which the boys do not arrive at before their voices perish, and small improvement of skill grows up in, till they come to man's estate. But both text and morality are against it, and the Roman issue of castration is utterly unlawful, and is scandalous practice where ever it is used.

North's mention of 'text and morality' shows why boys, and not women or castrati, were recruited or were press-ganged by Captain Henry Cooke and others at the Restoration. Luckily for the tradition, despite North's pessimism and perhaps the influence on him of some fashionable eighteenth-century ideas elsewhere,[5] resistance to change triumphed and the standard of all-male choirs recovered.

Since England's established church was a strange mix of Catholic and Protestant, it stood between extremes. No record seems to exist of the creation of castrati singers in England. This practice seems to have been considered abhorrent with regard to English boys, however much the foreign product was admired. The Richard Champernowne rumour (see p. 41) reported by Drake, seems to have been either unknown to or dismissed by musicologists.

In the English theatrical world, there was a fashionable interest in the artificial male voice, and this had been apparent for a long time. Shakespeare, and others, make mention of eunuchs for effect. The rôle of the Eunuch in D'Avenant's *The Siege of Rhodes* (mentioned by Pepys, 2 July 1661) was not played by a castrato singer. Presumably, he was played by a 'normal' actor who used the higher reaches of his speaking voice, including falsetto.

Giovanni Francesco Grossi (1653–1697), also known as Siface, a Sistine Chapel castrato, certainly sang in the Popish Royal chapel at Whitehall. Evelyn commends his performance there, and his singing in the house of Samuel Pepys.[6] Siface was one of the first castrati heard in England; there is some muddle over the date of his first appearance. Westrup is not clear

---

[4] Roger North, *Musical Grammarian*, 1728

[5] For instance, the appearance in 1716 of Margarethe Kayser as the first female soloist to sing in a Hamburg church choir, when Mattheson introduced her personally

[6] John Evelyn, *Diary* for 30 January 1687 and 19 April 1687

about it, and seems to suggest 1679 and 1687, as if Siface's first visit and first performance were eight years apart. The majority of informed opinion agrees that Siface first sang in England in 1687. Nevertheless, as Westrup says: 'English singers contented themselves with cultivating the counter–tenor, and winning approbation without insulting nature'.[7]

It was to be 1707, with the advent of Valentino Urbani, before castrati appeared on the opera stage in England. Though Siface's visit had had little or no effect on the English theatrical or operatic counter–tenor tradition (though what are we to know of the influence on singing style?), in the person of Urbani there were ominous signs of changes to come.

The Italian invasion of the English concert world seems to have begun in a small way in 1693. The *London Gazette*[8] announced that Signor Tosi, celebrated author of a treatise on singing (*Opinioni de Cantori Antichi e Moderne*), gave a 'Consort of Musick' in Charles Street, Covent Garden, in April 1693. Apparently, it was so successful that he repeated the event, weekly, throughout the following winter. Pier Francesco Tosi was a castrato–contralto singer held in great esteem.

Whatever was happening on the secular stage and in musical society in London, the cathedral and collegiate world continued in strictly English style. The Chapel Royal did so too, but with some important differences, to which we will return.

Following the Restoration, the familiar male–voice trio form had re-established itself strongly. Restoration and later anthems and settings are notable for their short choruses, and often florid, lengthy solos and trios for counter–tenor, tenor, and bass. Out of this situation grew the second golden age for solo counter–tenor in England; one which would last until a gradual decline from the middle of the eighteenth century onwards.

The significance of three–part music seems to be connected with the ancient mystical quality of the number three itself. George Herbert (1593–1633) wrote:

> Consort both heart and lute
> And twist a song
> Pleasant and long!
> Or since all music is
> But three part vied,
> And multiplied;
> O let Thy blessed Spirit
> Bear a part,
> With his sweet art.

Perhaps 'pleasant and long' refers to the sinuous line so beloved of English art (see Appendix Seven). Herbert was a consort player: John Aubrey noted a report that Herbert 'had a very good hand on the lute, and that he set his own lyrics or sacred poems', so it is possible that he was also a singer.

It was once suggested that the counter–tenor voice actually originated at the Restoration because of the weakness of the boys, but this view was never very credible. The theory originated in 1879, when John Hullah argued in the first edition of Grove's *Dictionary* that

---

[7] J. A. Westrup, *Henry Purcell* (Dent, 1937), p. 97
[8] *London Gazette* for 3 April 1693 and 26 October 1693

counter-tenors were first brought in by Charles II, who regarded them as a substitute for the castrati he heard while in exile in France.

As we know, the French rather disliked castrati. They preferred their male high voices to be products of the normal larynx. It seems likely that Charles II heard castrati only in Paris or Versailles, or wherever the French court was in residence. He heard Italian opera, which had been brought there in 1647. He certainly must have heard counter-tenors – there called haute-contres – and the falsettists at the Court and Chapel of Louis XIV where, as Fétis[9] confirms, castrati also sang.

The contention is obvious. Charles II was exiled from England 1646 as a boy of sixteen. He took with him memories of the English court and of counter-tenors at his father's Chapel Royal, and elsewhere. Abroad, while in exile, he heard high male or quasi-male voices, and saw to it that he restored such voices to his Chapel Royal upon his Restoration in 1660. Some commentators have suggested that it was at this point that the French type of counter-tenor, the haute-contre, took over exclusively from the outmoded English singers, but it is actually more likely, for reasons discussed at the end of chapter three, that it was the high counter-tenor – the 'high contra' and not the low counter-tenor – which was re-established from France. An examination of the records and lists relating to the Chapel Royal, London, suggests that if there was any change at all it did not involve a new voice or totally new vocal techniques – the advent of Damascene and Boucher notwithstanding. It brought, first at the Chapel Royal, new manners and new styles, and some new music which involved theatricality and flamboyance. There was increasing French influence generally;[10] Italian culture too was influential,[11] yet much of the old Chapel Royal foundation was re-established.

It is not always realised that today's shrunken musical establishment at the Chapel Royal which consists of ten Children, six Gentlemen, Organist and Sub-Organist, does not at all reflect the Foundation's considerable size and daily duties in previous centuries. The Chapel Royal was part of the Court Music, which included a large number of trumpeters and various wind-instrumentalists, drummers, viol players, lutenists, virginalists, violinists and even French dancing masters. Gentlemen of the Chapel Royal were sometimes appointed and listed as composers and instrumentalists too, in a complex system of pluralities. There were about thirty Gentlemen in total but, as we noted before, not all of them sang or played on every occasion. Though normally, today, the choir sings one service per week and there are few extra duties, services in the seventeenth century were sung twice daily as in a cathedral or collegiate church. Various studies of the records of the establishment at this period confirm the fact.[12]

Charles II certainly instituted some changes at the Restoration, notably the employment of a string band of twenty-four violin players. However, earlier species of instruments were also re-employed, and this fact implies that a totally new concept of music was not instituted, with dramatic changes to the style of singing and all that this would have implied for the counter-tenor. It appears that a real 'restoration' took place alongside some innovation. A number of the pre-Commonwealth Gentlemen were re-appointed, including only two of the counter-

[9] François Joseph Fétis (1774–1871), *Histoire Générale de la Musique* (1869–1876, unfinished), quoted by Hough, op. cit., p. 5, without exact citation
[10] See Ashbee, *R.E.C.M.*, vol. I, p. 150
[11] Ashbee, op. cit., p. 222
[12] See Ashbee, *Lists of Payments to the King's Musick in the Reign of Charles II ...* (Ashbee, 1981) and *R.E.C.M.*, passim. Also David Baldwin, *The Chapel Royal, Ancient and Modern* (Duckworth, 1990), passim

tenors, Thomas Pierce and Henry Lawes, the others being presumably by this time too aged rather than out of fashion. Lawes became Composer of the Private Musick for Lutes and Voices,[13] but he died in 1662.

In the provinces, the accent seems to have been on restoration rather than innovation, as may be seen from the Durham Cathedral music list for June 1680 in Part Two, chapter 13, pp. 262–3.

It is not usually realised that well before the time of the Civil War the Royal musicians included players of violins, a generic term for the violin family of instruments, and players of viols. The rolls of the establishment show eight violins and five viols, listed together with various other instruments.[14] We return to deeper implications of this situation later.

Two counter–tenors brought up as Children of the Chapel later returned as Gentlemen: Michael Wise (1648–1687) and William Turner (1651–1739), both composers. Wise, a versatile organist and singer, described as 'a counter tenor from Salisbury', was admitted 6 January 1676 into the place of Raphael Courteville[15] (composer of the hymn tune 'St James') and Turner on 15 July 1672, in place of Cooke. Turner was employed as 'Of lute and voice', not in Cooke's place as Master of the Children. It is absolutely clear from the records that to take another man's place on his resignation or death did not mean necessarily that the replacement was of the same voice part or official position. Place–juggling and internal politics seem to have been much involved.

At the time of James II's Coronation, Wise was suspended from the Chapel, probably because of characteristically troublesome conduct. In 1687 he became almoner and choirmaster at St Paul's Cathedral, but he still visited Salisbury where his wife had remained. After a quarrel with her, he left the house and was killed in a brawl with a night–watchman.

Of Turner, Burney later said: 'His treble voice settled to the pitch of a counter–tenor – a circumstance which so seldom happens that if it be cultivated, the possessor is sure of employment.'[16]

We may notice 'settled' and 'so seldom'. Perhaps the word 'immediately' inserted after 'settled' helps to explain this statement; or, possibly, Burney may have been thinking of the tenor–altino type. Alternatively, we may note David Wulstan's valuable observation in the 1960s:[17]

> There is yet another characteristic which the best contemporary altos share: the extremely gradual rate at which their voices broke. Singers whose voices broke more rapidly find greater difficulty in producing the typical 'counter––tenor' tone. This is one or several reasons which make research into the vocal aspect of puberty overdue ... this question is directly relevant to conditions in the sixteenth century. So ... the subject of pubertal change requires at least some consideration.

---

[13] Ashbee, *R.E.C.M.*, vol. I, p. 17

[14] Ashbee, *R.E.C.M.*, vol. III, p. 157

[15] Ashbee, *R.E.C.M.*, vol V, p. 70

[16] Charles Burney, *A General History of Music*, quoted by Hough, op. cit., p. 8

[17] David Wulstan, *Vocal colour in English sixteenth–century polyphony*, (originally published by the Plainsong and Medieval Music Society, 1966), p. 25; see also his *Tudor Music* (Cambridge University Press, 1992), pp. 223–5

The terms used throughout the records and lists for boys whose voices had gone, are almost identical with those used concerning Turner: '£30 by the year for the keeping of William Turner, one of the Children of the Chapel, *whose voice is changed and is gone from the Chapel*, beginning at 25th March, 1666.'[18] Though his voice changed gradually (as is still these days more usual than not) there was obviously a point past which the boy was deemed to have matured into young counter-tenor, if we are to believe the implications of Burney's description of him. Like Wise, experience at Salisbury prepared Turner for appointment at the age of twenty-six to the Chapel Royal.

Like other counter-tenors, he also sang on the stage and what we would call the concert platform. He was in *The Tempest* (presumably the opera by Pietro Reggio) in 1674.

The famous alto, or haute-contre, Alexander Damascene (Demascene, or Damzen) was seemingly of protestant French origin, though probably born in Italy. (The Arab implication of his surname – from Damascus? – might be significant.) He settled and sang in England from 1682, and was to take the greatly lamented Henry Purcell's place at the Chapel Royal in 1695; he was a prolific writer of songs, and died 14 July 1719. Yet Zimmerman[19] has identified Damascene as bass soloist in the first, and possibly also the second, performance of Purcell's ode *Hail, Bright Cecilia* in 1692 and 1694. A refusal on the part of singers (and indeed sometimes instrumentalists) to be pigeon-holed runs through these and other early records. Zimmerman even reports Turner as the tenor soloist on the same occasions.

According to Fétis,

These haute-contre singers sing the part next below the treble in operas.[20]

Thus, they were normally singers of the alto part. It is important to remember this in relation to the term 'haute-contre'.

In 1692, when there was a vacant lay-vicarship at Salisbury

'...the Young Man from Winchester...was judged...a very serviceable person for the Quire for that he Sang a good Counter tenour, and with good skill'. The 'young man' was therefore elected, and so established a family link with Salisbury Cathedral which still continues. The name of the young man was John Corfe.[21]

John Abell (1650–1720) is a famous name, a court favourite, one of whom we know much. He has been thought to have been one of the Children of the Chapel Royal. Certainly he was later appointed a Gentleman, both as singer and lutenist. He is also listed as player of the 'gitarr'. In addition, he was a Gentleman of the Roman Catholic Chapel of James II in Whitehall Palace, established in 1686. This establishment included a number of other Chapel Royal men. One of them was the counter-tenor Pordage referred to by Evelyn; see below. It

---

[18] Ashbee, *R.E.C.M.*, vol. I, p.76

[19] Franklin Zimmerman, *Henry Purcell, 1659–1695, His Life and Times* (Macmillan/St. Martin's Press, 1967), p. 241

[20] Fétis, op. cit., quoted by Hough, p. 6

[21] Suzanne Eward, *The Corfe Family at Salisbury* (F.C.M. Annual Report, April 1989), p. 32

included Italian castrati and French musicians.[22] Abell was renowned widely for his alto singing; he also sang abroad, notably in Cassel from 1698 to 1699. He returned to England as a stage singer and published collections of songs. Abell usually accompanied himself on the lute, and this fact raises the question of Abell's solo repertoire other than his own compositions: it presumably included classic lute songs of three–quarters of a century before or selections from anthologies, even the humorous songs from *Pills to Purge Melancholy*. It would seem that, despite what we often read today, not all earlier singers sang only music fashionable at the time. Evelyn wrote in his diary:[23]

> After supper came in the famous trebble Mr.Abell, newly return'd from Italy.
> I have never heard a more excellent voice, and would have sworne it was a
> Woman's it was so high & so well & skillfully manag'd...

Not for the first time, we may wonder at the use of the word 'treble'. Nobody would claim that Abell, aged thirty–one, had a treble voice, yet he was not a castrato. The term is surely used loosely, meaning 'high', and perhaps suggests a piping tone. We may note the allusion to a woman's voice. Unless Abell sounded like some of today's counter–tenors (good, but in timbre rather effeminate), Evelyn is telling us something of the ease and skill with which Abell sang. Congreve wrote of him:[24]

> Abell is here: has a cold at present, and is always whimsical, so that when he
> will sing or not upon the stage are things very disputable, but he certainly
> sings beyond all creatures upon earth, and I have heard him very often both
> abroad and since he came over.

We return to Abell later, in a discussion of 'secret service' matters, and a fuller account of him is contained in Appendix Ten.

Other English male high singers were welcomed abroad, for Evelyn says:[25]

> I din'd at my Lord Sutherland's invited to heare that celebrated Mr Pordage,
> newly come from Rome, his singing was after the Venetian Recitative, as
> masterly as could be, & with an excellent voice both Treble and base ...
> Pordage is a Priest as Mr. Bernard Howard told me in private.

This could mean that he sang in, or across, two registers; and/or that (apparently like Damascene) that he sang both bass and alto songs. Like Abell, Pordage was a singing–man at James II's Roman Catholic Chapel in Whitehall. He was also a priest, while Abell was a Roman Catholic layman. The Roman Catholicism and Italian experience of both singers would seem particularly apposite.

---

[22] Ashbee, *R.E.C.M.*, vol. II, pp. 16–17

[23] 27 January 1682

[24] William Congreve, *Literary Relics*, 1792; letter dated 10 December 1700

[25] *Diary*, op. cit., 27 January 1685

John Weldon (1676–1736), the composer, was another counter-tenor Gentleman, as well as Organist, of the Chapel Royal.[26]

We now move abroad again, momentarily, and in doing so we will break (not for the first or last time) the broadly chronological order of this account. Though this may upset those who prefer to see the alto or counter-tenor in English isolation, unconnected with main Continental usage and tradition, the present author subscribes to the currently unfashionable view that the French haute-contre at this period certainly involved the use of falsetto techniques and that he was the equivalent of English (low?) counter-tenor, and Italian contralto-tenor. Tomeoni (1755–1820) wrote of the haute-contre that the French tended to put them on the stage and that the Italians kept them in the church.[27]

The Italian falsettist (the term used for a singer who mostly restricts himself to pure head-register) was probably the equivalent of the English high counter-tenor, and the Bach-falsettist discussed later. We therefore include mention of the following as being members of the counter-tenor family.

Antonio Lotti (c1667–1740), the composer, was a boy chorister in the Doge's Chapel, Venice, and a member of the Confraternita Musicale di Santa Cecilia by 1687. In 1689, he was appointed 'cantore di contra alto', with a salary of one hundred ducats.[28] Unless he was (secretly) a castrato, he seems to have been in the direct tradition of Morales, Victoria, Escobedo and Soto. The influence of the original Spanish falsettists had established the Italian church's falsetto tradition or had strengthened an earlier secular one. We might suspect it did both.

In the French Chapelle Royale, use of the haute-contre continued strongly. François Couperin le Grand (1668–1733), for example, was writing for this voice. Considering the great influence that French culture and music in particular had on Charles II of England, there are interesting parallels and contrasts to be drawn between the musical usage of France and England in the late seventeenth century and beyond, despite increasing German influence in England during the eighteenth century.

The names of Couperin's singers at the Chapelle Royale are given in his *Oeuvres Complètes* (Oiseau Lyre). One name that appears there is a M. du Four, a counter-tenor, alto or haute-contre. He was evidently of some accomplishment.[29]

Another notable name, outside Couperin's time, is that of Joseph Le Gros; Burney refers thus to him:[30]

> M. Richer ... has a most charming tenor voice – but having only French music to sing, it was thrown away ... M. le Gros with a very fine counter-tenor voice becomes by his constant performance in the French serious opera more and more intollerable every day.'

---

[26] Ashbee, *R.E.C.M.*, vol. II, pp. 103 and 147

[27] Tomeoni, *Theorie de la Musique Vocale*, 1799

[28] Grove's *Dictionary*, 4th edn, under 'Lotti'

[29] See Hough, 'The Historical Significance of the Counter-Tenor', p. 16

[30] Charles Burney, *Musical Tours of Europe*, ed. Scholes, 1959, i, p. 310

Quite apart from the back-handed compliment, Le Gros presents something of a puzzle for musicologists. He is surely the Joseph Le Gros whose début was in 1764, and who eventually sang in Gluck's French operas, and whose corpulence which made his name rather apt eventually forced him to abandon the stage in 1783 in favour of management.

Further discussion is later made of the haute-contre, but articles and letters in *The Musical Times* in the mid-1970s[31] and René Jacobs's paper[32] are recommended for further study. One is drawn again to the conclusion that either the male vocal spectrum was considerably more varied in France and certain other European countries than in England, or that many misunderstandings, or the pre-occupations of musicologists with minutiae, make it seem so.

Le Gros was an haute-contre. He was therefore an alto, say some – the most recent being Ank Reinders who stated[33] without reservation that haute-contre was the French name for the falsetto voice. The current majority of commentators would say tenor; nothing is clear-cut.

We should remind ourselves that even the later haute-contre should be seen as a member of the counter-tenor extended family. Other famous haute-contres include Langez, Botelou, Rousseau, Jélyotte, Lainez and Dufrenoy. The celebrated Pierre de Jélyotte (1713-1797) was a leading singer of that range on the French stage in his day. Marmontel, admittedly a friend of the singer, wrote[34] that he possessed:

> ... the most outstanding voice one could hear, either by its volume and fullness, or by the piercing impact of its silvery tone. He was neither handsome nor well-built, but to appear more handsome he had only to sing; one could say that he charmed the eyes at the same time as the ears.

Like the English counter-tenors, Jélyotte appeared with castrati on occasions: with Farinelli and Caffarelli, for example. He was Colin in *Le Devin du Village* by J.J. Rousseau, and sang in revivals of works by Lully and Rameau. A statue of him by Ducuing was unveiled at Pau in 1900.

Thomas-Louis Bourgeois (1676-c1750) was another important French singer of alto range. In her *Companion to Baroque Music*,[35] Julie Anne Sadie describes him as a 'gifted counter-tenor' and a 'rather slender composer of cantatas and divertissements'. He was both a singer and a musical director – he was maître de musique at Strasbourg Cathedral (1701) and later at Toul, after which he returned to Paris in 1708 and sang at the Opéra and took brief engagements in provincial France and the Low Countries. His name is to be found in copies of some of Rameau's cantatas.

The haute-contre subject is very complicated. It has an obvious bearing on the counter-tenor, as we use the term today.

---

[31] Articles by Frances Killingley, Mary Cyr and Neal Zaslaw and letters from Killingley, Hill and Cyr in *The Musical Times* between March 1973 and March 1974; see also fn. 31 to p. 235

[32] René Jacobs, 'The Controversy Concerning the Timbre of the Countertenor', *Alte Musik Praxis und Reflexion* (Amadeus Verlag, 1983)

[33] Lecture at the 1990 International Seminar on the Care of the Professional Voice at the Ferens Institute of Otolaryngology, Middlesex Hospital, London

[34] Hough, op. cit., p. 17; translation by Carol Marcetteau, 1987. See the third edition of Grove's *Dictionary* for useful biographical details

[35] (Dent, 1990), p. 109

Henry Purcell (1659–1695), attributed to Kneller

Though the general opinion is that he was a counter–tenor, there is argument about the singing voice of the great Henry Purcell (1659-1695). Like Damascene, he seems to have sung bass on at least one occasion. Not only is he shown among them in illustrations to Francis Sandford's *History of the Coronation of James II and Queen Mary* (1687) but his name is clearly listed among the basses next to Gostling's. Sandford provides a complete roster of the most important singers and musicians employed at Westminster Abbey and the Chapel Royal, together with deputies where appropriate. These lists identify beyond question the various musicians shown in the superb illustrative plates he published.

Singing a variety of usually indifferent light baritone is often a choice for the counter–tenor today, but there are those who would claim that Purcell was a tenor, and may have walked with the basses at the coronation so that the procession might appear symmetrical, but this seems unlikely, as engravings also show that they did not usually bother too much about this. Alternatively, because Staggins, Blow (deputised–for by Forcer because he attended primarily as a composer) and Child are also noted as basses, Purcell might have attended in one of his other official capacities, and walked with the basses for convenience. He might well have possessed a voice of good quality throughout its (undefined) range, and hence could sing alto, tenor or bass. (To have such powers is by no means unique today and, because of seven–teenth–century vocal techniques, perhaps was more common then. However, many singers and pundits in the twentieth century find it difficult to accept that a singer need not possess a specialised voice in the modern sense.)

In 1692, Purcell is reported to have sung with distinction the superb, but low–pitched, 'Tis Nature's Voice' alto solo in the first performance of his own ode for St Cecilia's Day, *Hail, Bright Cecilia*. Because to propose that Purcell was not a counter–tenor would be rather like suggesting that J.S. Bach was not an organist, the matter should be pursued at some length.

A contributor to the *Gentleman's Journal* of November 1692 reported:[36]

> The following Ode was admirably set to music by Mr Henry Purcell, and performed twice [in that month] with universal applause, particularly the second stanza, which was sung with incredible graces by Mr Purcell himself.

According to the same journal, the Cecilian ode was repeated with similar success in January 1694. Dr H. Watkins Shaw[37] puts forward a currently fashionable alternative to the once commonly accepted interpretation of this report: that because they were mentioned at all, the graces were not added by the (unidentified) singer, but (unusually for the period) were composed by the composer himself. This is interesting, but seems unlikely for reasons which are to be explained shortly.

Though Purcell had written 'Mr Pate' by this solo in the manuscript score, Pate may well have been indisposed for the first performance. This circumstance would have made the reviewer's use of the phrase 'sung...by Purcell himself' especially apposite. A letter which replied to Shaw's suggestion raised rather different speculations.[38] But, perhaps because of

---

[36] *Gentleman's Journal or Monthly Miscellany*, November 1692
[37] Dr Harold Watkins Shaw, *The Musical Times*, March 1983, p. 166
[38] *The Musical Times*, August 1983, p. 472

Dr W. H. Cummings's rather shadowy reputation in recent decades, Shaw seems to have over-looked or dismissed Cummings's findings of 1881:[39]

> The air which Purcell 'sang with incredible graces' we are able to identify by means of various separate publications of the song. The title of one copy printed in 1692 or 1693 reads thus, 'Tis Nature's Voice (Ode for St. Cecilia's Day), a song set by Mr. H. Purcell, and sung by himself at St. Cecilia's Feast in 1692, the words by N. Brady.'

The present author has not been able to examine this copy (which Simon R. Hill confirms is of the song only and not the complete work), but we may note with interest Cummings's use of 'printed' after 'title', and his repetition of the phrase with which we are concerned. Cummings was not always reliable. If the word had been 'written', we would have had to ask when? If the inscription occurs on a copy printed contemporaneously with the date of the first performance it would seem to clinch the matter. A chance to examine the copy to which Cummings refers would be welcome.

(William Hayman Cummings (1831–1915) was originally an alto but later a tenor singer. He sang at The Temple Church from 1853 to 1867, and was a Gentleman of the Chapel Royal from 1865 to *c*1872. He was appointed Principal of the Guildhall School of Music in 1896. He seems to have made a number of enemies, including Arnold Dolmetsch, and has been regarded as unreliable by the musicological establishment for decades. It may be that the time has now come for at least some re-appraisal of him in his late nineteenth-century context.)

More intriguing still, there is a transposed version (done by Purcell?) of the top part only of the duet 'Hark Each Tree', from the same 1692 ode. Transposition makes the piece suitable for low counter-tenor. (See Appendix Seven, 'The Male High Voice as Artistic, Visionary and Symbolic Phenomenon'.)

Seventeenth-century usage regarding appoggiaturas and graces is covered usefully by Tosi and repays our attention. It is surely apposite to the Purcell case:[40]

> If the scholar be well instructed in this, the appoggiaturas will become so familiar to him by continual practice that by the time he is come out of his first lessons he will laugh at those composers that mark them, with a design either to be thought modern or to show that they understand the art of singing better than the singers. If [composers] have this superiority over them, why do they not write down even the graces (which are more difficult and more essential than the appoggiaturas)? But if they mark them that they may acquire the glorious name of a *virtuoso alla moda* or a 'composer in the new style' they ought at least to know that the addition of one note costs little trouble and less study. Poor *Italy*! Pray tell me: do not the singers nowadays know where the appoggiaturas are to be made, unless they are pointed at with a finger? In my time their own knowledge showed it them. Eternal shame to him who first introduced these foreign puerilities into our nation, renowned

---

[39] W. H. Cummings, *Henry Purcell* (Samson Low, Marston & Co. Ltd., 1881), p. 66

[40] Pier Francesco Tosi, *Observations on the Florid Song, c*1730 (modern edn, Pilkington, Stainer & Bell, 1987), p. 13

for teaching others the greater part of the polite arts, particularly that of singing! Oh, how greater weakness in those that follow the example! Oh, injurious insult to your modern singers, who submit to instructions fit for children! Let us imitate the foreigners in those things only where they excel.

Mr G. [Galliard, Tosi's London editor:] In all the modern Italian compositions the appoggiaturas are marked, supposing the singers to be ignorant where to place them. The French use them for their lessons on the harpsichord, &c, but seldom for the voice.

Tosi's *Opinioni de'cantori antichi e moderni* was published in 1723. It was reissued in an English translation in 1730, and is a treatise which should 'be regarded as an authoritative guide to the late 17th and early 18th centuries in all matters of embellishment and interpretation: to the Baroque style proper', as Pilkington, the modern editor, puts in his preface. 'As a renowned exponent of the old bel canto style', he says, 'he was naturally critical of the 'moderns' but nevertheless his views were thought worth publishing in translations right up to the late 1750s'.[41]

Purcell's own attitude to singers' gracing songs is recorded. Cummings records the following anecdote by Tony Aston, in his *Brief Supplement to Colley Cibber*:[42]

As Mr. Verbruggen had nature for his directness in acting, so had a known singer, Jemmy Bowen, the same in music. He, when practising a song set by Mr. Purcell, some of the musick told him to grace and run a division in such a place. 'O let him alone,' said Mr. Purcell; 'he will grace it more naturally than you or I can teach him.'

This surely indicates that graces were not written out.

Included in his posthumous *A Choice Collection of Lessons* (1697), and transcribed in a modern edition,[43] are Purcell's own 'Rules for Graces'. These (though related to the keyboard) together with Tosi's opinions, Cummings's information and the Bowen/Purcell anecdote surely answer all questions regarding 'Tis Nature's Voice', as sung with 'graces by Purcell himself'. However, if still it be argued that, despite convention, graces were in this instance written out, the phrase in question could be explained as meaning either that the composer, as soloist, had inserted (further) graces as he went along, as was customary, or that he was singing those already written and printed in his own text.

Another portrait and aspect of Purcell as a singer–composer comes to us by way of Cummings. He writes[44] of the opera *Dido and Aeneas* that:

There is a tradition that the part of Belinda (or Anna), written for alto voice, was sung and acted by Purcell himself. In 1794, S. Harding published a portrait of "Henry Purcell, musician and <u>actor</u>", copied from the original in

---

[41] Tosi, op. cit., preface. See also W. Dean, ed. *G. F. Handel: Three Ornamented Arias* (London, 1976) and W. Dean, 'Vocal Embellishment in a Handel Aria', *Studies in Eighteenth Century Music: a Tribute to Karl Geiringer*, ed. H. C. Robbins Landon (New York, 1970), pp. 151–9

[42] Cummings, op. cit., p. 67

[43] Howard Ferguson, *Keyboard Interpretation* (Oxford University Press, 1974), p. 116

[44] Cummings, op. cit., p. 33 fn.

Dulwich College. I have made a diligent search for the portrait without
success. – W. H. C.

We presume that Cummings, in using the word 'published', is referring to Harding's engraved
version of the portrait. Purcell might well have been an actor but it seems at first unlikely that
he would have appeared in *Dido*. For one thing, Charles II had decreed in 1662 that men were
no longer to be allowed to imitate women on the stage, at least in serious rôles – this
command was later ignored and then overtaken by the sexual ambiguities of eighteenth–
century theatre. For another, in the traditional view, *Dido* was written for a Chelsea girls'
school. On the other hand, recent research[45] has suggested that it originated five years before,
and was revived for Chelsea. Whatever the case, it is possible that Purcell took rehearsals and
occasionally supplied the part of Belinda in his alto voice. Alternatively, he may have sung
the Sorceress part in his chest–voice and so caused the apparent confusion. Indeed, he may
well have sung both parts, and caused even more.

In their article,[46] Price and Cholij suggest an intriguing 'bass sorceress' scenario, too
involved to discuss in depth. Their thesis should be studied in detail, but they suggest the
possibility that a bass–baritone's (a 'Mr Wiltshire') singing the Sorceress opens up the idea of
a counter–tenor's singing Belinda/Anna. Could it therefore have been Purcell himself, or have
the names somehow become confused and the subject forgotten in the intervening centuries?
Cummings edited the Purcell Society's first edition of *Dido and Aeneas* in 1889, and for this
he used the first–ever printed edition of the opera – a so–called 'concert version' by Macfarren,
published in 1841. In turn, Macfarren seems to have been popularising and publishing a
version based on four related eighteenth–century manuscripts, the earliest being of 1784. One,
of 1787, was linked closely with an earlier manuscript in the hands of John Hindle, the
counter–tenor. This conflated eighteenth–century version of *Dido* has a bass Sorceress, a tenor
Sailor and First Attendant, in addition to transposing Belinda (called Anna, exclusively) down
an octave, into counter–tenor.

Price and Cholij also point out that evidence has emerged recently to suggest that a bass
Sorceress in *Dido and Aeneas* can be traced back to within eleven years of the 1689 Chelsea
performance. This closeness to the original date seems highly relevant. (Development of the
male sorceress or witch was a feature taken up by pantomime.) The part of Anna is placed
very low in the alto clef. The tessitura is that of a low counter–tenor. The rôles of (Anna)
Belinda and Sorceress (or Witch) were written originally for soprano and what would today
be termed a mezzo–soprano.

Macfarren's version of the duet between Anna and An Attendant ('Fear No Danger') is
identical in style and pitch to Purcell's counter–tenor duets. It includes a figured bass and
resembles the familiar Purcellian A.T.B. trio; indeed the piece appears as a men's glee–trio in
early eighteenth–century collections. (Later in the century, it was included as a three–part glee
for men, in a pastiche called *The Prophet* of 1788).[47] These glee collections, which originated
not long after Purcell's death in 1695, include 'Fear No Danger' not solely, perhaps, because
of its lively tune but because it is stylistically similar to Purcell's trios.

[45] It has been suggested that Blow's *Venus and Adonis* and Purcell's *Dido* were written as
companion pieces (they have a similar cast)
[46] Price and Cholij, 'Dido's Bass Sorceress', *The Musical Times*, November 1986, pp. 615–8
[47] Fiske, *English Theatre Music of the Eighteenth Century* (O.U.P.), p. 540

Perhaps Cummings is correct even regarding Chelsea; for, other than in rehearsal, Purcell might also have supplied Anna/Belinda in performance, deputizing for an indisposed young soloist. (At the première of Macbeth, given in 1606 before James I, the boy actor playing Lady Macbeth was struck by a fever, and Shakespeare himself is said to have taken over the part at short notice.) If *Dido* was first given elsewhere, and as early as 1684, then there would be raised intriguing speculations about who might have commissioned the work, for whom and where.

If Purcell was involved personally in gender reversal on stage, could he have conceived the second version of Mopsa, involving the counter-tenor Mr Pate 'in Woman's habit', in *The Fairy Queen* because of his experience with Belinda and the Sorceress? Probably not directly. Mopsa's real ancestry lies in classical theatre, Medieval farce and the traditional, inveterate vocal mimicry of women by men. Purcell's 'Corydon and Mopsa' duet incorporates an existing popular comic form. Mopsa's opening phrase is 'Why how now, Sir Clown, what makes you so bold?' The pert or scornful maiden (often made grotesque), and clownish or wanton lover were stock figures in popular, often bawdy, ballads in England and in variants on the continent. Shakespeare, for example, included a 'Clown and Mopsa' comic scene in *The Winter's Tale*, Act 4, scene 4. Other characters were Autolycus and Dorcas; she, like all Shakespeare's female characters, was played by a man, youth or boy. Mopsa, Dorcas and Autolycus sing a three-part 'dialogue' song. In seventeenth-century Roman opera, which barred women from the stage, a tenor took the stock part of an old woman, while a bass took that of an old man; but what sort of voice was the tenor? This stock comic couple became very popular.

Purcell's Mopsa, played by 'Mr Pate' (John Pate) sang his duet with the character Corydon, taken by the bass 'Mr Reading', in 1692. He is also recorded as having sung the song allotted to 'Summer' in the same work. Cummings tells of altogether another kind of duo, when they were involved in a riot at the Dog Tavern, Drury Lane, in 1695. They were both dismissed from the Playhouse, and later reinstated.[48] Pate, again dressed 'in drag' (as we might say today), took the part of the Wife to Leveridge's Clown in the after-piece to *The Island Princess* in 1699. It was a comic and suggestive dialogue in the 'Corydon and Mopsa' mould. (Leveridge also doubled the rôles of Pluto and First Witch in the pantomime *Harlequin Sorcerer* at Lincoln's Inn Fields theatre in 1725.[49] It is quite possible that he sang them using different voices.)

Leveridge worked the 'theatrical jigg' in Dublin for some time. He became familiar with the urban theatrical music repertory there. As Joan Rimmer explains: 'Theatrical jiggs were after-pieces and entr'actes; whether in the apparently older sung and danced form, or in the later sung dialogue form, their essence was to present a dramatic situation or relationship, generally comical, often lewd, and not necessarily related in any way to the main piece'.[50] The reader interested to know in more detail about the jigg or jig, and related song-drama,

---

[48] Cummings, op. cit., p. 63

[49] Fiske, op. cit., p. 81

[50] Joan Rimmer, 'Carole, Rondeau and Branle in Ireland, 1300-1800', *Dance Research*, VIII/,2, Autumn 1990, p. 37

farce–jigs, dialogue–ballads, jests and novella plots, and their relevance to our topic, should study Baskervill's work on the subject.[51]

Pate was evidently fond of, and successful in, such rôles. He sang in Purcell and Dryden's *The Indian Emperor* of 1691–2, and sang the song 'I looked and saw in the Book of Fate', playing the part of Kalib as a woman. He was involved, too, in 'A Dialogue Between a Town Sharper and his Hostess' with Leveridge. The music, published in D'Urfey's *Pills to Purge Melancholy*, was by Daniel Purcell.

Apart from a fondness for comic drag rôles, Pate seems to have been additionally wayward and prone to trouble. In 1700, he was in serious difficulties. Luttrell's diary[52] records:

> Letters from France say, that Mr. Pate, who belonged to the playhouse here and sung so fine, is committed to the Bastile at Paris for killing a man, and that he is condemned to be broke on the wheel.

It would seem that he managed to escape or had been pardoned because he was certainly in London again three years later. A Drury Lane concert announcement stated in 1703 that 'Mr Pate (having recover'd his Voice) will perform several songs in Italian and English.'

(As late as 1851, Mayhew was to report a visit to a temporary 'theatre' in a broad street near Smithfield Market, London. It was set up for street traders and the lower end of the working poor. Entertainment was of a crude character: 'There was one scene yet to come, that was perfect in its wickedness. A ballet began between a man dressed up as a woman and a country clown. The most disgusting attitudes were struck, the most immoral acts represented, without one dissenting voice.'[53] We return to trans–sexual rôle–play on the stage at various points in this work.)

Evelyn mentions Pate, just returned from Italy, but apparently misnames him:[54]

> I dined at Mr Pepyss, where I heard that rare voice of Mr <u>Pule</u>, who was lately come from <u>Italy</u>, reputed the most excellent singer, ever England had: He sung indeede many rare Italian Recitatives, (etc) & several compositions of the last Mr Pursal, esteemed the best composer of any Englishman hitherto:

Handwriting being what it is, it has been suggested by Hough and others that 'Pule' is almost certainly 'Pate', and in fact the 1959 Oxford University Press edition of Evelyn's *Diary* has 'Pate' without question. A John Pate was buried in Hampstead Churchyard, 14 January 1704. The burial register described him as 'belonging to ye old Playhouse'. Though it has not been possible to examine Evelyn's original entry, it seems likely that 'Pate' was 'Pule'. The meaning of 'pule' is to cry, or weep. The languishing tone available to the counter–tenor may have encouraged a mis–reading of Evelyn's writing into an unintended but appropriate pun.

---

[51] Baskervill, *The Elizabethan Jig* (University of Chicago, 1929; Dover edn 1965), especially ch. 4, pp. 174, 180 (fn. 4), 203 (regarding Pate, Daniel Purcell and D'Urfey), 208 (fn. 1, referring to 'Mr Bowman and Mr Dogget in Womens Cloaths'), 209 (fn. 1) and, especially, p. 210

[52] Baldwin and Wilson, 'Alfred Deller, John Freeman and Mr Pate', *Music and Letters*, 1969, p. 107

[53] Mayhew, op. cit., p. 28

[54] *Diary*, 30 May 1698

Purcell composed eight songs in 1688 for a comedy by D'Urfey, *The Fool's Preferment, or The Three Dukes of Constable*. Among these was the well–known song 'I'll Sail upon the Dog Star'; they were sung by a William Mountford, of whom Colley Cibber (1671–1757) wrote:[55]

> William Mountford sang a clear counter–tenor and had a melodious warbling throat .... His voice was clear, full, and melodious.

Mountford, it would seem, was a low–ranged counter–tenor, and a favourite actor and singer with the public. He was also a dramatic author and enjoyed an appropriately dramatic life and death:[56]

> His career was brought to an untimely end in his thirty second year by Lord Mohun and Captain Hill, who murdered him in revenge for the part he took in preventing the abduction of the celebrated actress, Mrs. Bracegirdle.

According to Evelyn's Diary for 4 February 1693, Lord Mohun was acquitted. Zimmerman[57] gives a fuller account of the case. Mountford seems to have been a friend of Purcell.

To the sensitive, the presence of other favourite altos of the period may be felt in manuscripts and printed copies, though they are named only occasionally. We do know the four counter–tenor soloists who took part in the first performance of Purcell's ode for the birthday of the Duke of Gloucester (*Who can from Joy Refrain?*, 1695); they were Damascene, Robert, Turner and Howell. John Howell is a great name, styled by Purcell himself as 'the high countra–tenor' who 'takes the high D with agility'.[58] One of his appointments was as a Gentleman of the Chapel Royal, admitted as 'private musician of the voice' in 1697.[59] The Purcell Society edition tells us:[60]

> Mr. John Howell, a celebrated counter–tenor singer, who took part in many performances of Purcell's works, notably the '*Cecilia Ode*', 1692. He was appointed Epistoler in their Majesties' Chapel Royal, by Warrant from the Right Reverend the Lord Bishop of London, Dean of the Chapel[,] on the 1st October, 1694; and by virtue of four Warrants from the Dean, was sworn Gentleman of the Chapel, in full place, in the room of Mr. Bowcher, December 10th, 1695. He died July 5th [*sic*], 1708.

The 1692 ode requires first and second solo counter–tenors. Howell's range would seem to have been better suited to the higher part. *The London Gazette* for 29 December 1698 announced that 'On Wednesday next will be performed at York buildings, Mr. Daniel Purcell's

[55] Colley Cibber, *Apology for the Life of Mr. Colley Cibber, Comedian* (1740), quoted in Cummings, op. cit., p. 47; new edn, J. C. Nimmo, 1889
[56] Cummings, loc. cit.
[57] Zimmerman, op. cit., pp. 216–8
[58] Hough, op. cit., p. 9
[59] Ashbee, *R.E.C.M.*, vol. II, pp. 59–61
[60] quoted Hough, op. cit., p. 9. He and/or The Purcell Society misprinted the date of Howell's death

musick, made for last St. Cecilia's Feast, for the benefit of Mr. Howell and Mr. Shore, with an additional of new vocal and instrumental musick.' (John Shore was a famous trumpeter, who was also a lutenist and a member of the Chapel Royal Musick and the inventor of the tuning fork.)

Simon R. Hill has confirmed that Howell is buried in the south–east corner of the crypt of St Paul's Cathedral and that his grave is inscribed:

HERE LYES INTERR'D Ye BODY / OF Mr IOHN HOWELL WHO / FROM HIS YOUTH WAS EDUCATED IN / Ye DIVINE SERVICE OF Ye CHURCH & / BLESS'D Wth A VOICE SUITABLE TO / THIS EMPLOYMENT.
HE HAD Ye HONOUR TO SERVE KING / WILLIAM & QUEEN MARY & / HER PRESENT MAJESTY QUEEN / ANNE AS GENTLEMAN OF THE / CHAPEL ROYALL WITH GREAT / APPROBATION. HE WAS ALSO ONE OF / Ye GENTLEMEN OF Ye CHOIRE IN Ye / COLLEGIATE CHURCH OF ST PETERS / WESTMINSTER & IN THIS OF ST / PAULES. HE DEPARTED THIS LIFE / IULY Ye 16 1708 IN Ye 38TH YEAR / OF HIS AGE.

We have scant knowledge of the 'Mr Bowcher' (otherwise known as Boucher, or more usually, Bouchier) whose name appears on Purcell's scores, and whose Chapel Royal place was taken by Howell in 1695. Josias Boucher seems to have been of French birth, like Damascene. He may have arrived from France after the Restoration. Equally, his family may have lived in England for a few generations. In Canterbury Cathedral, on the wall of the Huguenots' Chapel in the undercroft, there is a definitive list of protestant families who found refuge in Canterbury during the French persecution of the Huguenots in the middle of the sixteenth century. The name Labouchere is included in this list. Sir Frederick Bridge[61] also mentions a 'Mr Labouchere', who lived in a house abutting the cloisters of Westminster Abbey in the late nineteeth century.

'La bouchère' means 'the butcher's wife', or 'female butcher'. There are still many Bouchers, Bouchiers, Bowshers (and other variants) in East Kent, and a Thomas Bourchier was Archbishop of Canterbury from 1454 to 1486. (An added coincidence, one of many to be encountered during the course of this work, is that *bouche* means 'mouth', 'lips', 'tongue', or 'voice'.) Could Josias Boucher have been a Canterbury or Rochester chorister and/or lay clerk, before going to the Chapel Royal?

John Freeman (1666–1736), a Gentleman of the Chapel Royal who was admitted to full place 30 December 1702, was another favourite solo alto for whom Purcell wrote much.

Francis Hughes (1666/7–1744) is an important singer who appears often in connection with Purcell, and later with Handel's scores for the Chapel Royal. He was eventually first (or senior) high voice of the Chapel. John Hawkins is quoted[62] as reporting that Hughes's strong counter–tenor voice could 'with ease' break a drinking glass. It is not clear whether this was a rhetorical or factual claim. Donald Burrows[63] points us to what seems to be another, less happy, aspect of Hughes:[64]

[61] Frederick Bridge, *A Westminster Pilgrim* (Novello/Hutchinson, 1918), pp. 166–7
[62] In Grove's *Dictionary*, 6th edn, p. 766
[63] D. Burrows, 'Handel and the 1727 Coronation', *The Musical Times*, CXVIII, 1977, pp. 46 ff.
[64] Chapter Minutes, Westminster Abbey, 14 November 1727

Order'd. That an Action be brought against Hues in the Name of the Dean
for Assalting and refusing his Ldp Entrance into the Choir the day of the
Performance of Musick there against their Majties Coronation.

A happier reference to him dates from 1708:[65]

Francis Hughes held two places simultaneously from 1730 because of 'his
extraordinary skill in singing and his great usefulness to the choir in the
performance of verse anthems'.

Could Hughes be the singer 'of the King's Chappell' in this next reference? Dean Swift of St
Patrick's Cathedral, Dublin, was having difficulty in filling two vacancies (of two years'
standing) in his cathedral choir. He wrote to his friend, Dr Arbuthnot in London, and Arbuthnot replied: 'It is mightly hard to gett such a sort of Voice. Ther is an excellent one at the
King's Chappell, but he will not go. The top one in the world is in Bristol Quire, and I beleive
[sic] might be manag'd'. Frank Ll. Harrison, who was himself a chorister of St Patrick's Cathedral, thought that one of or both these vacancies was for a counter–tenor. If so, who the
Bristol singer was is difficult to conjecture; but he at the Chapel Royal may well have been
Hughes or the equally renowned Elford. If Swift wanted particularly distinctive or distinguished singers, he may have been prepared to allow two–year vacancies in his cathedral choir.

The first of a succession of castrati had arrived here in the late seventeenth century.
Though there was no real challenge to the English counter–tenors at first, the castrati's
invasion intensified at the start of the eighteenth century. Hughes's experience is a case in
point. We know that he was Ormondo in *Arsinoe* (1705), that he was in *Camilla* (1706), and
that he played Sir Henry in *Rosamund* in 1707; but in December 1707 the great Hughes,
instead of taking the male lead, was relegated to be the understudy of Valentino Urbani, the
castrato, as Orontes in *Thomyris*, a part described as 'a countra–tenor'! Burney gives us useful
detail:[66]

But before a character is given of the great foreign singers who arrived here
after the Italian opera was firmly established in this country, it is justice to
say something of the English singers, who were able by their performance to
excite curiosity, give pleasure and set censure at defiance, when the opera was
in its infancy, and regarded by some as an idiot, and by others as a shapeless
monster ...
... Mr Hughes had been a favourite singer at concerts, and between the acts
of plays. For several years he was assigned the part of first man, in the first
opera that ever was performed on our stage in the Italian manner. His voice
was a counter–tenor, as we are told in the dramatis personae of *Thomyris*;
and, indeed, as the compass of his songs discovers. He continued to perform
the first part till the arrival of Valentini, after which no further mention is
made of him, either in opera or concert annals.

---

[65] David Baldwin, *The Chapel Royal, Ancient and Modern* (Duckworth, 1990), p. 416, quoting from
The Old Chapel Royal Cheque Book

[66] Charles Burney, *A General History of Music* (1776–1789; modern edn Mercer, 1935/Dover
1957), p. 666

The celebrated Richard Elford (sworn as Gentleman 10 November 1702 and who died 1714; of whom more later – see also Appendix Two), preceded Hughes as first high voice of the Chapel. The two were Handel's earlier choices as principal alto soloists since both were established before he arrived in England.

The part of David in *Saul* was originally sung by a Mr Russell, of whom we have no further knowledge. Walter Powell (1697–1744) is a more celebrated counter–tenor name; of whom more later.

The Irish counter–tenor, William Lamb, of Christ Church Cathedral, Dublin, is not only known to have been one of the original *Messiah* soloists but also as another temperamental counter–tenor: a man with a violent temper. W.H. Grindle[67] describes one instance:

> [The vicars–choral, and certain organists of the cathedral] ... were from time to time guilty of verbal and even physical abuse. Such instances of mis–conduct usually took place outside the cathedral. However, there were occasions on which emotions overcame respect for the consecrated building and its sacred ceremonies. In March 1737 John Church, then a stipendiary at Christ Church Cathedral, registered a complaint against one of his peers, William Lamb who had allegedly abused him, using 'opprobrious language' and had 'threatened to beat him in a violent manner in the time of divine service in the church'. Both were called and examined by the Dean and Chapter; Lamb was found guilty and a fairly standard sequence of disciplinary procedures was followed. Lamb was ordered to apologise to Church in the presence of the assembled body, and a first monition was issued. Having failed to comply with this order, Lamb was 'suspended for such obstinacy and misbehaviour during the dean's pleasure'. By 15th April Lamb and Church had been reconciled, and the latter applied to the Dean and Chapter for a pardon for his colleague. 'Both having received the holy communion together', it was agreed that Lamb's suspension should be lifted 'provided Lamb make his submission to the chapter for his disobedience to them'.

A real reconciliation must have been achieved, for the Reverend John Church, tenor, was one of Lamb's fellow soloists in the first performance of *Messiah* five years later.

When using English counter–tenor singers as soloists, Handel wrote that he thought them 'equal to the Italians' (the castrati).[68] He numbered counter–tenors among his friends, including Thomas Barrow, a Chapel Royal counter–tenor. Barrow had been a Child of the Chapel Royal and was a Gentleman from 1746, and a music copyist. In his biographical notes, Edward Rimbault wrote:[69]

> His voice was a high, loud counter–tenor. He was leader of the altos in the Oratorios, while under the management of Handel; this great composer admiring him for the strength of his voice and his steadiness. Barrow was a

---

[67] W. H. Grindle, *Irish Cathedral Music* (The Institute of Irish Studies, The Queen's University of Belfast, 1989), p. 41

[68] Frederic Hodgson, 'The Contemporary Alto', *The Musical Times*, April 1965, p. 294

[69] Edward Rimbault, *Cathedral Music*, 1847, vol. 1

good musician, and wrote several anthems and chants, besides the excellent Service. He died in the year 1789.

Another of Handel's friends was William Savage, who was both solo counter–tenor on the stage and a Chapel Royal bass. Nevertheless, Handel continued to help erode the traditional

position of the counter–tenor. It was part of the beginning of a long, fashionable period of English musical self–effacement. Handel, who had settled permanently in England, exerted enormous influence; in opera it was always towards the Italian style. Consequently, his imported castrati took over the operatic scene as celebrities, even prima donnas, and left the less demanding solo work, and all chorus work, to English counter–tenors. Handel's part in the establishment of English oratorio, however, was less influenced by his Italian experience than by Purcell and the English tradition. Nonetheless, he did begin to substitute women for men in alto solos both in opera and oratorio. This was not part of the English tradition.

In fact, Handel's approach to the designation of soloists was unusual. It is known that he intended his alto solos to be sung either by castrati or by counter–tenors, but they were sung more and more frequently by women as time went on.

Thomas Barrow; from a painting in the Chapel Royal Archive.

Mrs Cibber, the celebrated actress, who had developed a moderate but effective singing voice and certainly had exploited her undoubtedly superb platform presence, shared the alto solos with male singers in the first performance of *Messiah* in Dublin, on the 13th of April, 1742. All the solo arias for each voice were shared:[70]

> It is thought that for the first and/or subsequent performances, Signora Avoglio and Mrs Maclaine shared the soprano solo parts; Mrs Cibber, William Lamb(e) and Joseph Ward the contralto part; James Baileys and John Church the tenor; and John Hill and John Mason the bass. All the men except Mason (who was only in the service of Christ Church Cathedral) were members of both cathedrals.

---

[70] H. C. Robbins Landon, *Handel and his World* (Weidenfeld & Nicholson, 1984), p. 187

The counter–tenors of the two cathedral choirs provided the alto line in the chorus.

Both Harold Watkins Shaw[71] and Richard Luckett[72] have given useful indications of how these solos were allocated in other early performances. Robbins Landon continues:[73]

> Mrs Cibber's performance of 'He was despised' must have been magnificent (we must remember she was a great actress); it is reported that the Rev Dr Delany was moved to shout, after hearing it, 'Woman, for this thy sins be forgiven thee!'

Robbins Landon does not report his source, commenting only that the story might be apocryphal. Richard Luckett, however, suggests a possible origin.[74] There is certainly an appropriate feeling of Handelian theatrical rhetoric about it. Apparently, Burney said that her voice was 'but a thread', but agreed with the general view that her singing depended on expression at least as much as vocal quality.[75] It seems probable that her engagement as a vocal soloist was inspired by her great fame as an actress and well–publicised life–style, but her inclusion proved totally justified.

It is interesting to note Robbins Landon's general use of the Italian term contralto in place of (male) alto. This follows the style of earlier continental and occasional eighteenth–century secular English practice. Despite Dr Delany's and Dr Robbins Landon's[76] opinions of Mrs Cibber's performance of 'He Was Despised', the fact is that generally the range and style of writing by Handel for altos are so clearly masculine – not surprisingly, for often they were those of heroes – that however beautiful their voice few modern contraltos sound totally convincing. It is possible that the female contraltos of Handel's day had developed a different style – more masculine, which imitated counter–tenors – and it appears that Mrs Cibber's voice was 'mezzo–soprano rather than true alto'.[77]

In the second half of the eighteenth century in theatrical, operatic and stage music female contraltos displaced castrati (who were by then fewer in number in England) more often than did counter–tenors (who were also fewer). It seems probable that the style of these operatic contraltos had been influenced increasingly by the more flamboyant theatricality of the evirati, who were certainly not known for their masculinity, but for their sexual ambiguity. From this came the development of an intrinsically feminine contralto style as we know it today, and works were written with the feminine voice and genius in mind. By the middle of the nineteenth century, an essentially operatic style of solo singing evolved into what is regarded today as the norm.

During the eighteenth century, when the highest male voices and castrati were gradually being replaced by women in opera, oratorio and salon, it seems likely that (jealousy temporarily jettisoned?) the old order taught and trained the new. It seems possible that in the same way that the castrato Mustafà taught Madam Calvé at the end of the nineteenth century

---

[71] In his Introduction to his edition of *Messiah* (Novello, 1959)

[72] Richard Luckett, *Handel's Messiah, A Celebration* (Gollancz, 1992), ch. 5

[73] Robbins Landon, op. cit., p. 187

[74] Luckett, op. cit., pp. 128–9

[75] Fiske, op. cit., pp. 624–5

[76] Op. cit., p. 202

[77] Richard Luckett, op. cit., p. 130 (quoting the opinion of Charles Burney)

so eighteenth–century castrati, and probably counter–tenors, handed on style and vocal expertise to contraltos. There is more than one way of making a living through singing, and changes of fashion seem likely to have provided a new way for counter–tenors to do so.

The more masculine–sounding contralto (which might have evolved from the platform or oratorio counter–tenor, not the operatic counter–tenor or castrato?) survived and flourished in later oratorio. Dame Clara Butt was a stentorian member of this line. The most recent celebrity of this type in England was the superb Kathleen Ferrier, and some American 'blues' singers (like Bessie Smith) have demonstrated the same kind of tone, even if used rather differently.

Extremely rarely, a contralto is discovered to have much the same timbre and vocal presence as one type of counter–tenor we know today, with uncanny effect; indeed, Ferrier and Deller resembled each other in the middle ranges of their voices. It is the result of a rare physiological phenomenon. As this must also have happened in the eighteenth century, we may imagine this rarity contributing to the bewildering vocal terminology of the time. Today, one such is the Italian contralto, Adriana Lazzarini. Her style, delivery and the masculine quality of tone throughout her vocal range could be the envy of many counter–tenors. She seems to personify, almost in a psychic way, an eighteenth–century female contralto who acquired the positive style and sound of the counter–tenor, and thus contributed to his gradual disappearance from the secular stage for generations.

There were even occasions, during the eighteenth century, when women were styled counter–tenor, just as some were styled musici (castrati)! They were even engaged on occasions to sing male rôles, and castrati, suitably disguised, often sang female rôles. Androgyny was conventional. As early as 1702, Mrs Bracegirdle played Acis as a breeches part in Eccles' *Acis and Galatea*.[78] Yet in France, Rameau's comedie-ballet *Platée* seems to have raised some eyebrows as early as 1745, because the female rôle of Platée was written for and sung by an haute-contre, Jélyotte. Eventually, and for some decades, the terms counter–tenor and musici became over-generalized. Male alto was even used for castrato. The resultant ambiguities no doubt intrigued concert and opera–goers at the time, and perhaps this was the planned effect. 'Baroque' means 'strange', 'absurd' or 'distorted', and though 'baroque' is a modern term for the period it describes it well. The eighteenth century is associated with fantasy, yet it was also the Age of Reason. It produced Strawberry Hill Gothick as well as the Royal Crescent at Bath.

For examples of ambiguity we might look at two of Handel's operatic cast lists. The first is for *Admeto*, first performed in 1727 in London:[79]

Admeto	Signor Senesino, alto
Alceste	Signora Faustina, mezzo–soprano
Ercole	Signor Boschi, bass
Orindo	Signora Dotti, contralto
Trasimede	Signor Baldi, counter–tenor
Antigona	Signora Cuzzoni, soprano
Meraspe	Signor Palmerini, bass

[78] Fiske, op. cit., p. 14
[79] Robbins Landon, op. cit., p. 106

Baldi sang in operas by Handel, Bononcini and others in London from 1725 to 1728. Unless he was a disguised or indeed undisguised but malapropian castrato, he was some sort of falsettist and demonstrated the survival of the genre in Italy. He is not listed, as we might expect, as a contralto but as a counter-tenor in the English fashion. He seems to have been an excellent singer, overshadowed only by Senesino, who monopolised the leading parts. 'Orindo' seems to have been a 'breeches' part in this production. The description of Signora Dotti as a contralto represents an early use of the term as applied to the female low voice. Was Palmerini an English bass in disguise? Senesino, the celebrated castrato-contralto (as we would call him today), is also termed alto in the title rôle of *Ottone*, first performed 12 January 1723.[80]

A second illustration of confusing eighteenth-century vocal terminology is taken from the cast list of singers for Handel's Subscription Operas in 1729, which include: 'Antonia Margherita Merighi, a contralto profundo ... Anna Strada, soprano ...'. In the *Daily Journal*, London 2 July 1729, there are: '... Signora Merighi, a Woman of a very fine Presence, an excellent Actress, and a very good Singer – A counter-tenor ... Senora Strada, who hath a very fine Treble Voice, a Person of singular Merit. Signor Annibal Pio Fabri, a most excellent Tenor, and a fine Voice ... His wife, who performs a Man's Part exceeding well ... Signora Bartoldi, who has a very fine Treble voice; she is also a very genteel Actress, both in Men and Women's Parts ...'

Theatrical transvestism increased as the century progressed, as the reader can discover from Winton Dean's book *Handel's Dramatic Oratorios and Masques* (O.U.P., 1959) and Otto Deutsch's *Handel. A Documentary Biography* (Black, 1955). It continued into the first decades of the nineteenth century when women sang male rôles; as for instance, Maria Malibran (1806–1836) did in Rossini's *Othello*.

Sexual ambiguity on stage reached back to classical drama. Shakespeare's plays are also full of it. Originally, there was added spice: in the early theatre, female rôles were played by boys or youths. Some of this impact has been lost today, although such transvestism is an important part of theatrical make-believe. Before castrati were heard in England in the seventeenth century, women had taken male parts in parodies of English operas or semi-operas, the main female rôle being taken by a male comedian. One can easily see the relationship of the famous comic duet between Corydon and Mopsa to these opera parodies. Also, we can glimpse affinities with English pantomime, with its Principal Boy, and Dame or Widow Twankey tradition. Today's Hinge and Bracket and Dame Edna Everage are the modern counterparts of Mopsa. The ancient Greeks and Romans had their own versions, and so did seventeenth-century Roman opera. An early version of the Pantomime Dame was present in medieval mimes, hoodening and mummery plays. This well-loved comedy character seems to be important in our culture. Pantomime began as opera, and was not for children but adults. In pantomime, we still have elements of opera, masque and serious drama allied with bawdy humour, satire and mimicry. It was and still should be a world of the impossible: of topsy-turvy and transformation. It also provides evidence of earlier singers' being ready to sing the widest possible vocal range and to take several voice-parts.

In Gerald Frow's book, *Oh, Yes It Is!* we read:[81]

---

[80] Robbins Landon, op. cit., p. 101
[81] Gerald Frow, *Oh, Yes It Is! A History of Pantomime* (BBC Publications, 1985), pp. 95–6

... so successful was *Olympic Revels* [at Madame Lucy Elizabeth (née Bartolozzi) at Vestris' Royal Olympic Theatre] that later the same year [1830] [James Robinson] Planche provided Madame [Vestris] with a companion-piece, called *Olympic Devils* or, *Orpheus and Eurydice*. Vestris herself essayed a breeches part as Orpheus (described as 'the Thracian thrummer'), and the piece opened at the Olympic on Boxing Day. It was generally held to be livelier than its predecessor, its dialogue and lyrics being even more amusing. As an example of its exuberance [*sic*] and literary 'funning' one might take the scene in which Charon, the ferryman of the River Styx, discovers that Cerberus, the three-headed guard-dog of the Infernal Regions, has suddenly started speaking and ends up singing a quartette with him:

Charon:	Why, Cerberus! You've found a tongue I vow,
	And can say something more than 'bow-wow-wow!'
Cerberus:	Ay, thanks to Orpheus, I've three tongues found.
Charon:	One of 'em talks dog-Latin, I'll be bound.
	But wherefore Orpheus thanks? Responde cur?
Cerberus:	Why, ere he came and made this mighty stir,
	I was a three thick wooden-headed dog,
	With but a bark like any other log.
	Now as I am described – and by no dunce –
	I really feel 'three gentlemen at once!'
	And ever since I heard him play and sing,
	I've sat and warbled, sir, like anything.
Charon:	You mean you've howled some doggerel to the moon.
Cerberus:	No, sir; I sing I say – and sing in tune!
Charon:	A *bark*-a-role, of course.
Cerberus:	No, sir, a glee.
Charon:	You take the *treble*, then?
Cerberus:	I take all three[.]
	My voice is tenor – counter-tenor – bass.
Charon:	Let's try a quartette then, if that's the case.
Cerberus:	With you, forsooth?
Charon:	Oblige me by beginning one –
	I've seen a dancing dog, but never a singing one!

Quartette – Cerberus & Charon – 'Begone Dull Care'

Cerberus:	Begone, dull Charon! pry'thee begone from me!
	Thou'rt too dull, Charon, ever to sing a glee.
	Long time thou hast been ferrying here,
	And souls from far dost bring;
	But thou know'st dull Charon,
	Little of sol-fa-ing.
	I range with care through all the keys –
	My compass – octaves three!
	My voice can rove from A above,
	Down, down to double D.

Charon: Begone, dull cur! shall such a land–lubber as thee,
Pretend, dull cur! to talk of a compass to me?
I'm the son of Nox,
And a compass should box,
When thou wert a blind puppy.
So avast, dull cur! I'm a vast deal 'cuter than thee.
For I will bet my crazy bark
Against your own crack'd three,
That no–one can go to the D below,
If I didn't go to C.

The sexual ambiguity of the castrato was different. During the eighteenth century, even at the height of the castrati's ascendancy, there was seldom more than one in any single English opera production. He was the star.

Handel seems to have written only two solo rôles specifically for castrati in all his oratorios. He left his musical options open. It is also of interest that he only employed one real soprano–castrato: Giacomo Conti, as Meleagro in *Atalanta*, 1736. The rôle included the only 'top' C6 that Handel wrote for any singer.

An engraving on page 94 shows the counter–tenor, George Mattocks, as Achilles, in *Achilles in Pettycoats* in 1773. This demonstrates that even in the late eighteenth century not only were counter–tenors still appearing on stage, but that some were involved in trans–sexual oddities of the period, like other singers. In this particular case, the sexual twist was doubled.

Examples of the switching of rôles from male to female and vice–versa include Maurice Greene's *Florimel*, a pastoral of 1737. In one version, in which Act II was written by William Boyce when Greene's pupil, the hero Myrtillo was sung by a counter–tenor, but two other versions have Myrtillo as a 'breeches' part for a soprano, transposed to a different key. Greene himself seems to have approved both versions.[82] It was performed in a concert version, with male soloists exclusively, at the Three Choirs Festival of 1745, in the Boothall, Gloucester.[83]

As early as 1737, stage mockery had been made of Italian opera and castrati. The counter–tenor, Thomas Solway, dressed like Farinelli, played in *The Dragon of Wantley*, a popular and long–running burlesque. Such ridicule helped the decline of Italian opera in London, though not that of the castrati themselves until much later in the century. However, when the castrati finally lost favour and began to be the subject of ridicule, it has been suggested that men began to feel reluctant to sing counter–tenor because of them:[84]

But the establishment of the castrati deprived perfectly normal men of their pleasure in singing counter–tenor, for they found themselves viewed with the same amused and patronizing contempt as the castrati, but without the compensation of an equally heroic and profitable voice. In our own time the renaissance of the counter–tenor soloist is still bedevilled by the unease such singing occasions in some circles, an unease born of the triumphs of Nicolini. It would scarcely have been understood before 1700.

---

[82] Fiske, op. cit., pp. 177–8
[83] Daniel Lysons, *A History of the Meetings of the Three Choirs* (Gloucester, 1812), p. 169
[84] Fiske, op. cit., p. 55

There is some truth in this opinion, but one might doubt that fear of confusion with castrati could have affected more than a sizeable minority, however significant in terms of popular fashion, until the very end of the eighteenth century and the beginning of the nineteenth century. There is an account of Rossini himself singing falsetto in 1824 before George IV at Brighton Pavilion.[85]

We are often encouraged today by those who would seek to minimalize his importance (some even argue that he never existed outside the English choir stall) to think that the counter–tenor disappeared from secular view in the early eighteenth century. As we have seen, nothing could be further from the truth. The evidence is that there were plenty of counter–tenors on the English secular scene throughout the eighteenth century, even if the voice gradually became less fashionable.

It is strange that Fiske seems to discount entirely the continued presence of solo and ensemble counter–tenors in English ecclesiastical, academic and glee–club circles, all of which were traditional strongholds for the male high voice in England. In fact, he rather contradicts himself: ' The probability is that throughout eighteenth century Europe, falsetto singing was commoner than has been realised, and that it began to die out everywhere at much the same time.'[86] Elsewhere in his book, Fiske suggests that in the eighteenth century use of falsetto varied in solo singing on the Continent from country to country, and from tradition to tradition. Certainly, there is a large corpus of seventeenth and eighteenth–century music by European composers, clearly intended for counter–tenor voice ranges or as a favoured option.

Competition in the employment of castrati and solo counter–tenors is well–documented and by no means rare. For example, although the castrato Senesino had been engaged for the specially–composed part of Joad in *Athalia* in 1733, Handel dismissed him shortly before the first performance in Oxford and engaged Walter Powell, the English counter–tenor (1697–1744) instead.[87]

Lysons[88] makes particular mention of Powell:

> Though the memory of Mr. Powell does not appear to be recorded in any musical publication, or to be known to the professional men of the day, I find, upon inquiry, that it is not yet forgotten in the University of Oxford, where some of the senior members recollect their seniors were used to talk of the extraordinary vocal powers of Walter Powell, and to relate various anecdotes concerning him. He was a member of the choirs of Christ Church and other Colleges, was first one of the yeomen, and afterwards, one of the esquire beadles, and was the principal male oratorio singer when Handel presided at the Act, and the celebrated Strada sang there, in the month of July, 1733. On this occasion, his singing was so much admired that he was immediately afterwards appointed one of the gentlemen of the Chapel Royal: the general idea is that his voice was a fine counter–tenor.

[85] Ibid., p. 272
[86] Fiske, loc. cit.
[87] Hough, op. cit., p. 14 and Robbins Landon, op. cit., p. 142
[88] Lysons, op. cit., p. 165

The Gloucester Journal reported in 1733 that 'the famous Mr. Powell of Oxford did the meeting the honour of singing in the Cathedral on both days'.[89] It was announced in the papers in 1734[90] that the steward had procured the best hands, and that 'he had a promise of the most celebrated English voice to adorn the church music'.[91]

In Powell's obituary in *The Gentleman's Magazine* it was said that he was esteemed to have the best voice in England. The following lines were written by a gentleman of Oxford University, on hearing of his death:[92]

> Is Powell dead? Then all the earth
> Prepare to meet its fate:
> To sing the everlasting birth
> The Choir of Heav'n's complete.

Edward Rimbault (1816–1876), the musical historian and organist, says in a footnote:[93]

> A tradition is still extant in the University, that, on his deathbed, a short time before his decease, he sang an anthem, with the full powers of his voice, and with the most animated enthusiasm.

An English sense of humour might appreciate the full tragi–comic potential of this scene, in which perhaps Powell exercised his own sense of humour (or sense of occasion) for the last time in this life.

The counter–tenor Russell mentioned earlier may be the Russell in Smollett's satire *Advice* (1746–1747), described as 'A famous mimic and singer, engaged by certain ladies of quality, who engaged him to set up a puppet show in opposition to the oratorios of Handel ....' As Hough wrote:[94] 'If these men are identical, Russell must have been particularly mercenary after singing under Handel in 1739. The fickle instigators of the counter–attraction deserted him, and after seeing the interior of Newgate he ended his days in Bedlam.' We note yet another counter–tenor link with prison life.

The Chapel Royal continued to be known for the quality of its men singers. Two notable counter–tenors, Bayly and Mence, appeared in the 1740s. They seemed to have been thought to have been vocally complementary. Bayly had the higher voice; one apparently more lyrical but less agile than that of Mence. Greene used their characteristic voices in solo movements in his *Te Deum* of 1745. Handel featured their singular qualities in the *Peace Anthem* and the parallel revival of the *Caroline Te Deum*.[95] Donald Burrows has written in useful detail on these and on Handel's relationship with the alto voices of the Chapel Royal.[96]

---

[89] *The Gloucester Journal*, in a 'Report on the Meeting of the Three Choirs' quoted by Hough, op. cit., p. 15, without exact citation

[90] Quoted by Hough, op. cit., p. 15, without exact citation

[91] Lysons, op. cit., p. 166

[92] *The Gentleman's Magazine* for 1744, quoted by Hough, op. cit., without exact citation

[93] Quoted by Hough, op. cit., p. 15, without exact citation

[94] Hough, op. cit., p. 15 and fn.; also Schoelcher, p. 293

[95] Donald Burrows, *Handel and the English Chapel Royal* (Open University, 1981), p. 42

[96] Ibid., passim

As in the case of *Florimel*, the exclusively male world of Chapel Royal, cathedral and academe continued to influence the stage on rare occasions. Boyce's *The Secular Masque* was written in the early 1740s apparently for an all–male cast. The choruses in it are all scored for Alto, Tenor and Bass, and the vocal range of the solo goddesses Diana and Venus is exactly suitable for counter–tenors. (James Bowman played Venus in a production by Opera da Camera in London in 1971.) Fiske suggests that this is one version of a work otherwise sung in transposition by sopranos, not (female) contraltos, because the latter did not exist as such at this date.[97] This is the received viewpoint, but the Handel opera cast list (page 77) includes a female contralto – described thus – in 1727.

The rôle of the Boetian prince Athamas in Handel's *Semele* was sung in 1744 by Daniel Sullivan. He was evidently a good singer but (like Mattocks) may not have been as good an actor. In the same year, the day after a performance of *Samson*, Mrs Delany, writing in a letter to Mrs Dewes about a proposed performance of *Joseph and his Brethren*:[98]

> ...upon the whole, it went off very well, but not better than last year. *Joseph*, I believe will be next Friday, but Handel is mightily out of humour with it, for Sullivan, who is to sing Joseph, is a block with a very fine voice, and Beard has no voice at all.

Mr Brent, an alto soloist and dancing master, and father of the soprano Charlotte Brent, originally sang the rôle of Hamor in *Jephtha* in 1752. The part requires an outstanding voice.

So in England, throughout most of the eighteenth century, counter–tenors of different varieties and specialities seem to have continued to appear with success and some renown. As might be expected, many seem to have been based in cathedral, royal or collegiate choirs.

> Price had been some years a member of the choir at Gloucester; he had a fine counter–tenor voice and was particularly remarkable for singing the air in Milton's *L'Allegro* which describes Laughter 'holding both his sides'. In this air, without losing sight of musical correctness, he worked himself up to so hearty and so natural a laugh, that few of his auditors could avoid partaking of his apparent merriment. The late Signor Rauzzini was singularly affected the first time of his hearing it at the Meeting of the Three Choirs. Dr William Hayes, from whom it is probable that Price learnt it, was remarkable for singing this air.[99]

An Italian counter–tenor, Corri, was performing with success in Edinburgh ten years later; his appearances demonstrate again the fallacy of the argument that castrati had pushed continental falsetto–singers into extinction. From 1770, Signor and Signora Domenico Corri from Rome were favourite singers in Edinburgh and well patronised by the nobility. Robert Burns's friend, the poet James Thomson, says that the Signor had a falsetto voice which he

[97] Fiske, op. cit., p. 212
[98] Robbins Landon, op. cit., p. 211
[99] Lysons, op. cit., pp. 190–1

managed with great skill and taste.[100] Dr Burney also reports on Domenico Corri in a letter from Rome dated 2 September 1770:[101]

> The day after my arrival at his Grace the Duke of Dorset's, I heard Signor
> Celestini, the principal violin here ... He was ably seconded by Signor Corri,
> who is an ingenious composer and sings in very good taste.

Corri was a pupil of the great singing teacher Niccolo Porpora from 1763 to 1767. Hough reports[102] an account of the Corri Family in *St. Cecilia's Hall in the Niddry Wynd* by David Fraser Harris; the Hall was where the Musical Society of Edinburgh held its concerts. The actress Adrienne Corri, an expert on the painter Thomas Gainsborough, seems to have some connection with the Corri family of musicians, though she quotes Venice as their city of origin.[103] Three arias from Gluck's *Orfeo* were published in an interpretation by the castrato, Guadagni, in Corri's *A Select Collection of the Most Admir'd Songs* of 1788.

In 1775 Thomas Linley wrote the famous opera *The Duenna* in collaboration with Sheridan. Later productions seem to have cast the hero Don Jerome as a tenor because of the occasional high vocal-range of the rôle (something which would happen today); yet it seems to have been written for the counter-tenor Leoni. T. J. Walsh, who has researched valuable additions to our knowledge of him certainly discusses the rôle as if it was composed for the counter-tenor,[104] but Fiske does not, mentioning Leoni only briefly and regarding the rôle as for a baritone with falsetto higher notes. (There are several high G4s.) As will be seen later, in one way both Walsh and Fiske are right, but Walsh's deeper research into Leoni himself encourages confidence in his findings and judgements on this singer. Certainly, Fiske recognised that these falsetto notes are essential in the Duenna trio. He underlines that it is no solution for Don Jerome to be sung by a modern tenor. We might note this further example that the A.T.B. trio was still alive on the secular stage.

Because Leoni lived and sang at a time when the stage counter-tenor was in gentle decline and because we have useful detail on him, his career and voice merit further examination. We shall deal with the purely historical aspects here.

He was Jewish (his real name was Myer Lyon) and he was probably born in Frankfurt--am-Main. He was an exceptional boy singer. His reputation was such that he obtained a post as a young cantor at the synagogue in Duke's Place, Aldgate, London. Success there led to an introduction to David Garrick, who arranged for him to appear at Drury Lane Theatre. His first appearance there was on 13 December 1760 and he was 'received with great applause'.[105] He seems to have semi-Italianized his name to Michael Leoni at this time, though by then he could have been only about fifteen or sixteen years old. In a letter, written 12 October 1760, Garrick refers to him as 'ye boy Leoni'.[106]

[100] Quoted by Hough, op. cit., p. 18

[101] Charles Burney, *Journal...*

[102] Op. cit., p. 17 fn.

[103] Adrienne Corri, *The Search for Gainsborough* (Cape 1984), p. 66

[104] T. J. Walsh, *Opera in Dublin, 1705–1797* (Dublin, 1973), chapter 14, pp. 230–1

[105] *The London Stage, 1660–1800* (Carbondale, Illinois, 1962), part IV, vol. II, p. 830

[106] *The Letters of David Garrick*, ed. David M. Little and George M. Kahrl (Oxford University Press, 1963), vol. 1, p. 330

It would seem likely that a subsequent five–year gap in his theatrical career was for the purpose of vocal adjustment and, presumably, further training to become an adult singer. He appears to have kept his post at the synagogue. In October 1775 he returned to the stage as Arbaces in Arne's *Artaxerxes* at Covent Garden, in a part originally written for a contralto castrato. (There are two castrato rôles in *Artaxerxes*, and it is not clear who took the other in this production.) Walsh confirms that his most famous rôle was that of Don Carlos, in the opera *The Duenna*, which he performed at the same theatre for an exceptionally long run. He also reports that his Dublin début was 'probably' at the Rotunda Gardens on 13 June 1777.[107] There are a number of useful and illuminating reviews of his singing and stage performances which we refer to in the discussion in Part Two of the vocal techniques of the counter–tenor. He was still singing in theatres and concerts in London in 1788, and possibly later. Eventually he emigrated to Kingston, Jamaica, to a post as Chazan (cantor) at a synagogue. He died there *c*1800. Leoni's voice and career in many ways exemplify the stage counter–tenor in the later eighteenth century.

Our second interest in *The Duenna* is that the counter–tenor George Mattocks is known to have played the part of Ferdinand in at least one other production of the opera. This underlines that the male high voice, with its use of falsetto, could still be heard on the later eighteenth–century stage.

---

5 Bach and Germany

We have seen that the counter–tenor, by whatever name, was a European voice. Yet it is not always realised that Germany also possessed a flourishing adult male alto tradition. The employment of the counter-tenor range in the German states until some time in the later eighteenth century seems in many respects to have paralleled that obtaining in England, and indeed also in France, Italy and the Low Countries.

Confusion exists, nevertheless, over the use of altos by J.S. Bach.[1] Such confusion is rather surprising because even if we cannot know the tonal quality of Bach's choirs we do have a clear idea of their complements. Boys sang the soprano line, and three main varieties of voice were available for the alto – not of course necessarily in a single choir. One of these, in solo and chorus, was broadly speaking he who in England would be termed counter–tenor, and whose written tessituras indicate adult male voices of slightly varying type. In some German choirs, however, alto parts were also sung by boys or youths. In addition, castrati were employed there much more widely than in England and sang soprano and alto solo and chorus parts. They were employed in both Lutheran and Catholic choirs as well as in opera and secular music.

Many German solo alto arias, including those of Bach, seem high even when allowance is made for the effect of modern pitches which have raised their apparent pitch about a semi-tone. Specialist high falsettists could have coped well at Bach's pitch (some today can do so, even at modern pitch), and castrati or boys would have had no problems. There are also numerous examples of A.T.B. trios and some complete works which are clearly written for men's voices: the alto part of which often has a lower tessitura. Examine, for example, the A.T.B. cantata *Aperite Mihi Portas Justitiae* by Buxtehude, the Danish–born composer whose working life was spent in the extreme north of Germany.

Particularly in Bach's Leipzig cantatas, some alto arias may have been meant for boys with unmutated or newly mutated voices; but the style of the musical writing and the evidence of the existence of high, mature male altos (some of whom we know by name) in many of his musical forces suggest that it is clear that Bach and other Kapellmeisters would have used these for solo work, and not merely in the choruses.

Bach's dealings with singers and choirs give a glimpse of German practice of the period. The Weimar Kapelle was a small choir and one upon which in its full ensemble Bach seems to have made only modest demands: often he doubled the voices with instruments in elaborate

---

[1] C. Sanford Terry, *Bach* (O.U.P., 1928), pp. 35, 45, 49, 91–4, 164, 201 and 203; also 2nd edn (O.U.P., 1967). This book still provides a sound starting point for enquiries into alti in eighteenth–century Germany.

chorus sections. In six out of twenty-one cantatas written for Weimar, the full choir sings only a simple chorale and in three others there is no chorus at all. His cautious use of the boys' voices suggests that older soloists dealt with the bulk of the music and that the alto solos were sung by mature voices.

In 1700, the Kapelle included one Adam Emanuel Weldige (or Weldig) as falsettist and Master of the Pages. Terry wrote: 'Weldige ... may be added to the number of Bach's close friends'.[2] The composer is likely to have written solos for him; to discover exactly which solos would make intriguing study; Terry thought that Weldige took 'Pales' in *Was mir behaght* (BWV 208, today transcribed for popular use as 'Sheep may Safely Graze'): a rôle too high unless he were a soprano falsettist.[3] He may well have been exactly this. It would appear that Weldige was appointed on the death of Daniel Dobricht, also a falsettist.

In the choir, besides a tenorist and two bassists, there were two altists. There is still general disagreement on the exact definition of falsettists and altists. Whether altists were sometimes men or always boys, and whether Weldige was in fact singing in the choir at the time or merely training the Weimar boys remains unclear. Hough was concerned with the distinction between falsettists and altists:[4]

> In 1714 the singers comprised boys, and two men on each of the three underparts, altists being stated. Late in 1716, there were six singing boys, two falsettists, one altist, two tenorists, and two bassists ... the possibilities of these singers are seen in cantatas written for the Weimar Kapelle. For the Cothen Kapelle a descantist ... was engaged in 1718 and in 1719, Ginacini a male descantist who received more [money] than two horn players for the first Brandenburg Concerto. Both these singers may have been sopranists from the opera houses, but the Rudolfstadt descantist may have been a good falsettist.

In 1714, the 'boys' might have had mutated (broken) voices or were youths; though, in 1716, the implication is that the six 'singing boys' had un-mutated voices.

Hough, by proposing a difference between falsettist and altist seems to suggest that there was a difference between these voices equivalent to supposed English falsetto alto and true counter-tenor voices; a view that has attracted some English commentators in recent decades. It is of course possible that falsettist and altist corresponded with the high and low English counter-tenor voices. Another possibility is that altists were always unmutated if they were elderly boys, and were never counter-tenors – true or otherwise. Alternatively, falsettists could have been male mezzo-soprano or soprano singers who sang either the line above the altists – a second treble part – or even sang the top line with the treble boys, leaving the alto to altists – unmutated boys, or mutated youths.

The Musical Times for February 1974 (p. 128) contained a letter on the subject by three youthful experts. One of these, Robert Jones, subsequently took a soprano part in Cavalli *Pompeo Magno* at the age of seventeen-and-a-half and later became a choral scholar at Christ Church, Oxford. (The present author could easily have sung that rôle at that age.)

A Bach document which sets out the musical qualifications for choral vacancies stipulates: '8 sopranists, all fourteen or under. 2 altists – one fourteen, one sixteen, "has a passable alto

---

[2] Op. cit., 1st edn, p. 94
[3] Hough, 'The Historical Significance of the Counter Tenor', p. 17 fn.
[4] Hough, op. cit., p. 17; his précis of Terry, op. cit., ch. 5

voice" ...' The document is signed by J. S. Bach, as Musical Director and Cantor.[5] Were some of Bach's altos not necessarily elderly boys, near or undergoing vocal mutation, but in fact boys with highly–developed chest voices, after the continental manner of today? Was the position of falsettist sometimes a single voice engaged primarily to teach the boys their parts, as in early sixteenth–century England, where the Earl of Northumberland's household Master of the Children was a counter–tenor?

Certainly, a Beamtenstaat for 1700 (when opera was still performed by Weimar's ducal Kapelle, of which Bach was a member) includes as altists Josef Friedrich Bang (Hough instead gives 'Ganz') and Josef Petrus Martini.[6] Bang also held the post of Instructor of the Duke's nephews. The falsettist Weldige is placed directly above the two altists mentioned. The list is clearly in order of vocal range: soprano (three 'prime donne' sopranos) to bass.

It is sometimes suggested that while Handel could call upon highly skilled and often famous singers for his arias, Bach had to rely on home–spun talent of mediocre attainment: mere boys and youths. This seems an unlikely statement. Particularly at Weimar, excellent operatic singers, including altos, were available. The Thomaschule choir at Leipzig seems to have been a giant body of sixty–one boys, aged between eleven and – before Bach's time – seventeen, divided between four churches.[7] In large boys' choirs, like Leipzig's, all under-parts appear to have been supplied by older boys and youths, and this practice gave rise to the popular idea today of 'the Bach choir'. While Bach was Cantor, the upper age limit for the boys rose as high as twenty–one, and this late age must be a significant factor to be taken into account in any consideration of the vocal type and quality of his altos, tenors and basses.

The choir at Weimar (twelve voices, men and boys) loosely relates to Joshua Rifkin's recent experimental recordings and concerts of large Bach works using such small ensembles, including counter–tenors, though employing women – not boy – sopranos. The reader is advised to examine the research of Joshua Rifkin on Bach choir sizes, and to consider Rifkin's direction of various performances, notably of the *B minor Mass*[8] (which was not of course written for Weimar but for performance in Catholic east Germany). On paper, Weimar resembles a miniature English Chapel Royal at the time of King Henry VIII. The proportions of voices in this choir and indeed in most of Bach's choirs of which we know their size suggests that the altos were equal in tone and output to the tenors and basses. The balance therefore suggests that the altists possessed adult voices.

In at least one choir, we also have an instrumental stipulation for three of the men:[9]

Court of Celle / 1663   Memorandum / by the court organist Wolfgang Wessnitzer on the personnel of the well-appointed Capelle
1. Director
2. An Alto   capable of playing the viol in
   A Tenor   French music.
   A Bass

[5] Terry, op. cit., p. 197–8
[6] Ibid., p. 91
[7] Ibid., p. 201
[8] Joshua Rifkin, 'Bach's Chorus', *The Musical Times*, November 1982, pp. 747–754; a reply to this under the same title by Robert L. Marshall in January 1983, pp. 19–22, and a response by Rifkin (March 1983)
[9] From Terry, op. cit., p. 49

... 10. Two choirboys.

Apparently, Bach called in students to help his Leipzig boy altos in performances of his large-scale works. He seems also to have arranged to stiffen his choir with a bass, tenor and a mature alto; his 1730 documents of requirements for church music state:[10]

> ... stipendia were provided for a vocal Bass, Tenor and Alto, and for a few instrumentalists, particularly two string players, thus enlarging the resources for performing concerted music in church.

In a Leipzig memorandum,[11] Bach writes recommendations for each church choir:

> There must belong, at least, three trebles, three alti, three tenors, and as many basses [as a minimum] ... a motet may be sung with at least two voices to each part ...

In that part of Europe, by the middle of the eighteenth century, some protestant choirs, opera choruses and soloists must have been in confusion, sexually if not musically. Marpurg records:[12]

> *Gotha, chamber and chapel:* Two female singers: one male soprano, one male alto, one tenor, two basses ...
> *Breslau, Bishop's Chapel*: Five male singers (including two sopranos and one alto) ...
> *Paris, opera*: Eight female solo singers, four male altos, one tenor, seven baritones, choruses of seventeen women and twenty-one men ...
> *1755 Paris, Concerts Spirituels*: Many of whom also belong to the opera ... four female and four male solo singers, choir of six females and six male sopranos, six male altos, seven tenors, five high basses, eight low basses ...
> *1756 Dresden, King's Chapel*: Five female, six male sopranos, one female and three male altos, three tenors, four basses ...
> *Mannheim Court Chapel*: Three female and three male sopranos, two male altos, three tenors, two basses ...
> *1757 Schwarzberg-Rudolfstadt Chapel*: One female and one male soprano, one male alto, one tenor (the Kapellmeister), one bass ...
> *Anhalt-Zerbst Chapel*: One male soprano, one male alto, one tenor ...
> *Salzburg, Archbishop's Music*: Solo singers, five male sopranos (three vacant), three tenors, two basses, with additions from the choir; fifteen boy singers, their prefect and their preceptor, three male altos, nine tenors, nine basses (Chorherren) and one male alto, three tenors, four basses ...

Despite the use of the term 'male', it is not clear whether these male altos were exclusively castrati, natural voices or that the alto line was shared between both types.

---

[10] Terry, op. cit., p. 203
[11] Quoted in full by Spitta in *Bach* (English translation, London, 1884–5), vol. II, p. 240
[12] Friedrich Wilhelm Marpurg, *Historisch Kritische Beytrage* (Berlin 1754)

The male sopranos may have been castrati, but this is not certain. High falsettists seem to have been available to supplement their ranks, if necessary; a vocal type, we are again persuaded, which survived far longer on the continent of Europe than is often supposed. We are used to the notion that the highest French male voice was always an haute–contre, not a falsettist, the term invariably used in contra–distinction. An 1889 comment,[13] that 'soprano falsettists were once common enough in France' may therefore surprise some readers. It may also seem surprising that in some French mixed choirs until the beginning of the twentieth century, falsettists supplemented female sopranos and contraltos. Toscanini once used ten fal-settists in a performance of Verdi's *Requiem*.[14] We shall see that soprano– or mezzo–falset-tists were once common in other European countries.

It would seem that, for example, in Germany (except in Roman Catholic cathedrals and churches) as the eighteenth century progressed, there was an increasing temptation to incorporate women singers gradually, either on purpose to replace boys or castrati or reluctantly because the latter were less easy to obtain. Yet even Bach was reprimanded at Arnstadt (where he was organist from 1703 to 1707) for inviting his future wife to sing in the organ loft of the empty Lutheran church, though this may have been because the church was empty. The church elders no doubt wondered what the not–yet–Bachs got up to without a chaperone!

In protestant choirs which had once included castrato–contralti, it is possible, even prob-able, that women sang some alto solos on occasions from the later eighteenth century onwards. These protestant choirs would tend to have been like those in the private chapels of kings, bishops or princelets. As might be expected, opera–house choruses were in advance in their employment of women as altos.

Other than his six years at Cothen, a post which involved no church music, Bach was the Cantor (Director) of all–male choirs. Because he wrote no operas and seems to have written little non–sacred vocal music (only a few secular cantatas survive, mostly for musical forces directed by himself), it would seem unlikely that any alto solos or parts, particularly in his church music, were written for female singers. Certain solo cantatas, like *Vergnügte Ruh, beliebte Seelenlust* (no. 170), or alto arias in other works might have been written for and sung by a castrato or a falsettist like Weldige, for whom they seem eminently suitable. They could also have been sung by a boy or boys. Normally this would depend on their technical difficulty, the tonal quality Bach desired or the solo voices and instrumental forces available, or even the director–composer's preference on the occasion. On the other hand, it seems that Bach was always conscious of the lack of rehearsal time for the trebles. Like those written for and at Weimar, the Leipzig cantatas contain few and modest choruses. It is likely, therefore, that more mature solo voices were used for many arias and they were sung either by members of the teaching staff or by students who were probably comparable in competence to a present–day university choral scholar. It is interesting that no less an authority than J. A. Westrup failed to underline this:[15]

> Ears which [today] are accustomed to hearing alto solos sung by a female
> contralto or mezzo–soprano might find it difficult to accommodate themselves

---

[13] In *Harper's Magazine* for 1889, LXXVII, p. 73
[14] René Jacobs, 'The Controversy Concerning the Timbre of the Countertenor', p. 304
[15] Westrup, op. cit., p. 39

to the tone of a boy who was too old to be a soprano and too young to be a baritone.

We do not suggest, of course, that such a boy as Westrup describes was incapable of producing excellent singing.

We return to what the term falsettist really denoted in eighteenth-century Germany, and indeed elsewhere. To consider him as an exclusively (high?) falsetto singer seems convincing, initially. The mature altist (the term means merely alto or altus) could be defined respectively as a part-user of falsetto, the two-register counter-tenor or indeed the powerfully-voiced specialist low head-register singer. Certainly, it should include the tenor-altino. (There is discussion of technical matters in Part Two.) Of course, certain arias could have been sung by a falsettist, or an altist. Attention also falls on many of the so-called high tenor recitatives and arias which, using the tenor technique of the period, would have been sung using falsetto when desired or needed.

From all these varieties of alto came the specialist adult male alto soloist for whom arias such as 'Es is vollbracht' from the *St John Passion* or the 'Agnus Dei' from the *B minor Mass* were written. It is reiterated that the Bach-alto question: 'What kind of altos did Bach use?', has long been argued over. It still is.[16]

---

[16] See *The Musical Times* for February 1974, p. 128, for further investigation of the 'Bach altos'

6 Slow Slip from Fashion

For reasons easily understood, churches in Roman Catholic countries tended to retain male alti and castrati far longer than those of Protestant persuasion. In most churches of the Reformation which supported choirs, the use of women's voices accelerated throughout the later eighteenth and nineteenth centuries. This diversification has helped confusion to arise concerning the complement of choirs in Germany – a country with co-existing Roman Catholic and Protestant traditions.

Fading of the solo counter-tenor in England began in the most obvious way: a slow change of musical and cultural fashion. By around 1800, counter-tenors found themselves in a much worse situation than a century before, though there must have seemed at least some hope for the future. English audiences had been enjoying opera without castrati since the 1750s, though these singers had subsequently appeared in oratorio. In England at least, despite the successfully established female contraltos, there remained some work for solo counter-tenors, especially in the provinces. There was also work in choruses, and still some theatrical employment: not much in opera, but more in the various milieu which involved 'old fashioned' music or was connected with oratorios or with festivals, in cathedrals, and the performance of academic exercises.

George Mattocks (c1738–1804; mentioned above) was a noted theatrical counter-tenor. He began as a boy actor/singer, and continued his adult singing career at Covent Garden from 1758 to 1780. He enjoyed a notorious private life and although he seems to have been an indifferent actor with an unmanly appearance he was a fine singer. One commentator wrote: 'We are often led to imagine, that we are listening to the notes of a castrato, than to those of a British singer'.[1] Mattocks sang mainly in falsetto. In *Thespis*, Hugh Kelly summed him up as:[2] '... one whose tender strain, so delicately clear, steals, ever honied, on the heaviest ear, with sweet toned softness exquisitely warms. Fires without force, and without vigour charms.' He and his wife, Isabella (née Hallam), sang as a duo for many seasons. His last season at Covent Garden was in 1783 to 1784.

Productions of the *Beggar's Opera* continued. In 1777, one included a new scene with Macheath suffering retribution in the prison hulks near Woolwich. It is noteworthy for two reasons: first, that Macheath was played by a woman (Mrs Farrel, described as a 'counter tenor' by *The Morning Post*)[3] and, second, that we again here have an apparent link of the counter-tenor – albeit with sex-change – with a prison scene.

---

[1] *The Theatrical Biographer*, quoted Fiske, op. cit., p. 634
[2] Hugh Kelly, *Thespis*, quoted Fiske (E.T.M. 18) op. cit., p. 634
[3] Fiske, op. cit., pp. 402 and 628

94

The History of the Counter-Tenor

In fact, during the last quarter of the eighteenth century, there was an increasing tendency for actresses to play Macheath. Transvestism, of course, was rife in many plays, operas and other entertainments. One production of the *Beggar's Opera* in 1781 included reversal of all rôles, in a way which reminds one of the later 'heroic' – castrato-inspired? – pantomime Principal Boy. The bass, Bannister, sang the part of Polly 'with inconsistent falsetto' in one production,[4] and this recalls Mattocks who, in a bewildering double sexual reversal on stage, took the rôle of Achilles, dressed as a woman.

Mr Mattocks as 'Achilles in Petty-coats',
at Covent Garden, 1779

The Enraged Musician of 1788 attempted to bring alive the famous Hogarth print of a noisy London street, with falsetto singing at its start and later some street-cries. It is likely that many cries would have involved falsetto so that a link was thus formed with Gibbons, Weelkes and Dering, though the musical style surrounding these cries was markedly different.

In 1790, and in quite another context, Dr Samuel Arnold, describing William Hine in 1790 (1687–1730, more organist and composer than singer, it would seem) wrote: 'He sang elegantly in a feigned voice'.[5] (We address the question of 'feigned' elsewhere.)

John Dyne was a distinguished alto and a composer of glees. He was sworn as a gentleman of the Chapel Royal in 1772 and appointed a lay-vicar of Westminster Abbey in 1779. Dyne was one of the soloists at the Handel Commemoration concerts in Westminster Abbey in 1784, but committed suicide in 1788.

Charles Knyvett (1751–1822), formerly a chorister of Westminster Abbey, became a noted alto of his day. He was another of the alto soloists at the Handel Commemoration of 1784 and was a Gentleman of the Chapel Royal from 1786 to 1808, and from 1796 he was Organist to the Chapel. He was considered 'one of the best singers of glees' and 'perhaps the best catch singer in England'.[6] His son, William Knyvett (1779–1856), was also a noted alto and was described as 'outstanding' by Hough.[7]

[4] Op. cit., p. 406
[5] Arnold, *Cathedral Music*, vol. 3, p. 226
[6] Edward Pine, *The Westminster Abbey Singers* (Dobson, 1953), pp. 148–9; he refers to Parke's *Musical Memoirs*
[7] Hough, op. cit., p. 18. See also Grove's *Dictionary*, 3rd edn, vol. III, pp. 39–40, for biographical details of the Knyvetts

Charles Smart Evans (1778–1849) was a chorister of the Chapel Royal. After his voice-change, he developed into an unusually fine alto. He was a composer of glees, anthems and motets. Evans was for some years organist of St Paul's, Covent Garden, and he sang in the choir of the Portuguese Ambassador's (Roman Catholic) Chapel in South Audley Street, Grosvenor Square (now the Grosvenor Chapel).

John Hindle (1761–1796) was another celebrated counter-tenor of the time. He was appointed a lay-vicar of Westminster Abbey in 1785; he sang before the Royal Family at the Worcester Musical Festival of 1788 and often at the London Vocal Concerts in 1791 and 1792 with Charles Knyvett. He composed many glees and songs. Hindle's name is associated with the conflated eighteenth-century manuscript version of *Dido and Aeneas* referred to earlier.

By PARTICULAR DESIRE.
For the Benefit of Miss CATLEY.
At the Theatre-Royal, Covent-Garden,
This present TUESDAY, MARCH 21, 1775,
(For the LAST TIME of performing it THIS SEASON)
LOVE in a VILLAGE.
Justice Woodcock, by Mr. SHUTER,
Hawthorn by Mr. REINHOLD,
Young Meadows by Mr. MATTOCKS
Sir W. Meadows by Mr. QUICK,
Eustace, Mr. YOUNG, Hodge, Mr. DUNSTALL,
Deborah, Mrs. PITT, Margery, Mrs. BAKER,
Lucinda by Mrs. MATTOCKS,
Rosetta by Miss CATLEY.
End of the Piece, " The Soldier tir'd of War's Alarms,"
From the Opera of ARTAXERXES,
By Miss CATLEY.
End of the Opera, Rural Merriment, by Mr. ALDRIDGE, Mrs. STEPHENS, &c.
To which will be added
The GOLDEN PIPPIN.
In which is Sung, " Guardian Angels," by Miss CATLEY.
Jupiter by Mr. REINHOLD,
Paris by Mr. MATTOCKS,
Momus by Mr. QUICK,
Mercury by Mr. DU-BELLAMY,
Venus by Miss BROWN,
Pallas by Mrs. BAKER, Iris by Miss VALOIS,
Juno by Miss CATLEY.
To conclude with
" All I ask of mortal Man, is to love me while he can,"
From COMUS.
Part of the Pit will be laid into the Boxes, where Servants will be allowed to keep Places.
On Thursday, The Ninth Night, for the AUTHOR,
CLEONICE, PRINCESS of BITHYNIA.

Theatre posters can be deceptive – Mattocks was a prominent stage counter-tenor during the later part of the eighteenth century

The Academy of Antient Musick was formed in 1710 in London by Dr Pepusch, Gates, King, Dr Greene and Galliard, and it merged with the King's Concerts of Antient Musick after 1731. Various distinguished musicians were members, though apparently not Handel. It became extinct in 1792. Counter-tenors were both members and performers at the Academy;

not surprisingly, in view of its aim of keeping alive the taste for earlier styles of music. Charles Knyvett sang there, and so did John Immyns (1700–64). He was an alto, reports Hough,[8] and an active member of the Academy. He was one of the last lutenists to the Chapel Royal, and he founded The Madrigal Society in 1741.

During the eighteenth century glee and glee clubs proliferated. They provided entertainment for male voices, first in small groups and then in larger ensembles. Extensive solos and trios for men's voices were still being written for cathedral singers; glees were their secular counterpart – male 'sing-songs' had been popular throughout the century.

Cathedral counter–tenors still obtained engagements on the concert–stage, if not (it would seem) in many major opera productions, by the end of the century. One, though, who had a Covent Garden contract was John Saville (1735–1803). This famous Lichfield Cathedral alto lay–vicar and much–travelled secular solo singer introduces an important name and various points for discussion. He appeared at Gloucester in 1790:[9]

> In Mr Saville's triumphant songs, 'O Thou that Tellest', and 'O Death Where is Thy Sting ?' his voice was clear, sweet and powerful as we ever remember to have heard it, and they were given all his animated expression. His indignant scorn in 'Thou Shalt Break Them in Pieces' was very fine.

The last sentence in this letter to the *Gloucester Journal* has long been used as ammunition by those who contend that altos and counter–tenors are separate voices. It has also caused many people much puzzlement, because it refers to a tenor aria. At first, one is tempted to wonder whether the writer had confused the voice of Saville with that of the tenor, Spreay, as he had presumably written the letter either from memory or from notes. Another possibility is that 'Thou Shalt Break Them' might have been performed by Saville in a higher key especially for the occasion. At first it seems unlikely; though Handel himself was happy to transpose (even re–compose) other arias to accommodate particular singers in different performances of *Messiah*, the practice should surely have died with him.

The probable answer is simple, and is provided by Lysons. He reports authoritatively that:[10]

> The performance at Gloucester, in 1790, consisted wholly of *selections* [author's italics] (chiefly from Handel), except the masque of *Acis and Galatea* on the first evening.... Mr Saville ... appeared at the Meeting of the Three Choirs for the first time this year, as principal counter–tenor. The other principal singers were Spreay ...

It appears, therefore, that the letter–writer referred not to a complete performance of *Messiah*, but to a concert at which selections were performed from various works by Handel. If Saville sang this tenor aria out of its usual context it could quite easily have been in a key transposed for the occasion. It would make a fine declamatory aria for counter–tenor and there was no reason at all why Saville should not have sung it as a vehicle for his own voice. (In his early days, Deller did the same to fine effect with certain Purcell songs written originally for tenor

---

[8] Ibid., p. 18
[9] *Gloucester Journal*, 19 September 1791
[10] Lysons, *History of the Meetings of the Three Choirs* (Gloucester, 1812), p. 230

or soprano. Early music purists frown on this now, but transposition of individual songs or arias has been a long–established practice with singers of all voice–ranges.

If, on the other hand, Saville did sing 'Thou Shalt Break Them in Pieces' at the normal tenor pitch, he must have had the technique to do so. While observing that he was presumably a low counter–tenor of some kind, we cannot escape the fact that had he been a 'tenor' his technique would have been based on falsetto head–notes anyway. He could therefore have dealt with both 'O Thou That Tellest' and 'Thou Shalt Break Them'. (Saville's life is further detailed in Appendix Three.)

To underline the fact that altos could sing tenor arias, the alto William Lambe sang not only the recitative 'Behold a Virgin Shall Conceive' (presumably followed by the aria 'O Thou that Tellest') at the first performance of *Messiah* in Dublin in 1742, but he seems also to have sung the tenor recitative 'He That Dwelleth in Heaven'. Since this immediately precedes 'Thou Shalt Break Them', he would also have sung the aria.[11]

Writing in 1889, John S. Bumpus refers to the important cathedral composer and singer, Jonathan Battishill (1738-1801):[12]

Battishill was one of the professionals engaged to sing at the private concerts given by those marvellous boys Charles and Samuel Wesley at the house of their father, the Rev. Charles Wesley, in Chesterfield Street, Marylebone. In after years, Samuel Wesley was wont to relate that Battishill's singing was 'very engaging, energetic and commanding' and that it was 'a high treat to hear him take part in a duet of Handel's or a canzonet of Travers's, or sing any one of Purcell's songs or anthems'. His voice was a fine counter tenor.

Jonathan Battishill
(1738–1901)

Rimbault[13] records that the voice of Sir John Goss's uncle, John Jeremiah Goss, was a 'pure' alto of beautiful quality. In 1808, he was appointed a Gentleman of the Chapel Royal and at about the same time as vicar–choral at both St Paul's Cathedral and Westminster Abbey. His skill and taste in part–singing were remarkable. He was for many years the principal alto at the Meetings of the Three Choirs (The Three Choirs Festival) and was also a noted teacher of singing.

The word 'pure' may mean tonally ethereal or unblemished or indicate a sound totally natural. A 'pure' alto could therefore be either the once familiar round–voiced cathedral falsetto–alto or a more pharyngeally–supported voice. Is Sainsbury's *Dictionary*, which gives him as 'not a falsettist' (whatever the term really means), to be taken at face value? Words are liable to be manipulated to support a particular argument. Often, interpretation is based on current usage. Therefore, bearing Rimbault's epithet 'pure alto' in mind, one might be able to interpret a notice of his singing in Cornwall:[14]

---

[11] D. W. Kennan, '*The Messiah* in Dublin' (Hinrichsen's *Musical Year Book*, 1952), vol. VII, p. 466

[12] J. S. Bumpus, *A History of English Cathedral Music* (Werner Laurie, 1890), pp. 325–6

[13] Quoted by Hough, op. cit., p. 19, where he mistakenly puts 'father'; he corrected this in a letter to the author, 3 June 1991

[14] *The Royal Cornwall Gazette* for 13 August 1806

> Mr Goss's fine *contr-alto* was exceedingly adored by the *dilettanti*, and both
> pleased and astonished those who were unaccustomed to that tone and
> compass ...

His engagement was to take part in the Truro Grand Festival, directed by Ashleys, Managers
[*sic*] of Oratorios at the Theatre Royal, Covent Garden. Mozart's version of *Messiah* was
included in the festival, and Goss sang the alto solos in this, together with miscellaneous
selections in other concerts.

The following year he was referred to as 'Goss, a favourite counter-tenor at the Vocal
Concerts in London ... [who] appeared at the meeting this year for the first time (1807).'[15]
He returned for the 1809 Truro Festival, when he sang in Handel's *Dettingen Te Deum, Judas
Maccabeus* and *Messiah*, and in three other concerts. A review (short, because international
affairs predominated at the time) pronounced that Goss was 'excellent'.[16]

At Norwich in the early nineteenth century, the minor canons were a musical group and
sang with the cathedral choir. An anonymous ear-witness writes:[17]

> Well do I remember the delight with which I used to listen to the service in
> Norwich Cathedral, when the Minor Canons, eight in number, filed off to
> their stalls, Precentor Millard at their head, whose admirable style and correct
> taste as a singer I have never heard surpassed, Browne's majestic tenor;
> Whittingham's sweet alto, and Hansell's sonorous bass; while Walker's silvery
> tones and admirable recitation found their way into every corner of the huge
> building ...

Outside cathedrals and academic institutions, cold winds were blowing for counter-tenors, but
Lysons's history of the Three Choirs festivals, and the accounts of the Truro Festival confirm
that there was still demand for, and supply of, solo counter-tenors from London and
elsewhere.

Records of the Truro Festival reward detailed examination. The 1813 festival included the
counter-tenor 'Mr Garbett', who was listed with two sopranos, a tenor and a bass. There was
no complete *Messiah* that year, but these performers had certainly sung it at the other venues,
where Garbett performed 'Behold a Virgin Shall Conceive', 'O Thou that Tellest', 'He was
Despised' and the duet 'O Death Where is Thy Sting?'. He did not sing 'But Who May Abide'
and 'He Shall Feed his Flock', which were taken by the ladies – it is not clear in which
versions. In true liberal fashion, Madame Catallani, soprano, sang the tenor aria 'Every Valley'
and seemingly anything else she fancied, rather as the male soprano Guarducci sang most of
the tenor's pieces in London in 1767 under the direction of J.C. Smith the younger.[18]

Truro programmes survive to show that Garbett took part in the following works:

Winds Gently Whisper	A.T.B. glee by Whitaker
Disdainful of Danger	A.T.B. trio by Whitaker
'O God Wash Thou Me'	aria by Ciampi

---

[15] Lysons, op. cit., p. 248
[16] *Royal Cornwall Gazette*, 28 August 1809
[17] Quoted by Bumpus, op. cit., p. 355
[18] Richard Luckett, *Handel's Messiah, A Celebration* (Gollancz, 1992) p. 189

'Thou Shalt Bring Them In'	aria from *Israel in Egypt* by Handel
'Blessed is He'	quartet from 'Regina' [*sic* – printer's error for *Requiem*] by Mozart
The Wolf	A.T.B. glee by Shield, arranged Magrath
Faithless Emma	[a song?]
'O Thou That Tellest'	aria from *Messiah* by Handel
'He Shall Feed His Flock'	aria from *Messiah* by Handel

Apparently, 'Mr Garbett's songs, 'O Thou That Tellest' and 'He Shall Feed His Flock' were admirably executed', and 'Mozart's sublime quartett, 'Blessed is He', was sung in a most solemn and impressive manner by Miss Nash, and Messrs Garbett, Magrath, and Comer'.[19]

The Truro Festivals were something of a grand 'roadshow'. Few local players or singers were involved and the orchestra and chorus seem mostly to have been London–based. Every other year the Ashleys of Covent Garden toured the West Country, spending one week each at Bristol, Taunton, Exeter, Plymouth and Truro. In the intervening years they toured other regions.

Further recent research by Patrick Johns has yielded a clutch of important Truro reviews. Unless the singer concerned possessed a particularly controversial technique, they seem to demonstrate the vicissitudes which the solo counter–tenor, and his image, were undergoing by the third decade of the nineteenth century:

> A new voice in Mr Penphraze was introduced ... we have not yet seen his equal on the Truro boards. His voice (a counter–tenor) is not very powerful, but possesses much flexibility and sweetness, and his studies have been properly directed.[20]

> Mr Penphraze continues to delight all who possess a taste for higher refinements of the vocal art – his talent places him far above many who make much *noise* in the musical world.[21]

> Penphraze sang that beautiful song "Said a Smile to a Tear" in which he made some pretty turns; but we would advise this young actor to study, if he may be allowed the expression, the emphasis of music, a more distinct expression of the words, and to be less lavish of the trill and the run, of which he appears to be the perfect master, in important passages of his songs.[22]

> Mr Penfraze [*sic*], it appears to us, is only half understood in Truro – he would never otherwise sing without an encore. We, however, seriously recommend him to study a more intelligible enunciation.[23]

---

[19] *Royal Cornwall Gazette*, 4 September 1813

[20] *West Briton*, 9 November 1827

[21] *West Briton*, 23 November 1827

[22] *The Royal Cornwall Gazette*, 27 November 1827

[23] *West Briton*, 7 December 1827

At the request that 'ALL'S WELL' might be sung, Miss Campbell and Mr
Penphraze stepped forward.... the well-known duet at length commenced but
proved an abortive attempt. Miss Campbell might have succeeded but for the
strange tones and ludicrous gestures of Penphraze, which produced a sensible
effect on the risible muscles of the audience. Why was not Miller sent on to
sing the second [part]? His manly English voice would have been more
suitable for this favourite duet, and better supported the lady.[24]

Between 7 December 1829 and 5 January 1828, the *West Briton* critic does not mention
Penphraze. A performance of 'All's Well' (with no performers named) and the rest of the
evening, are described as 'unremarkable'.

'When Thy Bosom Heaves a Sigh'... really was very well sung, Miss
Campbell never displayed her vocal talent to so much advantage, and Mr
Penphraze gave his part with much sweetness.[25]

After the play, that charming duet 'When Thy Bosom Heaves A Sigh' was
sung by Miss Campbell and Mr Penphraze but with no better success than
'All's Well'. It is much against the lady to be so matched; their voices will
never harmonise. She executed her part in good style, but the lower notes of
her companion scarcely reached the side boxes, and his upper notes defy
description. He should sing alone, when he may rise to *alt* or *super alt* if he
pleases, hat and all, and enjoy his shake ad libitum, so we have no more
duets.[26]

Mr Penphraze sang with sweetness and execution. Respecting the treatment
this excellent vocalist has received in Truro, we cannot refrain from saying
a few words.... That which is not understood is unlikely to be appreciated ...
what chance has a singer – a fine Counter Tenor (of astonishing compass) –
has of becoming a favorite in a provincial theatre; especially where there be
an orchestral leader who manifests on all occasions every possible hostility
towards him. We recommend Mr Penphraze, notwithstanding the jeers to
which he has been subjected, by a small part of the auditory, to cultivate his
talent with assiduity – to study music, and, with a manly contempt of his
enemies, firmly cherish the hope that his future fame will ere long cause them
to regret the endeavour to crush the aspirings of a real, though unappreciated,
talent.[27]

Penphraze enacted *Count Basset* with his usual ability – could it be possible
that the sprightly Jenny was in danger from such a suitor? – but enough – our
prescription it seems disagrees with this choleric patient, who has much to
learn and to forget, before he will become even a tolerable actor. With regard

[24] *Royal Cornwall Gazette*, 5 January 1828
[25] *West Briton*, 11 January 1828
[26] *Royal Cornwall Gazette*, 12 January 1828
[27] *West Briton*, 18 January 1828

to the enconium pronounced upon his voice and singing by a neighbouring critic – *chacun à son metier et son gout* – we can only repeat that the effect of all that is ascribed to him when he sings in conjunction with another is lost upon the *million*, this scientific judge himself being perhaps the only one in that number who is sufficiently refined to enjoy it.[28]

It seems that the singers in these concerts were expected to take the occasional rôle as a supporting actor. They certainly performed songs before and after 'straight' plays and some ballad–opera amusements.

There is no mention of Penphraze in reviews in the *Royal Cornwall Gazette* between 27 November 1827 and 5 January 1828. Judging from concert advertisements it appears he did not contribute to every week's offerings. He was clearly a talking point in Truro and apparently a figure of fun for much of his audience. In these reviews may be discerned a man who represented a solo voice type with a vocal and musical technique which was quickly passing from fashion; there may have been changes in public taste since the performances of Goss in 1809 and Garbett in 1813. He was accused of an 'un–English' over–ornamented style (too eighteenth–century? foppish? unmasculine? not sturdy enough?) and of possessing a ludicrous acting–style. The complaint of poor enunciation may have referred to a bel canto emphasis on beautiful tone rather than clarity of words. We may note, too, that the orchestral leader exhibited hostility towards him rather as, notoriously, Alfred Deller would encounter it almost a century and a half later.

Even by the 1830s, it is clear that though there were counter–tenors who expected to be offered secular employment as soloists, they were not always obtaining it. A plaintive letter appeared in *The Musical World* in 1836[29] whose object was, its writer said:

> to draw your attention to a situation in which myself, and others who have the misfortune of being denominated counter–tenor singers, are placed by the introduction of female contraltos in most of the festivals and concerts instead of the legitimate altos. For instance, not one of us is engaged at the forth–coming festivals at the Exeter Hall.

This must refer to solo counter–tenors because there were still substantial numbers of chorus altos in the Crystal Palace Handel Festival Choirs until the end of the century.

Lord Mount Edgcumbe's account of the Handel Commemoration in 1834 had included:[30]

> There being no good counter–tenor, the song 'He was Despised', which is generally given to that voice, was given to a female contralto.

This might initially seem to be surprising. There were professional counter–tenors who were required to perform solo work in the London cathedral choirs. It is likely, however, that by

---

[28] *Royal Cornwall Gazette*, 19 January 1828
[29] Quoted by Hardwick, *A Singularity of Voice* (Proteus, 1980), pp. 91–2 without exact citation. *The Musical World* was published between 1836 and 1891.
[30] Edgcumbe, *Musical Reminiscences* (fourth edn, London, 1834), p. 281

this date their presence as soloists on the concert platform was beginning to appear unfashionable, even in Handel's oratorio. Percy Scholes wrote:[31]

> Mendelssohn gave the contralto prominence by writing solos for Madame Sainton Dolby in *Elijah* (1847), and since then, solos for that voice have been a recognised feature in oratorio composition, the alto voice falling more and more into the background, even in chorus work.

He was only too correct, though the solo contralto (outside oratorio) was successful before Mendelssohn. Scholes continued, presumably with Dr Charles Burney's comprehensive tome on the first Handel Festival open at his side:[32]

> In the great Westminster Abbey Handel Commemoration Festival of 1784, there [had been] ... in the chorus forty five altos [listed as 'counter–tenors'], with not a single contralto (not from any objection to the appearance of women in the cathedral, since there were such among the sopranos).

A careful study of the illustration of the 1784 Handel Commemoration choir reveals a few women in the front ranks of first and second altos; by that date and in this context, this may seem remarkable. In fact these are the mere six sopranos who were employed, the rest of the fifty–three trebles being boys, and who were accommodated in front of the altos. In the third row of the trebles there seem to be two male figures. It is unlikely that these are the two (soprano) castrato soloists, Signors Pacchierotti and Bartolini, because they are to be seen in the front row. It is most unlikely that they are the boys' supervisors. Three of the soloists were counter–tenors, who thus made a total of forty–eight persons with this voice in the choral forces.

The Choir and Orchestra, Handel Commemoration of 1784 (detail)

---

[31] Percy Scholes, *The Oxford Companion to Music* (ninth edn, O.U.P., 1955), p. 27
[32] Loc. cit.

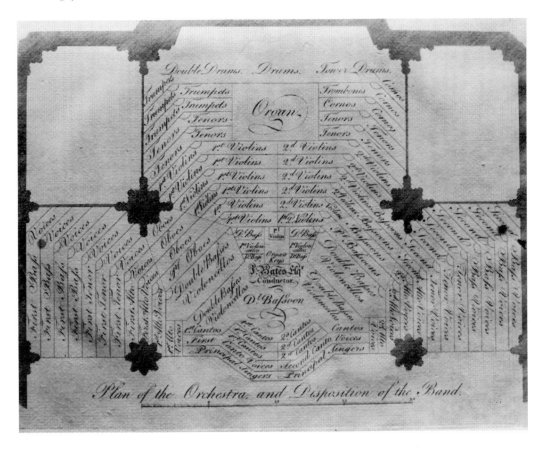

Handel Commemoration: Plan of the Orchestra and Disposition of the Band

It is illuminating to continue to examine subsequent Handel Festival performances. In the first Great Handel Festival at the Crystal Palace (by then moved to Sydenham) in 1859, the choir consisted of two thousand seven hundred and sixty–five persons (accompanied by four hundred and sixty players) of which four hundred and nineteen were altos and three hundred were contraltos. It sounds rather impressive, but there were no solo altos; the solo contralto reigned supreme. *The Musical Times* review[33] of the event speaks of 'The alto voice – well defined throughout ... large number of male voices ... ladies not powerful enough in lower register'. This could suggest that the writer (and presumably critics generally) expected altos to use their chest register. It could also mean that there was an acute shortage of genuine contraltos in the Festival Choir. Probably, many so–called were really second sopranos.

In 1883, the Leeds Festival Chorus still included forty–two altos but only seventeen contraltos.

Percy Scholes wrote that 'Apparently there was at this period a definite movement set on foot in favour of contraltos as against altos, for in June 1884, a protesting letter in *The*

---

[33] 1859

Musical Times insisted that it was a great mistake to do away with altos'.[34] The complete letter is interesting but Scholes quoted only part of it; for some reason, he did not include the part starting with the phrase 'Curiously enough'. It is worth including – it speaks volumes:[35]

> I ... protest against the gradual disuse of the 'alto' voice in our leading choral societies. It is, I think, a very great mistake to do away with altos and substitute contraltos in oratorio music, at all events. Curiously enough, in one of our most celebrated choirs this is gradually being done, as I am informed, through the conductor holding the opinion of ladies' superiority, while he himself is an alto, and has had several relatives in the profession with that voice. Hoping my protest will avail to lessen this (as I conceive) injustice to a very useful and beautiful voice ...

In the next Leeds Festival Chorus (1886), we find only sixteen altos as against fifty-seven contraltos.

The numbers of altos diminished further. In the Crystal Palace Handel Commemoration Festival Choir of 1900, there were only seventy-three altos whereas previously, in 1859, there had been four hundred and nineteen. By 1903, the number of altos in the same choir was to shrink to twenty-three in a gathering still presumably of traditional size overall. A review in 1903 rather curiously said: 'The alto part, sweet in quality, might have been strengthened by a larger number of male altos, there being only twenty-three "bearded altos" as Mendelssohn called them, on the Handel orchestra'.[36] [*sic*]

Further into the twentieth century, seventy-one contraltos were to appear in the Norwich Festival Choir of 1924, and not one alto – not even from the cathedral choir. Percy Scholes's phrase summed it up poignantly: 'Thus in 140 years we have a swing over from oratorio choirs with not a single contralto to oratorio choirs with not a single alto.'[37] So the 1884 letter of protest in *The Musical Times* was ignored just as, twenty-eight years before, in 1856, the letter to *The Musical World* had also been ignored.

Cathedral music *per se* had a sheltered existence and, though almost all serious alto solo work had gradually faded during the nineteenth century, there had been plenty to do in cathedral, church, and glee club. It would seem that opportunity had lingered longer for him in the glades of Academe, a world more conservative perhaps because of its historical links with the cloister. Describing the installation of a new Chancellor at the University of Cambridge in 1835, Bumpus writes:[38]

> ... the task of composing an Ode fell upon [Thomas Attwood] Walmisley. The performance took place in the Senate House, the exponents of the solo parts being Malibran, Terrail (a favourite alto of enormous bulk), Braham, Henry Phillips, and John Parry ...

---

[34] Percy Scholes, 'The Decline of the Male Alto' in *Mirror of Music*, 1947, vol. 1, p. 57 (and *O.C.M.*, p. 27)

[35] *The Musical Times*, vol. 15 no. 496, June 1884, pp. 360–1

[36] *The Musical Times*, July 1903, p. 475

[37] Percy Scholes, *O.C.M.*, p. 27

[38] Bumpus, op. cit., p. 467

(Note the word 'favourite'.) However, in 1847, the Installation Ode, also by Walmisley, was written for the contralto, Charlotte Helen Sainton Dolby.

Performance of the Installation Ode, Cambridge, 1847

The Purcell Commemoration Choir in Westminster Abbey, assembled and conducted by the staunch Purcellian Sir Frederick Bridge, contained in 1895 only eighteen altos as against forty–four contraltos. We know, however, that the alto solos were taken by men, lay–vicars of the Abbey choir.[39]

As Romantic influences had gathered momentum, so the tessitura of alto parts had begun to rise, especially under the influence of foreign composers like Mendelssohn. By the middle of the nineteenth century, not only had secular alto solos become the almost exclusive province of the female contralto but secular chorus alto parts were going the same way.

---

[39] 'Official Programme for the Purcell Bi–Centenary Commemoration Service' (Novello), for Thursday 21 November 1895

*Example 14. The nineteenth–century 'alto' solo with a high tessitura,
from 'Lord, I Flee to Thee for Refuge', Mendelssohn (1809–1847)*

Despite this, Balfe's opera *The Bohemian Girl*, provides a notable exception. Michael Balfe (1808–1870) was a well–known operatic baritone singer. Though thoroughly Romantic in musical style, *The Bohemian Girl* demonstrates a fascinating last flourish of English eight-eenth–century chorus designation. Although, previously, English operatic and stage music has been considered by most writers to have been totally bereft of counter–tenors by the first few decades of the nineteenth century at the very latest, this opera, produced in 1843 at Drury Lane Theatre, London, specifically included male altos as an important part of the choral forces even when the solo rôles were taken by conventional voice types. It contains three A.T.B. choruses (of 90, 19 and 91 bars respectively) of masculine characters: Nobles and Hunters. The alto tessitura was that of the classical counter–tenor; indeed the part (labelled alto) was written, like that of the tenor, in octave G Clef. We return to this work later.

Nevertheless, composers now wrote most opera and oratorio alto lines much higher on average; in anticipation, in opera at any rate, of female voices. (Compare the chorus–alto tessitura in Purcell and Handel with those in later operatic works or oratorios by Mendelssohn and Brahms, for example.) The alto part was now often unsuited to and uncomfortable – sometimes even impossible – for the male alto, a condition exacerbated by a general and relentless rise in orchestral pitch from the 1840s to the present day.

Cathedral music was affected eventually, to some extent; but kept at first to its own brand of Romanticism in the character of Samuel Sebastian Wesley (1810–1876) who was steeped in the English tradition. He wrote always for male choirs which included counter–tenors. The first of the following examples, from his anthem, *Let Us Lift Up Our Heart*, in its original 1853 version. This may be compared with a relatively modern edition intended for parish choirs in the 1930s. A footnote to this edition (* *this may either be quietly sung by contraltos or left to the tenors and basses*) indicated by a small asterisk in bar 9, at the alto entry, gives us another, secondary, point of interest. At this time, *c*1933, the editors obviously expected there to be either no altos or, at least, only ineffective ones. There seems to be no suggestion that chest– or basic–voice should be used. Clearly, contraltos were expected to be present, who would, of course, not shrink from using theirs!

*Examples 15 and 16. The opening section of 'Let Us Lift Up Our Heart',
S. S. Wesley; editions of 1853 (above) and c1933 (below)*

Advertisements for voices in musical journals indicate a definite dichotomy. *The Musical Times* of 1859 advertised for sopranos and a contralto for a London church and for a contra-alto and basso for a parish church in Manchester. It is not clear whether contra-alto refers to a female contralto. It would seem possible that the evangelical wing preferred contraltos as being nearer in spirit to Nonconformist practice.

The nineteenth century is known in English ecclesiastical history, above all, for the flowering of the Oxford Movement. One of its many musical consequences was a move to establish or, sometimes, to restore traditional male choirs. Advertisements for male altos to fill vacancies in these choirs are very numerous. The cathedral world went on as before. Durham Cathedral advertised for 'a counter-tenor singer to the vacant place'.[40]

We have some vivid details of the four altos within the Westminster Abbey choral foundation in the late nineteenth century. Apparently, the two singers on the Cantoris side of the choir were a wine merchant named Birch who travelled up from Brighton each day for the services, and John Foster who '... as a small boy had stood on William IV's dining table to sing to the guests ... He (Foster) was particularly fond of Tallis and Gibbons and used to say to the boys that Farrant's "If Ye Love Me" was one of the finest pieces of church music'.[41] Pine was perhaps mistaken about William IV's table because Foster was a chorister at St George's Chapel, Windsor, from 1841 to 1847, during Queen Victoria's reign.[42] Whether it was Foster or Pine who mistook Farrant for Tallis, we cannot be sure, but clearly Foster was in no doubt (even in the later nineteenth century) about the most suitable choral repertoire for his particular voice range and type. He sang in the choir for the coronation of Edward VII in 1902; his long life was therefore concurrent with the years of the alto's decline.

Pine[43] describes the two Decani altos at Westminster thus: 'Sexton and Schartau, both possessing good voices, but not liked by the boys, who objected to their singing the solos which they regarded as their due'. Clearly, Decani was the favoured side for higher alto solo-work, of which there must have been a generous amount, to judge by the boys' reaction. 'Sexton possessed black 'mutton-chop' whiskers and a heavy black moustache, and used to sing out of the side of his mouth. The boys considered he "looked like a tom-cat and sounded like one"; but it is doubtful whether they were very good judges.'[44] Singing from the side of the mouth suggests that altos even in the important choir of Westminster Abbey were probably self trained, or at least had not enjoyed the usual comprehensive vocal training presumably undertaken by their tenor and bass peers. Alternatively, it could suggest that such a technique was Sexton's method of hearing himself among over-loud tenors and basses.

Sir Henry Wood had the highest praise for the male-voice quartet 'The Meister Glee Singers', of which Sexton was the alto, when they sang for the 1899 Promenade Concerts.[45]

Contrary to some of today's notions, there were occasional surfacings of secular music by important earlier English composers in the middle of last century, and some of it was performed in well-known places. At the Theatre Royal, Drury Lane, London, there was a

---

[40] *The Musical Times* for September 1858, p. 297

[41] Pine, op. cit., p. 231

[42] See Lady Elvey, *The Life and Reminiscences of Sir George Elvey* (Sampson, Low, Marston & Co. Ltd, 1894) and Neville Wridgway, *The Choristers of St. George's Chapel* (Charles Luff and Co. Ltd, 1980), for full accounts of the event

[43] Pine, op. cit., p. 232

[44] Loc. cit.

[45] Henry Wood, *My Life of Music* (Gollancz, 1938), p. 180

production of a play *The Patrician's Daughter* by J. Westland Marston with a prologue by Charles Dickens. On the same bill[46] (as an afterpiece) was a production of Purcell's *King Arthur*.

Printed programmes also exist for concerts of what is known today as 'early music'. One of these includes,[47] in a 'Concert of Ancient Music', on Wednesday 21 April 1841:

King Arthur	Purcell
Military Symphony	[Haydn?]
Song and Chorus:	'Come if You Dare'.

The proceedings were declared to be 'Under the Direction of the First Duke of Wellington'. The song is performed today by a conventional tenor, but the tessitura is suited to a low counter–tenor. The Wellesleys were amateur musicians from the same stock as the Wesleys, and the Duke of Wellington was related to the Earl of Mornington.

The Drury Lane playbill gives no year, but the date was Saturday 16 December, seemingly some time in the 1840s. Our chief interest would be not so much to welcome the appearance of a Purcell demi–opera (or, in the second case, excerpts from one) at this unlikely period, but to ascertain, if possible, whether the opera cast list or concert contained a counter–tenor, or whether a tenor was substituted. However, the cast list follows the usual infuriating theatrical practice of omitting all vocal designation.

In a corner of Elgar's birthplace at Broadheath, near Worcester, hangs a framed concert poster. It advertises Mr H. Lane's Farewell Concert in the Music Hall, Worcester, 18 April 1876, which included items given by an instrumental ensemble in which the young Elgar played the violin. The vocalists are listed:

Miss Edwards
Master Box
Mr Gillham
Mr Pugh
Mr H. Lane
Mr Gummery
Mr J. D. Price
Mr Bennett

We might assume that some of the male singers were cathedral lay–clerks. Their voices are not given, but the printed programme helps us reconstruct them to some extent.

Miss Edwards seems to have been a soprano or mezzo–soprano and Master Box was perhaps a cathedral chorister. Mr Gillham was obviously the alto, as he sang the top part in a Mendelssohn glee with Pugh, Lane and Price and the second part in what seems to be another Mendelssohn glee, and the top line in *Dame Durden*, a humorous trio by Henry Harrington, M. D. (1727–1816). Two Hatton part–songs are listed, and these were probably sung by the same combinations of A.T.T.B. or S.A.T.B. voices. Two items include the boy with three of the men, including Gillham on the second line; nowhere does the soprano sing

---

[46] Displayed in The Dickens House Museum, Broadstairs, Kent
[47] A bound copy is displayed in Stratfield Saye, Hampshire, the country house of the Duke of Wellington

with the ensemble. Like some of the men, her contribution comprises solo and duet material. Apart from the boy, Gillham is the only singer not given a solo or duet.

From nearly twenty years later there comes another illuminating example of one of the few secular activities available to altos other than private or semi–private glee–club singing. An advertisement for a bazaar in aid of the fund for a new vicarage for the parish of St Thomas, Finsbury Park included a Grand Concert to be held on 13 November 1894 at 8.30 p.m. In this Mr Ernest Marriott, alto (St Paul's Cathedral), Mr W. H. Stevenson, baritone, Mr Douglas St Aubyn, tenor (St Mary, Stoke Newington), and Mr Vernon Taylor, bass (St Paul's Cathedral), who formed the Amphion Quartet, were billed as a main attraction.[48] The evening may have included solos, perhaps ballads, from some of the gentlemen. If so, as in the case of Gillham, it would seem unlikely, though not impossible, that Marriott sang one.

He and his Chapel Royal, cathedral, and collegiate alto peers throughout England were the linear descendants at least of Abell, Howell and Hughes. How sad that even the best of the late–Victorian altos were unlikely to be engaged outside cathedral, church or glee club for anything more exciting than an Islington Bazaar! Stevenson, St Aubyn and Taylor were, no doubt, singers heavily engaged elsewhere. Islington, for them, was probably a bit of additional fun. For poor Marriott and his contemporary counter–tenors, glee–singing may well have been almost the only work outside the cathedral that was available. Co–incidentally, it is interesting that there is also mention of a 'March in B flat, introducing the air of The Bailiff's Daughter of Islington.... [It] has been specially composed for the occasion by Mr Munro Davison.'[49] Davison, referred to later, was a well–known alto and was the assistant choir–master at The Temple Church from 1893 to 1927.

There is another highly revealing reference to Marriott in a valuable book of lectures.[50] He was included among several singers engaged to provide a small choir to demonstrate one of a series of important talks at the Music Loan Exhibition of the Worshipful Company of Musicians at Fishmongers' Hall, London Bridge, in June and July, 1904. The lecture in question was 'Our Cathedral Composers and Their Works', given by G. F. Huntley, Mus. Doc. The singers were listed: there were four (named) boy choristers, seven named gentlemen, headed by J. Sarjeant and E. Marriott (these noted as 'of St Paul's Cathedral') and 'other members of the Choir of St Peter's, Eaton Square', London. Most revealingly, there was a Mrs G. F. Huntley, A.R.C.M., contralto. Her name suggests why she and not another contralto was there. The music given ranged from Gibbons to Stanford. The only item likely to have been sung by Mrs Huntley was: 'Alto Solo from *Hear, O Thou Shepherd* – Walmisley', a well–known cathedral anthem of the nineteenth century.

Despite the presence of professionals from St Paul's cathedral, for whose vocal type the solo was definitely written, it would appear to have been sung by a singer for whose vocal type it manifestly was not. That this took place in a lecture and programme which purported to give an accurate account and demonstration of a unique English art–form is extraordinary. The exhibition and lecture series included the use of 'authentic' instruments and seems to have been a musicological event of great importance, so the inclusion of a contralto (however talented a singer) instead of an alto was as unfortunate as, in the particular circumstances, it should have been unlikely – even in 1904. This was not the only odd aspect of the exhibition

---

[48] Handbook of a Grand Bazaar to be held in the Athenaeum, Highbury New Park, Islington, London, 1894, p. 54

[49] Ibid., p. 40

[50] *English Music, 1604–1904* (Walter Scott Publishing Co., London, 1906), p. 293

and the lecture series. No less a pioneer performer, musicologist and instrument maker than Arnold Dolmetsch was excluded.

Counter–tenor singers of this period must have found the situation galling and occasionally hurtful when, on rare occasions, they attempted to sing solo songs on stage or in a salon. In 1889, George Bernard Shaw wrote:[51]

> Thackeray students will remember that when Colonel Newcome returned from India, and obliged a convivial circle by singing a ballad in a counter–tenor voice with florid ornaments in the taste of his own heyday, he was astonished to find everybody laughing at him. But I myself have seen a singer – a young man – appear before an audience of "the classes" in a blue evening coat with brass buttons, and gravely sing a song by Mendelssohn in an alto voice.

There seems no reason to consider the possibility that the 'young man' may have been an older boy (with changed voice) of the famous Bluecoat School, then still in London. Shaw would not have associated the singing of a youth with that of Thackeray's Newcome. Shaw continued, underlining the alto's effect on the Mendlessohn song:[52]

> The effect was by no means disagreeable; but it was so strange and unexpected that the room positively vibrated with suppressed laughter. The same thing would happen at one of Messrs Boosey's ballad concerts if an alto were engaged; though downstairs, at the Christy Minstrels, an alto, black with burnt cork, might at the same moment be piping away as a matter of course, to an audience quite familiar with his voice. Thus to some people the man alto is an everyday phenomenon, whilst to others he is either a Thackerayan tradition or an extravagant novelty.

We note again the tendency for audiences of more popular music to accept happily what more serious audiences find bizarre, and we note once more the use of falsetto in black, or quasi-black, music.

Several reasons have been given for the decline of the secular solo counter–tenor. What should be the most obvious of these needs to be emphasised. The unique timbre of the classical counter–tenor does not normally suit music of the Romantic school any more than this music suits the voice; one may as well play Mendelssohn's *Songs without Words* on a harpsichord. The change of musical style is surely also the main reason for the warmer, rounder and more mellow sound that most male altos seem to have made by the later nine–teenth century and the first part of the twentieth. We must remember that the untutored or semi–tutored singer attempting falsetto tends to make a mellower sound more readily. There is, of course, a wealth of difference between this and the rich beauty of properly–trained altos of the Romantic school.

The terminology used, as the tone of tenors and altos gradually diverged, also changed; alto seemed more appropriate than counter–tenor. As the vocal pedagogy which followed Gilbert–

---

[51] George Bernard Shaw, *London Music in 1888–9 as Heard by Corno di Bassetto (Later Known as Bernard Shaw ...)* (Constable & Co., 1937), p. 240
[52] Loc. cit.

Louis Duprez took hold (see Part Two), the alto voice began to be the only male voice left which employed pure head-register tone.

No small wonder then that many alto voices of the Romantic period seem to have been thought unsuited for performance of much of the earlier solo repertoire, where that repertoire was known or recognized. One view today is that the counter-tenor or alto of this period was like many modern breeds of dog, in that some of its original characteristics had become blurred or been bred out in other interests. Kenneth R. Long put this received view clearly, if rather drastically:[53]

> There was still all the difference in the world between the astonishing brilliance, agility and clarity of the Restoration counter-tenor, and the sepulchral wordless hooting of the 19th century cathedral alto. Vocally, no doubt, the alto voice and the counter-tenor amount to the same thing: but there is a world of difference in mental approach.

Long cannot, of course, have heard a nineteenth-century cathedral alto; but we can discern his meaning.

There is, however, an alternative view of nineteenth-century alto timbre. We have a clearly accurate description of the voice of William Windsor (1860-1954), an alto and all-round musician, who sang consecutively in some important London church choirs. A testimonial written in 1891 by Thomas Pettit, a professor of the Guildhall School of Music and organist and choirmaster of St Peter's, Cranley Gardens, London, reads: 'Mr Windsor's voice is very useful in a choir; it has a good compass, nearly two octaves; the upper part is a bright tone, and the lower part goes down as a 'light tenor'.'[54] This description of an alto's vocal tone quality, so unlike that usually considered the late nineteenth-century norm, provokes further questions. If Windsor's voice was of a type familiar at the time, should it encourage an adjustment in what we have previously thought to have been typical then, or, because Windsor found only moderate success, did he possess a technique and sound which was becoming unfashionable? Was his voice more like a classical type of counter-tenor which was again to be much sought by the middle of the twentieth century?

For centuries, most parish churches had enjoyed the dubious benefits of very mixed gallery choirs and *ad hoc* ensembles of yokels or stout-hearted citizens. The few especially important medieval parish churches which had boasted salaried singers, in some form, seem to have lost them at the Reformation.

By the last third of the nineteenth century, the influence of the Oxford Movement had brought all-male choirs to almost every parish church in the land, robed in imitation of the cathedral choir. However large these choirs were, they would often at the start have been weak, musically. But Windsor was potentially of cathedral standard, and he is a good example of a London-based, experienced alto hoping to enter cathedral work. Pettit's testimonial was one of several supporting Windsor's application for a vicar-choralship at St Paul's Cathedral. It is not known exactly why he was unsuccessful, except that his rejection letter stresses the extremely high standard of the auditionees generally. He settled for Lincoln's Inn Chapel choir (perhaps broadly comparable in that period with that of The Temple Church, its sister Inn of Court) and he continued to sing there until the age of eighty.

---

[53] Kenneth R. Long, *The Music of the English Church* (Hodder & Stoughton, 1972), p. 271
[54] Windsor's papers are in the possession of Mrs A. S. Young, his grand-daughter

Windsor's vocal type might have been one of the second category described by George Bernard Shaw in 1889:[55]

> ... adult male alto and counter–tenor singers, though no longer as common as they once were, are still to be heard in all directions singing the parts specially written for their kind of voice by the composers of the great English schools: not the second–hand Handels and Mendelssohns of the past century and a half, but the writers of the glees, madrigals, and motets and services which are the true English musical classics.

Shaw appears to speak of two distinctly different voices, alto and counter–tenor. When writing of the singing of Colonel Newcome and the young man in blue, he uses 'counter–tenor' for one and 'alto' for the other. It is still possible, however, that he considered the terms as interchangeable:[56]

> Nowadays, however, since the opera and the concert platform offer golden opportunities to a tenor or a baritone, whereas an alto or counter–tenor is confined to the choir or the glee quartet all his life, a promising choir boy gets rid of his treble as soon as Nature permits him. The effect of this in diminishing the number of adult altos must be considerable.

Contrasting tonal qualities may have been the basis for Shaw's possible distinction between alto and counter–tenor. It is likely that various alto timbres were present in most choirs, then as now. In passing, we may note that Shaw's assessment of the boy's psychology is still broadly correct and that boys generally, and choristers often, still come to abhor the mark of immaturity in their treble voices, both in speaking and singing.

Some notable Oxford Movement choirs have continued with distinction to the present day; for instance that at Leeds Parish Church. The splendid choral foundations of St Michael's College, Tenbury, and All Saints, Margaret Street, London, which boasted important all–male choirs, are alas no more. They are much missed.

In some instances, the movement towards establishing a proper choral tradition actually restored an important choir after many wretched years of musical neglect or total absence. What is recorded of those re–establishments can help us discern the contemporary attitude to the counter–tenor and his part in the vocal tradition of this country.

Though there is no available evidence that The Temple Church, London, possessed a properly established choir in medieval times, it is unlikely that a foundation of such importance never included one. There is, by contrast, no doubt that there was a full choral foundation to supply the Chapel Royal, Hampton Court Palace, in its hey–day. Both re–foundations have been documented, so that it is possible to trace the employment of counter–tenors in them.

David Lewer's study of the Temple tradition is full of fascinating detail. An authentically constituted choir at The Temple Church was re–founded in 1842. The proposed choir at the opening service was to be six or eight boys and one each of alto, tenor and bass. Though it did not seem to happen in the event, the use of a second alto was suggested 'which is

---

[55] Shaw, loc. cit
[56] Loc. cit.

necessary, as six boys would render one alto inaudible'.[57] In the event, the choir at the opening service was different. In papers concerning it, John Calvert, a deputy bass lay-vicar of St Paul's Cathedral and the newly-appointed Master of the Temple Choir, used the terms alto and counter-tenor interchangeably. Principal counter-tenors appointed were Enoch Hawkins of St Paul's Cathedral and Thomas Young of the Foundling Hospital: theirs was an early example of job-sharing in that they sang in alternate months. Hawkins evidently had a fine reputation; he died at the early age of fifty and was buried in the cloisters of Westminster Abbey. Bumpus wrote 'that he was the first counter-tenor of his day'.[58] Young also had a good reputation.

In 1843, William Burge, Q. C., published a book called *On the Choral Service of the Anglo-Catholic Church*. The Temple Church re-foundation was regarded as 'high-church' at that time, but it maintained an early version of high-churchmanship which was later overtaken by liturgical development. Burge mentions the composition of choirs: that there should be at least a bass, a tenor, a counter-tenor (alto) and four boys on each side. [The bracketed '(alto)' is his.] In cathedrals there should be more altos, he says.[59] The Temple had an unusual system from the beginning: one principal of each voice, alto, tenor and bass was backed by a second singer. This system ceased during Walford Davies's tenure as organist.

Thomas Young (1809-1872) was a Canterbury man: first a chorister, then a lay-clerk of the cathedral there (1831-36). He was appointed to the choir of Westminster Abbey in 1836, then to the Foundling Hospital, London (where the 'choir' consisted of six singers: two sopranos, two altos, a tenor and a bass) and was appointed to The Temple in 1842. He was back in Canterbury during 1847 (where a new business venture of his failed) and he returned to The Temple Church in 1848 where he stayed until his death in 1872. Lewer reported that:[60]

> Young was an excellent solo singer, and was successor in public favour to Knyvett and Machin, being the last male alto soloist of eminence. As such, he was frequently heard at the concerts of the Antient and Sacred Harmonic Society, in London. For him, the Society revived [Handel's] *Jephtha* and *Athalia*, and in the 1845 Worcester Meeting [of the Three Choirs] he sang in a revival of Purcell's *Jubilate*.

Young sang with the Society for ten years and first appeared for them in 1837 to take the solo work in Handel's *Dettingen Te Deum* and Mozart's *Twelfth Mass*. In *Jeptha* and *Athalia* he took the parts of Hamor and Joad respectively. We may note the phrase 'public favour' with interest. Is Lewer overstating matters, or were there still alto soloists to be heard and enjoyed by the general public in the mid-nineteenth century?

David Lewer's documentation of The Temple Church Choir and the relevant sections of Frances Killingley's research into the counter-tenor question, begin to throw light into previously obscure corners of decades of alto singing. James Brown, at The Temple Church from 1873 to 1884 had, according to a contemporary, 'an unusually fine alto voice with the timbre of a trumpet'. Also at The Temple Church, from 1884 to 1929, was Haydn Grover, who

---

[57] David Lewer, *A Spiritual Song* (The Templars Union, 1961), p. 100
[58] Letter to *The Musical Times*, 1 May 1902
[59] Quoted by Lewer, op. cit., p. 123
[60] Ibid., p. 137; see also Grove's *Dictionary* (fifth edn) and Hough, op. cit., p. 19

was described by a contemporary of his as having 'a counter-tenor voice of real beauty'.[61] Munro Davison's memoirs also should be sought out; he sang alto at The Temple Church from 1893 to 1927. As we have seen, Davison was also a minor composer and he was the assistant choirmaster – shades of 'Master of Ye Children a Counter Tenour'! 'His book is extremely interesting if a little egotistical', comments Frances Killingley. 'In it, Davison says: "My voice at sixteen had gradually changed to a counter-tenor."' This is of concern when considering the age of pubertal voice-change and its relevance to the development of the counter-tenor voice. Interestingly, Davison took a singing diploma and chose as his test piece none other than 'Then Shall the Righteous Shine Forth', the tenor aria from *Elijah*, transposed up a semitone. The examiner was no less than Sims Reeves, the famous tenor who, according to Davison, gave him a mark of 98 per cent![62] This is particularly interesting in view of Reeves's remarks on falsetto (see page 196) – when is falsetto not falsetto? Davison was also a noted teacher of alto singers.

Lewer reports what he calls an amusing 'alto-cation' in The Temple Church between Brown and his successor, Walter Coward.[63] He also gives an instructive glimpse of Haydn Grover: 'Haydn Grover, the new cantoris alto, had a high, thin voice, which he jerked out with an upward thrust of his lower jaw – much to the amusement of the boys and the astonishment of those who heard his performance for the first time.'[64] This, it could be maintained, might not be so much a hint of what some might see as suspect technique but, when taken with the description above of Brown's 'trumpet-timbred' voice, it suggests rather an interesting possibility, that not all Victorian altos sounded mellow. Some might go farther and credit Grover with something of a Renaissance singing-technique.[65] We might also remember that Grover was supposed to have had 'a voice of real beauty'! On Good Friday, 1889, Walter Coward sang 'He Was Despised' during the service. A chorister who heard him then wrote later: 'Surely one of the best-ever altos'.[66]

The other choir re-established in the middle of the nineteenth century was that of the Chapel Royal, Hampton Court Palace. Its problems of recruitment indicate that while competent and even very good altos were easily available in London and for cathedrals outside the capital, a choir of such obvious kudos which, like that at The Temple Church, sang only on Sundays, found them only with difficulty despite its proximity to London. Its 'official' choir – that of the Chapel Royal (based in Whitehall until 1698, when the chapel was burnt down and at St James's Palace thereafter) – had seldom been heard there since 1737, when Hampton Court had ceased to be occupied by the reigning monarch. In the 1830s and 1840s, a new, indigenous choral foundation was proposed and eventually established. Perhaps it was thereby returned to something like Wolsey's original foundation of 1514; he had employed a choir of sixteen boys and sixteen singing men in a manner befitting the private chapel of a Cardinal (cf. the Earl of Northumberland's foundation at Leckingfield).

---

[61] Ibid., p. 220

[62] Frances Killingley, letter to the author, 10 July 1984; see also Frederic Hodgson's letter to *The Musical Times*, July 1983, p. 409

[63] Lewer, op. cit., pp. 188–9

[64] Ibid., p. 187

[65] See Mauro Uberti, 'Vocal Techniques in the Second Half of the 16th Century', *Early Music*, vol. 9 no. 4, October 1981, pp. 485–495

[66] Lewer, op. cit., p. 203

Since its re-foundation, except for a slight hiatus in the 1960s, Hampton Court Chapel Royal choir has continued as an all-male ensemble with counter-tenors to the present day. During the 1920s and '30s, the Hampton Court Gentlemen were London singers – many from the colleges of music, we are told by an ex-chorister – but these were mostly tenors and basses. Counter-tenors were in short supply, and unavailable from colleges of music, it would seem. They were therefore either local men or ex-choristers trained as adult altos. This seems likely to have been the case since re-establishment. (The present author's love-affair with the male high voice began when he was a parish church chorister and heard James Atherton, ex-chorister and later an alto there, sing the alto part in the 'verses' of Purcell's *Rejoice in the Lord Alway*.)

Thurston Dart was also a chorister there, where his father was an alto. Dart senior seems to have had a fine voice. Apparently, in his time at Hampton Court there were two (men) altos. They were supplemented by the occasional ex-treble chorister, 'in training' next to them. Mr Atkins, a schoolmaster at Kingston Grammar School, whence some of the boy-choristers came (others, including Thurston Dart, came from Hampton Grammar School), is reported to have been of mediocre standard, but Dart senior, according to one of the 'trainees', 'had a glorious voice, not unlike that of Alfred Deller'.[67] Dr Phillips, newly arrived as organist in 1931, appeared to be unimpressed by his supplementary teenage altos and he imported some 'professional altos' to replace them[68] – one presumably to sing alongside Atkins.

In 1901, a notable and completely new choir was constituted, with counter-tenors, when Westminster's Roman Catholic cathedral was opened. Its foundation included a traditional English choir with a choir school. The organist and choirmaster, the distinguished Richard R. Terry, is said to have possessed and used a good alto voice himself, though later he confessed to having ruined it while training boys. Ben Millett, who made a number of solo records of a sentimental sort, was a Westminster Cathedral alto of this first period. (His work is noted further in the Interlude, pp. 131–3.) The choir soon became famous for its performances of polyphonic music. It was only much later that boy altos were established permanently by George Malcolm, though Richard R. Terry had had no alternative but to use them during much of the first world war. Today, the alto line is as George Malcolm left it: boys plus one counter-tenor.

It seems, despite Lewer's comment on Young (footnote 76), that from the middle of the nineteenth century until the mid-1940s, the mere idea of the very high solo male voice was amusing to many. It was an attitude formed from Freudian or folk memory of castrati; an irritating bug-bear which refuses to die completely even today.

Solo falsettists occasionally appeared as curiosities on music-hall bills. Charlie Chaplin's mother was a soubrette on the variety stage, and she appears in a printed programme which still exists, dated 8 February 1896, for a concert at Hatcham Liberal Club, New Cross, London. It is reproduced in Chaplin's autobiography.[69] Also in the list of artistes is 'R.W. Dredge – Male Soprano'. It is highly unlikely that Dredge was a castrato.

Various 'turns' and eventually even early recordings of ballads were the ignominious cul-de-sacs in which counter-tenors of varying type had become trapped. Gramophone records exist of strangely ambiguous 'Irish' tenors and unusual, high, light solo male voices – always singing best-forgotten novelty material.

---

[67] John Duffill, in a letter to the author, 20 June 1985
[68] Loc. cit.
[69] Charles Chaplin, *My Early Years* (The Bodley Head), pl. 2

Soon we may have to modify, even if only slightly, our idea of the post–eighteenth century, pre–Deller alto. Though not widely known, the term counter–tenor was not forgotten. As we have seen, George Bernard Shaw used the term, and he seems to have had a secret admiration for the counter–tenor, which he sometimes appears to think is identical with 'alto' and sometimes not. In 1894, he described an Arnold Dolmetsch concert in Dulwich of music from the sixteenth century:[70]

> I hope, therefore, that Mr Dolmetsch will dig up plenty of genuine medieval music for us.... The quality of the performances, which has always been surprisingly good, considering the strangeness of the instruments, continues to improve. The vocal music is still the main difficulty. The singers, with their heads full of modern "effects", shew but a feeble sense of the accuracy of intonation and tenderness of expression required by the pure vocal harmonies of the old school.

What the 'effects' were, we can only guess, but judging by the date (1894) they may have been an excessive vibrato because Shaw refers to inaccurate intonation and hints at lack of sensitivity. Part of his review appears to be concerned with unaccompanied ensemble singing, as can be seen from his next sentence:[71]

> Without a piano to knock their songs into them they seemed at a loss; and the only vocalist whom I felt inclined to congratulate was the counter–tenor, the peculiarity of whose voice had saved him from the lot of the drawing–room songster.

A few years ago, Frances Killingley wrote of the identity of Shaw's counter–tenor: 'We do not know his name for certain; it was either Lawrence Fryer or Walter Shiner. G. B. S. was obviously impressed with the experience.'[72] In *Man and Superman*,[73] Shaw writes:

> "Ah, here you are, my friend", says Don Juan to the Statue, "Why don't you learn to sing the splendid music Mozart has written for you?" The Statue replies: "Unluckily, he has written it for a bass voice. Mine is a counter–tenor."

(Shaw was concerned in this context to evoke a supernatural atmosphere. The Statue is of a ghostly, old but majestic Spaniard.)

From time to time, there were faint stirrings of interest in authentic musical performance. Unfortunately, the musical public was unused to timbres, instruments and styles other than those of nineteenth–century Europe, especially of Germany. Even Shaw, as a music critic, often fulminated in his writings of this period against the influential vocal training offered at the Royal Academy of Music, in which Manuel Garcia was still dominant. (We discuss Garcia

---

[70] George Bernard Shaw, op. cit., 7 February 1894
[71] Loc. cit.
[72] Frances Killingley, letter to the author, 10 July 1984
[73] *Man and Superman* (1901–1903), act III

later.) Clearly, Shaw disagreed with nineteenth–century Italian ideas of singing and with Garcia's pedagogy, which often appeared alienated from musicianship.

Even for immediately pre–nineteenth–century music there was little urge to re–create or seriously re–examine the musical conditions of the past. The philosopher, Nietzsche (1844–1900), remarked perceptively that 'the really historical performance would talk to ghosts';[74] the poignancy of which *aperçu* has a probably unintended poetic air about it.

Arnold Dolmetsch continued to 'dig up' early music. On 26 January 1901, his ensemble of viols performed Gibbons's verse–anthem *This is the Record of John*. We are not told the singer's name or vocal type, whether counter–tenor or tenor, but Dolmetsch is reported by Campbell[75] to have claimed that he 're–discovered the classic method of singing' in relation to this concert. Nevertheless, rather surprisingly, Dolmetsch does not seem to be recorded as having developed this idea, certainly with regard to the counter–tenor. The century of Darwin's *The Origin of Species* ended with the counter–tenor in limbo.

DENEULAIN   147 STRAND, W.C.

William Windsor (1860–1954)

---

[74] Cited in Frederick Dorian, *The History of Music in Performance* (New York, 1942), p. 313
[75] Margaret Campbell, *Dolmetsch: the Man and his Work* (Hamish Hamilton, 1975), p. 138

7 Life in Limbo

As we have seen, there were some distinguished altos in cathedral and academic circles: men of repute who, though seldom singing solo elsewhere for lack of opportunity, were justly celebrated in their own milieu. Mention will be made of a few early twentieth–century names, but we begin by discussing an important work with which a little-known alto soloist was associated.

Constant Lambert's *The Rio Grande* (1929) appears to be the first major English 'secular' composition for about one hundred years to have been written with a counter–tenor soloist in mind. In the 1930 recording, conducted by the composer, the soloist is Albert Whitehead, alto; he is a singer with tone and technique very much of his generation. Had Lambert lived longer (he died in 1951), he might well have done more for the quickening counter–tenor revival. Obviously he liked and chose to use the voice – he conducted Deller's first BBC radio broadcast – even when represented at a rather ordinary level in the 1930 *Rio Grande* recording. Lambert's choice of a solo alto for this composition bears some examination.

His setting of a poem by Sacheverell Sitwell is a work for piano and orchestra (without woodwind but with extensive percussion) and chorus with alto soloist. It evokes a South American seaport on a carnival day. Lambert seemed fascinated by hot seaports:[1]

> There was the heat, the proximity of the sea, and above all the picturesqueness and variety of these ports, where one could watch almost any aspect of the human comedy being acted out with a complete lack of inhibition.

Though famed for his lively heterosexuality, he wrote from the picturesque squalor of Marseilles in 1930: 'I feel rather like Walt Whitman – all races, all colours, all creeds, all sexes ...'[2] No doubt he felt that the employment of a male alto helped to evoke the louche atmosphere of *The Rio Grande*.

When it became a ballet, Lambert devised additions to the scenario which did not relate to the words of the poem, but concerned the amorous adventures of a Creole girl. Lambert said in a programme note: 'the [additional] theme is suggested by the music'.[3] Careful study of references to this work, and the fact that Lambert was sympathetic to early music, particularly Purcell's, show that it is likely that the alto solo was always originally intended

---

[1] Richard Shead, *Constant Lambert* (Simon Publications, 1973), p. 78
[2] Ibid., p. 79
[3] Ibid., p. 72

for a man, despite the feminine theme added to the ballet. There is also a seventeenth- or eighteenth-century trans-sexual quality about such a casting. Certainly, a high falsetto soloist fits well with the sea-going, Spanish and negro aspects of the music, and its suggestions of sexual licence. Indeed, Lambert wrote:[4]

> I want to do The Rio Grande with a negro choir. I have always had negro voices in mind for this piece, as the idea for the music came from seeing Florence Mills in "Dover Street to Dixie" and from some of the music in "Blackbirds".

Presumably, Lambert meant that the extended version of the music came from seeing Florence Mills. He was keen to have the work performed widely but it was not the kind of piece that English choral societies were used to. For a while it featured in concert programmes but, perhaps predictably, the choirs which sang the music found it hard to capture its essential style. Anyway:[5]

> The closing passage was usually marred by the presence of a contralto, resplendent in evening gown and all too obtrusive, on the platform beside the conductor.

Other altos or counter-tenors were making records but, like those of Ben Millett, mentioned earlier, they were mostly of ballads and ephemera. Many of these singers came from backgrounds other than the English cathedral.

The Chapel Royal choir in 1937, with Clarke and Hawkins
(middle row: extreme left and extreme right)

---

[4] Ibid., p. 74
[5] Ibid., p. 76

Hatherley Clarke, of the Chapel Royal (St James's), was one of the very few who recorded ballads and was a serious soloist outside cathedral and glee circles. He was widely known in the 1920s and '30s. A fuller account of him is included later. Another with a fine (later, distinguished) reputation, though much younger than Clarke, is Frederic Hodgson who while at Lichfield Cathedral sang with the BBC Midland Singers during the 1940s in Birmingham. He did some solo broadcasts with BBC Regional Radio and with the BBC Radio Third Programme. He was appointed to St George's Chapel, Windsor, in 1956 and later became a Gentleman of the Chapel Royal at St James's Palace. 'Nobby' Clark, at Ely until the late 1950s, was a similarly–celebrated cathedral alto. Others are mentioned later.

Reginald Forwood, chorister and then tenor lay clerk of Canterbury, confirms that the alto Donald Reid (a member of the Canterbury family of Reids, all connected with cathedral music there) returned from Canada in the mid–1930s to broadcast on 'the wireless'. Apparently, the broadcast was relayed from the concert hall at Broadcasting House, London. Forwood thought the performance likely to have been of oratorio, and that Reid was engaged as a solo, and certainly not an ensemble, alto.

The idea that altos were awaiting their chance to stage a triumphant general return to the serious secular platform is perhaps an over–simplification. A recovery seemed a forlorn hope until solo altos regained an appropriately secular style – and more panache. Even, dare it be said, more self–respect; for instance, despite the beauty of his voice and his wide reputation, Nobby Clark was always puzzled that people came to hear him. 'It's not even a real voice', he would say. There had to be one man vocally outstandingly different, and indeed tough enough to take on the prejudice of many decades. In the 1930s, despite Clarke, the young Hodgson, Clark and others, there seemed to be no sign of that man.

Percy Scholes wrote in 1938:[6]

> The real alto being now so rare, it is becoming common to speak of contraltos
> as altos ...

The woeful lack of the more brilliant toned and virtuoso solo alto voice, essential for the performance not only of Purcell but most early music, had been noted and lamented by many. E. H. Fellowes had asked, in 1919, what could be done about the awkward but essential alto parts in sixteenth– and seventeenth–century madrigals? Interestingly, he seemed to consider that the altos of his time could manage well enough, and of course this music does not always demand a virtuoso solo alto. Fellowes had no illusions; for him, counter–tenor equalled male alto, and vice versa. He wrote the following with mixed groups of voices in mind; at the time they did not normally include counter–tenors:[7]

> For practical purposes with modern singers a serious difficulty is presented by
> the awkward compass of the inner voice–parts of much of this music, both
> sacred and secular, though the difficulty is much mitigated when male altos
> are available. For the alto–parts sometimes extend for a compass of nearly
> two octaves, ranging for an octave on either side of middle C.
>   And the tenor–parts often lie very high, yet too low for female alto
> singers. It seems probable that in Elizabethan days male singers made very

---

[6] Percy Scholes, *Oxford Companion of Music* (9th edn, O.U.P., 1955), p. 27
[7] E. H. Fellowes, *English Madrigal Composers* (O.U.P., 1919), pp. 69–70

free use of the <u>falsetto</u> register. In order to meet this very real difficulty some editors have introduced drastic emendations into the text; such a course of action is inexcusable unless adequate annotation is printed which may enable the student to perceive the exact form of the composer's text, and may also make it possible to perform the music in its original design when circumstances admit of it. In Wilby's *Sweet Honey–sucking Bees*, where two counter–tenor voices of equal compass are employed, the difficulty has been met in most reprints by a wholesale rearrangement of these two voice–parts without annotation, but it might be overcome by transposing the music down a tone; while if counter–tenors are available, the parts, as they stand in the original text, are exactly suitable for that class of voice. In many instances this type of difficulty can be solved by the readjustment of a single phrase and sometimes of no more than one note. Another plan is to include a few alto voices [female] among the tenors, and <u>vice versa</u>. But all such minor matters are best left to the judgement of conductors, who must be guided by their own individual requirements, acting always on a wise discretion and with due reverence for the composer's text.

From this time on, Tudor music slowly began to be part of the repertoire of the more discerning parish church choir. Problems concerning the alto part were similar to those encountered in madrigal societies, but there were two more difficulties: the supply of male altos and, in many churches, the now permanently mixed alto/contralto line. Whereas the average madrigal society did not try to recruit male altos, possibly through ignorance of their historical place, the average church choir, knowing that this was the correct voice for the repertoire, usually instead bewailed their scarcity. When the alto part was taken by women only, or by both men and women, the resulting sound was inappropriate and the effect on musical authenticity and effectiveness detrimental.

Twenty–five years later, by the end of the second world war, the situation in many parish churches was worse. Not one but two horrific world wars had taken choirmen away, many never to return. Society had changed and was threatening to change further. More contraltos (and indeed adult women and girl sopranos) had been welcomed into an increasing number of previously all–male church choirs. The situation was beginning to resemble that in choral societies several decades before. Professional cathedral choirs and glee–quartet altos survived successfully, however.

The occasional introduction earlier in the century of authentic early instruments into experimental attempts at re–presenting early opera was uneven and often bizarre, even if well–intentioned.[8] Continuing stirrings of a desire to present early music using instruments and voices for which it was written inspired Edward Dent's production of Purcell's *The Fairy Queen* in 1920. The baritone Clive Carey sang the important alto solos in falsetto. Whether his performance was poor or merely unfamiliar to both audience and critic (perhaps H. C. Colles?), *The Times* remarked that 'he looked and sounded every bit as absurd as the original Mr Pate in woman's habit.'[9]

Despite this and other sporadic attempts to present more authentic performances of opera and other areas of early music activity – chamber orchestras with baroque instrumentation

[8] Harry Haskell, *The Early Music Revival: A History* (Thames and Hudson, 1988), esp. pp. 130–5
[9] Ibid., p. 107

were active in France and Germany during the first decade of the twentieth century – the music critic of *The Times* continued to be hostile. Reviewing the London Festival Opera Company's *Giulio Cesare* in 1930, he complained that 'The male alto representative of Nirenius should not have been allowed on the stage at all. He merely emphasized the tendency to allow the opera to degenerate into absurdity.'[10] Again, we do not have a true picture of the standard of performance, neither are we told who the singer was. We note also that it appears that the title rôle was not taken by a counter–tenor in place of the contralto–castrato of the original.

We may be certain that the general standard of solo counter–tenors of the period, whenever they might be heard, was not to the taste of A. K. Holland. Unlike Fellowes who in 1919 had been discussing the purely ensemble voice, Holland was concerned in 1932 with the lack of virtuoso solo alto or counter–tenor:[11]

> ...a rather grave problem, applying equally to his anthems and his dramatic pieces, is the use of the alto voice in so much of Purcell's most difficult music. Purcell has had, in the course of time, almost every conceivable kind of bad luck, serving to hinder the performance of his music and the growth of a practical tradition. But this misfortune has lain more heavily upon him than any other. Had he been himself a tenor instead of an alto, we might not have had quite so much of his work pitched in this particular register, though there is no doubt that the male alto, besides being inevitable in cathedral music and particularly in the verse–anthems of the time, was a very popular solo voice in Purcell's day. Nowadays it is scarcely cultivated outside the sphere of male voice choirs, if we except the type of falsetto which usually does duty for it in church. 'Feigned voices', as Matthew Locke tells us, were not unknown in Purcell's day. Yet the male alto (or counter–tenor) is a real voice and a traditionally English one. Apart from the fact that in colour and texture it differs from the contralto, it has, or should have, a compass that is at once higher than the tenor and lower than the female alto voice, so that for contraltos much of Purcell's music lies in an awkward tessitura besides requiring an agility which few contraltos possess. But the problem ought to be faced and not evaded. Alto voices are not incapable of development. The difficulty is one which is met with frequently in the case of the madrigals and wholesale re-arrangement or transposition will not solve it. The older composers wrote for a wide range of voices. The study of Purcell would certainly tend to do away with the vogue of the nondescript type of voice which modern English composers in their vocal music seem so often to encourage. The characteristic English voice of today is a mezzo–soprano or a baritone, when it is not a tenor that is a baritone forced up. Purcell wrote for real sopranos and real basses and in his inner parts used the fullest range of voice. A diagrammatic analysis of some of his typical songs would probably reveal the fact that his music demands not merely a wide compass but a fairly prevalent use of the more extreme and characteristic levels of the voice.

[10] *The Times*, 7 January 1930
[11] A. K. Holland, *Henry Purcell, the English Musical Tradition* (Penguin, 1933), pp. 124–5

There were other laments, equally strong. In 1937, John Hough's paper to the Royal Musical Association, 'The Historical Significance of the Counter–Tenor', was important. We discuss the 'falsetto versus high–tenor argument' in detail elsewhere, and much of Hough's lecture was concerned with this matter. Probably this was because in 1937 it puzzled most people that the altos then to be heard were either weak or were strong but inappropriate in tone when used for music written for them in earlier centuries.

During questions at the end of the lecture, Professor J. A. Westrup, an authority on the music of Purcell, remarked: 'One would not naturally assume from hearing modern [1937] counter–tenors that much of the music of Purcell's period was so virile in quality. Thoroughly manly songs were sung then by counter–tenors. What has happened to the voice in the meantime?'[12] His question might have been echoed by many concerned with the effective performance of pre–Romantic music. In his answer, Hough, himself an alto, stated his view that the counter–tenor is a naturally high tenor, virile in tone, and that the alto voice, though it can be very beautiful, is merely a mellow falsetto.

It is interesting to learn that Hough's lecture, demonstration and subsequently published paper, were not quite as they might seem. The circumstances surrounding the whole enterprise appear to have been jinxed. Fortunately, John Hough has been able to describe something of the background to what was destined to prove an important occasion:[13]

> Delivering that paper ... was a traumatic experience. The Secretary of the R.M.A. at that time, the late Rupert Erlebach (who worked on the Eton MS then), kindly arranged for a seventeenth century spinet to be on the platform for a rehearsal of the musical illustrations just before the meeting. The instrument was a third lower than usual pitch, and I had to transpose, sing, and direct my friends twice over.
>
> Sir Percy Buck and Canon Galpin were very kind, although nobody real-ised the difficulty I encountered....
>
> Much against the grain, in order to afford time for the discussion (a non sequitur affair rightly discontinued long since) I had to reduce my original (lost during War II when I was overseas), and this explains the short, swift changes from period to period, much truncated.
>
> Afterwards, at Lincoln College, Oxford, I gave my work verbatim in two sessions of the D'Avenant Literary Society....

In a subsequent letter, John Hough elaborated on the circumstances of the lecture and about himself and alto singers of repute of that date:[14]

> ... That fearful situation in which I found myself, with an antique spinet a third below present pitch. (The RCO never demands more than a tone transposition up or down in the tests.) My work was lost during the war years after the truncation of 1937. It was not easy cutting my original down to fit the time, with desultory discussion to follow. Before pursuing any question

[12] Hough, op. cit., p. 22
[13] John Hough, letter to the author, 17 January 1991
[14] John Hough, letter to the author, 24 January 1991

to some logical answer, another followed, and others after. It needed yet more transposing to come to some conclusion!

But that happened so long ago, and the kindest encouragement remains a happy memory of an otherwise very painful experience....

I sang alto after voice break, and cycled from Walsall to Lichfield to hear the services when Frederic Hodgson was there, and at that time I browsed through the anthems of our cathedral composers as well as the operas of Handel.

A lot of nonsense was spoken and written some time later, as if there were no singers before Deller. If you look through <u>Musical Times</u> at the end of the 19th century, you will find innumerable advertisements of male voice quartets among others, and there was many an excellent voice in the cathedral choirs (and town churches – Leeds had Briggs who painted [the portrait of] S. S. Wesley)... .

The singing men were returning from the Forces – George Richardson, mellifluous <u>falset</u> of Magdalen, who sang 'Acquaint Thyself' with the rigorous semitones section, the whole in G (from F) when the organist came to grief transposing. (It can be very tricky sometimes in the modulations, as I have experienced playing a flat wind instrument accompanied by some of the greatest!) Hetterley sang a well–turned solo at the House [Christ Church], and Frank Speakman (breeder of black cocker spaniels) was the alto opposite when I sang for H.K. Andrews as requested [at New College]. When diffi-culties arose through illness and otherwise, I was called into the three choirs and sang a verse (from MS. single lines in the chant books!)

Duncan Thomson asked me to help him to an alto L.R.A.M. which he gained and sang opposite Alfred Deller in St. Paul's... .

It would seem that Jack Westrup was not totally convinced by the jinxed 1937 lecture or by the answers to the questions. He, together with Frank Ll. Harrison, later edited Collins *Music Encyclopaedia*, in which there occur highly revealing entries:[15]

> *Alto 1* Lit. 'high' L. The highest adult male voice, now employed mainly in church choirs and male–voice choirs. The range of the voice is roughly two octaves from

> though the lower notes lack resonance. The upper part of the compass is made possible by the cultivation of the falsetto voice. In 17th–century England the alto (also known as counter tenor) was popular as a solo voice.
> *Counter Tenor*: The highest male voice (also known as alto), produced by using the head register. English composers of the late 17th century frequently

---

[15] *Collins Music Encyclopaedia*, ed. Westrup and Harrison (Collins, 1959); this was extensively revised in 1976, but with no changes to these entries; it is now entitled *Collins Encyclopaedia of Music*

wrote solos for this voice which demand not only a mastery of expression but also a brilliant ringing tone.

Contra Tenor: In 14th and early 15th century music the name for a part with roughly the same range as a tenor, which it often crosses. In the course of the 15th century a distinction developed between contra tenor altus (high contra tenor) and contra tenor bassus (low contra tenor) with a prevailing range respectively above and below the tenor. Those terms were subsequently reduced to altus (alto) and bassus (bass).

It is ironic that within six years of Hough's paper the revival was to begin. E. H. Fellowes, in his famous study *English Cathedral Music* (1941), seems still to be mourning the lost virtuoso alto, never realising he had only two years more to wait:[16]

> Tudway's reference to the exceptional excellence of the men's voices at Whitehall is significant. Among the basses was the famous John Gostling, for whose extra-ordinary compass Purcell and others wrote passages that are sometimes grotesque. But the altos must have been exceptionally good. Michael Wise was one who was evidently outstanding; William Child was another, and there were many more. The composers at the Chapel Royal had these singers in their minds when they wrote not only solos, but the numberless verses for men's voices with the altos at the top. Tudway was right; it is still a mistake to attempt to perform this music and much of that of the following century, unless adequate voices, especially altos, are available. Very seldom is a good balance of tone secured in the verse passages in modern performances, and it is idle to pretend that much of the music of the Restoration composers and later, which looks so good on paper, has any real artistic value when the trios, and, still worse, the alto and bass duets, are rendered with such a want of balance of tone as they often are. The effect is often made more intolerable by a kind of false tradition that all verse passages of this sort must be taken at a slow tempo, and after a short pause following the previous movement.

Small all-male ensembles which included counter-tenors were not totally exclusive to the British Isles at this period. During the 1920s and 1930s, a German-Jewish group, the 'Comedian Harmonists', were recording light vocal music brilliantly. They included at least one counter-tenor, a tenor-altino. Tragically, some of the six members did not survive Hitler's anti-semitism and the war.

James Phelan, for many years alto, and later tenor, baritone and then bass (from which department he finally made his retirement) in the then all-male choir of Brompton Oratory, London, recalled[17] that in the 1930s it was occasionally possible to hear a counter-tenor with a particular variety of what we would now call 'modern' timbre. One such singer was Roland Plumtree, whose voice belied his nick-name 'Plum' in that it was distinctly un-plummy, but high and rather mezzo-soprano in tone; it was produced from a 'forward position', as singers would term it, using vibrato. Phelan reports that Plumtree's voice had a bright, semi-feminine

---

[16] E. H. Fellowes, *English Cathedral Music* (Methuen, 1941), p. 135
[17] In a conversation between James Phelan and the author, October 1991

quality and was quite different from the usual alto of the day. It would have been suited to the Oratory choir, from which he retired in the 1950s. Unlike Phelan, he did not lose his head–voice singing high with the boys.

The situation in which the counter–tenor or alto found himself at this period was ambiguous. While recognised fully in his English ecclesiastical strongholds and in a few other arenas, none of them were now properly connected with the secular mainstream, normal and respectable worlds of concerts and oratorio, opera, music college or vocal pedagogy. The term 'limbo' springs to mind. It has a number of connotations, of which perhaps the most apposite here is 'an imaginary place for lost or forgotten persons'.

The male high voice was resting there, awaiting the re–appearance of the secular virtuoso solo counter–tenor.

INTERLUDE: Male high voices recorded and forgotten, c1904–c1934

Hitherto, the ballad, in the sense of a sentimental drawing–room song of the later nineteenth and early twentieth centuries, has been under–explored for early recorded evidence of the male high voice.

As we have seen, during the nineteenth and early twentieth centuries there was little solo work in serious secular music for male high voices. The conventional tenor was 'king', yet even during the long twilight decades some reputable altos were working within the traditional British (mostly English) all–male cathedral choirs. What has not generally been realised is that a few such singers, together with others from well outside English cathedral, church or glee–club traditions, made gramophone recordings which provide ample evidence of styles of voice production used by counter–tenors, whatever they called themselves, from about 1904 to the mid–1930s.

They sang the standard repertoire of ballads and popular songs common, for essentially commercial reasons, to all types of voice in those days. However, all other varieties of voice were also employed in more serious music, both in recordings and on the concert platform. Though this was not usually so regarding the counter–tenor, Hatherley Clarke seems to have been the main exception. Ben Millett at least also recorded a little Dvořák and Elgar.

A market existed for novelty items sung by unusual voices which included falsettists or strange, high so–called tenors. They were not always designated vocally in any way except sometimes by odd titles like 'Voice in a Million' (Colman). 'Tiny' Winters, well–known because he possessed what would popularly be considered 'a woman's voice', sang with the Lew Stone Band in London in the 1930s. (This novelty–market still exists in the world of popular music.) Cliff Edwards ('Ukulele Ike'), well–known for the song 'When You Wish Upon a Star', fitted this description. 'Tiny Tim', an American entertainer with what would now be called 'camp' falsetto, startled audiences in the 1960s. In more recent years, Roy Orbison proved to be a tenor–altino singing in a popular style.

To some extent, the old–fashioned ballad and its singers (some employing head–voice effects) live on in popular music in disguise. A group called 'The Communards', with their lead singer, Jimmy Somerville, is an example. The late Freddie Mercury, lead singer of the group 'Queen', had an extensive, high head–voice range.

Barney Hoskyns has written an excellent account of the male high voice as used in mainly American popular music during the last two decades.[1] His book is an absorbing and vivid study of the varied effects of the human voice on audiences.

---

[1] Barney Hoskins, *From a Whisper to a Scream* (Fontana, 1991), Chapter X

Essentially, commercial music has always been more indulgent, unfussy and unstuffy, and eager to embrace the unusual for obviously commercial reasons: on behalf of a market with few (consciously) pre–conceived ideas except a requirement for entertainment and novelty.

In the sphere of folk–music, certain singers employ head–voice. John Jacob Niles, the American 'Hill Billy' singer, is an excellent example. His voice is a fine tenor–altino. A recently re–issued recording[2] collects a number of early recordings of singers, mostly of ballads, and presents their contrasting singing styles and standards, ranges and high voice-types. This compact disc offers valuable insights. Inevitably, the vocal style of the singers is dated and the original recordings are worn, but the more discerning ear should be able to ignore this.

The interested reader would need to search 'junk' shops and advertise in magazines to acquire originals of these early records but they are not all impossibly rare. To forestall the natural objection that such primitively recorded sound will be useless for realistic assessment – let alone for pleasurable listening – we should read Julian Gardiner:[3]

> The acoustic method does not give an accurate idea ... of old singers' voices. To ensure good reproduction they had to move nearer the microphone in soft passages, and away from it in loud ones. It is this imbalance which accounts for much of our dissatisfaction when listening carefully to them. I need hardly say that in other respects the old recordings are admirable and provide an object lesson in bel canto, clean and gentle attack, and musical phrasing.

While this object lesson could not be claimed in the performance of all these ballads and light offerings, Gardiner's comments are useful. Such imbalance, of course, is most at risk on operatic records and often those of serious music generally, but, unless the singer wished to develop it, the average ballad did not normally require great dynamic or large range. Luckily, therefore, that one real deficiency need not concern us.

In terms of fidelity, the octave from C4 to B4 or C5 was recognised as being the best for acoustic–recording methods. Together with the short playing time of early recordings (which required less stamina of the singer), this helps to explain the apparently generous proportion, early in the twentieth century, of genuinely high tenors (of the type with which we have been familiar since about 1840) compared to what could be called, euphemistically, second tenors.

Not only do singers on the Pavilion re–issue vary in standard and style but together they represent the variety of male voices singing at high pitch in the late nineteenth and earlier twentieth centuries. Nine of them are considered in some detail in Appendix Five; regarding the always thorny matter of nomenclature, a table is included there of the various record companies and their own classification of these and other recorded male high voices.

Will Oakland's cylinders were advertised with publicity leaflets. One, dated 1912, reads:

> Mr. Oakland is a favorite among Edison artists and is one of the foremost counter–tenors now before the public ...

---

[2] 'Chime on, beautiful Bells', Pavilion Records (Compact Disc, Opal 9348), compiled and with sleeve–notes by Peter Giles
[3] Julian Gardiner, *A Guide to Good Singing and Speech* (Cassell, 1968), p. 144

Other than Jose, we might speculate on who might constitute the rest of the counter-tenor population of the United States! However, the phraseology on this leaflet seems to be additional evidence that use of the high solo male voice was far from rare. It also suggests that the average record buyer, almost more than the classical music-lover during this period, was expected to be familiar with the term counter-tenor as one denoting a male voice higher than, and different from, the ordinary tenor.

Though it includes music of more enduring worth, the compact disc under discussion presents some of the many ballads and other material of minimal merit recorded by these singers and others during the period. It is a shame that their proper repertoire was waiting for them, often unknown and mostly unsung – or being sung by the wrong voices at probably the wrong pitch.

The polite and often beautiful style of Clarke, Hawkins, Millett and Whitehead (inevitably tailored to the English cathedral world of the time, and conditioned by it) is in marked contrast to the more secular sound of Colman, Oakland and Jose. It is tantalising to conjecture what impact voices like those of Colman and Oakland, trained imaginatively and knowledgeably, would have had on the world of early music today.

Jose is a different case. If, after appropriate training, he were singing today, Pavarotti, Carreras and Domingo would be hard put to match him in the operatic world. However, his heavy production, even of thrilling high notes, seems unlikely to have been able to produce the brilliant agility required by the historical counter-tenor repertoire. Suitable training might have released a lighter tone, just as the rather antediluvian style of Hawkins, for example, though based on correct historical usage, would need to have been much modified for convincing performance of Purcell.

The term counter-tenor, even in England half-forgotten in the world of serious music during this period, need not have been totally unknown in the United States, as Stubbs's monograph *The Male Alto or Counter-Tenor Voice* was published there in 1908. It might well have appeared at just the right moment. There was a need to label these unconventional male high voices commercially but Jose, who was often billed as a counter-tenor, was recording before 1908. Perhaps certain singers influenced Stubbs?

Alternatively, in the United States, the term might have survived – just – almost as a distant folk-memory for a male voice higher than a tenor, hence the early labelling of the superb, ultra-high tenor, Jose, as counter-tenor.

Of Coombs and Romain, one can only assume from the evidence of these recordings that these earth-bound tenors, especially Romain, were entitled counter-tenor for essentially commercial reasons or that both were labelled wrongly on the discs.

It is a puzzle why the recorded evidence of these high male voices, Coombs and Romain emphatically excluded, did not encourage those in the world of serious secular music to explore the possibility of employing some of them in what we now call early music. Arnold Dolmetsch, for example, does not seem to have given these singers a first glance, let alone a second. Their recordings remind us, tantalisingly, of what might have been.

Alfred Deller

8 The Revival

Alfred Deller (1912–1979) will for ever personify the resurgence of a fine tradition, not only in Britain but throughout the whole English–speaking world and continental Europe. This self–taught, superb artist was responsible, single–handedly at first, through his incredible voice and sound, and instinctive style, for the re–establishment of solo counter–tenor singing in the serious, mainstream concert world. The story of the discovery of Deller by Michael Tippett in the choir of Canterbury Cathedral can be enjoyed in Deller's official biography.[1]

Deller eventually sang Purcell's 'Music for a While' to Tippett in the Song Room in Canterbury Cathedral in 1943. 'For me in that moment', according to Tippett, 'the centuries rolled back.'[2] In a recent BBC broadcast, Sir Michael Tippett added:

> It was quite clear to me that this was the voice which Purcell wrote for. I had been at that time drawn more and more to Purcell, and more and more to Purcell performances. I had wondered how on earth I would discover this voice which could do those florid vocalisations with the clarity which was obviously part of it.

Earlier, Tippett had described Deller's voice thus:[3]

> The counter–tenor is a male alto of what would be regarded now as exceptional range and facility. It was the voice for which Bach wrote many of the alto solos in the Church cantatas; and Purcell, who himself sang countertenor, gave to it some of his best airs and ensembles. To my ear it has a peculiarly musical sound because almost no emotional irrelevancies distract us from the absolutely pure musical quality of the production. It is like no other sound in music, and few other musical sounds are so intrinsically musical.

It is fitting that he discovered the virtuoso solo counter–tenor in Canterbury Cathedral, where Leonel Power and Thomas Tallis were once on the musical foundation, where William Byrd and John Ward had similar associations awaiting further research, and where Orlando Gibbons is buried. Thomas Young, whose salient biographical dates mirror Deller's a century before, was born in the city and began his career in the choir.

---

[1] Michael and Mollie Hardwick, *A Singularity of Voice* (Proteus, 2nd edn 1980)
[2] Op. cit., p. 74
[3] Quoted Hardwick, op. cit., p. 75

Canterbury Cathedral Song Room (1981),
where Michael Tippett first heard Alfred Deller in 1943

As we have seen, most counter–tenors, though not always very strong specimens, had been hidden away in quartets or choirs or had featured on 'light' or 'novelty' records. Tippett was not hearing a unique register, but a unique artist: the pre–nineteenth–century solo alto.

Yet it is appropriate to comment that the story of the dramatic discovery of the 'first counter–tenor for one hundred and fifty years' may have been a little over–played. Within that time, there must have been counter–tenor voices with Deller's potential. If so, obviously, their owners lacked his almost 'psychic' early music style. Even re–processed, the primitive recordings which do exist of earlier counter–tenors can hardly do them justice but, even taking this into consideration, one still feels instinctively that few of them could have possessed Deller's magic. Whatever the case, he was the right man heard at the right time. It seems inexplicable that, when he was appointed to the Canterbury Cathedral choir in 1939, he had already been turned down by the Lincoln and Salisbury cathedral choirs.

In 1944, *The Times'* critic (presumably not H. C. Colles), reviewing the Morley College concert at which Deller made his London début, wrote:[4]

> Mr Alfred Deller of Canterbury, in the anthem, and in an air, made familiar
> by Dr Whittaker as 'Music Shall Now Proclaim' (Music for A While), but
> sung in its original pitch, showed by the purity of his voice and of the style
> how it was that the seventeenth and eighteenth centuries came to attach so
> much value to the high male voice.

---

[4] *The Times* for 24 October 1944, possibly written by Frank Howes, the paper's chief music critic
     from 1943 to 1960 and lecturer at the Royal College of Music

It is not certain that the song *was* sung at *original* pitch, but the review reads as a piece of history. The concert was the real start for Deller and the start of a movement. Antony Hopkins recalled that[5]

> In 1944, a Purcell concert was given at Morley College under Michael Tippett's inspired and inspiring direction. For us who sang in the Morley Choir, the whole period was a revelation, introducing us to music by Purcell, Gibbons, Weelkes, Monteverdi and Gesualdo, that in those days was completely unknown to the general musical public.
>
> The discovery of Deller's voice and interpretative talent was a godsend to Tippett. Deller was frequently involved in the concerts, either in a group of solos or taking the arias in some choral work.
>
> On one such occasion the programme was supposed to include an elaborate duet for two countertenors, which particular title now escapes me. I had something of a freak voice (I once sang 'One Fine Day' on stage at Sadler's Wells only a semitone down!) and could sing alto, tenor or bass as required. I was duly enlisted to sing the second part with Deller, and we had great fun doing it.
>
> Afterwards, Engel Lund, a noted singer of folk songs, asked me how long I had been studying with Deller. "Never had a singing lesson in my life!" I replied with absolute truth, and to her considerable surprise.

It is interesting too that Deller was also self-trained.

The tenor, Lawrence Watts, not only emphasises Deller's determination to succeed and that his success was no accident but also reveals that he was light-heartedly aware of his importance:[6]

> Alfred Deller, Eric Barnes and I were appointed vicars-choral at St. Paul's Cathedral on January 1st, 1947. In those early days, Alfred was already getting some interesting radio broadcasts, notably on the BBC Third Programme. He was involved in a concert given by Anthony Bernard with the London Chamber Singers and Orchestra during the first few weeks of 1947. It was after this broadcast (in which I was involved as a member of the Chamber Singers) that Alfred said to me "Lawrie, I intend to put the counter-tenor voice on the concert platform in complete equality with all the other solo voices." This is exactly what he did within the next decade.

Deller was not embarrassed by a second incident:

> I well remember an occasion when a young counter-tenor who was a choral scholar at Westminster Abbey came to St. Paul's as a deputy for the first time. Alfred was showing him the ropes in the vestry – which cassock and surplice to wear, and how to sign in the deputy book to be sure of his fee. Alfred said: "By the way, my name is Deller". The young singer took a step backwards,

---

[5] Antony Hopkins, in a letter to the author, 15 November 1991
[6] Lawrence Watts, in conversation with the author, and in a subsequent letter, 28 April 1991

and clasping his hands to his breast exclaimed "How marvellous!" Alfred turned to the rest of us and said "You see?".

To the present author's total surprise and delight, that choral scholar has now been revealed as Charles Cleall! (By a further co—incidence, an editor of this book was at about this time singing in the Decani boys' choir—stalls in front of Alfred Deller, Gerald English and Maurice Bevan.)

Deller's first radio broadcast was a studio performance for the BBC Home Service of Purcell's *Hail Bright Cecilia*, conducted by Constant Lambert. The alto Albert Whitehead may be recalled as having performed in Lambert's *Rio Grande* in 1930. The alto Charles Whitehead sang with Deller in the BBC Third Programme's inaugural broadcast on 29 September 1946. Thus there is a continued coincidence of names round Deller, and another small puzzle: in Purcell's *Come Ye Sons of Art*, both Whitehead and Lambert Wilkinson of St Paul's Cathedral are listed as being second counter—tenor in 'Sound the Trumpet'.[7] A very young man named Charles Whitehead appears on a 1947 Chapel Royal group photograph (not reproduced here), next to Hatherley Clarke.

Deller had to overcome the most extraordinary prejudices. Many upsetting comments came his way, the most notorious being the time when he was waiting to go onto the platform of the Royal Festival Hall in the 1950s. He was standing by Sir Malcolm Sargent with the orchestra's leader – whom Deller has been too kind to name. The leader said to Sargent within Deller's hearing: 'I see we've got the bearded lady with us.' Apparently, Sargent, epitome of the English Gentleman, affected not to hear this, and is said merely to have brushed some imaginary dust off his sleeve.

It is easy with hindsight to remark that, after all, it was only a matter of time before a singer great enough came forward to re—establish this vital voice in the revival of authentic performance of early and pre—Romantic music. It is undeniable that Deller's task was difficult, initially – even with Tippett and the BBC Third Programme to help him. Most of the musical establishment, trained, still entrenched in and watched over by prestigious music colleges, simply ignored him; his biography is recommended for an account of his struggles for recognition. Selling the idea of the renascent solo (or indeed choral) male alto to choral societies and music clubs in the 1940s and '50s, when most committees were likely to be blissfully unaware of the true history of the alto, must have seemed an impossible task.

With Deller's death in 1979, an era ended: one filled with the excitement of great pioneer work. J. B. Steane, writing in 1974 as if Deller had retired by then – though he never did retire, but sang well until his quite sudden death in Bologna – summed up his impact upon the musical public:[8]

> ... over the last twenty years or so they have learnt to accept the voice of the counter—tenor as a regular part of the musical fare ... Alfred Deller's great gifts were luckily at hand at just the right time to give a lead, inspire new interest and virtually to found a school ... he gave some incomparable performances of songs by Dowland and Purcell. Of its kind his voice was unusually full—bodied and vibrant. He could float it very beautifully, but many altos and falsettists can do this. Where (as far as I know) he is still unique is

[7] Michael and Mollie Hardwick, op. cit., p. 100, and *Radio Times*, 29 December 1946
[8] J. B. Steane, *The Grand Tradition* (Duckworth, 1974), pp. 521-2

in his strong resonance; also of course, in the style which though often imitated was entirely his own. Ornate in its fondness for crescendos, sudden pianos, emphases ... knowledge of voice colourings ... most at home in Purcell ... erotic languor ... gentle mystical swing ... the minor–keyed languishing chromatic comforts ... When the poets spoke of making delicious moan and so forth, they must have had singing something like Deller's in mind. He could catch Elizabethan melancholy ... in Dowland's 'In darkness let me dwell' we hear something essentially stronger than melancholy ... a quite exceptional artist, who ... brought volumes of old music to the light of imaginative performance ... his resonant voice matching the sonority of the viols ... folk songs ... wealth of music from tavern songs to Monteverdi with his Consort, a fine body of singers ... strongly directed. Benjamin Britten paid his tribute with Oberon's music in *A Midsummer Night's Dream* which Deller recorded, using his full voice for this often aggressive part, and luxuriating in the Purcellian solo 'I know a bank'.

Thurston Dart, whose interest and ultimate career in early music and musicology must have been at least partly influenced by his father's alto voice, commented on Deller:[9]

> Another obsolete voice, the solo male alto or counter–tenor, has become familiar again during the last decade through the artistry of Alfred Deller. The tradition of counter–tenor singing in English cathedral choirs has never been broken since the earliest times, but solo counter–tenors of Deller's calibre must always have been rare. The voice itself seems to have been an especially English one – Purcell and Henry Lawes were both counter–tenors – and its distinctive tone colour is an essential part of English choral music.

During the late 1940s and early 1950s, Deller's brilliance inspired others to follow, notably John Whitworth, Grayston Burgess and Owen Wynne in England and Russell Oberlin in the USA. The influence a great artist can have on others, especially budding voices, is hardly surprising. Grayston Burgess was Head Chorister at Canterbury and sang with Deller there before Deller left for the London musical scene. He treasures the occasion when Deller first performed Vaughan Williams's 'Valiant for Truth' when Tippett was in the congregation.

Deller, Whitworth and Burgess (and later, to some extent, Oberlin or his influence) established what Burgess has called the 'alternative' alto sound in English male choral and ensemble music. Gradually, its impact increased, and the older style began to sound dated and tame. By the time of the joint Purcell/Handel Commemoration in 1958, the solo counter–tenor was re–established in England if not yet throughout the British Isles. Re–established, yes, but popular in a wide sense, not yet.

---

[9] Thurston Dart, *The Interpretation of Music* (Dent, 1954), p. 49

John Whitworth (1921–), who played a prominent part in the revival,
Owen Wynne (1926–); and Russell Oberlin (1928–),
who pioneered the revival in the United States of America

Even as the re–establishment of the solo counter–tenor was being consolidated by fine performances from a handful of singers, the 1957 British film comedy *Lucky Jim* appeared, based on the novel by Kingsley Amis. Our interest is in its 'silly–falsetto' theme song. The range chosen was the median of the average classical counter–tenor: G3 to A4. Though performed in burlesque, droll fashion, the technique was a parody of that historical voice. Was this coincidence? A counter–tenor renaissance was happening in England at the time. The film's setting was a red–brick university apeing the ancient foundations. The traditional academic setting is one of a number of totally appropriate counter–tenor environments. (Another is ecclesiastical. The song 'Lucky Jim' can be sung, successfully, as an Anglican chant for men's voices! Also, the words 'O Lucky Jim, How I Envy Him!' have especially comic overtones when sung insinuatingly in falsetto.) When the silly–falsetto voice finishes, a chorus of 'machismo–toned' tenors enters abruptly, one degree lower in pitch, as if to emphasize that what has been heard is a joke: these are real men! In the film, Jim Dixon (Ian Carmichael) is a disaster–prone lecturer. The falsetto–theme seems to echo his persona: some-one tragically, but comically, out of step with the normal.

We should not be over–sensitive. The film was, and still is, hilarious! According to the credits, the falsetto was supplied by Al Fernhead. It was actually very apt! (Must the slight similarity between the names Al Fernhead and Albert Whitehead be purely coincidental?)

The 1958 Purcell/Handel Commemoration was based in London. A comprehensive bro-chure published in conjunction with it included various articles on each composer and his works. It also listed the London events in detail. Interesting and revealing conclusions may be drawn. Out of a total of forty–two concerts (including some which were repeated), eleven involved solo counter–tenors. The main multi–performance events were:

The Tempest, Purcell	Seventeen performances at the 'Old Vic', with low counter–tenor part taken by a conventional tenor
Samson, Handel	Three performances at Covent Garden, one solo alto part taken by a woman
Dido and Aeneas, Purcell	Three performances in the Great Hall of Hampton Court. (In the preparation of which, Cummings's comments – see pp. 67–68 – might have been noticed.)
Semele, Handel	Three performances at Sadlers Wells, with the counter–tenor Grayston Burgess

However, if we take these operas as of one performance each (four in total), the Festival totalled twenty main musical events. Of these, only nine involved solo counter–tenor work.

The brochure listed a number of centres throughout Britain where other Purcell and Handel works were performed as part of the Commemoration. It would be interesting to know how many included counter–tenors in works where the voice was specified or expected originally – for instance in:

> *Acis and Galatea; Alexander's Feast; L'Allegro, il Penseroso ed il Moderato; Belshazzar; Dido and Aeneas; The Fairy Queen; Israel in Egypt; Jephtha; Joshua; Judas Maccabaeus; King Arthur; Messiah; Orlando; St John Passion; Saul; Semele; Solomon; Xerxes*

Solo counter–tenors listed in the Festival Brochure were Deller, Whitworth, Burgess and Pearmain. (1995 will mark another Purcell Commemoration, and comparisons with the former may be revealing.)

The Times music critic, writing in 1960, was vaguely interested but neutral:[10]

> The curiously sudden revival of the counter–tenor voice is another vagary of taste, added by scholarship which demands authentic performances of Purcell, who liked and used the voice. It is to be distinguished from the male alto,

---

[10] *The Times*, 'The Voice and its Vagaries', 24 June 1960

which is a baritone's falsetto, and its tessitura lies a fifth higher than the tenor's – Britten writes Oberon's part up to D. A generation ago, the voice was unknown outside books, and certainly unheard: now counter–tenors multiply, and there are even attempts to revive the sound of the male soprano (though without surgery).

From the standpoint of the 1990s we can survey more than forty years which have followed the renaissance of the solo counter–tenor. We are able to see how successful it has been in various musical spheres. 1943 now seems ancient history in many ways. Much prejudice against the highest male voice has faded – or rather it has shifted its emphasis. We discuss this later.

Opera seemed most likely to welcome the re–emergence of counter–tenor or alto voice, especially because the performance of very early opera had been handicapped without this voice, both as regards its musical effect and because of difference in stage 'presence' of a male rather than female singer. In addition, rôles were written for castrati which were and are well within the range of a large–voiced counter–tenor, with no need for transposition. Gluck's *Orfeo* is an example, and Handel's *Julius Caesar* is definitely suitable for such a voice. We might recall that many of Handel's so–called castrato rôles were written with both voices as options.

Regarding higher castrato parts, it used to be thought that they could be taken by counter–tenors only if a slight transposition downwards was made, and there seemed little hope of genuine soprano–castrato arias being sung by male voices without it. However, since 1982, the incredible sopranists, Randall Wong and Aris Christofellis, have appeared; there are also reports of Oleg Ryaberts. These men sing the soprano rôles without the need of transposition, and there must be others. The highly–developed, more average–ranged, so–called 'falsettist' retains much of the essence of the eunuchoid voice too.

Randall Wong (1955–)

Until recent years, transposition, or the use of a female mezzo–soprano or the employment of a tenor or baritone singing one octave lower, seemed the operatic establishment's only answers to the problem of performing originally castrato rôles today. As Robert Donington wrote, after first advising use of a counter–tenor as a substitute:[11]

---

[11] Robert Donington, *The Interpretation of Early Music* (Faber, 1963, revised 1975), p. 524

One alternative is the transposition to a low octave. In Handel operas, this has the unfortunate consequence of dropping the voice deep as a tenor (or still worse as a baritone) into an orchestration composed by Handel to support a soprano or alto part. A female voice may well be the best compromise, and *can be* [author's italics] musically although not quite dramatically satisfactory.

Another important aspect of using the expert, high falsettist, is that of androgyny. Sexual ambiguity is so much part of the essential artificiality of early (and indeed some later) opera. In castrato rôles, in addition to other considerations, the sexual twist is strangely lessened when a female singer, however accomplished, is employed.

Anything more than half-hearted use of counter-tenors or indeed slightly lower-ranged singers usually billed tenor or haute-contre (such as Cuénod, who has been a distinguished singer of his range since before the war) took a long time to happen in post-war operatic productions. The conservatism of the opera world, even among some of those purporting to stage authentic performances, was considerable. Other than prejudice, one problem was that singers of other vocal categories were then of conventional type, trained to match large orchestral forces, despite the date and style of the early operas being performed. Despite also the availability of Alfred Deller, Whitworth, Burgess, Oberlin, Bridger, Pearmain and Wynne, from the mid–1950s onwards and of Mitchell, Bowman, Brett, Jacobs (Belgium), Mark Deller, Esswood, Ferrante (USA), Brown and Tatnell, from the 1960s, the operatic establishment did not take much interest in them for some years. Of course, it is arguable that not all possessed appropriate voice–sizes and stage–craft, or the then currently acceptable operatic style. They tended to have their specialisms.

Perceval Bridger (1919–1970) and James Bowman (1941–)

René Jacobs (1946–) and Paul Esswood (as Ottone; 1942–)

Steven Rickards (1956–) and Michael Chance (1955–)

Though it took time to have maximum effect, the turning–point in contemporary opera was Britten's *A Midsummer Night's Dream* (1960) in which the rôle of Oberon was written for Deller.

Smith, Davis, York Skinner, James, Penrose, Collins (USA), Messana (USA), Sage (France), Crighton (Canada), Gentry (Canada), Hill, and Cheng–Jim surfaced in the 1970s.

In the 1980s and 1990s, we have seen the names of Martin–Oliver, Ledroit (like many French and other continental male high voices, billed either as counter–tenor or haute–contre), Royall, Cunningham (Canada), Visse (France), Lesne (France), Vandersteene (Belgium), Gay, Robson, Stafford, Chance, Minter (USA), Rickards (USA), Dooley (USA), Gall (USA), Cordier, Wilson, Ragin (USA), Wong (USA, and billed sopranist); Clapton, Christofellis (Greece, and billed sopranist); Kowalski (originally East Germany), Köhler (Germany) and Popken (Hungary). This list could never be complete.

Jochen Kowalski

In 1971, a promising mature English male–soprano, Richard Crane, seemed about to enter the scene, but little more seems to have been heard of him. It is to be hoped that Oleg Ryaberts, the youthful Russian also billed male–soprano, is more successful. Apparently, a young English sopranist, Michael Aspinall, is beginning to make his name in Rome, notably at the Teatro Ghione.

There was, and certainly is now, no excuse for non–employment of contrasting and appropriate high male voices by opera producers and casting directors. Undeniably, there is a growing number of such singers on which to call for pre–Romantic and modern works. It is gratifying that counter–tenors/haute–contres are being used increasingly. The healthy influence of the early music movement has affected orchestral size and type. More care is taken 'across the (vocal) board' to cast singers with voices of appropriate type. Matters have improved, even since 1981.

Rodney Milnes wrote of the Wexford Festival in January of that year:[12]

> Reactionary elements muttered about the unsuitability of the counter–tenor voice to Handel's castrato roles, and I could not disagree more violently. John Angelo Messana's singing of the title role was something of a milestone in the continuing process of the emergence of the counter–tenor in *opera seria*. His phrasing was extremely expressive, and he fielded more variety of tone colour and dynamic than many of his *confrères* could muster. His delivery of the long finale of the second act, a sequence of glowing genius, held the audience breathless. All right, it might not have worked at Covent Garden, but we were not at Covent Garden. Mr Messana's powerful stage presence was both exploited and controlled ...

Until the 1980s, with some exceptions such as Benjamin Britten (*A Midsummer Night's Dream*), Alan Ridout (*The Pardoner's Tale*) and Peter Maxwell Davies (*Taverner*), modern opera composers rather held back from writing rôles for counter–tenors. It has been suggested that perhaps composers have felt that the counter–tenor, by its very nature, does not reflect the contemporary world. In 1965, Frederic Hodgson, in one of two important articles in *The Musical Times*,[13] had pointed out that:

> Most modern composers seem to fight shy of writing for the solo alto, and the Britten/Oberon problem raises questions as to what comprehension they have of the potentialities and peculiarities of this voice. After the question of writing specifically for the alto had been put to a famous song–writer, he gave the ambiguous reply that it was difficult to find 'suitable words' for an alto! Another composer made play on a verse of the Psalms: 'I do not exercise myself in great matters which are "too high" for me!'

There seems little, if any, counter–tenor participation in modern light opera, stage, or film musicals, though popular–style singers sometimes employ head–voice without being billed under any particular vocal designation.

There should have been early success in opera's close cousin, oratorio. Ebenezer Prout's edition of *Messiah* (1902), restored the extended and now customarily used version of 'But Who May Abide?' to the alto voice. It was a move not generally successful at the time in returning the aria to its correct octave or of persuading musical directors to employ a high male voice or even a medium–to–low female voice for it.

Several decades later, soon after the second world war, John Tobin's annual 'authentic' (or 'historically–aware') versions of *Messiah* first in 1950 at St Paul's Cathedral[14], and sub-

---

[12] Rodney Milnes, *Opera*, January 1981

[13] Frederic Hodgson, 'The Contemporary Alto', *The Musical Times*, April 1965, p. 294

[14] The part played by the organist of St Paul's, John Dykes Bower, not only in assisting Alfred Deller (whom he appointed and whose consort singing he encouraged) but also in encouraging John Tobin, and Maurice Bevan, Andrew Pearmain and other editor/singers of early music, by

sequently at the Royal Festival Hall, London, were an inspiration. Compared with other performances of *Messiah* at the time, they seemed to be convincing in vocal–assignment, style, orchestration and ornamentation, although the chorus altos were mostly inauthentic contraltos. A counter–tenor always took the alto solos, including 'But Who May Abide?', and a second joined him from the chorus for the duet version of 'How Beautiful are the Feet'. Tobin's excellent 1965 score of *Messiah* for the Halle Handel Edition is still available.

Dr Harold Watkins Shaw's performing edition of *Messiah* was published in 1959. Like that of Tobin, it argued that solos originally written for the castrato Guadagni should be sung by a counter–tenor. However, he did allow for versions using a contralto. This is appropriate, if not so exciting dramatically, in view of later Handelian practice and some of the original performances of the oratorio. Dr Shaw's second edition appeared in 1992 as did another excellent version edited by Dr Donald Burrows.[15]

To hear arias usually associated with bass or contralto sung by counter–tenor can be like experiencing an old painting without dulled varnish. Recordings have appeared with Deller, Bowman, Oberlin, Esswood, Brett, Jacobs, James's and Chance's brilliant accounts of the *Messiah* arias; many of them are still obtainable. More will surely follow. It can therefore be said that, since the 1950s, pre–nineteenth–century oratorio, opera, cantata and similar forms have again become fruitful fields for counter–tenors.

Interest has also re–opened into male high voices of the pre–Deller decades. More research, and early ballad–recordings of altos like Hatherley Clarke (who was remembered particularly for superb performances as solo alto in Bach's *St John Passion* in the 1920s and 1930s, unfortunately not recorded) tempt some qualifying of opinion about past standards. If we acknowledge the deadening effect of primitive technology on the legendary reputations of a few noted altos of the past, we might wonder if the shortage of strong, positive voices was quite as acute as many have supposed.

Today, there seems to be no problem. Solo counter–tenors of all types are often to be heard in recordings, broadcasting, on concert platform and stage and increasingly on television.

The general public still enjoys the lighter offerings of, say, The King's Singers (with two counter–tenors and no sopranos to mask them) but seems apprehensive of the serious solo counter–tenor. Encouragingly, however, specialist television music programmes – particularly of early and contemporary opera – are beginning to feature him more often. Counter–tenors would seem to be here to stay, barring any cultural about–turns or social pressures. Their re–introduction into mainstream secular ensemble music happened naturally. It followed the example of the five–voice Golden Age Singers. Deller's was the sole voice of alto range.

Then came the excellent Deller Consort (1950), a similar group but directed by Deller himself. (John Whitworth replaced Deller in the Golden Age Singers in 1953, and Mark Deller was to replace his father when Alfred died in 1979.) Other ensembles followed, notably The Ambrosian Consort which also included John Whitworth. Most were concerned with early music – madrigals, motets and concert performances of early church music.

---

performing their editions and by his playing continuo in early authentic performances, should not be forgotten; nor his exemplary playing of Bach on the remarkable organ of 1953 at the Festival Hall when scarcely any other cathedral organist knew what to do with such an instrument

[15] A review of these which included a comparison of them with Tobin's edition was published in *The Musical Times*, November 1992, p. 577

The Deller Consort rehearsing in Boughton Aluph church, Kent, 1968

Initially, in many renascent counter-tenor mixed-voice vocal groups, the counter-tenor was surrounded by (otherwise often excellent) voices of inappropriate style. This highlighted the counter-tenor's contribution. 'Deller was miles ahead of many of his collaborators – the other singers in his consort came from the "normal" world of music, and it showed.'[16]

Male-voice quartets, or small ensembles (an honourable if by the 1940s rather stuffy-sounding survival of a great tradition) sang with a style and repertoire by then largely Romantic. Nevertheless, they began to be transformed by the new virile alto sound and capability. John Whitworth's excellent Well-Tempered Singers, for example, made exciting and emphatically not lugubrious listening. Groups today include The King's Singers, The Scholars (who started with two counter-tenors but have since replaced one with a mezzo-soprano), and the quite outstanding Hilliard Ensemble. There are also Cantabile, The Light Blues, and many others, including the only trio, Canterbury Clerkes.

Counter-tenors performing in small vocal ensemble have therefore been very successful. Male-voice quartets and glee singers were long established and other mixed, small specialist groups could quite easily adjust to re-inclusion of counter-tenors. Much of their original musical literature clearly demanded a male alto line. Contemporary composers and arrangers, too, have been active in writing for ensembles which include altos.

Grayston Burgess (1932–) directing The Purcell Consort of Voices, 1968

Several mixed or all-male groups were originally brought together and/or directed by counter-tenors. These included The Deller Consort, The Well-Tempered Singers (Whitworth), The Northern Consort (Wynne), The Purcell Consort of Voices (Burgess), the original Clerkes of Oxenford (Wulstan) and, later, Canterbury Clerkes (Giles). Many others, some of which

---

[16] Cohen and Snitzer, *The Extra-ordinary Revival of Early Music* (Reprise, 1989), p. 76 ('Singers, or the Main Difficulty')

included instrumentalists, seemed built round the counter—tenor, like the earlier Ambrosian Consort (Whitworth; directed by Denis Stevens), New York Pro Musica (Oberlin; directed by Noah Greenberg), St George's Canzona (Derek Harrison; directed by John Sothcott), Pro Cantione Antiqua (Mitchell; directed by Bruno Turner). Similarly, The King's Singers (originally Perrin and Hulme), The Scholars (Dixon), The Tallis Scholars (originally Harre-Jones and Bright), The Hilliard Ensemble (James), The Landini Consort (Richard Hill), The Toronto Consort (Crighton) and other one—voice and/or instrument—per—part groups, abound.

Ensembles based on instruments and one or two voices which include counter—tenors have flourished, though at present musical fashion seems to be shifting. The superb Early Music Consort of London (directed by David Munrow) featured the brilliant James Bowman. The group began in the late 1960s, and ended with Munrow's tragically early death in 1976. In recent years, the excellent King's Consort (directed by Robert King) has featured Bowman regularly and Michael Chance occasionally.

Post—war solo voices and small ensembles are not the whole story. As an example, there is a hauntingly lovely, but distant, early recorded performance of Byrd's 'Have Mercy on Me, O Lord' sung by St John's College choir, Cambridge, under Dr Cyril Rootham *c*1930, accompanied by an anonymous consort of viols. There is little difference between distant altos and distant viols – they are of similar timbre (surely as intended): edgy, yet sonorous.[17]

English cathedral choirs, and their treatment of the repertoire, have been almost transformed by the modern counter—tenor movement. Mostly, we now hear firm, ringing, properly—trained voices, able to cope well with the original musical literature. No longer, except in unusual cases, are counter—tenor solos like Gibbons's 'This is the Record of John' given to a tenor. Of course, any difficulty in obtaining a counter—tenor voice with a convincing timbre and range in these choirs will probably result in reversion of important solo work to a modern type of tenor.

The tone of boys' voices has changed, too. There is a different attitude to blend: the vocal parts are now equal, more in the Classical tradition than Romantic, though some choirs retain an over—prominent treble line. English cathedral choirs now tend to sound exciting, if sometimes rather insensitive. Once, most of them sounded super—sensitive, vaguely lovely or merely mellow. Certainly, there are occasions now when one hears an otherwise good contemporary choir tackling, for instance, S. S. Wesley, one wishes for some more appropriate tonal adjustment.

Some larger ensembles, like The Ambrosian Singers (founded by Denis Stevens and John McCarthy), The Renaissance Singers (first directed by Michael Howard and then by John Whitworth) and Cantores in Ecclesia (director, Michael Howard) in the recent past, The Clerkes of Oxenford (director, David Wulstan), The Sixteen (director, Harry Christophers), The Monteverdi Choir (director, John Eliot Gardiner) and certain smaller groups today which enlarge to perform bigger works, use counter—tenors in the alto part, at least in pre-nineteenth—century works.

In the 1950s, an interesting experiment was tried by The Renaissance Singers (the Howard/Whitworth ensemble, not to be confused with the chamber choir of the same name today) with the object of recreating the sound of the sixteenth—century Sistine Chapel choir. In this trial, (unlike one essayed by a particular mixed—voice ensemble of today, which purports to have the same aim), falsettists were correctly used for the soprano line exclusively.

---

[17] HMV B 2448, 78 r.p.m. disc

Lower counter–tenors sang the alto. Perceval Bridger was the principal soprano involved. Their concerts had a stunning impact, and some records and broadcasts were made, but the soprano aspect of the experiment was ultimately only partially successful in live performance. John Whitworth wrote:[18]

> ... I think the system broke down mainly because they had to sing two hour recitals almost without a break. The sound was quite thrilling before the voices began to tire, which they unfortunately did after about half an hour, and one was left wondering how good it would be if the system had about ten years or so of tradition behind it.

The smaller ensemble Pro Musica Antiqua later followed the Renaissance Singers' example, though not usually attempting works with the highest soprano parts. The American group, Chanticleer, which includes the male sopranist Randall Wong, however, starts where The Renaissance Singers paused. The Gabrieli Consort and Players have also made a strong impact.

Today, Michael Howard must surely wish that Wong, Christofellis, Crane and Ryaberts had been available then. Together with Bridger and the others, the sound would have been truly magnificent.

Other than in Tobin's London Choral Society in the post–war years, the counter–tenor has not yet seriously re–penetrated the secular chorus. In the Three Choirs Festival Chorus, though, the cathedral choirs of Gloucester, Hereford and Worcester themselves were the originators and founder members, and still remain the kernel of the massed mixed choir. Barry Still explains how this originally all–male chorus was slowly but steadily augmented:[19]

> Early in Festival history, a few ladies were 'imported' from the North, then members of other cathedral or collegiate bodies were invited, with the aim of giving extra strength to the choral forces. For the fashion was developing for more robust and opulent interpretations of the Baroque repertoire than could be attempted by the three cathedral choirs alone. (Even in 1835, the orchestra numbered seventy–one, the choral body one hundred and nineteen.) Taste has turned a somersault in some ways, as this year's Messiah at Gloucester testifies – cathedral choir with chamber orchestra!

An extremely rare form of the already rare tenor–altino voice must be included among the counter–tenor family. Russell Oberlin, a distinguished singer of the tenor–altino type, is one reason for the search, in the United States of the 1950s and '60s, for a different breed of solo counter–tenor.

---

[18] John Whitworth, 'The Solo Counter-Tenor and its Repertoire in England' (*English Church Music*, the journal of the Royal School of Church Music, 1965), p. 38. See also the reviews of the concerts in *The Times*, Friday 3 April 1959 under the title of 'The Re–emergence of the Adult Male Soprano'

[19] Barry Still, 'The Three Choirs Festival and the Three Cathedral Choirs', *Friends of Cathedral Music Annual Report*, April 1977, p. 11

After Deller had begun the revival in England in the late 1940s and early '50s, followed closely by Whitworth, Oberlin became known in America as a soloist, teacher and member of New York Pro Musica Antiqua. Like Deller and Whitworth, he broadcast, recorded and gave recitals and concerts to audiences for most of whom the solo counter–tenor was utterly new.

Deller toured the United States and Canada, Oberlin came to England and Whitworth went to America as a member of the Golden Age Singers. Because each had his own distinctive timbre, it began to be suggested that the term counter–tenor was right for one but surely not the other. Few thought that there could be a valid generic name for so many and various types of singer at much the same high pitch. It is unquestionable that the Oberlin type of voice (which many claim is exclusively identical to the haute–contre once common in France) is very rare indeed. It seems also to be a voice of no great longevity, though this is not necessarily because of a shorter life–span in eighteenth–century France: Jélyotte lived from 1713 to 1797, and though Le Gros lived from 1739 only to 1793 he was (appropriately) hugely overweight throughout his life and had to retire from the stage at the age of 44. These and other factors suggest strongly that the Oberlin variety of voice alone could not have been the voice–type which, for example, comprised the extensive French haute–contre population and provided easily half the adult male singers in every English medieval, Tudor and seventeenth–century collegiate and cathedral choir.

Though thenafter the ratio of voices became more equal, counter–tenors held their places in these foundations and those on the European mainland and in opera choruses and cantata choirs of the seventeenth and eighteenth centuries. This fact further increases the unlikelihood that enough of the rare tenor–altino voice–type could have been found to populate the alto part of these choirs exclusively and to provide solo singers as well. The truth is that variety has always been the genius of the counter–tenor family.

We should consider reasons for Russell Oberlin's original success in America other than his excellent artistry and his rarity value. In the 1950s, anything nominally male but which seemed to smack of effeminacy, musical or otherwise, must have seemed suspect in a country which boasted heroic baseball giants and the 'all–American hero' tradition. No wonder that, when he appeared, the American solo counter–tenor (despite in Oberlin's case, having a rather effete sound–quality) tended to maintain that his voice was exclusively a very high, rare tenor. Oberlin could certainly demonstrate a tenor–like lower register, though it sounded unusual.

As if to emphasize their distinct viewpoint, Americans tend to use 'countertenor' as one word, perhaps to nullify any suggestion of two distinct registers. Another reason may be more nearly to equate countertenor with contratenor, with the aim of emphasising a healthy and authentic pedigree (and why not?), but there seems little basis for the view that the original contratenor was always, or ever, a single–register singer. Of course, no one form of title – single, compound or hyphenated – is more correct than another; early usage varied too. However, perhaps in imitation of a perceived English tradition, Richard Jose's American records, made round the turn of this century, mostly hyphenate the term counter–tenor.

Americans seem shy of the word alto when applied to a man. It would appear that, originally, they wanted no part of the feminine assciations with the term, or indeed of links with the English cathedral tradition or (perhaps through ignorance) of the European falsetto tradition. In much of Europe and America, with its once–predominant German Protestant musical tradition, alto had become (and is still) associated with (a) a low, mature, female voice – strangely, in many countries they prefer to dock the prefix 'contra' – and (b) a low–pitched boy's or girl's voice. For much of the musical world, therefore, alto is now paradoxically associated not with high but with low pitch. It has a low, feminine or child–like connotation, or a combination of all three.

Many American singers, teachers and authorities, however much they admired the artistry and technique of Deller and Whitworth and, later, Bowman, Esswood and the younger men, seem to have regarded them merely as developed falsettists and, as such, questionable.

In England, the renaissance of the secular solo alto voice happened because, in the person of Alfred Deller, it returned from the mainly ecclesiastical shadows. For most decades since the war, all or nearly all English solo counter–tenors, like Deller himself, came from a cathedral, collegiate or church choral background. Many still do. Most had been boy choristers; if, like Deller, they were in a parish church they had remained there to sing alto when their treble voices faded. This often happened at an incredibly late age. Frequently, too, it was not their voices but their mature bulk and worried choir–masters which had dictated the move.

It was, and is, different for cathedral choristers. When they are about thirteen and a half years old they must leave to move to senior school whether or not their voices have gone. Because physical treblehood ends earlier than ever (in the opinion of the author, partly because of a change in treble training–technique), cathedral choirs are often deprived of excellent boys six months or even a year earlier than necessary. These former choristers usually move straight into a 'public' (that is, private) or senior school choir; some are still functioning as mature trebles, but most move to alto, tenor or bass parts in due course. Some lose or abandon their singing voices altogether but many continue singing in some sphere at least. Some reappear, aged eighteen–plus, as choral scholars in university college choirs or in those cathedral choirs which offer a limited number of choral scholarships to undergraduates.

As Julian Gardiner and others have pointed out before and since, good male voices are invariably those which never broke but which gradually deepened so that at no time were their possessors incapable of singing. Those who settle as altos have seldom sung at any other pitch. Thus they are specialists from the start: potential solo counter–tenors, if nature has been kind and training good. David Wulstan has written usefully on various aspects of vocal mutation.[20] This ecclesiastical and/or university background, therefore, has been the main source of English counter–tenors for centuries: an advantage and, sometimes, a disadvantage. Until recently, few if any of them were never choristers, lay–clerks, choral scholars, parish choirmen or some combination of these. The background to the English male choir tradition was the single–sex school and the influence of the originally all–male world of the university college. There was nothing odd, unusual, or effeminate in men's singing alto in these musical circles and never had been. It was the norm.

The coming of co–education to our ancient, and not so ancient, schools is now beginning to have an unfortunate – and predictable – effect on trebles and young potential counter–tenors when they are at a self–conscious age. It was particularly noticeable that some schools which, once noted as a source of male high voices, were found after becoming co–educational to be no longer prolific suppliers of young counter–tenors or of university choral scholarships in that voice. (This takes into account the already worrying decrease in the number of schools which encourage and promote good singing in all voice–ranges. There is, of course, a resulting detrimental effect on the numbers of emerging singers, professional and amateur, nation–wide.)

---

[20] David Wulstan, *Tudor Music* (C.U.P., 1992), pp. 215–225

As we have seen, the situation for the emergent counter–tenor in 'secular' music had differed from that of cathedral music and the academic world for many years. Until about 1957, when Trinity College of Music, London, established places for counter–tenors (though a reliable but unofficial source reports that counter–tenors were being given tuition and taking diploma examinations there in 1949), most colleges of music ran no courses which admitted or welcomed counter–tenors, though the Royal Academy of Music had allowed for 'male alto' in its Associateship examination when others did not. There can surely have been few candidates – unfortunately, the voice seems to have been more self–taught than taught. Because most colleges trained no altos and did not recognise the voice officially, there were no purely college–trained altos until much later, when prejudice had been worn down. Paul Esswood was one of the first distinguished counter–tenor singers to emerge from an 'official' background. The situation has developed much since Esswood's time as a student. Excellent altos trained at music colleges are now well in evidence on concert platforms.

Turning again to the United States, we can see immediately that a different situation would obtain. There were, and are, choirs of men and boys on the English pattern but these are few in a vast country. Fewer still are as yet recognised as outstanding, though at least one name must be singled out – that of St Thomas's Church, Fifth Avenue, New York City, which is excellent and comparable to some of the best choirs in England today. However, the tradition itself in America could be considered precarious. Of course, it is very recent by European standards. The situation should mature and develop if it can survive today's inevitable pressures and attacks. These are not, perhaps, pressures based on accusations of élitism as they currently are in Britain but (as also in Britain), they are theological and sociological pressures, and those initiated by feminism. The same comments could be applied to the Canadian, Australian, and New Zealand traditions of male cathedral and church choirs.

The American secular 'boy–choir', often based on a German model, is not quite the same animal. It is usually larger and has boy altos. The author's impression is that, as in (later) German practice, this boy alto is not intended or encouraged to remain in the choir as a young counter–tenor but to move to tenor or bass and then to leave. Other than those emerging from choirs like St Thomas's, New York, transatlantic solo counter–tenors, like Oberlin, seem far more likely to have emerged from within a mixed–choir background, or from a college training; almost certainly from the tenor, or possibly baritone line, the alto being occupied exclusively by women. If he came from a large secular boy–choir he seems likely to have been a tenor immediately before deciding to sing counter–tenor. When these young men found themselves with a potential head–voice – the alto range – it was probably a pleasant but sometimes bewildering bonus. It is possible that many never sang as choral altos or even as trebles at all. They may have had a vocally unsophisticated childhood and to have begun musical vocal life as young adults. Of course, as always, there are notable exceptions.

One American (counter–) tenor to emerge in the 1960s, Willard Cobb, trained first at Oberlin Conservatoire, then at Trinity College of Music, London. He sang recitals in London and made broadcasts and then, dropping out of English sight, appeared as a tenor in continental Europe; he now lives in the United States. Another fine counter–tenor, John Ferrante, who seems not to sing on the European side of the Atlantic, has also sung as a tenor. He may be heard, for instance, in some of the humorous 'P. D. Q. Bach' recordings. Like Cobb, his style employs falsetto, which he admits with no self–consciousness.

There have been exciting developments in recent years. Earlier we listed some of the excellent new American counter–tenors. There is also a small but thriving young Canadian counter–tenor scene from which we can expect much. It should be pointed out that the reception given to indigenous counter-tenors of quality in either country is not yet always enthusiastic. There is still much misunderstanding from the public there just as there is in parts of Europe.

Since Alfred Deller's early days, English solo counter-tenors have continued to enjoy success on the American continent despite the same reactions of non-comprehension, even dislike, in some areas. There is, perhaps, a tendency for an artist's overseas origin to influence his reception. Some might explain the popularity of visiting English counter-tenors in North America, and in parts of Europe today, as parallel to the reception of Italian castrati in eighteenth-century England. Visiting celebrities are one thing, but native 'oddities' quite another.

We might recall, however, that the English have never been associated with extremes. Americans have, and often are. Hence, it is likely that if it became fashionable in the United States the counter-tenor scene could 'rocket' for a time to an extent which at present seems unlikely to happen in Britain. In the same way, if ever castrato singers could return, in a changed cultural climate, they would probably enjoy truly astronomical success in North America. On the other hand, American influences are so powerful today that the British (traditionally susceptible to cultural influence from abroad) would no doubt be persuaded by them.

The foregoing broadly chronological historical account, together with the more detailed discussion of some important and colourful personalities in the appendices, should have prepared the reader for the second part of this work. In that part we will be exploring the vocal techniques of the counter-tenor in his differing varieties and consequently need to re-examine certain historical periods in more detail. We will also need to ask questions about future prospects for the male high voice.

Part Two

TECHNIQUE

He is made one with nature: there is heard
His voice in all her music, from the moan
Of thunder, to the song of night's sweet bird

Shelley: 'Adonais', XLII

O stay and hear your true love's coming
That can sing both high and low

Shakespeare: 'Twelfth Night', II

5

The Vocal Mechanism

The human voice, regardless of its tessitura, behaves like most other musical instruments. It needs vibration to produce sound–waves, and resonators to amplify them.

Musical instruments use a variety of wave–producers – strings, single reeds, double reeds, sharp edges or (in brass instruments) the lips. Their resonators usually employ a captive body of air set in motion by a surface (in stringed instruments) or a column of air (in woodwind instruments). Solid resonators are used in some instruments: for example, the xylophone. The human voice is based variously on several of these principles.

Phonation is begun simultaneously by a pair of vocal folds caused to vibrate, or, more perceptively, wave or undulate, by air passing between them from the lungs. Tone is produced above the larynx, by various resonators: cranial cavities, the pharynx, and the mouth.

Some maintain that human voice production has almost as much in common with the method used by stringed instruments as with that of woodwind. Others disagree, considering that the passage of air along a tube is the very hallmark of woodwind. However, stringed instruments have a fixed body of air of constant size to produce resonance, while woodwind players vary the length and therefore the volume of the column of air by covering or un-covering holes along the body of their instruments.

Though the volume varies from individual to individual, the pharynx or mouth, with minor variation, seems to have a fixed volume within each person. By contrast, members of the violin family, for instance, have different sized sound–boxes, but a viola cannot shrink to a violin's size, or swell to that of a 'cello, though even within one particular species of instrument, proportion, size – internal and external – and construction will vary slightly. But the human instrument can vary slightly more the size and shape of some resonators, simply because muscle is elastic so that some adjustment of mouth, pharynx and larynx height can be made. It is undeniable that many singers use the differing cranial cavities in various ways.

We have seen that sound waves are caused by something vibrating or fluctuating. Reed instruments rely on the rapid opening and closing of a small aperture provided by the reed's pressing on the mouthpiece (as in the clarinet), or on another piece of reed (as in the oboe). Flute and recorder rely on air eddying either side of an edge, and brass instruments depend on the vibration of their players' lips. Except by changing the length of the vibrating air column, woodwind and brass instruments are unable to change pitch except by overblowing to produce notes only of their harmonic series. Stringed instruments, though, have four methods of varying pitch which are directly analogous with the voice. They are: (i) the thickness of strings, (ii) the tension of strings, (iii) the harmonics of strings, and (iv) the length of strings.

The thickness of the string determines what notes may be played. The thicker the string, the lower the note, and vice versa. Though, in theory, a thick string and a thin string can produce the same notes, in practice a high note from a thick string would require very high tension, and a low note from a thin string under low tension would be rather weak and die away rapidly. The several strings of a musical instrument are therefore chosen to produce an optimum sound over each of their ranges. The tension on a string will vary the pitch of the note within certain limits – it has to be sufficient to make the string taut yet not enough to cause it to break. The greater the tension, the higher the note, and the tension of the strings is adjusted by means of the tuning pegs. The harmonic used can increase the frequency of a note by an integral factor: a change integral to aliquot – meaning, sustainable of division without a remainder. (Some high–quality pianos have aliquot strings which are not struck, but sound sympathetically, adding important harmonics to each note.)

Normally, the fundamental, the first or lowest note of the harmonic series, is used:

Even so, by plucking or bowing in different positions, or by using a finger to produce other nodes, other harmonics may be obtained:

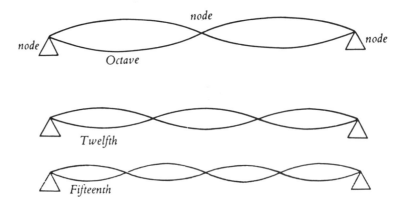

and so on.

Harmonics

This principle is used in the fretted clavichord, where one string may be used to produce two or three different notes, depending on where the tangents strike the string.

Nevertheless, though these three methods may be used to change the pitch of a note for a given length of string, none could be used for the actual playing of music because of the practical disadvantages. The exception is the clavichord, which, however, is almost inaudible except to its player. For practical music–making, the fourth category (length and tension of string) are the essential points.

Progressively shortening the length of a taut string, as in the action of a finger moving along the frets of a guitar finger–board, will result in a progressive raising of the pitch of the note produced. But, when applied to the voice, this analogy is misleading: stretching of the vocal folds raises pitch. This is infinitely variable – we are not restricted to the harmonics – and a choice of string–thicknesses will give the musician a sufficient range of notes on which to play. So it is with the voice, but resonating cavities are the final determinants of tone–quality; their use, some researchers would maintain, qualifies effective vocal range to some extent.

In the end, it has to be admitted that the human vocal organ is unique in its subtle mixture of powers. If we have to continue to relate it to artificial musical instruments, the clavi–organum – the combined pipe organ and harpsichord (crude though it is, when compared to the larynx) – though this seems at first to be a strange instrument to choose, is nonetheless a useful analogy, though even this parallel is not very satisfactory. For our illustration, the organ in question must possess reed–stops. Contained, therefore, in one instrument are flue pipes, reed pipes and plucked (though not bowed) strings. No single instrument can match the human vocal tract for sophistication and subtle versatility, though the claviorganum possesses no fewer than three of the important sound–producing elements possessed by the human voice. Of the others, the voice has the ability to change string–length, like the violin family.

The various types of voice – soprano, treble, alto, tenor, bass, etc. – are *related* to the length and character of the vocal folds, but not exclusively. A boy's vocal folds are short and thin, and hence capable of rapid vibration and high notes. The same is true of a girl's, though, by common consent, the boy of the same age can usually command more power and resonance, probably because of differences in muscle–tone and natural, gender–based psychology. By her mid–teens, the girl who has persisted with her singing has normally caught up, though by then the boy's voice has changed.

At puberty, the boy's folds thicken and become longer. The larynx becomes visually more prominent. Because the folds take some time to enlarge, and the muscles therein need time to develop, the voice 'breaks', and sometimes becomes unmanageable for a short time. Another definition of the word 'break' is to 'begin a new era', as in (i) day break, (ii) fresh start, new life, or even (iii) lucky break. The final quality of the vocal folds will determine the tessitura of the adult basic– or chest–voice.

Women's voices, from soprano to contralto, do not differ much, if at all, from men's in the manner of producing sound–waves. Tone–quality, however, is another matter. We shall look at this later in the chapter, especially where it must be taken into account in the debate on the use of women's voices in early music.

In either speech or song, the vocal folds fluctuate at the fundamental (see page 163). Change of pitch is made by the muscles within the folds tightening them and thinning out the edges – by pulling fold–material out of the way of the passing air. As with a violin string, there is a lower and upper limit to the possible notes produced. At their upper level, the muscles reach the limits of their strength, and can produce no more tension. At their lower, the muscles lose all tension, and become ineffective. At this point, any analogy with strings breaks down, and in fact must be reversed.

The vocal folds are two short strips of muscular, fibrous tissue, covered with squamous epithelium (tough, elastic, connecting tissue); they project like shelves into the air–stream at the top of the trachea or wind–pipe. They are not strings, but seem to act like the lips of the bugler, with a narrow slit between them. The folds, however, have a means of adjustment whereby the frequency of the vibrations may be varied. In this way, vocal folds act more like lips than reeds.

The folds in the adult male are about an inch long (25mm); less than this in women and children. They are situated in the larynx, which is a cartilaginous box (visible, especially in men, as the 'Adam's apple' at the front of the throat). The larynx is made up of two cartilages – the thyroid and the cricoid – and two small cartilages – the arytenoids. The cartilages are held together by ligaments and muscles, which, nonetheless, permit some movement. The vocal folds are attached to the thyroid cartilage at the front (anterior) and cricoid at the rear (posterior) of the larynx. The arytenoid cartilages are embedded in the vocal folds at their posterior end, but the full length of the fold can still be used for vibration.

The simplified diagram opposite depicts what happens in sound initiation. Muscles attached to the outside of the larynx can cause it to move higher or lower in the throat, and can put more tension in the folds themselves by acting in opposition on the thyroid and arytenoid cartilages. This tension will give a higher range of notes, but used badly can cause strain; yet the larynx should be free to move as it wishes in a relaxed way during phonation.

During normal singing, the vocal folds, which are wedge–shaped in section, are properly held parallel automatically, with a very narrow opening between them. Air from the lungs, passing through this slit (the glottis) causes the folds or vocal ligaments (*plica vocalis*) to wave and fluctuate in the flow, opening and closing rapidly. Video–recorded images, using a fibre–optic stroboscope, reveal a motion almost reminiscent of a rapidly–moving sea anemone. Air therefore passes through in a series of distinct 'puffs' which produce a moving and ascending column.

Frequency is controlled by movements previously described. Lower notes are produced by slackening and thickening the *plica vocalis* muscles in the vocal folds, and separating the arytenoid cartilages. This may allow leakage of air directly through the glottis, since the folds will tend to bow in the middle. The result is a rather 'breathy' tone, and is why it is difficult for most people to sing very low notes loudly.

To increase the frequency of the vibrations (hence, the pitch of the note), three events must take place. The arytenoid cartilages must move closer together, keeping the folds as parallel as possible, and the *vocalis* muscles in the folds must increase their tension, and thin the edges of the folds. When the singer has reached the upper limit of his basic–voice, something must happen to facilitate higher notes. He will make a 'gear–change' to his upper register, or head–voice, usually described as falsetto. This last is an unfortunate term, implying, as it does, an unnatural use. It is nothing of the sort. Theoretically, every voice–type has the ability to produce this mode, but of course in a naturally light voice (lyric soprano, treble, and some tenors) the changeover can hardly be noticed – which, incidentally, lessens the dramatic potential of the voice. Musical fashion plays no small part in our attitude towards all this.

Nowadays, the tendency is to smooth over the change as much as possible. Large, operatic female voices often continue to demonstrate clear register shifts which have as their basis some kind of chest to falsetto change. Even now, the public seems happy to accept this as the norm, though Clara Butt would have to modify her rather startling technique today. Traditionally, since at least the middle of the nineteenth century, many cognoscenti seem knowingly to have maintained this odd double standard: that while women and boys have clearly–defined head voices, men have voix mixte and falsetto. Head–voice applied to a man is almost always taken to denote 'mixed–voice'. Crude though these false distinctions may seem, and mistaken, they are stated in or implied by more than a few textbooks. No less an authority than Kate Emil–Behnke seems to have assented to this double standard.[1] On the

---

[1] K. Emil–Behnke, *The Technique of Singing* (Williams & Norgate, 1945), ch. 21, passim

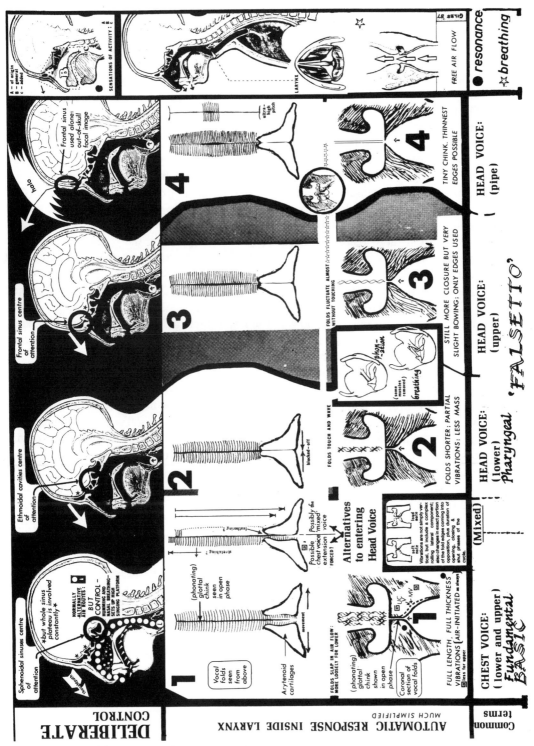

The relationship between the cranial cavities and the glottis

other hand, some, like Cornelius L. Reid, employ the term falsetto for both male and female, while frowning on its use.[2]

The anatomical reason for the usual falsetto voice seems quite simple, as the diagram shows. At the 'gear–change', the arytenoid cartilages press together, and prevent the posterior third of the vocal folds vibrating. Further shortenings from the closed posterior end towards the middle of the folds, and from the anterior end, give pure upper falsetto and an even higher range. On the other hand, V.E. Negus, F.R.C.S., argued in 1927[3] that in at least one mode of falsetto, the vocal folds actually lengthened.

When the laryngeal muscles have adjusted themselves to their maximum efficiency (and this is a purely automatic movement) but are then used wrongly, a mortifying phenomenon can result. The singer attempts a note, and all that is emitted is air, or a note begins and is cut abruptly, or cracks. The cause is air pressure from the lungs being too strong for the vocal folds to hold their shape; they distort and buckle and allow air to escape directly to the mouth. (In the case of air loss when low notes are sung, slackness of the folds causes the loss.) Cracking will occur more readily in an untrained voice in which the folds have not been accustomed to hold themselves perfectly parallel, and resonation and tonal–focus are not understood.

It is important to have a proper understanding of the use of the various resonating cranial cavities – indeed, of all the resonators. Their use will lessen strain and over–tension. Volume does not depend solely on raw lung–power. The raw volume able to be produced by a singer might seem to be directly proportional to the power of his lungs. An adult female soprano usually has a larger lung capacity and chest musculature than a boy. (If boys sing with trained women singers with large voices, they tend to be swamped, and this is one of the reasons why mixed choirs of boys and women are usually unsuccessful.) The Italian castrati gained their reputation for powerful, brilliant singing from a combination of unusually large men's lung power which energized vocal folds of a size similar to those in boys. Tonal brilliance, or the lack of it, can modify basic volume greatly; much depends on the use of the many cranial resonators. Body size is certainly not the most important contributor to vocal power.

Tone quality is a difficult matter to assess objectively. It is easy enough to distinguish between the sounds produced by an oboe, a piano, and a clarinet; but to describe their essential differences is another matter. Terms such as 'reedy' and 'sensuous' are subjective; the only way to analyse sounds is to listen, and then assess the intensity of the fundamental note and its overtones. For scientific analysis and precise measurement, one would need to use cathode–ray oscilloscopes, acoustic spectrometers, and the like.

To produce sound at all, vibrations or undulations of the vocal folds, and particularly the oscillations of the air column above the larynx – an air movement which *en route* from the lungs, began the larangeal undulations in the first instance – must be amplified. Earlier, we saw that, just as a violin has a sound–box under the strings, so the human voice has the pharynx and mouth above the vocal folds together with the cranial cavities. The sizes and shapes of all these will largely determine the quality of sounds produced in which certain overtones may be augmented and others diminished.

One school of thought claims (or claimed until recently) that the sinuses and cranial cavities have no effect whatsoever on emerging sound, despite the fact that many singers and teachers of singing claim to use them. It is also conventional opinion that, during singing, the

[2] Cornelius L. Reid, *The Free Voice* (Joseph Patelson Music House, 1965), ch. 4, passim
[3] Grove's *Dictionary*, 3rd edn, 1927, vol. II, p. 194

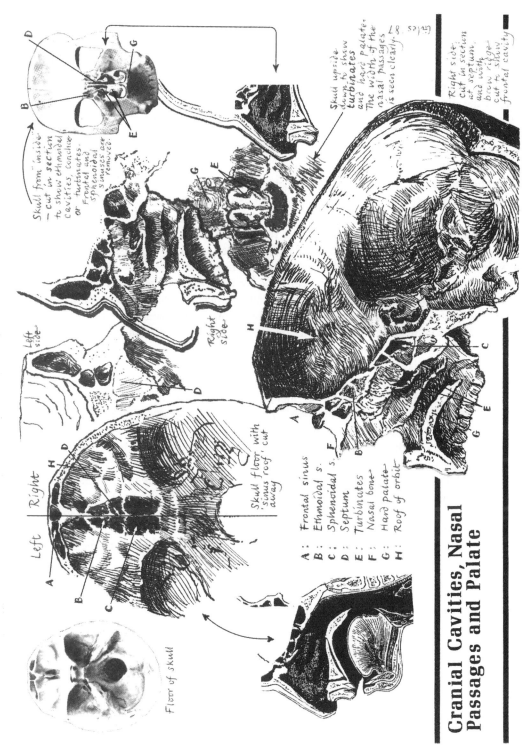

Skull from inside – cut in section to show ethmoidal cavities, conchae or turbinates. Frontal and sphenoidal sinuses are removed.

Left side

Right side

Skull floor with 'sinus roof' cut away

Skull upside down to show turbinates and hard palate. The width of the nasal passages is seen clearly.

Right side in section at septum and with brow ridge cut to show frontal cavity.

Left   Right

Floor of skull

A: Frontal sinus
B: Ethmoidal s.
C: Sphenoidal s.
D: Septum
E: Turbinates
F: Nasal bone
G: Hard palate
H: Roof of orbit

Cranial Cavities, Nasal Passages and Palate

Cranial cavities, nasal passages and palate

uvula and palate close off these cavities from the mouth and that, therefore, no air can reach them or the nasal cavities during phonation. Hence, it is said, sinuses cannot be brought into use as proper resonators, or in any way connect with the primary resonators of mouth and pharynx. However, a second group admits that the sinuses do act as secondary resonators, that sound waves can travel through the tissue of the palate and that they set up minimal resonance within the sinuses.[4] Usually, it is claimed by this group that this effect is felt only by the singer and not by the audience. It is explained that the sinuses can be used to help monitor the sound for the singer's own benefit, but that any effect the sinuses have on the emerging tone is illusory.

A third school of thought claims that the employment of the sinuses by the singer helps to produce the voice and that this has a considerable effect on emission of tone from the head. No less an authority than Charles Kennedy Scott was of this third school of thought, while the equally important theorist and teacher, Ernest George White, argued that the sinuses are the actual source and seat of vocal sound. We return to White later, but Scott wrote a masterly account[5] (which should be studied) of the crucial role played by the nasal and sinus cavities in voice-production, though he stopped short of White's view.

The term imposto is said to have been used by the early Italian singing teachers and has been revived in her own teaching by Lucie Manen. Imposto relates to the vocal quality of the bel canto school, which opines that tone-quality is not solely produced by the mechanism of the larynx and its resonator, the pharynx, but includes the exploitation of the nasal passages behind the bridge of the nose.

Some theoreticians, including White, go further, arguing that the sinuses are the actual source of vocal tone. We might note that a growing section of the vocal and medical establishment seems more willing to incline towards some of these unconventional or alternative ideas, or at least be open-minded on the subject. The author recently had to undergo an operation to remove a small section of the left nasal bone which blocked the air-duct; Alan Ardouin, the ear, nose and throat surgeon involved, warned that there was a slight chance of the operation's affecting the tonal quality of the author's voice. No such change actually resulted, but the significance of this instance lies in the authority of the person who made the suggestion.

There is an interesting theory that Australian aborigines have much less resonance in their speech than most other races, owing to the small size of their sinuses. On the other hand, the 'coo-ee' call of the aborigine to communicate over long distances should be mentioned, perhaps because smaller sinuses help to produce higher pitch and ultra-high falsetto tone more easily.

The position and adjustment of the velum (the soft palate) are crucial in the consideration of the sinus-tone theory of vocal production. The most effective counter-tenors seem (automatically?) to manipulate the velum more than most singers, but other voices could and should derive advantage from using it. Some factors which appear to be connected with this point are

[4] See Gordon Troup, 'On the Effect of the Nasal Tract and Sinuses in Singing: or, Should the Velum be Open on all Vowels? (A Preliminary Report)'. *Journal of the Ernest George White Society*, vol. 5, no. 2, 1988, pp. 7–10

[5] Charles Kennedy Scott, *The Fundamentals of Singing* (Cassell, 1954), pp. 23–29

touched on by Rebecca Stewart in her discussion of French and Italian languages, singing-technique, and Josquin des Prez.[6]

A singer suffering from a catarrhal blocking above the mouth soon notices the reduced resonance in his voice. In 1909, Ernest George White first argued that the main sinuses are an almost horizontal system of tone-originating cavities (which others would term 'resonation-chambers') which are semi-interconnecting, and must be employed as part of the integrated vocal organ. They are also of differing capacity and volume, and each main sinus area has its own function.[7] White's thesis[8] should be studied in its entirety. The similarity of myriad skull cavities at different levels with the complex spaces and structure of a vaulted, tribuned, multi-columned cathedral or abbey church might suggest that much earlier singers were unconsciously influenced by their surroundings and adopted some such vocal approach. Certainly, as we have noted elsewhere, tenor and bass unison singing, particularly of plain-song, creates harmonics and overtones in a large and resonant building. This effect can un-cannily give the impression that there are also counter-tenors singing at the octave above.

The School of Sinus Tone (The Ernest George White Society), of which Arthur Hewlett is a senior preceptor, trains all voices to use the advantages of sinus production and control. Hewlett writes: 'A man using only his frontal sinuses produces a treble-like tone, the so-called falsetto, which in general is used in performance only by male altos.'[9]

Sinus resonation could well be the key to the amazing extension of upward range of the Spanish falsettists. The attractive nasal resonances of many Hispanic language-sounds might suggest a parallel with forward, frontal-sinus tone. High vocal range would be likely. There is an obvious likelihood of links with Moorish and Arab practice: the result of the Moorish occupation of the Spanish peninsula between 711 and 1492.

The English tenor, Frank Titterton, well-known between the two world wars, was one of John Whitworth's teachers. From Whitworth's account, Titterton would seem to have sympathised with the ideas behind sinus-tone production, though it is not known whether he completely agreed with White's full theory. John Whitworth explains that, in counter-tenor vocal production, a balance must be achieved between an edgy sinus-element – an almost buzzing sensation in the nose, across the cheekbones and behind the front teeth – and rounder tone resonating in the mouth and oro-pharynx, the naso-pharynx, and above the curved soft palate in the higher cranial cavities. His explanation seems to confirm the importance of velum position in his own manner of production. Constant, subtle adjustment of the velum would help to obtain Whitworth's characteristic 'mixed' tone – both edgy and rounded.

At this point, it is advantageous to take a first look at what the important singer-teacher, Edgar Herbert-Caesari, had to say about falsetto in its two varieties. In point of fact, he did not seem to consider what is frequently called 'middle-falsetto' to be falsetto at all, but what he called 'pharyngeal voice'. In view of the recent revelations of the behaviour of the vocal folds, he was justified, just as he was in view of our investigation into Renaissance vocal terminology and practice. By 'falsetto', he seems invariably to have been referring to upper-falsetto alone.

---

[6] Rebecca Stewart, *A ... Study of Male Vocal Types ... in the Music of Josquin des Prez* (Tijdschrift van de Vereniging voor Nederlandse Muziekgeschiednis, deel XXXXV – 1/2, 1985), p. 148
[7] Ernest George White, *Science and Singing* (Dent & Sons Ltd., 1909), passim
[8] White, op. cit., 4th edn (Dent, 1938), and White, *Sinus Tone Production* (Dent 1938, repr. 1951)
[9] Arthur Hewlett, *Think Afresh about the Voice* (E. G. White Society, 1970; new edn, Thames Publishing, 1987), p. 56

Herbert–Caesari explains first that pharyngeal voice or mechanism is situated between the basic and falsetto mechanisms. He does not specify either oro–pharyngeal or naso–pharyngeal; these two areas are closely located but distinct. As will become apparent in later discussions, it would seem that by 'pharyngeal' Herbert–Caesari meant that mode of vocal production which feels and sounds as if it emanates from the pharyngeal area generally. We will continue to employ this useful term on this basis, though it seems possible to claim that the naso–pharyngeal sensation is felt mostly in medium and high notes, and that oro–pharyngeal is strongly felt in lower.

Herbert–Caesari suggests that the student would find it easier to envisage the three main mechanisms as:

> Three horizontal layers, superimposed, three *depths* of the vocal cords' mechanism producing three different tonal qualities, each of which is characteristic and quite distinct from the others. Taken by itself, the pharyngeal voice, without any admixture of basic or of falsetto, has a certain quality of steely intensity which is the reverse of beautiful particularly when produced forte. Mixed, however, with either the basic or the falsetto (and, better still, with both simultaneously), it assumes very considerable importance.[10]

```
◄─ FALSETTO
◄─ PHARYNGEAL
◄─ BASIC
```

(after Herbert–Caesari)

We might note that beauty could be said to be in the ear and aesthetic of the listener.

The technique described is not restricted to the male voice; just as the female voice has registers and upper–falsetto, so it has middle–falsetto. It is, however, says Herbert–Caesari, 'built into' the larynx in a different manner, 'into the back half of the vocal cords,'[11] while in the male it is in the front. 'Women', he says, 'have no pharyngeal on their head–notes'.[12]

The expertly developed upper–falsetto – like that of Alfred Deller's voice – is often produced with a raised larynx. Whether the larynx should be at a fixed, artificially low level, or be natural and free moving during singing, has been in contention for many years.[13] Until recent decades, most vocal–training has been based on a fixed, low–positioned larynx.

The concept of an 'ideal' laryngeal position seems to have owed much to the demands of great volume and the pursuing of more 'Romantic' and full, usually dark, tonal quality. Despite this, according to Sundberg, a low, fixed larynx does the opposite, and (by occasioning the singer's characteristic pattern of harmonic formants) gives phenomenal brightness.[14] But the

---

[10] E. Herbert–Caesari, *The Voice of the Mind* (Robert Hale, 2nd edn 1963), p. 335

[11] Ibid, p. 346

[12] Ibid., p. 347

[13] See Kate Emil–Behnke, op. cit., p. 104, and Mauro Uberti 'Vocal Techniques in Italy in the second half of the 16th century', *Early Music* (October 1981), pp. 486 ff.

[14] See Johan Sundberg, *The Science of the Singing Voice* (Northern Illinois University Press; London, 1 Gower Street; 1987), particularly pp. 101–140

present author's observation and experience, and those of others, make these findings seem somewhat puzzling. Perhaps it has to do with vocal type and gender. Certainly, this can be inferred from Sundberg's pages. We will return to him later, for he raises a number of important points.

Stewart writes thus of laryngeal position related to register–change:[15]

> In combination with the tongue, lips and velum, a raised and somewhat forwardly tilted larynx makes the masking of the vocal break and the matching of the falsetto and modal registers much easier... . It now remains to examine the subject in relation to Josquin's French–orientated works. As is known, the higher–pitched French male voice habitually and unobtrusively switches from this modal to his falsetto register while speaking, using the very muscles required in the change of register while singing. (*Note*: although outside the limitations of this study, the Spanish language also requires the male to use his falsetto, often to give additional emphasis to a statement. This may partially explain the significant number of Spanish falsettists in the Papal chapel, especially during the first half of the sixteenth century, when the Franco–Flemish sopranos were becoming less popular.)

Berton Coffin reminds us, in an enlightened comprehensive investigation, that the larynx must be allowed, indeed encouraged, to shift for particular tone colours and effects.[16] High and low larynx positions are not seen as 'wrong' or 'right', but as part of a set of subtle adjustments to be made in strict conjunction with specific vowel–colours and timbres. His book should be read. Deller often used what Coffin calls the 'whistle' register (*vogelstimme*, or bird–voice) and 'dimple falsetto', which involve a high larynx position. Of the whistle register, Manuel Garcia said:[17]

> The lips of the glottis are stretched, and perfectly, though gently, touch one another, while the space between the vocal tendons is considerably lessened. In this state of the organ, the least pressure of air will rush through a minute aperture of the glottis, which, however narrow, serves to produce the most rapid beats with extreme facility. The pressure of the air, however, should be very slight, when the aperture of the glottis is to be minute.

Mauro Uberti's *Early Music* article, referred to earlier, is valuable, but postulates a few controversial points. What is convincing, though, is Uberti's contention that use by earlier singers of a higher and lighter laryngeal position might well have encouraged them to force the vocal folds together in their quest for increasing volume and power, and thus produced vocal strain. (This and its full implications are returned to later.)

A permanent lowering of the larynx in conjunction with other adjustments to produce voix sombrée, or veiled voice, would change the character of the vocal sound and would produce a fuller, darker 'Romantic' tonal quality in addition to easing the singer's task in his or her

---

[15] Stewart, op. cit., p. 151

[16] Berton Coffin, *Overtones of Bel Canto* (Scarecrow Press, New Jersey, 1980), p. 195

[17] Manuel Garcia, *New Compendious Treatise on the Art of Singing* (mod. edn, Da Capo Press, 1972 & 1975, ed. Donald W. Pasche), p. 7

quest for additional volume. Advocates of this new method promoted this as the only correct technique, and any other was seen by them as a wrong one which their rightness had super-seded and corrected.

If we take upper–falsetto as 'the first layer' mechanism, to engage the 'second' – that which is responsible for the so-called pharyngeal voice –

> The folds approximate [i.e., come closer together] considerably more than they do when producing (upper) falsetto. As the pharyngeal mechanism comes into action, the feeling is one of flexible firmness and resistance (that are lacking in [the upper, or undeveloped] falsetto). Being the second 'layer', it is, as a tonal sensation, slightly lower than the falsetto; and by this we mean that it has slightly more vertical depth, definitely more substance, and is more lifelike [i.e., is more akin to the basic or fundamental or chest voice].[18]

Normally, when one sings an ascending scale in fundamental voice, pharyngeal and upper falsetto registers come into play at about the same pitch or frequency, irrespective of the vocal type of the singer. The usual tenor or baritone would expect to engage them or employ mixed voice at a point no higher than:

A soprano, mezzo–soprano or contralto change register in the same area, because, though written an octave higher, the tenor's high F4 is acoustically on the first space of the treble clef. The counter–tenor, however, is free to engage or maintain pharyngeal or falsetto at a lower point, if he wishes, because the tessitura he has to maintain is higher than the tenor's.

It is essential that all voices employ all available tone–producers and resonators, however it might be explained. Between the extremes of the views held by what could be called the conventional laryngeal school and those of proponents of sinus–tone production lie many shades of opinion. As in most human endeavours or areas of activity, the adoption of a happy balance is probably the most beneficial. However, it should be pointed out that it is best to avoid any pre-occupation with or over–consciousness of the larynx while singing. The athlete does not consider the action of his muscles while competing. Whatever his views on voice production might be, the singer would be well advised to concentrate on the use of his resonators. No vocal harm but rather great benefit can come as a result of this; not something which can be said of pre-occupation with the larynx.

We shall return to these schools of thought and to the implications for performance, performing conditions and arenas, both past and present; but before moving to more detail, the following revealing examples of phonation, resonation and sound–conduction through bone should be pondered.

---

[18] Herbert–Caesari, op. cit., p. 338

The first example, the African kissar, is a type of lyre which is made from two animal horns attached horizontally to the back of an open–topped human skull. The skull, with its top sliced off, acts as a sound–box in a manner impossible in life when it is filled with brain tissue. Nonetheless, the kissar helps to demonstrate a truth: that the various other cranial cavities, closed–off, semi–connected, or open to each other, can add valuable tonal qualities in both live and dead skulls. As regards dead skulls: if they were stopped along their length, that portion of the kissar's strings which project into the space behind the empty, open–topped brain cavity would produce a different volume and quality to those immediately above the open top itself. In turn, the portions of strings nearer the front, over the sinus–system, might well vary in their effect from the section suspended above the 'floor' of the skull; particularly as the six or so tuned strings are stretched over the front rim of the skull and deep into the eye–sockets where they are secured. In addition to the vibrations caused by strings suspended above a resonating cavity, physical vibrations of the strings themselves are transmitted directly into the rim of the skull and thence into the very structure of the frontal sinuses – and even beyond these into the rest of the system. Incidentally, strings and skull combined perhaps serve to remind us of the claviorganum.

The 'Kissar': an African lyre made from a skull and animal horn
(Giles, after Launder/Rogers/Worth)

The second example is from Siberia. An American recording, 'Tuva Voices from the Center of Asia',[19] of tribesmen and women demonstrating mostly vocal techniques in speech, 'song', animal–imitations, tribal chant and assorted sound effects. It is remarkable that during many of the items, unmistakeable use is made of the sinuses separately from the vocal folds, using a technique unknown to the sophisticated West. In many cases, a strong, graty, deeply guttural

---

[19] Smithsonian/Folkways Records (Washington DC), cd SF 40017

sound emanates from the vocal folds, while a high, bright, harmonic response seems to sound from the sinuses and cranial cavities. The recording is at least aural evidence that the cranial cavities not only contribute to vocal sound, but that there are techniques known to primitive peoples which allow vibrational activity within these cavities. The air–flow induced vibrations within the larynx can be isolated.

These thoughts, and the kissar (this inverted model of vibration–sources and varying resonators) are useful images to take into the next chapter.

1	2	3	4
– upper			
Chest voice – lower or register	Head voice (lower) or register	Head voice (upper) or register	Small register
Mainly sphenoidal– production	Mainly ethnoidal– production	Mainly frontal– sinus production	Pure frontal– sinus voice
Lower register	Upper register	Falsetto	Pipe voice
Thick voice – upper – lower	Thin voice (lower)	Thin voice (upper)	Falsetissimo
Pulse	Modal	Loft	Small bore
Basic voice	Pharyngeal voice	Super falsetto	Bird voice
Natural voice	Middle falsetto	Upper falsetto	Whistle register
Full voice	Medium register	Fine register	Dimple falsetto
Long reed	Throat voice	Mode 3	Flute
Mode	Narrowed voice		Mode 4
Mode 1	'Witch' voice		Bell register
Fundamental	Marginal voice		
	Short reed		
	Mode 2		

The register jungle

10 More on Registers and Range

We have seen that voice comes into being as a result of several elements: (i) the lungs and windpipe, or trachea, (ii) the larynx, the miraculous but tiny organ about which there is so much argument and (iii) the essential resonators and cavities which transform its air–originated rhythmic undulations into vocal tone.

Our chief interest at present is in the counter–tenor's use and exploitation of the vocal instrument, technically and historically. Here and elsewhere in the book, we should remember that, until the end of the eighteenth century, it is likely that, in most musical periods, the majority of singers and teachers would not understand our obsession with the seamless voice. They knew about registers and employed and exploited them. Certain earlier theorists, of course, wrote about them variously.

Some eminent teachers of voice deny that true head–voice (not mixed voice) and falsetto are one and the same. They deny that they require the same use, physiologically, of the vocal folds. Kate Emil–Behnke, for example, gave a masterly description in 1945 of the action and workings of the vocal folds in chest–register (upper and lower), medium–register (she never used the term pharyngeal – or middle falsetto – for reasons later explained) and head–register. She described the thinning of the folds for medium–register and the employment of between half and two–thirds of the folds for head–register, and then stated: 'If a man sings a high note so softly as to eliminate all tension of the vocal ligaments, he will probably sing falsetto, a mechanism which is useless, offering no foundation from which to develop.'[1]

Other equally odd views will be quoted during the present work. It is of interest that this was not Kate's father's opinion. Emil Behnke wrote:[2]

> How widespread is this mistaken notion that the use of the falsetto is entirely contrary to art ... we hear frequently enough in the expressions of individuals when some unlucky tenor happens to get caught on one of these tabooed falsetto tones. Thus, the school founded by Duprez, important in itself, has called into life a manner of singing, the ruinous consequences of which we see daily.

How had the term 'falsetto' and its use in singing, either alone or with basic–voice, become scorned? However it is explained, the change of attitude towards it seems to be connected with the fading of bel canto methods, the lost art of the beautiful voice taught by the 'old Italian

---

[1] Kate Emil–Behnke, *The Technique of Singing* (Williams and Norgate, 1945), p. 108
[2] Emil Behnke, *The Mechanism of the Human Voice* (Curwen, 1888), p. 6 (partly quoting Castell)

school' which, under the influence of Gilbert–Louis Duprez (1806–96), lost ground from the middle of the nineteenth century onwards. When the great voice teacher, Manuel Garcia, invented the laryngoscope (perfected in 1854), much speculation, excitement and curiosity were aroused regarding the scientifically provable mechanics of vocal function. Very soon, there developed a quite definite intent – almost an obsession – to control the larynx directly during phonation. Because the larynx could be seen easily (in the male throat), it became the centre of scientific attention and investigation. The result of this has been chaos and continual nostalgia for the lost 'golden age of singing'.

Early teaching and its traditions clearly worked, because they were based on principles and practice handed down by example and authoritative word of mouth. But, with the advance of scientific technology based only or principally on study of the larynx, proponents of bel canto methods were left without support. Though clearly and demonstrably right by result, they could not prove their methods scientifically. As Cornelius L. Reid explains:[3]

> In the meantime, a new generation of teachers came along to confront a world in a process of change; a world which created in every area of life uncertainty and confusion. Some found it expedient to adopt a pseudo–scientific jargon, but the majority tried to remain faithful to a tradition which was in the process of slipping away from them without their being aware of it. Vocal pedagogy, and the functional principles upon which it rested, thus struggled against the contrary currents of two worlds, neither of which was clearly defined nor concrete.

It is therefore of the utmost importance for us to look back to these old pre–scientific methods, for there we shall find the historical technique which produced the counter–tenor in its various aliases; but, unlike earlier teachers, we can also use modern scientific method where this is helpful, or necessary for explanation.

Vocal theorists considered registers for many centuries. Generally, authorities have agreed that the human voice seems to be divided into two distinct sections. Before the Renaissance, they were termed *vox integra* and *vox ficta* respectively. Later, they were more positively known as *voce di petto* (voice of the chest), and *voce di testa* (voice of the head).

Teachers began to realise that the two mechanisms shared a direct functional relationship, and that, for the greater good of the singing voice, they should be united – or, at least, that a technique should be developed which allowed uniting to take place. To allow for differences of qualities and timbres, new names appeared. The *voce di testa* began to be associated with the terms *mezzo falso*, or half–falsetto, and the *voce di finte* or feigned voice. (The word feigned has proved unfortunate, for it suggests to many today a counterfeit, a cheating, an unnatural voice.) Joining the two main mechanisms has become one of the first concerns of the establishment of a correct general vocal technique.

It is the nature of the joining which causes most disagreement. Is it a dovetail or a splice? Is one wrong and the other right? Are both right in different ways, different circumstances and historical contexts? The 'break' still remains the *bête noire* of most aspiring singers.

Mezzo falso is half falsetto: therefore, most would conclude, half head–voice, and half *voce di petto*, chest–voice. The French describe the two together as the *voix mixte*, or mixed–voice,

---

[3] Cornelius L. Reid, *The Free Voice* (Joseph Patelson Music House, 1965), p. 40

but middle–falsetto or pharyngeal voice (discussed in detail later) could claim to be the mezzo falso – half-falsetto – too. It fits both description and function. Pharyngeal is half-falsetto, though it is not quite mixed–voice as understood today. As will emerge more clearly later, mixed–voice or *voix mixte* is created when the singer employs his fundamental register togther with what is loosely termed falsetto on every note (so 'spliced') in a sung passage involving higher notes. Pharyngeal is half-falsetto, because it is neither true fundamental voice nor pure falsetto.

Be that as it may; as time passed, mezzo falso began to be called, merely, head–voice; so, whereas at one time head–voice was synonymous with falsetto, the term head–voice began to indicate a mixture, on each note, of falsetto and chest–register. Even then, falsetto was always the dominating element.

Oddly, this later term, head–voice (often, by the late eighteenth century and early nineteenth century a 'mixed' voice for tenors and basses) became thought of, eventually, as the only legitimate technique for higher notes, and falsetto became discredited. The concept of 'falseness' became so firmly fixed in association with falsetto that the latter was even considered, quite wrongly, for many years to be a product of the false or vestibular folds. (In this connexion, it is of interest to note that in Stainer and Barrett's *Dictionary*,[4] the authors state that 'The purring of the cat is produced by vibrations of the false vocal cords, which are well developed; the true vocal cords are small, and have no membranous part.') So though head–voice originally meant a developed, strong falsetto, this fact became completely forgotten.

Reid provides useful, though simplified tables (here edited slightly):

14th Century				*15th to 19th Centuries*
				Falsetto
*1 Vox Ficta	*1	Voce di Testa		Mezzo Falso
		or	combined	'Head' Voice
		Falsetto	to become	Voce di Finte
				Voix Mixte
*2 Vox Integra	*2	Voce di Petto		Chest Voice
		or		
		Chest Voice		

*Each of these two mechanisms divided by the 'break'.

Terminology pertaining to registers

Falsetto–derived tones were cultivated for the purpose of obscuring the break between the two register mechanisms. In reality, they represent a combined, or co–ordinated, registration in which both mechanisms form participating elements. The preponderance of balance, however, was always made to lean toward the upper of the two registers. With the passing of time, these conditions of blended registration came to be looked on as being initiated by resonance – a tragic misconception.

---

[4] Stainer and Barrett, *Dictionary of Musical Terms* (Novello, c1890)

Registers

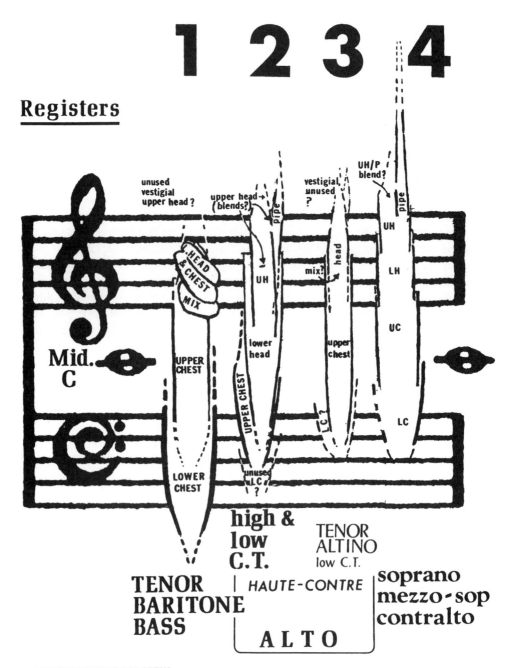

TENOR BARITONE BASS

high & low C.T.

HAUTE-CONTRE

TENOR ALTINO low C.T.

soprano mezzo-sop contralto

ALTO

THE CONVENTIONAL VIEW

A general guide to male and female registration, shown compositely, isolating the counter-tenor types. Notice the overlapping and ranges, but remember that individual voices may possess slight variations. The author has met and heard at least one singer who could demonstrate, throughout the ranges indicated here, totally convincing ability in every male voice type. His timbre was genuine and beautiful in every area in which he chose to perform. Though such powers are a rarity, human vocal equipment is a miracle of adaptability and versatility.

Registration, Equalization

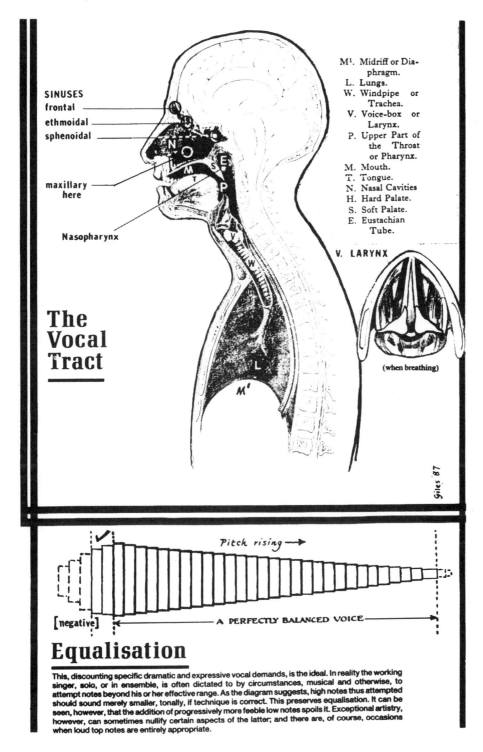

SINUSES
frontal
ethmoidal
sphenoidal

maxillary
here

Nasopharynx

M¹. Midriff or Dia-
     phragm.
L. Lungs.
W. Windpipe or
     Trachea.
V. Voice-box or
     Larynx.
P. Upper Part of
     the Throat
     or Pharynx.
M. Mouth.
T. Tongue.
N. Nasal Cavities
H. Hard Palate.
S. Soft Palate.
E. Eustachian
     Tube.

V. LARYNX

(when breathing)

**The
Vocal
Tract**

Giles 87

Pitch rising →

[negative]

A PERFECTLY BALANCED VOICE

Equalisation

This, discounting specific dramatic and expressive vocal demands, is the ideal. In reality the working singer, solo, or in ensemble, is often dictated to by circumstances, musical and otherwise, to attempt notes beyond his or her effective range. As the diagram suggests, high notes thus attempted should sound merely smaller, tonally, if technique is correct. This preserves equalisation. It can be seen, however, that the addition of progressively more feeble low notes spoils it. Exceptional artistry, however, can sometimes nullify certain aspects of the latter; and there are, of course, occasions when loud top notes are entirely appropriate.

and the Vocal Tract

By the close of the nineteenth century, chest–voice and falsetto gradually came to be re-garded as isolated and unrelated entities whose functional importance was destructive rather than constructive.

Group 1	*Group 2*
*1 Falsetto	1 Falsetto
2 Head Voice	2 Concepts of 'placement'
Upper Voice	a. 'high'
Voix Mixte	b. 'low'
	c. 'forward'
	d. 'back'
	e. 'up and over'
	f. 'in the masque'
	g. 'focus'
3 Middle Voice	3 Breath Control
	a. 'support of tone'
	b. 'sing on the breath'
4 Lower Voice	4 Tonal 'covering'
5 Chest–Voice	

Twentieth–century terminology

Group 1 *These two mechanisms are no longer recognised as presenting an opportunity for combined action to account for head–voice or voix mixte. Terms 'upper', 'middle', and 'lower' refer to a tonal change, not a register. Falsetto neglected and left unused. Chest–voice rarely employed, if ever.

Group 2 Registration in all forms denied, with falsetto considered an oddity, and chest–register an abomination. Because this error led, inevitably, to 'pushing', tone–qualities began to sound too 'open' and 'shouty' in the upper range. Thus, there developed an obvious need to refine the technique; a need which was met by 'covering'. A covered technique always distorts the vowel, and promotes tonal impurity.[5]

As has been described earlier, the head–voice or falsetto register, like other extremely high pitches, is initiated by thinning, or vibration of merely the edges of the vocal folds, but, for one form of 'head–voice/falsetto', it is produced mostly by shortening them. This 'alto mechanism', as it has been called, is brought into play at some stage in the ascending scale of both so–called falsettist and so–called tenor altino (discussed later). The alto singer would normally expect to enter head–register earlier, or employ it at a lower point in his overall range, than the voice–type called tenor, for the obvious reason that the tessitura the alto singer has to maintain is usually higher, and the average tenor singer has a lighter fundamental upper–chest range and timbre than the average light baritone singer. It is a matter of vocal

---

[5] Reid, op. cit., pp. 32–3

convenience and ease. Both these varieties of male voice possess the need (depending on the range and tessitura of the specific piece of music) for a chest–to–head–register change, however difficult for the listener to pick out. Of course, an alto may choose to stay within head–register exclusively, extending and developing it downwards, just as modern tenors often push chest–voice upwards.

Unless they wish to limit their ranges purposely, all voices, male and female, possess, at some point, the need for some kind of chest–to–head switch, however easy, 'natural' or disguised. At first, we might consider that some tenor altinos enter head register (or begin to use mixed–voice) early if their vocal folds are smaller and shorter. On the other hand, most light tenor vocal folds seem not to be shorter, but merely more elastic and lighter than heldentenor, baritone or bass folds. If tenor–altino folds are merely slighter or thinner even than normal tenor folds, further stretching of basic–voice would bestow an even higher change–point into head– or mixed–voice. (It should be remembered that, normally, the more basic–voice is used in any mixed–voice, the further from counter–tenor tone and timbre the result will be.) So it would seem that we have two hypotheses: either (i) tenor–altino folds are ultra–rare, shorter and smaller than normal tenor folds, or (ii) tenor–altino folds are ultra–rare, slighter, and must stretch ultra–long and ultra–thin. Perhaps an amalgamation of the two hypotheses reflects the real situation? Such a combination of rare physiological factors in one voice underlines the extreme rarity of the true tenor–altino. Hence, not many Russell Oberlins appear on the scene.

In 1880, Emil Behnke wrote:[6]

> It is true that the vocal ligaments of a soprano are sometimes longer than those of a contralto, just as the ligaments of those of a tenor are occasionally longer than those of a bass. But I maintain that the longer ligaments of sopranos and tenors are correspondingly thinner, and that their tension is greater, owing to the ring shield or stretching muscles being more powerful than their opponents, the shield–pyramid muscles. Where this is the case, the ligaments are more slanting than they would be otherwise, and the conse-quence of this is that less power of blast [an unfortunate term for, and concept of, phonation] is required to make them speak. With this mechanism, the higher registers are very readily united with the lower ones, and the voices so produced are of a light and flexible kind. Where, on the contrary, the vocal ligaments of contraltos and basses are comparatively short, they are also thick in proportion, and the shield pyramid muscles are more powerful than the opposing ring–shield muscles, so that there is less tension. I shall be asked how I can prove this tension theory, and my reply is this: The diameter of the vocal ligaments depends in a large measure on the magnitude of the shield–muscles. If, therefore, the ligaments are exceptionally thick, the muscles just named must of necessity be very powerful, and can easily resist the pulling of the ring–shield muscles. If, on the contrary, the ligaments are exceptionally thin, it is equally certain that the shield–pyramid muscles are weak in proportion, and then the stretching muscles can easily overcome their resistance.

---

[6] Emil Behnke, op. cit., pp. 66–7

Charles Cleall puts it thus:[7]

> When the folds are approximated for phonation:
> Elongation: lessens their mass
>   increases their elasticity
>   changes their contour
> Shortening: increases their mass
>   lessens their elasticity
>   restores their contour
>
> Many orthodox teachers today believe that the folds shorten for high notes. In fact, they do the opposite – or, rather (and this a crucial point), the opposite is done to them; they are pulled out long by muscles outside themselves. In chest voice, thryo–arytenoideus muscle contracts; but, as pitch rises, thyro–arytenoidus relaxes, and the outside muscles: crico–thyroideus at one end, and crico–arytenoideus at the other: tense instead ... .
>
> So longer folds *do* produce higher notes, by being pulled out long and thin, like a stretched elastic band. Basses have folds which are massive, thick, and relatively inflexible (probably because of a high level of testosterone in their blood). Tenors may have folds of the same or greater length, but (again, probably because of a lower level of testosterone in their blood) of markedly greater flexibility, adducting fewer fibres, and therefore a thinner, faster-vibrating fold.

Of course, in one sense, the counter–tenor's folds do shorten for high notes: they are shortened by a shutting of part of their total length. It seems possible that the theory of fold–shortening, or possession of shorter folds *per se*, for higher voices, and certainly for higher–pitched notes, originated with the conclusions of early theorists and teachers, researched via extensive practical experience, observation of the behaviour of instruments, especially stringed ones, inspired guess and/or illegal dissection.

Because all high notes were once sung employing falsetto mechanism in various ways (the definition of what constitutes 'high' depending on individual voice–type and the tessitura demanded by a particular song), this reasonable theory, that shorter folds produced higher notes and therefore higher voices *per se*, was established. This theory, which was correctly based as far as it went, worked until matters were muddied by the advent of 'scientific vocal methodology', which, owing to technology then thought advanced but now considered primitive, identified laryngeal action which, though genuine, seemed partly at odds with the earlier theory. The truth is of course that Garcia's laryngoscope could see only part of the reality. It has taken over one hundred years since his time for a more complete explanation to achieve the right balance: for both theories were 'correct' but not exclusively so.

Ardran and Wulstan's short article of 1967 was included as an appendix in the first edition of Alfred Deller's biography, *A Singularity of Voice*. This and other valuable material was

---

[7] In an unpublished analysis (1971) of Arthur Hewlett's *Think Afresh about the Voice* (1970, repr. Thames Publishing, 1989)

eventually expanded and used in David Wulstan's book *Tudor Music*.[8] In 1967, Ardran and Wulstan wrote that slow–motion cinematography had not yet given the sort of incontrovertible evidence needed on the workings of the head– or falsetto–register. (Though in fact useful insight had been obtained in 1940.[9]) They therefore initiated a series of investigations into the behaviour of the larynx to determine common factors in the falsetto production of all altos. This was to include a bass singing ordinary, undeveloped falsetto, and ranged through various differing vocal types to a singer of strong counter–tenor tone using his head voice. The idea was to investigate whether the laryngeal mechanisms used were the same in all cases, and, if not, how they differed.

Five male volunteers were chosen: some very good singers with what is usually considered counter–tenor tone, one a bass with a 'hooty' alto sound and the rest with tone between these extremes. Each man's neck was radiographed in a lateral projection, during quiet breathing. All the necks were fully relaxed and revealed a wide laryngeal airway with the vocal folds up–turned into the laryngeal ventricles. The result was that only a small amount of air remained in the anterior of the ventricles. Wulstan continued (in his 1985 version):[10]

> When the note a (220 Hz.; [A3]) was sung in the 'chest' register to the vowel 'ah', all the subjects showed the appearances of a vocalized larynx, that is to say, there were prominent air–filled ventricles delineating the vocal folds over practically the whole of their length, and there was evidence of the stretching of the vocal folds by the cricothyroid muscles both from the position of the laryngeal cartilages, and also from the shape of the airway. When exactly the same note was sung in the falsetto voice, all the subjects showed the same type of change: the air content of the laryngeal ventricles was reduced, indicating that a shorter length (shorter by about a quarter to a third) of vocal fold was free to vibrate. In each instance there was evidence that the cricothyroid muscles were not contracting so vigorously, and there was therefore less stretching of the vocal folds. All the subjects showed a narrowing of the laryngeal vestibule from front to back, which was associated with the backward bowing of the intralaryngeal portion of the epiglottis and its ligament. Other studies have shown that this is associated with the reduction of tension on the false vocal folds, allowing them to bulge medially. This effect can be seen on radiographs printed in Ardran and Wulstan (1967) which showed (1) the subject producing the note in chest voice and (2) the same note sung falsetto. Two sets of pictures contrasted (a), a subject with the so–called countertenor voice, with (b), a bass producing a hooty type of falsetto. The pictures of the production of (a) and (b) are identical.

In 1967, Ardran and Wulstan stated:[11]

---

[8] Ardran and Wulstan, 'The Alto or Counter Tenor Voice', *Music & Letters*, 1967, XLVIII, pp. 17–22; also David Wulstan, *Tudor Music* (O.U.P., 1985)
[9] 'High–speed motion picture of the human vocal cords', Bell Telephone Company, 1940
[10] Wulstan, *Tudor Music*, pp. 222–3
[11] Ardran and Wulstan, op. cit., pp. 17–22

It is suggested then, that when singing the same note falsetto as in the chest register, a shorter length only, in the middle of the vocal folds, is free to vibrate. Associated with this, there is evidence of a reduction in tension on the vocal folds. The backward bowing of the epiglottis is associated with a decrease in the distance between the body of the hyoid bone and the thyroid cartilage, and in some instances with the relative backward movement of the hyoid as well. We believe that it is the movement of the hyoid bone relative to the thyroid cartilage which is capable of moving the epiglottis and its associated tissues so that it can alter the tension on the false vocal cords, which allows them to bulge inwards and effectively damp the vocal folds: for the vocal folds cannot vibrate adequately unless associated with an air–filled laryngeal ventrical.

Recently, however, excellent papers by three British authorities, Welch, Sergeant and MacCurtain, have appeared in the United States;[12] and in 1989, the German ear, nose and throat surgeon Dr Volker Barth, working in England with English counter–tenors, performed experiments (the results as yet unpublished) in which he used a fibre–optic stroboscope inserted up the nose and down through the pharynx, and video–recorded televisual electronic technology. The British/American papers and Dr Barth's demonstrations all substantiate, or support independently, the present author's view (strongly maintained for more than a decade) that the so–called middle (or pharyngeal) counter–tenor head–voice – what has long been called middle–falsetto – *actually uses the full length of the folds*. Only the arytenoid cartilages are closed. The higher notes of this mode of use or mechanism seem to require some elongation of the folds.

Of particular pertinence are:[13]

> *Furthermore, it may be conjectured that, through training and consistent use, these countertenors have transformed their 'falsetto' register into their 'modal' register*, and:[14] There are characteristic differences between the Lx waveforms for modal and falsetto singing. However, some bass/baritones and tenors were able to maintain 'modal' shapes in their falsetto singing, and some countertenors have falsetto waveforms with modal characteristics. It is suggested that such similarities are a product of common features in professional training.

All this seems largely inconsistent with Ardran and Wulstan's 1967 theory.

We have seen that vocal folds are often compared with violin strings which when tightened raise the pitch of a note. But the range of pitch is limited by this method of tuning, so the violinist stops the string somewhere along its length with his finger. The tension remains exactly the same, but the pitch rises because the string is shorter. Not only is it possible to use this analogy for one use of the vocal–fold mechanism but, in addition, there is in the laryngeal

---

[12] Welch, Sergeant and MacCurtain, (a) 'Some Physical Characteristics of the Male Falsetto Voice', *Journal of Voice*, vol. 2, no. 2, pp. 151–163; (b) 'Xeroradiographic–Electrolaryngographic Analysis of Male Vocal Registers', *Journal of Voice*, vol. 3, no. 3, pp. 244–256

[13] Welch, Sergeant and MacCurtain, paper (a) cit., p. 162

[14] Welch, Sergeant and MacCurtain, paper (b) cit., p. 256

fold a lessening of tension, so that the pitch of the resultant note can remain identical, if desired. This explains how singers can move from chest to falsetto registers easily, and without tension, if they are able to control the falsetto mechanism with no effort.

All this, Ardran and Wulstan maintained, underlines that head– and falsetto–registers are one and the same and, however good or bad or however incompetent, there is no fundamental difference between the laryngeal mechanism of one alto compared with another.[15] This description would seem to have been an over–simplification. In 1967, they appear to have overlooked the existence of two main forms of falsetto: upper and so–called middle or pharyngeal voice. Wulstan modified this view in 1985.[16] Certainly, upper–falsetto, used alone, and probably badly produced, is the most usual production employed by poorly trained or untrained alto singers.

We referred earlier to the extension of falsetto or head register downwards. Many English counter–tenors, especially since Deller, have used this technique effectively, but those who, to put it idiomatically, 'change gear' (like Whitworth, Bowman and others) have developed matching head and upper–chest registers in historically correct fashion. The change in mode is not apparent or made over–important unless appropriate musically. Jacobs uses this technique. Some singers, like Oberlin, seem to do this unconsciously, but because it is an unconscious and ultra–gentle transition, it does not necessarily mean that the transition does not exist. Ardran and Wulstan expressed it well in 1967:[17]

> Here the analogy of the 'gear change', a phrase used by almost every alto, is a good one: a car with a crash gear box almost invariably gives an audible change. Less skill is required with a synchromesh gear box unless it is faulty. Another type of singer corresponds to the automatic gear box: here changes are made without effort, but a trained listener can detect the point of change in most cases. The last type of singer has an undetectable change, like the torque–converter on rather expensive cars. But, in common with all the other types, the torque converter box works to the same end: there must be a gear change (except, of course, in the case of altos using falsetto exclusively), however gradual it may be, and no matter how involuntary.

The analogy may be made even more apt. Considerable choice is available when selecting a 'gear': 'sense of urgency', fuel economy ('petrol' becomes 'air' analogously), convenience, engine–wear, pragmatism; all these are factors. The present author developed these and associated ideas in 1982. In fact, by the mid–1980s, Wulstan himself had further thoughts:[18]

> This change may be patent, or virtually imperceptible; here an analogy with the gear–change mechanism of a car is useful. There are many types of transmission, the crash gear–box, synchro–mesh, automatic and continuously variable systems, offering a series of increasingly smooth changes in which the involvement of the operator is progressively lessened. But the amount of effort required of the driver is irrelevant, as is whether or not the gear–change

---

[15] Ardran and Wulstan, op. cit., p. 194
[16] Wulstan, op. cit., p. 244
[17] Ardran and Wulstan, op. cit., p. 21
[18] Wulstan, op. cit., pp. 221–2

is noticeable: however gradual or smooth it may be, there must be a gear–change in order to maintain a reasonable ratio of road to engine speeds. Racing the engine too fast or labouring it too slowly in high gear will eventually result in mechanical failure. The same is true of the voice – although the relatively small vocal folds are able to stretch or loosen themselves to produce an astounding variety of pitches, their tensile capacity is not limitless; as with the engine, a gear–change is necessary to prevent impairment of the mechanism.

Reid uses the pianoforte as an illustration:[19]

> Examination of ... the piano immediately discloses ... two different kinds of stringing have been used. For tones extending from the lower middle to the top the strings are made of thin steel, for the lowest two octaves, steel strings are wrapped with heavy copper wire. Thus, bass notes on the piano are not only longer, but thicker and of different metal. Regardless of this difference, the piano has a smoothly graduated tonal scale with no point of mechanical transition detectable to the ear. A major transition is made, but the gradation is engineered so as to pass unobserved.

So, despite different mechanisms in chest and head, correct approaches to resonance and adjustment led to smooth vocal transition and, of course, to more choices of vocal colour. Reid reminds us that, in today's normal parlance: 'Calling one of the vocal registers the 'head' voice is a trifle misleading. Many teachers use the term 'head' to describe what they believe to be a type of resonance. The 'head–voice' is not 'head resonance'.[20] In other words, vocal–fold position initiates register, the results and sensations of which are resonated and produced above the larynx, and felt in the head, as Sundberg[21] makes so clear.

We have established an important point. It is the resonators which, to produce vocal tone, are all–important to air whose vibrations are the result of passing through the glottis. Like any other register, falsetto has no genuine vocal strength in itself. The auditory result of air moving through vocal folds and vibrating thereafter, can be compared with that of an old–fashioned gramophone needle held onto the record merely by the fingers. Connect the vibrations to resonator chambers, and we hear the full range of the sounds which lie within the record.

Before moving on, let us look at some relevant points which arise from Sundberg's *The Science of the Singing Voice* because, other than its undoubted value as a textbook, in it is a useful explanation of the singing voice. A shifting in position of the 'conventional' scientific viewpoint on voice as a phenomenon can sometimes be discerned. By implication, this shifting could affect how we consider earlier singing techniques, especially that of the counter–tenor.

Laryngeal position has been discussed previously. At first, Sundberg seems to follow the conventional obligatory line: that all properly trained, professional singers employ a low–larynx technique, though for ordinary, even loud speech, these same singers use an instinctively free–moving larynx. Given that singing and speech use the same instrument and that, frequently, the speech of a singer is rich, inherently resonant, and carries effortlessly (the

---

[19] Reid, op. cit., pp. 33–39
[20] Ibid., p. 40
[21] In *The Science of the Singing Voice* (Northern Illinois University Press, 1987), passim

superb bass, Willard White, is also an actor with fine, colourful speaking voice clearly related to his singing–tone), this seems strange.

Sundberg appears to have tested or consulted mainly (even exclusively) mainstream operatic singers. It is therefore almost axiomatic that such singers were trained in mid–nineteenth or post–nineteenth–century method. He underlines that the chief reason for the development of the low–larynx technique was to find a singer's formant which could compete against a loud, large orchestra.[22] We know that this developed mainly during the nineteenth century, and that the quest for such power has continued since.

He confirms the usual, conventional view that larynx lowering is of paramount importance to male singers,[23] but (a point particularly pertinent to counter–tenors) that females often or usually employ a shift in larynx–height for pitch changes.[24] His admission that tenors tend to adopt a slightly higher laryngeal position than baritones or basses is of particular significance,[25] because this is compatible with a still higher position for many well–produced counter–tenor voices.

Higher, lighter male voices are likely to find a higher laryngeal position than does a deep contralto. When questioning present received (and convenient) thinking, it should be remembered that because in most cases, the female larynx is hardly noticeable from the exterior and its position is unlikely to be obvious, monitored or analysed. It is therefore here suggested that the female's laryngeal position is not the constant pre–occupation it has become in male voice production.

Possibly connected with the gender of the writer to be quoted, and in case we are tempted to think that all late nineteenth– and early twentieth–century authorities insisted on a fixed, low–laryngeal technique, consider Kate Emil–Behnke's thoughts:[26]

> Commence on a low note and sing an ascending scale slowly. It will be found that the larynx rises slightly with each note. Now sing the scale again, keeping the larynx low and fixed in the position of the first note. As the pitch rises, more and more effort will be experienced, and the tone will deteriorate in quality, till finally it will probably 'crack' and break off, though the singer knows that he ought to be able to sing higher. Sing the scale again, allowing the larynx the freedom to move as it wishes. The tone will be pleasant, and a higher pitch will probably be reached with ease. It should be mentioned in passing that the larynx, if allowed freedom of movement, will commence each successive register at a slightly lower level than that at which the previous register ended. This adjustment will take place automatically, given the requisite mobility. Consideration of these points will make it abundantly clear that the habit of singing with a low, fixed larynx is unnatural and dangerous, for it is a violation of physiology.

[22] Sundberg, op. cit., pp. 123–4
[23] Ibid., p. 132
[24] Ibid., pp. 128–132
[25] Ibid., p. 112
[26] Kate Emil–Behnke, op. cit., p. 104

Sir Peter Pears, in a short Foreword to Hewlett's *Think Afresh About the Voice*, made the thought–provoking statement:[27]

> In different 'schools' a different emphasis is put on a certain sound, or a certain part of the vocal machine.
>
> When I was young the emphasis seemed to be almost exclusively on the raising of the soft palate and the lowering of the larynx. Indeed, at my very first lesson I was encouraged to press the Adam's Apple down with my finger. I had heard of Ernest White's books but was told not to bother about them. That, unhappily, was the attitude towards White's pioneer work in those days. Since then, quite recently, I have read them, and found them most interesting and helpful. The sinuses can be seen in their true perspective ...

Sundberg writes:[28]

> This is *not* to say that it is impossible to generate vowels with a singer's formant *without* [the present author's emphasis] a lowering of the larynx. The individual shape of the pharynx and larynx may very well be such that there is no need for lowering the larynx in order to obtain a singer's formant. Also, there may be other articulatory and phonatory configurations that generate it. Wang (1983), investigating ten tenor singers representing Chinese opera traditions and the type of singing often used in performing medieval music, found that singing with a strong singer's formant occurred even when these singers did not lower their larynxes.

Mention of Chinese opera, and (European) medieval music might evoke shared vocal practices which survived in Europe until the early to middle nineteenth century, which we shall be exploring further.

Sundberg's consideration of the differences of mouth and pharynx proportions between male and female is intriguing,[29] as is his underlining that, despite everything, vocal differences between the sexes are not yet fully understood. Women generally have shorter pharynxes than men, and tenors shorter pharynxes than basses.[30] The female tends therefore to have a larger development of the head–voice than the male, and the tenor – at least, potentially, because of nineteenth– and twentieth–century training methods – a higher–ranged development of head–voice than a bass. This is greatly to over–simplify the matter, and omits consideration of the character of the vocal folds and the contribution of the cranial cavities; but it serves as a useful illustration. Because raising the larynx shortens the pharynx, it can be seen that this tends to produce or enhance lighter, higher voices. A light pre–nineteenth century tenor is therefore likely to have sung with a higher laryngeal position than a deep contralto trained using nineteenth–century methods. We might also deduce that, because of the smaller space within the pharyngeal cavity, the rising and vibrating air column finds its

[27] Hewlett, op. cit., p. v
[28] Sundberg, op. cit., pp. 121–2
[29] Ibid., pp. 102 ff.
[30] Ibid., p. 115

way into, or affects, the complete system of cranial cavities, especially the ethmoid and frontal sinuses and nasal passages.

Vocal differences between the sexes are certainly compounded when we reflect that, looked at in one way, the counter-tenor has a vocal range which possesses tonal quality with an ambiguous character, in that it sounds quasi-male but is broadly at female pitch. Sundberg, however, writes[31] that the counter-tenor '... who is a male singer singing alto parts certainly sounds more female than male, although his vocal-tract dimensions would offer him a male selection of formant frequencies. The voice-source difference between falsetto and modal register may very well add to the female voice timbre.'

We may disagree that the counter-tenor sounds more female than male, for Sundberg's judgement must be determined by the types and variety of counter-tenor singers he has studied. Certainly, his work is valuable and should be examined, though it is well to remember that Sundberg uses 'alto' for 'contralto', without exception or explanation, which is confusing to those who correctly associate the term 'alto' principally or exclusively with a male singer.

We now return to the perennial dispute over what constitutes the counter-tenor and what the alto voice, for there are those who maintain that they are separate.

Tenors-altino usually claim that their higher, lighter chest-voices and smooth transition into head-voice (if, indeed, they admit to any separation at all) makes them different from the other main high voice type. Most appear to claim that the 'real' counter-tenor is clearly, and exclusively, a species of tenor [*sic*] voice, and that singers who use either only head-voice or the 'synchromesh gear-box', by this reasoning, are denoted 'male altos'.

It must be infuriating to conventional tenors of modest vocal gifts and little historical awareness to hear many an untrained alto negotiate high notes with enviable ease and, often, full and rich tone, even if without 'squillo'. ('Squillo' seems to be a useful idiomatic term in the United States for the inherent 'ring' of a well-produced voice. It is sometimes called the 'ring-ping'.)[32]

Which, it may be asked, is the most natural instrument? A simple one which operates easily or one needing acquired operational skill? The answers to the first question usually depend on pre-conceived ideas about voice. Whatever the case, many conventionally-trained tenors regard those called counter-tenors or male altos as voices 'tuppence short of a shilling'.

In fact, many counter-tenors argue just as emphatically that most tenors-altino are not counter-tenors at all, but very high tenors. They claim that counter-tenor altus, the voice type finally reached by the early sixteenth century, is purely a head-voice, and stayed as one. It is difficult to imagine such a hard-and-fast rule obtaining at any period before the nineteenth century, but it is possible to conceive of an exclusively head-voice singer in the sixteenth century.

Another opinion maintains, despite strong indications to the contrary, that the exclusively head-voice singer does not date from the sixteenth century but first developed, at least in England, in the latter half of the seventeenth century, for reasons which might have been discerned already. What is certain is that, in the late nineteenth century and into the twentieth, it was the norm for altos to use both head- and chest-registers, with further intrinsic adjustments. Dr A. H. D. Prendergast, writing in 1900, demonstrates this clearly:[33]

---

[31] Ibid., p. 105

[32] See Stefan Zucker, *Samples from 'Opera Fanatic'* (privately printed leaflet, 1989)

[33] Dr A.H.D. Prendergast, 'The Man's Alto in Church Music', *Zeitschrift der Internationen Musikgesellschaft*, Heft 11, p. 332

It is certain that even in the lowest register the chest notes are modified or veiled, in other words that some operation occurs in the throat by which the vocal cords giving chest notes are not allowed to vibrate to their full extent. The highest register is caused by some more decided limitation, or as it were pinching, of the vocal cords, so as to give an entirely new quality. The middle register, covering the 'break', is caused by a compromise between the two modes of emission, and is as everyone knows difficult to manage.

Dr Prendergast goes on to reinforce what he says about singing across the register change, having already shown familiarity with traditional use of two modes of falsetto and the chest-register. 'Modified or veiled' obviously refers to upper chest–register or light, basic–voice employed with maximum head resonance. (One is tempted to think that, when descending the scale, earlier singers did not delay inevitable change to basic–voice until the last possible moment, as often seems the case today, but used an unselfconscious 'area of transition' correctly.)

Prendergast describes the register change at about a third higher than that of most altos today: 'The ordinary compass of a man's alto voice in this country is from fiddle G to C in the middle of the treble clef. The best notes are from B flat to B flat. The break is between Middle C and the E above.'[34] This seems to suggest that, in 1900, the more sophisticated English alto, in spirit at least, was in touch with one aspect of a more European tradition and with what obtained in earlier light baritone and tenor technique and in the French haute–contre and the Italian contralto–tenor, all of whom used some sort of a chest to head–register [*sic*] technique. It is interesting to know that Prendergast himself was an alto, and was listed in that section of the Purcell Commemoration Choir in Westminster Abbey in 1895.

Alfred Deller's own view, just over sixty–five years later, is well explained in his biography:[35]

> There are generally recognised to be two types of counter–tenor voice. The first, and more usual, is where the fundamental voice is baritone or bass, and the head voice, or so–called falsetto, is developed to the maximum range. My own voice is of this type. You produce this head voice naturally, and you work on it as you would on any other voice. But, if you wish, you can still sing off the chest, so to speak. Purcell was a counter–tenor of great ability; he also sang bass in the Chapel Royal choir.
>
> The other type of counter–tenor is essentially a high tenor who can either dispense with falsetto entirely, or use it for the top fourth or fifth of the compass, without perceptible break. Some people say this is the true counter tenor; others, that it isn't counter–tenor at all, but merely a very high, light tenor. Certainly, some singers one hears who are billed as counter–tenors seem to be just tenors with exceptionally high range.

The point is sometimes made that, if the counter–tenor who possesses a tenor basic–voice moves into pure head–voice to sing alto, it is usually at a higher pitch: at about F4 or even G4. The counter–tenor with a baritonal basic–voice, who uses 'through technique', usually

---

[34] Ibid., p. 332
[35] Hardwick, *A Singularity of Voice* (2nd edn, Proteus, 1980), pp. 78–9

moves into pure head–voice at about B3 or C4. We should never forget, however, that these 'shifts' are in, or should be regarded as being in, areas of transition, i.e., in the *ponticello*. The actual moment of change is, properly, variable.

Tenors wishing to sing alto often strongly imply that they make this change because they choose to employ pure head–voice timbre (which they will probably call 'falsetto') and most certainly not because they cannot maintain basic–voice at the higher pitch and tessitura suitable for classical alto parts. This is not always true. Frequently an element of 'one–upmanship' is involved.

It is also assumed automatically that, in order to sing the alto part at all, the baritone must enter head–voice as early as possible or start in it and remain in it, avoiding all use of basic voice. Nevertheless, though 'early as possible' and 'avoiding use of all basic voice' are not always true, both of these assumptions are often used as bases for forming value judgements about possible differences between altos and counter–tenors. The word 'tenor' makes rational judgement difficult for, as we have seen, the original term 'tenor' had no meaning, strictly speaking, as a term of tonal description. However, it is understandable that most people today expect any title including 'tenor' to resemble what has come to be associated with that word.

The genuine tenor–altino is not merely a tenor who can 'squeeze out a bit of alto' from the point past which he finds it impossible or difficult to sing in or maintain a high–pitched part in basic–voice without forcing. Like Oberlin (and Jacobs?), the tenor–altino variety of counter–tenor is a natural alto–tenor of light, high–pitched voice who moves into head–voice at an easy point in his range where it suits him. He is also a genuine counter–tenor who happens to move into head–voice at a lower point where it suits him, but from a light though more baritonal–timbred basic–voice.

The most important factor when discussing the counter–tenor, and the one which provokes most argument, concerns the 'break' or register change and its use or non–use. Register negotiation is traditionally the *bête noire* of all singers. Today, because most male voices use a different technique, it is mainly women who must deal with fundamental register change constantly, as most must always have been obliged to do, because the musical demands made on their voices are awkward for their vocal physiology. Indeed, because the need is self–evident and inter–register usage is commonplace, most manage the necessary transitions well, with training.

We are not surprised or automatically put off that heavier female voices have more obvious register changes. Why should we be surprised or worried if the same is true of male voices? In any case, not all heavier male voices produce surprising or unattractive register changes.

In a British television broadcast performance in 1991 of *Carmina Burana*, for which no counter–tenor soloist was engaged, the baritone Thomas Allen sang in the most beautiful and convincing pure head–voice for whole phrases. In many ways, it was more successful even than the tenor Frank Lopardo's rendering of the 'Song of the Roasted Swan', in which he, too, moved into pure head–voice. Both singers gave an excellent idea of traditional, general male-voice technique before the first decades of the nineteenth century.

Most modern tenors, particularly those with voices of the large operatic variety, avoid confrontation with pure head–voice as much as possible by extending their chest- or quasi-chest voice upwards. 'Mixed-voice' is the nearest to it that they allow themselves to go in normal circumstances. Indeed, many have lost any pure head–voice they may have possessed. Likewise, most baritones and basses have long since abandoned historical practice regarding high notes.

For the counter–tenor, fear seems to change to aversion of a rather illogical kind, when one considers essentially historical voice production procedure. This fear is not confined to the singers themselves. It is present in many musical directors. Also, the *bête noire* becomes strangely transplanted to many sophisticated listeners, most of whom should know better. It is surprising how many are not aware of the historical background: that how, with training, register change, properly negotiated, is a valuable extension of the counter–tenor's range, dramatic contrast, and colour; and the same goes for other voices. Indeed, this is true even of certain orchestral instruments whose various ranges and interesting timbres were smoothed out during the nineteenth century: the clarinet, for example. The problem should fade when more counter–tenors, and their teachers, approach their training with this in mind and do not shirk the issue by avoiding their lower register altogether.

The second point of importance connected with the 'break' and its existence or non–existence, is a quality or description often associated with the title 'true counter–tenor'. In these rare cases, it is claimed, the subject usually speaks and sings extremely lightly and has little, if any, downward singing range below about D3. While there are rare cases of such singers, the descriptive phrase often used about such a singer is: 'He couldn't sing anything else'. What does it really mean? One good counter–tenor, with whose voice and technique the author was once very familiar, but who shall remain anonymous, has a speaking and fundamental singing voice best described as 'raspy'. Certainly, as a counter–tenor, he could not sing anything else, in the sense that only his head–voice was usable. Any other sung sound he attempted to make was dreadful. In fact, many good altos or counter–tenors make an unpleasant or totally ineffective noise in what remains of their chest or basic singing voices. Others do possess the classic well-adjusted 'other' voice to be used when they please.

Some young, high counter–tenors who take, or sometimes grate, their head–register down to F3/E3/D3 often seem likely either to impair or alter their speaking and basic singing voices, or they reveal in them an already existing under–development which may have resulted from a badly negotiated adolescent voice change. Despite convincing auditory evidence to the contrary, some apparently well adjusted basic–voices can sometimes have poor or almost non–existent head–voice or falsetto. In theory, this should not be possible because good production should embrace the whole voice.

Some counter–tenors have a mediocre but vaguely serviceable baritonal or 'second tenor' timbre of voice with a very short and stunted range which shows little trace of the considerable skills demonstrated in their head–registers. Their speaking voices sound full, tonally even, but neither totally focused nor one hundred per cent efficient. The phrase 'he couldn't sing anything else' can therefore be applied in more than one way. The truth is that the human voice can be utterly unpredictable.

Some years ago, the author heard an ordinary, completely untutored 'non–singer' (in that he did not consider himself a singer at all) in an industrial pottery workshop, who produced the most glorious rich head–voice 'for fun' when imitating Kathleen Ferrier. The 'non–singer' was astounded when the author confessed admiration for it.

Attitudes to head– and chest–register change have varied over the centuries. Ardran and Wulstan were maintaining in 1967 that the two–register voice, while being needed in sixteenth–century music (and, by implication, in earlier music), seems not so clearly useful by the time of Purcell:[36]

---

[36] Ardran and Wulstan, op. cit., p. 18

Distinction between the compasses of full and verse passages is indeed the reverse of that found in the early part of the sixteenth century. Whereas the chorus parts (in Restoration music) are of normal compass, the solo parts are extended either to a high or to a low tessitura. This suggests that the falsetto was now being cultivated for the low register, and the chest voice was abandoned; this resulted in the division of counter–tenor voices into two specialist classes: the high and low counter–tenors.

It is an interesting and attractive theory, though Jacobs's arguments (discussed later), that the Baroque counter–tenor used fundamental voice for his lower or even lower–middle notes seem equally valid. Of course, Jacobs was seeking to draw a distinction between church and stage singing.

Unfortunately, misunderstanding of Ardran and Wulstan's statement of 1967 may have helped form the fashion current in 1992 for considering the Purcellian counter–tenor as either falsetto alto or a high tenor of our modern lyric type. It is fashionable to support the latter idea at present. Yet, as we have seen, all male voices used falsetto or had the accepted, normal option of employing it. However, certain musicologists continue to claim that the 'true counter–tenor', *ipso facto*, used no falsetto at all, of any variety.

David Wulstan wrote in 1985:[37]

Apart from one or two pieces, the *Eton Choirbook* displays little differentiation in range between one countertenor part and another; indeed in earlier music there is little distinction in the compasses of the countertenor and tenor, which suggests that chest and head registers were used in both voices. However, the difference between the compasses of these voices soon becomes more obvious, suggesting a progressively greater concentration on the falsetto register by the countertenor. The tone would naturally change, and become more 'edgy' (Butler's 'sweet shrill voice'). This development would result in the difference between the falsetto and chest registers being harder to conceal. This circumstance is reflected in the generally rather higher compasses of post–Reformation alto parts, and also in the way composers tended to avoid very low notes in exposed verses. The bottom limit seems to have been low *a'flat* [A♭3] unless some such phrase as 'out of the deep' or 'he hath put down' called for exceptional treatment, in which case the limit could be as much as a fourth lower. Even *a'flat* seems to have caused some difficulty, for various sources of Gibbons' 'This is the record of John' (cf. EECM 3, pp.222–3) show changes from the original *a'flat* to *c'* [A♭3 to C4]. Here the problem was probably caused by the difficult vowels with high lower formants on the words 'Christ', 'no' and 'Lord'.

In Purcell's time the solo parts are markedly different, some descending as low as *e* or *d* [E3 or D3], others hardly going below *c* [presumably C4], and the upper limit of the range also differed accordingly. Thus singers such as Turner and Howell were distinguished as a 'low countertenor' or 'high countertenor' respectively. It seems overwhelmingly probable that by this

---

[37] Wulstan, op. cit., pp. 243–4

means falsetto was used exclusively; where a low range is demanded consistently it is possible to develop a powerful low falsetto. Byrd, in his Latin music, occasionally makes a distinction between first and second alto. But the idea of low and high falsetto registers being exploited solo, is most strikingly demonstrated in the work of Tomkins, which shows quite different characteristics in comparison with the earlier technique. Although both low and high notes are often required in verses, they do not normally occur in the same part. For example, in 'Who can tell', there are alternative passages (cf. EECM 9, p.56 ff.) which show that a command of low and high registers in Verse passages was not necessarily expected. So the change towards the use of two types of solo alto seems to have been taking place at about Butler's time, which might possibly explain why he complains about 'a right voice' being 'too rare'; perhaps he did not approve of the new technique.

There is of course, an intriguing possibility. It is arguable that, though tenors, baritones and high counter–tenors all used falsetto techniques as a matter of course, one type of low counter–tenor – if, as is often claimed at present, he were arguably the equivalent of today's light, lyric tenor voice – could have avoided it until he reached the upper limit of classical low counter–tenor repertoire in which an easy tessitura would have helped him avoid falsetto production of any variety altogether. Such avoidance would certainly make him rare, judged by earlier universal usage.

Jacobs, writing in 1983, also after the publication of the author's *The Counter–Tenor*, demonstrates a middle view.[38] He argues that use of head–voice alone was not a technique used by the seventeenth– and eighteenth–century counter–tenor; not even the 'high' type. Neither does Jacobs give any support to the 'tenor lobby' who, as we have seen, argue that falsetto was never used at all and that counter–tenors and haute–contres were merely the highest variety of the light, lyric tenors we can hear now. Jacobs, however, argues that all counter–tenors and haute–contres used falsetto and their chest–voice; even singers whom we would regard as high–range counter–tenors today. His is a well–researched, extremely useful piece of writing with most of which one can have little real disagreement. (One debatable point concerns definition. Jacobs defines 'falsettist' as one who uses head–voice exclusively.)

In the 1970s, no less an authority on early music than Robert Donington seemed unclear about the counter–tenor question. He wrote of the castrato modern performance problem:[39]

> Thus our substitution of a female soprano, mezzo–soprano, or contralto, though it is what Handel himself did when short of a castrato, is inevitably a mis-representation. A good counter–tenor (i.e., a male alto) makes a plausible substitute, if he has power and agility enough.

Illogically, further down the same page, Donington defined male alto and counter–tenor differently and ambiguously. His text reads rather strangely:[40]

---

[38] Jacobs, *The Controversy Concerning the Timbre of the Countertenor*, passim
[39] Robert Donington, *The Interpretation of Early Music* (Faber, 1975), p. 524
[40] Donington, loc. cit.

(a) A male alto is a bass or baritone singing high parts in a falsetto voice, apparently produced by using only the edges of the vocal cords.
(b) The counter–tenor is a natural voice often of extremely high tessitura, light and more or less unchested yet masculine in quality. The range is from g to d or even e". [G3 to D5 or even E5]
(c) A normal tenor may sometimes go extremely high, as in the magnificent voice and musicianship of Hugues Cuénod.

It would seem that Donington was tempted to define (a) and (b) separately as a result of having been misled by the tonal variation and vocal idiosyncrasies of individual singers: something which can be bewildering. Unfortunately, he did not seem to realise that Cuénod himself admits openly that his higher notes are [middle] falsetto. Also, Donington appears to have overlooked the fact that Handel's practice was not always to substitute a female singer for a castrato, when necessary: altos or counter–tenors were used too, in oratorio and opera in England and probably elsewhere.

Donington modified his views, it appears, seven years later, in a new book published in the same year as *The Counter–Tenor*. In addition to providing a succinct account of vocal production and varieties of voice, he explained, after discussing castrati and recordings of Moreschi in particular:[41]

His voice, in spite of its feminine tessitura, sounds remarkably masculine – far more so than any boy soprano – and far more dramatically so even than the best of counter–tenors, who can, of course, be perfectly masculine people: natural basses or more or less high tenors using an exceptional register (from about f' to c" [F4–C5]) by bringing only a portion of their vocal cords into vibration. Under the alternative name of cathedral altos, they have in England never died out, but have been brought back only recently (first by Alfred Deller) to their pristine virtuosity. They have also been called *falsetti*, though there is nothing false about them to justify the term; or singers of the head (*testo*) as opposed to the chest (*petto*), more reasonably, since that is certainly the register which they so exceptionally exploit.

Nevertheless, in the same book, he seems unclear about early tenor technique, appearing to imply that the Romantic *tenore robusto* or *Heldentenor* inhabited the Baroque stage.

Before some arbitrary twentieth–century date (perhaps 1930?), all or most professional altos seem to have employed basic plus head–register as their normal technique, to judge from early recordings. If, as some writers of recent years claim, the pre–nineteenth–century counter–tenor soloist was a light tenor, with or without pure head–voice added, altos who employed only head–voice could have mingled with, then taken over from, tenors as sole employers of true head–voice, when the latter began to forsake it in the middle of the nineteenth century. Was it, therefore, perhaps after about 1930 that altos began (or resumed?) the use of head–register only? This certainly seems possible; one might recall the accusations of critics of that time who complained of 'weakness of lower notes' and so on.

---

[41] Robert Donington, *Music and its Instruments* (Methuen, 1982), pp. 172–3

Later, when Deller appeared on the scene, he proved these critics splendidly wrong: lower head–voice notes could ring. It is thought–provoking that he may have been the first singer since the sixteenth century to take a properly–developed head–register down to the depths. Deller could therefore have been re–establishing, if not an earlier norm, at least an earlier frequently–employed option.

Various early theorists stress that the ideal was to unite the registers by integrating head with chest–voice. Usually, the accepted interpretation of these pronouncements has been the *voix mixte*, in which falsetto – pure head–voice – is engulfed and loses its identity. Many teachers, including sinus–tone practitioners, talk of the need to train the voice from high–pitched, gentle, soft notes, downwards towards the heavier area and never the other way round.

Could the English interpretation of the phrase 'taking head–voice down into the chest' have varied from the Continental? In other words, 'taking it into' is taken to mean into the area, displacing the use of chest–register at that point? Could this have been in contrast to Continental practice, which took it down to blend and splice with the chest–register as it went; or, in earlier practice, to form a 'dovetail joint'? It is possible. Could the English method have been that used throughout Europe before the Renaissance? Could it have survived in England, while the rest of Europe went its own way? Many maintain this view, which has given rise to the idea that the counter–tenor is a peculiarly English voice which never existed beyond the shores of England.

It should be discerned that this 'exclusively English voice', as an explanation of the counter–tenor, is mistaken. The concept of an English exclusively head–voice counter–tenor in the sixteenth and early seventeenth centuries is attractive until one reflects more deeply on the historical development we have traced earlier. However, it too remains possible.

Uberti's paper on sixteenth–century Italian vocal techniques[42] will be considered later, but it is mentioned now because its content has some relevance in any discussion of English practice. It is also appropriate to later discussion of tenor technique. There are occasions when one is unlucky enough to encounter a voice which demonstrates only too well the commonly held view of falsetto: a weak, amorphous, false voice. It therefore seems useful, at intervals, to remind ourselves that the term 'falsetto' is a misnomer, though an undeveloped voice can be weak–toned (yet not automatically unattractive) and incapable of anything more than a mellow, gentle tone with neither 'ring' nor resonance enough to hold its own against other developed voices.

All that is known or can be inferred of Medieval, Renaissance, and later musical practice suggests that such a sound would be quickly smothered by anything more than a gentle and quiet accompaniment. It could not possibly be heard against most instruments and voices in low or medium range without proper focus and resonance. (Other undeveloped registers can share this characteristic.) Resonators focus the tone; they amplify, change and produce it as a mature voice on an equal footing with other voices. Nevertheless, because the fundamental or basic–voice is exercised daily during speech (however badly it is produced) it is inevitably stronger and more advanced than the little–used higher vocal registers. It is easy to see therefore how the legend of weakness, falseness and unnaturalness which is associated with falsetto persists in common parlance. The sheer ringing power and brilliance possible with correct use of all the resonators, as with all voice ranges, is ignored or not acknowledged. A

---

[42] Mauro Uberti, 'Vocal Techniques in Italy in the Second Half of the 16th Century', *Early Music*,
    October 1981, pp. 486–95

natural quality is present in genuine head–voice or falsetto, but the legend persists; so, what really is natural?

Let us be quite clear: for what the term 'natural' is worth, the chest or basic and fundamental voice is the only truly 'natural' voice, approximating as it does to the pitch of the speaking voice. This applies to women as well as men. Even the chest–voice is not, as is often supposed, one register, but two: lower and upper. On average, upper chest–voice is usually tenable with general ease, up to about E4 in men and F4 in women, depending on the individual larynx. Some fundamental voices, of course, end a tone or two lower. Others may be encouraged, pushed or forced higher than E4 and F4. Add the head–voice and we have a crude description of the vocal organ in both men and women. (Some teachers insist that, whereas women possess three registers – head, medium and chest – men only have two. This is not so; these three registers are available to men.)

Most modern teachers would probably claim, if pushed, that medium register is upper chest. Yet, considered differently, pharyngeal is that medium register. This is totally in line with Renaissance vocal theory, discussed later.

If only basic–voice is completely natural, it follows that the head–voice is always to an extent a developed voice, although we know that falsetto capability is present in almost every adult larynx to some degree. This suggests that the use of falsetto is more 'natural' alone than in the *voix mixte* – a startling idea for some! It is useful to read what vocal authorities, and writers about the voice, past and present, write about falsetto, though we should be especially cautious about the references which automatically equate falsetto with falso.

Anthony Frisell states that:[43]

> In its undeveloped state the head register is often referred to as the falsetto. Many think of it as a carry over from the child's boy soprano voice and unrelated to the matured male voice. Nothing could be further from the truth. The misconception is due to lack of technical knowledge for developing and uniting its quality and action with the lower register. The upper register is often referred to as the head voice and the mixed voice. The lyric voices are more familiar with the falsetto than the dramatic ones. However, both must utilize the register in the same manner. Qualities both associate with it are soprano–like, flutey, lyric, soft and sweet. These terms only describe the register's undeveloped condition and fail to indicate the power that is acquired with advanced development.

Lilli Lehmann stated:[44]

> Most male singers – tenors especially – consider it beneath them, generally, indeed unnatural or ridiculous to use the falsetto, which is part of all male voices ... . They do not understand how to make use of its assistance ... . Of its proper application they have not the remotest conception.

[43] Anthony Frisell, *The Tenor Voice* (Bruce Humphries, Boston, 1964), pp. 18–19
[44] Lilli Lehmann, *How to Sing* (New York Macmillan Co., 1902 and 1914), pp. 165–6

E. Davidson Palmer:[45]

> The term 'falsetto' is a most misleading one, and its indiscriminate use has been mischievous in the extreme. The man who invented it has much to answer for. He has caused right to be mistaken for wrong, and wrong to be mistaken for right ... what is false appear to be true, and what is true appear to be false. Had it been his desire to do all the injury in his power to the male voices of his own and succeeding generations, he could not, by the exercise of the utmost ingenuity have devised means better calculated to accomplish his purpose .... *The way to get rid of falsetto is to use it.* Let it alone and it will assuredly remain. It may grow weaker, but so long as voice of any kind remains, it will never disappear. Use it judiciously and perseveringly and in course of time it will lose its falsetto character and become firm and sonorous. It will then no longer sound strange and artificial, but will have the true manly quality and will seem to be what it really is, the natural voice. Wherever a separate falsetto register exists, it, and it alone, is the rightly produced voice. Its extremely high notes, however, are not the notes to practise upon.

Herbert–Caesari:[46]

> The term *falsetto* (diminutive of the Italian *falso*, false) means 'false little voice'; by itself it is worthless for purposes of vocal expression. The old Italian School used to call it *falsettino di testa*, 'false little head voice', because, as a sensation, it seems to be generated high up in the head cavities. By no means is it a false voice, as the tone is generated by the thread–like upper edges of the vocal cords which, in order to produce the so–called falsetto, separate much more than is the case for the production of either the pharyngeal or normal tone. And because of the greater space or slit between the cords while producing the falsetto, a much greater quantity of breath is expended, in that not all of it is employed in producing tone (as is, or should be, the case with normal tone) but escapes through the slit, thereby 'diluting' the product. It is a 'head' voice, but of a pale, insignificant, breathy sort: the tone is anaemic and static. Most voices, male and female, are able to produce falsetto. But some basses, and baritones of the heavier calibres, apparently do not seem able to produce it at all. In its usually undeveloped state, the falsetto is weak, and has little tension–resistance (due to the separation of the cords). We hold the falsetto tone in contempt only when it is produced by itself.

It is suggested that for Herbert–Caesari's 'falsetto' we should read 'undeveloped *upper* falsetto', for it is simply not true that all upper head–voice (by our definition) or 'falsetto' (by Herbert–Caesari's) is produced in the manner he describes, with 'breathy' tone, but many of his other

---

[45] E. Davidson Palmer, *Manual of Voice Training*, quoted by Ernest George White in *Science and Singing* (1909; 1938 edn), p. 52

[46] E. Herbert–Caesari, *The Voice of the Mind* (Robert Hale, 1951), p. 338

observations are useful. As suggested earlier, his employment of the term 'pharyngeal' for developed lower–falsetto is valuable.

Sims Reeves, the great Victorian English tenor, was unequivocal about falsetto. Some of his views are surprising and even totally untrue:[47]

> As the term implies, falsetto is a false voice. It is produced by a coup di glottis – that is, by a sudden, forceful shock of the voice. A falsetto note, to give a startling effect, must be high, and must be attacked from a chest voice lower in the scale. Any attempt to add vibrato to falsetto will at once result in the production of a nondescript tone of very bad quality. It is impossible to make a crescendo on a falsetto note – it may swell out a very little, but a full, genuine crescendo cannot be done. This fact will help the learner to distinguish between the head register and falsetto. I consider falsetto to be merely an illegitimate way of getting an effect which, at best, is only vulgar; good voices never have occasion to adopt such an inartistic trick. Bass voices usually have the best falsetto tones.

(Ernest George White was equally dismissive of Reeves and his opinions: '... one must admit that all his utterances are not exactly great flights of wisdom, even for a shilling! For example: "Male voices consist of tenors, baritones and basses." The poor alto was evidently forgotten!'[48])

Alessandro Moreschi, the last castrato, employed a technique similar to that castigated by Reeves. His recordings demonstrate quite clearly head–notes which are attacked from a chest-note lower in the scale.

Deller's biographers, Michael and Mollie Hardwick, commented colourfully on falsetto:[49]

> Much of the modern neglect of falsetto may be due to the cult of the ringing tenor, who, in accordance with one of the many dubious conventions of Italian opera, must attack his high notes at full bellow, or be derided for a ninny. Falsetto was valued by earlier generations of Italian singers; even the castrati used it to extend their range, and Farinelli's incredible ability to span three octaves certainly owed something to it.

Stubbs wrote:[50]

> Now if the falsetto was an unnatural and injurious production it seems incredible that the greatest teachers of singing the world has ever known failed to make that discovery.

Though it contains a few internally–conflicting arguments, Stubbs's monograph should be studied; it has a particular interest because of its date.

---

[47] Sims Reeves, *On the Art of Singing* (Chappell & Co. Ltd., 2nd edn 1901), pp. 5–6

[48] E. G. White, *Sinus Tone Production* (Dent, 1909), p. 9

[49] Hardwick, op. cit., second edn (1980), p. 79

[50] G. Edward Stubbs, *The Adult Male Alto or Counter Tenor Voice* (Gray, New York, 1908), p. 34

In 1957, Grove's *Dictionary*[51] defined falsetto as:

> A particular form of sound production at the larynx sometimes adopted by male singers and in the majority of cases employed only when it is desired to reach a note above the ordinary range of the individual voice. By some singers falsetto is habitually adopted, as in singing alto, and in such cases tones of wide range, extending to a comparatively low pitch and of powerful volume, may be produced. But in most instances the tones of this mechanism are high–pitched, of feeble volume, of short duration and of poor quality.

We should note that, unlike Owen Jander's article in *The New Grove Dictionary of Music and Musicians* of 1981, Denis Stevens in the 1957 edition made a distinction between the Deller type of counter–tenor and falsetto. The whole counter–tenor essay should be studied. Its perception is admirable, although (as is the case with most commentators) even so distinguished a musicologist as Stevens fails to suggest the possibility of more than one mode of falsetto. His meaning, however, is clear:

> A male alto is not necessarily a counter–tenor, for the alto voice is more often than not a bass voice singing falsetto, whereas a true counter–tenor of high range is a naturally produced voice, using head resonance – that is with a high and free position of the larynx. As the high counter–tenor must be clearly distinguished from the alto, by reason of its great difference in timbre, so the low counter–tenor must be distinguished from the tenor, whose tessitura it very nearly approaches. Here again it is largely a question of timbre, the low counter–tenor possessing a lighter and more melliflous quality than the 'tenor robusto' or 'Helden tenor'. The tone quality of the high counter–tenor is difficult to describe but it is an essentially masculine voice, and at its best is clear, flexible and incisive. It may be described as a fistular voice supported by resonance, whereas the falsetto male alto (by contrast weak and effiminate) is not so supported.
>
> The high counter–tenor with its range of a twelfth or thirteenth (G – D (E)) is indeed something of a rarity. In recent years it has been successfully revived in England, notably by Alfred Deller.

Following a conventional description of falsetto, V. E. Negus, F.R.C.S., hinted grudgingly in 1927[52] that

> other mechanisms of falsetto have been described [but not mentioned by Negus], but the explanation given above [i.e., in his falsetto article] fits with practical description.

---

[51] Fifth edn, pp. 13–14
[52] Grove's *Dictionary* (3rd edn, 1927), p. 194

Percy Scholes wrote:[53]

> Falsetto. The head voice in adults, an unnatural effect producable by practice (as distinct from the voice of a castrato produced by means of a surgical operation). The male alto sings falsetto. Falsettist is a falsetto singer. Counter–tenor – see alto voice.

Scholes was less dismissive in his entry under 'alto voice',[54] almost as if the alto singer has to some extent redeemed by artistry the unnatural basis of his vocal production.

Herbert–Caesari was highly perceptive:[55]

> As the Old School used to say, the *falsetto* is the pile of the *pharyngeal carpet*. The pharyngeal puts life, lustre and intensity into both the falsetto and the basic; this is particularly true of the tenor's high notes. Falsetto is the velvet cloak for the steely pharyngeal, and the latter provides a solid base for the falsetto.

W. H. Griffiths wrote:[56]

> The falsetto (head–voice) – i.e., the 'upper thin' register in men – comprises some of the most rare and beautiful tones in the male voice, and their culture denotes supreme art.

Kristin Linklater, in a book of far–reaching insight into the 'world of voice', wrote:[57]

> Falsetto work increases the elasticity and strength of the vocal folds and the breathing muscles. (This part of the range can be referred to as the 'loft register'.) It is useful for both men's and women's voices because the whole range will benefit from such strengthening if it is done as the final part of a well–balanced workout on the voice.

She continues, more specifically:[58]

> Men are no longer as culturally averse to experimenting with the falsetto part of their voices as they used to be, although some still make a subconscious protest at its unmanliness by being unable to find it. Similarly, many women [singers of serious music] still seem to feel subconsciously that chest resonance is not for them, preferring the 'feminine' appeal of their upper register. A man can compete easily with a woman's soprano range and develop at least two octaves in a falsetto that is mellow and unforced. For

---

[53] Percy Scholes, *The Oxford Companion to Music* (O.U.P., 9th edn, 1955), p. 345
[54] Scholes, op. cit., p. 27
[55] Herbert–Caesari, op. cit., p. 352
[56] W. H. Griffiths, *The Mixed Voice and the Registers* (Curwen, 2nd edn, 1905) p. vi
[57] Kristin Linklater, *Freeing the Natural Voice* (Drama Book Publishers, New York, 1976), p. 118
[58] Loc. cit.

both men and women, work in the high, falsetto, skull–resonating area
develops flexibility and strength in the rest of the voice.

The *Oxford English Dictionary* entry under 'falsetto' should also be studied.

Herbert–Caesari, Stubbs, Lehmann, Davidson Palmer, Hardwick, Frisell and Linklater put
their fingers on the situation exactly; but for Sims Reeves and Kate Emil–Behnke all falsetto
was an undesirable state produced in the head–register by slackness in the vocal ligaments.
They seem to have overlooked the difference between a collapsed falsetto and a properly
produced supported falsetto mechanism which is an integral part of, and even produces,
medium/middle/pharyngeal and upper, or pure, head–voice.

For Reeves and Kate Emil–Behnke, the word falsetto was itself derogatory and an object
of scorn; yet remove the word and use instead middle– and head–register when studying Kate
Emil–Behnke and she, like her father, can be thoroughly recommended to the student counter-
tenor. In addition, study Sims Reeves carefully, but interpret him in similar fashion to Kate
Emil–Behnke's work.

In the 1950s, it was unrewarding to search for any reference to the counter–tenor voice in
books on technique and utterly vain to hope for reference to modern singers of this type. One
would have thought that by the early 1960s the purely historical rôle, at least, of the
counter–tenor would have been quite clear, but no less a writer than Percy M. Young made
two odd errors in his 1962 book, *The Choral Tradition*. These were that Byrd's *Mass for
Three Voices* was scored for 'contralto, tenor and bass' (as he puts it in the main text) and for
'soprano, alto and bass' (in the Index of principal works). The second instance may well have
been an editorial fault (or a suggestion for a pitch variation?). The only explanation for the
first, other than outright error, is that Young may have been thinking of the practice, in pre-
nineteenth–century Italy, to use 'contralto', correctly, for the natural male alto or counter–tenor.
In English music, of course, other than by Handel and the Italian Opera in eighteenth–century
London, contralto never seems to have been used for male singers. Oddly, Young almost
always used 'contralto', not 'alto', in his many other quoted examples of English early music.
The unsuspecting reader, therefore, could be greatly misled.

In 1973, Kurt Pahlen wrote:[59]

> Alfred Deller is a counter–tenor, a rare class akin to the coloratura soprano
> among women's voices. But, since the repertoire for this voice is extremely
> limited, it has necessitated the rediscovery of long–forgotten works or the
> performance of modern compositions which have sometimes offered reward-
> ing tasks for Deller: for example, Orff's *Carmina Burana*, and Britten's *A
> Midsummer Night's Dream*.

The situation has improved slightly in the usually ultra–conservative world of vocal textbook
writing. There is nearly always at least some references to be found to the counter–tenor,
though some authors are damning and some damn with faint praise. It is still difficult to find
anything very enthusiastic. A notable exception is Linklater's admirably–entitled book *Freeing
the Natural Voice*:[60]

---

[59] Kurt Pahlen, *Great Singers* (W.H. Allen, 1973), p. 222
[60] Linklater, op. cit., p. 117

The first objective in working to free the top of the range is to remove doubts, fears and unfamiliarity. The quality of the sound is irrelevant, although,as the vocal folds strengthen and the throat frees, you develop excellent rare material for a soprano or tenor voice and rich counter–tenor quality.

Medical books on laryngology can be of interest to the enquirer into counter–tenors. In one such work, A. S. Khambata contributes a wealth of information and ideas on vocal possibilities from this point of view. He suggests that the counter–tenor voice is peculiarly English, but continues with somewhat grudging praise:[61]

> This rather specialised category of male voice is perhaps a by–blow of the original castrati soprani and contralti, but it has lingered on through ... cathedral singing in this country ... [He mentions Deller as the catalyst to the new movement] ... The speaking and so–called normal singing voice of this breed of singer is generally of a baritone colour, the particular characteristic of the counter–tenor voice being a well–developed falsetto which is extended down–wards into the chest–register.

Khambata goes on to say that, in his opinion, the counter–tenor is best heard in a medium–sized concert hall. He considers it too small a voice for the larger spaces of a conventional opera house, but he seems not to be very familiar with the vocal tone of most modern solo counter–tenors:[62]

> The use of the falsetto in such a manner tends to produce characteristic hooting qualities in the voice, but there are notable exceptions, particularly that admirable singer, James Bowman.

One would think that in knowing Bowman's tonal quality, Khambata would also be aware of his enormous tonal power, but other than the odd arguable point (for instance, the English counter–tenor is not a 'modern derivative' of the castrato), even this slightly qualified enthusiasm in an important book is refreshing when we consider the vitriolic views of Kay (see pp. 321–3). There is a cool look in *The Voice and Its Disorders* by Margaret Greene, a medical textbook which has a chapter on 'abnormal mutation' (an alarming heading!) in the course of which she writes:[63]

> Natural tenor singers are occasionally found to have a freak vocal range, able to sing with facility in the falsetto register. The peculiar thin and silvery voice of the counter–tenor always has a certain vogue. The fluty, rather haunting quality of the voice is due to reinforcement of a limited range of overtones in contrast to the deep baritone or bass voice which is enriched by a wider range of harmonics. Alfred Deller has popularised counter–tenor singing in

[61] A. S. Khambata, "The Phenomenal Voice", in *Music and the Brain* (ed. Critchley and Hewson, Heinemann, 1977), p. 76
[62] Ibid., p. 76
[63] Margaret Greene, *The Voice and its Disorders* (Pitman, 3rd edn, 1972), p. 220

our time. The voice of the male falsetto–singer is rather richer in harmonics
than that of the boy by reason of the larger adult resonators.

Greene's work contains a wealth of information which, though not normally essential for the development of the singing voice, serves to support and amplify our knowledge of voice as an instrument. Perhaps we should at least find comfort in the fact that if Greene's book had been written before the advent of Deller an equivalent paragraph would probably not have been merely a little condescending but almost certainly scornful.

The medical word for falsetto, in speech and generically, is 'pubephonia': the production of the unchanged voice of a boy (though the term 'unchanged' is inaccurate in this context) when one is physically capable of the changed voice of a man. The cause of pubephonia is the subconscious use of the musculature which elicits the 'child voice'. It is common in deaf youths and in many Indian youths (for complex psycho–sexually based reasons) who need expert help in breaking through to the adult male fundamental voice.

We conclude this chapter, and prepare for the next, by quoting Roland Tatnell's paper written in 1965:[64]

> What exactly then, is meant by 'falsetto'? Physiologically, it is that sound produced by vibration of the extreme membranous edges of the vocal cords (as opposed to their vibration as a whole in the case of ordinary phonation), and characterized in the voices of altos and counter–tenors; etymologically, that word which derives from *falsus*, the past participle of the Latin verb *fallere* – to deceive – and which, in Italian, is the diminutive of *falso* – or false. Elaboration upon the unfortunate connotations 'feigned', and 'artificial' lies outside the scope of this discussion. Suffice it to point out that the human voice, is the Human Voice. Attempts to isolate that part of the whole mechanism not *customarily* employed, and to write it off as 'false', or 'unnatural', may be dismissed as illogical and plainly ridiculous. The association between this sound and 'falseness' most probably originated from the antagonistic attitude of the early medieval monastic mind, shocked to hear a voice hitherto regarded as secular, and apparently feminine, in an environment totally sacred and masculine.
>
> That it seemed 'unnatural' for a man to sing like a woman, was an accusation levelled repeatedly by many a prominent divine, in a futile attempt to stamp out the practice.

---

[64] Roland Stuart Tatnell, 'Falsetto Practice: A Brief Survey', (*The Consort*, 1965), p. 31

11 The New Music: Renaissance Vocal Theorists

The revival of arts and letters during the fifteenth and sixteenth centuries is usually regarded as having begun as a result of the capture of Constantinople in 1453 by the Ottoman Turks. It seems likely that this event was the last straw for the Greek scholars who had already begun to re–migrate to Italy; at any rate, the remaining humanists left at that point taking with them their Greek and Roman manuscripts and other impedimenta of great learning.

The effects of this were far–reaching, and the impact of the Renaissance has never faded totally; it affects us today, not least in the world of vocal theory and vocal production. That historic event has been described as 'the victory of healthy humanism over medieval religious superstition' and this may be the key to the attitude of some Renaissance writers and theorists to the human voice, its training and repertoire.

Late–Medieval, pre–Renaissance humanism was the passion of scholars. It was not an ideology, and did not preach a gospel of Man–over–God. Mostly, it was a way of thinking. Renaissance humanism was rather different. By contrast, those who read pre–Christian, Classical texts were encouraged to reshape and remould their fifteenth- and sixteenth–century lives by their interpretation.

Some humanists took a purely scholarly interest in Greek music, with the consequence that they felt little urge to transform music of their own time as a result of studying that of ancient Greece. Others believed that their contemporary music was vastly inferior. They wished to alter it, radically and permanently. Yet others took a middle position, feeling that their own music had reached a new state of perfection, but that it could be improved still further because it was still inferior in certain ways to that of the ancient Greeks.

The nature of Classical studies in music was markedly different from that of other subjects. Very few specimens of actual Greek music were known, or easily deciphered. Scholars were forced to speculate on its true nature largely on the basis of theoretical treatises. Some of these became generally available only towards the middle of the sixteenth century. An important part of the resulting hunger in Italy for the Graeco/Roman past involved a rekindling of love of Classical architecture and sculpture was satisfied amid the semi–buried ruins of Imperial Rome, where objects could be found, handled and seen among the damaged or fragmented stone masterpieces. The sagacious builders of Renaissance Rome quarried stone for the Vatican from the ruins of the Coliseum.

Music itself, of course, is a renaissance: it must be continually recreated to be heard and to be experienced. It cannot be seen except on paper or parchment – poor substitutes. The artists of the Italian Renaissance movement handled shattered antique sculpture and surveyed glorious ruins. They saw in this desecration the descent of a once–glorious civilisation into medieval licence, crudity and barbarism, but after this night of the soul they expected and worked towards a sunrise.

Many Renaissance musical theorists, therefore, must have seen their rôle not merely as restorers, but crusaders and improvers, whose aim, in the most extreme cases, was to banish all that remained of what they considered crude (Ars Nova) music; the Renaissance was essentially a movement which powerfully attempted to recreate an urban[e] civilisation based on a supposed Greek city–state model.

The Renaissance may be divided into four periods. It is useful to list some key composers and therefore musical styles from each, while remembering that it became a wider European movement, and that responses to it displayed somewhat varied national characteristics.

1 Early Renaissance 1420–1490:   Power to Ockeghem
2 High Renaissance 1490–1520:   Josquin to Mouton
3 High Renaissance 1520–1560:   Gombert to The Council of Trent
4 Late Renaissance 1560–1600:   Palestrina to Byrd

Reflecting on the Renaissance in general, and vocal technique in particular, we may note that what C. E. Montague called 'a [Classical] Greek liking for moderation' seems to have been mixed with the Italian penchant for excess, via the (ancient) Roman. As in most fields of creative, artistic activity, the results of this mixture in the fifteenth and sixteenth centuries became a happy compromise. Montague wrote: 'The Greeks had a ruse of saying much less than they meant, in the hope that their hearer's mind would make good even more than the large discount which they had deducted from the truth.'[1]

Indeed, it could be claimed that one method of assertion is hearty understatement.

Much of our modern interpretation (and it *is* interpretation) of vocal theory of the period is based on what a few Renaissance writers are recorded as having thought, advised, promoted or dictated.

Denis Stevens was in no doubt, in 1960, about the favoured voice ranges in the Early Renaissance period:[2]

As art–song became more supple, more ready a vehicle for the sister art of poetry ... the vocal line favoured the alto or tenor ranges ...

Stevens also wrote of Renaissance Spanish song, apropos the 'Cacionero de Palacio:[3]

The prevalence of songs for higher voices should not blind the reader to the fact that the male alto or countertenor voice was much cultivated in Spain, and textural bienséance demands that many of these villancicos be sung by a man. There are few examples of an exceptionally high range for male alto (though it is fairly certain that pitch was lower in the fifteenth century than today)

We should bear in mind the influence of foreign composers and musicians generally – French, Flemish and English – in fifteenth–century Italy. From 1440 onwards, non–Italian composers

---

[1] C.E. Montague, *A Writer's Notes on his Trade* (Chatto & Windus, 1930; Pelican, 1949), pp. 46–7
[2] *A History of Song*, ed. Stevens (Hutchinson, 1960), p. 68
[3] Ibid., p. 73

were in demand for employment in both court and cloister, as Stevens noted:[4]

> It would be tempting to hazard a guess that secular songs with Italian texts, unattributed and unclaimed amongst this great mass of material, might be the work of native Italian composers; but we know too well that the northerners were quick to learn both the language and the poetry of their southern hosts, so that many a ballata unsigned in the manuscripts may be the work of Dufay or Ciconia.

The vocal ranges used by Flemish and Franco–Flemish composers such as these suggest the likely musical culture of the singers who were active in Italy at this time.

No doubt Stevens was at least as familiar in 1960 with the work of the Renaissance theorists as are younger commentators of today, but he seems to be at odds with them in his support of the idea that much music was performed by the male alto or counter–tenor. Today it is common for the theorists to be interpreted differently with regard to falsetto, feigned voice and head voice. Most of the musicologists, directors and singers today who dismiss both falsetto (as a blanket term) and feigned voice – usually thinking them to be one and the same – do so on the apparent final, unarguable authority of Caccini (1550–1610) and a few others. It is as well to quote Caccini immediately:

> 'Faked' voices cannot give rise to the nobility of good singing, which comes from a natural voice suited to all the notes.[5]

Another, rather lumpen, translation gives:

> From the falsetto voice no nobility of good singing can arise; than comes from natural voice, through the whole range, able to be controlled at will, [and] with the breath used only to demonstrate of all the best mastery of all the best a[e]ffects necessary to this most noble manner of singing.[6]

This statement from an important composer and singer, linked with utterances by a handful of other theorists, seems so clear, so direct. Are such directives or advice always what they appear to be? Possibly not. The phrase 'It all depends on what you mean by falsetto', comes to mind. We should remember that Caccini, possessed personal preferences and dislikes, and that he was part of a trend, a fashion. Moreover, he was theorizing and recommending ways of approaching the 'new music', and writing of his hopes for the future, including his own as a singer/composer. In the preface of *Le Nuove Musiche*, he declared that it had been his object to write a type of music to be sung to the archlute in which one could, as it were, 'talk in music' (*in armonia favellare*), acknowledging the primacy of the text in the process of composition.[7]

While we might applaud a composer for being so sensitive to his text, we should not overlook the significant point: that Caccini had *natural* utterance as one of his first considerations.

---

[4] Ibid., p. 96
[5] Guilio Caccini, *Le Nuove Musiche* (Florence, 1601–2) f. Ca r
[6] Caccini, op. cit., ed. Hitchcock (modern edn, A–R Editions Inc., Madison), p. 56
[7] Ibid., p. 44

It was to reflect the everyday, normal human condition as opposed to the exalted, poetic, religious, spiritual, allegorical, 'artificial' style or styles. Yet his perception of perfection, and Renaissance ideals based on Classical values, also lay behind his aims. It is arguable that, though related, Caccini's exhortation does not necessarily amount to the same as Monteverdi's *Seconda Prattica*, used to describe music which is 'commanded by the words', rather than the reverse which he called *Prima Prattica*.[8] Certainly, Monteverdi applied and transformed the ideas behind *Le Nuove Musiche* with unusual ingenuity and artistic insight.

A feigned voice – assuming for the moment that the term is supposed to apply to falsetto in all its varieties – could not reasonably be described as 'normal, usual utterance' for 'talking in music'. Caccini seems to have attacked falsettists (in one or other shades of meaning) as (un)dramatic secular performers, for reasons which can be discerned[9] even if not always agreed with. Despite Caccini, falsettists continued to exist both in and out of church; one has only to recall Coryate's famous reference to the superb falsettist at a Venetian feast. This is but one indication that his recommendations about secular singing were not always taken up, even in late Renaissance or early Baroque Italy. When we reflect that it was and is the source and powerhouse of the artificial and fantastic, and of illusory opera, the long–term failure of the strict theorists is not surprising.

We may point to some slight similarity between Caccini's 'talking in music' and mid–to–late twentieth–century 'pop culture', in which supposedly ordinary 'normal utterance' without frills and clever vocal tricks is the criterion: a demand for the popular, natural, basic and down–to–earth. Human nature being as it is, alongside ordinariness soon develop contrast, fantasy and novelty. Factions then adopt one or the other. Inevitably, a middle ground develops while extremes become more extreme. It is no new phenomenon. Hence, still within the perceived trend there is a wide degree of co–existence, before fashion twists again. Even as Caccini was writing his strictures, the fantastic castrati, who used *all* vocal–registers and variation possible, were in the process of conquering the church choir–gallery, followed closely by stage and 'concert' platform.

Mauro Uberti, an authority on early singing, referred to the question of registers, head–voice and falsetto, in his generally excellent article of 1981.[10] The apparently all-embracing dislike of falsetto (head–voice) which Uberti reports as expressed by the theorists Zacconi and Caccini seems to be inconsistent with the views of Maffei and Vicentino. This is hardly surprising; the four were not exact contemporaries. It is salutary also to study Rebecca Stewart's 'A Physiological and Linguistic Study of Male Vocal Types, Timbres and Techniques in the Music of Josquin des Prez'.[11] Josquin lived from $c1440-1550$. Stewart's paper leaves no doubt of the importance, indeed indispensability, of falsetto to Renaissance voice–production, though it seems clear that in some ways northern European practice differed somewhat from southern.

We should look back, momentarily, to the 'springboard' from which later Renaissance writing and practice came. During the middle–to–late fifteenth century, the Early Renaissance, northern European and northern Italian vocal techniques included singing in more than one register: trebles (boys) were to sing very high, and the sound was to be 'suave, sweet and

[8] See Mauro Uberti, *Early Music*, October 1981, p. 492
[9] See note 5 and Caccini ed. Hitchcock, op. cit., p. 45 fn. 12
[10] Uberti, op. cit., pp. 486–95
[11] Rebecca Stewart, *In Principio erat Verbum*, passim

sufficient'.[12] It seems obvious that 'singing in more than one register' includes pure head–voice or falsetto. (The reference to men's voices is dated 1469, and that to boys' technique 1536.) Only three decades later, Maffei seems to be referring to the full use of all registers in the virtuoso voice, in the secular vocal tradition:[13]

> Because when you say that the virtuoso voice [voce passeggiata] is 'small' and trained with the intention of pleasing the ear, it is made different from the small voice heard in laughter ... which ... is not educated ....Such a voice ... is reduced to the flexible, consisting as it does in going from bass to *alt* and descending from *alt* to bass with the diminutions and orderly repercussions of the air ....To those to whom Nature has not given the soft and pliant throat ... these rules of mine may be useful to them only a little or not at all.

'The soft and pliant throat' suggests one which allows the easy transition from one register to another, from the deepest to the very highest notes, without forcing the fundamental voice beyond its comfortable limit.

On the other hand, it should be borne in mind that, in attempting to interpret all (including later) Renaissance theorists' views on head–voice or falsetto, it is obvious that direct quotation is not enough. We are removed by several centuries from the nuances of their original meanings. As with most surviving objective evidence, or essentially subjective personal description from the past, we have to interpret its thinking, context and experience, with the mind, perception and imagination of our own time. It is hardly new to suggest that taking the simplest phrase or apparent meaning at a superficial level will not do. Therefore, although after the widest possible consideration of such documents, all commentators and interpreters, including the present author, must hypothesize using direct quotation, it is essential to reserve some judgement throughout; to be ready, as the saying goes, 'to take it with a pinch of salt'.

For example, though he appears to be writing in general terms of head–voice, falsetto or feigned voice, Zacconi (1555–1627) might well have been referring ruefully to experience with a particular singer or singers as he wrote:[14]

> molti hanno voce detta voce di testa; la quale è da cantanti produtta con un certo suono frangibile, e il frangente è una certa cosa che per ogni poco si sente; e però si avertiscono a moderarglila; sì perchè non abbiano da superare gli altri; sì anche perchè la detta voce di testa il più delle volte offende ...

> Many have what is called a head voice, which is produced by singers with a certain fragile sound, and breaking is a certain thing which every so often is heard; and yet let them be advised to moderate it in order not to outstrip the others and also because this 'head–voice' is usually offensive.

---

[12] Ibid., pp. 125–6
[13] Ibid., p. 134, quoting MacClintock , p. 44
[14] Ludovico Zacconi, *Practtica di Musica* (Venice, 1592), quoted by Uberti, op. cit., p. 493 (translated by Mark Lindley)

This might be paraphrased:

> Many or most singers have head-voice. Sometimes it is produced with an
> uncertain wavering quality which can occasionally be heard to crack. In order
> to stop this, they force it and drown (or take attention from?) other singers.
> This type of head-voice is usually offensive.

'Breaking', by which, presumably, is meant a quasi-pathological rupture in the flow of sound,
is a phenomenon which does not happen in well-trained and properly-controlled voices today,
of whatever range or type, and probably did not happen in Zacconi's time either. We should
notice his further warning about forced high notes, a defect as common then as now, and his
advice that 'Similmente nel cantar piano nelle alte non si debbano forzare se commodamente
non vi arivano: perche meglio è di fingerle, ò di taccerle ...' ('In singing high notes quietly one
should not force them if they do not come out conveniently; because it is better to fake or
omit them.')[15]

A paraphrase of this might be: 'If you can't sing high notes quietly, then don't force them,
but either sing something else (*fingerle*) or leave them out.' This meaning is far from a dismissal of head-voice as offensive. It is about the art of singing (or not singing) high notes
quietly; even about the preferred employment of properly developed controlled head-voice for
the higher range. Advice on omitting inconvenient high notes would suggest that Zacconi is
referring to ensemble singing, perhaps by amateur or untrained singers. A soloist might take
a lower note, but could hardly omit it altogether. When we turn to Chrysander's translation of
the same theorist, we learn:[16]

> According to Zacconi, writing in 1592, the contratenori, or 'voci mezzani'
> (middle voices) "are partly chest and partly head voices. They receive their
> names because of the effect produced, as if they are half the first type and
> half the second. It is said, however, that when they sing more in the chest
> than in the head, they are even more beautiful."

Zacconi's advice seems to conflict with Caccini's; his text proves that it was considered an
advantage to possess the ability to unite chest-voice and falsetto and to be able to sing with
both chest and falsetto in the same range so that both registers overlap. His comment that
'singing in the chest than in the head [voice]' can be 'even more beautiful' brings to mind the
lovely warm quality of John Whitworth's chest-notes. They colour his head-notes in a
marvellous manner.

Maffei is usually interpreted as recommending an extremely limited range for *camera*
singers, which implies that they were advised not to extend into different registers. This can
be applied both ways. Presumably, if the singer was already in head-voice, either exclusively
or in part, for the purpose of singing alto or soprano, he was being advised not to extend into
chest-voice. However, Maffei seems to have regarded soloists differently:[17]

---

[15] Loc. cit.

[16] Chrysander, quoted by Stewart, op. cit., p. 108

[17] Maffei (Bridgman 18), quoted Stewart, op. cit., p. 104

> One finds some singers who sing bass [today's baritone], tenor and every other voice with great ease, and decorating and diminishing with the throat, make passages, now in the bass, now in the middle, now in the high – all beautiful to hear.

Upon which Stewart comments:

> Although Maffei cites extreme examples of the phenomenon, it is clear that singers were expected to use both their modal and falsetto registers, if at all possible, and to do so with considerable technical proficiency.

Jacobs quotes a different translation which ends

> ... now in the bass, now in the mezzo, now in the alto – all beautiful to hear'.[18]

The differences regarding register–change therefore seem to have been not only between *camera, cappella* or *chiesa* and solo singing, but between amateur (frequently untrained?) and professional vocalists. Though this requires wider and deeper consideration than is possible here, we look at it briefly.

Nicola Vicentino (1511–1572) advised, like the later Maffei:[19]

> ... per commodita de i cantanti, & acciò che ogni voce commune possi contare la sua parte commoditamente ... mai si dè aggiognere righa alcuna, alle cinque righe, ne di sotto, ne di sopra, in nissuna parte, ne manco mutar chiavi ...

> ... for the convenience of singers and in order that every common voice can sing its part commodiously ... no ledger lines should ever be added to the five lines of the stave, neither above nor below, in any voice–part; nor indeed should the clefs be changed ...

This restriction of each voice to moderate territory seems to suggest that, like Maffei, Vicentino did not advise ordinary singers (presumably those in amateur ensembles) to change registers at all. Again, this is not the same as advising against the use of head–voice totally. Employment of the appropriate clef would automatically ensure that composer and singer did not need to use ledger lines. If the singer happened to be using head–voice at the time, Vicentino's strictures would still have been appropriate. He continued: 'questa commodità sarà communa, si alle voci buone, come a quelle non troppo gagliarde & potenti ...' ('This convenience will suit good voices as well as those which are not very elegant and powerful...')[20] Elsewhere, he implied that 'good voices' (professional singers or amateurs of superior gifts?) were capable of, and used to, greater vocal extension; but, in his recommended limits, he seemed to be safeguarding effective employment of voice and possibly clarity of text.

---

[18] Jacobs, 'The Controversy Regarding the Timbre of the Countertenor', p. 302

[19] Nicola Vicentino, *L'antica musica ridotta alla moderna prattica* (Rome, 1555), quoted Uberti, op. cit., p. 491

[20] Quoted by Uberti, loc. cit.

Vicentino appears to be one of the first to differentiate vocally between *camera, cappella* and, by implication, solo styles.

Judging by the modestly–ranged voice parts in some choral and ensemble music of the period, for a time, an extremely restricted range for individual ensemble singers seems to have been established successfully, following the ideas of the Renaissance theorists; not merely in Italy, but also in the Low Countries, for example. Nevertheless, many choral works of the period reveal wider ranging voice parts or awkwardly–pitched voice parts which appear to require register negotiation. Such vocal lines are likely to have been awkward then to singers of (purposely?) restricted range, as these same vocal lines often are today. It is therefore also germane to speculate that, where there were two or three singers to each vocal part, each with his own territorial and tonal speciality (as in some examples of Josquin, where many of these parts, particularly the inner voices, often ranged over two octaves), a highly effective single vocal line of great range would have resulted.

Some Italian Renaissance theorists seem to contradict others; but many modern commentators, when considering the use of falsetto, or pure head–voice techniques involving falsetto, have since decided that, collated, interpreted and summarized, the theorists' conclusion is that head–voice, used alone or at all, was and is inappropriately dull and featureless for solo work for stage and other secular use (though perhaps suitable for church performance). A few commentators seem, however, to give tacit acquiescence to the idea that falsetto might have been used for secular ensemble singing. Certainly, if used unimaginatively, head–voice (like any other vocal register) can lack variety of colour. Unless it is made part of a wider vocal spectrum – either through use of all available resonators, and/or, if used with the broader tones of chest–register, with all the extra colour that this can bestow – it can indeed be underexpressive. In this, we can perhaps discern something of Elster Kay's modern complaint regarding unvaried tonal quality. If we today interpret the theorists' head–voice as *upper* head–voice, then *voce mezzana*, or middle–voice, becomes lower head–voice: pharyngeal in our terminology. In the twentieth–century (post–Duprez) context, *voce mezzana*, middle or medium voice, seems to us to be head–voice; but if the theorists and generations who followed considered it (rightly) not absolutely pure head–voice, but middle–voice, probably with a change of mode between its own lower and upper areas of operation, this makes sense of the notion of a weaker, thinner register (called 'feigned' above all this). Perhaps it was this vocal area, which for the moment we shall call 'upper–falsetto', which was disliked for secular use by the fashionable Renaissance theorists. Yet the highly–developed upper–falsetto could hardly be considered weak. Was their 'feigned voice' what we term 'pipe–voice'?

The sixteenth–century light bass, wrote Rebecca Stewart[21]

> in addition to his 'normal' voice, also sang in his 'mezzo–soprano' register. This is supported by Vicentino, writing albeit somewhat conservatively in 1555, who mentions a written gamut of twenty–one notes, from F2 to E5, including his head–voice, as being the standard vocal range of the 'bass'.
>
> Perhaps the most convincing argument for the absence of the [true] bass voice [in ensemble of this period] is shown in the music itself: to accommodate the bass [of today], all other voice types must shift one [part] down [in today's performances], destroying both the light and transparent

---

[21] Rebecca Stewart, op. cit., p. 106

quality of the music *and the carefully conceived function of the contratenor as a double register 'instrument'.* [The present author's emphasis underlines both essential truth and useful images.]

We can discern, then, that blanket or 'knee–jerk' pronouncements by certain modern writers, musicologists, singers, or musical directors to the effect that all early theorists banned the use of falsetto seem to be unsubstantiated. The key phrase here seems to be: 'It all depends on what you mean by falsetto'.

As part of the Renaissance of learning, Italians 'discovered' their own language during the fifteenth century. Previously, Latin and French had been the international languages of composers living in Italy. The dominance of French influence there started to fade at the start of the sixteenth century. Italian and Italian–Latin began to usurp it, an example which eventually influenced the rest of western Europe.

Stewart analyses the effects this had on French and Italian singing techniques.[22] We can see how this can be applied to the development of the counter–tenor. Some, including Stewart, opine that the art of singing underwent a complete transformation between, say, Conrad von Zabern in 1474, and Guilio Caccini in 1601. If it did, that change does not seem to have been permanent in every regard. There was, of course, varied vocal orientation across countries affected by Renaissance influences. The differing techniques used for French 'closed' and Italian 'open' vowels, for example, were never reconciled.

Our chief interest is in head–voice and the use of falsetto. French vocal orientation contrasts revealingly here with Italian. In the middle–to–late fifteenth century, Zabern wrote:[23]

A particularly striking crudity is that of singing the high notes with a loud tone, indeed with full lung power.... The lower notes are to be sung entirely from the chest [with full resonance, he implies], the middle ones with moderate strength, the high ones with a soft voice.

... Sing with a delicate tone in the upper register.... In this fashion one can also sing without fatigue and can sing higher than would be possible with full voice.

Finck wrote:[24]

... the higher a voice rises the quieter and lovelier should the note be sung. The more it descends, the richer the sound ...

Once again we are made aware of the effects of native language on singing techniques:[25]

Note: In French, accents are of height and length. They are not essentially dynamic. Therefore, the equation of height with softness. Furthermore, the forward placement of the sound virtually precludes the use of a pleasantly loud dynamic in the higher register of the voice. The lower registers are

---

[22] Ibid., p. 131 and 136–40, and passim
[23] Quoted by Stewart, as translated by MacClintock (15) and Dyer (219), op. cit., p. 131
[24] Quoted by Stewart, as translated by MacClintock (62), loc. cit.
[25] Loc. cit.

naturally fuller. In his observation on delicacy of tone combined with upward extension of the range, Conrad implies the use of falsetto for specially high passages. Easy bridging of the register gap is characteristic of French singing as well as of the French language.

Maffei wrote:[26]

> I say that even though the deep and the high voices are different from the large and the small, that is no reason why they should not exist together, for it often happens that the same voice is large and deep, large and high, deep and small, high and small.

Stewart comments:[27]

> ... although Caccini is unduly harsh on the falsetto sound (to him synonymous with a high, weak and breathy sound), he clearly reflects Maffei's view that a voice should be dynamically flexible in its entire range. This is a basic characteristic of the Italian language: accents are of a dynamic nature, whatever the height.

Caccini and the sixteenth-century theorists, hoping for future developments, were also commenting on past and present practices, some but certainly not all of which they endorsed. They did not always agree; no doubt they posed and postulated at times, like critics and writers of any age. The Florentine *Camerata* is an example: it began to meet *c*1580 and existed for about fifteen years, aiming to search the past for Classical Graeco-Roman traditions in music and the arts generally. It was a scholarly yet progressive and reforming group, of which Caccini was a member; its ideal was taken from the Ancient Greeks, 'seeing that in every science and every art we are enlightened by writings'.[28] Plato and Aristotle advocated voices which were neither too sharp nor too dull, but clear, even, moderate and flexible.

Nevertheless, the *Camerata* theorists depended on the written word, like all researchers before the era of recorded sound. In their case, they had to decipher problematical manuscripts; in addition, it is important to remember that, though the Camerata were experimenters, theory preceded practice. Under the umbrella of what we might now call a search for authenticity, this group, perhaps like certain present-day early music researchers, theorists and musical directors, while claiming to seek truth by returning to fundamental practice, seem to have taken the truths which they approved and manipulated them to reflect their own current ideas of reform. Again, as is similarly seen today, the probability is that a small number of singers of Camerata-approved type appeared and re-appeared in musically-fashionable venues, giving the illusion of a widespread and undeniably-established change of technique. It would have seemed like a crusade, but we should reflect, perhaps, that crusades or 'party-lines' are not always well-advised, do not always succeed, and even when they seem successful are not always permanent. One is inclined to wonder how effective a strict party-line in vocal-usage could have been in the various Italian states.

---

[26] MacClintock's translation (41-2), quoted Stewart, loc.cit.
[27] Loc. cit.
[28] Caccini, *Le Nuove Musiche*, (A-R Editions, Inc.), p. 48

Since Caccini was a famous tenor singer, his outlook may have paralleled the vocal ambitions of some of today's singers of all voice–types in that he may have been promoting his own vocal characteristics, interests and strengths. His own head–voice might have been weaker than he would have wished; consequently, he not only advised singers against the use of that vocal area but also carefully pitched his songs within the limits of the fundamental tenor voice so that it need not be employed. There is a sprinkling of F4s in the collection, most of which are no longer than a quaver in length. (It is even possible that a few songs, like 'Fortunato augellino', could have been sung up an octave in head–voice alone by established high–voice singers who ignored Caccini's edict, or by castrati; at this pitch it is extremely effective.)

The *Camerata* were decidedly against polyphonic music, because it neither renders words with clarity nor expresses emotion with enough subtlety or impact. One of their aims was to imitate Greek tragedy, using music of a style which allowed for maximum clarity of words and 'natural' delivery. Jacopo Peri wrote:[29]

> I am convinced that the ancient Greeks and Romans (who, according to many, sang their tragedies in their entirety) had used a harmony surpassing that of ordinary speech, but falling so far below the melody of song as to take an intermediate form ... I thought that this kind of speech ... lying between the slow and suspended movements of song and the swift and rapid movements of speech could be adapted to my purpose.

The first composers of opera, like Caccini and Peri, though singers themselves, were not really attempting to glorify the art of singing in their music for the theatre. Speech–song (*parlar cantando*) which they employed for their own interpretation of the Orpheus story, for example, served rather to intensify the drama for the audience. Of course, each singer–interpreter had to possess great vocal ability, as Della Valle wrote:[30]

> In order to be in a position to express the desired feelings, to make the sense of the words clear, to be able by the timbre and inflexion of the voice to indicate charm, grief, tenderness or boldness.

This drama–music ideal was to produce in a short time at least one masterpiece, Monteverdi's *Orfeo* (1607), which shows convincingly that the '*rappresentativo*' style was suited to the creation and maintenance of dramatic tension throughout an extended work.

However, for lesser composers, sustained dramatic intensity was to prove too demanding, and for the public too unentertaining. Instead, dramas were created which were purely visual works, with hundreds of singers and actors, many theatrical effects and extravagant scenery. In 1642, Monteverdi himself was to achieve the apotheosis of this in probably his greatest opera, *L'Incoronazione de Poppea*.

Various commentators have felt that the *parlar cantando* style of Peri and Caccini led directly to that of Monteverdi, appointed *Maestro di Cappella* at St Mark's, Venice in 1613, and that this music–drama ideal evoked his masterpiece *L'Orfeo* of 1607. They argue that this important work demonstrates convincingly that the *rappresentativo* style was in fact suitable

---

[29] In the Foreword to his opera *Euridice*, 1600
[30] Pietro Della Valle, *Discourse on the Music of our Time*

for the creation and maintenance of dramatic tension throughout an extended work. But this style needed an extra touch of genius and a sense of theatre, as Robbins Landon points out:[31]

> *Orfeo*, though of course owing its physical existence to the efforts of the Florentine 'camerata', is a far cry from the earlier music of Peri and Caccini. When the thrilling trumpet toccata which opens *Orfeo* first sounded at Mantua on the 22nd February, 1607, the cognoscenti (led by the hereditary Prince Francesco) knew that they were hearing a new kind of opera: instead of Peri's thin accompaniment of harpsichord and two or three strings, there was a rich a mighty orchestra, some forty strong; choruses delighted the ear and ballets the eye; Florentine recitative, Gabrieli–like intermediums for wind–band, songful ariosos and madrigalian choral textures succeeded one another with breathtaking virtuosity.

For the rest of the seventeenth century, opera would remain affected by the concept of *dramma in musica*, with its music largely subordinated to the text. At the start of the next century, a change was to take place: bel canto opera, in which male and female singers would become, in the manner familiar today, the central features in musical theatre, had arrived. Composer and librettist would provide music and words with which star soloists could communicate to their audience myriad emotions by the subtlety of their execution, coloratura and carefully ordered gesture. The balance between spectacle and plot, recitative and song, was to move to other extremes and the old *Camerata* ideal forgotten. The audience would flock to hear beautiful singing, above all, and the singer became dictator. Yet certain aspects of *Camerata*–thought were to survive, in which essential human qualities could be revealed on the stage. Gluck's *Orfeo* was to reflect this, in 1762.

We may discern that the restraint which certain Renaissance theorists and composers sought to impose on secular singing was probably patchy in its effects and, in time, it fell away. The full potential of the human voice in all its varieties, ranges, colours and registers, could not remain suppressed for long; if indeed they were suppressed as much as has been supposed.

Stewart's paper, referred to earlier, encapsulates previously–missed aspects of early singing techniques; though, like several other musicologists or writers considered in this book, we might question a few of her conclusions. She concludes, for example, that the Franco/Flemish contratenor and alto voices of Josquin's period (1445–1521) were closely related, but distinct. She may be correct, but the thrust and detail of her interpretation and reasoning do no more than point to *specialisations* within the seemingly kaleidoscopical male vocal ranges and timbres during the late fifteenth and early sixteenth centuries. Because both Stewart's suggested 'contratenor' and 'alto' used extensive head–voice or falsetto, we may feel that here are what would later be termed 'high contra' and 'low contra' (eventually changed in England to 'counter'), and later still, first altus or alto and second altus or alto. She suggests that 'the psychological starting and return points' for alto would be falsetto; for contratenor it would be the fundamental or basic–voice. She confirms that both alto and contratenor types used two registers as the norm, but fails to explain why the alto or (eventual) contralto part or voice is so termed. Study of her chart of male voice–ranges (1450–1550)[32] is recommended:

---

[31] H.C. Robbins Landon, *Music in Venice* (Thames and Hudson, 1991), p. 80
[32] Stewart, op. cit., p. 105

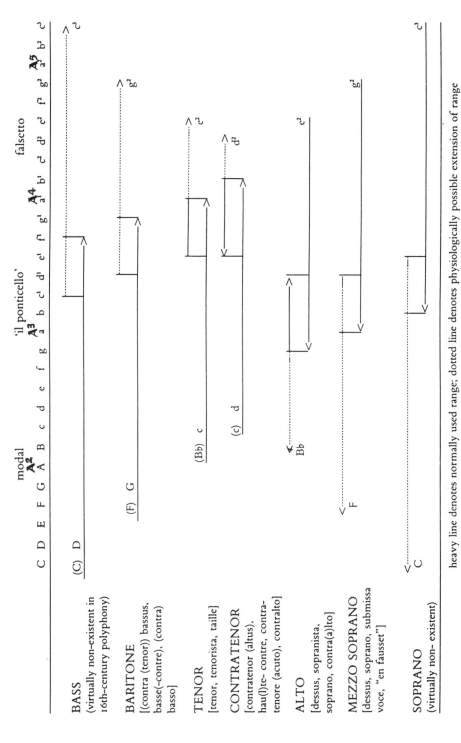

An Explanation of Male Vocal Ranges, applied to Polyphony, 1450–1550

These male voice ranges are shown exactly as she gives them. The soprano is falsetto–based, and does not refer to castrati.

Referring to the above chart, Stewart has since written:[33]

> Of course, other factors are important, such as early training, later training in both registers, the thickness of the vocal folds, even one's native language. (I have a sixteen–year–old mutated soprano who has had to learn to speak in a non-'North Holland' manner just in order to preserve his flexibility in the higher register. His speaking voice is of a low baritone nature.... In this part of the Netherlands the men speak with much air and force – hence the lack of higher falsettists.)

Stewart's chart confirms that there should be no artificial limiting of vocal range. Thus, the suggestion of extreme restriction, often perpetrated by some musicologists and musical directors today when justifying certain performance practices in early music, would seem to have no justification. The contemporaneous directives and pronouncements of Maffei, Vicentino, Caccini and Zacconi, taken at face value, do not seem to have applied in France and the Low Countries. The fact that Josquin's later works show more Italian influence, and require a more Italian technique, should not obscure matters.[34] Many of the best singers in Italy at that time were Flemish or Franco–Flemish.

Some of the vocal ranges which Stewart so usefully demonstrates may occasion surprise in some quarters. It becomes apparent that in the Low Countries and in other parts of continental Europe the male vocal scene was part of an extremely comprehensive system with a complexity which does not seem to have existed in England to the same degree. Despite this, it might still be argued that, during the Late Renaissance period and beyond, the various Italian city states, North and South, stood firmly together in their avoidance and dislike of male head–voice and falsetto (though they differed from other European practice). If this was indeed the case (however unlikely it may now seem), the impact of the castrati's arrival must have changed thinking and practice fundamentally. That they used an extensive vocal range and myriad vocal colours is undeniable.

It seems far more likely that castrato vocal technique was an apotheosis of an already existing methodology and pedagogy. (Coryate's account of the Venetian falsettist strongly suggests this was so.) The methodology would seem to have included the use of pure head–voice.

In England, Renaissance ideas such as architectural Classicism took late root: and, though far–reaching and influential, did not remain omnipotent for long. But even the survival of the Gothic in English architecture, in parallel with Classicism, is not in itself a reason to equate the counter–tenor, and the tradition of male voice production from which he emerged, as simply an analogue or vocal equivalent of the Medieval Gothic: a vocal phenomenon which, in the years after the Renaissance continued in England alone while the rest of the continent developed vocal production rather differently.

From her researches, Stewart concludes that, largely owing to physiological factors, the average French male voice was (and is) a high baritone; the Italian's voice was what we would now call a tenor; the Flemish singer a lower baritone; and the German and English singer was

---

[33] Stewart, in letter to the author, 11 April 1992
[34] Stewart, op. cit., pp. 167–8, and passim

and is more likely to be a low baritone or bass.[35] Some of her conclusions are perhaps surprising. Undoubtedly, she is referring to the fundamental voice. (Incidentally, she not only seems to endorse the viewpoint that the boy high treble was a phenomenon confined to England,[36] but also to confirm that high treble singing was common in Franco–Flemish choir schools.)[37]

Her understanding and summary of the origin and timbres of falsetto, and the mechanisms which cause it, and of resonators, are slightly at odds with the author's views and seemingly those of some others; however, she notes the influence which native language has on singing:[38]

> Italian language requires ... steady ... constant resonance during speech; the French language requires ... ebb and flow of resonance. Given the same vocal fold length, therefore, an Italian tenor will prefer to continue singing in his more resonant modal register for as long as possible before going into his falsetto, while the French tenor will use his 'ebb' to cross over into his less resonant falsetto at a lower point.

Even Richard Miller, the arch–opponent of the use of falsetto, admits that, in the modern French school of singing, 'the falsetto sometimes comprises the entire upper range of the tenor voice, and a considerable portion of the upper range of the light baritone, as well'.[39]

Stewart agrees that the French haute–contre, who like many counter–tenors today, used light fundamental plus falsetto, sang with bright tone and a rather highly–positioned larynx, tilted forward. This technique lightens the tension of *musculus vocalis*. It helps the *crico–thyroid* muscles to stretch the vocal folds, thus facilitating an earlier passage into falsetto. As long as the dynamic level is moderate, and rather bright and forward vowels are produced, movement into falsetto is easy and unobtrusive.

This is yet another indication that obsession with the upper extension of basic–voice, helped by a fixed, low–positioned larynx during phonation, is a much later phenomenon. It produced the *voix sombrée*, or 'sombre voice' (a useful descriptive term) which seems to have originated in the nineteenth century.

Though our chief interest is in head–voice, we should not overlook the entirely proper importance attached to fundamental voice. Reference to it often brings forth comment on the other vocal registers. Donington's discussion[40] of vocal matters in early music is an important and useful, though sometimes contradictory, source of information. In summing up, he writes:

> There can be no *bel canto* without an excellent chest voice to colour the bottom register and to blend upwards into the medium and head registers above.

---

[35] Ibid., p. 103
[36] Ibid., p. 106
[37] Ibid., p. 125
[38] Ibid., p. 103
[39] Richard Miller, *English, French, German and Italian Techniques of Singing* (Scarecrow Press, Metuchen, NJ), p. 108
[40] Robert Donington, *The Interpretation of Early Music* (Faber, repr. 1975), pp. 516–526

If his interpretation of the following passage (using square brackets) is correct, it demonstrates Monteverdi's attitude to the use of all vocal registers:

> A fine voice, strong and long [sustained] and singing in the chest, he reached all places [in the voice] very well'.[41]

Another revealing passage concerning Monteverdi's vocal style and the operatic taste of the time, comes from Harman and Milner:[42]

> *Poppea* ... although it was much admired for the brilliance of its characterization, its genuine passion, and the quality of its music, operatic taste, whetted by typical Venetian fare, preferred the sensuousness of pure melody, the excitement of coloratura (virtuoso) singing, and the fascination of gorgeous and variegated spectacles to the more profound, subtle, and hence less easily appreciated (or created) art, wherein music and drama achieve some kind of balance.

A testimonial which dates from the middle of the eighteenth century reminds us that the basic principles of early vocal technique had continued over centuries: ' [Paita's tenor voice] would not have been by nature so fine and even, if he himself, through art, had not known how to join the chest voice with the head voice.'[43]

Stewart's view seems mostly to agree with those of the present author: that (many) heavy bass voices and certainly the heavy tenor vocal types we know today are usually ineffective falsettists – if they possess tenable falsetto or head–voice at all. It must be admitted, however, that some 'real' basses are able to engage the pharyngeal register. The largest vocal folds have a correspondingly generous capability (when they lose a third of their length) to produce a large, natural falsetto, but certain basses possess enough elasticity in the *vocalis* muscles to thin them to help produce good, ringing, pharyngeal tone. Once again, we are reminded of the dangers of attempting to lay down hard rules about the essential versatility and unpredictability of human vocal physiology.

It seems fair to suggest that voices not only evolved but were trained to sing existing voice parts; yet one problem today concerns our perception and expectation. As previously noted, when considering many medium voice ranges in music scores, our eyes see a part which stays mainly in the area C3–C4/D4, but which comes out of it to explore a relatively high tessitura up to B4. But the fifteenth–century contratenor who dwelt happily in what we think of as the regions of the chest–voice, and moved from this into falsetto when necessary, is certainly not the lyric tenor of today.

Alto singers who spent most of their time in head–voice (though the range may not have been much higher than contratenor), but occasionally moved into chest–voice where necessary, were (and still are) of much the same vocal type as the earlier contra–tenor. To an extent, the singer chose (and can still choose) his ground.

---

[41] Donington, op. cit., p. 523, quoting Monteverdi's letter of 9 June 1610 to the Duke of Mantua

[42] Alec Harman and Anthony Milner, *Late Renaissance and Baroque Music*: Man and his Music (Barrie and Jenkins, 1988), p. 388

[43] Joachim Quantz, *Autobiography (1754)* in Marpurg's *Historische–kritische Beytrage, I* (Berlin, 1755), pp. 231–2

12 Feigned Voice: Tosi and Garcia

Francesco Tosi (1653–1732), in his important *Opinioni de'cantori antichi e moderni*, shows what had happened to Caccini's recommendation to avoid the feigned voice, after a generation – or three. This Italian singer, teacher and author answers the objections to the use of 'feigned'; both the term and voice.

Our largest quotation is from 'Observations for One who Teaches a Soprano'. That observations for this voice should open his treatise is not surprising, because he was a castrato singer. Though he was a contralto, not a soprano, his treatise dates from when the castrato coloratura soprano was undisputed emperor of singers. The English version of Tosi's work is notably entitled *Observations on the Florid Song*, but the treatise seems to be suitable, and intended, for singers of all voice types. It was certainly popular. In the English version (published in 1743), the original was not only translated by John Ernest Galliard ('Mr G'), but commented on by him, at intervals, in clearly–identified paragraphs. So we have two levels or varieties of explanation apparently only twenty years apart. (The useful observations of Michael Pilkington, the modern editor, make a third level.)

Tosi was born in 1653. Since his book was first published as late as 1723, it reflects a lifetime of experience as well as an inheritance of an established tradition. He travelled much, sang and taught widely, and worked in England for some time; all this underlines the importance to us of this treatise.

A   *Tosi (1. 21)* A diligent Master, knowing that a [castrato] soprano, without the Falsetto, is constrained to sing within the narrow compass of a few notes, ought not only to endeavour to help him to it, but also to leave no Means untried, so to unite the feigned and the natural voice that they may not be distinguished; for if they do not perfectly unite, the Voice will be of diverse Registers and must consequently lose its beauty. The extent of the full natural voice terminates generally on the fourth–space C, or on the fifth–line D, and there the feigned voice becomes of use, as well in going up to the high notes as returning to the natural voice: the difficulty consists in uniting them. Let the master therefore consider of what moment the correction of this defect is, which ruins the scholar if he overlooks it. Among the women one hears sometimes a soprano entirely *di petto*, but among the male sex it would be a great rarity, should they preserve it after having past the age of puberty. Whoever would be curious to discover the feigned voice of one who has the art to disguise it, let him take notice that the artist sounds the vowel 'i' ['ee'] or 'e' ['ay'] with more strength and less fatigue than the vowel 'a' ['ah'], on the high notes.

Pilkington In referring to 'lines' and 'spaces', Tosi is using the soprano clef (*c* on the bottom line), not the treble. He clearly considers the falsetto a normal part of the male voice, as did most eighteenth–century teachers. In referring to sopranos who sing entirely '*di petto*' he is thinking of women not men, who can sometimes (as Nares and others suggest) blend the two registers 'so as to be imperceptible'. The vowel sounds referred to by Tosi are of course Italian.[44]

B   *Tosi (1. 18)* Let the master attend with great care to the voice of the scholar, which, whether it be *di petto* or *di testa*, should always come forth neat and clear ...

Galliard[45] *Voce di petto* is a full voice, which comes from the breast by strength, and is the most sonorous and impressive. *Voce di testa* comes more from the throat than from the breast and is capable of more volubility. Falsetto is a feigned voice which is entirely formed in the throat, has more volubility than any, but [is] of no substance.

C   *Tosi (1. 20)* Many masters put their scholars to sing the contralto not knowing how to help them to the falsetto, or to avoid the trouble of finding it.

Pilkington It seems clear that 'falsetto' means the same as '*di testa*', and that most singing teachers of the time agreed. James Nares, writing later in the century, maintained that 'after the scholar has gained good intonation, and some management of his voice, the master should make him acquainted with the compass of his voice, showing him where his *voce di petto* ends, and where to cultivate the falsetto or *voce di testa*, and instruct him how they should be joined, so as to be imperceptible, without which the pleasing variety will be lost.' (*A Treatise on Singing*, London *c*1780.)[46]

D   *Tosi (1. 22)*[47] The *voce di testa* has a great volubility, more of the high than the lower notes, and has a quick shake [= trill], but [is] subject to be lost for want of strength.

One could spend much time discussing the full implications of the above; but we must content ourselves with a few observations.

1 Tosi and Galliard's '*voce di testa*' seems to be our pharyngeal or middle–falsetto; see B and D.
2 Galliard's understanding of '*falsetto*' is of a voice produced similarly to '*voce di*

[44] Pier Francesco Tosi, *Opinioni de' cantori antichi e moderni*, 1723; trans. Galliard, (London, 1743) as *Observations on Florid Song*, ed. Pilkington (Stainer and Bell, 1987), p. 6
[45] Ibid., p. 5
[46] Ibid., pp. 5–6
[47] Ibid., p. 6

testa', but termed '*feigned voice*' because it is totally weightless and '*voluble*'. '*Feigned*' could equal '*false*', because it is assessable as a sensation disconnected from normal, bodily vibration; see B. This seems to equate with our '*upper–falsetto*' or pipe-voice. It also parallels Caccini's dislike of it (apparently, though he does not say so exactly, on the grounds that, because it is disembodied in tone, it is *ipso facto* unnatural). He also objected to it on other grounds.

3 Nares (1780) reiterates Tosi's stressing of the importance of joining and using both 'head' and 'chest' (*di testa* and *di petto*) in an effective way; see A and C.

4 It would appear that (Tosi's) feigned voice was expected to be used alone for certain high passages, for Tosi talks of its disguise and discovery; see A.

5 Though Galliard does not agree with B, some might argue that '*feigned voice*', often used as a convenient alternative blanket–term for 'falsetto', might well include both *voce di testa* and (upper) *falsetto*. It is therefore an unfortunate generic term. Certainly, it is possible that earlier, loose usage of the term '*feigned voice*' has been, and still is, responsible for regrettable misunderstanding. Caccini's dictats, taken at face value, affect certain well–meaning but sometimes mistaken musical directors and singers today. Unfortunately, most do not seem to be as familiar with Tosi's.

6 Tosi discusses briefly the range of the full natural voice, and that of the feigned voice; see A. Though his references appear to be to notes of the soprano clef, it is interesting that, taken at our tenor pitch (with a treble clef transposed one octave down), Tosi's 'C or D' fit well with the changeover area for most through–voice counter–tenors of today. We should note that Tosi considered the use of falsetto important for non–castrato students – i.e., the great majority of singers.

7 Pilkington's note after A is thought–provoking. Writing in the twentieth century, he obviously expects women to blend registers, 'end on', as it were; but does not expect the need to arise for male singers in the same way. For them, instead of the 'dovetail', he assumes the 'spliced joint'. Also, he seems to overlook the fact that castrati extensively used falsetto too: a common misunderstanding today.

8 Though the idea was known in the eighteenth century, we must surely smile at the idea of the '*natural*' voice in a castrato (A), because the castrato's condition is so inherently artificial.

9 In A, Tosi notes the rarity (or its rare employment) in the eighteenth century of the entirely *di petto* (chest, or fundamental) voice by male singers; presumably these included the castrato soprano, though Pilkington seems to have overlooked this possibility.

Much hinges on the meaning of falsetto and falsettist. As seen earlier, this particular problem of definition is not confined to discussion of the Renaissance period. For example, René Jacobs's interpretation of falsettist is of a voice which employs falsetto exclusively and does not use basic–register. The Baroque falsettist, he argues, was strictly an ecclesiastical singer, a *voce finta*: a feigned or unnatural voice. He confirms that if a falsettist develops and uses his chest–register to blend with and overlap his falsetto, he is no longer a falsettist with a feigned voice but (referring to Bacilly[48]) a 'natural' voice and, therefore, a counter–tenor.[49]

---

[48] Benigne de Bacilly, *Remarques Curieuses sur l'Art de Bien Chanter* (Paris, 1679), quoted by Jacobs in 'The Controversy Concerning the Timbre of the Countertenor', p. 295. See also Mary Cyr, 'On performing 18th–century Haute–contre Roles', *The Musical Times*, 1974, pp. 291–5

Jacobs's views are those of an excellent counter–tenor singer, conductor and knowledgeable theorist. It is easy to be sympathetic with them; they are persuasive when studied in their entirety. There are, of course, a few points about which we may disagree. One is that, after much experience of hearing fine, natural–toned, almost quasi–chest pharyngeal–register singing, it is difficult to accept the idea that *only* if this is linked to and employed with the fundamental voice (a joint not 'spliced' but 'dovetailed'), can the singer be considered a counter–tenor, not a *voce finta* or feigned voice.

The highest male voice, which includes but certainly does not consist solely of, upper–falsetto (presumably 'feigned' voice), approximates in pitch to many medium female voices. It frequently exceeds them tonally, and in carrying power. In late Renaissance Italy, women's voices were beginning to be welcomed in selected secular circumstances. This process continued and developed in the seventeenth century. During the eighteenth century, as the castrati waned, women's voices were to become equal in favour to those of men in various European countries. How likely is it that a skilled and often powerful male voice or mode of production, in certain respects at least broadly comparable with that of women, would be that which was warned against or dismissed by various Renaissance (and later) writers and theorists? (In most such warnings, there is no accusation of effeminacy. There are, however, criticisms of vocal unreliability, feebleness, and falseness.) When used alone, can the glorious, developed, often powerful ringing of a properly–trained and produced head–voice, which includes pharyngeal register (capable of strong low range, yet also high) really be that warned against, or dismissed, as a 'feigned voice'? Is it likely? Surely not.

However, Jacobs's arguments, albeit mostly concerned with the Baroque period (though late–Renaissance and early–Baroque overlap), are persuasive. Certain early theorists and musical commentators can be interpreted, collectively, as forming a basis for his view. Of course, interpretation, etymology and philology of past and present words, like statistics, have a habit of being 'all things to all men'. They can sometimes be used to support diametrically opposed arguments.

After carefully considering variously–dated descriptions of the feigned voice, it seems possible now to venture some definitions. It was perhaps a term used either for (i) a soft, undeveloped falsetto, or (ii) a falsetto used with poor technique (for example, with wasted breath), or (iii) the employment of upper–falsetto too low in the singer's vocal compass to be effective, or (iv) a combination of these. Though often vaguely pleasant in timbre, there is indeed an unnatural quality, a falseness, about all these, certainly enough to cause Caccini's strong recommendation to avoid them. A fifth possibility is that 'feigned' equals a voice 'substituted' for a soprano (castrato or female). Clearly, Giovanni Camillo Maffei, in his *Lettere* on singing (1562; the first knowledgeable account of singing) considered feigned voice as a vocal effect produceable by a bass who was able to 'feign' or simulate a voice called falsetto as a substitute for a soprano 'per mancamento di soprano fingesse la voce, chiamata falsetto.'[50] This is not the same as an accusation of effeminacy.

There are, in fact, many references to the tonal quality of a feigned voice as being attractive. Reviewers and ear–witnesses of the past by no means always used the term as one of abuse – often just the opposite; so 'with feigned voice' was not automatically an insulting

---

[49] René Jacobs, op. cit., p. 305

[50] Nanio Bridgman, 'Giovanni Camillo Maffei et sa lettre sur le chant', *R & M* (1956), 3; repr. in English in *Readings in the History of Music in Performance*, ed. Carol McClintock (Indiana, 1979)

description of a technique, or of a singer. Indeed, the words 'feigned' and 'fiction' appear to be close in meaning, but they are not, philologically. *Musica Ficta* appears to denote 'feigned music', for we think of the modern meaning of 'fiction', actually a sub–meaning. The word's primary meaning is 'formed, fashioned, adjusted': a perfect term to denote a musical device or interpretation. We should therefore consider, by its context, whether or not an earlier writer who uses 'feigned voice' is concerned to deprecate, or merely to acknowledge, a commonly used and accepted vocal technique.

Sometimes, changes in spelling can muddle matters. Derivation and exact meaning can be obscured. English orthography was far from standardized until the later nineteenth century. 'Fain', for example, is defined by *Chambers's Etymological Dictionary* (1959) as: 'glad or joyful: content for want of better (to): compelled (to) ... gladly. 'Fane' is defined as 'a temple', or shrine – an ancient place of worship. Who can be sure that all users of the term 'feigned voice' in the past meant what we now might think they meant?

However, the most useful point of all which could be made when associating 'feigned' with 'voice' concerns a probable confusion not yet considered here, but long established, widely acquiesced in and promoted until misunderstanding was and is still almost complete. We have already noted that obscurity, mis–reading and misunderstanding is sometimes the result of faulty translation (as in Tosi, which is in English mediated to us only via Galliard), or because of subsequent shifts in meanings and usage. In other circumstances, the association may happen through apparent misunderstanding by a widely influential, comparatively recent authority whose views and writings, and those authorities of his persuasion, still affect us today. Tosi's work has long been familiar only to historians, musicologists and early–music specialists (though this situation is changing). By contrast, the work of the nineteenth–century vocal authority, Manuel Garcia (1805–1906), because of his long life and his books (on which most modern vocal teaching is based) and because of his important invention of the laryngo-scope in about 1840 – indeed his pivotal position which looked back to earlier practice and forward to modern vocal pedagogy – is very familiar today to all involved in the sustained study of the voice. Garcia's researches into vocal physiology and technique[51] in the middle of the nineteenth century were not only highly influential, but – as with Darwin's theories in *The Origin of Species* (1853) – any major questioning of his findings is still highly inadvisable; both works will always retain their important places in history.

Garcia's *Traité*, in its English version, begins[52] by revealing that he broadly confirms historical practice and usage but later he made some significant differences which were to influence future vocal pedagogy heavily. Of particular significance for us, he first states that, in both male and female, the falsetto lies *between* chest- and head–voices – that is:

Head (voce di testa)
Falsetto (faussetto)
Chest (voce di petto)

It seems highly significant, bearing in mind the adjustments in perceptions of vocal pedagogy and practice by the late nineteenth century, that in 1895 Garcia revised his listed order as on the next page:

---

[51] Notably *Memoire sur la voix humaine* (1840) and *Traité complet de la chant* (1847)
[52] *The Art of Singing*, pp. 3–4

Falsetto
Head
Chest

During the course of his paper, 'The Controversy Concerning the Timbre of the Countertenor' (1983),[53] the first few pages of which are concerned with Garcia, René Jacobs explored the significance of Garcia's first listed order, and other related matters. (Our particular reason for quoting Jacobs, rather than Garcia himself in this instance, and noting Jacobs's citing of von Zabern and de Moravia, will become apparent in due course.)

Jacobs refers to the original French version of Garcia's *Traité*:

> According to Garcia, men and women have the same registers: the *voix pleine* or *voix de poitrine* (hereby noted 'Vdp'); the *voix de fausset* ('Vdf'); and the *voix de tête* ('Vdt'). Although men have a much more developed chest voice than women, women have a greater developed head voice. The middle register of both, however, the Vdf, is very similar.

Jacobs's paper provides pitch and ranges, but this diagram should suffice here:

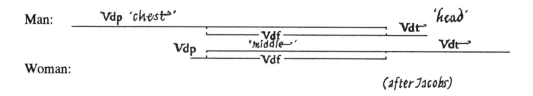

Man:

Woman:

(after Jacobs)

Jacobs continues:

> There is a 'break' between the Vdp and the Vdf because different mechanisms correspond to the two registers. But, between the Vdf and the Vdt the pass–agio is smooth and less problematic – both registers correspond to the same mechanism, so there is only a change of resonance. Thus at the end of his life Garcia spoke of two registers (the Vdp and the *voix de fausset–tête* ('Vdf–t') instead of three.[54]

[Therefore: Falsetto–head
            Chest   – the implications for twentieth–century modes of thought and vocal pedagogy are obvious, as is the misunderstanding on which they are based.]

Centuries before Garcia, Conrad von Zabern in *De modo bene cantandi choralem cantum* (Mainz, 1474) wrote that a good singer uses his voice in three degrees ('trivarie'): 'resonantly' (*grossius*) and 'trumpet–like' (*tubalius*)

---

[53] In particular, pp. 290–1

[54] Manuel Garcia, *Traité complet* ..., preface to vol. 1: 'Rapport sur le memoire de M. Garcia presenté a l'Academie des Sciences' (Paris, 1857), pp. xii, 8 and 11

for low notes, 'moderately' (*medio modo*) in the middle range, and 'more delicately' (*subtilius*) for the high notes – even more so the higher the chant ascends ... An organ whether large, moderate or small in size has three kinds of pipes: large, medium, and small. The large pipes sound the lower notes of the chant, the medium–size ones the middle notes and the little ones the upper notes of the chant. The sound (resonant, medium, and high–pitched or delicate) of these tubes or pipes can be said to be threefold. Since, however, a man has only a single windpipe through which the voice passes, which must supply for the diversity of the many organ pipes, some large and some small, how mistaken it would be to attempt to imitate the diversity by a uniform use of the voice[55] ('uniformae vocis usus': the twentieth–century ideal of some teachers, the *Einregister*). [Once again we meet the monochrome dream.]

The *vox plena* or *valida*, *vox media* and *vox subtiliata* termed by von Zabern correspond respectively to the *vox pectoris*, *vox gutturis* and the *vox capitis* described by Hieronymus De Moravia, the first writer on the voice to connect resonance changes with registers.[56] I am convinced that Garcia's *voix de fausset* is referring to the *vox gutturis*: *fausset*, often written in the eighteenth century as *faucet*, derived from the Latin *fauces* meaning throat, not from *falsus*.

In considering the relationship of 'falsus' with 'falsetto', and therefore 'false' with 'feigned', as suggested earlier, use of the term 'feigned–voice' seems to have been based originally on a philological confusion which bred a simplistic, misleading and mistaken conclusion in which the 'real' voice is contrasted with the 'false' voice. The inference is clear.

It is significant that the American and Canadian word for 'tap' is 'faucet'. There are obvious links with 'fauces' – which means the area between the mouth cavity and the pharynx. The term 'throat' voice, i.e., a voice between 'chest' and 'head', must then have seemed a logical even if now we might consider it unfortunate because the throat is actually a narrow tube and the image this presents to the singer is psychologically unhelpful. However, apart from this psychological drawback, the image of the faucet is useful for our purposes. If the reader imagines a normal tap (or the faucet itself, actually a fireman's tap on the street, or the tap in a barrel) in side–section, there is a clear resemblance to a throat and mouth (albeit with drooping lips!) above which is a 'head' topped by a twistable 'handle' used to turn the tap on and off. The easy flow of water (or beer) through the faucet resembles the basic movement of air through the fauces, in speaking and singing, though the use of the other cranial cavities is here discounted for the sake of convenience.

Garcia's complete text, if examined carefully, though continuing to mislead in its own interpretation of 'falsetto', actually reinforces the likelihood that the seeming dismissal of all falsetto or feigned voice by some Renaissance theorists was not as it might seem. Their understanding of these terms was not Garcia's. What today is generally known as falsetto –

[55] Karl–Werner Gumpel, *Die Musiktraktate Conrade von Zabern* (Mainz–Wiesbaden, 1956), trans. into English by Joseph Dyer in *Early Music*

[56] Hieronymous de Moravia, *Tractatus de musica*, (Regensburg–Freiburg, 1934), vol. 2 (*Freiburger Studien zur Musikwissenschaft 2*), trans. into German by Bernhard Ulrich, *Die Grundsatze der Stimmbildung wahrend der A–cappella–Periode und der Zeit des Aufkommens der Oper 1474–1640* (Leipzig, 1910), p. 93

since the mid–nineteenth–century, any mode which does not employ fundamental voice – was probably the *voce mezzana* or the medium register, possibly linked, 'end–on' or 'dove–tailed', with the fundamental voice – a technique used with great success, for example, by John Whitworth. The head–voice referred to by the Renaissance theorists was probably upper falsetto or 'pipe–voice', used alone, inappropriately, or badly.

Regarding the question of the 'natural' voice in singing or speaking, in drama or opera, Barry Humphries, as the comic character Dame Edna Everage, has proved it possible to speak strongly and convincingly in *voce mezzana*; that is, in his pharyngeal or medium register.

We have seen that the whole Renaissance movement was essentially a revival which aimed to displace what was considered a long and regrettable period of barbarism which had followed the collapse of Classical civilization. Those aspects of the Renaissance which could be considered essentially reformist in spirit and intention might perhaps be compared to influential nineteenth–century thinking in political and social spheres, as well as in those of singing and voice–production.

It is tempting to see the Renaissance theorists, if not the *Camerata*, in political terms: almost as musical equivalents to Karl Marx and his followers. Like him, they theorized, pronounced and sought passionately to influence a scene they considered unsatisfactory and uneven: out of order, out of control and without an acceptable system. Some of Marx's powerful ideas and principles, though never universally accepted, will probably remain to benefit (or even bedevil) mankind, but the strict authoritarian régimes his followers sought to impose could not and may not succeed ultimately. It may have been so with the Renaissance vocal reformers, aspects of whose writings might even be compared, loosely, to the earlier worries, preoccupations and complaints of St Bernard of Clairvaux, Aelred of Rievaulx, and John of Salisbury, in the twelfth and thirteenth centuries; would–be reformers all.

The Renaissance was a new order with the energy of a new broom: the musical glories, intricacies and subtleties of the late Medieval *Ars Nova* were discounted and, to a large extent, dismissed. (An attractive concept for the late twentieth–century mind could be to equate the Renaissance imposition of order, or convergent thinking, with the male ethos, and Medieval High Gothic, or divergent thinking, with that of the female genius, but perhaps nothing is so clear cut!)

Some might even argue that there is a possible parallel between the teeming nineteenth century, with its masses of poor and its powerful capitalist forces, and late Medieval Europe. Certainly, we could relate the aims of the Renaissance theorists with Garcia and other nineteenth–century bringers of a new vocal order, parallel with the sweeping–in of a new age. But humanity does not always react neatly, evenly, predictably and gratefully. The residual and well–tried richness of tradition often survives and triumphs, though influenced and slightly changed for ever.

Some stances taken by the *Camerata* exemplify this process. Apart from their over–restriction of the singer and actor's stage and vocal style, their anti–polyphonic crusade faded. Polyphony was too firmly established to be abolished totally. Monody proved lacking in melodic interest and texture (monody = monotony?) though its influence was never totally lost.

To summarize, there is a strongly–held viewpoint that, on the (apparently) unarguable evidence of the Renaissance theorists, new Italian vocal techniques which banished all secular use of falsetto made a major and permanent break with the medieval past. Some commentators seem to go further. They appear to claim that this sixteenth and early seventeenth–century vocal revolution rivals in impact that of the nineteenth. In fact, the implication is that the sixteenth– and seventeenth–centuries' revolution was the one significant movement which established the basis for the worthwhile male vocal technique which has continued to the present day. Little mention is usually made of the effects or otherwise of this or any vocal revolution on the female voice, and only lip–service is paid to the changes in male voice production which occurred in the 1840s. These changes are regarded as being connected mainly with demands for increased volume, so that 'light' tenors developed into 'heavy' tenors, and similar things happened to other voice–types. Put simply, everyone had to sing louder or be swamped by the orchestra – or they had to retire.

The basis for an opposing view of the impact of the Renaissance on music and voice production seems to have been proposed in a perceptive recent article by Christopher Page. Though he is discussing musical composition rather than vocal performance and technique, he supports the view that the Renaissance, in terms of music, was of less import than in the other arts:[57]

> Now it so happens that musicology is a very young discipline, and like all young things it is independent. For many decades musicologists have been occupied with huge tasks: editing the many hundreds of compositions that have survived from the Middle Ages; tracing the origin and development of various styles; establishing who the composers were and where they worked. As a result, broader questions of cultural history have been neglected.
>
> Musicologists have borrowed the concept of a 'Renaissance' in the fifteenth century from their colleagues working on the history of art and of literature, but does 'the Renaissance' really make sense in the musical context? Most of the truly influential music of the fifteenth century was composed not in Italy, regarded as the cradle of the Renaissance by art–historians, but in Huizinga's 'expiring' Gothic realm of England, France and Flanders. To make matters worse, there is virtually nothing in the history of fifteenth–century music which can be interpreted in terms of a 'rebirth' of classical learning, which is what the concept of a 'Renaissance' is designed to express.

The distance between the two concepts of fifteenth–century Medieval music as either 'a pinnacle of sophistication' or alternatively as 'country–bumpkin' music is vast. Any championing of the incredible achievements of pre-Renaissance music, which must have *overlapped* music of the Renaissance period, implies also a correspondingly high standard of accomplished performance. This further implies that, particularly outside Italy but no doubt also inside it, vocal technique was likely to have continued essentially as before. If this were so, it supports the idea that it is probable that there were no really major changes in voice production principles in Europe until the early decades of the nineteenth century.

Throughout the centuries, though new ideas came and went and were either taken up and absorbed into 'received' knowledge or were discarded or were never established at all, it seems likely that the broad corpus of vocal *modus operandi* stretched and twisted with only minor adjustments from sophisticated late Medieval to the late eighteenth century. Thus, the nineteenth century truly marked the coming of vocal revolution, mainly in the realm of the male voice.

---

[57] Christopher Page, 'A View of the 'Waning' Middle Ages', *Leading Notes* (National Early Music Association), vol. II, no. 2, July 1992, p. 20; based on a chapter in Page, *Discarding Images: Music and Culture in Medieval France* (O.U.P., 1993)

13 The Falsetto Family: the Counter–Tenor and the Tenor

The tone of totally undeveloped falsetto is usually soft, fluty, pleasant and rather weak – the sound popularly associated with the term 'falsetto'.[1] If this vocal capability already has a reasonable upward range, it is most unlikely that falsetto notes below C4 (middle C) will be audible except from close by. The correct training of other vocal areas, however, can help unused falsetto lying above and parallel to them. Many baritones, tenors and lighter tenors may well find a counter–tenor head–voice awaiting use and further development. Such a discovery is thought by most enlightened singing teachers to show that vocal development already achieved is along the correct lines.

Many put it another way, and say that if head or falsetto voice is understood and produced properly, other vocal registers will be produced properly too. Therefore, why is this production so important to other vocal types? How can what seems to be a soft and limited head–voice be developed correctly? How may its tonal potential brighten and widen other ranges and registers?

As suggested earlier, falsetto or 'pure' or head–voice embraces not one register, but two – pharyngeal, or 'middle–falsetto', and 'upper–falsetto'. The latter is easily encountered and produced by most men. Even when it is undeveloped, it makes the singer feel detached and aerified, with a sensation of a position disproportionately higher than the chest- or basic–voice far below. When taken down to C4 (where upper falsetto used alone will be especially weak – that is, in the area where not only pharyngeal but upper chest lie waiting), upper falsetto feels separated from chest by a gulf. The singer has a feeling of buoyant flexibility: he is free to pirouette vocally like a skater on ice. All vocal weight has gone. He exists in the free world of the head.

By contrast, pharyngeal or 'middle falsetto' (sometimes called mezzo–falso), feels quite definitely related to chest–voice, even though in itself it has some falsetto quality. It, and upper chest–voice overlap each other. Pharyngeal voice is the source of the power, edge, ring and essentially masculine timbre of the mature, developed counter–tenor singer. The properly produced tenor voice also uses something of this production, in its mixed state, as should high baritone. Nevertheless, many tenors and baritones are unaware, not only of their employment of it, but of its very existence within them.

As we have previously noted, pharyngeal voice uses the same edges of the vocal folds as does upper falsetto, but the folds are now completely aligned and use is made of about two-

---

[1] From this point, all reference to 'falsetto', or 'head–voice', unless clearly and purposely differentiated between, is used generically, and is intended to denote vocal production which does not involve fundamental register

thirds of their length, taking into account the extension supplied by the abducted arytenoid cartilages. Without the latter, the folds are in fact used along their full length, as opposed to pure upper falsetto, in which approximately one–third is used. Pharyngeal voice requires more diaphragmatic breath support than upper–falsetto. As Anthony Frisell says:[2]

> Its flexibility is limited by its attachment to the chest register, and the physical demands [in] producing it are greater than the detached falsetto and the singer senses both register characteristics in his throat simultaneously'.

Usually, pharyngeal voice cannot be obtained or developed by the beginner, but must be found after full development of upper falsetto *or* properly–produced fundamental voice. The essential character of the whole falsetto range changes with continuous exercising. At first, the original soft, lyric timbre often turns into a rather piercing, sometimes unpleasant sound. The reason is that the first exchange of power from the chest–register has taken place. We then await roundness and polish to join it. Though but a transitory stage, this piercing quality is never completely banished, but is mixed and coloured by other, added qualities. It was nicely termed the 'witch voice' by early Italian singing teachers.

Stainer and Barrett[3] wrote, in an amusing and interesting entry under 'Larynx':

> The Gibbon has a well–developed larynx, and alone of all the apes can sing a complete octave; moreover the quality of its notes is decidedly musical.

They go on to describe and to analyse the constitution of the gibbon's sophisticated cry:

> overpowering and deafening: it consists of a repetition of the syllables oo–ah ... extremely brilliant shake ... quality of notes is very musical.... The gibbon's voice is certainly much more powerful than that of any singer I have heard ... the quality is like that of a very powerful male alto ...

The article possesses material both thought–provoking and humorous. The latter quality may or may not be unintentional but, as Frederic Hodgson noted, it is difficult not to prevent oneself thinking of *This is the Record of John* (especially 'What Art Thou Then?') as sung in (what else?) Gibbons's setting by certain counter–tenors we have heard! Hodgson,[4] always alert for the witty and/or bizarre, brought the author's attention to yet another animal analogy with the counter–tenor; not for the first or last time, humour can make significant points. The following occured in a newspaper article about 'canine songsters' whose efforts evoke various human voice–ranges and types:[5]

> Herbie, yet another Welsh springer [spaniel] ... enjoys watching television. His favourite programme is 'All Creatures Great and Small', but for some reason he never sings to its theme. His voice, a sophisticated counter–tenor, is in the tradition of the Italian opera *castrati*, and he wears a red bandana as he

---

[2] Anthony Frisell, *The Baritone Voice* (Crescendo Publishing Co., Boston USA, 1973), p. 14
[3] Stainer and Barrett, *Dictionary of Musical Terms*, (Novello, c1890), p. 266
[4] In a letter to the author, 6 November 1990
[5] Celia Haddon, 'The Howl Story', *The Daily Telegraph*, 12 October 1991

sings... . This kind of howl is different to a distress howl ... it's a
pack–gathering howl, like the ones used by wolves.

Wolves employ a quite audible 'fundamental' mode of 'voice' from which they click into an
equally audible 'falsetto' mode as the howl ascends in pitch. They raise their heads, presumably
to facilitate a characteristic hollow resonance. The highest vertebrates do not possess vocal
folds in the human fashion (though most mammals do have under–developed larynxes) but
usually possess sinuses which, owing to greatly differing skull forms, vary in size and
character.[6]

When the 'witch voice' is finally tempered, and the full beauty of finished pharyngeal voice
has been revealed,

> the singer acquires security in the area of the register's break, and passing
> from one register to the other (in both ascending and descending directions)
> while maintaining full resonating quality is no longer a problem. The middle-
> falsetto is operative throughout the range.[7]

According to Herbert–Caesari, the term 'pharyngeal–voice' derives from the Italian *voce faringea*, and was used much in the old Italian school of singing to describe the tone of a peculiar
and distinctive mechanism. Its strength and use are that it can be engaged alone, or in
combination with the basic– or chest–voice, or upper falsetto – or, indeed, with both together.
Thus, it is a link and it forges together the chest and upper head–voices: a true 'medium'
register, essential for all voices except, perhaps, for the (falsetto) male soprano. We should
note that Frisell also employs the term 'pharyngeal'.[8] The use of this vocal register is ancient,
certainly three hundred years old, including the bel canto era, but now the knowledge of it,
in 'conventional' singing, seems to be possessed by few; yet most modern counter–tenors often
instinctively use it continually. Some trace of it remained throughout the counter–tenor's long
years in the shadows and the best singers probably used it. Herbert–Caesari wrote in 1951:[9]

> The male alto, heard in churches and choirs in England, employs mainly the
> pharyngeal, which for lack of real schooling never attains, however, perfection
> of development.

We can only assume that, when he wrote this, Herbert–Caesari was unaware of Deller's voice
and technique – at that time it had achieved full maturity – yet, up to the end of the nineteenth
century, Italian tenor and baritone singers were trained to use *voce faringea*. Specialist users
were traditionally known as 'contraltos'. Though apparently not used in England before the
eighteenth century (or much after it), in Italy (and generally) the term 'contralto' could signify
a male or female voice. This male 'contralto' (not the castrato–contralto) was the nominal
descendant of lower contra–tenor altus.

In the first part of the nineteenth century, when male vocal methods and fashion began to
change with some speed, the new generations of secular tenors mostly abandoned this ancient

[6] See E.G.White, *Science and Singing*, 3rd edn (Dent, 1938), pp. 86–96
[7] Anthony Frisell, *The Tenor Voice* (Bruce Humphries, Boston, 1964), p. 23
[8] Frisell, *The Baritone Voice*, p. 22
[9] Herbert–Caesari, *The Voice of the Mind*, 2nd edn (Hale, 1951), p. 337

technique. Those high voices who specialised in it (the majority of whom emanated from an ecclesiastical vocal background, though they also sang elsewhere) were often termed not 'tenors', but 'contraltos'. The higher voices could, and did, sing the alto part in important Italian cathedral and church choirs, like that of the Sistine Chapel. A quotation from Rockstro (1927)[10] follows which discusses the male–soprano range in addition to that of the alto. After commenting that 'the trained soprano falsetto which needs no accident to produce it is not yet extinct', Rockstro added a footnote: '... these (foregoing) statements are founded on information supplied to us by gentlemen resident in Rome, whose high position and long experience render their evidence more than ordinarily trustworthy, and he continued:

> Italian choirmasters draw a careful distinction between the different voices they employ. The Voce bianca [white voice] or *naturale* is by no means uncommon, but produces only contralto singers [i.e., male contralto]. The true adult [male] soprano, *arte fatta* (made by method, i.e., not by operation), is an excessively rare voice, produced rather in the head than in the chest or throat, and lasting, generally, to the astonishment of the uninitiated hearer, who cannot understand its co–existence with a long white beard ...

To this, Rockstro added another footnote: 'In Adami da Bolsena's *Osservazzione* (Roma, 1711) will be found numerous portraits of soprani and contralti with long beards – many of them priests'.

It is well to point out for the benefit of some readers in the last decade of this secularized twentieth century, that reference to church singing here or elsewhere in this work, is not intended to suggest that ecclesiastical singing employment is unimportant, or be dismissive. Until recent decades, considerable and deserved prestige was attached to important professional cathedral or church choral appointments, both in the United Kingdom and abroad. To some extent, this situation still obtains.

It appears likely that the Italian contralti possessed the basic–voices of either 'tenors altino', or were developed 'second–tenors' or 'light baritones', together with full–toned pharyngeal and head development. The title 'counter–tenor' for these singers, it seems, was not used in Italy at that date. (However, see the totally Italian cast in London for Handel's *Admeto* as performed 31 January 1727, page 77). Garcia allowed for a male voice termed 'contraltino', and described it as 'light'. The term 'contralto' seems to have embraced the entire counter–tenor family.

The 'contralto tenor' used a form of falsetto. Herbert–Caesari[11] wrote that the term 'falsetto' was:

> Something applied to ... tenor vocalists because the latter's head–voice was an ad–mixture of pharyngeal and falsetto. When exercised to the maximum (over a period of about four years, depending on the individual voice of course) these two mechanisms, properly amalgamated, are capable of producing a head voice of extraordinary power.

It is worth emphasizing that, by 'falsetto', Herbert–Caesari seems to mean upper–falsetto. He underlines the importance of vocal maturity in the development of the full–range head–voice.

---

[10] W.S.Rockstro, Grove's *Dictionary,* 3rd edn, p. 778
[11] Op. cit., p. 334

The nationality and training of Herbert–Caesari's own teacher seem apposite here. Herbert–Caesari tells us that he was the celebrated Giovan Riccardo Daviesi (1839–1921), the greatest contralto–tenor singer of the Sistine Chapel in the nineteenth century. But there is some puzzlement over Daviesi.[12] Apparently, Daviesi was born in Rome of English parents who died when he was six, leaving him to be brought up in the Ospizio San Michele. He became a singer in St John Lateran; then in the Cappella Giulia, and finally in the Sistina. Frances Killingley[13] comments:

> He also seems to have travelled a lot; he had a triumphant success in England (no particulars about exactly when or where and no mention of him in *The Musical Times* that I could discover). He became, successively, Director of the Conservatory of Irkutsk, and of the Moscow Conservatoire. (We have a lot of Russian material in University of Essex Library – it's one of our specialities – and the Russian departmental librarian and I searched in vain for any trace of a conservatory in Irkutsk. His name does not appear in the list of directors of the Moscow Conservatoire.) A footnote in Herbert Caesari's *Voice of the Mind*, page 336, says he spent seven years in Irkutsk – perhaps he actually spent seven years somewhere he did not want people to know about. It is all very intriguing anyway.

One wonders whether the 'conservatory' in Irkutsk was a modest, semi–private institution? Elsa Scammell adds:[14]

> Daviesi became noted for his teaching; but Domenico Mustafà, [castrato] soprano himself, was without doubt the greatest teacher of singing in the ecclesiastical style in the 19th century. Daviesi, originally an Englishman, [or Welshman?], was presumably a counter–tenor, though listed as contralto in the Sistine list. (Caesari's daughter, Alma, has no other details). Alberto de Angelis copied all this from Schmidl. Caesari must have got his information about Daviesi from the elderly teacher, Mustafà, who had given it to Schmidl.

It is certainly intriguing, not irrelevant nor unique that a musician of English or Welsh descent should Italianize his name; we might recall Coperario and Palmerini.

Herbert–Caesari is able to quote three extensive press reports of Daviesi. In the first, an account of the grand performance (in memory of the composer) of Rossini's *Requiem Mass* on 14 September 1869 in Lucca Cathedral:[15]

> The principal part of the Mass is written for the 'contralto', and was sung on this occasion by Giovan Riccardo Daviesi, the distinguished 'contralto' of the Papal Choir. This young artist is beyond doubt the rising star of Italy. The extension, strength and purity of his voice, the extreme sweetness and

---

[12] Herbert–Caesari, op. cit., pp. 334-6 (fn.) and the entry (under Daviesi) in Schmidl, *Dizionario Universale dei Musicisti*

[13] Frances Killingley, letter to the author, 20 August 1981

[14] Undated letter to the author, *c*1981

[15] *Orpheus*, New York and Boston, 1 January 1870

marvellous flexibility, the clearness of utterance, the exquisite finish and depth of feeling and expression, places him at a height that admits of no rival.

The rest of the report talks glowingly of the possible visit of Daviesi to America. The second press cutting is an extract from a Roman journal:[16]

> Giovan Riccardo Daviesi, born in Rome, April 12th, 1839, was undoubtedly the greatest 'contralto' ever heard in the Roman churches. He was a pupil of the 'Schola Cantorum' of St Michele. He was first engaged for the Cappella Pia Lateranense, then for the Cappella Giulia, and finally in March, 1864, when nearly twenty–five years old, for the Cappella Sistina.

The third report concerns his death:[17]

> Yesterday, at 7 pm, Giovan Riccardo Daviesi, teacher of singing, passed away. With the demise of Daviesi, Rome loses one of her greatest singers and teachers.... After the fall of Rome in 1870, he repaired to London in order to continue his medical studies under the famous throat specialist, Sir Morell Mackenzie. Subsequently he opened a school of singing there, but shortly afterwards was recalled to Italy by the Vatican. He finally settled in Milan as a teacher of singing. Daviesi was also an excellent composer. At sixty years of age he was engaged as Director of Vocal Studies in the Conservatorium of Irkutsk, Siberia, where he remained seven years and then went to Moscow. On returning to Italy he settled in Rome. He associated with the most famous composers and singers of his time. He was an intimate friend of Liszt, and of Rossini with whom he lived for some time in Paris, and also of Frezzolini, the celebrated soprano. Gounod, after hearing Daviesi sing in Paris approached him, saying 'Est–ce que vous être peintre, Monsieur?' ('Are you a painter, Sir?'), and on his replying in the negative and demanding the reason for such a curious question, Gounod replied, 'Parce–que vous chantez avec de couleur' ('Because you sing with so much colour') ...

When one recalls the presence of soprano castrati in the same Papal Choir in the nineteenth century, one realises that something of the traditional Sistine 'sound' had survived there against the odds, in much the same manner as in English cathedrals. Franz Xavier Haberl (1840–1910) noted that the alto parts were still sung by the 'high tenors' in the Papal choirs, and in the Anglican church choir. We know, of course, that not only were his 'high tenors' not tenors in the modern meaning of the term, but that modern–style tenors did not sing the alto part in English choirs. Haberl's phrase begs the question, 'What is a high tenor?' We should remember that 'high tenor' is the nearest that German musical terminology of his time could get to 'counter–tenor'. So yet again, contralto–tenors and counter–tenors seem to be linked. 'High tenors' of the past used falsetto. While the fashion in tenor–range singing had largely changed across Europe, male singers of the alto part had retained the early techniques, so that English and Italian choir–altos and even any surviving castrato–contralti seem to have been compar-

---

[16] *Musica*, 28 February 1918
[17] *La Tribuna* (Rome), 10 July 1921

able in technique if not always in standard.

The Sistine castrati were by now heard almost exclusively in their ecclesiastical surroundings, like the English alti; yet, as Herbert–Caesari and some news–cuttings of the time report, the Italian male contralti–naturali were not only acceptable in the secular world, but even celebrated in it. However, is this statement merely a student's hero–worship of his teacher? This Frances Killingley[18] seems to think possible:

> I cannot believe that they [contralto-tenors] were accepted and celebrated in the secular world – we would have heard something about them if they had been. Even the great Daviesi seems to have left no traces outside the writings of Herbert–Caesari.

However, it would seem that Killingley was unaware of the press reports quoted above, or knew them to have been found spurious in that Herbert–Caesari could have originated or embroidered them – which is most unlikely.

It has been suggested by some that the title 'contralto' for male singers derived simply from their vocal resemblance to the female contralto or, arguably, even came about because of the similarity in the upper range to the castrato–contralto – a voice which still existed in nineteenth–century Italy.

There is even a theory that the term 'contralto-tenor' was Herbert–Caesari's own invention. Even if it were, his suggestion that contralto-tenors were so called because their tone and range resembled the female contralto is incorrect. 'Contralto' was simply an ancient title for alto in Italy which referred to the voice–part immediately above the tenor's. 'Contra–alto', according to Zarlino in sixteenth–century Italy, 'some call *contratenore*, some *contralto*, and others call it simply *alto*'. Thus, castrati and women were the interlopers who annexed the description. Counter–tenors appearing in Italy today are sometimes termed *contraltista*. In Monteverdi's time, contraltos were certainly normal males: not even castrati, let alone women.

Of male voices, Tomeoni wrote, 'Nature gives contralto, tenor, baritone, and bass'.[19] It may surprise many to read that in the eighteenth century there was frequent criticism of Italian singers for their habitual employment of falsetto. We may ask 'Of which variety?'; see Mary Cyr, at footnote 21. A late nineteenth–century reference to a secular solo tenor declares that 'The Italian Tenor ... is an incomparable falsettist.'[20] Though not referring by name to a 'contralto', this reference seems to confirm that even by this date certain tenor singers, even Italians, used pure head–voice. In France, as in England, the term 'contralto' had become exclusively female by the middle of the nineteenth century. Haute–contre ('high–contra') was the usual title of the highest male voice in France. The following 1867 *Encyclopaedie* reference is discussing its rarity by that date:[21]

---

[18] Letter to the author, 20 August, 1981

[19] Tomeoni, *Theorie de la Musique Vocale*, 1799

[20] *Daily News*, 28 July 1892

[21] *Encyclopaedie*, 1867. See also Frances Killingley, '"Haute-contre" – alto or tenor?', *Music and Letters*, 1, iv, 1973, pp. 256–7; 'The Haute-contre', *The Musical Times*, CXV, 1974, p. 217; Neal Zaslaw, 'The Enigma of the Haute-Contre', *The Musical Times*, CXV, 1974, pp. 939–941; and Mary Cyr, 'On Performing 18th-century Haute-Contre Roles', *The Musical Times*, CXV, 1974, pp. 291–5

Haute-contre.

A man's voice higher than that of the tenor, and a little more inclined to harshness, but more extended or lower than the woman's voice called contralto. These voices are called in Italy *tenor-contraltino.* One hardly ever finds them in France, except in Toulouse and its environs, where they are becoming very rare, and one is often obliged to have certain rôles in old operas, those of Gluck for example, sung by women, which were written originally for haute-contre voices.

Despite the apparent authority of the *Encyclopaedie,* its entries can be misleading. As far as is known, the only haute-contre rôle (thus designated) which has been sung by a woman (Pauline Viardot-Garcia, mezzo-soprano) is that of Orfeo in Gluck's *Orphée,* during the 1830s and 1840s. This was performed in the hybrid Berlioz edition which restored the pitch of the original version written for castrato.

The often-quoted harshness in tone of at least the later haute-contre singers and Herbert-Caesari's description of the 'steely' quality of the pharyngeal voice, and the piercing, even sometimes unpleasant, quality of 'witch voice' (falsetto in metamorphosis), referred to by the early Italian singing teachers, all seem likely to be closely related, or even to be one and the same.

Because he wrote in the middle of the twentieth century, Herbert-Caesari now represents a useful link between the 1990s and the singing world of a century before. His links with the elusive Daviesi, and the falsetto techniques of that time (by whatever name), imbue his remarks with some significance. We must remember that, though he was undoubtedly a legatee of the past, Herbert-Caesari was also a child of his age. We need to examine some of his phraseology with care, but through him we can more than glimpse the vocal practices of the preceding three centuries.

A well-documented article published in 1969[22] discussed the counter-tenor question through the medium of three important singers, Deller, Freeman and Pate, and two Shakespearian operas in which, separated by three centuries, they sang: Britten's *A Midsummer Night's Dream,* and Purcell's *The Fairy Queen.* The general thesis of Baldwin and Wilson is that, because the Britten counter-tenor solos are approximately a major third higher than the Purcell parts, then they were *ipso facto* written with different voices in mind: a reiteration of the old 'falsetto-alto versus high tenor' argument which ignores the major change in tenor technique which has taken place since Purcell's time. Their article contains in microcosm many of the arguments used by those who maintain that counter-tenors were always high tenors, as we understand the term now. It incidentally suggests support for a view that, if it occurred at all, the secular use of falsetto, always termed 'alto' in England, was a vocal aberration in an off-shore island. The article also served as a starting point for later published discussion of similar views.

The choice of two Shakespearian operas and of particular singers is apparently significant and logical. What could be more revealing? Yet the comparisons are not as clear-cut as they seem to be at first. Britten wrote the rôle of Oberon for Deller. It is not by any means certain that Purcell wrote the counter-tenor solos in *The Fairy Queen* for Freeman and Pate, though

---

[22] Olive Baldwin and Thelma Wilson, 'Alfred Deller, John Freeman and Mr Pate', *Music and Letters,* 1969, vol. 50, p. 103. See also the same authors' 'Purcell's Counter-tenors', *Musical Opinion,* August 1966

it is possible he did. It would appear that Freeman was a counter–tenor under contract to the company which first performed it and that Pate, apparently a free–lance singer, also could well have sung with this company. Britten would seem to have chosen the excellent upper–falsetto and 'pipe voice' of Deller for its special ethereal quality. His writing includes excellently-calculated effects which employ excursions into strong pharyngeal territory, but the disembodied tone of upper–falsetto has exactly the right supernatural quality for Oberon.

In *The Fairy Queen*, Purcell writes mainly for the pharyngeal register – happily the most effective range of low counter–tenor of either type – perhaps because the use of upper chest with the pharyngeal voice has much the same effect as the contrast of pharyngeal with upper-falsetto in the Britten work; in other words, each low counter–tenor type exploits two main contrasting timbres. Britten was concerned to build a particular vocal and dramatic character, but Purcell seems to have written more generally: no singer was asked to portray one character throughout.

Baldwin and Wilson also suggested that the Purcell counter–tenor solos are nearly impossible for the modern type of counter–tenor. In too many cases, they may be right, but how wrong their view can be is demonstrated by hearing the recording[23] of *The Fairy Queen* (in the Britten–Pears edition) which features Bowman, Brett, Partridge and Pears. Through careful adjustment on the part of the singers, there is little variation in the effect of some of the solos as rendered by these superb artists. In others, the different voices express what Purcell probably intended: a similar but not an identical sound, with contrasting head–tones: brilliant, tender and powerful.

However effective Partridge and Pears might be, a conclusion that the seventeenth–century tenor employed a traditional part–falsetto technique seems inescapable: the contrasting palette of head–voice colours is potentially great. This is surely what composers expected. The modern lyric tenor, given sensitivity, willingness, and an ability to use minimum basic voice in his higher notes, may well approach the correct sound but, even if he does not go quite this far, the sensitive contemporary tenor artist should be able to produce suitably adjusted tonal colour to complement the head notes of the counter–tenor singer with whom, or even instead of whom, he performs.

Nicolai Gedda's 1961 recording[24] of 'Je Crois Entendre' from Act 1 of Bizet's *Les Pêcheurs de Perles* should be heard. This beautiful performance, in which Gedda uses pure head–voice (i.e., falsetto) for the top third of his range, well illustrates one version of the effect Purcell was probably expecting to hear. Were Baldwin and Wilson, writing eight years after this recording, suggesting a Gedda–like tenor? Perhaps, or perhaps not....

The Baldwin and Wilson article also states that English pitch (by inaccurate implication, a single pitch, employed nation–wide since the latter part of the seventeenth century) has risen since Purcell's day. If it has, which seventeenth–century pitch has risen? Again, if 'it' has risen, has it done so very significantly? The question of variable pitch, as we shall see, is one which has labyrinthine complexities. Their article is concerned that there are very few tenor solos in *The Fairy Queen*, and they wonder how tenor soloists could be engaged for only two solos, and a trio which involves one tenor only. They suggest that the counter–tenors were also the tenor soloists. This may well have been so, but not quite as Baldwin and Wilson imply, and we return to this matter shortly. It is quite possible that the tenor soloists may have been specially drawn from the semi–chorus for those few numbers. In fact, there is a theory that

---

[23] Decca SET 499–500
[24] EMI TC EMX 2114

all soloists were drawn from, and returned to, the chorus at this time, as in seventeenth- and eighteenth-century stage music or opera the term or instruction 'chorus' appears often to have meant that all the soloists sang together. At other times, all members of the company not otherwise employed, even the instrumentalists, seem to have been used to swell the vocal sound.

Their article concludes by referring to Anthony Lewis's recording[25] of the Purcell work in which Pears is heard against a (modern) trumpet, singing the counter-tenor solo 'Thus the Gloomy World', which he performs very well. Baldwin and Wilson seem to suggest that, because of the volume required to balance a trumpet or, by implication, a modern operatic orchestra, the opera's counter-tenor solos should all be allocated to tenors. In fact, the tone and volume of a modern orchestral trumpet, as used in that recording, is one thing and the light trumpet of Purcell's day, now heard increasingly in 'historically aware' performances, is quite another.

It is significant that Baldwin and Wilson fail to mention how Whitworth, who sings most of the rest of the alto solos makes a sound comparable in timbre to that of Pears during the central section of the piece. Whitworth was using pharyngeal production and Pears used mixed voice. Both used light fundamental register for the lower notes. Rather ironically, John Whitworth was indisposed on the day that this particular and important solo was due to be recorded, and recording time ran out; but his recording of 'Yes Xsansi' should be heard. Sadly, a young high counter-tenor was used for the famous 'Corydon and Mopsa' duet: a bad lapse of judgement. He totally lacked the low range essential in this piece, and used no comic characterisation. In all respects, the performance is unsatisfactory and provides us with another object lesson. Yet if, as Baldwin and Wilson advocate, a modern-style lyric tenor sings this and all counter-tenor solos, then though the vocal range may be covered perfectly well, the comic possibilities of Mopsa remain as unrealised as they are in the Anthony Lewis recording. Extensive use of falsetto head-voice is essential, for reasons which are obvious. If ever a part demonstrated by its style and range that it required a counter-tenor, preferably not a tenor-altino and certainly not a high counter-tenor with feeble lower range, this is surely it. An ordinary modern tenor is unlikely to achieve the bizarre effect which Purcell, without doubt, envisaged. Mr Pate 'in woman's habit' must surely have employed all the special head-voice effects possible, with maximum comic result.

In 1990, a recording (generously reviewed[26]) of *The Fairy Queen* appeared, directed by William Christie. Tenors, not counter-tenors, were employed, though the excellent Charles Daniels, sometimes billed elsewhere as alto, was one such tenor. The 'Corydon and Mopsa' duet sounded tame and missed the point. As if conscious of this, the 'high' tenor, Jean-Paul Fouchecourt, actually sang one or two phrases in falsetto, an octave higher than written. Curtis Price reviewed the recording[27] rather differently, writing that

> The famous dialogue between Corydon and Mopsa in Act 3 ... is curiously underplayed by Deletre and Jean-Paul Fouchecourt. In this, Purcell's second version, a countertenor replaces the original soprano; it is [was] a send-up of the first production and could therefore be more in the manner of Dame Edna.

[25] L'Oiseau-Lyre OLS 123
[26] *The Musical Times*, July 1990, p. 374
[27] *Early Music*, August 1990, vol. XVIII, no. 3, p. 496

Price also took issue with Christie over the choice of an extremely low pitch and a number of other aspects of the recording. The pitch chosen was A4 = 392 Hz; *The Musical Times* reviewer was happily convinced by this abnormally low pitch, and wrote: 'A thoroughly convincing response to recent research'. Yet even A4 = 415 Hz, the usual 'baroque' pitch employed today, is probably a little too low.

Bruce Wood, who wrote the detailed and informative programme note for the 1991 recording by Harry Christophers of *The Fairy Queen*, agreed totally with Price but also shared the view that 'counter-tenor' parts were written for tenors. Indeed he called John Pate a tenor and even joined those who, from time to time, have claimed that all partly or exclusively pure head-voice singing, that is by counter-tenors, was largely introduced into England in the late seventeenth century:[28] '... falsetto-production (a technique which seems not to have been common in England before the late-1680s) ...'

We should reflect further on Purcell's choice of the counter-tenor for the 'Song of the Chinese Man' in *The Fairy Queen*: 'Yes, Xsansi'. Such choice would seem highly significant, given that traditional Chinese opera employed falsettists. Purcell seems to have been concerned to give the music a 'Chinese' flavour, but we cannot know why he wrote the song for low counter-tenor and not a high one; except that this preserved the dramatic contrast between the Chinese man and a Chinese Woman? No doubt the singer's vocal tone would have been adjusted to sound 'oriental'. (As if co-incidentally to underline the oriental predeliction for male high head-voice, the present author encountered a seemingly instinctive and addictive falsetto-humming Chinese steward on a ferry between Sheerness and Vlissengen in February 1993. Unfortunately, he proved to speak no English.)

It would seem that the longing of an influential lobby for an ultra-high 'real' tenor to be established as the seventeenth-century English counter-tenor is based on a sideways and backwards glance across the Channel at an apparent French tradition. A surprising weight of vocal opinion and sometimes performance (even in France!) still considers the haute-contre to be a particularly high, modern-style and not always light, lyric tenor. Mindful of French influence in England after the Restoration, there is an understandable temptation on the part of this lobby, which seems to include Baldwin and Wilson (and more recently Price and Wood?) to assume that the English counter-tenor too was a modern high tenor; thus compounding the error.

As we have seen, the cultivation of what today we term the 'real' tenor seems not to have existed before the end of the eighteenth century; some would claim rather earlier in Italy. The large operatic tenor voice was unknown before the nineteenth century. We are left with the 'falsetto-tenor' (always a misleading term) which was the norm, especially in France, but in England too. Purcell's lower counter-tenors must have been of similar timbre and type. They would have employed often audible but certainly not unattractive register changes, just like Whitworth, Jacobs, Bowman, or indeed, Cuénod (discussed later), Gedda and Daniels. Even tenors who employ apparent mixed-voice for their upper notes, like Peter Pears or Richard Lewis or those who sound as if they use *voix-mixte* predominated by thinned fundamental voice, like Rogers, Elliot or Covey-Crump might have been called upon. We can glimpse a situation where counter-tenor and tenor soloists could indeed be interchangeable.

Herta Piper-Ziethen, in her article,[29] occasionally refers to the counter-tenor as a

---

[28] Bruce Wood, review of recording of Purcell's *Odes* in *The Musical Times*, July 1990, pp. 489–90
[29] Herta Piper-Ziethen, 'Alto Naturale, oder: von der Kunst des Falsettierens', *Fono/forum*, July 1974, p. 607

'falsetto−singing tenor' and maintains that his Italian title was 'tenorino' (an alternative title for 'male contralto'). Frances Killingley considers this to be another instance of the Germanic habit of using 'tenor' in the general sense of 'high' male voice (alto being there used for low boys' or female voices). She reminds us again of a quotation of Haberl in which he calls English male altos 'high tenors'[30] and cites this as a probable source of the confusion about the haute−contre.

One distinguished conductor was interviewed[31] about a revised production of Gluck's *Orfeo* (or *Orphée*) which, we may note, was composed only a few decades after Purcell's death. After stating categorically that the haute−contre was a very high tenor (presumably he used the words in its modern sense), the conductor was asked whether he had considered looking for such a voice for the part. He replied, 'Certainly I've considered it, but so far have always rejected it. Most of the haute−contres I have heard sound to me as if they have got themselves caught in a mincing machine....' One might wonder which singers he had heard and might reflect that perhaps they were indeed high lyric tenors of the modern type who were attempting a tessitura beyond comfort for singer and listener. On the other hand, it may be possible that he simply dislikes the haute−contre's timbre. To describe superlative artists like Oberlin, Jacobs, or Cuénod (with whom he worked at Glyndebourne) in such an insulting and ignorant way is astonishing.

Hugues Cuénod, the veteran Swiss 'high tenor', has been a celebrated interpreter of haute−contre rôles. In January 1982, he confessed on BBC Radio Three's programme 'Music Weekly' to being really not a tenor at all, but a baritone with 'a very easy falsetto'. (Had his career begun later, and had he lived in either Britain or America, it is possible that Cuénod would never have called himself a tenor and would now be credited with the haute−contre or low counter−tenor revival.) Another natural baritone who seems to have developed his pharyngeal voice and proceeded through it to become a tenor was the celebrated Sims Reeves (1818–1900). Kate Emil−Behnke[32] explains how, and in what context, Sims Reeves's transformation occurred:

> No student must expect to overcome register trouble unaided. Expert advice should always be sought. One safe rule may, however, be laid down. Never practise in the early stages of training from below upwards but from above downwards. It must not, however, be imagined that the Head register itself can be carried down throughout the entire compass of the voice. The idea that this is so is due to confusing cause and effect. But at least it can be said that no harm can result from the attempt. Madame Calvé is a case in point. Many will remember a sensational change which took place in her voice. Her singing of Carmen will never be forgotten by those who heard it. She was regarded as one of the finest mezzo sopranos of her time. Her voice was rich and full and of heavy calibre. Then, suddenly, she electrified the musical world by appearing as Marguerite in *Faust*, and her voice had become a pure,

[30] F.X. Haberl, quoted in *Concerning the Principles of Voice Training during the A Capella Period and until the Beginning of Opera* (Bernard Ulrich, Minneapolis Pro Musica Press, 1973, p. 224). Originally published as *Die Grundsatze der Strimmbildung Wahrend der Acappella−Period und zur Zeit des aufkommes der Oper, 1474–1640* (Leipzig, 1910)

[31] *The Times*, 24 June 1982

[32] Kate Emil−Behnke, *The Technique of Singing* (Williams & Norgate, 1945), pp. 106–109

high soprano of exquisite quality. She came to discuss the matter with me and to seek further information. Here is what she told me. She had long been convinced that she possessed the potentialities of high notes which for reasons she could not fathom she was unable to reach. Everywhere she sought guidance, but in vain. Then one day she sat listening to rarely exquisite singing in the Sistine Chapel in Rome. Not only were the high voices pure and sweet, but their upper tones had the light, carrying vibrancy the secret of which she was convinced was what she needed to know. At the close of the service she determined to seek an interview with the Music Director [the castrato, Mustafà]. She sent her card to him and was soon discussing her problem. How, she asked, were those soft, 'carrying' high notes, so effortless and pure, produced, and how was that same floating quality maintained right down to the lowest notes?

The answer was that during the entire period of training no loud singing was permitted. All practice was carried out pianissimo; there was systematic practice of humming, and the tone characteristics of the high notes were brought down throughout the entire compass. Calvé worked patiently for many months on these lines, with the result I have related. But though she had obtained her desire her keen sense of logic was not satisfied, and this was her reason for consulting me. How, she wanted to know, could she be carrying her Head down thoughout her entire compass, when she was fully aware that at a certain point she must necessarily pass into the Medium and then into the Chest register!... As was there stated, each register obtains, or should obtain, special reinforcement from and in different sounding-boards and sounding-chambers. Anyone may convince himself of this by placing one hand firmly, flat, on the upper part of the chest whilst singing in the Chest register. Strong vibration will be felt there. On passing to higher notes these vibrations cease. The reinforcement of the Medium and Head registers is much less tangible, but though it cannot be felt by hand, the singer who has it is fully aware of the co-vibrations in the nasal cavity and the head, and he will be very sure that without them the high notes will necessarily be 'poor' and lacking in ring! So definite are they in the head that it is not difficult to understand the supposition that the mechanism of the Head voice is being carried down through the whole voice when these co-vibrations continue – and this capacity may be there, inherent and integral in some cases. Such are exceptional. These co-vibrations must usually be brought about by long and patient work. This was so in the great tenor, Sims Reeves, with whom as a very young girl I had the privilege of studying Oratorio and old English ballads, and who told me of his experience in this connection.

During the first few years of his professional career he sang as a baritone, in Opera as well as on the concert platform. He, like Calvé, was convinced that he had the potentiality of high notes. So he used his voice delicately, never 'stressing' the Chest register, and practised in the upper part of his compass very softly, always bringing the light timbre *down*, instead of trying to reach high notes in ascent. Gradually and very slowly his high notes came, finally blending with the lower part of his voice which he had been so rigorously keeping to a small volume; eventually becoming, as students of the history of singers of the past know, a lyric tenor, with a voice of rare beauty. If he could have stopped all other singing while he was working at his high register – as did David Bispham – he would have reached his goal sooner, but for financial reasons he was obliged to continue singing professionally as a baritone, which materially increased the difficulty. Only those who have attempted the task under such conditions will be able to appreciate the patience and perseverance that he had exercised.

It may be further pointed out that the masculine voice is confronted with a far greater difficulty in this connection than is the feminine. If a man sings a high note so softly as to eliminate all tension of the vocal ligaments he will probably sing in falsetto, a mechanism which is useless, offering no foundation from which to develop. [This sentence urgently requires the discussion and important qualifications variously featured earlier.] If he has been in the habit of singing with undue weight in the Chest register, or, if he has carried the mechanism of the lower half of it up, to the exclusion of the upper half, he will not be able to adjust to the finer degree of tension and vibration for high notes. Then, when he tries to sing them quite softly – which is essential for their development – they slip into falsetto, for the gap between low and high is too great to be bridged. Hence it may be necessary in many cases to cease using the Chest register for a time. I have known of many instances where there was either not the requisite patience to carry out the work needed, or where the necessity of earning a living precluded it, and the attempt has been abandoned. The result is usually a mediocre voice, for if it really be a tenor it will – limited to the range of a baritone – not have the characteristic 'solidity' and weight of tone. There is far too much tendency to class a voice by its compass and not by its timbre, consequently there are many indifferent baritones who might be fine tenors.

Other than in the use of the actual word 'falsetto', her explanation is absolutely in line with the present author's. Thus, it seems that until at least his mid–development, Reeves (whether he recognised it or not) was probably a low counter–tenor. As a young man, we are told, he had singing lessons from a counter–tenor and a bass. It would appear that, trained originally in what must have been late eighteenth–century techniques, he developed slowly into a full nineteenth–century style of tenor (though, predictably, the latter ultimately proved limiting to his higher range).

It would appear that Cuénod has retained that variety of technique which Sims Reeves used, passed through, and ultimately disowned. Cuénod seems to have had some affinity with the counter–tenors, Freeman and Pate. Reflecting on this possibility should help us to understand much about the pre–nineteenth–century tenor and low counter–tenor.

We might now first consider the fine tenor, or possibly counter–tenor, Richard Jose (1862–1941), in the present context. (Appendix Four includes his biographical details, and the 'Interlude' in Part One discusses his relationship with the world of the late nineteenth and early twentieth–century ballad.) Joseph Pengelly, a champion of this Cornish–American singer, has researched him, and supervised a re–issued recording of some of his early cylinders and discs. He seems to maintain that Jose was not only a 'true' counter–tenor, but the true counter–tenor; implying that his tenor technique makes virtually all other counter–tenors into mere 'male altos'. (Pengelly makes a strict, even puritanical, distinction between the two.)

Richard James Jose (1862–1941)

We have previously discussed and described early tenor–falsetto technique, and its relationship with that of counter–tenor. We should now review Jose's late–nineteenth–century method. Apart from his obvious importance individually to the debate, he represents, if not the popular idea of the counter–tenor today, the 'gut reaction' of many to a voice–type described by its terminology as a type of tenor: for to many a tenor is a high, powerful, Pavarotti–toned voice. To them, this means that a counter–tenor must be the same, but astonishingly higher and therefore even more astonishingly dramatic.

After making allowances for early acoustic recording apparatus (1903–1909), study of Jose's recordings gives the listener the strong impression of:

1   Immense power throughout the whole range.
2   Imperceptible register–changes, except for the top few notes in 'overdrive'.
3   An 'overdrive' which apparently sometimes approached pure pharyngeal, used very high.
4   The tonal heaviness which makes him seem unlikely to be able to manage agile, historic counter–tenor arias of great rapidity with melisma throughout the range, even in 'overdrive'.

Sheer effort is noticeable in his recordings. It is partly that which is needed to record at all at that date (though not all singers sound so power–bound); but his non–legato singing suggests a pushing technique, which would make the fast runs of Purcell, for example, very difficult – perhaps impossible. Admittedly, ballads and similar material do not usually require agility, or stretch the vocal technique: most are slow or very slow; but one feels that other early–recorded counter–tenors like Clarke could have negotiated fast runs if need be.

Why did Jose cease recording relatively early in life? When did he finally retire from live performance? According to Pengelly, he re–emerged on early radio to enjoy nostalgic popularity. So Jose, though he was a superb, unusually high tenor, does not appear to have been either the usual Purcellian style of tenor or counter–tenor; but a later personification, perhaps, of the immediately–pre–Duprez tenor, who used vestiges of late eighteenth– and early nineteenth–century vocal production. In fact, his voice represented something of a pushing to the limits of pre–Duprez methods.

Early this century, cognate with Jose's active career and recordings, Griffiths's treatise on singing[33] appeared, which expounded much good sense. His prefaces to the first and second editions (1904 and 1905) contain a fascinating reaction against the almost exclusively medical and physiologically-based teaching of the period; yet of course he was also a man of his time. After nearly a century of research and practice, some of his arguments need qualification or answer. (For instance, he uses the term 'forcing' as a natural procedure; such a term is worrying today.) He should be studied. It is interesting that, in his opinion alto and counter-tenor were separate voices. Like the present author, he explains something of the varieties of falsetto and head-voice.

Griffiths includes photographs of himself, in profile, head and neck, demonstrating laryngeal position during phonation in different areas of the voice. It is noteworthy that the larynx is shown to occupy a medium, or medium-high position, according to the pitch and register in use. The implication is that it is expected to take appropriate positions and not to stay jammed down as low as possible at all times. This instruction, and the photographic examples make him unusual for his date, though his tilted-back head position is typical of the period. He also lists the female low voice as 'The Counter or Contra-Alto'. This term reveals some awareness of the pedigree of the title 'contralto', as extended to include female singers in the eighteenth century.

His (not unique) employment of the terms 'Lower Thick, Upper Thick, Lower Thin, Upper Thin, and Small' to describe registers or areas of the voice, are useful. His total acceptance of the importance of falsetto as a crucial part of vocal structure makes him a teacher of note, though his charts do not always seem to demonstrate the apparent meaning of his text. He speaks warmly of male-alto singing, even as he differentiates between falsetto alto and counter-tenor alto. For him, surprisingly at this time, the former uses no basic-voice whatsoever, but the latter does. In this respect, his views are similar to those of René Jacobs today. Griffiths differs in that he claims that falsetto cannot be joined to basic-voice.

However, this summary is simplistic. Though his conclusions are not always ours, and occasionally he seems to contradict himself, he demonstrates an awareness of singing techniques earlier than those of his own period. In short, much though not all he expounds, seems to be classical teaching. There are links, for example, with Kate Emil-Behnke's views a generation or so later and, in our own time, with Rebecca Stewart's, though they are differently expressed. Herbert-Caesari's position is not quite compatible with these.

Griffiths mentions several times that (in his terms) it is often difficult to tell falsetto-alto and counter-tenor apart. His statement is all the more remarkable by its date: 1904. Despite his opinion on falsetto-alto and counter-tenor/alto, it is obvious that he did not expect the late nineteenth- and early twentieth-century tenor to resemble the counter-tenor tonally. He relates counter-tenor to 'alto'. It would be intriguing to hear his reaction to appropriate singers of today.

Much of the argument of those of the 'Baldwin and Wilson persuasion' about the Purcellian counter-tenor is grounded on the interchangeabilty of counter-tenor and tenor. Based on what

---

[33] W.H. Griffiths, *The Mixed Voice and the Registers* (Curwen, 1904). Preferably, the second edition should be studied; it is subtitled 'A Manual for the Development of Male Voices, with Original Diagrams and Vocal Studies; also an Analysis of the Male Alto and the Boy Soprano Voices'. Griffiths is listed on the title-page as author of *The Human Voice, its Cultivation and Preservation*, Late Voice Lecturer to Lancashire and Cheshire County Councils; Speech Lecturer to the Church of England Training College, Liverpool, &c.

we know of seventeenth–century falsetto–tenor technique, this is perfectly reasonable (though one suspects that Baldwin and Wilson were making an opposing point). Therefore, the alto solos in *The Fairy Queen* were written for either a low counter–tenor of one type or another, or even a high counter–tenor with the greatly–extended strong head and pharyngeal–range downwards, and little or no use of chest–voice. Freeman and Pate were probably performers of one of these types.

A truly superb recording[34] of John Blow's *Ode on the Death of Mr Henry Purcell*, for two counter–tenors, two flutes and continuo, should be referred to here. The range of both counter–tenor parts approximates to the counter–tenor ranges demanded in *The Fairy Queen*, and in this recording the first counter–tenor part is taken by René Jacobs, the second by James Bowman. There is little difference between the voices and indeed it is difficult to tell them apart. It follows that to give counter–tenor solos to tenors today is correct only if, in seventeenth–century style, they use a genuine head–voice or possibly an extremely light mix for their higher notes. A few are beginning to.

Earlier, we saw that in many instances Purcell wrote for unusually high basses. We may now see why. They used their head–voices, possibly in mixed state, or in what we could term pharyngeal form: the ancient and proved method. The great Purcellian bass, John Gostling, had enormous range. His deep chest–notes were surely never weakened by stretching them high above the stave – which usually happens today. Gostling must have used his head–voice. In a discussion of Charles Bannister, the eighteenth–century bass and his son, John, also a bass, Roger Fiske[35] quotes sources which indicate the traditional method, presumably used by Gostling about a century earlier. Of Charles it was said that 'His voice was a strong clear bass, with one of the most extensive falsettos ever heard', and of John that 'His voice united in extraordinary perfection the extremes of deep bass and high–toned falsetto'.

As we have noted, a Bannister even played the part of Polly in *The Beggar's Opera* 'with inconsistent falsetto', says Fiske.[36] Lilli Lehmann comments:[37]

> I regard it, however, as absolutely necessary for the artist to give consideration to his falsetto, that he may include it among his *known* [my italic] resources. Neither a bass nor a baritone should neglect to give it the proper attention, and both should learn to use it as one of their most important auxiliary forces.

A fine early music specialist bass of today, David Thomas, uses what sounds like a *voix mixte* which seems to approach pure head–voice.

The counter–tenor is in a similar position, but in reverse (as it were). His important auxiliary force is his use of basic–voice. He is a specialist head–voice singer, and, unless he is a tenor–altino, he will usually engage middle falsetto at a lower point in the scale. This is necessary, because he has usually to maintain a much higher tessitura than tenor or baritone.

---

[34] Philips (LP) 6675 016, directed by Gustav Leonhardt
[35] Fiske, *English Theatre Music of the 18th Century* (O.U.P., 1973), p. 271
[36] Op. cit., p. 406
[37] Lilli Lehmann, in *Meine Gesangkunst* (1900), published in English as *How to Sing* (1903), pp. 174 and 177

It is interesting to recall that according to Prendergast (in 1900), nineteenth–century altos, at least by the close, engaged head–voice between C4 and E4. This may have been traditional usage, or perhaps from lack of weighty–enough development of the lower head–voice – or middle falsetto. It may have become necessary because of demands for excessive volume.

The average two–register counter–tenor, depending on his basic–voice quality, and on the volume needed for the size of performance–space and acoustic, would expect today to engage pharyngeal at about B3/C4, and use it for forte singing mixed with upper–falsetto to about the B♭4 above. Beyond that, pure head–voice is predominant and, though there may not be much obvious difference in the tone of a skilled singer, an equally skilled singer, like Deller, may choose deliberately to emphasize the change of timbre for musical effect and coloration. At other times, upper–falsetto will be retained lower than B♭4, probably in works requiring a soft, mezzo–voce, cantabile tone or when the other vocal parts, too, are low in their range.

In his music for English singers especially, Handel wrote alto parts of classical tessitura. Donald Burrows[38] noted Handel's obvious expectation that head–voice would be used, whether exclusively or as part of a through–voice technique:

> The consistent use of the fifth between d' [D4] and a' [A4] as the *centre* of the voice for alto soloists, which Handel's Chapel–Royal music shares with the music by contemporary, native–born Chapel composers, also supports the extensive employment of falsetto techniques.

The usual well–trained one–register high counter–tenor will find that his effective range will be within the extremes marked (1):

The low counter–tenor seems to have used a variation of this technique, and to have enjoyed a slightly lower vocal median. Richard Elford's range, marked (2), is often cited as ammunition by the 'tenor' lobby. The nearest which most commentators will come to accepting his being a counter–tenor (as we understand the title today) is to describe him as a puzzlingly–low counter–tenor, and to change the subject. As we have seen, the distinguished Francis Hughes's voice was a high counter–tenor; his colleague, Elford, was clearly an equally distinguished, but undoubtedly low counter–tenor. They sang together in trios in Handel's *Utrecht Jubilate* with Gates, the bass. John Hough, in *The Historical Significance of the Counter–Tenor*,[39] has taken this to suggest that the alto duets which occur in works like Maurice Greene's *God is Our Hope and Strength* are really written for alto and high tenor – it being his view that Elford was really a very high tenor (as he terms it, 'a true counter-tenor'). Strangely, a few lines later, Hough says:[40] 'The composers of the period still observe the distinction of 'high countra–tenor' and the ordinary high tenor of the Restoration period.'

---

[38] Donald Burrows, 'Handel and the English Chapel Royal', (Open University, 1981), p. 41
[39] Hough, pp. 13–14
[40] Loc. cit.; see also Burrows, op. cit., pp. 40–43

Earlier, he had noted that the present day sharp distinction between alto and tenor voices was [then] almost non–existent:

> The counter–tenor making use of his higher notes and blending them to his bass or baritone compass, if a falsetto alto; or the tenor using his high voice judiciously. The easy production of the alto rather points to the former practice ... .

Hough's suggestion in 1937 of using a tenor if a 'true' counter–tenor is not available, is based on what seems to be a fundamental contradiction in his paper: for, having stated the opposite, he seems to argue that altos do not sing over the break with any real success, or even at all, and that counter–tenors have no break.

Is there a valid distinction to be made between the two voices? The terms are historically interchangeable; a low counter–tenor of the John Whitworth type deals well with the lower parts of the Maurice Greene anthem mentioned above, which Hough apparently thinks unsuitable for an alto.

At (2) above, it will be noticed that Elford's, to some puzzling, low counter–tenor range A2 to B4 is bounded at the top by the ending of middle–falsetto register. If he chose not to use upper–falsetto, this would grow weaker through extensive use of pharyngeal with chest–register. This does not happen if the chest–register is employed almost full time, as with specialist baritone or bass singers, unless it is stretched too high in pitch and/or is badly produced.

The well–trained baritone's pharyngeal voice is often excellent, but he still regards himself as a baritone because that is his speciality. There is a well–documented historical example of this. Deutsch prints a letter (written by a lady) after a performance of Handel's opera *Lotario*, in 1729:[41]

> There is also a bass from Hamburg [Riemschneider], whose voice is more of a natural Contralto than a bass. He sings sweetly in his throat and nose ...

We have already seen that baritones with good pharyngeal capability sang on the eighteenth–century stage, and that this was a well–established and normal technique. Richard Elford was probably one such singer. In 1967, Ardran and Wulstan did not seem to have considered that possibility:[42]

> Freaks undoubtedly did exist from time to time, but they cannot be regarded as the norm. The fact that Elford had a range as low as A at the bottom of the Bass Stave is a musicological red herring, for either Elford was a tenor, as Mr Hodgson suggests, in which case he should not have called himself a counter–tenor, or, more likely, this note was falsetto. It is not an impossible note to reach in this way, but to sing it in performance would make Elford very unusual.

---

[41] Quoted in H. Robbins Landon, *Handel and his World* (Weidenfeld & Nicolson, 1984), p. 136
[42] Ardran and Wulstan, 'The Alto or Countertenor Voice', *Music and Letters*, p. 196. See also Burrows, op. cit., pp. 41–2

One is tempted to add that it would also have made Elford inaudible; it would seem most unlikely that he used a falsetto 'bass' A2 in performance. Such a note would hardly be used normally; though, if he sang baritone–parts as well on occasion, he would have opportunity to bring his A2 into play. His strangely modest top note (B4) suggests that extensive pharyngeal development could well have lost him first the quality, and eventually the use in public, of his upper falsetto.

Brian Crosby confirms that Elford sang tenor at Durham. However, in the modern meaning of the term, he was not a tenor at all. If Elford saw himself as tenor, as Ardran and Wulstan thought possible, and Hodgson believed, why has he come down to us as a counter–tenor? Perhaps he ordinarily sang the tenor part in chorus, but enjoyed singing counter–tenor in solos or ensemble parts (a phenomenon not unknown in the twentieth century, though it usually involves glorification of high chest–voice singing, with the use of much head–resonance). Elford would thus become known as a counter–tenor much as those tenors today who are really 'forced–up' baritones are referred to as tenors because they choose to sing tenor and sound heroic – which (in a sense) they are – because they use fundamental voice only. Most tenors, of course, do not possess a usable bass A2. While seventeenth–century and modern tenor technique differs for high notes, seemingly, the equivalent low range capability and technique cannot have altered.

Hodgson reports[43] that a song by Croft:

'To Celia's Spinet' [was] said to have been written for Elford. Certainly, he sang it in the opera *The Lying Lover*, in 1703. I broadcast this song with spinet accompaniment from Birmingham in 1947. It had not been sung for over two hundred years, and it seems it has not been sung since.

Hodgson's normally exclusively head–voice technique would seem to be markedly different from Elford's 'through–voice' style. This underlines once again the perfectly acceptable overlapping of indigenous repertoire which is possible in the counter–tenor family.

There are two other possibilities regarding Elford. First, research is now in progress to ascertain whether Durham pitch in the later seventeenth century was higher than that of the Chapel Royal, London. If it was, it is possible that Elford's 'tenor' at Durham would have felt more like the second counter–tenor part at the Chapel Royal. In any case, the technique to sing both tenor and alto was basically the same. 'To Celia's Spinet' has an original range of G3 to A♭4 and includes rapid demi–semi–quaver melismas and runs in the upper area of the voice which require pure head–register vocalisation. The song also includes low passages for which use of fundamental voice would have been advantageous, but not obligatory.

Second, Simon R. Hill challenges Elford's possession of a 'bottom A' [A2][44] as

a misconception that has become one of the main bases of the whole 'Countertenor equals Tenor' heresy. I know of *no evidence* that Elford sang as low as bottom A [A2], nor that he had a range of more than two octaves. Of the music composed for him or that he is known to have sung, nothing has

---

[43] Frederic Hodgson, in a letter to the author, December 1991. The song is included in Volume Two of *Songs for Countertenors* (Thames Publishing, 1992), transposed up a tone to D minor, a key more convenient for the average singer

[44] Simon R. Hill, in a letter to the author, 9 January 1993

a range of more than two octaves, and that range was almost certainly *c–c''* [C3–C5]. For the most part, he seems not to have sung much lower than *f* [F3] (see Handel's Chapel Royal anthems) or *e* [E3] – a fairly normal range, very similar to the pre–Commonwealth period!

Example 17. An excerpt from the Nunc Dimittis of the
Second Service by Byrd (verse S.S.A.A.),
transposed up a minor third

Example 18. An excerpt from Purcell's Magnificat
in G minor (transposed); high and low trios

So, even if Elford's 'bottom A' proves to have been apocryphal, one is tempted to remark that C3 still seems likely to have been ineffective in pure head–voice, unless unaccompanied; see Appendix Two for a further essay by Simon Hill on the subject.

Few yet seem ready to accept the theory that there is a 'counter–tenor family of voices'. Writers and commentators have argued for a black–and–white definition of counter–tenor range and voice type for many decades. In 1980, Wulstan expounded a theory which related counter–tenor register change to expediency, and to certain special effects. It may be asked: are special effects and register changes both related to expediency? or is register change related to expediency as well as to special effects? It seems likely that there was no consistent rule. The physiological situation which obtained at any given time was exploited by human ingenuity for the utmost artistic expression.

In 1967,[45] Ardran and Wulstan suggested that, in sixteenth– and *early* seventeenth–century music, a comparison of exposed passages for verse (solo, duet, trio or quartet, or occasionally more voices) with full sections or full anthems often reveals a clear contrast in the ranges expected of the alto in two different situations. They suggest that though E♭3 is reasonably commonplace in full sections, A♭3 is normally the lowest note in exposed verse passages, except for special effects. (Presumably we are to assume allowance has been made for sixteenth– and seventeenth–century pitches.) They conclude that composers of the period deliberately limited certain solo sections (or, by implication, single voice participation in verse sections restricted to two, three or a few solo voices) to the falsetto register, expecting the 'gear change' to be used in unexposed passages.

While this might have been the case in some instances, a study of the double treble and double counter–tenor verse in the Nunc Dimittis of Byrd's *Second Service* reveals a well-known exception to this hypothesis. There are other examples, such as the S.S.A. verse in Byrd's *Salve Sancte Parens*.

S.S.A. trio passages in Purcell's music constantly remind us that the 'low–stepping' alto part is in fact harmonically a bass part. The usefulness of a strong fundamental voice for the lower third of the range required is at once obvious; though the quasi–fundamental quality of a good low pharyngeal technique can be similarly effective.

To limit solo sections to the falsetto–register would be wise, suggested Ardran and Wulstan, because many altos are not skilled at undetectable register changes. This statement seems to overlook the fact that pre–nineteenth–century singers used register changes without any evident trace of self-consciousness. Certainly, one of the 'special effects' to which they refer can be found in the verse anthem, *Out of the deep*, by Thomas Morley, 'for A Countertenor a lone', which was (incidentally) still in the repertoire at Durham in the late seventeenth century, and was performed there on Friday 4th June 1680. (See the music list on page 262.) Whether the counter–tenor's lower notes were doubled by accompaniment or not, is a 'red herring'. If the register change was thus partially obscured, so be it. If not, slight differences in vocal quality would not have been considered surprising or worrying; in fact, they were probably encouraged for tonal variety and, sometimes, for word–painting.

In using blended chest tones for the first phrase, the solo counter–tenor would underline the meaning of the text in a powerful way, especially with a full and powerful second phrase following this and a more resigned third phrase. Alternatively, a gradual emergence of counter

---

[45] Ardran and Wulstan, op. cit., p.192. See also Wulstan, *Tudor Music*, pp. 243–4

Example 19. Morley, 'Out of the Deepe', from John Barnard's
The First Book of Selected Church Musick, 1641

–tenor head–voice from a low, quiet and light start would be equally dramatic and effective. As now, it was capable of either interpretation in Morley's time.

Out   of   the   deep   have I   call – ed   to   Thee   O   Lord   Lord, hear

Example 20. The opening of 'Out of the Deep(e)',
transposed up a minor third

A proved and successful technique is likely to have been used to the full. It seems likely that the traditional register change (upper–fundamental to head voice) remained part of the counter–tenor's and tenor's usual techniques. It was an option totally acceptable for use in solo work and in both verse and full sections of choral works, just as it can be today.

Bernard Rose, in discussing Thomas Tomkins's counter–tenor parts (which are later than Byrd's but almost contemporaneous with Morley's and similar in range to both, and several decades earlier than Elford), seems to imply that he believed that seventeenth–century altos probably used no falsetto. This undisputed expert on Thomas Tomkins writes:[46]

> In Tomkins's *Musica Deo Sacra*, for example, the range of the counter–tenor is from bottom E flat to C, a thirteenth above (this is at modern, transposed pitch). There is no documentary description of the type of voice production which was used by this counter–tenor. It was a much favoured voice – this is evident from the fact that most five–part works are for SSATB, and that many of the finest verses are for counter–tenor. The normal counter–tenor of today, who tends to sing falsetto, can manage the higher notes of this wide range but is very ineffectual in the lower part. There can be little doubt that he was either a very high tenor such as the present American singer, Mr Oberlin, or a bass with a high and probably strident top octave. With the mellifluous falsetto–alto of today it is vital that he should learn to sing the lower notes in his low speaking voice, and effect an unnoticeable 'gear–change' round about the B flat below middle C, otherwise much of the finest music of the period just does not 'come off'. Obviously, if one has a really high tenor in one's choir, it is far better that he should sing the big alto verses than a falsetto–alto who does not possess a good low register.

Dr Rose is right in that it is vital to use a singer whose lower notes can be heard. The early seventeenth–century alto would always have been heard. An alto with a properly and appropriately produced voice is, of course, just as much a counter–tenor as the tenor–altino. Dr Rose's meaning, regarding the 'bass with a high and probably strident top octave', seems obscure. Presumably, he means a 'falsetto' head–voice. If so, in one way, he might be right, though why 'probably strident' it is difficult to tell.

---

[46] Bernard Rose, 'The Interpretation of 16th–Century Music' or 'Vocal Pitch in Sixteenth– and Seventeenth–Century Music', *English Church Music* (R.S.C.M., 1965), p. 30

The rare, apparently unique counter–tenor of Russell Oberlin is most certainly based on an abnormally high tenor, of neither modern nor what seems to be general pre–nineteenth-century type. Oberlin himself claims not to use 'falsetto-tones' (notes), which lie untouched at the top of his range. We may suspect that he is referring to 'pipe' or even 'collapsed' falsetto. Whatever the case, his upper notes resemble Paul Esswood's. Incidentally, we should doubt that all tenors–altino could have possessed amazing voices like Oberlin's; his timbre is far too rarely encountered.

It is a fact of experience that if it is used in a particular way pharyngeal voice can weaken upper–falsetto, while itself attaining considerable strength. An experiment with this production for a few weeks produced in the present author's voice a noticeable weakening of previously 'floated' and easy upper notes from B4 upwards. If that mode of production had been continued, a fixed range similar to Elford's would have resulted. In his later years as a soloist, John Whitworth seemed to have Elford's range exactly. As, arguably, might have Purcell; the arguments over his voice have not yet been resolved.

Ardran and Wulstan, in appearing to suggest that Purcell was a low counter–tenor, and sharing the view that he could sing some sort of bass, underlined the traditional relationship of alto and bass:[47]

> This [singing bass] is by no means a unique occurrence, and, in any case, all counter–tenors are able to sing bass of some sort, even if the quality differs.

Yet, in his various writings, Wulstan does not seem to take into account the close relationship that all male voice ranges had and have with falsetto – but here he maintains that all counter–tenors are able to sing some sort of bass. Even this overlooks the fact that although a basic tenor voice can sing a light baritone the genuine tenor–altino, like Oberlin, could not.

It seems reasonable to suppose that because a fundamental tenor voice is rarer than a baritone/bass voice, the counter–tenor population would have comprised more of the latter than the former.

The solo passages referred to by Dr Wulstan (page 251), and Dr Rose's comments on Tomkins's alto parts (see page 253), now seem to have their answer from what is known of earlier, surviving, general male falsetto vocal-practice. The Purcell?/Elford/Saville (and indeed, in our day, Whitworth or Jacobs) type of full–range, two–register counter–tenor were written for in secular and sacred music throughout the seventeenth and eighteenth centuries. This concurs with Jacobs's statement that 'a good alto is never a one–register voice'[48]; but the possibility that unusual, rare, or even freakish voices surfaced from time to time cannot be ignored.

The fact remains that head–register alone contains two or three sub–registers. Jacobs, quite rightly, calls these 'different colours', but they are probably caused by a slight shift of mechanism as well as of resonator. This makes them 'sub–register' changes. It is therefore arguable that the multi–register voice can be employed without the use of chest–register; its use being only one of several vocal options. Jacobs's contention is generally valid: that, broadly speaking, the historical counter–tenor seems to have been required to use basic–voice, in addition to head–voice, at least on occasion, whatever his speciality.

---

[47] Op. cit., p. 18
[48] René Jacobs, 'The Controversy Surrounding the Timbre of the Countertenor', p. 306

Since it seems clear that universal counter–tenor techniques existed, it may well be that different arenas of vocal activity are likely to have influenced the way in which they were employed. Jacobs argues that the Baroque secular counter–tenor was an exclusively head– and chest–voice, a 'through–range' singer. By implication, he differentiates between the secular counter–tenor and the church singer. The stage counter–tenor Michael Leoni (*c*1756–*c*1800) was trained in the Jewish synagogue; a specialised art which perhaps resulted in a stage style unusual at that date.

Initially, it would seem that his excessive falsetto, which was becoming rarer, caused the comment that 'His tone of voice was that which by the cognoscenti is termed a falsetto'.[49] This might be taken at face value to mean that employment of falsetto on stage was almost unknown by the later eighteenth century. However, because of what we know of the tenor technique which survived into the first decades of the nineteenth century, it is more likely that the writer meant by 'falsetto' upper pure head–voice, not the variety of falsetto called 'middle' or pharyngeal. A few years later than 1803, it might well have been necessary to explain the use of upper falsetto if employed on the stage. Certainly, a new generation of 'cognoscenti' had arrived by then and, as in any age, they were busily concerned to make their critical impact.

Descriptions of Leoni's vocal tone make interesting study. 'Its effect resembled the flute part of an organ with the tremor stop upon it', said one.[50] Another wrote:[51] 'The truth is, that Leoni has in reality, *no voice at all* – his tones being neither *vocal* nor *instrumental*. They have a peculiarity of sound in them that we never heard before. When he stood before us on the Stage, the voice did not seem to proceed from his lips, but fell into our ears as if it had descended from the clouds. This rendered it a matter more of curiosity than delight; and his admirers therefore, lay mostly among the female part of his audiences, who are ever well pleased when their curiosity is satisfied.'

Sheridan, in advising Thomas Linley on the composition of *The Duenna*, wrote of Leoni:[52] 'I should tell you that he sings nothing well, but in a plaintive or pastoral style; and his voice is such as appears to me to be hurt by much accompaniment'.

Michael Leoni in 'The Duenna', 1775

---

[49] *The Monthly Mirror*, London, July 1803, in a footnote to an article on John Braham

[50] James Boaden, *Memoirs of the Life of John Philip Kemble* (London, 1825), vol. one, p. 397

[51] *The Westminster Magazine*, London, June 1777; a 'Critique on the Theatrical Merits of Mr Leoni', quoted by Walsh, *Music in Dublin, 1705–1797*

[52] George Hogarth, *Memoirs of the Musical Drama* (London, 1838), vol. II, p. 430

This last sounds as if Leoni's voice was too weak to balance well against an orchestra in an indifferent or difficult theatre acoustic. His first appearance at Covent Garden produced a mixed review:[53].

> In the songs his taste and execution was [sic] manifest; and when it is considered he sings in a feigned voice, admiration cannot be carried too high. In the pathetic he evinced a feeling superior to any performer since Tenducci. He executed the divisions with a degree of neatness and articulation, that could not fail of giving delight to a cultivated ear.... However, the total absence of any ability as an actor rendered his recitatives tedious and insipid.

In these accounts and reviews, we can glimpse the effect that Leoni's technique produced upon late eighteenth– and early nineteenth–century opinion. We can also see that, even in the late eighteenth century, castrati (in the person of Tenducci) were still evoked as excellent singers, and that counter–tenors such as Leoni were thought comparable to them.

Fiske's comprehensive book throws especial light on procedure regarding stage songs, especially in ballad operas. He makes the point that almost all ballad opera songs seem intended for high voices; their top notes are seldom lower than F4, and quite often there is [sic] G4 or even A4;[54]

> Yet singing actors with untrained voices can have been no more inclined to sing tenor in the 1730s than they are today. In modern productions of *The Beggar's Opera* nearly all the airs are transposed down, some of them by as much as a fourth or fifth.... Male singers expected to have to sing their top notes falsetto.... Because of this, baritones and even basses could manage notes which today look possible only for tenors. When the castrati became the rage, baritones continued to toy with falsetto because men had so sung for generations, either occasionally or regularly.

Fiske is generally right, but his phrase 'toy with falsetto' is misleading. Singers were not playing at it, but using traditional head–voice techniques. Of course, theatres today are not always renowned as places for the display of excellent singing technique, and it is likely to have been that case also in the eighteenth century. Fiske also reminds us that:[55]

> It does seem that the key in which ballad opera airs were printed was sometimes of the publisher's choosing, for it is suspicious that the tunes should so often be in whatever key results in the fewest leger lines.

We may reflect on this thought in relation to other areas of early music.

Fiske bears out much of what we already know; but it is here presented to underline our thesis that the last 150 years are not remarkable for the eclipsing (and uneclipsing) of the counter–tenor so much as for a fundamental change of singing technique for male voices, particularly the bass and tenor. Fiske, while discussing the universal use of falsetto production

---

[53] *General Evening Post*, London, 17/19 October 1775
[54] Op. cit., pp. 119–120
[55] Loc. cit.

for higher notes, tells us of a minor singer called Robert Owenson (1744–1812) who was told by Arne in about 1771 that he had:[56]

> One of the finest baritones he ever heard, and particularly susceptible of that quality of intonation then so much admired and now so out of fashion, the falcetto.

Both baritones and tenors sang their high notes falsetto, for Charles Dibdin (1754–1814, ?tenor singer and composer for the stage) wrote of the bass Richard Leveridge (1671–1758) and the tenor John Beard (1716–1791) as 'having given way to the use of effeminacy and falsetto'. Though the force of this remark is dimmed somewhat because Dibdin could hardly have been in a position to criticise Leveridge at first hand, it is of interest for its pejorative undertones. (Leveridge, incidentally, was known for his stage impersonations of castrati, using his falsetto.) Nevertheless, until the 1790s, it is clear that the public found in [upper?] falsetto–singing something to admire rather than condemn. Handel was still writing for solo counter–tenors in 1744, in *Joseph and His Brethren*. Despite the views of some commentators today, the distinguished counter–tenor, John Saville (fifty–four in 1790) an alto lay–vicar at Lichfield, must have used pharyngeal production, at least.

Notwithstanding Dibdin's views, and the turns of fashion, it is worth bearing in mind that falsetto head–voice technique was to continue to be used here and abroad into the nineteenth century. It refused to fade, though much Italian operatic training seems to have eschewed it by this period. But – yet again – it all depends on what is meant by falsetto.

An Irishman, the tenor Michael Kelly (1762–1826), who sang for Mozart and 'had been educated for five years in Italy', was described thus:[57]

> His voice had amazing power and steadiness; his compass was extraordinary. In vigorous passages he never cheated the ear with the feeble wailings of falsetto, but sprung upon the ascending fifth with a sustaining energy, that often electrified an audience.

Though this critique appears initially to deprecate falsetto totally, it seems that, even for Kelly (see below), 'traditional' falsetto–use had been and probably still was appropriate for other effects.

The generic term 'falsetto' includes various different modes of production, one of which, of course, is pharyngeal. This register is usually entered into by tenors and baritones at D4 or E4. Fiske, though he does not use the term pharyngeal, agrees with this, and states that baritone songs – no doubt of the bluff, heavy variety – were often purposely kept below this pitch in order to avoid any falsetto timbre. His findings confirm that normal tenors 'changed' at about the same point. Thus, most male voices could extend their potential and sing as counter–tenors, *if they wished* and if their voices had the right quality.

No doubt, by the middle of the eighteenth century, even theatre singers specialized as tenors, baritones, and counter–tenors; but head–voice was in universal use. The singer used it whenever he encountered the appropriate point in his vocal scale.

---

[56] Fiske, op. cit., p. 270 fn.
[57] *The Quarterly Review*, 1826, vol. XXXIV, no. LXVII, p. 242

Example 21. Excerpt from 'Music for a while',
Purcell (Oedipus, 1692), in eighteenth-century format

Fiske includes some details of the techniques used by individual tenors of the period:[58]

> Shield wrote C's and D's for both Incledon and Johnstone, the leading Covent
> Garden tenors towards the end of the century. Examples can be found in
> *Fontainebleau* and *The Woodman*. In *The Choleric Fathers* (1785) Johnstone
> even had a high E. His falsetto was praised by both Kelly and O'Keefe. *The
> Thespian* for September 1793 found it 'pleasingly expressive', though the
> writer was worried by the jerk between his natural and counter-tenor qual-
> ities. Most people seem to have accepted the jerk as inevitable.

The Musical Quarterly, 1818, has an article on Incledon which states:[59]

> He had a voice of uncommon power, both in the natural and the falsette. The
> former was from A[2] to G[4], a compass of about fourteen notes; the latter
> he could use from D[4] to E[5] or F[5], or about ten notes.... His falsette was
> rich, sweet and brilliant, but totally unlike the other. He took it without pre-
> paration, according to circumstances, either about D, E, or F, or ascending an
> octave, which was his most frequent custom.

We can see from this, and implications elsewhere, that even for an important singer like
Incledon, there was little attempt or suggestion of the desirability to blend the two registers.
As Fiske says:[60]

> We today accept falsetto notes from some of our tenors when these notes are
> both high and soft, but we expect the singer to conceal the change in quality
> so far as his skill allows, and in theory we regard it as a small weakness that
> he should resort to falsetto at all. This is not a viewpoint of any antiquity.

It is difficult to agree with Fiske's rather oddly truncated statement on the same page that the
falsetto range of a baritone, 'was naturally lower and smaller than that of a tenor'.

Today there are very occasional performances and a few recordings of minor English
operas or semi-operas of the eighteenth century, such as *Rosina* by William Shield (1748–
1829). Productions seem to give most rôles which reach into falsetto to tenors exclusively,
thus creating little variety of timbre. The original intention was to perform them with different
types and weights of voice: bass, baritone, tenor – and presumably counter-tenor 'in reverse'.
So today, 'the only solution is for our singers to cultivate falsetto once more'.[61]

In the light of what we may discern about eighteenth-century vocal range and stage
custom, we may now see some extra significance in the reproduction of the famous counter-
tenor solo 'Music for a While', from Purcell's masque *Oedipus*, in an eighteenth-century
edition. It will readily be seen that, though it was published for an 'Alto Ten:' (a low counter-
tenor or a seventeenth-century falsetto-tenor), a modern high tenor could take it, even if he
would not give the effect for which Purcell wrote. The late seventeenth-century original was

---

[58] Fiske, op. cit., p. 271
[59] Quoted Fiske, loc. cit.
[60] Loc. cit.
[61] Loc. cit.

The late seventeenth–century original was written in alto clef; this edition, a few decades later, is still in C minor, but uses the G clef in order to invite alto or tenor. Some ambiguity of voice–parts seems to appeal to the English psyche.

The English tendency not to take their music seriously on occasions could best be epitomized in the persons of John Liptrott Hatton (1809–1886) and William Hawes (1785–1846). Hatton was an entertainer, raconteur, musician and serious composer. He is now remembered mainly for some favourite glees. Hawes was Master of the Children of the Chapel Royal, who boarded at his house. He was also a lay–vicar of Westminster Abbey, and at one time he housed the Abbey boys also. He was a prominent member of the London musical world of his time. Amongst other activities of great and amusing diversity, he 'was remarkable', so John S. Bumpus[62] tell us, 'for natural flexibility of a somewhat uncultivated voice – a circumstance which elicited the joke of Tom Cooke that he could take alto, tenor or bass *indifferently*'. Hawes, and musical wits like him, seem to most of us now to be the lunatic fringe. Probably Hawes should have lived a hundred years earlier. Perhaps he demonstrates that to specialize, but also to be adaptable and imaginative, cannot be a bad thing.

This adaptability, this almost 'composite' vocal capability, the full advantages of which cannot be enjoyed in the twentieth century with its pigeon–holed and restricted vocal system, were well used in the past. William Savage (1720–1789) comes to mind: he was one of Handel's intimate friends: a member of the Academy of Antient Musick, the Noblemen and Gentlemen's Catch Club, and the Beef Steak Club. When he was a Child of the Chapel Royal, he was the boy soloist for Handel in the opera *Alcina*, 1735, and seems to have sung as a young solo counter–tenor in *Giustino* in 1737 and *Faramondo* in 1738, and as a counter–tenor in other operas and oratorios, including *Messiah* in 1743. He is known to have sung tenor in choruses, and was a bass at the Chapel Royal. He was also a teacher of singing. Burney described Savage as: 'a powerful and not unpleasant bass', and Stevens insisted that he had 'a pleasant voice of two octaves' and had 'a clear articulation, perfect intonation, great volubility of voice, and chaste and good expression'.

Since the twentieth–century post–war revival, specialist high counter–tenors have claimed most attention – at least, until recent years. In England, it seems to have been mainly secular demands which had first encouraged great upward–extension to be used in Elizabethan stage or concert music, for example, and by men like Abell, Howell and Hughes in the seventeenth and early eighteenth centuries. Howell sang the high first part of 'Sound the Trumpet', from Purcell's *Come Ye Sons of Art*: a part of high tessitura and which hits several E5s. Deputising for castrati would have developed higher ranges, too: a need which probably never arose in English ecclesiastical surroundings, because boys were usually present.

Yet, during the later eighteenth century, despite Leoni (and no doubt a few others), as the castrati faded, the theatre's need for high falsetto singing seems to have faded too. For the most part, women's voices had replaced both falsetto and castrato singing in the majority of secular arenas. In any case, the theatrical counter–tenor had tended to be represented more by the falsetto–tenor type than before. Then, when male–alto stage rôles or rôles of ambiguous gender in the seventeenth– or eighteenth–century style began to fade, the only singers left using pure head–voice were counter–tenors unconnected with the stage or falsetto tenors still singing on it. When eventually the falsetto–tenors faded, the process was complete.

[62] *A History of English Cathedral Music* (Werner Laurie, *c*1900), p. 429

Before the nineteenth century, as Fiske says: 'The counter–tenor voice had been cultivated at the expense of what we would regard as the true tenor',[63] but during that century, the situation changed, markedly. Not only did the modern style of tenor take over the rôle of male high voice completely in most vocal genres but the idea of vocal adaptability itself disappeared. Specialization took over to the extent that it has for so long been normal that modern puzzlement at the idea of a composite male voice able to deal with varying demands of range, register, timbre and tessitura is perfectly understandable.

A few decades ago, any intention to achieve a wide vocal range by 'metamorphosis' as a powerful factor in vocal development, in addition to natural physiological endowments to be exploited sympathetically, came as a surprise. (To some extent it still does.) *The Times* music critic wrote in 1960:[64]

> The vocal cords, though a small organ, are infinitely adaptable provided their owner will limit their infinity to one thing at a time. No one can sing both high and low ... if a man finds that his vocal cords are adjustable to high notes he can cultivate that end of his range and become a counter–tenor, just as Per Contrarium a trumpeter or hornist cannot be expected to play Bach's high solo parts if his normal work is ordinary orchestral playing where the tessitura is anything from a fifth to an octave lower.

Therefore, in introducing *intention* as an important element, both historically and psychologically, we are not only suggesting a situation in which mind needs to overcome matter but also matter over mind. To use an architectural metaphor, this is because structure determines function, and function eventually determines structure. For, once intention has been successful, range is surely prescribed and tone and style follow. *The Times* critic continues:

> All these musical faculties depend on elasticity of tissue ... . The vocal cords, like the trumpeter's lips, cannot be both tense and loose. The singer's pitch range is of course primarily given by nature: a low bass is not convertible into a high tenor or a light soprano into a deep contralto, but short of that the muscular adjustment of the larynx can with practice produce almost anything desired, if there is a model to imitate ... . Men who would be undistinguished baritones astonish the world by singing whole Handel opera roles in the soprano range.

Because, in both secular and sacred music, pre–nineteenth–century singers seem to have been more versatile (vocally, if not in repertoire) than most would wish to be today, we should note one important difference between the worlds of secular and sacred singing. In general, theatre singers sang mainly new or recently composed works. The 'concert platform' demanded a similar approach.

The university and academic milieu also required singers to perform freshly–written works too, as in the Oxford Act;[65] but the situation was not comparable; 'newness' was not the

---

[63] Fiske, op. cit., p. 56

[64] 'The Voice and its Vagaries', *The Times*, 24 June 1960; possibly written by Frank Howes, chief music critic, 1943–1960

[65] See Susan Wollenberg, 'Music in 18th–Century Oxford', *PRMA*, vol. 108, 1982

prime or most important factor. The church approach to repertoire, in cathedral choirs and parallel foundations, was a compromise. A large corpus of traditional cathedral music formed the basis for the daily repertory, and though new music was constantly being written, it did not compare with our present–day repertory which ranges widely from the twelfth century to the late twentieth.

Some foundations were perhaps more traditional than others. The 1680 music list from Durham Cathedral shows that only twenty years after the Restoration there is nothing instantly recognisable as being of Restoration date and style, though there are a few unfamiliar names.

June	Morninge	Eueninge: Service: 1680
(Tusday:1)	[O. Gibbons] short service	[O.] Gibbons: [short] Eueninge service
	(Behold) [now praise the Lord] [R.] Allinsons	[Ravenscroft]: O lett me heare thy louinge kindness
(Wed:2)	[Byrd's] (s)hort service	Birds: short service Almighty god ye fountaine [T. Tomkins]
(Thursday:3)	[R. Farrant's] (sho)rt service [The Lord bless] us: R. White]	[R.] Farrants: Eueninge service O lord yu hast searched me out [Batten]
(Fryday:4)	(Childs in D so) l re	Childs in D sol re Out of the deep [Full anthem]: Morley
Satt(erd:5)	[Pattrick's short] service (Deliver me fro)m mine Enemies [would be Byrd; should be R. Parsons]	Patterick: Eueninge service God standeth in the congregation [Read]
Sunday:(6)	[Bryne's short] (s)ervice	Brynes: Eueninge service Holy lord god Almighty: Battins
Munday:7	[J. Farrant's in D] (s)ol re Arise [O Lord]: Tallis	[J.] Farrants in D sol re Blessed be thy name o God [Tallis]
Tusday:8	[?Nicholls short]service O	Nichols: Eueninge service Let god Arise: tow Basses: wards
Wed:9	Wil(kes shor)t service	Fosters second service o how gloryous art thou o God [R. White]
Thursday:10	Childs B(enedici)tie [in Gamut] O pray for (the pe)ace: Nichols	Childs: Eueninge service [in Gamut] If the lord himselfe: [Edw.] Smiths
Fryday:11	Fosters: (secon)d service	Fosters: second Eueninge service O God the proud [Byrd]
Satterd:12	Wilkinsons (sho)rt service O lord give (ear) [Byrd]	Reads: short service When the lord turned: Fosters
Sunday:13	Tallis: short (ser)vice I will magnifi(e t)he[e] o lord: Hooper	Tallis: Eueninge service I will alwayes Give thanks: [W.] Kings
Munday:14	Shaws: short (se)rvice O pray for the (p)eace: Childs	Shaws Eueninge service I call and cry [Tallis]

Tusday:15	Hilltons: shor(t) service Blessed by the (l)ord god: Childs	Hiltons short Eueninge service I will give thanks Nichols
Wed:16	Childs in F faut	Childs in F faut Save me o God [? Byrd; or Hilton, Portman – both *v*]
Thursday:17	Childs: in E:# O clap yor hands: Childs	Childs: in E:# Behold how good and Joyfull: Portman
Fryday:18	Loosemore short service	Loosemore short Eueninge service I lift my heart to thee [Tye]
Satterd:19	[T.] Tomkins short service Give laud vnto [the Lord] [J. Mundy]	[T.] Tomkins short service Call to remembrance [Hilton]
Sunday:20	Gibbons short servi(ce) o Give thanks Willi(am) [Tucker]	Battins 3 for vers praise the lord o my soule Battins
Munday:21	Strogers sh(ort service) o thou God (Almighty) [would be Mundy; should be Hooper]	Strogers short Eueninge service If the lord himselfe Foster
Tus(day):22	Childe	I will magnifie ye lord Pearson [R.] Hinde: o sing vnto the lord
Wed:(23)	[R. Farrant's short service]	[R.] Farrants short Almightie [and everlasting God] [O.] Gibbons
Thursd(ay:24)	[Parsons of Exeter] (O) sing [unto the Lord] Child	Persons of Exeter Vnto the[e] o lord Wilkinson
Fryda(y:25)	[Childs in D] sol re	Childs in D sol re O pray for the peace Nichols
(Satterd:26)	[Bryne's] (sh)ort (Behold) it is Christ [Hooper]	Bryne short o lord I bow the knees of my heart [W. Mundy]
(Sunday:27)	(Tal)lis short lift up your heads [O. Gibbons]	Tallis short We praise the[e] ô father [O. Gibbons]
(Munday:28)	Wilks short o how gloryous [R. White]	Nichols magnific(at) Blow vp the trumpet [Peerson]
(Tusday:29)	[W.] Mundays short If the lord himselfe: Foster	Reads [short] O God my heart prepared is [R.] H[ucheson]
(Wed:30)	Hiltons short Behold [how good and joyful] [J.] Hutchinson	Hiltons short o lord Let it be thy pleasu(re) [J. Hutchinson]

A month's music list at Durham Cathedral in 1680,
demonstrating the almost complete absence of works in the Restoration style

It may have been largely a matter of provinciality, for as a contrast, a list of services and anthems transcribed into Chapel Royal part–books between 1670 (January?) and Midsummer 1676 includes nineteen services, of which only seven seem to be of pre–Restoration date, and sixty–five anthems, of which only fifteen seem to be pre–Restoration.[66] A further list of services and anthems, of 12 February 1676–7 to 25 December 1680, tells us that of eleven pieces copied into the Chapel Royal books, three are of pre–Restoration date. There is another list of items torn out of 'Ye Childrens Bookes'. This list excludes composers, except in one case: surprisingly, that of 'Dr Blowes Service'. *Christ Riseing* could be by Byrd or Weelkes.[67]

So although today's interest in early music in the normal cathedral repertoire did not become properly established until the middle decades of the twentieth century, it is still clear that earlier ecclesiastical singers were required to perform works spanning two or three centuries. How they coped with the inherent changes of musical style is another matter. Perhaps they were not asked or encouraged to attempt style change very often. In any case, the archetypal lay–clerk or lay–vicar choral was notoriously stubborn and resistant to change. He was appointed to a free–hold post or stall and in many cases rejected any form of musical direction by the Organist who was himself often, according to ancient statute (as at Lichfield), merely one of the lay–vicars who had a stall in the quire but whose duties were to play and not sing. The modern lay–clerk or lay–vicar choral is a different animal and, though he may or may not boast a better singing technique than his predecessors, is far more likely to be receptive to suggestions that his style should be adjusted to match different musical periods.

The nineteenth– and earlier twentieth–century tenor

We have seen that prior to the development of (1) baritones who began to avoid head–voice, and (2) high, powerful, 'chesty', operatic tenors, all male voices employed much pharyngeal, often together with upper falsetto, in their normal vocal production. The counter–tenor or alto voice is part of an ancient family tree.

The hautre–contre should be included in the counter–tenor family. There has been confusion because the haute–contre overlapped the first development of the 'modern', i.e., nineteenth–century tenor. Some see the haute–contre as the very highest lyric tenor of today; no more, no less. Slightly differently, others claim that haute–contre was actually the pre–Romantic tenor. (Nevertheless, a distinction was always drawn between the two.) It therefore seems relevant that the celebrated haute–contre, Giovanni Davide (1790–1851) had a three–octave range, up to B♭5, high above the treble stave.[68] Stendhal said that though Davide was called tenor he was brilliant in his falsetto. He also remarked that Davide was the only such singer who approached the 'sensation delicieuse' of the soprano–castrato, Velluti. However, the mannered eighteenth–century style could not satisfy those who, in the nineteenth century, demanded heroic power.

Though considered a haute–contre by the new dramatic tenor, Duprez, Adolphe Nourrit (1802–1839) was a tenor and not a haute–contre although he used the earlier techniques:

---

[66] Andrew Ashbee, *R.E.C.M.*, vol. I, pp. 162–164
[67] Op. cit., pp. 193–294 [sic]
[68] Grove's *Dictionary*, 5th edn, p. 607

The writer of this article was a personal friend of Nourrit and heard him in nearly all his rôles which he created.... He used his falsetto with great skill, and was energetic without exhausting his powers.[69]

Of course, just as the counter–tenor seems to have changed or evolved variously from age to age, influenced by outside fashion, so his French equivalent, the haute–contre, must have so evolved and had, by the early nineteenth century, altered somewhat as a vocal type.

Certainly, Nourrit – idolized by the French public until the advent of Duprez – tried to change to the new *voix sombrée* style of production in what should have been mid–career, but turned out to be the end of it. It would seem he was partly successful, though he lamented 'I have only one colour at my disposal.... I hope that with time, I may be able to regain those fine nuances which are my true talent, and that variety of inflexion which I had to renounce in order to conform to the exigencies of Italian singing'.[70] Nourrit did not succeed, but killed himself, perhaps significantly in Naples, in 1839.

We have a valuable first–hand description of tenor technique immediately before the Romantic era quickened its momentum. It is of considerable interest to us, for obvious reasons. Writing to Bellini in 1831, when the part of Pollione was being composed for him, the famous tenor, Domenico Donzelli (1790–1873), said:[71]

> I do not consider it amiss if I give you some idea of the compass and general nature of my voice, for you will then know better how to write for it and I shall be sure of successfully interpreting in the dual interest of your music and my art. My compass is almost two octaves: from D to high C; I employ chest voice to G only, but up to this pitch I can sustain a vigorous declamation. From this G to high C, I employ a falsetto which, when used with art and strength, is extremely ornamental. I have adequate agility.

One can imagine the type of 'vigorous acclamation' which he described, using chest or fundament register to its absolute upward extreme in a manner familiar to us now, changing only when forced to by the vocal tessitura. Clearly, by falsetto from G to high C, he was referring to pharyngeal voice, possibly mixed with what we today know as upper–falsetto. Herbert–Caesari commented:[72]

> By 'chest voice' Donzelli meant the normal voice. In accordance with the training at that time, Donzelli used his normal voice up to F sharp or G, and then the pharyngeal–falsetto combination for the head notes. Several arias in Bellini's and Donizetti's operas include high D' natural, obviously intended to be sung with the pharyngeal–falsetto schooling.

Together with the ever greater importance of volume at that period, the rising of pitch itself must have had some schizoid effects on the male singer; the tenor in particular. Even while he was using ever more fundamental voice, pushing always higher for more volume, pitch

---

[69] M. Gustave Chouquet, quoted in Grove's *Dictionary*, 3rd edn (1927), vol. III, p. 664

[70] Quoted Jacobs, op. cit., p. 300

[71] Domenico Donzelli, quoted Herbert–Caesari, op. cit., p. 340 fn.

[72] Loc. cit.

itself was edging up. (It must have been tiring and bewildering: Sims Reeves was still complaining about rising pitch in the later nineteenth century.) Though head–voice was engaged at an ever higher point, Donzelli would have possessed a technique to pass into it, because of his classical method of training. In him, it could be argued, the scene was set for the next logical progression.

The famous tenor, Rubini (1795–1854, so roughly a contemporary of Donzelli) clearly possessed an eighteenth–century technique. He is known to have had an enormous range but a weak middle to his voice, and a powerful, 'freak' (so called) extension at its top. Yet he is reputed to have had a small voice, by later standards of assessment. Rubini, too, could be said to represent the transition in male vocal training, because his technique included two notable features of the Romantic and modern tenor. He invented the 'operatic sob', and sang using a conspicuously fast vibrato. As a result of the latter, at one period he was derided as a goat! His influence was great and lasting. It even extended to the cathedral tenor of the author's acquaintance, who was always allotted a particular solo which included the unforgettable sound of 'O Lahahahahm of God'!

No doubt many of the singers who had originally been trained to use it continued to employ head–voice, but they became increasingly out of fashion as the nineteenth century progressed. We have already seen that the notion that Italian tenors have always avoided entry into head–voice for as long as possible, or totally, is misleading. It is nevertheless true that many took to the new nineteenth–century techniques with enthusiasm, and because Italian influence was paramount, their effects on general tenor technique were great. The development of these techniques in Italy seems largely to have been due to a combination of the pre-eminence of Italian opera, and as we have seen, ever larger opera houses and increased musical volume.

It is therefore quite clear that, though today's muscular operatic tenors are a comparatively recent breed, seeds for their development were sown long ago. The irony is that it was not an Italian but a Frenchman, Duprez – from the land of the haute–contre – who was to be the first *tenore robusto*. The influence of this powerful type on the thinking of contemporary tenors of other varieties is still noticeable. Not many of today's tenors are likely to admit to regular use of falsetto of any sort, except Cuénod!

Even the lightest, most obvious falsetto–tenor will usually explain pure head–voice as anything but falsetto, possibly through ignorance of the several states or modes that falsetto possesses. Anthony Frisell says:[73]

> Present–day singers are expected to sing upper tones with a great amount of resonance drawn from the lower register, which limits their upper extension. If our present day tenors were to sing upper tones in a falsetto manner their production would be criticized as being false and unrelated to the natural voice. The castrati of the early 'Bel Canto' era were the only males to possess extreme ranges, due to their altered nature.... Recordings of [great tenors] ... reveal that none display any more than two octaves' range, with D flat above high C as the utmost top.

---

[73] Anthony Frisell, *The Tenor Voice*, p. 21. See also N.A. Punt, *The Singer's and Actor's Throat*, 3rd edn (Heinemann, 1979), p. 52

This is quite true. Even particular tenors renowned for abnormally high basic–voice singing did not, it seems, possess this facility for more than a brief part of their total singing careers. (One famous tenor of today is reputed to have a pre–recorded 'bank' of high notes ready for insertion into newly–recorded arias.) But even Frisell seems here to have overlooked that the castrati's phenomenal range was partly, even largely, due to falsetto techniques. Ironically, though lyric tenors use, or should use, pharyngeal mix, many either do not know (or do not wish to know) that they are using it. Frisell does not mention tessitura; a different matter from the occasional extremely high note.

Tenor rôles in the operas of Rossini, Bellini and Donizetti show that they were clearly written for voices trained in the old method: for *tenore di grazia*, or light, graceful tenors. Their tessitura and their melismas with phrases touching E5 or even F5 were never written to be delivered in so–called chest or basic mechanism, or to sound as if they were. To sing them in chest–voice is impossible.

Usually, authorities today who pooh–pooh the use of falsetto happily talk of 'head–voice', apparently without understanding how it identifies with the two main forms of falsetto production. Presumably, they do not consciously set themselves against what is, by common agreement, the most glorious era in the history of singing, yet they appear to preach against one of its basic tenets.

Duprez was the catalyst. He dominated the Paris Opéra in the decade 1837–1847, displacing Adolphe Nourrit, who had until then been an important Berlioz tenor. Duprez was originally a rather light lyric tenor who developed darker tones and great power in Italy, where he sang the rôle of Arnold in the Italian première of Rossini's *William Tell* (1831) and created the role of Edgardo in *Lucia di Lammermore* in 1835. Berlioz admired Duprez's developed 'Italian quality' of voice and preferred it to Nourrit's, but he soon came to doubt his sensitivity and artistic humility.[74]

Herbert–Caesari[75] tells us how the break with vocal tradition began. It was:

> initiated by the tenor Gilbert Duprez, whose success, however, was all too ephemeral. He is credited with being the first tenor to produce all the head notes, including the C and C sharp, with the normal voice (unmixed basic mechanism) ... . Duprez's vocal collapse [in his mid–forties] and eclipse are instructive under the circumstances. Might is not always right; and in this respect the following extract from *Cantanti Celebri del Secolo XIX* [Celebrated Singers of the Nineteenth Century], by the impresario Gino Monaldi, is illuminating.

Herbert–Caesari, whose teaching and writing advocated an approach far removed from that of Duprez, continues:

> Duprez through sheer willpower and determination became one of the most famous tenors in the world. In his case, Nature had not been lavish, his voice being both weak and dull; yet by dint of hard unremitting work he succeeded in making it exceptionally robust. After hearing Duprez in *William Tell*, Rossini complimented him with tears in his eyes: 'I weep because those who

[74] *The Memoirs of Hector Berlioz*, ed. David Cairns (Gollancz 1969), p. 670
[75] Herbert–Caesari, op. cit., p. 342 fn.

heard *William Tell* tonight sung by Duprez will not enjoy hearing it sung by
other tenors; but unfortunately, poor Duprez cannot last long'.

Whether Rossini's tears were the result of deep emotion or suppressed mirth is perhaps open
to question, for David Cairns reports[76] that Rossini 'likened the sound to the "squawk of a
capon having its throat cut" and considered that the note in question (the top C5 in Arnold's
aria in Act IV of *William Tell*) should be sung with head–voice, as Nourrit, the first Arnold,
had done'.

Certainly, Rossini's prediction came true. Duprez's voice seems to have declined rapidly
during the 1840s. Unfortunately, his technique was imitated and he became a popular and (in
that sense) successful teacher. It might be germane to reflect that not only do many 'heavy'
operatic tenors lose their voices relatively early but that many lose their lives early too –
though, ironically, Duprez (1806–1896) was exceptionally long–lived. The celebrated Russian
singing teacher, Panofka, declared of Duprez:[77]

> Duprez sang ... with a tenacity and energy worthy of a better cause; and who
> can deny that afterwards most tenors set themselves the task of imitating
> Duprez's mistakes, seeking nothing but the brutal force of the high C?... Who
> can deny that such tenors had to engage in an athletic contest with their
> voices, a struggle from which the voice came out second best? Who can deny
> that the sopranos, in order to compete with the '*tenori di forza*', were obliged
> to force their voices beyond the normal?

All this illustrates how the mid–nineteenth century vocal revolution established in most of the
serious singing world an ever more complete abhorrence of and scorn for falsetto. The
autobiography of the baritone David Franklin includes a salutary story of tragic misunderstanding of the working of the larynx:[78]

> There was just before the [1939–45] war an Italian teacher in London who
> announced in the concert columns that he was to hold a pupils' concert at the
> Wigmore Hall. The feature of this occasion was given star billing: 'A tenor
> will die on top C from *fff* to *ppp* – WITHOUT FALSETTO!' I was curious
> to see and hear this feat. He did nothing of the sort, poor fellow, though in
> the effort of making his decrescendo from *fff* to *ppp*, he did nearly strangle
> himself.

The story illustrates the lengths to which some singers will try to go to avoid using falsetto.
Even then, the singer in question obviously did not succeed. Duprez's legacy lingered then,
and lingers still.

The American tenor, Stefan Zucker, has an admirable ambition: to return to early
nineteenth–century bel canto singing. On recordings his enormous range sounds as if it
embraces the various register and sub–register changes discussed, with much ornamentation

---

[76] Loc. cit.

[77] Herbert–Caesari, op. cit., p. 342 fn.

[78] David Franklin, *Basso Cantante*, (Duckworth, 1969), pp. 65–70

and vocal fireworks. Zucker writes knowledgeably and convincingly, if egocentrically, and one can agree with much, though not all, of what he says.

He does not, however, share this author's view of the relationship of tenor to counter–tenor; neither (which is surprising, in view of his interest in historical practice) does he share the hardly unique view of falsetto early–tenor technique:[79]

> Falsetto was never used in opera except for buffo effects or parody. Tenors in the early 19th century sang their high notes in head voice, something different, although the terms were often used interchangeably.

It would seem that, not wishing his technique to be associated with 'falsetto', he rejects (or is unaware of) the several varieties of falsetto. He has founded a society, 'The Association for the Furtherment of Bel Canto', and a sporadic journal *Opera Fanatic*. Unfortunately, his own vocal performances and show business excesses are not the best advertisements for his excellent cause. To hear him sing 'Ah, mes amis ... Pour mon âme' from Donizetti's *La Fille du Régiment*, and 'Son geloso' from *La Sonnambula* by Bellini, is an experience not likely to be forgotten. His singing seems to be either hated, scorned, or loved – the former being predominant. According to his own writings, he has been labelled by reviewers as 'funnier than Florence Foster Jenkins' (the rather elderly, rich 'soprano' whose unintentionally hilarious offerings filled even Carnegie Hall, New York) or a 'newer and even more offensive version of Tiny Tim' (an American 'fey' falsettist popular in the 1960s) and 'this decade's camp sensation'; but he maintains that he has also been hailed as 'a male Joan Sutherland'.

Zucker is included in *The Guinness Book of World Records* as the world's highest–singing tenor: 'Stephan [*sic*] Zucker sang A in *alt*–altissimo for 3.8 seconds in the tenor rôle of Salvini in the world premiere of Bellini's *Adelson e Salvini*, in Carnegie Hall, in New York City, on November 12th, 1972'.[80] Examination of Zucker's writings is recommended; the brave–hearted should also seek out his recordings.

The medium– or heavy–voiced tenor, as popularly considered today, can be compared with sports or even a formula–one racing car. We may first think of the gear box, and the consequences of refusing to change up when the engine is working at its limit. There is decidedly more noise, more sense of speed, of high urgency. The vehicle is physically exciting to be in, though wear on engine and drive is increased. Comparison of a sports car and, say, a Rolls–Royce travelling at the same speed, is useful: the sports car generates excitement and exhilaration as opposed to smooth effortlessness in the other. Even if the sports car were to be driven more slowly than the Rolls–Royce, it would still feel more physically exciting. Only when the Rolls–Royce is taken to its own absolute limit would it be exciting. The post–Duprez, operatic tenor voice thrills audiences in a fashion similar to the effect of a fast sports or racing car on its driver and passengers.

---

[79] *Opera Fanatic*, number 2, Autumn 1986. See also an absorbing article by Zucker: 'Stefan Zucker, Rosina Woolf, Mayne Miller ...' in a booklet issued by The Association for the Furtherment of Bel Canto, 1981

[80] 1980 edn

The Illustrated London News reviewed Duprez in September 1847:[81]

> the supremacy of Duprez – his dramatic power and declamatory eloquence ... .
> The house rang with acclamations. Our recollection of this performance will
> be that of Duprez, and Duprez alone.

Duprez was the first 'tenor racing car'. Nothing has been quite the same since. His influence has helped reverse the intrinsic balance of all types and ranges of the human voice. From Renaissance to the early nineteenth century, the ideal was a voice whose usual tonal balance resembled a narrow triangle sitting firmly on its base. During the nineteenth century, the triangle became inverted. Since then, most voices have been trained to be top–heavy. (We may reflect that it was Deller's influence which helped point the way back to correct earlier technique, in this regard, for all voice ranges.)

The uninverted triangle 'ideal' was and is made possible by the use of either mixed–voice, or pharyngeal used alone. It may well be that, by the mid–nineteenth century, in the main, only church [counter–] tenors (the so–called contralti) employed pharyngeal–falsetto without any basic or normal voice on head–notes. It is, however, possible that (like Rubini) some operatic light tenors of the Rossini/Bellini/Donizetti era continued the traditional techniques while the rest produced their head–voice mostly using pharyngeal mode plus a modicum of basic–voice: *voix mixte*, in fact. The reasons are either that church or oratory acoustic does not usually need the same amount of sheer sound as a 'dry' theatre or that the style itself required something different.

Herbert–Caesari describes the rare truly natural voice: the totally untutored singer who can progress from basic through pharyngeal to (upper) falsetto and back with no discernible break in the mechanism:[82]

> In these particular cases nature has, through recondite circumstances
> completed her work – as sometimes she thinks fit to do, to show us one and
> all what a completely natural voice is, and how it operates, and what tonal
> effects it produces. On the other hand, she is generally very remiss in this
> sense and apparently is content to leave things in an unfinished state, albeit
> with full mechanical potentialities, under the assumption that man will exert
> himself to complete the work. Indeed it is far better so, for such industry,
> such striving, is creative of both art and the artist.

The present author has met and heard a few singers who, though mostly not untutored, could sing naturally and superbly in and through all registers: from low bass parts to those for high counter–tenor. We have seen earlier how the twentieth–century mind finds it difficult to accept any suggestion of a composite male voice able to sing in all male voice ranges and to use appropriate timbres.

Both its development and recognition seems to be as much a matter of psychology, training and/or cultural environment as physiology. It is usually overlooked that at least something of the 'composite male–voice' was still being employed in some non–operatic spheres, even during the nineteenth century. In 1842, during the re–establishment of the Temple Church

---

[81] No. 281, vol. XI, 18 September 1847, p. 202
[82] Op. cit., p. 347

choral tradition, F. W. Horncastle, of the Chapel Royal, 'the well–known concert singer and vocal teacher'[83] seems to have sung alto, tenor and bass in choral services on different occasions during 1842 and 1843. David Lewer reports that Horncastle had sung alto in one of the original rehearsals, but he was actually appointed as a tenor in the Temple choir when it was re–established with three men and six or eight boys.

Earlier mention has been made of W. H. Cummings who, like Sims Reeves, began as an alto and developed into a tenor. It is of special interest that Cummings had his first great success as a concert–tenor when he sang as a substitute for Reeves under Sir George Martin in Handel's *Judas Maccabeus* at the Exeter Hall, London. It is also significant that John Whitworth has tended to sing as a tenor rather than a counter–tenor over the last decade or so.

The truth is that the human voice can be incredibly adaptable, and as with the rest of the body, adjusts itself even as the cells are reproduced. Nevertheless, vocal folds which are light and inherently of a tenor character, have always been in the minority. Most tenor voices are at least partly 'acquired' voices. Taken on average, the male, world–wide, has a light baritone voice. Probably, it has always been so. Of course, certain countries acquire reputations for producing more than their reasonable share of one variety, like the Russian bass; but, besides climatic and possibly genetic reasons, usage and demand also build these reputations: so it is with the English counter–tenor tradition.

Many fine voices belong, tragically, to utterly unmusical persons, or perhaps to people who, by accident of birth or environment, are brought up to believe they are unmusical. The finest voice in the world, brought up where fine singing has no place, as likely as not will never be used. The weakest baritone voice, or, indeed, 'ineffective second tenor', may, in the possession of a musician, be capable of development into a superb counter–tenor.

Yet we have seen, too, many well–produced baritone and tenor voices have always been ready for use in the counter–tenor range. It is therefore intriguing that, for reasons connected (sometimes unconsciously) with Duprez and the nineteenth–century vocal 'revolution' in the male voice world, it is still true to say that the almost automatic twentieth–century assumption is that tenors must always have used and constantly sought to extend their higher basic–voice range, using *modern* tenor technique. It should now be clear that this was not so.

Acoustic, singer, posture and environment/buildings

In earlier centuries, as in England today, various counter–tenors are known to have worked and been celebrated in theatres and concert rooms as well as in churches, cathedrals, or Chapels Royal. There was, however, always something of a 'vocal divide' between secular and sacred. In England today this is becoming increasingly marked as many male singers who are members of élite historic ecclesiastical choral foundations appear to take little pride in the fact, and even own up to it with reluctance.

What if this divide, which operated variously across the male vocal spectrum, and to a greater or lesser extent in different countries, developed not only because of differences in singing environments but also through the demands and outcome of head position and stance, and the vocal technique and style that (partly?) resulted from these?

---

[83] *Musical World*, 19th January 1843. Quoted David Lewer, *A Spiritual Song* (The Templars' Union, London, 1951), p. 109

Wren's drawing of Drury Lane Theatre (designed in 1674), showing its moderate height (top)
La Scala Milan (built 1778), showing its immense height (left)
The Georgian Theatre, Richmond, built in 1788 (right)

Seventeenth– and eighteenth–century theatres, large and small

The characteristic forward head–tilt used in monks' plainsong is a posture which resulted in a sound quality that influenced church and formal singing for centuries. Gradually, the obvious demands of stage work would have dictated some modification in this stance; the later theatre–based counter-tenor, by whatever name, would need to have used more fundamental voice and to extend it higher first by a semitone, then another, to cope with the increasing sizes of auditoria and the position of audiences in boxes and tiered seating. This seems to have happened earlier in some countries, notably Italy, although, as we have seen, not all Italian tenors abandoned falsetto techniques.

We are never far from the demands of increasing volume. All voice-production is affected by singing environment, whether a 'resonance–riding' monastic light voice, using emptiness, space and stone vault; or a modern, secular, whispered or half–voice sung through microphone, with artificial balance and huge amplification; or an unamplified Wagnerian tenor or soprano on full bore, trying to dominate a giant orchestra. The composer, John Jeffreys, has complained about the sheer volume which seems to be thought necessary today by many solo singers, even when singing songs of small-scale or intimate character with piano accompaniment in a moderate–sized room. Tosi would have agreed:[84]

> IX.23 He should regulate his voice according to the place where he sings; for it would be the greatest absurdity not to make a difference between a small cabinet and a vast theatre.
>
> [Mr G.] There have been such who valued themselves for shaking a room, breaking the windows, and stunning the auditors with their voice.
>
> IX.24 He is still more to be blamed who, when singing in two, three or four parts, does so raise his voice as to drown his companions; for if it is not ignorance, it is something worse.

And so would Charles Cleall, who related the 'unison' comment of five choral contraltos on an absent sixth (1957): 'She leaves us no contribution to make'.

John Jeffreys made a highly revealing point concerning a lutenist and singer such as John Abell: the playing position of a lutenist is such that he usually sits with his head tilting down slightly over his instrument, probably with his music in front of him. This comment is worth pondering further: from such a head position (similar to that of the chanting monk) the singing voice is likely to have been produced naturally, using a large proportion of sinus–placed and pharyngeal activity. It would be difficult to raise the head often, anyway, for instrumental, physical and vocal reasons. Volume would not have been of great importance, but tonal variety, nuance, expression and the capacity to radiate tone with vocal ease to the edges of a moderate–sized room, would.

Though the lute itself continued as an accompanimental and continuo instrument, with a revival in the eighteenth century, the lutenist/singer's hey–day was past by the end of the seventeenth. The necessary head–position of such a singer continued only in the countries and cultures which used later developments of the lute and guitar for vocal accompaniment. In those places where continuous use was and is made of music copies, the head positions are level at the very least, and seldom tilted back. This is the case in small part–song and consort–singing, in madrigals and glees, in cathedral and church music, oratorio and most

---

[84] Tosi, op. cit., p. 67

secular choral music as well as in and solo-singing when the singer accompanies him or herself on a lute or similar instrument or at a keyboard.

Singing from memory, while acting on stage without a music copy, might have suggested the eventual development of a slightly different vocal technique. This seems especially likely as volume became important, then of equal concern with musical considerations during the later eighteenth century and into the nineteenth. In opera houses or theatres, with their often many-tiered galleries and boxes, the angle and position of the singer's head must have been modified for maximum contact with the widely-dispersed audience. This is certainly so today. As theatres and opera houses were built ever taller and larger inside, singers would surely have continued to sing, act and position themselves well for approval from the most important Royal or Ducal presence, which was likely to have been placed only marginally higher than the level of the stage; it was usually directly in front of it, a few rows back, or in a low first level of boxes. In a royal or ducal opera house or theatre, the courtiers and audience would be incidental to the performance, and in effect be 'overhearing' a private performance given to the royal party, in the same way as they attended choral service in the Chapel Royal.

In a non-royal theatre or one not aristocratically patronised, cast and audience appear to have had a freer relationship. Occupants of the boxes to the immediate left and right of the stage assumed a more intimate relationship with actors and singers. The design of a building has effects upon the technique(s) of singers: the stage height, the size of the proscenium arch, the extent of the apron, boxes, side-stages and the width and depth of orchestra pit are all highly relevant variables.

At a recent professional performance of Donizetti's *Don Pasquale*, most of the singers were overpowered by the orchestra of twenty-eight players who used modern instruments. The theatre, though modern and designed to include regular opera productions, bore much of the blame: there is no apron when the orchestra pit is in use. This admittedly deep pit is a relatively wide chasm across which the cast has to sing. The front of the stage is almost under the thin, flat proscenium arch. Fortunately, Donizetti's carefully-arranged orchestration, with 'gaps' through which voices could be heard, compensated to some extent; but whatever the orchestration, an orchestra of reasonable size and forward position can usually 'win' in the end, unless the singer is Wagnerian mega-soprano, and the conductor is ultra-sensitive and totally in control.

When it was built in 1876, Wagner's Bayreuth Festival Opera House was progressive and well thought out for singers. There are no prompter's box or galleries, and the orchestra and conductor are almost hidden under the stage in the enormous orchestra pit. Acoustic and balance are carefully considered. Gently raked curved lines of audience seating offer an excellent view and are well arranged for good hearing. Though they had to sing loudly, Wagner's experienced singers were given the maximum assistance to reach vocally over Wagner's huge orchestra. (In fact, there is also a Baroque opera house in Bayreuth with which contrasts are revealing.)

Built in 1778, La Scala, Milan, with its six tall tiers of boxes and balconies, is horseshoe-shaped and extremely lofty. This design was adopted and adapted widely for other opera-houses, though not concert halls for which it results in too short a reverberation time. At La Scala, however, the reverberation is 1.2 seconds. The sound quality is excellent, except for listeners at the rear of boxes, especially those boxes to the side of the auditorium.

In case it may be thought that all Italian opera houses boasted a traditional orchestra pit, we might consider this example of Venetian practice in the nineteenth century. Julian Budden wrote:[85]

> The stage had a large proscenium area which projected about four metres into the auditorium. There was no orchestral pit; the players were simply strung in front of the footlights ...

The shallow orchestra pit of the usual size and position was rejected when Wagner's opera house was built at Bayreuth, but unfortunately Wagner's healthy influence in this regard was not taken up universally. In fact, other than at Bayreuth, and more recently in Sydney, most opera house design has changed very little since the building of La Scala.

Reverberation or echo is unwelcome in opera houses and, in general, in theatres and concert halls not merely because it results in loss of clarity but because any blurring of the sound seems to lessen the impact of stage presence. In cathedrals or churches (other than preaching–houses), a totally different set of values is in operation. Spacious echo seems to evoke the presence of the Almighty. It offers aloof objectivity, other–worldliness of a kind unwelcome in the theatre, despite the inherent artificiality of stage tradition.

Early opera was attached to court ceremonial and aristocratic houses – a purely private affair. It originated with plays, masquerades and the like, for royal weddings, state visits and birthdays. Sometimes a theatre was especially built for it in the palace. At other times, it was part of a lavish entertainment out of doors, with a huge theatrical setting, purposely constructed.

Italian mid–seventeenth–century *serenata* performances in the open air were sometimes compromises in that often they were sung from music scores. These productions were frequently staged in front of simple scenery, or against backgrounds similar to those used for oratorios. Advantage was taken of natural settings: courtyards, loggias, pavilions, lakes or elegant, landscaped grounds. Such exterior settings, combined with a need to keep the face unmasked by the music, is likely to have required adjustments of head position and singing technique. Though the performance was outdoors, it seems unlikely that the audience was large, except for special events, so any serious question about extra volume probably did not arise. Also, we may assume that an acoustically advantageous position was selected.

When opera moved into the public domain, more patrons needed to be accommodated. The first commercial opera house opened in Venice in 1637. Competition among nobles who staged opera seems to have encouraged the building of ever–larger houses. Comic opera was first performed in inexpensive theatres for ordinary people or taken by travelling companies to halls and private houses. It lacked the grand trappings of its heroic counterpart. The mid–eighteenth century was an important period for small travelling opera companies, who performed wherever they could.

The differing conventions or species of opera seem to have affected theatre architecture, design, and vocal technique so that, until the eighteenth century, most performing spaces generally had fewer and/or lower tiers, boxes or galleries. Performing venues until the end of the seventeenth century tended to be considerably smaller than those which were to be developed in the following centuries.

---

[85] Quoted by H. Robbins Landon, *Music in Venice* (Thames & Hudson, 1991), p. 164

In the earliest opera-houses there existed nothing like a modern orchestra. As late as 1660, Cavalli, composing for the Teatro SS. Giovanni e Paolo in Venice, required only two violins, two violas, a bass stringed instrument, with some keyboard instruments (organs and harpsichords) and two instruments of the lute family. This modest ensemble had its parallels all over Europe at this period; it gave a gratifyingly light but subtle and flexible accompaniment to the singers. In addition to these considerations we should remember that even where a larger instrumental ensemble, band or orchestra was employed, in Venice and elsewhere, there were careful conventions in operation concerning its use. Instrumental accompaniment was varied according to the character and progress of the plot: violins were used for a lament and bassoons and trombones to evoke the netherworld. The full orchestra was not supposed to play when somebody was singing (this should be remembered when other examples of mid-to-late seventeenth-century accompaniments are considered – in the English Chapel Royal, for example), though passages depicting magic, sleep, or the underworld were regarded as exceptions. Recitatives were probably accompanied by the director on a separate harpsichord.

The increase in volume required by the nineteenth century and the ever higher tiers, boxes and galleries, combined with the move from static, formal opera acting styles, seem to have begun the demand for a strange phenomenon in singing position with the face slightly raised towards the higher audience, yet also with a tucked-in chin and a head rather sunken into neck, and neck into shoulders. Tone produced had to be ever louder, yet without the sharply varied timbres of the past. *Voix sombrée* was and is capable of heavy, often booming power, because the larynx is always used in a lower position. Thus, it opens the throat in a particular fashion, and the thoracic vertebrae are pressed into the rib-cage. Lowering the larynx cuts out overtones unwelcome in music of the Romantic and immediately post-Romantic period: overtones with frequencies above 5000 cycles per second,[86] or, according to Sundberg,[87] it causes the 2nd, 3rd, 4th and 5th formants to converge at about 3000 cycles. The voice does not acquire the sharp timbres normally caused by these high frequencies.

It is likely that changing demands of opera-style: 'artificial' evolving to 'natural'; 'non-acting', perhaps, to 'acting': might so have influenced such changes to both head and body position during singing that male vocal-production in particular would have simplified to some extent. Head held up, and twisted or contorted naturalistic-dramatic positions, would make certain techniques more difficult to monitor and control. (Despite encountering the same performing conditions as their male colleagues, though not in average singing at the same vocal tessitura, for physiological reasons it would appear that female vocal technique in serious singing altered less.)

Yet the audience's often fickle attention had to be kept. Various elements: music, singing, acting, stage design, audience-behaviour and seating; might well have combined, in different periods, to affect each other. In seventeenth-century opera, for example, musical embellishments reflected the lavish setting and decor of theatre and stage. Statuesque acting was part of a strict, formal convention, firmly established. The usually select audience was transfixed by delights and spectacle, visual and aural.

It is likely that, during the course of the eighteenth century, this continued in the performance of what today would be considered 'grand opera'. Other varieties, like the Ballad genre (Gay's *The Beggar's Opera*, for example) would have required a more 'down to earth'

---

[86] Fant, 1970

[87] Sundberg, *The Science of the Singing Voice* (University of Illinois Press, 1987), p. 121

style. The formal species of opera had to adjust its presentation and style as audiences and theatres became bigger, and a wider cross–section of the populace was admitted. Musical embellishments and decoration, vocal 'tricks', extravagant stage decor and acting style became essential in dominating the audience's attention. Volume increased in importance and artificial and exaggerated gestures began to develop. Of the former, Tosi wrote:[88]

> IX. 75 But when the audience is in no further expectation, and (as I may say) grows indolent, he will direct him to rouse them that instant with a grace.
> IX. 76 When they are again awake, he will direct him to return to his feigned simplicity, though it will no more be in his power to delude those that hear him (for with an impatient curiosity they already expect a second, and so on).

The effect of clothing and costume on singers' and actors' style seems relevant: not merely because of its design, but through its restrictions and physical feel. Most clothing of the past, on and off stage, was less comfortable than that in which most formal concert music, opera or modern opera is performed in the second half of the twentieth century. Together with other period factors, clothing could be claimed to have had an effect on posture, singing–style, voice–production, and musical approach. Certainly, it was and still is a part of the ethos of 'period' style.

During the nineteenth century, the increase in volume brought with it less graceful physical gestures and, indeed, usually less graceful music. Sophisticated musical embellishment and sensitivity began to fade. Yet, like for example the design of furniture, the heavy Victorian melodramatic stage style was actually rooted in eighteenth–century and earlier conventions, of 'Grand rhetorical Baroque statement or histrionic posturing ... dramatic exaggeration or virtuoso affectation', as Hitchcock puts it so vividly.[89] Ironically, with the coming of ever more realistic and less mannered plots and stage–settings, the acting style could not be as free in nature as it should have been because singing techniques had changed.

There now developed a combination of new, loud, increasingly stentorian singing and a somewhat restricted physical mobility and acting style. The latter now obtained for rather different reasons than that of the stylised artifice of earlier centuries. Additional volume would always have been needed in informal performances in the open air, barns or public house. Folk– and traditional songs would be given, not always without skill or sophistication, strictly from memory. Ballad singers and sellers, however, could have sung from the broadsheets they offered for sale. Town street–singing would have varied from crudely competitive, unsophist-icated roaring without music, to more clever 'glee singing' from music in carefully chosen corners.

Early chamber music in domestic (not court) circumstances was probably moderate or quiet in tone; not only because the instruments were quieter, but (unless the music were performed in large establishments enclosed in their own parks like Knole or Penshurst Place) because town houses were closely jammed together. Even those lived in by what we would now call the middle classes – professional men, or merchants – and their families lived cheek by jowl with their neighbours. As Zacconi wrote (of Venice):[90] 'Many singers learned to sing through

---

[88] Tosi, op. cit., p. 80
[89] Wiley H. Hitchcock, Introduction to *Le Nuove Musiche* (A–R Editions, 1970), p. 10
[90] Zacconi, *Prattica di Musica Utile*, 1597

Enclosed quires in English cathedrals: (top) Canterbury Cathedral Choir
singing the daily office, 1981, seen from the screen, looking east;
the author is nearest the camera on Decani men's row (right)
(lower) Norwich Cathedral quire, c1967, looking west.

soft singing in private houses, where shouting is abhorred ...'. This was the more understandable when we consider the tall Venetian buildings whose windows open opposite others on
echoing, narrow canals and 'calles' (tunnel–like, high–walled stone alleys). This topography
must have influenced volume and style of Venetian chamber singing to a large extent; no
wonder then that 'camera' singing resembled normal speech and encouraged rapidity and
fluency of ornamentation. In 1637, the Medici court chronicler wrote of the early days of the
'new music' that when Guilio Romano (Caccini) had invented *musica recitiva*: 'Si sceggievano
da principio le stanze piu piccole quasi stimassero le sale maggiori essere incapaci di godere
la dolcezza di quello stile!' ('From the beginning they chose the smaller rooms since they
considered that in the larger ones one could not enjoy the sweetness of the style.')[91]

In a medieval or later hall in England and in countries with similar architectural tradition,
paid performers in particular usually sang or played from gallery or 'screens top' (thus looking
down on audience or company), floor or slightly raised dais, but amateur domestic music-
making and madrigal–singing was generally performed at ground level.

The close proximity of singers round a table on which rests a single music book, printed
to face four sides should be visualized. Their tonal volume would be light, and their head
positions tilted forward, or level – books printed with each part facing outwards were more
common in England than in any other country. The dramatic madrigal (by Monteverdi, for
example) required some changes to this, with singers standing in special juxtapositions to
underline various aspects of the texts, perhaps with each holding a copy of the music.

Regarding posture and volume, clear–cut divisions are difficult when we recall that, from
the sixteenth century onwards, *chiesa* (church) singing, in Italy at least, was loud by comparison with intimate *camera* (chamber) singing. But would loud *chiesa* singing necessarily have
been all noise and little sophisticated technique, as some today would have us believe?
Probably not. Some 'terraced' dynamics would have been used. For *chiesa* performance,
singers would still have used correct vocal resonators and placements. If not, voices would
have suffered, particularly if, as in the Sistina, the choir sang every day. Vicentino states that
in churches 'one sings with a full voice with a multitude of singers'. As Wulstan comments:[92]
'This should not be taken to imply the sound of today's choral society: it merely points up the
difference between the forces and timbre of church music as opposed to the solo voices and
less sharply–focused tone used in chamber music'.

We should not overlook the acoustical implications for music performed in particular
cathedrals or churches or on the voices evolved in them. It is too simplistic to state that the
church style was always loud, and chamber style soft. A more restrained, almost intimate
camera style of singing (with a quasi–interlocutory character?) would have been sufficient for
those cathedrals and churches (especially monasteries) with high–screened, enclosed quires,
or even some open buildings with great and easy resonance.

English ecclesiastical choral style developed in monastic cathedrals and those churches or
secular cathedral or collegiate churches which imitated them. All possessed full sets of screens,
and virtually totally enclosed quires. This architectural influence and preference lingered on;
even the new St Paul's Cathedral, built at the end of the seventeenth century, was fitted out
originally with an enclosed quire. Abroad, in buildings where screens had not survived, either

[91] *Le Nouve Musiche*, page 10 of Introduction to Hitchcock edn
[92] Wulstan, *Tudor Music* (O.U.P., 1985), p. 247

London Printed for I.Walfh Serv.t in Ordinary to his Majefty at the Harp and Hoboy in
Catherine ftreet in the Strand and I.Hare at the Viol and Flute in Cornhill near
the Royal Exchange.

An idealized representation of The Chapel Royal, 1712,
from Weldon's 'Divine Harmony'
The choir is in the foreground, on each side

wholly or in part, normally the louder *chiesa* style would have been employed for performances to the whole building where the acoustic would not impossibly blur great volume.

A typically English compromise between *chiesa* and *camera* styles, with high treble parts
which soar effortlessly over high–screened quires, is still to be experienced and relished in
England today. Almost totally–enclosed quires, though certainly not unique to England, were,
and still are, particularly prevalent there – though the best surviving example of a quire
enclosed on all four sides is in fact to be found at St David's Cathedral in south–west Wales.

A jubé is defined as a construction which marks off the chancel or sanctuary of a church
from the rest of the interior. In its mature medieval form it consisted of three elements: a
screen (in England, the rood–screen), ranging from a solid partition to an open latticework;
a gallery or loft above (e.g., the rood–loft, and in England often an organ–loft); and a crucifix
(or rood). In most cases, the quire originally possessed canopied screens behind the stalls, but
some were swept away during revolution, innovation, and changes in ecclesiastical fashion.
From the seventeenth century onwards, the use of jubés declined. They obstructed the
favourite Baroque effect (followed by the Romantic concept) of a single dramatic vista. In the
early eighteenth century, grilles of open ironwork were substituted, especially in France and
elsewhere on the continent. An English example of a rare, only partially restored jubé is in
Lichfield Cathedral. The western quire screen there dates from the middle of the nineteenth
century, and consists of light, open metalwork. The stall canopies were never replaced, and
the curious result is a mixture of Basilican railed chancel and Gothic quire. The Lichfield
acoustic is now notoriously 'dry', but may not always have been so: a glass screen (designed
and erected by the cathedral's architect, Potter, at the same period as John Saville was in the
choir) completely closed off the nave from the quire, which at that time extended into the
eastern Lady Chapel, from 1800 until about 1845.

Common throughout Italy, in Basilican churches (as in St Clemente, Rome), the chancel
and quire is separated from nave only by a low railing. Sometimes, this scheme extends to a
low rail or wall behind the choir–seating or stalls on each side, producing a squat, open,
'flattened–jubé', shallow box (or egg–tray) effect. Clearly, the presence or absence of high
screens can affect the acoustic (and therefore, vocal technique) in a positive way. The
tendency of Italians and Germans, for example, to place singers in galleries rather than in
choir–stalls, might have further encouraged the medium–range voices – *voce mezzana*, low
counter–tenors or contralto–tenors – to use through–range techniques. (The Sistina choir sang
from the little choir–loft which projects from the south chancel wall, just inside the screen.)

While, for example, Italian singing–style and choir–placement varied and changed, was the
English continuation of enclosed quire singing primarily rooted in musical conservatism linked
partly with the sixteenth–century adoption of a secular quasi–madrigal or *camera* singing
style? It is feasible.

We might note, in passing, that a number of English greater churches, for example Westminster Abbey and Exeter Cathedral, have small balconies or galleries presumably intended
for special musical and vocal effects. The solid quire screen, or pulpitum, was another place
from which singers could reach a wider audience or create a dramatic impact.

We should consider the moderate size and the nearly open space of the Sistina and reflect
on Palestrina's masses, Allegri's famous *Miserere* and other music composed for it. With this
building and others like it in mind, we might therefore question the automatic assumption that
loud singing was necessarily the rule in all Italian churches. Consideration should also be
given to the small size of the Chapel Royal in Whitehall Palace, in London. According to one
surviving ground–plan it was about forty feet long. The other (by Vertue, c1670) suggests that

it may have been about seventy–five feet long and about thirty–five feet wide. Whichever was the case, while a *camera* style of singing would seem to have been more appropriate there, the new violin band, and a more dramatic style of music and performance at the Restoration, might well have encouraged something of a stylistic and dynamic compromise perhaps similar to most English cathedral choirs of today. The engraving on p. 280 shows the singing choir at the nearer (west) end; in front of them are long, angled music desks.

Much is made today of the general French influence on English Restoration music in 1660. The French Chapel Royal, notably at Sainte Chapelle, is something of a French Gothic cathedral in miniature: sans transepts, screenless (by the twentieth century), and possessing (in the top or main chapel) a generous acoustic even when full. The original chapel of the Palace of Westminster must have resembled this building; we may speculate on its possible acoustic.

Large voices are not needed at Sainte Chapelle. A small choir of moderate–sized voices (the day to day complement of the Chapels Royal of France or England), singing well within itself, suits it admirably. This should be borne in mind when considering the vocal size and character of haute–contre [*sic*] voices which sang there. Though organ and gallery under the western rose window have gone, it is possible to visualise singers stationed above (and behind?) the Dauphin and Dauphine, assuming that they sat at something approaching floor–level. Of course, they might have sat in a gallery.

Versailles: the Chapel Royal
(designed in 1710)

The Chapelle Royale at Versailles – a larger, more brilliant, early eighteenth–century architectural composition of great splendour with a generous acoustic – has an organ and choir gallery above the high altar. In this case, however, singers would have been singing at the same level as the royal family, because the royal gallery, entered from State Apartments on the first floor, is at the west end of the chapel. In its eastern gallery, the choir would have been both above and level with its hearers.

A homelier, English equivalent of the Versailles Chapelle Royale is at Hampton Court. Here, however, the choir sang and sings antiphonally, in traditional fashion, at ground level. There was no question of singing to a Royal gallery or pew, though the Royal Gallery is at first floor level at the west end, and is entered from the State Apartments. Much the same seems to have been true of the Chapel Royal, Whitehall Palace.

Oratorio began in Italy in churches but was also performed in halls before an aristocratic audience. It was virtually religious drama, or opera without stage setting. It is likely that singing from music score, and consideration of other lower head–position factors, positively encouraged a forward, high–placed vocal production. Singing in theatres, especially as building height and audience–size increased, would seem to have given no such encouragement; though, even today, the Italian vocal method is something of a compromise: usually a forward placing of the voice, though most frequently combined with a slightly back–tilted head position. It seems that, by the beginning of the nineteenth century, the tendency to tilt the head back was becoming an established method.

Pre–nineteenth–century (public) opera–houses and theatres in Britain, with the exception of Covent Garden, were, on the whole, smaller than many in Europe. Would less volume have been necessary than in many comparable performing spaces abroad? Would they have had the effect, in Britain, of allowing or encouraging use of pure head–voice for longer than in some other countries? It is an interesting idea.

The semi–private opera–houses and theatres of European kings and aristocracy, of course, were also smaller and more intimate. Did this affect the vocal technique of visiting singers, accustomed to much bigger arenas with larger orchestras? Could a volume–related parallel have existed between this variety of smaller, continental, private theatre and the average public theatre in Britain? (The projected Inigo Jones Theatre, planned to be part of the rebuilt Globe complex to be built on Bankside, London, should provide for actor and singer a useful indication of English seventeenth–century theatre conditions, in physical and architectural aspects at least. It is to be an elegant private theatre of the period, built to the great British architect's surviving design. It will however, obviously lack the sensory ambience of the time.)

An even more exciting pointer to the working environment of early theatres is of course provided by the famous Drottningholm Court Theatre in Sweden. Although it dates from 1766, it is essentially unchanged and is still in use today. An account of its rediscovery in the 1920s can be read in the first issue (September 1993) of *Early Music Today* magazine.

In theatre and opera houses, the chest/pure head–register change began to be unfashionable in male voices in the late eighteenth and early nineteenth centuries. Why? The hot, dusty, often claustrophobic, fume–ridden atmosphere (candle–oil/gas/human odours and perfumes) of public theatre or more plebian opera house boasted no air–conditioning, proper ventilation, or sanitation systems. There was also the peculiar odour of play–bills, vilely printed with the stickiest ink on poor paper, sold in as well as outside the theatre. It was an environment difficult and unpleasant in which to sing. A simpler basic technique which could cope better with worsening singing conditions of all kinds would have commended itself. (Not that poor singing environments were totally new, when one takes into account medieval stench, centuries of unwashed bodies, and open–sewered narrow streets, one might even consider the effect on the breathing of singers of earlier periods. Did this affect vocal writing–style?)

Elizabethan audiences were more like football crowds than modern theatre–goers. Dekker satirized their disruptive behaviour. He noted that the true gallant should arrive early enough to be seen ostentatiously playing cards or, better still, should make a 'grand entrance' by arriving almost, but not quite, late. The stage itself was the ideal place to sit in order to be seen. If the gallant grew bored, he could walk out in mid–performance, taking as many others from the 'stage–audience' group as possible. However, remaining in situ provided many other disruptive choices:[93]

> Marry, if either the company or indisposition of the weather bind you to sit
> it out; my counsel is then that you turn plain ape: take up a rush, and tickle
> the earnest ears of your fellow gallants, to make other fools fall a laughing;
> mew at passionate speeches; blare at merry; find fault with the music; whew
> at the Childrens action; whistle at the songs; laugh aloud in the midst of the
> most serious and saddest scene of the terriblest tragedy ... and, above all,
> curse the sharers.

Strong vocal tone would seem to have been essential in the Elizabethan theatre. Perhaps this encouraged counter–tenor techniques with maximum high head–voice employment. It also makes one wonder how much of the boy players' and singers' performance was actually heard.

If completed, the scheme to rebuild The Globe Theatre, like that of the Inigo Jones Theatre referred to earlier, will itself provide some answers, if not necessarily to this question. The original Globe was built in 1599, burnt down in 1613, quickly rebuilt, closed by the Puritans in 1642, and destroyed in 1644. If the archaeologists, researchers and architects have got it right, the Globe was perhaps larger than many people would imagine, and consisted of a broadly circular structure housing three decks of lowish galleries, with a totally protruding stage surrounded on three sides by the audience. Some of the audience were galleried almost behind the stage itself, which was fully canopied by a gabled roof. The centre of the theatre, the enclosure inside the 'ring' or 'pit' was open to the sky.

The musicians' gallery seems to have been on the middle level, behind the stage and under its large roof. Presumably, the musicians also included any singers not required on stage. It was helpful to singers and musical balance that the theatre 'band' was not like the familiar pit orchestra of today, in a group in front of the singer/actors on stage, but was behind them in a small gallery, enclosed on three sides. Quieter voices, like those of boy actor–singers, would have found this useful.

When we consider the overall noisy atmosphere in such a theatre, we cannot escape the notion that the apparently lowish range of many of the boy–actors' songs suggests that those 'boys' were either older boys with loud unmutated chest (fundamental) singing voices, or young counter–tenors of perhaps nineteen or twenty (choral–scholar age) whose fresh looks and youthful vocal timbre made them suitable to take the rôles of women on stage. Perhaps the young female rôles were divided amongst both types, while those of older women were taken by more mature actor–singers. (Not, of course, that all rôles, male or female, required singing.)

Examination of the Elizabethan theatre plan in general, and the Globe in particular, suggests that a fair proportion of the acting and singing seem to have been directed away from the pit and to the rear of the stage, because the 'Lords' Rooms' were so–situated, almost balancing the musicians' gallery. Of course, if the Lords' Rooms were not literally exclusively reserved for aristocratic or wealthy members of the audience, but were so named for other reasons, then this particular aspect of directional acting/singing would not have occurred. If, on the other hand, the Lords' Rooms were used by the élite members of the audience, then the

---

[93] Thomas Decker, 'Advice to the Gallant attending the Theatre who sits upon the rushes of the Stage', *The Gull's Hornbook*, 1609

theatre acoustic must have been better than we might otherwise imagine for the rest of the audience to hear properly. The gentle sound of the lute on stage might seem unlikely to have been easily audible, yet such lutes were used.

The rebuilt Globe will therefore help settle some questions, though the Elizabethan unruly audiences will not be present. Neither will boy actor/singers, nor will young counter–tenor actors, normally (unless for research purposes?) take the rôles of women.

The behaviour of audiences, of course, has always been inconsistent. Those at most court theatres tended to be quiet – unruly acclamation, crude signs of disapproval, and so on, were out of the question in the theatre of an opera–loving autocrat like Frederick the Great of Prussia. He sat at the front of the stalls for the best view. At the other extreme was Charles III of Naples who is reputed to have talked through half a performance and slept through the other.[94] This would surely have encouraged bad behaviour in the audience. Etiquette was less rigid still in Hanoverian England. Riots and unruly demonstrations could take place, even with royalty present.

The environment has changed; but, when full, the average theatre (even some opera houses) today is not often known for an acoustic truly helpful to singers. The orchestra pit is frequently too shallow; the apron does not protrude over it. It requires singers to perform across and through an accompaniment of considerable volume. This rules out any great contrasts of singing–dynamic. Today, of course, electronic amplification has come to the rescue in some types of production, though for other reasons this has not necessarily made much difference to contrasts in singing dynamics. It is still the singer's task first to create properly varied dynamics and vocal colours.

The familiar, crowded, old–fashioned British music hall can help us to imagine singing conditions in theatres of the past: not, however, the sanitized version, 'The Good Old Days', as seen on British television until recently. Mayhew describes a very different music–hall environment, probably somewhat akin to conditions in the Elizabethan playhouse, though lacking gallants:[95]

> On a good attractive night, the rush of costers to the threepenny gallery of the Coburg (better known as the "Vic") is peculiar and almost awful ... . The long zig–zag staircase that leads to the paybox is crowded to suffocation at least an hour before the theatre is opened; but ... the crowd will frequently collect as early as three o'clock in the afternoon ...
>
> The walls of the well–staircase having a remarkably fine echo, and the wooden floor of the steps serving as a sounding board, the shouting, whistling, and quarrelling of the impatient young costers is increased tenfold. If, as sometimes happens, a song with a chorus is started, the ears positively ache with the din ...
>
> To anyone unaccustomed to be pressed flat, it would be impossible to enter with the mob. To see the sight in the gallery, it is better to wait until the first piece is over. The ham–sandwich men and pig–trotter women will give you notice when the time is come, for, with the first clatter of the descending footsteps, they commence their cries ...

---

[94] Charles Burney, *Musical Tours*, vol. ii, pp. 164 and 207
[95] Henry Mayhew, *The Street Trader's Lot – London: 1851* (Reader's Union Edition, 1949), pp. 11–15

At each step up the well–staircase, the warmth and stench increase, until by the time one reaches the gallery doorway, a furnace–heat rushes out through the entrance that seems to force you backwards, whilst the odour positively prevents respiration. The mob on the landing, standing on tiptoe and closely wedged together, resists any civil attempt at gaining a glimpse of the stage, and yet a coster lad will rush up, elbow his way into the crowd, then jump up on to the shoulders of those before him ...

When the orchestra begins playing, before 'the gods' have settled into their seats, it is impossible to hear a note of music. The puffed–out cheeks of the trumpeters, and the raised drum–sticks tell you that the overture has commenced, but no tune is to be heard. An occasional burst of the full band being caught by gushes, as if a high wind were raging ...

Whilst the pieces are going on, brown, flat bottles are frequently raised to the mouth, and between the acts a man with a tin can, glittering in the gas–light, goes round crying, "Port–a–a–a–r! who's for port–a–a–a–r." As the heat increased, the faces grew bright red, every bonnet was taken off, and the ladies could be seen wiping the perspiration from their cheeks with the play–bills.... No delay between the pieces will be allowed ....

Admittedly, Mayhew is describing the lowest class of nineteenth–century music hall. It is easy to transfer these scenes to a house like the Theatre Royal, in Richmond, Yorkshire: a Georgian miniature.

What of the 'chicken–or–egg' character of noise? The following observations are taken from the author's note–book:

Recently, I was at a concert by a six–piece progressive jazz–group, led by a musician of some reputation, whose marvellous playing I admire greatly. On this occasion the equipment proved to include electronic instruments and huge amplification. We sat near the back of the modest–sized auditorium. The collective musicianship was considerable and enviable. Nevertheless, until the interval, the audience was subjected to volume which stunned and brutalised in the hard–walled hall. Some gave no appearance of minding; but my ears, and those of my companions, were rendered highly uncomfortable: mine were almost pain–areas. As usual, the musicians stood behind, or to the side of, the speakers. Despite admiring the musical skill, which was distorted by the din or trapped and battered behind the aural mayhem, we were tempted to leave before the interval. Nevertheless, fingers in ears to reduce the assault, we managed to survive until then.

During the break, the amplification was reduced; the effect was transformation. Detail began to emerge: intricate, marvellous, even beautiful. There was another consequence. Once the paralysing brutality of volume had been tempered, small pockets of the audience began to talk, a few loudly. Suddenly, it occurred to me that much of the reason for excessive volume has always lain in its ability to neutralize; simply to wipe out all opposition, and to make impossible the conversation of the less–musical, less–sensitive, or least–interested. Tragically, the gargantuan power of modern, sophisticated electronic amplification–systems not only does this; it can injure the hearing of the audience and of the musicians.

Theatrical and operatic performing conditions prevalent by the end of the eighteenth century therefore helps us discern another reason for the rise of instrumental and singing–volume in the first decades of the nineteenth century, with all that this implies for techniques and well–being of singers. Volume commands attention. It brooks no competition. It stuns. It brain–washes.

A perceptive later nineteenth–century singer's viewpoint offers food for meditation: 'The more music is deprived of intimacy, the more it will be lacking in true genius.'[96]

While considering the effects of environment and volume–demands on singers, we might reflect on the twentieth–century folk–revival scene, particularly because it often involves male high singing. There could be possible parallels between earlier theatre and modern folk–singing conditions, for it is noticeable that folk–singers tend to hand–cup their ear(s), either to hear the full subtlety of resonances in their head–cavities, or to hear at all in a noisy musical and/or conversational environment: in a folk club, public house or in the open air – or (more likely in the past) in or near the workplace. The habit appears to be of ancient, not recent, origin. While serious singers scorn 'ear–cupping' during public performance, it affords a helpful monitoring method during private rehearsal or recording–session. To take but one example: the operatic tenor, José Carreras, makes use of it.

Did eighteenth–century operatic and theatrical singers or nineteenth–century musical–hall artists, and various volume–beleaguered vocalists of the past, ever use the cupped–ear while performing so as to hear themselves in the engulfing din? It seems possible, in some circumstances.

'Grateful' or 'ungrateful' to the voice are apt and thought–provoking terms. The cooler, invariably damp, often spacious and resonant church or cathedral building is associated with the first description, though incense can affect those unused to it. In churches or cathedrals, there would have been no need to strive through an often ill–mannered, gabbling audience, and possibly its orchestral equivalent. The congregation would have remained silent, or nearly so, during choral and solo music. It seems therefore significant that, what could be called a 'liquid–larynx' quality (the technique needed to sustain an easy transition through the two main registers) is easier in most churches but more difficult in most theatres, particularly in some past performing conditions.

Often, today, if the singer attempts to employ earlier vocal technique in unsuitable performing conditions, he cannot hear himself although it is possible that he can be heard more than he realises. He is tempted continuously to adjust his technique or even to force it in search of volume, as happened in the past.

On the whole, by physiological chance, most serious female singers had, and have, no choice but to employ all or most available registers unless the range of the music is small. The result is that even celebrated divas can sometimes be heard today 'changing over' notice-ably. Nobody bothers much, of course; it is an intrinsic, often exciting part of the vocal instrument. By contrast, when volume began to be of the essence, male voices could 'brazen it out' and choose to ignore the traditional, sensitive, synchromesh system.

---

[96] Lilli Lehmann, *My Path Through Life* (New York, 1914), quoted in Lebrecht, *The Book of Musical Anecdotes* (Sphere Books, 1987), p. 252

(It is interesting to note that, except in a few cases, modern female 'pop' singers seem to avoid head–voice quite intentionally, perhaps because of its association with sophisticated and 'élite' singing traditions or because thay have the 'traditional' chest–voice technique of black female blues–singers in mind. It is possible that they are simply (unconsciously?) anxious to avoid what is currently considered to be a stereotyped, feminine rôle–model, or it may be a combination of all three factors. On the other hand, many of today's male 'pop' vocalists continue to explore the upper reaches and colours of their head–voices, also in conscious or unconscious imitation of black–music rôle–models. Thus there is a fair degree of vocal 'cross–dressing' in popular music at present.)

It seems likely that, as theatre and opera houses must have encouraged male singers to use basic–voice increasingly, it was also because, surrounded by huge accompaniment, the singer yearns to feel the voice, to experience vibration and sensation in his throat and even in his body. Earlier through–register techniques with lightness of voice and use of head–voice do not give this sensation. A buzz in the cranial cavities, upper gums, nasal passages, and the naso–pharynx, is not the same. No effort is experienced, no feeling of striving and winning against odds: sensations which, arguably, the style of nineteenth–century stage and operatic music encouraged. The effect of this on counter–tenor, contralto–tenor or tenor would have been to precipitate the movement between head–voice and upper–chest at even higher points in the scale.

Perusal of contemporary prints, drawings, paintings and sculpture is useful for indications of the stance and head positions of singers, but in some respects it is not always as helpful as it might promise. The visual artist has always been swayed and influenced by various factors: composition and design, flattery, social, visual and cultural convention, scale, clarity or his own intrinsic drawing ability – or sometimes lack of it. Some contemporaneous represent-ations, therefore, of singers and players may not appear to support these points. However, the observation of Luca della Robbia (1400–1482) in his famous marble relief of a group of singers in Florence is revealing; these are to be found in the cathedral and in the Museo di Santa Maria del Fiore.

The cathedral section is illustrated. Observe the jaw and mouth positions, and those of all heads (except that of one boy) as they sing from, or regard, the music–book. The exception has his head back. Perhaps the sculptor sought posit-ional contrast.

In the Museo section (not illustrated here), the position of the three main singers' heads as they sing from the long horizontal music scroll

A group of boy singers: a relief by Luca della Robbia
(1400–1482)

relates to those in the cathedral. Of the fourth and fifth singers (behind the front three), one appears to be barely able to see the music. His head is awkwardly bent backwards. The other's head tilts sideways, face on palm, and he seems to have lost interest, in the only too familiar manner of a boy! In both sections of this important marble relief, the sculptor demonstrates that he has observed singers directly and at first hand.

We have plenty of opportunities today. Also, since the early twentieth century, photographs taken during musical perform-ances are helpful for our purpose, but even they can mislead. In the photograph of Alfred Deller, it will be seen that his head is tilted slightly upwards. This seems to run against the foregoing theory, but Mark Deller has suggested to the author that his father was singing Purcell's 'Music For a While', to intimate accompaniment, in Boughton Aluph Church, Kent. The building is renowned for its excellent acoustic qualities. So, this hypothesis is offered: Deller always sang this song at high pitch, and his technique was to float, or 'pipe' much of it, quietly, in a very beautiful way. To do this, a singer uses not merely a frontal–sinus focus, but almost an 'out–of–skull' focal image: a 'halo' sound. Thus, the face is best lifted slightly, or at least kept level. To tilt the head down, even a little, makes this production more difficult.

Alfred Deller using 'pipe–voice'

In 1723, Tosi wrote a little on posture and related matter, also suggesting that the familiar Italian smile during singing is of well–established date:

> I.25 Let him take care, whilst he sings, that he gets a graceful posture and makes an agreeable appearance.
> I.26 Let him rigorously correct all grimaces and tricks of the head, the body, and particularly the mouth, which ought to be composed in a manner (if the sense of the words permit it) rather inclined to a smile than to too much gravity.[97]
> VI.27 When he studies his lesson at home, let him sometimes sing before a looking glass, not to be enamoured with his own person, but to avoid those convulsive motions of the body or the face (for so I call the grimaces of an affected singer) which, when once they have took footing, never leave him.[98]

---

[97] Tosi, op. cit., p. 7
[98] Ibid., p. 40

We read also a reminder that singers were expected to work from music, as well as from memory:

> IV.27 Let him never suffer the scholar to hold the music paper, in singing, before his face, that the sound of the voice may not be obstructed ... and to prevent him from being bashful.[99]

Tosi mourns the increasing practice of singing from memory:

> IV.32 In certain schools, books of church-music and madrigals lie buried in dust. A good master would wipe it off; for they are the most effectual means to make a scholar ready and sure. If singing was not for the most part performed by memory, as is customary in these days, I doubt whether certain professors could deserve the name of singers of the first rank.[100]

Despite some stiff-strutting modern male 'pop-singers', the musical content of whose performance paradoxically strives for ultimate informality, an informal relaxed stance or posture is usually related to equivalent vocal-style and vice-versa.

When pioneers of the British folk-revival of the latter part of the nineteenth century and the early part of the twentieth were researching and evolving a suitable vocal technique with which to recreate traditional music, they realised that anything similar to the modern 'serious' or 'operatic' approach would be out of place. This was not only, or even primarily, because formal singing-style seemed unsuited to informal music-making, but because the technique itself was too stiff, unyielding and even inadequate for the purpose. They needed a technique which could accommodate the subtle vocal twists, tweaks, turns and changes of vocal timbre which could be discerned in much surviving traditional folk music. This was difficult or impossible for most singers with a polite 'art-song' style of sophistication, plummy tone, and academic training. Folk-singing is, or can be, skilled; though often it is an art which conceals art. The world of serious singing could re-learn from the subtleties and tonal colours of some folk singers. When one listens to the best of such performers, one is often struck by their sophisticated and varied use of resonators, together with a thinner, brighter, often sinuous, 'heady' and 'forward' quality which some detractors might call nasal (but this is to misunderstand the term). This vocal approach allows easy agility in spontaneous note decoration and ornament. It also helps extend range.

Some singers from the serious, formal tradition appear to have realised this and learned from it. Many of the colours absent from the voices of their colleagues and peers can be heard in recordings of Alfred Deller, and the tenor, Wilfred Brown (though significantly, Deller was self-taught and virtually untouched by the then academic ideas of style). Both used in their technique what could be termed 'sinus-subtleties'. They were invaluable for contrasts and characterization. Both Deller and Brown (at one time a member of the Deller Consort) sang unaccompanied folk-songs beautifully, with no stuffy 'Wigmore Hall platform' element suitable for accompaniment by polite pianoforte. Neither seems to have used a cupped-ear while singing in public, though, as with other singers, who knows what went on in the recording studio?

---

[99] Ibid., p. 25
[100] Ibid., p. 27

Though no attempt has been made to include equally balanced representative views from the four main European schools of singing, here are but a few authorities or important pedagogues of the past hundred years who give advice on upper–body stance and head–position during phonation:

J.B. Faure (1898?): erect stance without being unnatural or stiff.

W.H. Griffiths (1904): head slightly tilted back and upwards.

E.G. White (1909): head level, natural balance. His advice relates to that given by *Butenschon & Børchgrevink* (b) when sitting to practise; and to that of *Dr Merebeth Bunch, 1978.*

Kate Emil–Behnke (1945): head level, chin in (but not down).

Charles Kennedy Scott (1950): head sits loosely into body, not stiffly on it. There is shortening and widening of the neck.

Butenschon & Børchgrevink (1962): two options of stance which originate from either (a), a dorsal method, or (b), a ventral method which relates to *White.*

Mauro Uberti (1981), writing about Renaissance singing technique: head level, jaw more forward than for Romantic *voix sombrée.*

Niven Miller (1990), on posture:

Those of us who are familiar with the Alexander Technique know exactly the benefits of good posture and a slack jaw. To start with, the position of the head. It must rest in a relaxed position, neither with chin up, nor chin down. Neither tilting to the right nor to the left nor, most emphatically, the whole head thrust forward. This is a very common fault, and when it is corrected spectacular results are often experienced. Pop singers stretch out to microphones as in Elton John's case, sitting at the piano with bottom out and neck stretched. We also have over–anxious singers stretching out to the audience. The whole body posture therefore must be brought into play, making sure the 'tail' is tucked in, which of course pulls in the 'tummy', sternum lightly raised with shoulder muscles very relaxed. Check that the head is not sticking out. 'The larynx is suspended in the neck by three groups of muscles, one pulling towards the breastbone, the second towards the jaw–bone and a third towards the base of the skull. Their greatest exertions are in non–phonatory activity, such as yawning, chewing, and swallowing. Their movements change the shape of the throat and mouth; the *buco-pharyngeal resonator'*. (William Vennard, *A series of four Electromyo-graphic Studies.*) These muscles are affected by the clavicular muscles on the shoulders. This is why the tightness of the shoulders affects the function of the larynx, and this is why it is so important to do shoulder–relaxation exercises such as one learns from Dalcroze Eurythmics; for example, raising the shoulders as high as they will go, then loosely dropping them. This can also be done with alternate shoulders and then by shaking the arms out to the fingertips.[101]

---

[101] *Singing* (the Journal of the Association of Teachers of Singing), vol. 1, no. 19, Winter 1990, p. 61

Historical variation of head–position and stance in performance–context

Though it must be admitted that so small a list makes for somewhat superficial and premature conclusions, it could be suggested from the foregoing alone, that:

> (a) for early music generally, the singer's ideal head position seems to have been face not turned up; but skull level, or tilted slightly forwards;
> (b) for bel canto, perhaps eighteenth- or even early nineteenth-century music, the singer's ideal position may have been with head level, chin slightly more forward than for (a);
> (c) in mainstream mid-nineteenth-century and most mainstream twentieth-century secular singing, the chin is slightly raised, yet tucked in, because the thoracic vertebrae are pressed forward into the rib cage. An ultra-lowered laryngeal technique is compatible with this.

The reader is advised also to consult other authorities on singing technique. A study of Richard Miller's book, *English, French, German and Italian Techniques of Singing* is advised.[102] This generally excellent book is recommended with some hesitation, because of many of the views, arguments and conclusions therein, in relation to falsetto, head-voice, and the counter-tenor. Richard Miller (who is not related to Niven Miller), who seems to base his conclusions, like Sundberg, on mainly operatic singers of the type familiar today, rejects totally any artistic use of falsetto, both now and in the past. Despite this, the work is important and useful. It sets out in fine detail differing ways in which the four main schools of singing approach vocal pedagogy. Nevertheless, readers should be warned: after digesting its massive information, take care not to suffer bewilderment. Miller does, however, offer useful glimpses of techniques used by male voices of four different important countries in the past, inasmuch as no national tendencies or techniques could have left any voice type or range, including the male high voice, untouched or uninfluenced.

Even contemporary laryngologists who use ever more sophisticated computer technology to diagnose problems seem to require a head-posture which is high enough during phonation. Thus, it would seem, the majority of singers investigated must use conventional modern technique. There can be little hope of what we shall call alternative, earlier technique being investigated, recorded and validated. (We might consider the various implications of this for the future.)

Alessandro Scarlatti is credited with the founding of the Neopolitan school of opera. Henceforth, Naples was considered to be the great training ground for Italian operatic singers and musicians. (It is interesting to reflect on its French, then Spanish-dominated history.) During the seventeenth and eighteenth centuries, there appears to have been a characteristic approach in Naples which not only affected singing-style but also, probably as a result, posture and stance – and hence, acting and movement. It involved what could be called a 'Neopolitan-jaw position'. (Further study of Uberti's article on early vocal-technique is recommended.) The natural accent of everyday speech and phonation in that city and area appears to have been a major factor.

'Hanging' the jaw slightly more forward during singing results in an immediately higher laryngeal position. A change is felt which results in a brighter, more instant, forward tonal quality suitable for pre-nineteenth century music. This continues to be so, even when the jaw

---

[102] The Scarecrow Press, Inc., Metuchen, New Jersey, 1977

is dropped further but remains in a rather forward position. The nineteenth- and twentieth-century *voix sombrée* position, i.e., with over-dropped and more backward jaw, encourages the larynx to descend to its limit automatically, thus imbuing the voice with a darker, powerful yet more mellow, tone quality.

It seems possible that, when a more upward facial position began to be adopted for singing, it was found more and more that for many singers – especially those with high ranges – a slightly forward jaw position, combined with greater volume, produced a hard, unyielding tone quality and strain. The adoption of a more backward–placed jaw and a corresponding slight downward shift in larynx–position might well have commended itself in conjunction with gratifying increase in apparent fullness of tone and volume to fulfil changing demands. At any rate, this ideal became the norm for over a century, until recent re–thinking on early music vocal techniques began to surface. Wulstan has written usefully on much of this matter.[103]

There was another relevant factor in the nineteenth–century transformation of singing technique. Demands for maximum volume affected the method of breathing. 'Full–depth' breathing of a type best suited to fullest possible capacity and greatest volume (and the mental attitude which goes with this) can make fast runs more difficult, in that it often encourages a visible and audible 'pumping', almost 'laughing', effect on vocal tone during the run. Though often tonally magnificent (considered from one point of view), it usually results in less speed and flexibility, and even in ponderosity.

Though proper breathing techniques must always have been used by successful professional singers over the centuries, lighter and brighter melismas were, and still are, better and easier if 'breathed from a high point'. Such an approach is better suited to the requirements of earlier music; it must be emphasised, though, that 'breathing high' is not shallow or inadequate breathing. The mental approach may well have been, and should be today, to think of voice, therefore (in one sense) and breath as emanating from the cranial cavities and that part of the vocal tract which is above the larynx. This required some degree of 'automatic pilot'-breathing. It might be objected that runs and roulades supplied by eighteenth–century composers would have needed a maximum amount of breath, but breath–capacity would have been sufficient if a good breathing–technique had been established during training. A runner does not monitor his legs and feet during a race.

It should also be borne in mind that extremes of embellishment, during the seventeenth and eighteenth centuries, must have required the freedom of the singer to place his or her head and bodily stance in position, or positions, most beneficial for executing ornaments and divisions. A commonly–employed posture developed during the nineteenth century, with the jaw tucked in, the head tipped back semi–permanently and pushed into the neck, the neck into shoulders, seems highly unlikely to have bestowed enough freedom for the vocal high–agility of previous centuries. Indeed, such vocal gymnastics would seem to have been neither much required, nor usually possible, by the end of the nineteenth century.

There are obvious significances in this for the counter–tenor; indeed for all singers as they approach music of various periods.

As a post–script, and also to underline the dangers of laying down clear rules about anything concerned with the creative arts, consider the following. Charles Dibdin (1745–1814), a singer/actor like Mrs Cibber, could be thought of as an exception to what proved the rule. His style of performance was totally unusual for his time in that it was absolutely natural. In

---

[103] Wulstan, op. cit., pp. 225–233

fact, it seems to have resembled a twentieth–century 'one–man' show. Eye–witness accounts relate how he would run onto the stage, chat and joke with the audience and then, seated at his harpsichord or spinet, perform as if to a group of friends. He would lean backwards and rarely refer to his music copy – he was near–sighted – and sing with simplicity and natural demeanour, with no attempt at ambitious ornament. His enunciation was ultra–clear. From 1789 onwards, he was also involved in 'table entertainment', in which a single performer sat behind a table to face the audience. Dibdin's entertainments featured song as the predominant ingredient, and he combined in himself the functions of author, composer, narrator, singer and accompanist: an 'all–round' entertainer.

Dibdin, with his 'basic' and natural style, is thought to have avoided all use of falsetto head–voice; but many of his songs, in company with other stage songs of the period (most of which, of course, were sung partly in head–voice), have sections which seem intended for falsetto as decoration, or ornament – often shortish descant–like effects over the melody already heard at least once, as perhaps in the final phrase of the lovely air *Tom Bowling*. Certainly, a counter–tenor like Whitworth, Jacobs or Lesne, with a good through–voice technique and an attractive quality in his fundamental register, could perform songs like *Tom Bowling* (and for that matter, George Butterworth's *Is My Team Ploughing?*) extremely effectively. Pure head–voice would be reserved for the 'descant' or 'special effect' passages. Such reflections form a useful introduction to the next chapter.

14 Towards Performance: Pitches, Ranges and Styles

The identification, in original sources, of specific songs or arias for counter–tenor is sometimes difficult. Even though it usually seems to be identified by the alto clef, the music looks sometimes absurdly low or impossibly high. Anyone who attempts to advise on the investigation of early pitches, is, of course, on a hiding to nothing from some quarter or another. Informed, differing opinions are legion. Where is it advisable to start? With Fellowes's important earlier twentieth–century work on English madrigal composers? With Wulstan? Donington? Ellis and Mendel? These and other authorities cite some further authorities and commentators, and cross–references abound. Unless he has already done so, the totally committed reader will need to investigate deeply and at length.

Possibly, for many readers, Wulstan's perception, or perhaps Hill's succinct essay will provide the best basic beginning.[1] Notwithstanding, we ourselves must grasp something of the nettle here, if (as is inevitable) rather too briefly, in order both to provide a general introduction to, and demonstrate the size of, the problem.

'Standards' for musical pitch, often called 'diapasons', are usually expressed today in relation to the note A4, but many people do not realise that existence of a universal pitch (and one connected to this note in particular) is a modern phenomenon. Though the tuning fork was invented by the trumpeter John Shore in 1711, wide variations continued. In a letter to the author, Ian Harwood wrote:[2]

> People are frequently surprised at how recent a universal pitch–standard is. When my father died, I found a box with four tuning forks: two at a' [A4], one at c"[C5], and one at g'[G4]; all at different pitches. He had needed them all as a 'jobbing conductor' of choirs, bands, and orchestras in the 1920's and 1930s! Only in 1939 was a'=440 eventually agreed as a European standard.

We make our assessments, of course, by Western criteria. A precise relation between notation and pitch is thought to have been used in China, the Solomon Islands and Brazil long before Europe.

---

[1] E.H. Fellowes, *The English Madrigal Composers*, 1921, pp. 70–75; Alexander J. Ellis and Arthur Mendel, *Studies in the History of Musical Pitch*, (Frits Knuf, Buren, 1968 edn); David Wulstan, *Tudor Music*, (O.U.P., 1985), particularly pp. 192–214, and 'Birdus tantum natus decorare magistrum', *Byrd Studies*, ed. Brown and Turbet, (C.U.P., 1992); Robert Donington, *The Interpretation of Early Music*, 1975 edn; Simon R. Hill, 'Further on Pitch', *Leading Notes*, (N.E.M.A.), issue 4, July 1992

[2] 30 July 1991

Pitch has an important and obvious effect on the performance of historical vocal music. We can be certain that the lowest parts in choral works for what could be considered the 'basic usual choral combination' (the rough equivalent of today's S.A.T.B.) were sung by a bass of some variety (a male voice employing mainly fundamental, chest-, or modal-register), and the highest usually by a treble or, later, a soprano. Inner parts are obviously less clear-cut in their ranges, and when today's altos and tenors are trained to use different techniques, are particularly affected by considerations of pitch-shifting.

Though at present, Frank Ll. Harrison's views are probably considered by some to be a little dated, others believe that his research and method in his specialist area still remain valid and valuable. In considering medieval choral pitch and vocal range, he discusses the Eton Choirbook (probably the most important manuscript in existence of English liturgical music from the end of the fifteenth century, preserved in Eton College) and the Old Hall manuscript (an extremely important manuscript of Mass sections and motets by named English composers, c1370–1420) thus:[3]

> The Eton music shows the extension in the range and pitch in choral music which came with writing five or more parts, with the highest parts for boy trebles and the lowest parts in the modern bass range. The written pitch of the Old Hall music and of that of Dunstable's time had tenor C [C3] as the lowest normal note, the B flat [B2] a tone below being rarely written. Though the actual pitch was partly a matter of convenience, it is clear that the range of polyphony until the second half of the fifteenth century corresponded to that of the tenor and counter tenor voices of today .... The regular compass of pieces in five or more parts in the Eton manuscript is twenty-two or twenty-three notes. The compass of each piece is given these terms in the manuscript, together with the number of voices, both in the index and at the head of the piece, probably to show which works needed trebles and which could be sung by men only or, with transposition, by boys only. A few five- and six-part antiphons keep within the range of fourteen or fifteen notes, but none of the four-part antiphons exceeds fifteen notes. Of the ten four-part Magnificats, only one of which remains complete, six had a range of twenty-one or twenty-two notes, one of seventeen, and three of fourteen. The sonority obtained from the wider range in the full sections and the greater possibilities of textural contrast in the solo sections were among the major 'discoveries' of the later medieval composers, whose liking for the sound of rich and full chords is also evident in the common practice of dividing one or more parts at important cadences.

Most vocal music of the sixteenth and seventeenth centuries was written and printed in a very narrow range of keys, and seldom with ambitious or extreme key signatures. Other than ease for the printer at a time when music, like type, was set up manually, this may well have been related to the tuning of the keyboard instruments likely to be used for rehearsal and/or accompaniment. They were tuned in meantone temperament, which provided about eight central or 'home' keys in which the essential chords contained intervals 'purer' than the equal

---

[3] Harrison *Music in Medieval England* (Routledge and Kegan Paul, 1958), p. 311

temperament system and therefore nearer to the intervals to which singers naturally tune them—
selves (when they have the chance) and which provide satisfying points of rest at the cadences.
In particular, meantone temperament provides harmonically pure major thirds, much narrower
than the thirds of equal temperament which are artificially placed very 'wide'. Conversely, the
minor thirds of meantone are apparently 'out of tune' (because of clashing harmonics) and
therefore appropriately anguished – as opposed to the minor thirds in equal temperament
which are inappropriately, and against the grain of the musical mode, more nearly in tune than
the major thirds. Certainly, in printed music and manuscript, the 'simpler keys' and less-
involved key signatures feature most often.

Guido d'Arezzo invented a system called Solmization to designate the degrees of the
diatonic scale. It was used to teach singing and sight–singing until 1600, after which it became
obsolete as use of chromaticism increased. Harwood reminds us of the importance and
influence of Solmization when he writes:[4]

> Remember the problems of sight–singing and note–naming that Morley's
> scholars get into when trying to go 'off the beaten track'. There was just no
> easy way to do it, and I think that this is one very good reason why they
> stuck to 'simple' keys (if one should even use the word 'key' in this context).

Of course, the question of 'simple keys' and keyboard pitch is itself highly complicated. In
England, organ pitch seems to have been a fourth higher than choir pitch in the sixteenth
century. Bernard Rose wrote in 1965:[5]

> Does the fact that 'a capella' choral music was not 'written down' in extreme
> keys necessarily prove that it was not 'sung' in extreme keys? When one
> realises that different pitches for different 'media' ran parallel throughout this
> period – church pitch, chamber pitch and so on – and that different parts of
> Europe used different pitches from each other – witness organ tuning – it
> would lead one to conclude that the expression 'absolute pitch' is a recent one
> and would have been an unlikely and an embarrassing attribute at that time.
> Surely it is possible that if a composer desired to have a piece sung in, say,
> A flat minor he would write it out in A minor and the director would hum A
> flat! Those of us who have daily experience with choirs know well that a
> choir will sing a piece better at a low pitch on one day and at a higher pitch
> on another day. So many factors affect singers – the time of day, temperature,
> atmosphere and the proximity of meals! My conclusion is, and here I am at
> variance with most scholars on the subject, that there is nothing sacrosanct
> about pitch in 'a capella' choral music of this period. Verse anthems and verse
> services are an entirely different matter, since the tuning of organs permitted
> the use of only certain keys.

Wulstan discusses the effects on choirs (and later on solo voices) of a static pitch in sacred
music. He marshalls the three main arguments usually put forward in favour of flexibility and

---

[4] Loc. cit.
[5] Dr Bernard Rose, ' The Interpretation of Sixteenth Century Church Music', *English Church Music*,
(R.S.C.M., 1965), p. 30

answers them point by point (here slightly paraphrased):[6]

> 1 Despite evidence that pitch was known to have vacillated in previous
> centuries, the same scholars adhere to the conviction that Tudor pitch was
> co–incidentally the same as the modern standard.
> 2 'Lack of evidence' (a favourite phrase) makes total certainty impossible.
> The fact that evidence, albeit somewhat complex, exists; is hardly the same
> as 'lacking' evidence. Lastly [and this relates to the Rose point of view]
> 3 'Since there was no tuning fork ... the pitch of vocal music would have
> been flexible, and would have been chosen to suit each piece.' The absence
> of fixed pitch, however, is no more proved by the lack of tuning forks than
> the absence of fixed time must be assumed prior to the invention of the clock.

The sun's rising and setting times are in fact slightly staggered, from one end of a country
even as small as England to the other. Before the coming of the railways, time was not in fact
standardised across the country: there was a difference in time of about ten minutes between
London and Bristol, for example.

It would seem that there were at least two main pitches in use in England alone, during the
sixteenth and early seventeenth centuries, but unaccompanied vocal music, as we have seen,
can be (and still can be) pitched where convenient on the day. Instrumental pitches are more
fixed; though not always totally. For example, though strings may be tuned variably, there is
an ideal string tension for each instrument from which its optimum tonal quality can be
obtained.

It is worth reporting that, in 1619, Praetorius found that the E strings of violins, then made
of gut, could not withstand for long a tuning of A4 = 455 cycles.[7] One might ask how such
a measurement of pitch was calculated, but surviving instruments are obviously valuable in
helping to ascertain the pitches of earlier periods. In addition, a paper by Harwood is
recommended.[8] Harwood, formerly a maker of early stringed instruments, researcher into early
music procedure, and counter–tenor singer, argues convincingly that two main pitch standards,
a fourth apart, were used for instruments in late–Elizabethan England, *c*1600. His own
researches support the view that, in effect, there were two sets of instruments for consort
music – which would also include singing voice(s), where called for. One set was at 'low'
pitch, about a tone below modern standard. The other, at 'high' pitch, was about a minor third
above it:[9]

> This happens to be the level advocated by one school of thought for English
> church music of the period, which must affect the argument with regard to the
> 'consort anthem' and other music for voices and viols. The lute song repertory,
> too, may have been available at two pitch levels to suit different voices.

When lute tuning and pitch are discussed, it should also be remembered that, like other

---

[6] Wulstan, *Tudor Music*, p. 194
[7] Wulstan, op. cit., p. 196
[8] Ian Harwood, 'A Case of Double Standards', *Early Music*, Oct. 1981, pp. 470–481
[9] Harwood, op. cit., p. 480

instruments, it varied somewhat from country to country,[10] and that lutenists seem likely to have had alternative instruments for alternative pitches.

Some scholars feel that a church pitch a minor third above the printed note of the sixteenth and seventeenth centuries seems too high, but Harwood's and Wulstan's separate researches support it convincingly. The low pitch of about a tone below our modern A4 = 440 Hz has, however, been seized on for most secular music from the early seventeenth century onwards. As Harwood explains, viols of different sizes existed for use when the higher pitch was desired. There seems little reason to suppose that they were used only in churches. They were for use, when convenient, in secular or domestic performance. Such usage as that now supported by musicologists of the same mind as Harwood would have remained more or less constant in a conservative country like England, until an important or dramatic change came about.

That event seems to have been the abolition of the monarchy and the establishment of the more austere Cromwellian régime in 1642. In 1660, the Restoration may well have been something of a cultural shock; but, as we have seen earlier, the event could not and did not change pitches, instruments, and repertoire overnight; it is more likely that it began a development. The usual view is that French influence at the court of Charles II brought with it a move towards the adoption of a lower musical pitch, notably at the Chapel Royal with its new string–band; but it would seem that the pitch used at the Chapel Royal, after the Restoration must have involved a compromise between old and new, 'low' and 'high'. ('Old' instruments may have been used in 'new' ways: a bass instrument at 'old' high pitch could be used for 'tenor–ranged' parts at 'new' lower pitch.)

The original pitches of the older instruments had come into being because by 1600 each musical centre had developed collections of instruments tuned to perhaps two or three different diapasons or pitches. Usually, these included a pitch for sacred music (termed 'Chor–T(h)on' by Praetorius), the diapason of an important local organ, and a pitch for chamber music (Praetorius's 'Cammer–T(h)on'): the pitch in use at the castle or palace of the local prince. Mendel[11] points us towards Bach's friend, J.G. Walther, in 1732, who defined Cammer–Ton as follows:

> Chamber pitch means: when a piece of concerted music is performed not at the old Choir or Cornet Pitch, but rather, mainly on account of the adult [male] sopranos, who cannot well sing in the highest range [therefore, surely not castrati, but falsetti], and also for the sake of the instruments so that the strings may hold better, a whole tone or even a minor third lower.

One's own experience of an ancient choral tradition demonstrates something of the practical problems that might have been encountered in Restoration England not only in the re–establishing of an earlier usage but also in accepting new ideas. The choir at the Chapel Royal included some new singers as well as men who had lost their employment (if not their pensions) only twenty years before. Which diapason triumphed? Were the new violins tuned to the (traditional?) pitch of the new Chapel Royal organ, or was the organ tuned to the pitch of the 'new' strings? It has been assumed that strings accompanied only the verse anthems, and that the rest of the choral service was accompanied on the organ, but it is a point of dis–

---

[10] Ibid., p. 137, on the 'French Lute'
[11] Ellis and Mendel, op. cit., p. 192

agreement that organ and strings were ever used together.

It seems that a *basso continuo*, at least, was supplied after the discontinuing of the full string band:[12]

> 8 March – Warrant appointing Francis Goodsens to play upon the bass violin in the Chapel Royal, noting "he hath in consert with ye Organ performed upon ye Base Violin in Our Royall Chappells to Our satisfaction"; fee of £40 a year, from 1 October 1711.

We may imagine the problems encountered if singers were asked to sing at different pitches when accompanied by organ, then strings, followed again by organ. In the Chapel Royal, during the years following the Restoration, the pitch of the 'new' violins and the 'old' viols must surely have been adjusted to the same level? If not, difficulties would have been likely, particularly if old and new instruments were used together.

The argument against this is that old and new ensembles were probably used separately: that the latest French-style compositions were played mostly by the violin band, while all other music was performed on the earlier consort and other instruments, in their great variety. On the other hand, though this 'apartheid' may have obtained on occasion, it seems unlikely always to have been so.[13] As a result, we may see that variable pitches, according to the instruments employed, are likely to have caused problems in adjustment for singers; both those blest with 'perfect pitch' (whatever that could have meant in the circumstances), and those without.

The last anthem that Purcell wrote with string accompaniment is thought to have been *O Sing Unto the Lord*, 1688. In 1689, William III ended the custom of using strings for the Sunday anthem(s). In normal circumstances, the violin band appears to have accompanied the Chapel Royal Choir on one day a week. Perhaps 'accompany' is not quite the right word: in most anthems, strings seem to have done little more than alternate with voices and organ and to reinforce the final chorus.

Judging from the positions of choir and string band in the admittedly rather fanciful engraving of 1712, we may see that the small size of the building (known to have been only about thirty feet wide and between forty and seventy feet long) and the close proximity of choir, band and congregation required no great volume. The Chapel Royal solo voices were seldom called on either to dominate a large ensemble of strings, with organ, or to fill a large building with sound. A moderate, even intimate style would have been sufficient.

Hearing yet not seeing certainly removes inappropriate visual distractions. A recent BBC radio broadcast of a recorded concert of Purcell's music for the Chapel Royal, originally given in the spacious acoustic of St John's Church, Smith Square, Westminster, brought the seventeenth century alive in a moving way. Though, ideally, it would have been most satisfactory to have been listening to the Chapel Royal Choir of today (suitably augmented, because there are only six Gentlemen on the Foundation now), the effect was satisfyingly authentic. Actually, seventeenth-century pluralities often meant that the same singers were both Gentlemen of the Chapel Royal and Lay-Vicars of Westminster Abbey (itself a Royal Peculiar), so in the event, the Choristers and Lay-Vicars of the Abbey, with a string band comprising authentic instruments, drew us powerfully into the seventeenth century.

---

[12] *R.E.C.M.*, vol. V, p. 102
[13] See Ashbee, *R.E.C.M.*, vol. I, p. 109, for an example: an account of court music at Windsor

The 'rightness' of this performance was due in no small manner to the fact that what was being heard was not one of today's exercises in reconstruction which invariably employs a small, anachronistically mixed, choir. Instead, we 'entered into' a performance which mirrored almost exactly the forces used originally. The Lay–Vicars of the Abbey, for example, were in view of their (Royal) peculiar office their almost direct descendants. In addition we were hearing Purcell, and being made highly conscious of his joint connection, boy and man, with both the Chapel Royal and Westminster Abbey. It was noteworthy that the pitch was A4=440, and that the early instruments were tuned to this with apparent ease and totally satisfactory effect. There are perfectly sound arguments for use of this pitch for this period of music, partly because it is a good compromise between the probable late seventeenth–century English secular pitch of approximately a quarter of a tone down from A=440, and the probable sacred pitch of the same period of between a semitone and a tone higher than A=440 (discussed later). Indeed, some authorities believe that, in the Restoration Chapel Royal, it was all much simpler than is often suggested; that, in meeting at a common pitch, both church and secular music were performed at what amounts to our modern pitch. Other scholars claim that English seventeenth–century secular music, both before and after the Restoration, is now played at a pitch about a semitone too low. This, they point out, seems to come about because many 'authentic' instruments used today are either genuine or reconstructed continental instruments, whose natural pitch was a semitone below today's. By an accident of history, it appears that fewer early English stringed instruments have survived. This is not so with wind instruments, such as hautboys, a fair number of which, by English makers, are extant.

As we have discerned, European instruments and pitches have differed among themselves, and from English pitches, at various periods. Nevertheless, it must be admitted that the effect of music played on 'authentic' instruments, of whatever origin, pitched a semitone lower than modern standard, or indeed at A=440, is usually superior to that obtainable on later Romantic instruments, tuned either to A=440 or, where possible, to a lower pitch. It seems that certain instruments were tuned higher or lower than what was 'normal' – whatever 'normal' is deemed to be. Cornetts, for example, sounded slightly more than a tone higher than their written music would suggest. Similarly, there is evidence that some English organs were slightly in excess of a semitone higher than the 'printed note'.

Research continues to explore whether or not the average secular pitch of Blow and Purcell differed markedly from that of Handel. English late seventeenth–century church pitch is thought by many scholars to have been high – up to one tone higher than the printed note, considered at our modern A4=440 level. Church pitch, in fact, had remained fairly steady (in the first half of the seventeenth century, it seems to have remained at its earlier level: a minor third above A4=440) but, although after the inhibitions and restrictions of the Commonwealth the 1660 Restoration must have felt like a fresh start, the reality must surely have been a clinging, or return, to a conservative and well–tried tradition.

Peter Phillips[14] wrote, in a passage equally appropriate to a discussion of composition, pitch and voices:

> England remained peculiarly exposed to the continent and, equally important, uncharacteristically receptive to what was going on there. Yet always what was imported was remoulded to suit the native view....

---

[14] Peter Phillips, *English Sacred Music, 1549–1649*, (Gimell, Oxford, 1991), final chapter

There is, however, a theory that when Handel and large numbers of other German–speaking musicians, instrumentalists and instrument makers came to England in the early eighteenth century, they brought with them a German pitch between a tone and semitone lower than our modern pitch. Whether it was this or a French pitch at some time in the late seventeenth century, the theory is that something encouraged 'English pitch' below A4=440. At the moment, judging by early–music performance practice today, most scholars seem to believe that mainstream opera, oratorio and other secular music of the eighteenth century was performed at a standard pitch a semitone down from that of today. Some directors would include church music in this, while others are even busy exploring the effects of extremely low pitches, at around A4=392, for Purcell's music.

Tosi[15] tells us (1723) that Lombardy pitch was about three quarters of a tone above our present standard. Roman pitch was about a minor third lower than that of Lombardy. The average pitch in eighteenth–century Northern Europe was about a quarter of a tone below the modern standard. The truth is that a single approach to the evaluation of pitch before about 1830 can only apply to a particular work, or corpus of works, written for a specific place within a particular period of time.

It is therefore merely for convenience today that what is now known as 'Baroque Pitch' is standardized as a semitone down, at A4=415. Some early tunings could have been as much as a tone lower than today's. However, research into the actual instruments is beginning to demonstrate that, for most works of the Baroque period, a drop of pitch by a semitone from today's standard is too great, and that a quarter-tone is probably more appropriate.[16]

Difficulty with old pitches is further complicated by the use of certain 'high' clefs which indicate that the music should be performed a fourth or fifth away from what is 'written'. The principle of transposition when 'high clefs' are used is precisely stated by Michael Praetorius in his *Syntagma Musicum*, vol iii, 1619. 'Chiavette' (which means changing clefs) involves the use of the tenor clef

for a bass part instead of

There was also the use of the G clef on the second line

for a soprano part instead of the usual

The idea was to avoid the need for ledger lines, but (because ledger line notes may well lie outside the effective compass of the voice) they were used also to indicate transposition down by a fourth or fifth. Therefore, a soprano part written in the G clef with this compass

---

[15] Tosi, *Opinioni...Observations on the Florid Song*, (modern edn, Stainer & Bell, 1987), pp. 7–8

[16] See Robert Rusk, 'Pitch Putsch', *Opera Fanatic*, 1989, pp. 49–52, and William Sumner, 'A History of Musical Pitch', *Music Book* (Hinrichsen, 1952), vol. VII, pp. 233–242

might possibly indicate that it was to be sung thus

with a similar transposition indicated by the chiavette of the other parts. We should not forget that the pitch from which the transposition is effected is not likely to have been our modern standard. Monteverdi is an example of a composer some of whose works are now thought to be associated with the chiavette device. It should be reiterated that the effects that pitch and clefs may have on all parts merit thorough study.

As has been suggested earlier, there are occasions when transposition in performance today of earlier music is made on the basis of convenience, and not on the grounds of historical pitch. 'Convenience' can be linked with, or applied to, several situations, but one of significance concerns the availability of suitable singers. The reasons for such availability, and of course the implied unavailability of other voices, has been suggested variously throughout this work; the performance of the liturgical Passion is one such example.

The large–scale Passion oratorio, like Bach's, is well-known, but its precursors are less familiar, and they reward investigation by students of the male high voice. Of particular interest in the present context is the liturgical passion sung on Palm Sunday and Good Friday in the Western Rite. The recitation of the Gospel Passion narratives in Holy Week is an extremely ancient usage. An earlier and more simple ritual was superseded in the twelfth century by one more complex and dramatic, in which the narrative was recited by three 'Deacons [*sic*] of the Passion', though in fact they were of various ecclesiastical ranks. The Deacon, who was a tenor (*media vox*) intoned the narrative text. The Priest was a bass (*bassa vox*), and intoned the utterances of Christ. The Sub–Deacon was an alto (*suprema vox*), and represented the people (the *turba*) and individual characters other than Christ. The male high voice was androgynous, in this case in its rôle as 'the crowd' and minor characters male or female.

The reciting note (*tonus currens Hauptton*) of each singer was the highest in the plainsong formula which was allotted to it:

Priest:	F3	Bass
Deacon:	C4	Tenor
Sub–Deacon:	F4	Alto

The complete compass of the three voices formed three tetrachords: an octave and a half:

Priest:	C3–F3 inclusive
Deacon:	F3–C4 inclusive
Sub–Deacon:	C4–F4 inclusive

This scheme survived into the sixteenth century, though the choir eventually took the *turba*, while the alto soloist continued to sing the parts of Pilate, Pilate's Wife and the minor characters.[17] Examination of Victoria's Passion settings (St Matthew's and St John's Gospels; 1585) for the traditional four-part *turba* (boys, or high falsettists and/or castrati?, together with A.T.B.), written for the choir of the Sistina, demonstrate this. Modern general performing editions, however, nearly always print the setting without making allowance for any pitch-changes. This results in a pitch probably about a minor third lower than expected by the composer; most likely not for musicological reasons, but either because when these modern editions originated, altos – counter-tenors – were not available or suitable; or that, at the time, priests were still used for these rôles and it would have been difficult to find good clerical high voices for Narrator, Pilate, and Pilate's Wife. If all the solo parts were sung by choir-members, a boy-alto, though he might have sounded vaguely convincing in the part of Pilate's Wife, would not have been at all appropriate for the rôle of Pilate himself.

It seems significant that the alto voice was chosen for Pilate. Though it may have been merely unavoidable, given the restrictions of the 'three-deacon' scheme, one is tempted to think that the timbre of the male high-voice was thought best to represent the traditionally slimy, evasive character of Pilate, at least as portrayed in the gospels. Modern liturgical performance of Victoria's setting, however, sung approximately a minor third too low, trans-forms alto into tenor, tenor to baritone, light bass to basso profundo, and makes the four-part music more suitable for A.A./T.B. (which is incorrect, however effective in this form).

Byrd wrote a Passion setting (*Turbarum Voces in Passione Domini Nostri Secundum Joannem*) which consists of a three-voice polyphonic *turba* only, seemingly to be sung with the passion tones of the Sarum Use,[18] which are very simple and extremely restricted in range. The Fellowes/Dart edition of 1958, transposed down one tone from Byrd's original,[19] concludes that the *turba* is for mens' voices, A.T.B., and proposes that the Evangelist is for tenor voice, and that Christ is to be represented by a bass. Thurston Dart's Introductory Note does not state the basis on which transposition is made: whether of historical pitch or vocal convenience.

Having read earlier of the origins of the contra-tenor part, the reader will no doubt recall how it has risen gradually from early medieval times when it did duty for a rudimentary bass and alto. This was a gradual process which assumed, in England, the name 'counter-tenor' as it went along. It arrived in the sixteenth century at what is considered a 'comfortable' alto range – i.e., a range which the average alto today enjoys most, it being based on, or success-fully singable in, extended head-voice. The upper range and tessitura rose much later, through Romantic influence. Though this was chiefly in secular music, eventually it was to variously influence the church-orientated composers, Stanford, Wood, Bairstow, Vaughan Williams (in one of his areas of composition) and Howells (yet see Example 22, p. 307).

The resulting tessitura of alto parts in twentieth-century English cathedral and church music is usually as high as is possible for most counter-tenors to manage; sometimes, it is decidedly uncomfortable. Yet, occasionally, cathedral composers still showed that they were conscious of the traditional rôle of the counter-tenor part.

---

[17] See C. Sanford Terry, 'Passion Music', in Grove's *Dictionary* ..., 3rd edn, 1927, pp. 72-79
[18] Trinity College, Cambridge, MS. B. 11.13 (from Lincoln, early fifteenth century)
[19] *Gradualia* of 1605 (Stainer & Bell, 1958)

*Example 22. Excerpt from 'I Sat down under His Shadow', Edward Bairstow (1874–1946)
which illustrates the traditional rôle of the contra- or counter-tenor part
employed in an anthem of the romantic style (1925)*

In October 1956, Stuart Humphry Ward, in a short article in *The Musical Times*,[20] pointed out that the modern alto part's tessitura can actually damage the young adult voice before it has matured enough to cope with a sometimes cruel range. This, in turn, spells doom when the singer has to deal with Classical counter–tenor parts – yet composers continue to write ever–higher alto parts. Ward pleaded for more lengthy vocal training to avoid this damage and added that modern composers might break the vicious circle by keeping alto tessituras down.

He took two excerpts from important works for alto, and demonstrated the change. We are not discussing a different voice, an abnormally high tenor with modern technique, as compared with an 'exclusive' falsettist but what is widely regarded as the pre–Romantic, traditional English cathedral and 'concert–platform' counter–tenor. The first example may have been sung by Purcell at its first performance; it matters not that Example 23 is probably for a low counter–tenor or second alto, and that Example 24 is for high or first alto, but some commentators might consider it important that Purcellian pitch might have been about a quarter tone below A=440, while Vaughan Williams wrote undeniably for A=440, or even higher – depending on the pitch of Canterbury's organ at that time.

Example 23. Excerpt from the alto solo 'Tis Nature's Voice', (top)
(Ode on St Cecilia's Day, 1692) Purcell.
Example 24. Excerpt from Te Deum in G (first–alto line) (middle)
R. Vaughan Williams, 1928.
Example 25. Excerpt from the duet 'Hark Each Tree' (first–bass part) (lowest)
(Ode on St Cecilia's Day, 1692) Purcell.

[20] Stuart H. Ward, 'The Male Alto in Church Music', *The Musical Times*, October 1956, p. 531

As Ward commented, the tessitura of the *Te Deum* is cruel, yet it is a work frequently performed by cathedral and similar choirs, and was in fact written for performance by Canterbury Cathedral Choir at Archbishop Lang's enthronement in 1928; it has been sung at several enthronements since. It is therefore clear that Vaughan Williams always intended it for altos, not women contraltos.

Which counter–tenors would wish to sing Purcellian solos immediately following the Vaughan Williams *Te Deum in G* or many compositions for male S.A.T.B. choir since? Not many, if they are honest! Who would care to reverse this? The examples given could be seen to support the point about many low counter–tenors' lack of upper–falsetto: Example 23 was either for full–strength pharyngeal voice alone, possibly plus fundamental voice (a 'dovetail-joint', probably as to be used in Example 25, despite its labelling as a 'bass' solo). Example 24 is for upper falsetto, with the added strength (since it is a *forte* passage) of pharyngeal support.

As Jacobs[21] has pointed out, the phrase 'passions to express' can hardly be brought out by a weak, low falsetto voice. Unless Purcell had his tongue in his cheek, one is first tempted to agree that the word–painting throughout the air in question is obviously planned to exploit a balance of fundamental voice plus falsetto (dovetailed, not spliced). Note, however, that strong pharyngeal tone can be equally effective low in pitch and, indeed, is capable of possessing passion. (The author can still remember being present at a stunning performance by Deller of this work in the mid–1950s in the BBC Broadcasting House concert hall for a Third Programme broadcast.) Many exclusively head–voice counter–tenors can make this air totally convincing and effective.

The currently fashionable suggestion is that, whoever first sang the air 'Tis Nature's Voice' (be it Purcell or Pate), he was a tenor. Most performances today which set out to prove this use a light tenor with modern technique but (remembering Purcell's unrivalled sensitivity to the nuances of the English language) it surely cannot be coincidence that he selected the counter–tenor, and his particular vocal characteristics, for Nicholas Brady's words:

> Tis nature's voice,
> Thro' all the moving wood, and creatures understood,
> The universal tongue, to none of all her numerous race unknown [.]
> > From her it learnt the mighty art,
> > To court the ear, or strike the heart,
> At once the passions to express and move [;],
> We hear, and straight we grieve or hate; rejoice or love [.]
> > In unseen chains it does the fancy bind,
> > At once it charms the sense, and captivates the mind.

The singer is required to personify the human voice – both male and female, not one or the other, but the 'universal utterance'. We should ask ourselves what sort of sound Purcell had in mind to bear this responsibility and to express the wittily planned *double entendre* of the opening line? We know, of course, that he composed the air for a male voice, but was it a voice of timbre both sexless and androgynous or one like our modern tenor: straightforward and unambiguously male? It is a point worth remembering when we come to assess certain 'authentic' or 'historically aware' performances of today.

---

[21] Jacobs, 'The Controversy Surrounding the Timbre of the Countertenor', p. 294

An inverse of this question is the rôle of The Angel in *The Dream of Gerontius*, which is also meant to be androgynous. Elgar wrote it for a contralto or mezzo–soprano; any suggestion of using a high counter–tenor for The Angel in a performance is unacceptable to most people, including the present author; though, purely for curiosity's sake, it would be interesting to hear a high male voice (like Wong or Christofellis) sing the part in rehearsal. Elgar's clear intention should, of course, be followed at all times in a public performance.

The style of Purcell's writing in 'Tis Nature's Voice' favours light, disembodied, head–voice effects with coloratura and rich effects in the lower register. The voice–type chosen is to represent the gamut of human emotions: 'In unseen chains it does the fancy bind, at once it charms the sense, and captivates the mind.' It cannot be claimed that no other voice type could do this if sung by an artist, but the delights of the counter–tenor's vocal qualities and potential seem particularly apposite.

We should reflect on points raised by 'Tis Nature's Voice' because much counter–tenor solo and verse singing in late seventeenth– and early eighteenth–century cathedral music demands an unchurchy vocal style.

One of the most interesting aspects of Ward's article was his random choice of ten works written for cathedral choirs (five older works and five newer) in order to compare the tessitura of alto part writing. Conscious of pitch differences which might divert the discussion, he pointed out that his inspection of the tessitura of other voice parts in the older works shows the fairness of his comparison. Purcell makes his bass soloist sing Example 25, from the same Ode as Example 23; both of these could have been performed at 'secular' pitch. The tenor lobby would take this point as further proof that counter–tenors were modern tenors, but compare the almost identical ranges of Example 23 and Example 25, and reflect that seventeenth–century pitch was probably only about a quarter of a tone lower than A=440.

There should be no problem in understanding how Purcell could take both counter–tenor and bass parts especially when written with a tessitura like these. As T. S. Eliot says of St Thomas Becket: 'There is no mystery about this man who takes a certain part in history'.

Here are Ward's conclusions.[22] He calculated the percentage duration of the alto part spent above A4 (A4=440) thus:

Vaughan Williams, *Te Deum in G*	37%
Howells, *'Collegium Regale' Magnificat*	25%
Stanford, *Jubilate in C*	21%
Bairstow, *Blessed City*	18%
Wood, *Jesu, the Very Thought*	17%
Palestrina, *Christe Redemptor*	7%
Purcell, *Ode on St Cecilia's Day*, 1692, 1st solo alto	6%
Byrd, Four–part *Mass*, omitting Credo and Gloria	3%
Blow, *Salvator Mundi*	one semiquaver B♭
Purcell, *Remember Not, Lord*	0%

Of the five modern works investigated, none descends lower than A♭3, whereas low Gs and Fs are not infrequent in the older works. If one wished to extend Ward's idea and to analyse a well-known collection of Tudor works, *The Oxford Book of Tudor Anthems* could be useful.

---

[22] Op. cit., p. 532

It must be said that, to some extent, we are in the hands of editors, but most editors today, acutely conscious of (other) musicologists looking over their shoulders, are generally scrupulous in their decisions, including those of pitch, even though there are differences of opinion, and they nearly always indicate the original printed or written pitch in modern editions. A few works give the alto or counter–tenor voice a part originally labelled with another name. Apparent tenor parts in these cases are often worthy of special study.

We should consider briefly the range and character of the two counter–tenor parts called for in the anthems included in the Oxford collection cited and many other works, including settings of the canticles and responses. Compositions with two alto parts (even, on occasion, three) are found in abundance until the Civil War: then, through Henry Purcell and William Croft (e.g., his *Te Deum*) to many of Handel's English choral works.

The almost inevitably double counter–tenor parts of the sixteenth and seventeenth centuries are not to be confused with the mid–fifteenth–century 'split' contra–tenor. The first is the direct result of the popularity of the high vocal register, but the second was a fifteenth–century logical division to exploit the possibilities of sub–tenor territory, when the two alto parts 'countered' each other, crossing and re–crossing continuously, and enriching the polyphonic texture. When there are double counter–tenor parts, we are accustomed today to think of Decani taking the higher and Cantoris the lower, and in verse work the same principle applying, but this is a relatively modern simplification of the real situation. In the early seventeenth century, Cantoris first counter–tenor was the principal voice. His 'partner', Cantoris second counter–tenor, sang the same part as Decani first counter–tenor, and *vice versa*. This was to ensure that, when the choir sang antiphonally in five parts, all five would be present on each side. Also, it meant that both counter–tenor parts were strong throughout their range.[23] This practice seems to have been in existence also for most of the sixteenth century but, as alto parts were formerly almost equal, crossing each other frequently, to a large extent their voices must have been 'equalized' too. Subsequently, it would appear that either the composers altered their style of writing and counter–tenors specialized – or, less probably, that the writing followed the development of the voices of the singers themselves. This may have varied from country to country:

> ... the English use of voices, whereby the shape of the musical outline is
> suited to vocal proclivities, rather than the voice having to follow the stonier
> path indicated by more abstract ideas.[24]

It should be remembered that choir sizes (relevant to any consideration of the allocation and doubling of voice parts) would have varied according to the importance of the foundation. Clearly, St Paul's Cathedral or the Chapel Royal would have had a larger number of available singers, but at Chichester (a modest provincial cathedral), when Thomas Weelkes was organist *c*1602–1623, the choir consisted of eight boys and eight lay–clerks. There were also four vicars–choral, but by this date they rarely sang with the choir. (At Chichester, and some other cathedrals, vicars–choral are the equivalent of minor canons, but in most cathedrals of the Old Foundation, the terms 'vicar–choral' or 'lay–vicars–choral' refer to singing–men only.) Knowing the usual assignment of vocal parts in cathedral music, we may assume that at Chichester, out of the eight lay–clerks, one might suppose that four would be counter–tenors

---

[23] See Wulstan, *Tudor Music*, p. 243
[24] Wulstan, *Byrd Studies*, p. 76

– two each side – to cope with the frequent antiphonal divisions requiring two altus parts; while two would be tenors and two basses; or perhaps a more flexible arrangement with three altos, three tenors and two basses: an arrangement which, if the tenors were sufficiently flexible and all voices were produced as 'through' voices, would have coped with all polyphonic demands. Unfortunately, such an arrangement and balance does not exist anywhere today.

Regarding choir–size today, anthems written for cathedrals or similar bodies are generally composed with forces of perhaps eighteen boys and between six and twelve men in mind. Until recently, anthems written by British composers for mixed or larger forces seem to be in the minority. However, in both cathedral and mixed choirs, the twentieth–century alto part has usually remained higher, with something of a late–nineteenth–century tessitura.

Tudor works, and (until recent years) most modern anthems, were written exclusively for traditional male choirs. Some twentieth–century sacred choral compositions, however, were intended, initially, for mixed church choirs.

The large, mixed–voice choral society had been in existence throughout the nineteenth century and had influenced choral writing style and vocal tessitura. Is it conceivable that part of the reason for the steadily rising pitch was that, in large–scale choral writing (in Mendelssohn's, for example) there was a search for higher choral harmonics? (Mendelssohn preferred the use of contraltos in his oratorios; though examination of his compositions which use both English and German texts, for smaller groups, even English cathedral–style choirs, often shows awareness of more traditional tessiture, and an alto range and character more appropriate to male singers.)

As contraltos displaced altos in choral societies and opera choruses, the different quality of the female voice, with a higher median, and in particular a lack of plangency or brightness until higher in the vocal range (if there), probably began to be apparent. It is possible that composers wishing to lighten the choral timbre would have been encouraged to write higher contralto parts. Like musical directors of the time, they probably welcomed rising pitch for its 'brightening' and apparent intensifying of choral and orchestral sound.

It is also tempting to think that rising pitch must gradually have encouraged altos in cathedral and church music to return to a practice put forward as the sole sixteenth–century (and earlier) English alto technique – that of using head–voice only, with basic–voice being more or less unemployed. However, several factors work against this:

> (a) Nineteenth–century cathedral and comparable choirs continued to sing seventeenth and eighteenth–century music, with its low alto verse and choral parts. It is thought that the few sixteenth–century pieces still in the repertoire were, like those of the seventeenth and eighteenth, sung at the visual pitch of the period of performance or that of the particular organ in situ – i.e., no minor third or other transposition was usually made. Strong tone and volume had become the order of the day. The reaction (what could be called the 'ecclesiastical camera' style), whether it was a return to earlier practice, or a new approach, was yet to come.
>
> (b) Early in the twentieth century, altos (who, like Hawkins and Clarke, can still be heard on recordings) used chest/head technique. Their formative years were in the nineteenth century. We have seen that, slightly earlier than Hawkins or Clarke, Dr A. H. Prendergast, and others, described this technique as normal.

(c) Frederic Hodgson tells the story about C. S. Simkins, the Windsor alto and musicologist: when Hodgson was first appointed to the choir in the 1950s, they found themselves comparing vocal techniques. Simkins, who was older and had a markedly different timbre from Hodgson, used a through–voice technique. 'Of course', said Simkins, 'I am an old–fashioned type of counter–tenor'. (Hodgson uses head–voice only.)

The Alto clef

Usually, alto parts are now printed in what is often a quite infuriating manner – the treble or G clef is employed, and this takes most earlier alto parts into a web of ledger lines. When one compares its use with the neater layout and instant legibility of the alto or C clef, one is left wondering why the C clef was ever abandoned.

One reason is surely expediency: the fewer clefs, the easier music reading became to the less skilled. In addition, women contraltos would probably prefer a treble clef for obvious reasons. A female singing the alto part would normally consider it a low voice, and think 'down' for it. Dropping below the stave for her has a psychological effect similar to that encountered by basses using the bass clef. As we have seen, the coming of the contralto produced a strong influence on choral writing and vocal disposition.

The alto clef had its drawbacks. Though, originally, singers used part–books, the later use of scores (championed by William Croft) highlighted the rather irritating similarity of alto and tenor parts placed on adjacent lines with similar clefs (see an example of this overleaf). Nevertheless, the C clef was useful to show a vocal line which could be sung either by a counter–tenor or by a tenor. Music type–setting with moveable type was made considerably more difficult if the compositer had to set many ledger lines. For the singer, perhaps the best reason for employment of the C clef was that it placed the alto part squarely into the stave. In addition, there was and is a psychological effect on the singer: the continuous use of the C clef induces the development of a tone–colour as a direct result of a 'high–looking' as opposed to a 'low–looking' part. John Whitworth, who sounds high and tenor–like even in a low alto part is a case in point.

Dr Prendergast (then organist of Winchester Cathedral) wrote of the alto clef:[25]

> Its disuse in England cannot be too strongly deplored. When the man's alto part is written in the G clef ... and in a score where the tenor is notated in the G clef an 8ve above, as is now the almost universal practice, the alto part has the appearance of being lower than the tenor part. There seems no reason why even where the G clef is used for the tenor, the C clef should not be retained for the man's alto. Every cathedral alto is quite familiar with the C clef.

Unfortunately, familiarity with C clef is no longer the norm.

It has been pointed out that a particular clef does not necessarily indicate a specific human voice. For example, in madrigal part–books it was common to find alien parts printed among

---

[25] A. H. D. Prendergast, 'The Man's Alto in Church Music', *Zeitschrift der Internationalen Musikgesellschaft*, 1900, p. 334

Example 26. A trio from 'Behold I Bring you Glad Tidings' (Purcell),
showing the confusion possible when C clefs are used on adjacent lines

those of the indigenous voice. Certainly, it is possible for one voice type to perform the part allotted to another, but we should remember that vocal compasses and clefs were not only known but described in written detail by such important men as Thomas Morley, in his famous treatise of 1597. Yet, even in Morley's writing, we may discern an ambiguity between alto and high tenor:

> The musicians also use to make some compositions for men onely to sing, in which case they never passe this compasse.

Altus   Tenor   Tenor   Bassus
          Primus   Secondus

> Now you must diligentlie marke that in which of all these compasses you make your musicke, you must not suffer any part to goe without the compasse of his rules, except one note at the most above or below, without it be upon an extremity for the ditties sake or in notes taken for Diapason in the base.[26]

Allowing for pitch changes, the following should help twentieth–century eyes and minds to envisage Morley's instructions (we have adjusted upwards by the customary minor third):

Alto   First tenor   Second tenor   Bass

Morley seems to suggest (see his original) that music for men only should normally be set in 'the lowe key' (low pitch), but contemporary examples of composition sometimes give a different impression.

    Observe from the examples shown:

1 That, to twentieth–century eyes, the alto looks a low part.

2 The bass appears baritonal, suggesting that its favourite low notes are to be thought of as 'diapason in the bass' – a special underpinning effect used occasionally. Also, its highest note occurs in the area where chest–voice ends. The extension into head–voice, essential for such passages as that of Example 25 (p. 308), is taken for granted. Though he was writing well after the death of Morley, it is suggested that the same principles apply to both composers.

3 That when Morley falls into line with fashionable Italian strictures ('you must not suffer any part to goe without the compasse of his rules') his remark about 'An extremity for the ditties sake' could mean 'to express the words'. Harwood points out that the 'dittie' means the words: i.e., those which are 'dit', as opposed to the notes, which are 'chanté'. Alternatively, could it hint that the composer might well decide to suspend Italian fashion to write in a more English manner? Doing so could extend the

---

[26] Thomas Morley, *A Plaine and Easie Introduction to Practicall Musick*, 1597 (mod. edn, Harman, 1952 repr. 1966), p. 275

part by several tones, up or down, momentarily.

4   That the first tenor could easily be a low counter–tenor part. While this could suggest that low alto–parts were sung by first tenors, the reverse is also possible: that 'high tenors' were sung by 'altos'. The range is nicely that of the alto. If, as we have seen, tenors sang with falsetto technique, by our convention they were altos. In truth, they were both.

5   In music for men's voices, at low pitch, there seems to be no suggestion by Morley of high falsetto singing in the Spanish/Italian manner, though we might expect him to have known of the Spanish falsetto–tradition.

It is possible that, despite first impressions, Morley was writing here not primarily of vocal, but musical compasses: that he was giving instructions or guide–lines to composers writing choral harmony and counterpoint. Though Morley's compasses are inevitably associated with known existing vocal usage, the eternal 'chicken–or–egg' question arises. Nevertheless, once again, we suggest that sixteenth–century singers were probably more versatile than most today.

Some scholars, however, are firm in their belief that Morley, and English practice, advocated a strictly adhered–to scheme for vocal compasses, with all that this implies. For further discussion and more detail of vocal ranges and designations, see Wulstan[27], in which Morley and Praetorius are compared, and a valuable chart supports his thesis. However, the more one examines the byzantine systems governing the use of pitch and clefs, and the historical reasons for their development, the more one is thankful that these conventions of intricate tranposition and multi–clefs were abandoned during the early–Baroque period.

An examination of a cross–section of the sixteenth–century vocal ensemble repertoire suggests two possibilities: that a rather restricted range for ensemble–singers was established successfully along the lines of some Renaissance theorists' ideas – not merely in Italy but also in Franco–Flemish countries; or that, especially in the case of Josquin, some of these parts were extensively ranged. Either singers were expected to employ 'through–range' techniques, or there were two or three moderately–ranged singers to each vocal part, each with his own strength: a highly–effective single vocal–line of great range would then have been available.

Composers often wrote for choirs, ensembles and singers they knew well, whether they were professional or amateur, sacred or secular, large, medium or small vocal ensembles. All these are likely to have influenced the ranges for which they wrote.

Needless reassignment?

The counter–tenor voice–type/range is now widely accepted as a solo instrument with original literature and as a vocal category for more general repertoire. Inevitably, there are still disagreements on the subject.

In recent years, it has begun to be apparent that certain English training methods are not producing counter–tenors with effective lower notes. They appear to be persuaded during training not only that a head–register is everything, but that extending it downwards is not as useful as upwards, to resemble a mezzo–soprano. Solo singers may be able to select their own repertoire, but the ensemble singer cannot. A very real problem occurs when a counter–tenor

[27] Wulstan, op. cit. pp. 210–4, and passim

with a weak lower voice, and no register–change, attempts, for example, a Purcell trio for A.T.B. He is swamped as easily as were too many of the 'woolly' altos commonly heard before the coming of Alfred Deller. This tempts the choir director or music editor to re–assign the alto part to a high tenor so that it will be heard more clearly. Sir John Stainer, when he edited the beautiful E minor Evening Service by Daniel Purcell, was presumably persuaded to do so because many Victorian altos lacked the vocal weight in their lower notes to balance his strong tenor and bass voices, particularly in the large open acoustic of St Paul's Cathedral.

Yet reassignment is happening again quite needlessly, even when a properly trained counter–tenor is available. Unless he is a specialist in the high–range voice, he should have the edge, resonance and pharyngeal strength as well as the solidity in his fundamental register to match a tenor and bass who wish to blend, however low a (genuine) counter–tenor part is written. The edition of Purcell's verse anthem, *Give Sentence With Me, O God*, published in 1977 in *The Musical Times*, included an accompanying scholarly article (i below) and an all–revealing footnote (and a consequentially incomplete top–voice clef?) at the end of the music itself (ii below) written by Eric van Tassel:[28]

> (i) Our edition of 'Give Sentence' in prescribing a tenor for the highest solo part (originally in the alto–clef, in the contratenor partbook), implicitly enters a brief (with reservations) on one side of the haute–contre/countertenor controversy which has been much aired in recent years.
>
> There are sound practical reasons for suspecting that the post–Restoration 'contratenor' soloist was often (though by no means always) not a falsettist but high, light tenor – a *haute–contre*, or Rimski–Korsakov's *tenore altino*. And the considerations that led me to transcribe the contratenor solo part of this anthem for such a tenor were essentially practical ones. (1) The highest note in the part is 'G' (reached only five times, always in passages favourable to a tenor's un–false voice), while it goes as low as F sharp (bars 22–3) and E (bar 99) in context where a falsettist could easily be swamped. (2) The two upper solo parts – frequently paired in thirds in the Monteverdian manner – quite often reach a cadence by an approach in which, again, a falsettist would risk being swamped by his tenor partner (cf. bars 15–6, 22–3, 28–9, 53–5, 98–9, 112–4, 121–3/125–7). (3) The falsettist would surely be at risk where the alto–clef part goes below the tenor (see especially bars 26–7 and 92–4).
>
> These tessituras are a not unusual feature in anthems of the period (parallels can be found elsewhere in Purcell, as also in Child, Humphrey, Blow, and others), and it is likely that a distinction was understood between high altos (falsettists, presumably), and low altos (*haute–contres* or something very like) – even though in most manuscripts both kinds of alto used the same notation.
>
> (ii) The highest solo part (top note G♯) was probably sung by a high tenor, and the modern clef has been chosen accordingly. This part could be sung by a male alto if he can balance the middle voice (without forcing) in passages where the two parts cross.

---

[28] Eric van Tassel, *The Musical Times*, 1977, p. 382

*Or Alto: see the editorial notes on the back page.

*Two extracts from 'The Musical Times', 1977, edition of
Purcell's anthem 'Give Sentence with me, O God' which demonstrate
the reallocation of voice–part from alto to tenor.
Example 27 (top) shows the normal tessitura of the counter–tenor part;
Example 28 (lower) demonstrates an unusual depth for this vocal part.*

It all sounds so reasonable at first; but note that no allowance has been made in this edition for (church) pitch variation since Purcell's time. Today's customary transposition upwards of about a tone for seventeenth–century church music would lighten the effect. Not that such a transposition should be strictly necessary. The only point at which the alto part actually touches low E is when in unison with the tenor (see Example 28).[29]

Much of Van Tassel's argument becomes academic when we remember that all voices, counter–tenor, tenor and bass, used falsetto head–voice as well as fundamental voice when they felt it appropriate. Today's coyness over such techniques would have been found puzzling in former times. However, if there was a 'right type' of tenor–altino, he can surely have been no more available than he is today. Indeed, there were fewer educated singers, in a smaller population in the seventeenth century. Do editors now expect tenors–altino, always rare in any period, suddenly to be available in every cathedral or collegiate choir which performs this music? In practice, it will be likely, today, that this alto verse part, re–labelled 'tenor', will be given to the usual tenor voice. Quite often (though not always), his timbre will be inappropriate and thick–toned and will have been made heavier because he has to sing louder, later music too. Permanent vibrato would thicken it further. He will not sound authentic but solid, opaque and quite un–Purcellian.

He may, of course, be able to adopt an 'early music tenor' style and technique – bland, light, vibrato–less and attractive but usually with no employment of true head–register. The effect, undoubtedly, will be much improved; but if these tenors could be persuaded and trained to take the next logical step (to use the head–voice), we should begin to hear something of what Purcell probably expected from one type of low counter–tenor. There is, of course, a very thin dividing line between unmixed head–voice and the most beautifully handled *voix mixte*, and we should remember superb tenors like Gerald English or Paul Elliott in this context.

The reluctance of some to accept that counter–tenors, even those who employ head–voice exclusively, might possess suitable timbre and tonal strength recurs from time to time, like malaria. Unfortunately, remembering the new young generation of English high counter–tenors, the point of view represented by Higgenbottom and Van Tassel might be thought understandable, even if its apparent dismissal of older, stronger–trained voices is regrettable. What is less understandable is that James Bowman's large voice and superb vocal skills, for example, were well–known by 1977, particularly in Oxford, and therefore Van Tassel, who had connections there, must have been aware of him. With the subtler, more sensitive singing we expect and usually hear in today's authentic or historically–aware performances (or at least those not designed to be heard during a promenade concert in the vastness of the Albert Hall!), our attitudes need to change.

Original instruments and scoring are now being considered more carefully for the accompaniment of counter–tenors, even in less–advanced musical circles. In 1959, it was the voice and not the power of modern instruments which was blamed for ineffective performance of Purcell:[30]

> 'I Call, I Call', is difficult to cast: it is in the alto clef in the original, but the
> alto voice seems unsuitable for such bold sentiments, and it is sung in this

[29] See also Van Tassell, 'English Church Music, c1660–1700', part one, *Early Music*, October 1978, pp. 572–8
[30] Nigel Fortune, notes with recording of Purcell's *King Arthur*, 1959

performance by a tenor [David Galliver], even though the tessitura is a trifle high.

Galliver, in fact, often sounds decidedly uncomfortable. How a counter–tenor could have been thought 'unsuitable' for this particular text is a mystery; John Whitworth was in the cast (and given only a fraction of his due solo work) and his timbre, with its virile low range, is especially suited to bold sentiments.

If tonal virility was not an issue, it was sometimes vocal weight. Of the then new Purcell Society edition of the scena *Saul and the Witch of Endor*, Jeremy Noble wrote in the early 1960s:[31]

> It is a pity, though, that the editors decided to print the counter–tenor part of Saul in the untransposed G clef, since few male altos carry the vocal weight for it, and fewer the dramatic weight; printed in a transposed G clef, it might have attracted the attention of a high light tenor or two, and I can't help thinking that this was the kind of voice Purcell had in mind.

Here is another noted musicologist who is apparently reluctant to hear the evidence around him – especially John Whitworth, who shortly afterwards recorded the part of Saul for EMI. 'Decided to print the counter–tenor part of Saul in the untransposed G clef', suggests that Noble was not thinking even of Oberlin – of whom, at the time, he may not have heard, and for whose range the work is well–suited – but of a normal lyric tenor who might find problems with this high part. Apparently, when at Oxford, Noble himself took Saul in a performance in the Music Club. His difficulties may well have influenced his thinking.

Bowman, Jacobs, Chance, Rickards, Kowalski, or some other counter–tenor of today with a good low register, or the tenor Charles Daniels, who has a versatile voice often similar in effect to theirs, should record what could be the definitive performance of *Saul and the Witch of Endor*. Once again, the choice of voice–type and timbres is significant for a particular work. It would seem likely that Purcell, as a counter–tenor himself (or at the very least a composer and singer familiar with the varied colours available to the counter–tenor), chose this range for Saul with care. The particular and varied tonal qualities associated with this voice–type and range suit the rôle and character of Saul, who was historically a colourful and psychologically complex individual: initially a brave and successful warrior–king, he developed schizophrenic symptoms, together with psychic sensitivities, jealousies and doubts, and eventually committed suicide.

The vocally–central placing of the rôle in the three–voice scena, as set by Purcell, seems skilfully to underline both the states of balance and imbalance. The Witch (high soprano) and the Ghost of Old Samuel (bass) are bisected vocally by Saul, the counter–tenor, a voice in itself characteristically split between two main registers. (This, of course, is a strength rather than a weakness, especially when the contrasting colours and ranges are used for dramatic effect.) Thus, during his encounter with the Witch and the Ghost of Samuel, in Endor, Saul is seen and heard in both low and high vocal–ranges (D3–B♭4). Balance is carefully maintained, and the style of the writing evokes this world and the next. Samuel tells him: 'Tomorrow, thou and thy son will be with me beneath', and Purcell's writing for Saul, with its

---

[31] Jeremy Noble, 'Purcell's Motets and Anthems', *The Musical Times*, March 1963, p. 200

depths and moderate heights, indeed suggests a future life in Hell with perhaps an occasional chastening visit to the world of the living.

A counter–tenor willing and able to exploit all these various tonal colours in his voice can express this; so too could a seventeenth–century style tenor of today, who is willing and able to use his various head–voice colours, employing more dovetail than splice technique. Certainly, it appears that ordinary lyric tenors still sing Saul more often than counter–tenors, which is a pity. Sadly, the work is not often performed. John Whitworth's strongly–sung version, at present unobtainable (which might be considered rather dated, almost totally because of the musical style of some of the other singers and instrumentalists), expresses many of the shades of meaning implicit in the rôle. Deller's, though not one of his best recordings, has many superb moments.

In *The Counter Tenor* (1982), it was suggested that, despite some progress, much prejudice still existed (often disguised) in spheres where it really mattered. This view may have been thought exaggerated by the then reader and still might be today, especially if that reader is familiar with Sir Michael Tippett's remarks in *A Singularity of Voice*:[32]

> But Deller had to face extra problems and overcome peculiar susceptibilities owing to the very nature of his voice. And again it is ironical to note that present day young people, hearing a lot of beat [music] where voices are high or low, quite irrespective of sex, and generally accepting our permissive society, where virility is no longer a he–man mythology, must find Deller's worries about his voice, as he talks of them in this book, quite outside their ken.

It is easier now to sympathize with Tippett's view, but one might still wonder whether such optimism seems premature. Not only is the music the voices sing that is increasingly the point of division (most of Tippett's 'young people' would not easily accept the usual counter–tenor repertoire) but there are still modern teachers of classical voice-production, singers and writers, who might question Tippett's view.

This said, it is to be hoped that the following could not be written today in any serious work on singing. This vitriolic passage, written in 1963 by Elster Kay (sometime choral scholar of King's College, Cambridge, no less) and, at the time of its publication at least, a singing teacher in Cambridge:

> *Falsetto.* This type of tone is now known by cinematography to be created by pressing together the greater part of the free vibrating edges of the cords causing a node, so that only a small length is free to oscillate, combined with very low breath compression in the larynx. In legitimate singing it has no place except for the occasional production of comic effects such as the imitation by men of women's voices. It is used by yodellers whose technique consists of singing low notes in *voce piena* and then by allowing the laryngeal inlet to fly wide open suddenly thus minimizing laryngeal breath compression, to cause an instantaneous change of the mode of cord vibration, at the same

---

[32] In the Foreword

time singing wide intervals, often of an octave, the upper note being in falsetto.

The sterile and emasculated quality of this type of tone is all too painfully familiar in England where it is to be heard in the form of so–called male altos in all church choirs, and frequently on the air in the form of again so–called 'counter–tenors'.

The male alto of medieval times was, like the male soprano, a castrato, not a falsettist. These men sang like women: that is, under full compression, resulting in *voce piena* tone. The modern male alto is a baritone who perpetually sings an octave above his normal compass using falsetto tone. There have been recently before the public one or two male sopranos of the same falsetto kind: these are presumably tenors who sing an octave above their normal compass using falsetto tones. So far, no professional success has attended the endeavours of any of these latter 'spuriosities'.

The vocalists (they are hardly to be described as singers), who nowadays are given the courtesy title of counter–tenors, are simply falsetto male altos who have the wit to develop a bright clear tone as contrasted with the dark, hooting tone of the traditional English cathedral alto. The excruciating mono-tony of the tone of these personages is due to their incomprehensibly obstinate refusal ever to use more than a single resonator adjustment. Their emasculated bleatings would be rendered the more curious if not the more agreeable were they to use all three resonator adjustments, which they perfectly well could. As it is we are faced with the painful choice of the screech of a night–jar, or the hoot of a sort of supersonic owl. The most that can be said for this new kind of noise is that it is less disagreeable than the traditional kind. The medieval counter–tenor was a light tenor (*tenore bianco*) who, on passing above his *tessitura* (at f' or g')[F4 or G4], immediately went into falsetto and by so doing was able to add five or six notes to his compass, singing up to g or a above the tenor high c. He was on his way to being a male falsetto soprano (not, of course, a castrato soprano). Such voices are rarely heard today, but they must exist in reasonable numbers. Handel and Purcell wrote for counter tenor. The best example of writing for this voice in modern music is the part of the Astrologer in Rimski–Korsakov's opera *Le Coq d'Or*.

It should be noted that falsetto tone can be used through the middle and upper thirds of the natural baritone or tenor compass and there is no reason why women should not sing falsetto if they were so mentally deranged as to wish to do so. [It is Hough's, together with many others', opinion that they *all* do.] Happily they never seem to be so afflicted, although many women who are not trained singers but who have strong virile speaking voices, invariably and involuntarily break into falsetto when they sing.

Children before puberty are not falsettists, although in England, especially in cathedral choirs, they are usually trained to emit tone of a falsetto timbre, by singing in the low adjustment and under low air compression. It is perfectly possible to train a treble (that is a child soprano) to sing under full compression and to produce tone which is well on the way to *voce piena*. In England this is almost never done but in the Sistine choir a majority of the boys usually sing in this way. This type of training is possible in the case of children falsettists as distinct from adults because in the child the cordal nodes are fixed and will not open when laryngeal air pressure is increased.[33]

This long and remarkable quotation occurs here so that the reader may be able to assess Kay's remarks with some knowledge of the physiological and historical background of the counter-tenor voice. Kay's simplistic, misguided view of falsetto technique, among other things, is remarkable. How could anybody, in 1963, have described Deller's vocalistic skills, for example, as 'excruciatingly monotonous'?

However, there is one point with which we should have some sympathy: that of the three resonator adjustments he mentions. It is important for singers to employ all available resonators. There were and are one–colour counter–tenors, but no more so than the monochrome tenors, contraltos, sopranos and basses who are often to be heard. Tonal variety is essential in all voice types.

An accusation of tonal monotony is nothing new. In view of Kay's own background and concern with church singing it should be noted that John Dowland, Thomas Morley and others also criticized the failure of church musicians to sing expressively.[34]

Although Kay has shown an inexcusable prejudice against altos, there may be at least a little (and only a little) more excuse for *The Times* music critic, then H. C. Colles, who wrote in 1945, before the modern revival was really under way in the person of Deller:[35]

> Handel must have chuckled to himself over our Cathedral Altos squawking in falsetto, but, if that was the sort of thing the English liked, they should have it. As a matter of fact, he began his *Ode for Queen Anne's Birthday* with a recitative in which the male alto was invited to do his worst, and he probably did.

Frederic Hodgson has commented of Colles's remarks:[36]

> This can be seen to contain nothing but prejudice when it is remembered that Handel soon made friends with English singers, among them such celebrated altos as Hughes, Powell and Barrow, who sang frequently for Handel, and who, by their great reputations, did anything but 'squawk in falsetto'!

Sometimes, of course, gentle, affectionate fun has been made of counter–tenors, but any worthwhile endeavour can withstand genuine fun at its expense. Think of the mirth the figure of the coloratura soprano has evoked at times; it does not matter. There have been so many truly great sopranos: who cares for those who cannot appreciate them? Is there not a comical side to every human activity?

Sir Frederick Bridge, Organist Emeritus of Westminster Abbey (known affectionately as 'Westminster Bridge'), told[37] of the dreadful old alto performing a recitative in Purcell's verse

---

[33] Elster Kay, *Bel Canto*, (Dobson, 1963), pp. 67–70

[34] Morley, op. cit.; see also Peter le Huray, *Music and the Reformation in England* (C.U.P.), passages quoted on pp. 124–5

[35] H.C. Colles, *Essays and Lectures*, (Oxford, 1945), p. 35

[36] Frederic Hodgson, 'The Contemporary Alto', *The Musical Times*, April 1965, p. 294

[37] Frederick Bridge, *A Westminster Pilgrim*, (Novello/Hutchinson, 1919), p. 80

anthem *Thy Word is a Lantern*, at the Chapel Royal. 'I suppose,' writes Bridge, 'with his cracked and comical voice, he somewhat annoyed an old Peer who sat immediately behind the choir and was rather given to thinking aloud. When the singer had finished his sentence, "The ungodly have laid a snare for me," the old Peer ejaculated, loudly enough to be heard by the choir, "I wish to Heaven they'd caught you!"'

Another story attributed to Bridge is about the bass phrase in S. S. Wesley's verse anthem *Ascribe Unto the Lord*: 'Noses have they and smell not'. Apparently, during a rehearsal, Bridge remarked to his choir: 'Well, the altos use theirs to sing through!' (This interesting reference to what has been termed (unfortunately) nasal resonance, in a musical age when such technique – properly used – was generally out of fashion, could be claimed to demonstrate a late nineteenth–century misunderstanding of earlier vocal techniques.)

Fun and malice differ, however. Deller's early concert–platform days produced so–called 'wit' from those who should have known better, like fellow musicians. One instance has been described, earlier. At another time, Deller had just left a Liverpool concert platform, when (yet another) orchestra leader said to him: 'If I got up to sing like that in public, my mother would disown me'.[38] The choice of the parent, mother, is significant. An example of journalistic malicious wit was reported in the Hardwick biography[39] of Deller:

> ... the eminent critic of one of our national daily newspapers, in writing up a performance of the Monteverdi Vespers at the Festival Hall, said something to the effect that 'the soloists included the countertenor Alfred Deller. This voice can best be described as the soulmate to Mr Hoffnung's tuba.' That may be funny, or it may not; but it can only be considered in the context of humour, and playing for cheap laughs. It has no value as music criticism at all, and yet it is the remark of a professional critic.

An anonymous music critic, writing in *The Times* in 1959[40] was equally jaundiced. Discussing the use of counter–tenors for alto solos in *Messiah*, and the unfamiliar re–allocation of certain arias for reasons of historical awareness, he begins soundly:

> Handel hardly ever played *The Messiah* twice alike. Everything depended on what singers he had available, and, since taste in singing was changing during the middle years of the century enough to enable him to modify in the oratorios the conventions that he observed in his Italian operas, we are not obliged, if we do not like the hooting of counter–tenors and falsetti, to make our performances as top–heavy with high voices as was fashionable in Handel's youth.

He is entitled to his preferences, but prejudice surfaces in surprising ways, and is not often acknowledged by its perpetrators.

As late as 1968, Julian Gardiner coolly admitted, by way of admiring the female chest–voice as used in folk, pop and light music, that he derived great pleasure from training

[38] M. Hardwick, op. cit., p. 149
[39] Ibid., reported without exact citation
[40] 'Editing Purcell and Handel', *The Times*, 24 June 1959

and listening to it, and:[41]

> That is more than I can say about counter–tenors! Maybe it is prejudice, but I am not alone in this. It is a deep–seated instinct, and runs parallel to our attitude towards transvestism on stage. A man masquerading as a woman is completely unacceptable except in broad farce. In contrast, the woman trans–vestist can be a delight to both eye and ear. Her long and honourable lineage takes in Cherubino, Quinquin, Oscar and Prince Orlofsky ... to say nothing of the glamorous principal boys of English pantomime. In the same way, if she uses it correctly, her chest–voice does nothing to detract from and probably emphasizes her sexual charm.

Would a woman agree with Gardiner's totally subjective point of view? Gardiner certainly had courage openly to acknowledge his prejudice and feelings. Objectively, it still remains un–reasonable.

A neat twist should be reported at this point. The 1968 edition of Gardiner's book, on the back of the jacket, displays an extensive advertisement for the first edition of *A Singularity of Voice*, Alfred Deller's biography! Such poetic justice! A humorist must have been lurking at Cassell's.

Vibrato: purl or plain?

Use or non–use of vibrato affects counter–tenors, like other voices. Vibrato should be seen not as concerning vocal production itself (a view put into practice by many singing teachers), but primarily as an aspect of musical style and embellishment.

It should not be a built–in, permanent tremulant, as on a cinema organ. It is not merely vocal wobble, brought about accidentally through the incorrect use of throat musculature, or uneven breath pressure. It should be a valuable, conscious effect and a response to the music and words. Its capability is developed during training. Total and continuous use of any form of pitch undulation in 'early' music of most periods is inappropriate. Some sort of undulation can be put into any vocal tone if wished. It is not an automatic phenomenon, and unless it is present because of bad habits it can be trained in. Similarly, ingrained, habitual vibrato can usually be removed by careful practice. The scientific investigation and perception of Johan Sundberg[42] provides a useful basis for study, in this respect.

The foregoing paragraphs set the scene, so to speak, for a fuller discussion. We now examine vibrato from two slightly differing viewpoints. The first is based loosely on apparent currently–held 'early–music movement' perception and practice; in which opinions on the use of vibrato range from 'sometimes' to 'never'.

Vibrato and tremolo seem to have been confused by theorists at different periods. What is nowadays called vibrato, but has been termed tremolo, properly controlled, should be thought–of as an ornamental effect switched on and off at will. Used continuously, as by most modern singers, it loses its charm and robs the music of its freshness. This is a special danger

---

[41] Julian Gardiner, *A Guide to Good Singing and Speaking* (Cassell, 1968), p. 229

[42] Johan Sundberg, *The Science of the Singing Voice* (Northern Illinois University Press, 1987), pp. 163–181

when performing early music. Thurston Dart was firm about modern misuse of the effect:[43]

> The incessant vibrato which has so regretably infected nine out of ten singers of the present day could not be obtained with the methods of breath-control taught by the finest eighteenth and nineteenth century singing teachers. The evidence of early recordings shows that even fifty years ago [Dart's book first appeared in 1954], it was used with the utmost care (though the tremolo seems to have been rather more common than it is today), and it is one of the greatest disfigurements of modern music performance.

Concerning sixteenth-century music, Wulstan wrote:[44]

> A blurred 'fruity' tone is incompatible with polyphonic singing. So is vibrato: in its various forms, it seems only slowly to be loosening its stranglehold upon singing style. To forsake it requires effort both because it appears to amplify the voice, and because intonation poses no problems when the margin of error is so obligingly wide.

In 1723, Tosi wrote:[45]

> 1.28 Let him learn to hold out the notes without a shrillness like a trumpet, or trembling; and if at the beginning [the master] made him hold out every note the length of two bars, the improvement would be the greater. Otherwise from the natural inclination that the beginner has to keep the voice in motion, and the trouble in holding it out, he will get a habit, and not be able to fix it, and will become subject to a fluttering in the manner of all those that sing in a very bad taste.

> [M.P.]: By 'fix it' Tosi means 'hold (the long note) firmly in place', not 'correct the error', a use of the expression introduced in the USA in the 19th century. This passage is a warning against excessive vibrato.

Some take this to mean that all vibrato is to be banished, but it appears likely that Tosi is advocating total vocal control, from which enviable state the singer may choose to introduce, then remove, ornamentation which may include strictly controlled vibrato when appropriate. (It is noticeable that some of the better jazz singers, 'crooners', and 'pop-singers' can start a long note without any trace of vibrato, then can add it, control its frequency, and remove it again. Why is this then so hard for most 'serious' singers?)

Garcia's important *Traité complet de l'art du chant* (1847) contains nothing about vibrato or tremolo, but plenty on steadiness of voice. In 1889, *The Musical Times* reported:[46]

[43] Thurston Dart, *The Interpretation of Music*, p. 50 fn.
[44] David Wulstan, *Vocal Colour in English 16th Century Polyphony*, P.M.M.S., p. 58. See also *Tudor Music*, (O.U.P.) p. 233
[45] Tosi, op. cit., p. 8
[46] 'Musical Times a hundred years ago', *The Musical Times*, March 1989 (on the first performance of Wagner's *Das Rheingold* in Budapest)

At last an occasion has been found for that vocal defect, the *tremolo*. The Rhine Maidens in New York are all 'wobblers' of a pronounced description, but they have a press friend who points out that, as they are supposed to be singing under water, the effect of their performance is realistic. So true is it that nothing has been created in vain.

At the end of the nineteenth century, the distinguished English Victorian tenor, Sims Reeves, counselled:[47]

It is scarcely necessary to describe the tremolo. Five out of every six modern singers are afflicted with it, and consequently there is a great deal of make–believe that the tremolo is a splendid vehicle for the expression of sentiment and passion. But experience soon proves that an audience never mistakes affectation – and tremolo is nothing else in effect – for sincerity; and the singer finds, when it is too late, that the tremolo has literally got him by the throat and he cannot get rid of it. This quivering of the voice, as if it were a jelly, may be due to a variety of causes. It may be caused by sheer affectation, or by unsteady breathing, or by fatigue, and occasionally by an elongated uvula. In the last–mentioned case a medical remedy must be found. Where, however, the tremolo is the result of mistaken ideas about the expression of sentiment, it must be rigorously corrected. In such work as recitative, declamation, and *canto largo*, the voice must be firm and steady as a rock. If the voice persists in trembling, even against the will of the singer, then resort must be had to the practice of long, single notes. These notes must be done without any *crescendo* – steady tones, sung alternatively *piano* and *mezzo forte*, and with a gentle, unwavering emission of the breath. Tremolo results very often from a wrong way of breathing; lack of sustaining power can be overcome by paying attention to the rules and suggestions already given. Another very important point in connection with this *tremolo* voice lies in the proper 'placing of the voice'. If the tone is not directed towards the front teeth, so that it may be felt to vibrate across the bridge of the nose, then the voice trembles because it is not properly placed. As a last word about tremolo, it may be pointed out that all great singers preserve their voices much longer than the average artists, and while the latter usually show the tremolo, the former invariably never do. The deduction may not satisfy logicians, but it is sufficient for students of singing.

Note that, for Reeves, tremolo (vibrato) is indulged in to express sentiment. We saw earlier that Rubini (1795–1854) is credited with inventing the practice of continuous vibrato; previously, singers reserved it for special effects of decoration and in passages or moments of heightened emotion. That was the classical approach. Though his technique was based on earlier principles, Rubini's continuous vibrato was conspicuous and fast. (Henriette Meric–Lalande (1798–1867) was the first woman to make a career with a Rubini–style vibrato.)

---

[47] Sims Reeves, *The Art of Singing* (Chappell, 1900), pp. 25–6

Clearly, Reeves disapproved of such use of vibrato, although he remained influenced by Duprez–inspired nineteenth–century stentorian techniques. Certainly, Reeves wrote perceptively, and from practical experience, but had only part of the truth. The myriad ornaments, graces and divisions performed expertly by classical singers of the seventeenth, eighteenth and early nineteenth centuries were so much cleverer than blanketing every phrase, every note, in unceasing vibrato. Vibrato existed as an honourable and lovely vocal effect. The twentiethcentury singer of Baroque music cannot, of course, merely jettison all vibrato without replacing it with the full treatment of ornaments and divisions with which the music was graced originally. In any case, to abandon vibrato completely and absolutely cannot be appropriate for Baroque music.

It should be borne in mind that, like other art–forms, music varied in style during the early, middle, and late–Baroque periods, so that the amount of vibrato employed varied too.

There are those (whom we shall call the 'vibrato lobby') who argue that a vibrato–less voice is colourless, while one with permanent vibrato possesses colour automatically. By so arguing, they confuse themselves and others; yet much of the latter viewpoint could be said to represent a large proportion of 'mainstream' musical thinking where advice on the use of vibrato ranges from 'continuously' to 'occasionally'.

The lobby for permanent vibrato regard it as essential. They claim it as the sole or main source of harmonic overtones. The opposing view to this is that hearing throughout song or aria what often amounts to several notes at once because of the amplitude of the vibrato can give the impression of overtones, but the well–produced voice should be the result of good production technique before the addition of vibrato, though it is true to say that continuous *voce bianca* – white, colourless voice – seems to be frowned on too. As a general guide, therefore, the singer is advised to keep vocal quality alive and pleasantly colourful without resorting to continuous pitch–wobble.

It may surprise many today, used to hearing carefully considered and sometimes bland 'historically–aware' performances of early music, that vibrato has a much longer history than is usually supposed. Pyscho–physiological phenomena suggest a deep–seated origin for it. When human or animal organisms are strongly affected emotionally by an outside stimulus, they often answer with a corresponding bodily response in which specific muscle groups are stimulated to shiver or to tremble. For instance, when we are anxious our hands begin to shake, and our voice can be affected. Laughter, sexual desire and crying all have their rhythmic varieties of trembling. Animals react in a broadly comparable fashion: frightened dogs shake all over, and trained canaries reportedly sing with discernable vibrato.[48]

This instinctive, automatic phenomenon which must have been present in our early human ancestors, remains within us all. Ecstasy, fear or other emotions must have caused rhythmic pulsations in those first human utterances. In similar fashion, ethnomusicological studies have shown discernible vibrato in the singing of unschooled or primitive native peoples.[49] The effect on the body of intense cold, too, cannot be overlooked. It therefore seems that vibrato is grounded in our pre–cultural biological nature.[50]

---

[48] Carl E. Seashore, *Psychology of the Vibrato in Voice and Instrument* (University of Iowa Studies, vol. III, 1936), pp. 58 and 140

[49] Loc. cit.

[50] Jochen Gartner, *The Vibrato* (Gustav Bosse Verlag, Regensburg, 1974; English translation, 1981), pp. 15–16 and passim

The first references to vibrato or tonal undulation appear in Greek culture,[51] in a treatise dated *c*350 BC, from the followers of Aristoxenos.[52] Written symbols (decorative neumes) in medieval documents which call for a type of 'staccato or vibrating of the voice'[53] first appear in about the tenth century. In the later Middle Ages, numerous ways are found to express musical ornamentation, like *crispatio* and *trepidatio*, which call for types of trill, often extended in length (not the simple trill of modern meaning). Also employed is the expression *reverberatio*, which roughly translated means 'striking' or 'vibrating'. Too much significance should not be attached to these references, but they could be said to allude to forms of vibrato.

There are detailed descriptions of the production and practical use of it in the treatises of Sylvestro Ganassi (1492–?) and Martin Agricola (1486–1556). Jacques Martin Hotteterre, C.P.E. Bach, Leopold Mozart, and others, wrote pedagogical works (or otherwise contributed to the subject) which contain many references to the use of vibrato.[54]

Agricola wrote:[55]

And if you wish a firm foundation
So learn to play with trembling breath;
For it is to singing most becoming,
And to piping most flattering.

Michael Praetorius (1571–1621) was concerned to introduce into Germany rules or ornamentation and teaching derived from Italian singing styles. He writes of vibrato several times;[56] that the singer must possess by nature 'a beautiful, lovely vibrating voice – but not as is occasionally the case in schools, but with particular moderation'.[57] His reference to schools clearly suggests some dissatisfaction with poorly produced vibrato, or overdone application of it:[58]

Therefore he is not satisfied with the supposition that a singer is 'gifted by God and nature with a special lovely vibrating voice', but he insists that this vibrato in addition must be brought forth with 'particular moderation'. In today's scientific terminology we would say more precisely: variable in amplitude and frequency.

Purcell and his contemporaries asked for special string effects which could be described as a *tremolando*, most famously in the 'Frost Scene' in *King Arthur*, in which the bass soloist and strings are both indicated to 'quiver' by Purcell. This is not vibrato, strictly speaking, but the effect is of 'vibration' and comparable to the contemporary Italian *trillo*.

Johann Mattheson (1681–1764), an early friend of Handel, was a celebrated tenor,

[51] Robert Haas, *Aufführungspraxis der Musik*, quoted Gartner, p. 25
[52] Gartner, op. cit., p. 16
[53] Seashore, op. cit., p. 8
[54] Gartner, op. cit., pp. 23–29
[55] Martin Agricola, *Musica Instrumentalis Deudsch*, fol VIr
[56] In *Syntagma Musicum*, vol. II, p. 68
[57] Ibid., p. 231
[58] Gartner, op. cit., p. 18

composer, critic and writer on musical matters. He writes:[59]

> The tremolo or Beben ('vibrate') of the voice is the most gentle motion possible on a single definite note, in the production of which the main action occurs in the epiglottis ('Oberzunglein') of the throat, moving in a very soft way to moderate the breath ...

Mattheson possessed detailed anatomical knowledge and he hypothesizes on the physiological basis for singers' vibrato. Regarding its importance and notation, he remarks:[60]

> One can indeed designate the places on which such a vibration or trembling should happen, but the actual manner in which it should be done cannot be taught by pencil and compass, but only by the ear.

Baroque artifice and cartouched style demands the ready availability of vibrato in solo singing and even occasionally in vocal ensemble.

Quite clearly, the various opposing foregoing viewpoints overlap at their centres. We must therefore beware of assuming that all vibrato is suspect, just as we should disbelieve those who proclaim that no well–produced voice can be without it. It has an honourable and ancient history. So has the knowledge of when and how to use it. It is possible that the adoption of a simpler and louder, even stentorian, vocal style probably at the time of the début of Duprez in the 1840s and at the abandonment of much of the 'old–fashioned' eighteenth–century vocal ornamentation and style, was in some way connected with Garcia's failure to mention vibrato in his famous treatise. Because it was not a part of the usual training of singers at that date, this would also account for the Wagner–connected criticism of vibrato in 1889, and Sims Reeves's warnings in 1900.

Other than Dame Clara Butt, there are many early recorded examples of a rigid, stentorian style, particularly of male voices, to be heard in secular vocal soloists late in the nineteenth century, but the influence of their tonal quality was still going strong in the first decades of the twentieth century in the choir of St George's Chapel, Windsor, particularly in the bass voices. This was largely due to the teaching and training originally imbued in them by Sir Walter Parratt (1841–1924). Windsor recordings of the late 1920s and early 1930s demonstrate this; for example, in a recording of S. S. Wesley's *Ascribe Unto the Lord*, directed by E. H. Fellowes.[61]

Rubini, and to a large extent Garcia himself, appear to have represented a transitional stage between earlier and newer modes of thinking. A continuous–vibrato style seems to have increased in favour once the strongest impact of the stentorian style had passed, and it continued to be used with enthusiasm in the very late nineteenth century and throughout much of the twentieth.

Not all modern singers are cursed with permanent, unthinking vibrato. Dietrich Fischer–Dieskau and Victoria de los Angeles are examples of pre–eminent artists who use maximum vocal colouration and a removable vibrato.

---

[59] Quoted by Gartner, op. cit., p. 22
[60] Johann Mattheson, *Der Volkhommone Capellmeister*, p. 114
[61] Columbia 9175 (AX 2273), 80 [sic] r.p.m.

Style

In the first two decades of the twentieth century, when experiments based on the relationship of colour to music were taking place, the chemist Wilhelm Ostwald (1853–1932) devised a colour system which sought to control and equalize and to ensure absolute, automatic blend throughout the painter's colour–range. In the event, the Ostwald system soon lost popularity, and all but vanished. Painters preferred freedom to choose and use the full, creative, imaginative range of effects possible; to resist any subjugation or abandonment of individual human choice and control, and to avoid the imposition of an artificial system on the wonder of colour.

There are parallels in sound: tuning in equal or unequal temperament; differing concepts of what constitutes blend and balance; infinite variations in vocal and instrumental timbres.

When examining the singer's repertoire today, one cannot ignore the sheer variety of music over at least nine centuries. It is unfortunately true that so many otherwise excellent singers, some counter–tenors included, still seem unwilling to adjust their vocal tone, colour and style sufficiently to make distinctions between, for example, a Britten canticle and an Elizabethan lute song or between Brahms lieder and a Gluck aria. As Julian Gardiner wrote:[62]

> The failure of teachers and performers to discriminate between music which is romantic or subjective, and music which is non–romantic or objective, results in their pumping false sentiment into non–romantic music which of its very nature demands a cool, sympathetic and exclusively musical approach. The old Italian arias for instance and the works of Bach, Handel, Haydn and Mozart do not demand the same intimate approach as the songs of Schumann and Fauré. Naturally all vocal music suggests a more subjective approach than does instrumental music. Nevertheless a great deal of the vocal repertoire is evocative; it calls for an active imagination and a sympathetic knowledge of the style and period of the composer, but no personal sentiment. For a teacher to tell a student to feel this kind of music is no more or less an invitation to tell musical lies. Any work of art which is predominantly objective must be performed with the keenest ear for tone quality and variations of colour, rhythm and tempo, and with a respectful though not necessarily reverent regard for traditional readings. A sympathetic and active imagination is needed also, but no more personal involvement than would be found in an actor who plays Macbeth.

To put it slightly differently, we know that the tone of any singer would obviously be conditioned by custom, accompaniment and style and type of music performed. A late six- teenth- or early seventeenth–century singer would have been expected to deal with crisp, clear, contrapuntal parts of equal importance in ensemble works and to be capable also of soft languishing tone when singing to a lute. He might also need ringing power against a band of instruments. Such a variety of sound should be available from a modern singer, not only in volume but also in character. Yet how many do cultivate a varied manner of vocal presentation?

---

[62] Gardiner, op. cit., p. 252

There are those who question any realistic possibility of knowing how earlier voices sounded. Certainly, vocal tone in the Middle Ages, for example, was utterly different from today's; it possibly had an Eastern quality, perhaps owing to the influence of the Crusades. (This is disputed by some authorities,[63] but it seems likely that near–Eastern, even Indian, influences on European music included a stylistic tendency to 'swoop' or, to use modern terminology, to employ considerable *portamento*; near–Eastern and Indian instruments (the sitar, for instance) suggest this possibility. The permanent sympathetic or drone strings of the sitar have an affinity with the European hurdy–gurdy. Even the English bagpipe seems to have possessed its drones only since the thirteenth century, towards the end of the times of the Crusades. The Scottish bagpipe employs a scale similar to certain scales commonly used in the near East.) The answer to doubters is surely that though written contemporary vocal description can only go so far (and it can be extremely valuable up to a point), we do have one powerful help in determining long–past vocal timbres: any surviving or accurately reconstructed early musical instruments.

Though very early playable unrestored specimens are rare, instruments, unlike the human larynx, do not utterly decay in a grave. Replicas of them can be built, and provided the player knows or can make an educated guess how to produce their sounds correctly, then instruments, especially wind instruments, are extremely valuable to singers because their timbres and those of voices have always been related. Yet conversely, in the 1950s, when wider concern first increased for 'authenticity' in performance, a *Times* music correspondent wrote:[64]

> The factor which has changed least during the intervening periods is probably the human voice. Assuming the possibility of ridding ourselves of the dubious benefit of Italianate voice production, a lot can be done to bridge the gap which would otherwise separate us from the thirteenth, fourteenth and fifteenth centuries. In this respect, the desirability for early music, of using a hall with a resonance time of six–nine seconds [is obvious] ...

We now know all too well the difficulties of modifying the human voice to produce timbres expected by an earlier age. Though there has now been some success, it is nevertheless, despite *The Times* correspondent, easier to begin with instrumental sound and contemporary description.

Books on musical style abound with excellent advice and with examples based on impeccable musicological research. Arguably, style is an amalgam of the physical limitations of a given period instrument, augmented by what is known through research, the arts, and essential *zeitgeist* of that period, plus physical human considerations like breathing capability, hand size and reach, and the like. From our knowledge of style and the tones available from any early instrument in playing order, or modern exact replicas, we may surely deduce a great deal about the voices which they once accompanied or in whose close proximity they were once played.

The human vocal organ is capable of tonal and stylistic variation in a way no other instrument can manage. Many singers, unless they are strict specialists, seem unaware of this or they ignore the possibilities more than two decades after Gardiner's book. They sing music of all periods beautifully but with an almost identical vocal approach which is therefore wrong for

---

[63] See Wulstan, op. cit., p. 232
[64] *The Times*, 'Austria's Bid to Revive the Study of Old Music', 14 June 1960

most of the music. Brian Trowell wrote in 1963:[65]

> We moderns can only hear the music of the Renaissance sung by voices whose training has been influenced by conditions unknown at that time – the need for one solo voice to carry over the sound of a large orchestra, for example, in theatre or concert hall.

There has been some improvement, of course. Increasingly, there are appropriately scaled performances in buildings of appropriate size – except in the Albert Hall!

Other than contemporary verbal description, and the sound of the instruments, the sound quality, particularly of Medieval and Renaissance singers, is usefully portrayed in painting and sculpture. The change to choral polyphony clearly initiated a change in vocal tone production. Early fifteenth–century paintings often portray singers with creased brows and strained features. Brian Trowell explained:[66]

> We sometimes see today such contorted features on our concert platforms, and they are associated with a strident, tightly–produced, nasal tone–colour. This appears to have been the noisy, penetrating sound which the Middle Ages enjoyed. If soloists were to be heard in the huge cathedrals of the Gothic era, there would certainly have been a tendency to strain. Later on, however, the faces become relaxed .... This suggests the modern approach of relaxed muscles and open throat. Vibrato, however, is condemned.

It would, however, be a mistake to describe all vocal tone before the middle of the fifteenth century as crude or barbaric. For one thing, the huge medieval cathedrals were usually multi-screened, which, as discussed earlier, must have encouraged a more controlled vocal technique and moderate volume during the singing of the Office, and probably during Mass and ritual processions. Some other events, like morality plays or other drama, may well have required louder singing.

We must remember that the visual artist's only method of suggesting the sound singers made is to exaggerate. It is not necessarily true that, because a depicted singer looks strained and tight, the throat of his live equivalent actually felt the strain. Clever vocalists can create deliberate tension in their tone for artistic reasons without the slightest physical effort. It is far more likely that tightly focused tone and skill, not crudity, projected the music of this period.

In any case, we must be aware here of possible differences in the vocal production of different countries. David Wulstan instanced that the faces in the stained glass of the fifteenth century Beauchamp Chapel of St Mary's Church, Warwick, show no trace of the tense production found in representations of continental singers of a similar date.[67] Although we are considering timbre before the fifteenth century, it is possible that certain national characteristics had developed regarding singing style before the soaring quality of the later English fifteenth–century school evolved.

There seems little doubt today that an acceleration of concern for appropriate techniques has been healthy. There has been progress even since the mid–1970s. An excellent record of

---

[65] Brian Trowell, *The Pelican History of Music* (1963), vol. 2, p. 60

[66] Loc. cit.

[67] Wulstan, op. cit., pp. 241–2

Mauchaut's *Messe de Notre Dame*, made in 1974 by the Purcell Choir, had a programme note by the director as follows:

> Much medieval music demands and contemporary professional singing techniques certainly include methods of rhythmic articulation and dynamic control which few singers trained by modern methods possess.

J. B. Steane, commenting on the same record, added:[68]

> If the singing of the choir is anything to go by, a 'pure', unvibrating tone is also required. Now, again it looks as if the extension to the singer's repertoire is likely to have some salutary effects upon singing methods. Just as the vocal lines of Stravinsky's songs or of Schonberg's 'Herzgewachse' forbid a spreading, unsteady tone (the notes have to be placed purely and accurately as by an instrument), so a medieval ballade or virelai (or a vocal–line in a choral work or part song) imposes a discipline. Where there is any unsteadiness, there intrudes something which sounds immediately anachronistic; and since melisma, elaborate and often strenuously rhythmical, is also a prominent feature, then the singer is compelled to dispense with aspirates – their habitual use, always regrettable, would be grotesque in this music.

Singers of the past were not burdened by the same problem. It was not lack of conscience but the fact that, especially in the secular sphere, they sang mostly contemporary music. The present age knows more music than any before it. In theory at least, it is the first in which, armed with knowledge, advanced research capabilities, ultra–sophisticated recording and communication, one might feel some confidence over how most music of the past should be performed. We have a responsibility not to ignore the fruits of this knowledge, but we should not rely on it totally; this is a matter that requires and will receive further exploration.

Nevertheless, it is true to say that stylistically no one voice can be all things to everybody. Each has its own predominating timbre and character. These can be varied to a reasonable degree, but not totally and not perpetually. Ultimately, the singer's decision is an aesthetic one: 'Is this musical work suitable for my voice, or *vice versa*? How convincing is my careful and considered judgement?'

So some stylistic specialisation must inevitably creep in, and why not? We have early music voices who should never (and probably do not ever) open a book of lieder, and lieder recitalists who should not try to sing Lully. There are some 'created' voices, especially those for esoteric performances of early music; few singers are so clearly specialist as the 'mezzo-soprano' Jantina Noorman, who has sung medieval music so effectively with Musica Reservata. (She has also sung the Witch in a recording of Purcell's *Dido and Aeneas*).[69] The use of inverted commas round 'mezzo–soprano' is necessary: anyone who has heard her voice, so perfect for medieval music, would understand that it is practically unacceptable for anything later in date except the more bizarre rôles, as Steane wrote:[70]

---

[68] J.B. Steane, *The Grand Tradition* (Duckworth, 1974), p. 520
[69] Chandos ABRD 1034
[70] Op. cit., pp. 521–2

One should really speak of 'voices', for she has two (maybe many more). One is a dulcet, piping sound, quite gentle and entirely without vibration; and when singing in this way she achieves exceptional precision in rapid ornamentation. That voice can be heard in Emilio de'Cavalieri's 'Godi turba mortal'. Then, in the same record, called Florentine Festival, she sings in some trios where one would not recognise the voice, which is itself revealed more fully in some anonymous dance songs. Here is the voice of a peasant, and the technique of a virtuoso: an uninhibited primitivism of tone, with the sophistication of modern musicianship.

On the other hand, there is a parallel to be drawn between singers and actors. Many of today's actors are allowed, or encouraged in training, to remain 'themselves'. No change of accent or essential persona is encouraged from one rôle to another. The actor often insists on this to 'preserve his personal integrity', his own essential character. But the true actor (not perhaps the star personality) must be able to transform himself as required by each rôle. It is the traditional ability of the good actor to do this. If not, his narrow specialisation can lead to self–imposed artistic limitation, or of course to the building up of a celebrated unique stage character.

Such considerations regarding acting teach singers a valuable lesson, for if there are different characters, colours and tones within all voice ranges, then surely there can be no cut–and–dried argument over the nature of counter–tenor sound? We can instantly know that a particular, individual voice suits Tallis but not Gluck, so different voices could all be excellent solo counter–tenors for particular purposes.

It is only partly a question of voice production. A rounded–falsetto alto may sound pleasant and appropriate in Romantic works, and even in certain lute songs, but he is perpetually handicapped should he attempt most Classical works without somehow altering not only his interpretation but also adjusting his production. If he does not, or cannot, adjust (even though he sings most of the classical counter–tenor range) it will be with tone so unlike what is and was required, that critics will claim that it is the wrong voice. He, they may retort, is 'only a male alto'. But it is the right voice–type, used inappropriately and by the wrong individual. The male alto, with some justification, has been called the Romantic version of the counter–tenor, but it must be repeated that the term alto is a perfectly proper alternative for counter–tenor and vice versa. 'Male', used before alto, is the oddity.

The character of the counter–tenor sound was a point at issue for a few decades; apart from the question of register–changes, or the lack of them, it was vocal timbre of what we might call 'Romantic' falsetto which seems to have worried the Americans, perhaps spearheaded by Oberlin. They are right to regard it with some suspicion when it is used in the wrong musical and vocal context – it is the whole reason why Deller was such a revelation in England.

The best contemporary English alto voices are no longer merely beautiful but lacking in ring, in *squillo* – therefore the Oberlin school's argument against most English counter–tenor tone quality cannot be sustained. However, there is still some mileage in their criticisms of some English counter–tenors today, in that the counter–tenor voice was never meant to be weak in its lower notes. Listen, however, to recordings of Whitworth, Brett and Bowman, and some of the younger men, for sheer tonal strength, through–range and fully supported sinus tone. Ironically, the fine American counter–tenor, John Angelo Messana, is so unlike the Oberlin school that his middle register apparently peters out below (middle) C4, perhaps because he specializes in the high, quasi–castrato repertoire. He seems to be an exception,

however; most younger American and continental European counter–tenors are now developing excellent through–range techniques.

A newspaper review from as long ago as 1960 mentions tone quality, and helps us divine
some of the original objections of the Oberlin school to Deller's idiosyncratic English
technique. The account in *The Times* of the first London performance of Britten's *A Mid–
summer Night's Dream*, contains two telling phrases which, we suggest, may ultimately be
seen as surprising:[71]

> The new Oberon, Mr Russell Oberlin, is gentler of voice and more mercurial
> of gesture and gait than Mr Deller ... but extremely musical. 'I Know a Bank'
> is here treated not as a soloist's showpiece but as part of the drama ...

'Gentler of voice' suggests weaker – subtle and effective, perhaps, but weaker. Listen to
Deller's recording of the rôle, in which he uses much contrast: first, heavy pharyngeal tone,
now thin upper–falsetto effect. It is strong stuff, judged by the complete recording of the
work, and by recordings of Oberlin. You can imagine what the reviewer meant; yet, by some
definitions, Deller is merely a male alto, and Oberlin a counter–tenor: supposedly that strong,
ringing, 'natural' voice, so different, it is claimed, from mere falsetto. These arguments, made
generally and usually without reference to specific singers have continued to flow back and
forth since. Oberlin, in fact, suffered vocal trouble while in this rôle and was replaced by
Grayston Burgess.

On the evidence of Oberlin's recordings, his upper range (the 'alto' areas), though agile and
beautifully–toned, do not really ring. It is the present author's contention that Deller's more
brilliant sound is not merely the result of highly–developed pharyngeal and cutting upper–
falsetto tone, but that it also came somehow both from ancient ecclesiastical acoustic and
ambience, and from an instinct for earlier secular tonal colourations; even, unconsciously, from
a psychic source.

> It occurs to me that, if not the origin, then something of the development of
> Deller's unique but influential sound must have been shaped by the Canter-
> bury acoustic, and later by that of St Paul's Cathedral, London. I never dis-
> cussed it with him, but I know from personal experience that the acoustic at
> Canterbury often encourages one to use less body in the alto tone; more light
> edge, and a thinner, brilliant, sound. Adjustment has to be made, as in many
> other buildings, for a broadcast or recording, and microphones are placed
> accordingly. Canterbury Cathedral's particular ambience favours high tones,
> but rather swallows lower voices. Thus, the cathedral choir really needs larger
> bass voices than many comparable buildings. (The famous Purcellian bass of
> enormous range, John Gostling, came from Canterbury.)[72]

By contrast with Deller, Whitworth was first a choral–scholar at King's College, Cambridge,
in its famous resonant acoustic, then a Lay–Vicar at Westminster Abbey, where the quire
acoustic, somewhat like that at Lichfield, is very dry. At Westminster, however, the quire is
enclosed, while another difference is that resonance is achievable but only at fortissimo, as the

---

[71] *The Times*, 'London Triumph for Britten's Dream', 11 June 1960
[72] Author's notebook, 1980

sound rises over the screens. Whitworth's tonal quality changed as a result of this acoustic. His fuller, trumpet–like tone–quality seems to have been at least partly the result of singing in the Abbey. A review in one of the London 'quality' newspapers reads:[73]

> Of the soloists, the counter–tenor, John Whitworth (Barak), as on former occasions, was an impressive curioso. A voice of that quality, and so equal throughout its register, I have not heard since Cambridge days when Mr Benton sang in King's College choir. Mr Whitworth is a true artist, as Jennifer Vyvyan is, and the two made a delightful thing of 'Why Do Thy Ardours?

Mr Benton was a lay–clerk in King's College Choir, before the advent of choral–scholars. Perhaps the reviewer meant 'range' not 'register', yet if he considered that Whitworth used only one register, in normal circumstances he would have been mistaken. The compliment paid to 'equality' of course is a particularly twentieth–century one, and Whitworth's variety of vocal colour was never as great as Deller's. Maine may have been writing 'against' Deller in this instance.

Singing in a dry quire, theatre, opera house or recording studio, necessitates a change of approach; yet something of one's instinctive timbre must remain. In Deller's case, the resonance was somehow trapped, magically, in his voice. In the case of Whitworth, this was less obvious; but probably the various timbres achieved by both singers were as much the result of skilful use of the cranial cavities as of cordal action and adjustment. Oberlin's dry technique sounds as if it is in direct contrast with those of Deller and Whitworth. (It would be intriguing to consider the hypothetical tone–quality of well–known counter–tenors of the past, like Saville of Lichfield, based on the setting in which they are known to have sung regularly, as well as the music associated with them.)

Properly resonated and produced, the English pharyngeally–based solo counter–tenor (depending on how he is trained) can be as crisp, clear, masculine and strong in tone as the light tenor–altino. At the same volume level, pharyngeal voice can sometimes carry more than lyric tenor in middle range and above. On both sides of the Atlantic, we can now hear excellent, ringing tone, and superb, 'through voice' counter–tenors are making an impact on concert platforms. The matter of nomenclature is raised occasionally, but is becoming less important.

It is perhaps appropriate here to recall the always quirky uncertainties of popularity. There have always been artists who have been denied their full acclaim. In some ways, Charles Brett seems to be today's equivalent of John Whitworth in the late 1950s and the 1960s. He is a counter–tenor whose voice, technique, approach and influence are so obviously right and totally convincing, yet who, though widely known, does not seem to receive the attention and recognition that is his due.

Returning to *The Times* review of Britten's *A Midsummer Night's Dream*: the phrase 'a soloist's showpiece' merely suggests that the two artists differed greatly in their interpretation. (Oberon/Oberlin: other than Deller's static acting, could there have been any unconscious influence at work in the minds of the Covent Garden authorities during the original 'Deller or Oberlin?' machinations[74] which even found subliminal echoes in *The Times* review? Probably not, but here a coincidental similarity of names enters the counter–tenor scene yet again.) Be that as it may, can we here glimpse the virtuoso solo counter–tenor of the past, as compared

---

[73] Cutting from unidentified newspaper; Basil Maine reviewing a performance of Handel's *Deborah*
[74] Hardwick, *A Singularity of Voice* (Proteus 1980), pp. 143–148

to the more modern technique of the light lyric tenor? Is this difference – that of stylistic familiarity – the real basis for varying preferences today? Perhaps; but both the truth and the irony is that both Deller and Oberlin are counter–tenors, and excellent ones. They display contrasting techniques, styles and origins. Many counter–tenors have since assumed the rôle of Oberon, but the singer about whom it can truly be claimed that he has for the rôle the combined qualities of Deller and Oberlin, is Charles Brett. He has Deller's delicacy in thin upper–falsetto and pipe–voice and rich pharyngeal middle–tones, yet possesses Oberlin's apparently effortless through–range technique and light upper–falsetto [sic], and can draw on a gentle but resonant fundamental register comparable to that of Oberlin.

Tonal quality is inevitably a subjective phenomenon. Frederic Hodgson, the distinguished alto and knowledgeable writer on the 'alto or counter–tenor' question, wrote in *The Musical Times* to lament the loss of what he terms 'real' alto tone:[75]

> This is recognisable in the full, mellifluous head voice, resembling that of the contralto, but with a quite definite masculine depth of quality, by which the bona–fide alto becomes something of a vocal paradox. There is nothing 'weak and effeminate' about the voice. It is neither 'fruity' nor 'hooty', and substantiation of its claim to be real alto is borne out by the fact that as it is chiefly on aesthetic and dramatic grounds any singer stands or falls, it cannot be argued that the cold, edgy type of voice so prevalent among many young contemporary singers, who sound all alike, is to be compared with the warm, rich and beautiful alto quality which has always met with unanimous acceptance. The difference is that one is a gimmick; the other a rare gift.

Fashion and usage being what they are, of the term 'unanimous acceptance' it is difficult to accept the qualification 'always', and the young contemporary singers 'sounding all alike' is surely no more the case than any other type of voice. Frederic Hodgson seems to have been mourning a particular ideal, one which was equally sought after by just as many altos in the past, perhaps between 1890 and 1940. In fact, since 1965, the wheel has turned slightly. Alto *voce bianca* is itself slightly suspect; though not yet soprano *voce bianca* – fashion plays its uneven part.

B. Forsyte Wright, in *The Musical Times* for November 1959, explained his view, which in part Frederic Hodgson (in 1965 at least) seemed to share: that the counter–tenor and alto voices are utterly different. Forsyte Wright wrote:[76]

> By way of contrast, the alto voice, which is still fairly common in Anglican Cathedral Choirs, is an artificial voice and in that sense 'falsetto'. Being relatively weak and unsupported by a full resonance, it has no great value for solo work, on account of its lack of power. It is very useful, however, for the purpose of harmony in the way it blends with boys' and men's natural voices.

Wulstan's view of the earlier alto is of interest here:[77]

---

[75] Frederic Hodgson, 'The Contemporary Alto', *The Musical Times*, April 1965, p. 293
[76] 'The Alto and Countertenor Voice', *Musical Times*, November 1959, p. 593
[77] Op. cit., p. 244

> The alto was therefore predominantly falsetto, a 'sweet, shrill voice' which was 'edgy' without being raucous. Its tone was not unlike that of the treble or castrato, but was dissimilar from that of the tenor. The change into chest register would have been masked in such a way that the lower notes would appear to be low in the voice, for otherwise there would be no point in setting a lower limit to the range.

We might well disagree with his statement that the alto always differed markedly in tone from the tenor; neither can we be sure that the alto endeavoured to suggest a low quality to his lower head–notes. The limits, top and bottom, of upper chest–voice form a basis for continuation into head–voice. High continued timbre and feeling could surely be as likely to have been thought important. The limits at the top, of upper fundamental voice form a basis for continuation into head–voice. A continued timbre and feeling of 'height', like the quality achieved so thrillingly by Whitworth, could have been considered equally important. The lower limit to the upper fundamental voice, i.e., that area in which the heavier, lower fundamental register begins to be predominant, is certainly felt by the singer and can be audible to the more sensitive members of the audience. Wulstan's point about 'setting a lower limit to the range' seems thus to be answered.

Wulstan was of course discussing the sixteenth–century situation, but for reasons which emerge during the course of the present work, we may feel that he was either partly mistaken or inadvertantly misleading. The voice could hardly have been shrill in the pharyngeal area, where there must have been some affinity with the tenor's tone. Certainly, the higher areas of the alto range can sound shrill – that is to say, piercing and high–pitched. It is possible that Wulstan had a now little–used definition of 'shrill' in mind: 'insisting on being heard'.[78]

What is most interesting is that Hodgson, Forsyte Wright and Wulstan are talking of the same voice, or at least of a voice based mainly on the same vocal production: the falsetto or head–voice. Yet nobody is surely going to accuse one of describing the alto and the others as describing something else. It would seem apposite that Wulstan was talking of usage in an earlier musical period and that Hodgson's and Forsyte Wright's views reflected the very best and the worst examples of the same alto voice as used in the Romantic period.[79]

Julian Gardiner (1969), seemed at first to agree with Frederic Hodgson, then more with Forsyte Wright, then *vice versa*. In his chapter on 'Mechanisms', talking of the alto mechanism in men's voices, he wrote:[80]

> An untrained baritone singing up the scale on these notes, comes to a point where he has a choice of doing two things. Either he can continue brazenly and uncomfortably up to G in his normal voice, or he can drift into falsetto. This is a noise which may be comic or pleasing, but either way will be ineffective, and quite inappropriate to the rest of his voice and to his own personality. The true alto mechanism is no breathy little pipe, but a tone of full–blooded contralto quality such as is heard in English cathedral choirs. In

---

[78] *Concise Oxford Dictionary* (O.U.P., 1929 edn)

[79] See the criticisms of Lowell Mason in his *Musical Letters from Abroad*, which includes accounts of the Birmingham, Norwich and Dusseldorf festivals of 1852 and New York, 1854. For uncomplimentary references to male altos, see the entries on pp. 206, 261, 281 and 309

[80] Gardiner, op. cit., pp. 217–8

Victorian days male altos were popular as soloists and as leaders of quartets, but times have changed and today they are seldom heard outside the cathedral stall. Nevertheless, in the training of men's voices the alto mechanism plays an important part which singers are unwise to neglect. In breath management and vocal cord approximation the technique is precisely the same as for the normal male voice. Tenors and basses are as a rule nothing like such good alto singers as baritones. Even so, however modest their range and tone quality, all singers should make use of what they have. No matter what strange sounds they produce, they will enormously increase the quality and the steadiness of their normal voice. Of course, if they start singing exclusively in the alto mechanism, their ordinary voices will soon disappear. Similarly women who habitually sing in chest lose their ordinary voices, while their chest notes acquire surprising depth and range. I am assuming however that my male readers have no intention of becoming cathedral altos, nor that my female readers aim to excel as night-club singers, so that in both cases they will use their extraordinary voices to promote their general well-being.

It is not possible to sing a truly legato descending scale of four notes in alto voice, unless a correct technical preparation and follow-through is maintained – and let it be clearly understood that alto invariably means alto and not a quavery little falsetto. No forward production specialist can manage it. A high centre of gravity, raised cheeks and chest, retracted jaw and contracted tongue muscles, all these are indispensable adjuncts for a true alto voice. It is indeed significant that the average cathedral alto has a much steadier and purer quality and a rounder tone than have his colleagues in the tenor and bass sections. The voice itself has little individuality and is decidedly limited in range and power; yet it seems to remain as good as new through fifty-odd years of cathedral services. This suggests that the male alto possesses an elixir of vocal life, but the explanation is much simpler. He cannot sing at all unless his technique is correct, and good technique keeps voices young.

Also, the late Colin Scull, ex-Gentleman of the Chapel Royal, St James's, wrote:[81]

> My old colleague Charles Hawkins, though he would not have been considered a counter-tenor in the present day use of the term, was singing adequately when he retired at eighty-two years. From a *Musical Times* letter, April 1943, I see that Henry Dutton retired from St Paul's on the 4th of April that year aged ninety. Even Deller sang to sixty-seven. [His age at death.]

Frederic Hodgson, then aged eighty, gave many a young singer a lesson in effortless breath control, beauty of tone, and vocal command, in a London recital in October 1987:[82]

> The singer provided living evidence of the longevity of a voice properly used, and an astonishing demonstration of the possibility of noiseless

---

[81] Letter to author, 1987
[82] Dr Graham Welch, *The Journal of the Ernest George White Society*, vol. 5, no. 1, 1987, p. 27

breathing and superb breath–control at the age of eighty years. The audience
was enchanted by Mr Hodgson's art ...

Gardiner's attitude was puzzling: his statements on altos or counter–tenors throughout his book change radically: first there is admiration, then grudging approval, but finally the absolute execration (his pages 813–4). But in the quotation above there seems more than enough contradiction to make the point. His remark about counter–tenors 'seldom being heard outside the cathedral choir stall' could not be true in 1968 unless by altos he did not intend to mean solo counter–tenors. Is he thereby implying recognition that the modern solo counter–tenor differs greatly in tone and timbre from the 'old–fashioned' Romantic cathedral alto? His highly critical and misleading remarks on the techniques of the alto in his last paragraph make extraordinary reading – unless they refer only to self–taught singers of mediocre gifts.

In 1967, Ardran and Wulstan wrote on alto tone:[83]

> If no historical justification can be found for distinguishing two different voices by the two terms – a conclusion that Mr Whitworth, in his article on the counter tenor voice [*English Church Music*, 1965], also reaches – what is the difference between the patently falsetto 'hoot' associated with the term 'male alto' and parish sextons, and the clear tone of singers usually called counter tenors, such as Alfred Deller? The fact that the two types of singer produce sounds of rather different quality cannot justify the use of two separate words unless a further range of terms, such as 'throttle–tenor' and 'bull–bass', are to be called into use to describe differences in voices other than the alto. Unless they are tenors rather than altos (in which case there is no historical or logical reason for describing them as either counter tenors or altos) all altos, however named, must produce their voices by the same basic mechanism. Such refinements in tone–colour as distinguish one singer from another must by a question of natural ability and/or training in the 'placing' of the voice, that is, the control of resonance. It is clearly the larynx that must be studied in order to determine the mechanism that is common to all altos ... . To sum up, the alto voice today is produced in basically the same way by all singers. Such differences as there are depend on good voice production as in any other voice. There can be no doubt that the classical alto produced his voice in the same way with various modifications in the finer points of techniques from period to period.

Most of this reads convincingly, for reasons given previously. Alfred Deller commented on the Ardran and Wulstan article (an Appendix to *A Singularity of Voice*) in these terms:[84]

> This is quite the most sensible thing I have read; but, in my opinion, the view that the alto voice today is produced in basically the same way by all singers, and that such differences as there are depend on good voice production as in any other voice, is an over–simplification. It is much more complex than that, not to say mysterious. I believe that with all first–rate – certainly with great

---

[83] Ardran and Wulstan, *Music and Letters*, January 1967, p. 19
[84] Hardwick, op. cit., p. 196

– voices, the possessor is physiologically and psychologically predisposed to
the making of the actual sound, the timbre and quality of the voice. Of course,
hard work is also necessary to acquire technique, but no amount of work will
produce a clarion sound from what Nature has (inscrutably) designated a
bugle.

A bugle is appropriate only to a bugle band and a clarion to a Baroque ensemble; but we can
share Deller's meaning.

*

It would be difficult if not impossible after so many pages to provide a summing–up satisfying
to all readers, but as a conclusion to this work, two important and controversial aspects of the
counter–tenor – perhaps the most important – should be re–introduced for further thought and
to put what has gone before into context. The first concerns vocal style, sacred and secular.

We have seen that not only in earlier periods such as that of the Tudors was the style of
sacred and secular music often similar, and sometimes even identical except for the texts, but
that consequently the vocal style which they demanded was also very similar. This obviously
casts doubt on the idea that the alto or counter–tenor in his ecclesiastical garb was a different
singer to the alto or counter–tenor wearing his secular hat. In musical periods when (on the
whole) ecclesiastical and secular styles differed, as in the nineteenth century (and indeed the
twentieth), those singers of all vocal categories who had a foot in both camps had perforce to
adjust their style daily or to specialize permanently; but there is no convincing reason to
conclude that not only vocal style, but also vocal production itself, had to be changed
intrinsically. Nevertheless, it seems impossible to deny that, from the later eighteenth century
onwards, one important, purposely–developed difference between singers of stage and opera
and those of cathedral or church lay, and often still lies, in the choice of vocal tonal character
and approach.

Though there have always been singers who could adjust and cross a 'style–divide'
convincingly, it seems undeniable that in England particularly (but not exclusively), the taking
part in the performance of choral services, especially during the last two centuries, has not
always encouraged singers to develop enough tone–colours in their general singing style. The
ecclesiastical environment has usually imposed a rather grave and serious tone–quality and
(apart from periodical fallings from grace!) has elicited a matching demeanour from singers
under the eyes of the Dean and Chapter, or other ecclesiastical authority. This understandable
gravity discouraged any possibility in the cathedral milieu of a lighter and multi–colourful
tonal approach – except in a few places, at certain periods. One obvious earlier example is the
secular theatricality of the Chapel Royal string band and vocal style in the years following the
Restoration of Charles II.

Alfred Deller's failure to obtain appointments as an alto lay–vicar at Lincoln and Salisbury
cathedrals in the late 1930s now becomes easier to understand. His carefully controlled
variable vocal colourings would have disconcerted most cathedral organists trained in the late
nineteenth century, apropos both solo alto work and then–current English Romantic concepts
of choral and ensemble blend. Deller's appointment by Gerald Knight to Canterbury was part
of the beginning of a slow stylistic change in English cathedral singing.

There has long been a link (in terms of performers, their musical style, and their singing
in some kind of uniform clothing) between cathedral, church, oratorio, (other than early

oratorio in Italy) and the sacred and secular customarily formal, formally–clad lieder recital. By contrast, the operatic or stage singer, usually in costume, has always inhabited a different, multi–coloured world of theatre – often fantasy-based and, as it might be phrased today, entertainment–orientated. This is one reason for the two main contrasting vocal–styles and appropriate demeanour.

It is significant that, even today, unless he changed his very secular style markedly, the excellent counter–tenor, Jochen Kowalski, would be unlikely to get (and probably would not want!) a post as an ecclesiastical singer in almost any English cathedral–style choir, possibly not even in the Sistina in Rome. Nevertheless, there are times when, as in Deller's case, a style such as Kowalski's would be totally appropriate for solo work in the ecclesiastical milieu.

The second important aspect of the counter–tenor debate which demands a reprise at the conclusion of this volume is that of the 'ponticello' or 'bridge area'; its use or avoidance in relation to the male voice. Once the two basic modes of voice, 'chest' and 'head' [*sic*] had been discovered by early man, it could not have been long before it was realised that the two voices actually overlapped. In this ponticello area, which varied from one individual to another, notes could be sung using either upper–chest or lower–head voice. Eventually, it was realised that not only could the singer choose between registers while he sang in this overlapping area, but that he could take one of a further set of options. He could choose to:

1 Stay in 'chest' and stop singing at its highest note, or return to lower notes.
2 Stay in 'head' and stop singing at its lowest note, or return to higher notes.
3 Move abruptly from 'chest' to 'head' at a convenient point.
4 Return abruptly from 'head' to 'chest' at a convenient point.
5 Try to disguise the different timbres of chest- and head–registers.
6 Accentuate the different timbres of chest- and head–registers for dramatic effect.
7 Try to disguise the actual movement from chest- to head–register and vice versa (the dovetail technique).
8 Accentuate the actual movement from 'chest' to 'head' and vice versa for dramatic effect.

Though these options remained (and indeed still remain today), at some point in the evolution of singing, it began to be realized that it might be possible to extend the fleeting overlap or 'mix' when making a smooth transition from 'chest' to 'head' or vice versa, to form a joint or mixed–voice for higher notes (the splice technique).

While this made the transition smoother, if adhered to stubbornly (e.g., retaining as much chest register in the mix as possible, even for the highest notes), it inevitably limited the higher range and tessitura, and though it was much easier to sing at this pitch than when attempting to use chest–register alone for these high notes or whole passages, it still remained more tiring than employing head–voice alone. (Nevertheless, as time passed, mixed–voice would be extended to cover as much of the old head–voice territory as possible, while chest–voice, used alone, would take care of the average working range of the particular music to be sung.)

Quite obviously, the singer who most enjoyed using his low voice (whom we would call a bass) would stay as long as possible in his chest/basic/fundamental register, while the singer who most enjoyed using his highest range (whom we would term a first alto or high counter–tenor) would use and remain in his head/falsetto register as long as possible. When singers wished to move into the 'new' area, the two main registers could be joined by using the earlier dovetail technique, or alternatively, the later splice technique. To effect actual transition between real 'chest' and true 'head' modes, the dovetail technique was most useful for greatest overall range, versatility, and dramatic effect for all singers. Those whom we would call baritones, tenors and low counter–tenors or second altos, who enjoyed working (variously) in the more middle areas, with briefer visits to the extremes than those made by basses or higher counter–tenors/first altos, also had the option of dovetail or splice as they moved through their range.

Today, the constant unnecessarily–controversial question about register change for counter–tenors remains, ranging from 'at which point?' to 'never'. This topic is that on which so many contemporary commentators base so many of their opposing entrenched positions.

It seems axiomatic that if the tenor singer uses only upper–fundamental register, or conventional *voix mixte* technique for high notes or high passages, he cannot be considered a counter–tenor. On the other hand, if, for his higher notes, the tenor moves from upper–fundamental almost immediately, without using mixed–voice more than momentarily (or perhaps for a tone or two) for the transition into pharyngeal/middle–falsetto/voce mezzana, in which he is happy to remain for whole vocal passages, he is employing a traditional low counter–tenor/tenor–altino/light baritone/earliest–tenor technique: in fact, the composite male voice method. If he spends, say, at least half his time in head–voice, he could be considered a low counter–tenor. The counter–tenor specialist who moves down from pharyngeal/middle–falsetto/voce mezzana into upper–fundamental without employing *voix mixte*, is using the same traditional technique. He too is a low counter–tenor.

The ponticello, or the bridge, is indeed an excellent analogy. The counter–tenor singer who employs it briefly, exploits one of its various possibilities – the convenience of choice: where in its length or territory to make his change to the next register? But what if he decides not to change at all? The high counter–tenor is the head–voice specialist with enough tonal strength in his lower pharyngeal not to need, or hardly to need, his true fundamental register *because he has converted his pharyngeal into a second fundamental register*.

Some would argue that though he chooses not to employ the ponticello mechanism, it is because it is there that the high counter–tenor can obtain strong enough tone for his musical and vocal purposes in the long 'tail' of the dovetail joint.

This is the nub of the matter. Use of genuine head–voice is the decider. A singer who never employs it should not be called a counter–tenor; but conversely, he who uses head–voice exclusively should be termed a high counter–tenor (given that he has extended and developed his range to cover the repertoire effectively). This is not of course to involve ourselves in discussion of singing standard and good or poor technique.

René Jacobs, and those who take his position in the debate, probably support most, if not all, the conclusions above, except the definition of the high counter–tenor. They are likely to say that he who uses no fundamental register at any point whatsoever is a falsettist, though most would add that falsettist is not a pejorative term. To that we could respond that the title falsettist is not a definition on which there is universal unequivocal agreement.

Surprisingly, there is lingering prejudice about the counter–tenor, and it can emanate from both the musically ill–informed and the musically knowledgeable. The present work has endeavoured to address both of these varieties but, in any case, musically ill–informed prejudice is weakening rapidly as a result of liberal ideas, the use of the male high–voice in popular music, and the general *zeitgeist* of the late twentieth century. As to more informed opinion (behind which prejudice can often hide): for many today who 'have a problem' when considering their reactions to the counter–tenor, his voice, his range, his *raison d'être*, it seems that it is somehow more 'respectable' if one can point to a tenor fundamental voice rather than that of even a light baritone. Apart from other considerations, 'counter-tenor' is so conveniently connected philologically with the familiar, dependable term 'tenor', in that one is satisfyingly seen as part of the other.

Rather more surprising is the idea which has begun to be 'put about', or dropped into sophisticated musical conversation or interview (sometimes by those who should know better), that the solo counter-tenor is not, after all, a historical voice-type of musical significance but that it was invented in the mid-twentieth century. It is said that the counter-tenor – by this or any other title – never existed outside the English cathedral choir stalls (if indeed it ever existed there at all until the mid-nineteenth century), much less provided important soloists in secular music during the sixteenth, seventeenth and eighteenth centuries in England and other European countries.

Such strange ideas may well reflect some sort of loss of confidence, or be born partly of a wearied reaction to the eternal controversies about defining the terms counter-tenor, alto and haute-contre, and, as a result, over which singers are which. Conversely, the idea may also be born of total confidence, and is a cavalier flourish to waft away all argument by crying 'Who cares what happened or did not happen in the past! The counter-tenor is a marvellous sound! Music develops. Let's enjoy the male high-voice now! Let's exploit it in new and exciting ways!'

The counter-tenor is indeed a marvellous sound, and this author also trumpets these fanfares for the future. But the future is not quite enough alone.

L. P. Hartley's famous phrase 'The past is a foreign country: they do things differently there' prefaced this work. If things were indeed done differently in the past – and the reader might agree that this was not necessarily the case vocally, except in terms of musical style – it is because music, as any other art-form, reflects the period, setting, and milieu in which it is composed and performed.

Differing requirements for vocal style, tone and range have therefore encouraged or dictated some change in all voice-categories throughout all ages. It therefore cannot be surprising that counter-tenors in solo and ensemble work have also varied somewhat in order to meet the demands of the age in which they serve. Though not all characteristics have always been present in every individual member, the counter-tenor, as a vocal family, has always possessed a variety of tonal and stylistic options: exciting, ringing, piercing, nasal or clear, and strong. Yet his palette of colour-options also included the delicate, the subtle and the languishing, the rich and mellifluous.

APPENDIX 1 The Nicholas Morgan mystery

Nicholas Morgan was a Chapel Royal counter–tenor in the middle of the sixteenth century. 'Nicolas Mauregan' was admitted to the choir of the French Chapel Royal, La Sainte–Chapelle, Paris, about 1583. That this was the same Nicholas Morgan sworn in 1566 into the English Chapel Royal there has seemed to be no doubt:[1]

> 1566 Hechins died the 9th daie of November Anno 9", and Nicholas Morgan was sworn in his place the 9th of December, A"10".

> 23 July 1583 Gift of 10 Crowns to 'a poor English cantor [singer]' who sang 'with the companions in the church here'.[2]

However, recent research seems to show that they cannot be the same man and that Brenet (in 1910) and Hough (in 1937) and others since, including the present author (in 1982), were mistaken.

One fact seems undeniable:

> 1581 Mr Morgan died the 9th maye, & Anthony Todd sworne Gent the 15th of maye in his Roome.[3]

Thurston Dart[4] suggests that Morgan was sworn at the Chapel Royal in 1567 and, seemingly without knowledge of his 'death' in 1581 (and his admittance to Sainte–Chapelle in 1583), he implies that Morgan sang at the Chapel Royal until 1582. According to Dart, he stayed at Sainte–Chapelle until 1586.

We therefore have a fascinating mystery. Is it really possible that there were two Nicholas Morgans, both counter–tenors or haute–contres, of the same period and nationality: one in the English Chapel Royal, who died in 1581, and the other in the French Chapelle, and who was very much alive in 1583? This seems unlikely. Yet, except that Morgan is recorded as having died in 1581, circumstantial evidence: the date, name and office of the royal singer, would indicate a move by him from London to Paris.

---

[1] Old Cheque (or Check) Book, Chapel Royal .....
[2] Michael Brenet, *Les Musiciens de la Sainte–Chapelle du Palais* (facsimile edn, Minkoff, 1973), p. 135 fn.; translation by David Stone, 1990
[3] Bodleian Library MS. D318, fols. 25–47
[4] Thurston Dart, 'English Musicians Abroad', Grove's *Dictionary*, 5th edn, p. 950

We must surely assume that the singer referred to by Brenet on 23 July,[5] 3 December 1583 and 8 March 1586[6] was the same man. In one of these references, there is a strong indication of the Parisian Mauregan's reasons for leaving England:[7]

> 3 December 1583 My lords 'have ordered the Receveur to give Nicolas Mauregan, a shamefully poor wretch, the sum of 10 crowns in consideration of the fact that he has been driven out and expelled from his native land for wishing to die a Catholic, and for not having wanted to follow the Huguenots. Joined to the fact that he goes every day to the church here to sing his part as counter-tenor [haute contre] ... coeur et à l'aigle'?

The term 'à l'aigle' has puzzled many, but after some enquiries (even including the author's visit to the gothic church of St. Martin in the town of L'Aigle, some 35 kilometres south of Paris) the phrase would seem likely to bear the simplest meaning: 'sing his part in quire and at the lectern (eagle)' – in other words as cantor. However, Charles Cleall has suggested: 'With a light heart' – a heart that takes wing like an eagle, or: 'To sing his part as counter-tenor from the heart', and 'rising up with wings, as an eagle'[8] or literally, 'from the heart, in the manner of an eagle'.

Just over two years after the entry dated 3 December 1583, we read:[9]

> 8 March 1586...the same day, a gift of 10 crowns, 'in alms, to Morgant, a poor English fugitive from his homeland through being a Catholic'.

Brenet believed this to have been Morgan and added, in a footnote:[10]

> Nicolas Mauregan, who had been singing at the Sainte-Chapelle and receiving alms from the canons since the 23 July, 1583, seems to have been the same as Nicholas Morgan, cantor in the Royal Chapel of England in 1566.

Before we consider this further, we should read the original French of Brenet's entries concerning Morgan which were translated above:

> p. 135. 23 juillet 1583. Don de 10 ecus a 'ung pauvre engles chantre' qui a chanté 'avec les compaignons en l'église de ceans'.

> p. 136. 3 decembre 1583. MM. 'ont ordonné au recepveur de donner à Nicolas Maregan, Anglois, pauvre honteux, la somme de 10 escuz en consideration de ce qu'il a esté chasé et explusé de sa patrie pour voulloir mourir catholique et pour n'avoir voullu suivre les huguenotz. Joinet qu'il se

---

[5] Brenet, p. 135
[6] Brenet, op. cit., p. 139
[7] Brenet, op. cit., p. 136
[8] Cf. Isaiah, ch. 40, p. 31
[9] Brenet, op. cit., p. 139
[10] Loc. cit.

range tous les jours à l'église de ceans pour chanter sa partie de haute–contre au coeur et à l'aigle.'

p. 136. 23 juin 1584. Aumone de 12 escuz à Nicolas Mauregan.

p. 139. 9 decembre 1585. Don de 10 ecus 'à l'anglais chantre', en forme d'aumone, 'et pour la residence actuelle et debvoir qu'il faict au service de la Ste Chappelle'.

p. 139. 8 mars 1586 ... 'Le même jour, don de 10 ecus, 'par aumone, à Morgant, pauvre engles fugitif de son pays pour estre catholique'.

It would seem just possible that, despite the written proof of his death, Nicholas Morgan, counter–tenor of the (English) Chapel Royal, did not in fact die in 1581 but, like Mauregan, fled to Paris as a religious exile. The fact that his death and the swearing of his successor are not recorded in the Chapel Royal Cheque Book would seem to be significant. Many who wished to remain Roman Catholic in a century of religious upheaval and persecution fled abroad, among them (for example) the composers Peter Philips and Richard Dering. The Cheque Book notes: '... 1583 Richard Morrice' ... 'Fledd beyond the Seaes'.[11] Others, no doubt, remained Catholics secretly. Tallis and Byrd managed to retain their Roman faith openly, while managing to keep their positions in the Queen's favour and in the Chapel Royal.

So was Morgan, officially dead in London, finally admitted to the Choir of Sainte–Chapelle after a difficult and poverty–stricken interval in Paris of about two years?

The *Musical Antiquary*, in 1913, painted an intriguing picture:[12]

Nicholas Morgan of the Chapel Royal. Among the Hatfield Papers, published by the Hist. Mss: Com. (vol V), there is a letter from John Dowland, the lutenist and composer, to Sir Robert Cecil, dated November 10, 1595, in which he says: 'Fifteen years since I was in France...and lay in Paris, where I fell acquainted with one Smith, a priest, and one Morgan, sometimes of Her Majesty's Chapel, one Verstigan who brake out of England, being apprehended, and one Moris, a Welshman, that was our porter, who is at Rome. These men thrust many idle toys into my head of religion, saying that the Papists' was the truth and ours in England all false, and I, being but young, their fair words over reached me and I believed with them,' &c. The whole letter was printed with valuable notes in "The Musical Times" for December, 1896 and February 1897 by Mr W. Barclay Squire, who discusses the possibility of Dowland's having confused Morgan with Morris, for Morris was a Gentleman of the Chapel Royal who 'fled beyond the seas' for the sake of his religion. Documents published since Mr Squire's article appeared enable us now to state that Dowland was perfectly correct, except in saying 'nearly fifteen years'; and that 'one Morgan' was Nicholas Morgan, a Gentleman of the Chapel Royal, who was sworn in the place of William Hechins or Huchins

[11] Old Chapel Royal Cheque Book
[12] W. H. Gratton Flood, 'Lists of the King's Musicians', *The Musical Antiquary*, October 1912 – July 1913, vol. IV, p. 59

on December 9, 10, Eliz. (i.e., 1567). He too fled for conscience' sake, apparently in the early summer of 1582, and found employment in Paris, where he was taken on as a stipendiary at the Sainte-Chapelle.

This seems to solve the question raised in Squire's article as to who was the companion of Thomas (or Richard) Morris in his flight. In July 1582, Cardinal Allen writes from Rheims of 'two notable musicians' then at Rouen but expected at Rheims. They were married men who had escaped from the Chapel of the Queen, to her great indignation. One was Morris, the 'finest musician in the place' [*sic*]; the other, however, was reported to be far superior to him. Morris went on to Rome and the other unnamed musician was doubtless Morgan who, as we have seen, remained in Paris.[13]

The case of Nicholas Morgan suggests another candidate for the still under-explored topic of the English singers and musicians of this time who lived, or settled permanently, in countries other than their own for political, religious or apparently innocent musical reasons. Dowland, however, returned to England to find a ready payment from the Secret Service funds of James I awaiting him.[14]

In the seventeenth century there was constant musical, though certainly not religious, co-operation and traffic between English and French Chapels Royal and similar establishments of other countries. Henrietta Maria, Charles I's Queen, had her own chapel in London, which included several Frenchmen. The young Pelham Humfrey, that most outstanding of Captain Cooke's boys at the Chapel Royal, was sent to France by Charles ll in 1664 to study the work of Lully and Louis XIV's twenty-four violins. Humfrey was given a £200 payment in the same year from the Secret Service fund 'to defray the charge of his journey into France and Italy'.[15] The over-large amount and the source of the money appear significant. We might recall Dowland and Abell in connection with the latter (see Appendix Ten) and remember that John Bull (1562–1628), organist variously of Hereford Cathedral and the Chapel Royal, is also suspected to have acted as a spy in the Royal service while abroad. He left England in 1613. 'John Bull, Doctor of Musicke, went beyond the seas without license and was admitted into the Archduke's Service'.[16] No definite reason has ever been established for Bull's leaving the country. It has been thought likely that he had become a Roman Catholic. He certainly became organist of Antwerp Cathedral in 1617.

Following the Gunpowder Plot in 1605, Roman Catholics were persecuted rigorously. For Bull to leave the Royal appointment of Organist of the Chapel Royal to become a Roman Catholic was every whit as unacceptable to King and Establishment as it would have been a few decades earlier, in Morgan's time. Such forced resignations from Royal service continued to happen decades later. John Smith, 'late of His Majesty's Private Musicke', had to resign in 1687 for being a Roman Catholic. Payment of stipend seems to have been granted in his case.[17] Depending on the occupant of the throne, the situation shifted between uneasy truce and near or actual persecution.

---

[13] Ibid., pp. 59–60 ('Notes and Queries')

[14] Christopher Hogwood, *Music at Court* (The Folio Society, London, 1977), p. 12

[15] Ibid., p. 12

[16] Old Chapel Royal Cheque Book

[17] Andrew Ashbee, *R.E.C.M.*, vol. I, pp. 289–90, and Vol. II, p. 20

Therefore, about a century earlier, had Morgan become an agent or spy? If so, his abrupt disappearance from the Chapel Royal and England could have been engineered to this purpose, and might even have involved a faked death.

A letter among the Molyneux Manuscripts[18] suggests another intriguing possibility: that Morgan, sent originally to Paris as a spy in the service of Queen Elizabeth, had become a double agent. He was again in England in 1591. There is a letter from the Lords of the Council to Sir William More, dated 14 June, 1591:[19]

> For the immediate discovery and arrest of "one Morgan sometymes of her maiesties chapell, an obstinate and seditious papist", who "hathe wandred in lurcking sorte up and down this great whyle from place to place, and is nowe thought to be in Sutton, either in or about Sir Henry Weston's howse, or at least yf he be not nowe there it is knowen that at tymes by startes he vseth to come thither in secret sorte, and perhaps not called by his right name.

Thurston Dart wrote that, after returning to England in 1591, Morgan or Mauregen 'entered the Jesuit College at St.–Omer in 1595, was ordained in 1605, became organist of the Convent of Benedictine nuns in Brussels (1608–11) and then moved to Louvain, where he became organist to the convent of Augustinian nuns from 1612 until his death, 3 August 1640.[20] He was named in Sebastian Westcote's will in 1582 (see p. 43). And yet Morgan died in 1581, in England!

What if Nicolas Mauregan, or Morgant, the exiled English singer were not the Morgan of the English Chapel Royal? A Nicholas Morgan is named as builder (i.e., first owner) of a sixteenth–century house near Rochester Cathedral in Kent. It was later made famous by Charles Dickens as Satis House in his novel *Great Expectations*. (The house is now restored and is owned by the entertainer Rod Hull.) The name Morgan was, and is, not especially common in England but is common in Wales. The population of England was much smaller in the sixteenth century, at about four million persons. Could this Morgan, the builder or commissioning first owner of 'Restoration House' (so called later as a result of associations with Charles II), be the same Morgan as the singer? It seems unlikely that a Gentleman of the Chapel Royal could have maintained his then daily duties in London while living in Rochester, though it is arguable that owning a house does not pre–suppose continuous occupation of it. In the seventeenth century, John Gostling managed to be both Gentleman of the Chapel Royal and a minor canon of Canterbury (appointed 1679 and from 1674–83 respectively), and Richard Elford (16?–1714) positively bathed in pluralities.

Could Morgan have been a lay–clerk at Rochester Cathedral? It is near both London and France, and though there is no mention of his name in the cathedral archives they are incomplete at this period. There is yet no evidence to connect Morgan the Chapel Royal or cathedral singer, or Mauregan of Sainte–Chapelle, or indeed the Welsh Catholic spy Thomas Morgan in Paris in the 1580s, with Morgan of Restoration House, Rochester, but the absence of records or evidence proves nothing, one way or the other.

The life of Nicholas Morgan, counter–tenor and haute–contre, seems likely to remain a mystery, but it has all the ingredients of which spy thrillers are made.

---

[18] At Loseley Park, Surrey

[19] Flood, op. cit., p. 60

[20] Dart, op. cit., p. 950

APPENDIX 2   Richard Elford and the Restoration counter-tenor

Elford or Elfford was a boy-chorister at Lincoln Cathedral. His first adult appointment was as a tenor at Durham (1695; full status 1698) followed by a quite remarkable collection of plurality appointments as counter-tenor at St George's Chapel, Windsor, (1701–1714), Eton College Chapel (1702–1710), the Chapel Royal, London (sworn as Gentleman, 10 November 1702, the place being made for him), St Paul's Cathedral and Westminster Abbey. In addition, he sang in and composed for the theatre. Other composers, like Weldon, wrote for what, in view of the demand for him across the London area, must have been Elford's truly outstanding voice.

Brian Crosby, formerly alto at Durham Cathedral, has researched Elford's career at Durham:[21]

> His name is the third in a list of four written inside the cover of a Durham Tenor Cantoris part-book. The first-named was indisputably a tenor. The second-named replaced the first one in the choir; and the fourth similiarly followed Elford – the doubt is whether Elford replaced anybody, for with him and another appointment made at the same time the number of lay-clerks increased.
>
> The details of his stay in Durham are as follows. He was appointed a probationer Singing Man on 20th July, 1695 (Acts 4, page 28), being raised to full status on 20th November 1698 (ibid., page 53). His tenure of the position, however, was brief, for a Chapter Minute dated 18th February 1689/9 [i.e., 1699] records: 'Mr Elford was admonished for neglecting ye Quire, & Singing in ye Playhouse and 7: Mar for his Manifest Contumacy was expell'd ye Choir, But Mar: 9 upon his Humble Submission was restored' (ibid., page 55). The original minute presumably went as far as 'Playhouse', the rest being added as the saga unfolded. It looks as if Elford left Durham shortly afterwards, for the Treasurer's Account Book for 1698–9 shows that on 11 February 1699 he drew in advance his salary due at the Feast of the Annunciation (25 March) and John the Baptist (24 June). That his salary, due at Michaelmas (29 September), was never claimed indicates he had vacated his position. As yet, I have not tried to discover whether any Durham theatre records for the period are extant.

---

[21] Brian Crosby, letter to the author, 28 November 1983

Roderick Williams, formerly baritone in the choirs of Eton College Chapel and Canterbury Cathedral, has researched him further:[22]

> Elford sang at Eton College, and St George's Chapel, Windsor. He was lured to St George's by promise of double salary, which presumably he received.
>
> The Chapter Acts of St George's, Windsor, record that, on 29th December 1701, Elford was chosen as clerk in place of Edward Morton deceased. (Morton was a counter–tenor.) He had been specially recommended by Princess (Anne?) and other influential people, and was to be given extra pay of £18 per annum (on top of his standard salary of £22 per annum. His 'subscription' is duly recorded in the Register Book on the same day. He subsequently appears in the Treasurer and Stewards' Book, receiving £40 per annum, only slightly less than the organist, Goldwyn (£44).
>
> At Eton, the College Audit Book records that Mr Elford was being paid £10 per quarter 'for his services in the choir' from the first quarter of 1702 onwards, despite his being sworn as Gentleman of the Chapel Royal in London, on 10th November 1702.
>
> All the clerks' places at Eton were filled, so he was a [paid] supernumerary [or deputy]. He continued to sing on this basis till the end of 1710. Clerks at Eton received a salary of either £17.6s.2d, or more usually (five out of eight places) £15.9s.6d. Most of the places were shared, so each got half pay; most of them were also clerks or petticanons at St George's.
>
> By 1709, the Chapter of St George's may have been regretting their extravagance, for the Chapter Acts record on November 3rd that, in view of the heavy expenses being incurred, a clerk's place is to be left vacant while Mr Elford is receiving £40 per annum. The Treasurer's Book continues to record his payment at this rate till the year 1714–1715, when we find 'Mr Elford deceased £11'.

Simon R. Hill kindly contributed the following:

> Over the past few years, a new 'orthodoxy' seems to have arisen which assumes, unquestioningly, that the Purcellian counter–tenor was (with the exception of a few voices such as Howell) simply a tenor. No evidence is ever adduced to support this assumption, nor, as far as I know, has any paper or article been presented on the subject.
>
> One piece of 'evidence' which must underlie this thinking is the often–repeated assertion that the singer Richard Elford (d. 1714) had a range of A–b' (A2–B4). This would derive from the apparent overall range of the solos in John Weldon's *Divine Harmony* (1712) which, as the title page tells us, were performed in the Chapel Royal 'by the late Famous Mr Richard Elford'. However, it must be remembered that (a) this set appeared some two years after Elford's death, (b) it is not a single work, but a collection of six individual works and (c) it was *published* – i.e., not put into circulation for

---

[22] Roderick Williams, letter to the author, 13 January 1991

performance by other counter–tenors, but for sale to the general public. As such, the publisher would seek to maximise his market by presenting them in keys and clefs which would make them accessible to as many voices as possible. (Though not strictly 'evidence', there is a manuscript source from 50 or so years later of four of these anthems, three in the alto clef, transposed up by a third or fourth.)

The piece with the widest range in the set is 'O praise the Lord', which has a <u>printed</u> range of a–a" (A2–A4) in treble clef. However, inspection of the music shows that the low a (A2) occurs only twice, in the final 'Allelujah', where it is the cadence note, approached by a fall of a fifth, easily accomplished by a 'gear change'. Otherwise, the lowest note in the piece is c' sharp (C♯3). The next widest range is represented by 'Have mercy on me', with a notated range of b flat to a' flat (B♭2–A♭4), but again, there is only one instance of the low b flat, where it is the cadence note, approached by a fall of a third. Otherwise, the lowest note is a c' (C3), and generally the lowest note in the piece is e' flat (E♭3).

Thus, the total range required to perform any one of these anthems is only two octaves, with falsetto needed for probably only an octave and a sixth. As to precisely what that range was, we must look at other works known to have been sung by Elford which are still extant in manuscript or in a form which leaves no doubt as to the original pitch.

Handel wrote several works with parts for Elford, including anthems for the Chapel Royal and the birthday ode for Queen Anne – these give him an overall range of f to c" (F3–C5). The solos allocated to him in Croft's D major *Te Deum* have a range of a to b' (A3–B4), while the quartet 'The Father of an Infinite Majesty', in which he sang the lowest part, has a range of f to g' (F3–G4) with two instances of bottom d (D3), both cadence notes approached by a fall of a fifth. Other works by Blow and Jeremiah Clarke give a range of d to b flat (D3–B♭4).

Burney states that most of the solo anthems in Croft's *Musica Sacra* were 'expressly composed' for Elford. Neither he nor Croft tells us which, but most of the alto solos in that publication lie within the range e to b' (E3–B4). 'Rejoice in the Lord' has a range of f to c" (F3–C5), while 'O Lord God of my Salvation' has a range of c to a' flat (C3–A♭4). However, in the latter work, the only two instances of the bottom c (C3) are both as a cadence note, approached by a fall of a minor third, and again could have been taken with a 'gear change'.

On the basis of this evidence, it would seem likely that Elford used a range of two octaves, c to c" (C3–C5), but with the bottom one or two notes probably negotiated by a 'gear change' – a <u>low</u> counter–tenor, certainly, but by no means unusual for a falsettist.

While on the subject of the 'tenor heresy', it might be worth mentioning two other instances, which have occasionally been cited in the past, of countertenors supposedly also singing as a tenor – those of Thomas Heywood and Thomas Richardson.

Heywood appears to have been a counter–tenor in the Chapel Royal from 1678/9 to 1688. (His voice is not stated in the Cheque Book, but he took the place of a counter–tenor, and is listed among the counter–tenors in Sandford's account of the 1685 coronation – though neither of these should be considered as incontrovertible 'evidence'). However, in a list of August 1685 confirming the personnel of the new king's Private Music, he is mentioned as a <u>tenor</u> (this is the famous list which seems to name twenty–three counter–tenors!). The answer is given by a later certificate (October), listing seven members of the violin band, of whom Heywood is one – obviously a player of the <u>tenor violin</u>! (He had already been a musician in ordinary for the lute since 1674). (It might be noted that twenty–one of the twenty–three counter–tenors were also violinists – players of the <u>haute–contre de violon</u>, no doubt.)

In the case of Thomas Richardson, we have the unequivocal declaration in the Cheque Book (1664) that he was 'to be sworne into the next place of a lay tenor or counter tenor that shall be voyd'. Five months later, he took the place of Henry Purcell (father of the composer, who was a counter–tenor), and on his death in 1712 was replaced by another counter–tenor. He was also listed with the counter–tenors in the 1685 coronation. There is no evidence that he actually *sang* as a tenor. It has been suggested in the past that the document of March 1663/4 might indicate a purely administrative ploy – it is certain that vacancies were not always filled by the same voice type (John Abell succeeded a bass!). Ideas of internal vocal balance were not necessarily the same as they are today, and in any case, of the thirty–two salaried Gentlemen of the Chapel, there would always be a number who, being in the job for life, were no longer actually singing. I would guess that, in 1664, there were not many basses in the choir but plenty of tenors, so that a good counter–tenor could be given a tenor place if it came vacant first.

Finally, it should be remembered that, even if incontrovertible evidence were to come to light of a singer who sang as both a tenor and a counter–tenor, this does not necessarily imply that he was a tenor rather than a falsettist. I know of three instances (one of them being myself) of falsettists who sang for some time as tenors, and who were accepted as such, before discovering their true identity!

356

APPENDIX 3 John Saville of Lichfield

John Saville (c1735–1803), a counter–tenor lay vicar–choral of Lichfield Cathedral and a solo singer of oratorio and secular works, lived in Vicars' Close, Lichfield. He was well known in his lifetime as a singer, but he is still vaguely known in Lichfield for his so–called 'platonic' thirty–year 'affair' with Anna Seward (c1742–1809), daughter of a residentary canon. It is an intriguing story which it is almost obligatory to tell in a book on counter–tenors.

An inherited legend in the Saville family tells of his great–grand–daughter's destroying family records which proved that the Savilles had connections with Oliver Cromwell.[23] He came to Lichfield from Ely in 1755, at about the age of nineteen, and served as a vicar–choral there until his death forty–eight years later. At Ely, Saville (or Savill) had been admitted as a chorister 24 June 1744, and was replaced by Robert Rayner on the same day in 1751. A John Savell was admitted a King's Scholar at the King's School, Ely, aged ten and a quarter, 4 April 1746, on the nomination of the Dean.[24]

John Saville the ex–chorister was admitted as lay–clerk 14 June 1754.[25] He left one year later. John Short was appointed in his place (14 June 1755) 'who was going to Litchfield'. If Saville the chorister was born in 1736, and he and John Savell, King's Scholar, were one, then Saville's chronology would then become:

Ely chorister, 1744, aged eight.
King's Scholar, 1746, aged ten and a quarter.
Replaced in choir, 1751, aged fifteen.
Ely lay–clerk, 1754, aged eighteen.
Lichfield lay–vicar, 1755, aged nineteen.

The Chapter Acts of Lichfield[26], which are housed in the cathedral library, tell us:

2 May 1755 before Rev. Thomas Smallbrooke, Canon Residentiary – Mr. John Saville the Younger was installed as Vicar Choral.

---

[23] Information via Hopkins, *Dr Johnson's Lichfield* (Peter Owen Ltd., 1956) from James R. Beard, esq., great–great–great–grandson of John Saville

[24] *The King's School, Ely* (ed. D. M. Owen and D. Thurley, Cambridge Antiquarian Records Society), vol. 5, 1982

[25] Dorothy Owen, in a private letter to the author, 16 May 1991, using as her source the contemporaneous list of the Ely foundation (EDC 2/23) now in the Cambridge University Library

[26] From Laithwaite, *via* Hopkins, op. cit., p. 236 fn.

We should note Saville's age upon his appointment. He must have been even then outstanding vocally. The designation 'the Younger' is interesting. Was Saville's father known in Lichfield?

The contrast between Ely and Lichfield must have been enormous for the young and ambitious Saville, who had trailed across the fen causeway from his damp, grey 'city'. Bleak Ely, with its magnificent, empty cathedral, vast and clammy, was a townlet bestrode by haunted giant: a place where by the eighteenth century little of significance went on. Saville's voice and musicianship had brought him to red–sandstoned, Georgian–brick, Lichfield. It was small but fashionable: associated with Dr Johnson, David Garrick and Erasmus Darwin; a city topped so beautifully by the modest–sized, elegant three–spired cathedral. Lichfield was a centre to which all important Mercian ways led and signposts pointed.

Lethargic Ely with its folk memories of pre–Reformation monks, superseded by then no doubt distant canons, but with its ever–present tradesmen and fen–folk, must have seemed worlds away from smart, cultured Lichfield, its genteel canons and puffed–up prebendaries, fashionable cognoscenti and refined, *à la mode* intellectuals and 'Blue–Stockings'. The new scene must have dazzled the youthful Saville. It seems likely that the effect of his voice and looks on Lichfield society was gradual, but their impact was to prove powerful on one Anna Seward, aged about thirteen when he arrived.[27]

It is from the letters of 'the Swan of Lichfield',[28] as she has has been called, as well as from the cathedral archives (and Saville's descendants) and the various mentions of him in other musical contexts that we know about this important eighteenth–century lay–vicar–choral and solo singer.

In view of his 'other' reputation, it should be stressed that, contrary to his official title, a cathedral vicar–choral is not necessarily in Holy Orders. In fact, Saville's position would be describable today as a professional singer in the cathedral choir, yet behind the term itself lie centuries of tradition. There are two varieties of vicar–choral: priest–vicars who are in Holy Orders, and lay–vicars who are not. Both deputise vicariously for canons and absent prebend-aries. (Priest–vicars are now few, and becoming fewer, in cathedrals generally. In some cathedrals, that is those which employ lay–clerks, these priests are termed minor canons.) It is not yet established which was Saville's prebendal stall at Lichfield. The Chapter Acts at the time of his appointment are now held at the Public Record Office, London.

An exclusive, collegiate atmosphere is still strong in the cathedral close at Lichfield. Harwood[29] wrote:

> The Vicars Choral was a specifically chartered corporation with a common hall, a mace, and a seal, from at least as early as 1240. These gentlemen were a lively bunch with ideas as to their rights and privileges. The Vicars Choral had a dust–up with the Dean and Chapter after the Restoration, when they called attention to the fact that they (who had numbered sixteen for over four hundred years) were now only six, and that three of their sixteen dwellings had been demolished beside their common hall. They pointed out that they

[27] For a vividly–written portrait of Lichfield at this time, see Hopkins, op. cit., passim
[28] *Works of Anna Seward*, ed. Walter Scott (Edinburgh, 1810) in three vols.; also unpublished materials, see Hopkins, op. cit., notes
[29] Revd Thomas Harwood, *History and Antiquities of the Church and of Lichfield* (London, 1806), pp. 271 ff.

kept Vicars' Close clean while the Great Close was filthy from swine being kept by the inhabitants.

By the 1960s, the ancient power of the Corporation had been long broken (chiefly by the Cathedrals Act of 1930), and the nine lay–vicars were, as they still are, stipendiary singers of the cathedral. Together with the sixteen boy–choristers, they form the cathedral choir. In such a tradition, continuity is important. Saville's house in Vicars' Close is at present occupied by Raymond Leang, alto, senior lay–vicar for many years and recently retired.

The author, lay–clerk at Ely Cathedral (1960–1964), was a lay–vicar–choral at Lichfield for three years (1964–1967) and lived in Vicars' Close, a few doors from Saville's house.

During the eighteenth century, a professional singer or instrumentalist did not enjoy high social standing, though the position of cathedral lay–vicar or lay–clerk possessed some prestige. As today, they undertook singing and other musical engagements outside.

Saville taught music privately and gave private and public concerts. He conducted oratorios (in which, often, he also sang the principal alto solos) in Shrewsbury, Birmingham, Manchester and various other towns and cities. He was under contract at Covent Garden, London. Nearer home, and less importantly, he was towards the end of his life in charge of the music for Lichfield Race Week.[30]

It has not yet been established exactly whom, when and where he married; though, in view of his age on leaving Ely, it seems likely that Saville met his wife, Mary, in Lichfield.

From 1765 to 1772, Saville, and his wife and children, lived in a corner house in the idyllic setting of Vicars' Close. Because of later demands of the choir school for yard–space, Saville's is now one of the very few houses there with private ground attached.

The atmosphere in this walled place above a corner of the dry moat still evokes something of the much–loved and carefully nurtured botanical garden which once it was. (In fact, Lichfield itself, despite the impact of the twentieth century, and 'subtopian' spread on its outskirts, retains much of its enclosed eighteenth–century atmosphere in its city centre.) Saville loved to study plants and flowers; his garden increasingly reflected this interest. A friend, Honora Sneyd, named it 'Damon's Bower', from a poem by Shenstone:[31]

> How blithely pass'd the summer's day!
> How bright was every flow'r!
> While friends arriv'd, in circles gay,
> To visit Damon's bow'r ...

Was there any subtle implication in the use of the words 'toward', as almost rhyming with 'Seward', and 'Close'? Perhaps not.

Though strictly speaking it comprises merely half the original, the single quadrangle now known as Vicars' Close is a half–timbered huddle of medieval houses, the earliest of which dates from the fourteenth century. The whole Vicars' Close is a substantial biddern, built in two modest–sized quadrangles, sub–divided by the reconstructed Vicars' Hall, itself long since divided into living accommodation. The second medieval quadrangle, greatly restored and refaced after damage sustained during the Civil War, appears to be Georgian. This impression

---

[30] *Aris's Birmingham Gazette*, 5 September 1796
[31] William Shenstone, *Verses Written toward the Close of the Year 1748*. Hopkins points out that Sneyd (deliberately?) mis–quoted the verse.

is superficial. Nevertheless, both quadrangles, especially that which includes Saville's house, remain much as he would have known them.

After the Reformation, the biddern had been divided internally into separate houses for married vicars-choral; the semi-communal life-style had come to an end. All vicars-choral had a right to live in these lodgings, which form the main part of the Cathedral Close.

Saville's House, seen from the back,
showing part of 'Damon's Bower', much altered

As we noted before, reminiscences of John Saville's name are still to be found in Lichfield; not so much from his prowess as a fine singer, but as the lay-vicar who had a scandalous affair, or intense platonic relationship (opinion is divided over which) for over thirty years with a canon's daughter. Saville was an attractive man. Hopkins tells us that, apparently, he had a fear of unpopularity though, in fact, he had no such problems in that direction – at least not with Anna Seward![32]

She was a few years younger than him. It is possible that he taught her the harpsichord. She first mentions him in a letter written in February 1764.[33] A group of musicians, amateur and professional, had assembled in the large drawing room of the Bishop's Palace: a fine room in which the youthful Samuel Johnson and young David Garrick had learned etiquette and social skills. Her letter tells how a particular gentleman had reported a connoisseur's claim that Handel's music lacked delicacy and tenderness. Anna Seward disagreed, mentioning a few of

---

[32] Hopkins, op. cit., p. 107
[33] Ibid., p. 108

her favourite arias: Return, O God of Hosts (from *Samson*), O Sleep, Why Dost Thou Leave Me? (*Semele*); and Father of Heaven (*Judas Maccabeus*). Saville, who was becoming known for his singing of Handel, supported her viewpoint. If Saville himself sang these arias, it should be noted that the first and third are for alto, and the second is for tenor.

An association between Saville and Seward blossomed. With other friends they began to visit beauty spots within reach of Lichfield. This small group, or clique, spent more and more time together. It does not seem to have included Saville's wife. Hopkins relates that they enjoyed impromptu concerts, in which, as would be expected, Saville took a leading part. They had poetry and other readings. Anna Seward reported that he possessed a vibrant and musical speaking-voice.[34]

'The Lichfield Circle', an exclusive cultural group connected with the Cathedral close comprised people of varying accomplishments. It included Dr Erasmus Darwin, the scientist and Anna Seward, the poetess, as representatives of their disciplines, and various other local luminaries.

> A frequent visitor was Richard Edgeworth, the 'gay philosopher' [*sic*], who took two of his wives from the circle.... As Mrs Sherwood (1775–1851) [née Mary Butt, who seems to have attended the circle and was to achieve some importance as the author of *The Fairchild Family*] remembered the Seward Circle, it was altogether what she would call 'correct'. Anna Seward's relation-ship with a Mr Saville, who was at odds with his wife, was regarded locally as equivocal. And yet – perhaps, she admits, it may have been only the glamour of youthful impressions – was there not a certain grace and charm about cultured society in those days which modern education [i.e., of the middle of the nineteenth century] did not foster? She cannot say whether the art of pleasing, so successfully cultivated by some of the women she remembers, had any solid value. As Miss Seward used it, it was of course to be condemned, and many of the Circle were no better than infidels. But even this infidelity lacked the plebian vulgarity of modern demonstrations .... In fact, such was the fascination of the Lichfield Circle that she could not wonder that her parents were 'unaware of the serpents that lurked under the flowers of that garden of intellectual delight'.[35]

We may note the possibly unintentionally apposite botanical imagery of the Mrs Sherwood's last sentence. Within the coterie there was a small clique comprising John Saville, Anna Seward, Honora Sneyd and John Andre. On 13 July 1771, Seward wrote to a friend: 'Il Penseroso Saville sighing and singing to us, sharing or imparting our enthusiasms ....'[36] John Milton's poetry, especially for obvious reasons *Il Penseroso*, provides clues not only to the sort of poetry likely to have been included in the group readings but also to the conceivable direction of Anna Seward's romantic imagination. A few lines seem particularly apposite on two counts: the first concerning the location of lovers' meeting and the second to provide an arguable basis for the view that the affair was platonic and spiritual:[37]

[34] ibid., pp. 109–110
[35] Muriel Jaeger, *Before Victoria* (Penguin Books, 1967), pp. 157–8
[36] Hopkins, op. cit., from an unpublished Seward letter, p. 112
[37] lines 27–42

Oft in glimmering Bowres, and glades
He met her, and in secret shades
Of woody Ida's inmost grove,
Whilst yet there was no fear of Jove.
Com pensive Nun, devout and pure,
Sober, stedfast, and demure,
All in a robe of darkest grain,
Flowing with majestick train,
And sable stole of Cipres Lawn,
Over thy decent shoulders drawn.
Com, but keep thy wonted state,
With eev'n step, and musing gate,
And looks commercing with the skies,
Thy rapt soul sitting in thine eyes:
There held in holy passion still,
Forget thy self to Marble ...

Of course, if Seward's use of the title *Il Penseroso* to describe Saville had been employed in conjunction with a reading or musical performance of the work, it could have been meant as a deliberate device to mislead her friend; what is called today a 'cover-up'. Whatever the case, a month after the letter of the 13th of July, Mrs Saville refused to allow Miss Seward into the house, and 'Damon's Bower' was visited by Anna for the last time on the 2nd of August, 1771.

There is no room here to describe fully the ensuing crisis within the small, claustrophobic cathedral community composed of cultured ecclesiastical and professional people, except to suggest that in many ways eighteenth-century society resembled our own, in that liberality and even licence appear to have been commonly accepted – except by Mary Saville. 'Live and let live' seems to have been surprisingly usual even though in this case reluctantly adhered to within an outwardly very conventional cathedral close. The Saville/Seward connection would certainly not have been tolerated by the church a few decades later. Hopkins writes:[38]

> The scandal in the Close reached a climax when Mr Saville, in 1773, left his wife, and moved to an adjoining house, a very small house with only one bedroom and a place for a servant to sleep. His wife seems to have remained in the Saville home next door with the two little girls, and Mr Saville appears to have financed both establishments. The husband and wife are said not to have been on speaking terms, though he shopped for her, and she saw to his laundry. In later years, there was a close bond between Saville and his daughter Elizabeth.

Despite the commonly accepted version of the story, that Anna Seward joined Saville in his new home, the truth is probably that she often visited him there. (Whether his pets: two dogs, two birds and one green frog, ever did so is not recorded.)

The Saville/Seward affair lasted more than thirty years, until Saville's death. The Close became used to it but approval, official or unofficial, was never and could never be bestowed.

---

[38] Hopkins, op. cit., pp. 114–115

To a large extent, Miss Seward seems to have been avoided socially, but she continued to write. Meanwhile, whatever attitude was displayed towards him – and that was likely to have ranged from semi–ostracism to grudging admiration – Saville maintained his cathedral singing duties, and his successful concert career. One imagines that the cathedral community and the ecclesiastical hierarchy and the church–based society surrounding it awaited the ending of this embarrassment, in their midst and of their own, with characteristic patience. No doubt the Dean and Chapter managed a wry, Anglican half–smile.

In addition to its literary, ecclesiastical and musical preoccupations, eighteenth–century Lichfield was a centre of botanical interest, whose central luminary was the eminent Dr Erasmus Darwin (1731–1802), grandfather of the even more famous Charles Darwin. Saville was influenced deeply by them.

Some time after separating from his wife and presumably his original garden, he leased a tract of land in Stowe parish, beside Stowe Pool, about half a mile from the cathedral close. One would imagine that, his two dogs had to be on their best behaviour if allowed there; indeed we might wonder about their effect on 'Damon's Bower'. Here he spent much of his free time, creating a second but larger and more comprehensive botanical garden where he was visited by other enthusiasts, including Darwin. The latter formed Lichfield Botanical Club. It consisted of but three members. Saville was invited to join them, but declined, apparently wishing to avoid the paperwork which he knew would be given him.[39]

John Saville, after a miniature by John Smart, 1770

It is comparatively rarely that we possess accurate portraits of counter-tenors of the distant past, but John Saville's case is different. A miniature of him, painted in 1770, depicts a handsome man in his early thirties, wearing a bright blue coat. He has a tidy, white–powdered wig with a long curl over each ear. His face is attractively–boned. The mouth is full, sensitive and well–formed as is the classical–looking nose. His eyebrows are rather heavy, and seem to grow slightly at odds with the line of the eyebrow or superciliary ridge. Saville's forehead is high and rather sloping. His almost sultry expression caused by the strong eyelids does not look arrogant, as Hopkins suggests.[40] The fine eyes are soft and deep, with a clear suggestion of potential passion. It is easy to envisage the effect he had on Anna Seward ...

---

[39] Ibid., p. 194
[40] Ibid., p. 107

... just as it is easy to imagine the effect his singing of Handel's O Death Where is Thy Sting? and Thou Shalt Break Them would have on an audience. Judging from his appearance and his reputation he must have had a powerful platform presence.

As can be imagined, after they had shared an illicit but public liaison for more than thirty years, with its attendant social problems, Saville's death at the age of sixty–seven or sixty–eight (there is some confusion) must have been a terrible blow to Anna Seward. Clearly to his memory, and certainly to her credit, she assumed responsibility for the financial support of his family. One wonders about the feelings of Mary, Saville's widow.

John Saville died 2 August 1803, apparently after a long illness. He never resigned his post, and continued to sing to the end. He had served as a lay–vicar–choral at Lichfield for forty–eight years, but the exact location of his grave is not clear. Anna Seward caused a monument to his memory to be erected in Lichfield Cathedral. It is a tablet on the west wall of the south transept, whose inscription is as follows:

Sacred to the Memory
of

JOHN SAVILLE

48 Years Vicar–Choral of this Cathedral.
Ob: Aug'sta. 2ndo 1803 AEta '67

Once in the Heart cold in yon narrow cell,
Did each mild grace, each ardent virtue dwell;
Kind and kind tears for other's want and woe.
For other's joy, the gratulating glow:
And skill to mark and eloquence to claim
For genius in each art, the palm of fame,
Ye choral Walls, ye lost the matchless song
When the last silence stiffen'd on that tongue
Ah! who may now your pealing anthems raise
In soul–pour'd tones of fervent prayer and praise?
Saville, thy lips, twice on thy final day,
Here breath'd, in health and hope, the sacred lay;
Short pangs, ere night, their fatal signal gave,
Quench'd the bright Sun for thee – and op'd the Grave!
Now from that graceful form and beaming face
Insatiate worms the lingering likeness chase,
But thy pure Spirit fled from pains and fears
To sinless–changeless–everlasting Spheres.
Sleep then, pale mortal Frame, in yon low shrine
"Till Angels wake thee with a note like thine".

'Yon narrow cell' and 'yon low shrine' might indicate that Saville lies beneath the paving of the transept. The verses to Saville have an unmistakable quality of personal loss and grief and, according to the Victoria County History, were written 'by his friend Anna Seward'.[41] Seward had also had a memorial erected to her family, notably her father, inside the North West Entry Door of the Nave. The arrangement of the inscription seems to suggest that the memorial was paid for and placed there by direction of Anna Seward's will, following her own death on the 25th of March, 1809. Nonetheless, the wry Anglican half–smile appears to have triumphed, for while she is commemorated at the head of the memorial, her name, Anna, is spelled 'Ann' as if purposely to confuse the reader, or to suggest ambiguity. If she were born 'Ann' but was known as 'Anna' throughout her family and among her social and literary circles, then an adjustment of her epitaph and last work (for it is likely that she wrote the Miltonesque verses which resemble those on Saville's memorial) could be seen as a subtle insult. If the missing 'a' was unintentional, it is strange that an elementary mistake by the sculptor in his first incised word was not corrected, or a new piece of marble taken.

Ann Seward died March 25th 1809 aged 63
by her order this tablet is erected
to the memory of her father
the Revd. Thomas Seward, M.A. Canon Residentiary of this Cathedral,
who died March 4th 1790, aged 81,
of her mother Elizabeth his wife, daughter of the Revd. John Hunter,
who died July 31st 1780, aged 68:
and of her sister Sarah their younger daughter,
who died June 13th 1784, aged 20.

AMID THESE AISLES, WHERE ONCE HIS PRECEPTS SHEW'D
THE HEAVENWARD PATH-WAY WHICH IN LIFE HE TROD,
THIS SIMPLE TABLET MARKS A FATHER'S BIER,
AND THOSE HE LOV'D IN LIFE, IN DEATH ARE NEAR;
FOR HIM, FOR THEM, A DAUGHTER BADE IT RISE,
MEMORIAL OF DOMESTIC CHARITIES.
STILL WOULD YOU KNOW WHY O'ER THE MARBLE SPREAD
IN FEMALE GRACE THE WILLOW DROOPS HER HEAD?
WHY ON HER BRANCHES SILENT AND UNSTRUNG,
THE MINSTREL HARP IS EMBLEMATIC HUNG?
WHAT POET'S VOICE LIES SMOTHER'D HERE IN DUST,
TILL WAK'D TO JOIN THE CHORUS OF THE JUST?
LO, ONE BRIEF LINE AND ANSWER SAD SUPPLIES,
HONOUR'D, BELOV'D, AND MOURN'D HERE SEWARD LIES.
HER WORTH, HER WARMTH OF HEART OUR SORROWS SAY
GO SEEK HER GENIUS IN HER LIVING LAY.

We may note the flattering nature of the final lines, and the employment of the word 'lay'. She used it in her verses for Saville to suggest that his lay, or song, was now stilled until angels woke him with 'note like thine', but in her own epitaph she preceeds 'lay' with 'living', in order to emphasize that the poetry she has left should be sought after by the reader.

---

[41] *Victoria History of the County of Stafford* (Constable, 1908), vol. XIV, p. 55

Saville's Will is lodged at the Probate Court, Birmingham. It was drawn up 9 February 1792, eleven years before his death, and proved 1 February 1804. He bequeathed:[42] 'To my wife Mary Saville all my property whatsoever and wheresoever, after lawful debts are paid, and after such of my papers and books as Anna Seward of the Close of the said Cathedral Church, spinster, shall choose to take for her own use.' Saville's proved estate was nearly six hundred pounds – a respectably large sum for the time.

In Seward's generous will, she left to Mrs Saville, with reversion to Mrs Saville's daughter Elizabeth Saville Smith, the house which she had bought for John Saville when, because of his failing health, he needed accomodation large enough for his daughter also. Anna Seward had managed to acquire this house because, though most Close property belonged to the Dean and Chapter, some was in private hands at this date. The building in question is now number 8 The Close.

She settled an annuity of one hundred pounds on Elizabeth Saville Smith, which, with a fifty–pound annuity she already received, supported her for life. Anna Seward left a trust fund for Saville's grand–daughter.

The story of Saville and Seward would make a fine novel or film. It is possible that Anna Seward, so immersed in literature, saw in their liason a romance and tragedy of the order of Dido and Aeneas, or Abelard and Héloise. Perhaps Milton's *Il Penseroso* in its entirety suggests Seward's rapt world most expressively – for one suspects that she drew Saville into, and made him an integral part of, her poetic vision, while she in turn was drawn into his distinguished musical milieu.

According to his epitaph, Saville sang at Matins and Evensong in the cathedral on his last day on this earth – indeed, it is said that he died soon after singing Evensong. The psalms allocated by the Book of Common Prayer to the second day's morning and evening services are full of appropriate imagery. Amongst the most apposite verses are from Psalm 13, verses 3 and 4:

> Consider and hear me O Lord my God:
>   Lighten mine eyes that I sleep not in death.
> Lest mine enemy say I have prevailed against him:
>   For if I be cast down they that trouble me will rejoice at it.

John Saville's life has come down to us in two ways: eminent counter–tenor and busy musician, and single–minded lover – a man apparently worn out by his various and wide–ranging labours, but, it would seem, with the glory of his superb organ intact.

---

[42] Ibid., p. 246

APPENDIX 4 Short biographies

These solo counter–tenors are representative of voices of outstanding quality and/or importance, all selected for particular aspects of vocal style. The following list is subjective and the
length and detail of each entry does not denote a scale or ratio of importance.

(Jack) Hatherley Clarke (1885–1975) was a Gentleman of the Chapel Royal, St James's
Palace, from 1934 until 1957, when he was succeeded by Colin Scull. Clarke toured widely
with his Gresham Singers. Probably the most celebrated male quartette between the wars (the
Comedian Harmonists were a sextet), they appeared at six Royal Command Performances, and
at a gala performance at the Paris Opéra. They made many records for the 'His Master's Voice'
label. The Gresham Singers were favourites of Lord Lonsdale (well known for his interest in
boxing, as well as his patronage of music, through his presentation of the Lonsdale Belt), who
used to entertain them nobly at Lowther Castle, and in his London house.

It is not known if Clarke sang as a boy, except that he appears to have sung in a parish
church choir. He studied singing for five years with Dr Churchill Sibley, a well–known
festival and concert organist in London. Clarke began his adult choir career at St Anne's,
Soho, London, and went on to St Margaret's, Westminster. He then became a lay–vicar at
Westminster Abbey. According to an article in *Church Times* in 1957, he sang the alto solos
in Bach's *St John Passion* more than a hundred times between 1910 and 1930, some of them
in the presence of Queen Alexandra. His solo records date from 1915 to 1925. Such was his
popularity that, in the late 1920s, his solo records for Zonophone were re–released on the
cheaper label 'Ariel' under the name of Herbert Ainsworth. All these records were acoustically
recorded. He was billed as a 'counter–tenor' on both labels. His records suggest that he
possessed an extensive high range with excellent upper falsetto easily to F4,[43] good
pharyngeal area and occasional use of upper chest–voice – all beautifully integrated. His style,
inevitably, sounds 'dated' to modern ears but the discerning can ignore this. Clarke is included
in the discussion in Chapter 8.

Alfred Deller (1912–1979). He was a parish church boy chorister and then an alto lay–clerk
at Canterbury Cathedral from 1939 and vicar-choral at St Paul's Cathedral, London, from
1947 until 1962. Largely self-taught, he used only head–voice in his prime. His earliest
records, made when he was thirty–seven, are remarkable. The music chosen features his
incredible upper sinus-tone: a dreamy, delicious sound with no vibrato, but with a piercing

---

[43] A. C. Payne, 'Hatherley Clarke', *Talking Machine News*, August 1916

edge, with the thinnest of rounding. As he grew older, this upper range gradually came down, but never left him. The lower, pharyngeal section of his head–voice was richly edgy and penetrating; he often used it with vibrato, and it was able to hold its own against a lyric tenor. It did not deteriorate with age. Benjamin Britten wrote the part of Oberon in his opera *A Midsummer Night's Dream* (1960) especially for him. He was the first counter–tenor of the revival to break new ground on the operatic stage, though his tenure of it was brief because of his weak acting. Several other composers wrote new works with his voice in mind.

Deller's voice was unique, but his style – copied but never surpassed – became for many an archetypal modern alto sound for two decades. He influenced a significant proportion of younger counter–tenors, and other voice types – indeed the early music movement to come. As a vocal type, he was originally a high counter–tenor but, later in his career, he used upper chest and middle registers increasingly. Though Deller seems to have possessed a large voice, he seldom used it loudly. As James Bowman has remarked, he was first and foremost a miniaturist, loving most of all the delicate lute–songs of the Elizabethans.

Perceval Bridger (1919–1970), was a parish church boy chorister and then an alto lay–clerk at Exeter Cathedral; later, at St George's Chapel, Windsor Castle. For a short time, he studied privately with E. Herbert–Caesari. Because of his early death, and the fact he made no solo recordings, he was never well known. He recorded a number of amateur tapes, of mediocre technical standard, and not always of characteristic music. They are unavailable to the general public. He may be heard in recordings of The Renaissance Singers after 1959, during the time that they included 'male sopranos'. Bridger is included here as a rare type of high counter–tenor – a sopranist in all but name. His voice represents a transitional stage between Romantic and Classical styles.

Of all the names here, his career was perhaps most affected by the early reluctance of opera management to use the high male voice for castrato parts, though he did appear in a few provincial productions. He had an amazing upward range which reached a comfortable C6, and he could sustain a far higher tessitura than most comparable singers. His tone was roundish, except for the highest notes, and very strong except for the lower head range. He used vibrato consistently, and sang mainly in upper falsetto. He appeared to have little pharyngeal capability despite his lessons with Herbert–Caesari. The implication of these facts is that his lower head–register was incapable of much pharyngeal development because of his extensive upward range. His fundamental voice was a light baritone or tenor, which he used occasionally for low notes. It is interesting to note that Caesari, ever Italian in outlook, advised him to train as a tenor. (We can never know whether Caesari meant he should train as a contralto–tenor.) Bridger would not hear of this. The result was his almost eunuchoid-sounding voice, with its great potential, which was sadly under–exploited.

John Whitworth (1921–), was an organ pupil at Ely Cathedral and choral scholar at King's College, Cambridge; then a lay–vicar at Westminster Abbey until 1971. He studied vocal production privately with the tenor Frank Titterton, then with Robert Poole. Whitworth uses both pharyngeal head–voice and upper chest–register, but apparently has little if any upper falsetto for use in an unmixed form. The resulting tone is fuller than Deller's and much more trumpet–like; one that rings like an extremely high lyric tenor on occasion. His superb blend of head to fundamental voice makes him a low counter–tenor of tremendous versatility. In early days, he sang second counter–tenor to Alfred Deller's first with artistically satisfying results; they also thus demonstrated the two main English vocal types. Whitworth uses vibrato very sparingly and judiciously. In tonal type and vocal production, he influenced many; he foreshadowed James Bowman's style to some extent, though Bowman uses more upper falsetto and so has a more extensive high range and can sustain a higher tessitura. Whitworth has been much involved in Medieval, Renaissance, sixteenth– and seventeenth–century music. His range and versatility are especially suited to the various types of contra–tenor parts.

In recent years he has become more of a tenor; he also sings baritone. Ringing alto head–notes, i.e., those with squillo, now start at about E4. Of distinguished modern counter–tenors, Whitworth perhaps best represents the composite male voice, probably like Damascene's in the seventeenth century, or Richard Elford's, who died in 1714.

Russell Oberlin (1928–), studied voice at the Juilliard School of Music, New York, 1951, and sang with New York Pro Musica for some years. He has a tenor–altino type of voice with an imperceptible blend of registers. His upper tone is extremely light, resembling a mezzo–soprano. His lower register is thinnish at the bottom but his voice is more substantial in its middle range. He is a versatile, technically excellent, singer, though his continuous use of vibrato often seems out of place in early works. An archetypal American counter–tenor, he has also sung as solo tenor, and is firm in his personal belief that his phenomenally rare voice type is the only true counter–tenor, all other kinds being 'male altos'. (He makes a clear distinction.) However, he is generous in his praise of Deller, Esswood and Bowman, for example; though (perhaps significantly) not of Whitworth. There is no hint of pure pharyngeal production in Oberlin's tone. Except for his decidedly modern technique, he, like Whitworth, fits well into the demands of medieval contra–tenor parts, but his lower 'tenor' finishes earlier and more thinly than Whitworth's 'baritone' and his upper head–voice has a higher range than that of Whitworth. He also sang on occasion as a lyric tenor.

He had a distinguished career singing the counter–tenor repertoire from Medieval to Modern. Several solo works (for instance, the counter–tenor part in Bernstein's *Chichester Psalms*) were written for him. Surprisingly, and regrettably, at the age of thirty–six he abandoned full–time singing for teaching.

James Bowman (1941–) was a boy chorister at Ely Cathedral, a choral scholar at New College, Oxford, and then an alto lay–vicar at Westminster Abbey for three years. To the knowledgeable listener, Bowman seems to be a 'Whitworth type' of counter–tenor (he indeed was influenced by Whitworth) with an excellent blend of head– and chest–registers, but with more developed pharyngeal capability upwards. His voice is basically a low counter–tenor with an extended higher range. His rich, sheer ringing power has ensured his frequent engagement for opera, and he was one of the first renascent counter–tenors to be regularly employed in the genre. One of his earliest first–rank engagements was as Oberon in Britten's *A Midsummer Night's Dream* in 1967. He was a founder member of David Munrow's Early Music Consort of London, in which his direct, trumpet–like tone matched the various early instruments superbly. He uses vibrato only where work and style demand it. He has been regarded as the leader of the second generation of modern solo counter–tenors, and his impact and influence have been great. A distinguished and exciting singer, he has performed every period of vocal music, except apparently to date, the Romantic.

Paul Esswood (1942–) studied voice with Gordon Clinton at The Royal College of Music, and was an alto lay–vicar at Westminster Abbey from 1964 to 1971. The first counter–tenor of distinction trained at a music college, Esswood's style and tone recall Oberlin's upper voice but without his 'chest–voice' extension downwards. Esswood is a high counter–tenor and seems to use only head–register. His technique suggests a gentle use of pharyngeal voice which blends perfectly with a highly–developed upper falsetto. He uses vibrato consistently. As with many subsequent college trained counter–tenors, it has been said by many who are accustomed to a more masculine timbre that there is an element of effeminacy in his overall vocal sound. This is not in any way to deprecate his virtuoso technique and musically sensitive performances. Like Bowman, Esswood has appeared with distinction in many operatic productions, for which his voice is highly suited. He was the first modern counter–tenor to sing at La Scala, Milan. His range has also stood him in good stead for the high Bach cantata alto parts, many of which he has recorded in Germany. In recent years, he has sung abroad more than in Britain.

René Jacobs (1946–) studied singing with Devos in Brussels and with Frateur in Antwerp. He was the first representative in Europe of the contemporary solo counter–tenor. Of important counter–tenors, Jacobs seems to have felt more than most the influence of, and affinity with, Alfred Deller's vocal style, except that Jacobs possesses a tenor fundamental voice.

Apparently, Deller persuaded this very fine Belgian singer to specialize in Renaissance and Baroque music. His Deller–like top register is well complemented by his tenor basic–voice. He takes both high and low counter–tenor parts. The pharyngeal area of his voice is strong and incisive, and he uses vibrato selectively. He has sung in all parts of the world. Besides taking part in early–music concerts, Jacobs has sung in and directed various excellent productions of early opera. In recent years, he has written on the subject of counter–tenor timbre (see the Bibliography). He has also increased his already considerable reputation as an excellent soloist in, for example, interpretations of haute–contre rôles.

Randall Wong (1955–) was born in Oaklands, California, USA and sang as a boy 'soprano'. He studied voice principally with Anna Carol Dudley. He had a long and thorough academic musical and early music education. He would appear to have started his solo singing career rather late, by present–day standards. He used to be billed 'sopranist', but at present prefers 'soprano', because the term 'sopranist' has not always received favour in the United States. He seldom undertakes parts with ordinary alto range. He has an incredible voice, of Bridger's range and upwards. Like Christofellis, his potential in operatic castrato and oratorio rôles is enormous. He has sung in many productions of Baroque opera. Recently, he has been featured in modern and 'alternative' opera. His voice is truly soprano–like and of great agility. He uses vibrato where appropriate musically and he employs a through–range technique involving upper chest– and head–registers, changing at about C3 or D3. His speaking voice, however, is unexpectedly deep. Wong has sung throughout the United States and in Europe. He is fourth–generation American Chinese; his grandfather sang high parts in Chinese opera.

Eight Male High Voices in early Recordings

These are featured, not as celebrated singers (though Jose might qualify as one), but as early–recorded examples of the counter–tenor family (with at least two possible exceptions) and are to be studied mainly in relation to the Interlude between Chapters Seven and Eight of this volume. The vocal terms used should be studied further in Part Two and the Glossary.

Richard Jose (1862–1941) was born in Cornwall and orphaned early in his life. He moved to the USA as a boy, where in due course he began his career. His voice has been described by one commentator as 'a tenor with a sort of over–drive'. Jose made about fifty early acoustic recordings. They suggest a fine but largely untrained tenor voice with powerful volume with extensive high range and without apparent use of pure head–register. He achieved popular acclaim in the USA. In 1906, his recording 'Silver Threads Among the Gold' was the biggest seller that the American recording industry had achieved before that date. He appeared at the gigantic Madison Square Garden Picture House and on Broadway. He toured the USA many times and was billed, variously, as 'tenor' or 'counter–tenor'. Caruso called him the world's greatest ballad singer.

Even taking into account the limitations of early recording, when compared with the other singers in this section, Jose sounds like a high modern operatic tenor of truly superb, natural vocal gifts, with a thrilling and unusually high range. His voice does not resemble a tenor–altino. His last recording was issued in 1909, but there was a re–issue of his recorded collection in 1927. Some Jose recordings are in the collection of the Royal Cornwall Museum, Truro. On the disc label of one, 'I Cannot Sing the Old Songs', is written 'To Lill. R J Jose. From Dick and Trace' (the last two letters are unclear). On the record sleeve is the label: 'PROPERTY OF – Therese S. Jose THE PONY EXPRESS 795 Sutter Street, San Francisco 9, Calif. Prospect 6–5346.'

Will Oakland (died 1954) was an American vaudeville, 'nigger–minstrel' (Dockstader's Minstrels) and radio singer with more than a touch of the 'Irish tenor' about his style. However, his real name was Herman(n) Heinrichs and he was a second–generation German–American. He was billed as a 'counter–tenor', and from the evidence of his recordings he was a fine tenor–altino. He sang mainly ballads and made his first cylinder of 'Silver Threads' in 1904. He continued to make discs and cylinders until about 1920. Some of his records were released in the United Kingdom and seem to have sold well, judging by the number of copies that still come to light. He was billed 'counter–tenor' even when he sang a whole piece in a modest tenor range. All his recordings were acoustic. He seems to have enjoyed a good reputation.

Frank Coombs, of whom no personal details are available at present, despite his billing as counter–tenor, sounds to have had a pleasant light lyric tenor voice of usual range. He made no evident use of pure head–voice, and seems to have used mixed–voice for high notes.

Manuel Romain, of whom no personal details are available at present, though listed as 'counter–tenor' sounds to have been a conventional tenor of mediocre range and gifts. A singer of ballads, his name and vocal designation seem to have been selected for commercial considerations. In fact, he was listed 'tenor' on his cylinder recordings. Perhaps his billing as 'counter–tenor' was in error? Whatever the case, it seems appropriate that, in 'Curse of an Aching Heart', he sings the phrase, 'You made me what I am today: I hope you're satisfied'.

Charles Hawkins (1883–1972) sang in the Chapel Royal choir from 1926 to 1969. A low counter–tenor of rather plummy, almost heavy contralto tone, judging from his records, he sounds to have had very little upper–falsetto. He used mainly pharyngeal production allied with upper chest–voice, together with a strong vibrato. Apparently, only two solo discs, electrically recorded, were released in England (1926), but he made some for the American market. These were still selling there in the 1960s. The two British records were re–makes of Oakland originals. Hawkins was billed as 'counter–tenor'. He was leader of The Salisbury Singers (a quartette, as it was often spelled), with whom he made many records for the Columbia label in the 1920s. He also sang for the Chapel Royal choral records of the period. He often performed ballads at concerts in the 1920s and 1930s. No details are to hand of his United States records, or when they were made.

Of **Ben Millett** few personal details are to hand at present, except that he was an alto at Westminster Cathedral, under Sir Richard Terry. Later he was soloist at the Church of the Immaculate Conception, Farm Street, London, in the 1920s and 1930s. He appears to have made just six records (some with the choir), all of Latin motets of a sweetly melodious type, all recorded acoustically. He was billed as an 'Alto Vocalist'. His technique seems to have involved a minimal amount of basic–voice with some middle–falsetto, but with extensive use of upper–falsetto range. He was served unevenly by the recording engineers of the time. Judging from his best recording, his was an attractive, very light high counter–tenor voice which enjoyed a good reputation. In the late 1930s (in 1939, according to Patrick Johns) it seems that George Malcolm engaged him to sing, but Millett failed to appear. At that date, the cause may have been either the outbreak of war or Millett's age.

Frank Colman, of whom no personal details are available at present, can be heard on ballad records made in the late 1920s and early 1930s. He had a startling and exciting voice of soprano range with a firm pharyngeal lower area and extensive upper–falsetto extending to at least B5 above the treble stave. His was an easy–sounding vocal production. Unfortunately, he seems to have had a short and limited career in which he sang mostly with the Maurice Winnick band. He was billed simply as a 'Voice in a Million' or sometimes as 'male soprano'. He made six electrically recorded discs.

Albert Whitehead, of whom no personal details are available at present, apparently made only one recording: the alto solo in Constant Lambert's *The Rio Grande*, for Columbia in 1930. He was billed as 'alto'. The discs were electrically recorded. From the evidence of this recording, he seems to have employed only upper falsetto voice. His style is dated but oddly attractive.

Reference should be made to pages 138 and 141 for discussion of the names 'Whitehead' and 'Fernhead' and the possible use of singers' pseudonyms.

Record companies operating before 1939 which employed high–voiced male singers:

Label:	Listed as 'male soprano':	Listed as 'counter–tenor':	Listed as 'alto':
Ariel		Herbert Ainsworth (Hatherley Clarke)	
Beltona		Joe O'Rourke	
Columbia (USA)		Will Oakland	
Columbia			Albert Whitehead
Decca	Frank Colman		
HMV			Ben Millett
Regal		Will Oakland Frank Coombs Charles Hawkins Manuel Romain	
Scala		James Llewellyn	
Victor (USA) (Victrola)		Richard Jose Will Oakland	
Zonophone	David Davies	Hatherley Clarke	

APPENDIX 5 Counter–tenors in choirs in Scotland, Wales and Ireland

The intrinsic musical cultures of the British Isles are all of ancient origin, but each culture possesses an individual character, in which strands of solo vocal folk traditions (with or without accompaniment) are present if not equally prominent. As in folk music generally, it seems likely that ancient Scottish, Welsh and Irish vocal usage, like the English, included exploration of all facets of vocal capability, including the production of what would later be called 'pure head–voice' or, less satisfactorily, 'falsetto'.

The story–telling, bardic, lay or minstrel classes of singers associated particularly with Wales and Ireland seem likely to have employed head–voice when appropriate. The 'Irish tenor', for example, because this vocal type is so characteristic of Ireland, seems likely to have had ancient origins. It is also a traditional male voice ideally suited to the highest part in male choral singing. There are indications that there was some sort of archaic association of Irish with Welsh harpers,[44] which would suggest that at least the early Welsh harpers, bards and singers would also have employed pure head–voice when it was felt to be appropriate in the telling of a musical story. Love of the solo voice does not necessarily prevent an equal love of harmony. The Welsh choral tradition is based on a characteristic instinct for part–singing. Indeed, any *ad hoc* gathering of the Welsh leads quickly to it. At the end of the twelfth century, Giraldus Cambrensis wrote of Welsh music the following often–quoted passage:[45]

> The Britons do not sing in unison like the inhabitants of other countries, but
> in many different parts. So that when a company of singers, among the
> common people, meet to sing, as is usual in this country, as many different
> parts are heard as there are performers, who all at length unite in consonance
> with organic sweetness.

In Medieval times, Scotland, Ireland and (to a lesser extent) Wales possessed their own abbey, collegiate and cathedral churches, each with its choral polyphonic tradition. England, however, with its renowned cathedral choirs, has to some extent stood apart musically since the Reformation.

Because religious practices have been rather different in Scotland since the Reformation, it would seem that chorus counter–tenors survived very tenuously, if at all. Until its decline

---

[44] See Grove's *Dictionary*, 3rd edn, vol. 5., p. 687

[45] Wooldridge, *Oxford History of Music*, vol. I, p. 162, quotes this passage from *Cambriae Descriptio*, cap. xiii, in Latin and English, and comments on its interpretation

in the sixteenth century, Scotland had a proud musical history, in court and church. Frank Ll. Harrison[46] mentions the Chapel Royal at Stirling which was made into a collegiate church in 1501 with 'a dean, sub–dean, sacrist, sixteen canons, sixteen prebends "skilled in singing", and six boy clerks "competently trained in singing or fit to be instructed therein".'

The Reformation hit particularly hard in the north, under the influence of John Knox. In 1601, when King James VI of Scotland became also James I of England and came south, what was left of Scottish court music petered out.

Though Wales possessed monastic and collegiate churches, it seems never to have enjoyed the grand Medieval and Renaissance musical tradition of both Scotland and England. Of the four ancient cathedral foundations in Wales, by the middle of the sixteenth century only St David's could (it would appear) maintain an adequate musical foundation. Most Welsh musicians then, like teachers now, were in England.

Since then cathedral choirs have survived better and with fewer breaks in the tradition than in Scotland. This is a result of the particular nature of the Reformation north of the England/ Scotland border. Various Scottish new or re-foundations in the Episcopalian cathedrals, for instance those at St Mary's Cathedral, Edinburgh, and Aberdeen Cathedral, use counter–tenors in the traditional manner, though St Mary's has now moved away from the tradition and prefers to use a mixed treble line of boys and girls. Glasgow Cathedral has a completely mixed choir.

Llandaff Cathedral choir has displaced St David's as the premier one in Wales. Today, four of the six foundations, modest though they are when compared with the major foundations in England, still support choirs on the authentic traditional pattern with boys only singing the top line, and male altos the second. A fifth cathedral uses boys as altos. Unfortunately, some years ago, it was thought necessary to admit girls to the St David's Cathedral choir. Thankfully, recently a separate boys' choir has been formed, presumably to sing with the men, thus restoring the ancient tradition. It seems likely that, with occasional blanks, there have always been counter–tenors (of all varieties) in Welsh cathedral choirs, broadly parallel with the English pattern.

An interesting sidelight on Welsh choral singing shines from 1903. Dr Roland Rogers, organist of Bangor Cathedral, was then credited with the discovery of the contralto voice in North Wales:[47]

> He conducted the celebrated Bethesda Choir which won £1000 in prizes at various Eisteddfodau and discovered the contralto in North Wales. Until then, the alto part in choruses was sung by boys whose voices were bordering on the 'breaking' point, and all the women sang soprano! He was quick to perceive that the beautiful deep–toned voices of Welsh women could be used with splendid effect in choral music, with results that are too well–known to need further comment.

---

[46] Frank Ll. Harrison, *Music in Medieval Britain* (Routledge and Kegan Paul, 1958), p. 26. Rogers, *Chapel Royal of Scotland*, and Farmer, *A History of Music in Scotland*, also include much detail on 'sang schules' and the like.

[47] *The Musical Times*, October 1903, pp. 649–650

Percy Scholes[48] was drawn to the conclusion that this signified a total absence of male altos in Wales until 'recently': that is, until about 1947. He wrote:

> Rogers was born in 1847, and died in 1927. It would seem from the above that the adult male alto, for centuries so common in English choirs, was unknown in Wales until recent times, and that the introduction of the contralto came much later than in England.

Of course, we must remember that, though it is a small country, there is a difference between the cultures of South and North Wales. Problems of communication between them were great until the twentieth century. Contact was often easier between adjoining counties of England and Wales.

Despite this, it seems unlikely that such a voice–conscious country could ignore the possibilities of the male head voice or falsetto. In fact, the actor–dramatist Emlyn Williams gives substance to this thought. As a boy, he lived over a public house. He writes of his boyhood memories:[49] 'Once, a voice sang jaunty Welsh songs in exquisite falsetto'. One swallow does not make a summer, but there is no mention of comical quality in the singing, or laughter or derision greeting it. The implication is that the voice was taken seriously.

Concerning the Welsh contralto, why had nobody previously thought of what now seems obvious: that some women possessed contralto voices clearly more suited to the alto part, not soprano, in a mixed choir? Especially so when that part is being maintained exclusively, at least according to *The Musical Times* in 1903, by the semi–broken voices of boys? Where, it might be asked, were those boys singing before reaching semi–puberty? With the women sopranos? It seems unlikely that this worked musically and even more unlikely that they would have begun their singing careers just before their boys' voices finished.

Did young girls sing before becoming women sopranos? If so, where? A secular vocal tradition which used only men, women and boys in this way seems curious historically. Were there children's choirs? Why was the alto part given to boys who, while possessing a rich strength at that point in their vocal lives, might lose it before the next concert? Some might ask, why had nobody thought of putting girls on the alto line too as insurance? (Older girls, presumably, as young girls usually have weaker–toned lower voices for various reasons.)

Various points arise indirectly from the account above of Rogers's innovations. Hidden within its lines, is there a hint of the remains of a secular Welsh all–male choral tradition of men and boys? How old a tradition is the totally adult male–voice choir in Wales? Was it really a product of the Industrial Revolution? Were the first tenors originally 'falsetto tenors'?

At any rate, during the nineteenth and early twentieth centuries, apart from any altos in cathedral and collegiate and abbey foundations, there must have been low counter–tenors singing with 'top' tenors in male–voice choirs who never heard the term 'counter–tenor' in their lives.

There is another possible interpretation of 'boys whose voices were bordering on breaking point'. Could they have been young counter–tenors, boys only in the sense of youths with recently–changed voices or 'cambiata' voices? Such an interpretation could parallel the English

---

[48] Percy Scholes, 'The Decline of the Male Alto and the Rise of the Contralto', *Mirror of Music*, 1947

[49] Emlyn Williams, *George, An Autobiography* (Hamish Hamilton, 1961; Reprint Society, 1962), p. 31

tradition of gradual vocal adjustment which produced beautifully mature boys' voices and, eventually, counter-tenors. In Welsh choirs, of course, this would help supply, in due course, a proportion of the tenor top line singers in male choruses. We might reflect on the apparent Welshness in origin, at least, of the important counter-tenor names of Morgan, Howell, Hughes, Price and Davies (Daviesi) – and in present times, Wynne and James.

Ireland was a different case: in the South its churches were mostly parochial Roman Catholic, and in the North, mostly fiercely 'congregational' and Protestant. The ubiquitous but thinly-spread Church of Ireland was stuck traditionally and precariously between them, and it was of course different musically. Most of its 'Anglican' cathedrals are tiny, but the two in Dublin seem to have preserved from medieval times what is considered the English style and repertoire of choral singing. Therefore, they must have enshrined the tradition of alto voices as a direct consequence.[50] After all, it was the joint choirs of Christ Church and St Patrick's cathedrals in Dublin which Handel chose to supply the chorus and most of the soloists when he gave the first performance of *Messiah* in 1742. Certainly, there were well-established counter-tenors there by that time. A letter of Handel's to Jennens described the first performances in his Dublin season late in the previous year. Referring to *L'Allegro, il Penseroso ed il Moderato*, he wrote on 29 December 1741:[51]

> ... I have form'd an other Tenor Voice which gives great Satisfaction, the Basses and Counter Tenors are very good, and the rest of the Chorus Singers (by my Direction) do exceeding well ...

Apart from the various Irish 'Anglican' cathedrals, and Séan Osborne (who lives and sings in the Netherlands), Ireland's high male-voice tradition appears to have come to be represented in the main by the 'Irish Tenor', arguably a member of the counter-tenor family. However, as we have noted, the ancient Celtic high-voiced singer, a traditional singer of lays, possessed a very high range and technique. These male high voices were probably of several varieties, especially given that the vocal tradition was based on self-tuition, imitation and essentially informal procedures. (Though it chiefly concerns England, we discuss folk music in more depth in Appendix Eight.)

Scotland, Wales and Ireland, not surprisingly, were slower than England in the acceptance of the 1940s revival of solo and chorus counter-tenors' singing outside Anglican cathedral choirs. The facts that the counter-tenor revival had begun in England and was a part of English culture might well have counted against its acceptability except in areas of particularly strong English influence.

---

[50] For an account of these choirs in the eighteenth century, see Harrison, 'Music, Poetry and Polity in the age of Swift' (Iris an dá chultúr, Eighteenth Century Ireland Society), vol. I, 1986, pp. 37–63

[51] Robbins Landon, *Handel and his World* (Wiedenfeld and Nicolson, 1984), p. 177

APPENDIX 6 An Exchange of Correspondence

Dr Brian Crosby, ex–alto lay clerk at Durham Cathedral, and Senior Master of Durham Chorister School, has generously given permission to publish his side of an exchange of letters in which he and the author took part in late 1983 and early 1984. They are slightly edited for inclusion here. The first letter had been one of the author's, which requested information on Richard Elford who was a lay–clerk at Durham before he moved to the Chapel Royal. The reply to this was as follows:

The Chorister School, Durham,
28th November, 1983.

Dear Mr Giles,

It may help you to understand some of my prejudices if I start on a personal note. It is over thirty years since my voice finally 'broke' at the ripe old age of nearly seventeen. I very much wanted to become a basso profundo, a not unreasonable aspiration, as I could get bass G whilst still a treble. However, after about three months of singing bass I had to give it up because it was hurting my throat (and it still does, if I attempt really to project my voice in that register). At that time Alfred Deller was making some fascinating noises on the radio, and I decided to see what I could do, because tenor was out of the question. I remember that A above middle C was all that I could manage, and even in my early days at university C above middle C was very much my limit. My contemporaries at college regarded it as a loud voice, which means it had developed, for when I first started I thought how ineffective it was. It is hard to be precise, but I think I tried to use what was left of my old treble voice: certainly I did not become a member of the counter–tenor school.

From the previous generation of Durham lay–clerks I have inherited an aversion to changes of register, not only in the case of altos and counter–tenors but also with tenors at the upper end of their range (when I joined the Durham choir, the Decani tenor used to go for his high C full throttle) and with trebles at the lower end of theirs.

In early September [1983], I asked a former bass lay–clerk (now aged 96) what sort of voice my predecessor had – my predecessor came in 1914! The answer was that he was 'a proper counter–tenor'. Needless to say, I asked for clarification. It was not a 'big' voice, but he was like a tenor moved up a little – and at no point did he alter the method in which he produced his voice. He particularly remembered the blend in the duet (with the lower part sung by a tenor) of Greene's *God is our Hope and Strength*.

I can only remember my predecessor's voice when he was in his late sixties, and by then it had mainly gone – when reciting the Creed below middle C it was like a boy's breaking voice, fluctuating uncontrollably from one octave to another – and yet he still had the artistry to manage his solos. I agree that he did not change register when in control of his voice. The same bass lay–clerk had strong views about the modern counter–tenor. I knew of them when I sang with him – he sang until he was 79 – and he was still of the same opinion when I met him. Indeed, he went so far as to say that the modern counter–tenor was a gimmick 'thought up by the BBC'! He also opined that Joe Lisle (mentioned in recent correspondence in *The Musical Times*) was a falsettist; and one of the choristers of those days (the 1910s) thinks likewise, and adds that Lisle had an obviously different voice when he went for his lower notes.

Because of all this, I prefer a quiet start to Morley's *Out of the Deep*, swelling out for 'Lord, hear my voice', using the same register throughout. Equally, I would expect to go up to treble D using the same production. Occasionally for it, and certainly for the E and F above it (e.g., the end of Dyson's Magnificat in D, and the duet in Mozart's *O God, when Thou Appearest*) I have a different production which I regard as falsetto.

I agree with you that the modern composers are making too great demands on the altos. Much seems to have been written with contraltos in mind. I have said that I do not like the shrieking involved, and that if I want to hear shrieking the seagulls at Hartlepool are good exponents of that art! But where modern writers would stretch us at one end, S. S. Wesley has us plumbing the depths with his Es below middle C in anthems and services.

But be that as it may, one serious point does emerge from all this, a point which was not touched upon in *The Musical Times* debate. Over the years, it has been my privilege to have beside me some excellent choral scholars. However, the fact remains that whenever they have been of the counter–tenor school I have difficulties over pitch and even over producing my voice. Trying to analyse it, it is almost as if the notes have been approached from different directions. I was aware of this by the early 1960s, and mentioned it to Owen Wynne, querying whether the counter–tenor approached notes from below and the alto from above. I wondered if you had any views or theories on this point.

Much of [the earlier book] *The Counter Tenor* seems to revolve round what Richard Elford's voice may or may not have been like. But even though it may be possible to determine what range he was required to sing, in the absence of any comments from people who actually heard him one can do no more than conjecture how he produced his voice. I have had an interest in Elford for some years now, ever since the Olive Baldwin/Thelma Wilson partnership contacted me about his stay in Durham. They described him as a 'counter–tenor', but I rejoined that I was not sure about this.

And now, a number of points which have occurred to me. I may have missed it in your book, but are you aware of the comment in Arnold's *Cathedral Music*, vol. 3, p. 226, about William Hine (1687–1730): 'He sang elegantly in a feigned voice'? Is it known what part he sang and, of course, what is meant by 'a feigned voice'?

Again, you may have referred to it or to a similar situation, but rightly or wrongly I have it at the back of my mind that there were no boys in the Peterhouse choir [Cambridge] of the late 1630s. The repertoire was very like that of Durham – not least because no fewer than seven Durham copyists are numbered among the scribes responsible for the Peterhouse manuscripts. If I am correct in my assumption, what sort of production would the men responsible for the top line have employed? Are they to be likened to the modern falsettists?

Equally, in terms of production (though it is somewhat irrelevant I fear) I find myself quite amazed to discover that at Durham prior to the present century the boys occasionally included characters aged nineteen and even twenty. I am sure of this, because not only do we have their signatures in the Treasurer's Account Books showing a tenure lasting ten years, but it has also been possible to discover their dates of birth. With only ten boys in the choir, there was hardly room to carry a passenger whilst he was waiting for a vacancy in the men's ranks. Again, at such an age their production must surely have not been 'natural'.

Yours sincerely,
Brian Crosby.

While it was being prepared for publication, small sections or phrases of the following reply were given square brackets: the result of subsequent reflection and regret at not expanding slightly and explaining better in the original letter.

3rd January, 1984

Dear Mr Crosby,

I was most interested to read of your experiences and ideas, and it all helps to add more to my own. To comment on your points – where they need or ask for comment –

(1) I am of the opinion that much of today's earlier breaking of voices is due to a change in training, to some extent; but perhaps more to <u>expectation</u> and extra–musical psychological pressure; <u>and even more than this, to a dislike amongst choir–masters and others, of mature treble tone.</u> In my opinion, the larger voices of the past, including the far past, were probably not crude, brazen and over–blown for their size but naturally big–toned because the boys continued long enough to be adolescent trebles with a good amount of new, quasi–adult head– and chest–voice in the mix! I say this despite the obvious earlier physical development of today. The latter is, in any case, not by any means even and universal, as you will know!

(2) I am not surprised that the Romantic school flourished in Durham and that your predecessors of all voices were steeped in its methods and in the ideals of training the male voice! I think that few people have realised the incredible changes which took place in male–voice training during the nineteenth and early twentieth centuries and up to the present day – which could not happen over–much in the sphere of women's voices by the very nature of things. We should look with interest at these changes.

It sounds as if you use a gentle 'pharyngeal' for much of your own range with most [mixed?] tone reserved for medium–to–high notes, plus upper–falsetto/super–falsetto/pure head–voice at the top. It would feel like a shift of mechanism, and is of course perfectly normal, just as the lower change, if you chose to use it, is perfectly normal. It all depends on what you <u>want</u> out of the voice, after all – or much of it does! [Brian Crosby's predecessor sounds to have had excellent, if light, low 'pharyngeal', or was a tenor–altino.]

(3) As to whether people should consider their range as if 'from above going down', or 'from below stretching up', I am now of the opinion that the traditional counter–tenor (in my terms) may have done neither. I know from much deliberation and my own experiences over the last few years, that the most rewarding approach is to work along a more horizontal plane, forward for higher–pitched notes, backward for the lower–pitched ones. [This is better thought–of as <u>fractionally less forward</u> for the lower–pitched notes.] You are right to bring up the question of mental image – it is quite crucial to the sound produced. [The traditional use of, and essential musical message given by, the alto clef is the nub.]

(4) About Elford, thanks for your information on him. *The Counter Tenor* was not really supposed to revolve round him personally, though I suppose it could be thought of that way. As I have now written notes for the projected enlarged, improved version [which has developed into the present work], I can perhaps do no better than quote from them: 'Brian Crosby confirms that Elford sang tenor at Durham. But my real point is that in the modern meaning of the term, he was not a <u>tenor</u> at all, and that, using seventeenth–century technique, he could take tenor and lower alto parts by means of the pharyngeal/chest combination, not because he had a modern tenor voice.'

(5) About the 'feigned voice', I have not said much in the book. [That is, in the original *The Counter Tenor*.] To me it suggests a perhaps weak undeveloped head–voice which is nevertheless used musically and attractively. The temptation is automatically to take 'feigned' as the opposite of 'true', and in modern terms this quickly and simplistically becomes synonymous with 'falsetto' (unnatural), as opposed to 'chest' (natural, normal, real!). It all relates to my pages 92–94 [in *The Counter Tenor*], and Reid's tables. The word 'true' is, in any case, capable of several interpretations, especially when one remembers how language shifts! I therefore rather skirted round 'feigned', deliberately.

(6) Regarding Peterhouse, I would hazard an opinion that in colleges without boy singers the top line would have been supplied by 'falsettists' in the best sense of the term. Pitch could be varied, of course – and was [probably] a variable animal anyway – and questions might be raised about the Peterhouse organ and/or viols, etc. After all, until recent co–education in Oxford and Cambridge colleges, some establishments only had tenor and bass choral scholars, didn't they? This suggests not an unbroken line of tenor/bass choir but more, I think, of some change in the fairly recent past to fit fashion, call it what you will. Archives of colleges need looking into. Why not do it? I'd be most interested. You might well find that light falsetto tenors [in choirs apparently comprising only tenor and bass voices] were the aliases of counter–tenors in the far past, and ordinary modern tenors in the years up to the greatest change of all!

I note your comment about 19–year–old Durham choristers! It fits well at my point (1), and raises speculation about Peterhouse choral scholars, aged 19, at point (6).

Once again, thank you for your help so far. I suspect that if we could meet we would have much to discuss!

Yours sincerely,
Peter Giles

APPENDIX 7 The Male High Voice as Artistic, Visionary and Symbolic Phenomenon

Before considering the deeper implications of this phenomenon, there is an intriguing hypothesis which could explain the almost uniquely unbroken survival of the counter–tenor in England.

Despite its original development as a European voice, how very English this voice seems to be! It possesses particular characteristics discernible also in other forms of expression. It is totally English in that at first some of these characteristics appear to be at odds with others.

In the mid–1950s, Nikolaus Pevsner wrote *The Englishness of English Art*, based on his Reith Lectures for BBC Radio.[52] He argued that English art has a peculiar and unique quality: a love of *line* – sinuous, sensuous, flowing and ever–present. It has pervaded English architecture: most Anglican cathedrals have extreme length but never extreme height (unlike French buildings). It is to be found in painting and drawing: linear–preoccupation pervades early illumination and illustration on vellum and, later, tonal areas of pure painting: for example, Gainsborough's almost cross–hatched solid–colour areas and Blake's voluptuous line which can now be seen in its context with his language: flowing subtleties of English prose and poetry. It is there in the music: idiosyncratic vocal lines as in, for example, a Tallis motet – with the accent on the individual journey of each vocal part which sometimes leads to 'strange' clashes a semitone apart, and is the chief characteristic of that marvellous flourish, the 'English cadence'.

 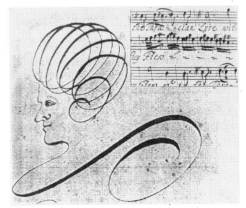

The characteristic English sinuous line: (i) mid–12th century illumination (left);
(ii) Purcell drawn by Purcell? (right)

---

[52] The Architectural Press, 1956

The second characteristic of English art is idiosyncrasy itself; a refusal to be bound by rationality. It has given rise, for example, to the writings of Edward Lear and Lewis Carroll, to the drawings by Richard Dadd, Rowland Emmett and Gerard Hoffnung, and to the comedy of The Goon Show and Monty Python's Flying Circus – all of these quirky and surrealist worlds, which co-exist oddly with the so-called traditional reserved English mien: the 'stiff upper lip' of recent times and colonial English 'phlegm'. This odd mix spawned, or was created by, the English eccentric. Even the brilliant invention, if not always the playing of, team games and sports – the majority of them were devised by English sportsmen – is surely an escape into an unreal world.

The third characteristic is common sense – something which certainly comes strangely after the second. A Chinese wrote: 'The spirit of the English people is more akin to the spirit of the Chinese people, for both nations are worshippers of realism and common sense. Both peoples have a profound distrust of logic and are profoundly suspicious of arguments that are too perfect.'[53]

The fourth characteristics are a love of tradition, and conservatism. Dunstable was a foremost composer in Europe during the fifteenth century primarily because he and other English composers were part of a conservative tradition. While European composers were desperately looking for the new, Dunstable was able to point the way as a result of an English independent line (yes, line!) which had valued discant and developed 'strange dissonances' which we now call 'thirds' and 'sixths'.

During the late sixteenth century, for example in lute-songs, and in the seventeenth century, in stage-music, French and Italian interest was centred almost entirely on vertical harmony (with melody and bass, plus 'filling' continuo). English conservatism meant that there was continued interest in 'line', which sprang from an horizontal approach to harmony. A tradition of writing polyphony survived healthily in both instrumental and vocal composition throughout the century.

The fifth characteristic is compromise. The English themselves are a compromise of convention and eccentricity. A counter-tenor's voice seems to be placed at the balance between 'natural' (commonplace, or usual) and 'unnatural' (or unusual). That this is so is emphasised by eighteenth-century English attitudes towards the 'super-star' operatic Italian castrati. Despite siren wooings of fickle high fashion and the tendency which still exists to welcome cultural invasion, the English then, especially outside the capital, quietly preferred the natural, home-grown counter-tenor to dazzling, foreign, artificial singers, most of whom – the castrati – were demonstrably superior, vocally. The English did not and do not like 'showy' voices, or at least not showy English ones; as showing off is thought an excess!

A voice can sing only a single line, but the male high voice is ultra-linear – it is not always a thin line, but it is essentially lithe. Decidedly 'other-worldly', it inhabits a strange sphere somewhere in the head, indefinably more so than falsetto.

A fascinating article entitled 'Purcell by Purcell?'[54] speculates on whether or not Purcell portrayed himself in a particular manuscript. (There is at least one precedent for it: five of the six part-books of John Taverner's mass *Gloria Tibi Trinitas* have decorative initials, all of which include the same portrait, probably that of Taverner himself.) In the manuscript there are ultra-linear flourishes of penmanship; there is the tantalizing possibility that the scribe might have been Purcell himself. The manuscript has a transposition of 'Hark Each Tree' from

[53] Lin Yutang (1895–1976), *This England*, Autumn 1989, p. 37
[54] *Radio Three Magazine* (BBC Publications, November 1982), Vol. 1, no. 2, pp. 14–15

Purcell's *Ode on St Cecilia's Day, 1692*. Arguably, in the original, he wrote for treble or high counter–tenor, and bass, in A minor. As the illustration on page 381 shows, it has only the top part, marked 'canto' – transposed a fifth higher into E minor. It could also be sung effectively one octave lower by a falsetto–tenor or lower counter–tenor. If the scribe was Purcell himself, was he suggesting a personal link with this composition and his own vocal type?

At the very least, the style of the draughtmanship of this flourish not only supports Pevsner's thesis but also enhances the links between English delineation and the counter–tenor. Aptly, its draughtsmanship and portrait also form a link with the 'lineament' and the 'distinctive features; facial characteristics' of the dictionary definitions.

The counter–tenor phenomenon is irrational – men do not usually sing as high as women – therefore how characteristic it is that the English would favour a voice which often does! English conservatism caused the counter–tenor's survival. His continued existence stemmed from English reluctance to embrace the new, and a refusal to recognise a battle lost.

Counter–tenors are a sensible compromise between normal and abnormal. Their singing pitch, their plangency and increasingly their vocal range, can resemble and now can well represent the voice of the castrati; but counter–tenors were, and are, free from un–English excess. Therefore, despite castrati, and the steady introduction of female contralti during the eighteenth century, it took time to freeze counter–tenors from concert–platforms. Even when this was accomplished, it was not a permanent exile.

In a country seldom celebrated for religious enthusiasm, though her music and musicians have always been tied to the church, the counter–tenor's retreat to the choirstalls and his subsequent victory against the odds are very English.

The English counter–tenor was a survival of an European preoccupation with a male high voice which had faded almost to extinction. What lay behind its near–worship in previous centuries?

It seems possible that the pre–occupation with this high voice reached its zenith from the sixteenth to the eighteenth centuries. It grew from a Medieval and Renaissance vision: a concept of heaven on earth as expressed by the architecture and ambience of the buildings of the Church Triumphant. Stained glass, twinkling aumbry lights, wall paintings, wondrous music, ceremonial and ritual, incense, mystique and mysticism, power and glory: these were unchallenged even by most kingly Courts.

It is arguable that the positioning in a gallery of singers, organ and sometimes instrumentalists, not only sought to enhance their musical effect but could be considered highly symbolic, and was not at all merely a method of tidying the choir away out of sight of the congregation (however ideal some traditions thought this might be). Though the priest at the high altar, representing Christ, is near ground level (albeit often elevated by steps), the mystical, coloured vault soaring brilliantly over the sacred space inside a mighty church represented heaven and infinity. In France, the attempt to achieve the highest vault possible culminated in the sublimity, and initial over–reaching, of Beauvais Cathedral's choir vault. Many vaults were painted with 'glories' and stars; the most magnificent of these were situated above the high altars or the saints' shrines behind them.

Special choir galleries and balconies, splendid in appearance, were often placed high above the worshippers, as in the naves of Wells and Exeter. The celestial sounds emanating from these lofts, even those placed at a moderate height, must have seemed to originate in paradise itself. This was certainly true of the Sistine Chapel, celebrated for centuries for its high voices, though – paradoxically – the small south gallery customarily used by the Papal choir is not of great altitude.

The church building, in addition to being the earthly embodiment of heaven, was probably considered a tripartite model in which the wondrous vault represented the firmament and God, ground level representing earth and man, with mazes and other floor patterns that symbolised his life's search for truth, and the crypt which lay below the stone floor echoing the infernal regions and physical death. Thus we see the significance and importance attached to the disembodied, high voice and its ultimate development, the song of the angels, the highest vocal art. The sexlessness of the castrati added even greater significance to this concept.

The English tradition in which the choir was placed antiphonally at ground level in the ritual quire is based on the monks' 'use' and their singing of the regular daily offices. It is possible that this placing may have encouraged the development of a more ethereal treble tone than that which obtained on the continent. A choir placed in a gallery, usually at the side or back of the building, particularly when that building is resonant, has an inherent, purely musical advantage. Height and distance imbue magic, but something is lost when the singers are not visually and tangibly present and the choir is not a part of the liturgical ritual.

Before the invention of recording, reverberation was the only means of prolonging sounds. High voices best exploit the miracle of echoes. The ethereal sound of the 'angelic choir', as it pervaded the void and entered ears, minds, imaginations and hearts of minute men and women below, must have brought heaven as near earth as the lofty, spreading vault.

Until we in the West can free ourselves from our twentieth-century, earthly, body-bound philosophy, we seem fated to glimpse only a little of the high holiness and magic which, consciously or unconsciously, permeated much artistic creativity in previous centuries and which were the ideals of the nineteenth-century medievalists.

In most pre-twentieth-century serious vocal music and even in some lighter fare, there was an almost constant reminder of an 'upward-search'. There was a yearning for the gods, or God, and a need to sing to, emulate, aspire to, a higher plane, whether Heaven or Parnassus, where dwelt super-beings in the image of whom the human was created. Even secular love-songs were usually couched in appropriate language. Take for example the song *My Goddess Celia* by George Munro, written in the eighteenth century but slightly sanitized by its 1899 editor, H. Lane Wilson, as *My Lovely Celia*. Munro, who wrote the words of the song as well as its music, entreats his 'Goddess Celia, Heavenly Fair' to let him gaze on her bright eyes 'where melting beams so oft arise ... O take me dying to your arms' – words which call to mind many paintings of rapt, religious swoon with eyes upturned to the heavens. The parallels between sacred and secular love were not new, and can be found in late sixteenth- and seventeenth-century English songs.

Lighter varieties of opera, like Offenbach's *Orpheus in the Underworld* and comparable light-theatrical vocal music, often made light or mock of the 'upward search', but the idea remained, if only in the ether. The 'God-search' seems always to have been present in human beings and their culture in some form. Use of high voices, and even an obsession with them, seems to be an integral part of the process. The all-embracing, authoritarian hierarchy of the Church has been a spiritual, (sometimes) benevolent dictatorship. Its schematic secular equivalent was the world of the pre-modern Theatre. Each presented a mythology – Christian and Classical respectively, though the Church would not have acknowledged theirs as such! Both church and theatre employed the visual, aural, literary and physical arts, and received totally appropriate responses, even obeisance, from them. Mere mortals searching for Heaven or Parnassus, however dimly they perceived these, could thus go some way towards recreating either or even both on earth. The high voice, male and female, was part of this quest for paradise.

APPENDIX 8 English Folk and Traditional Music and the Male High Voice

There is some discussion of folk–singing technique in Chapter 13 (page 290), but there needs to be some deeper consideration of its ethno–musical and ritualistic origins.

In pre–history, music, magic, dance and religion were virtually synonymous. The most primitive forms of religion are death and ancestor cults. Like many more sophisticated religions, they involve belief in spirits, ghosts, and the supernatural. The use of male head–voice or falsetto, the 'disembodied voice', had and still has an instinctive natural and obvious affinity with many primitive societies and cultures.

Ancient folksong and ritual, secular liturgy and religious liturgy, all share a common root. There are significant and audible links between folk–song and liturgical chant, pagan and Christian (oral and written traditions respectively) though these are usually either ignored or given only slight notice. The common idea that folk–song developed from plainsong is totally misleading. In fact, they have a joint origin. Religion and every–day life have been separated only in modern 'sophisticated' societies and their philosophy.

It is sometimes suggested that most genuine British–derived folk–song from the British Isles is not harmonic in character. Even if this were true, it does not necessarily mean 'never harmonized': for example, Joan Rimmer's researches into Irish folk music suggest the occasional employment of simple or simplistic harmony. English folk–melody, too, in simple unison interspersed with short burdens, choruses or refrains in primitive organum–like harmony seems to have links with plainsong and organum. Most English folk–songs are in instinctive Dorian or Mixolydian modes. It seems likely that, far from being an exclusively ecclesiastical musical invention or development, what we call organum (which must have involved use of pure head–voice when required by the tessitura) was probably more the formalized application of a pre–existing informal musical usage. The employment of organum in folk–music, therefore, was probably ancient instinct.

Even when consideration of the subject of ancient folk music is restricted to European traditions, there arise many rich possibilities which could impinge on our subject but which are mostly too intricate to explore here. These tangential matters might include a consideration of the ancient mysticism of the figure '3' (some musical and vocal aspects of which have previously been mentioned) and the idea that folk–ballads form a ritual song–story cycle which may have been part of, or have influenced, Medieval mystery plays.

Another, perhaps a surprising one in view of usual practice today, is that of folk–dance. The folk–music authority Bob Stewart has written: 'Many ballads within our folk–tradition may have had dance associated with them. If they imply ritual meaning, the refrain–line may

386

be suggestive of mimetic action.[55] His writings are recommended for further reading.

Consideration of English folk–music and folk–dance leads quickly to the Morris tradition and to its ancient links with ritual magic, music and significant physical movement. It has also symbolic and intricate meaning, procedure and practice. Fertility, purification, pre–Christian 'mother–earth' liturgy and mythology were, and are, all expressed in various modes and rôles – sexual and otherwise.

One school of thought argues that Morris dancing has come to us as a mixture of two main continental European folk traditions, originating in diverse and very different cultures. (The proper exploration of any possible links with falsetto singing in these cultures is certainly a subject for research.) The other view is that Morris is an exclusively native Anglo–Welsh tradition, is pre–Christian, and is very ancient in origin. We will consider this idea briefly because the employment of falsetto was extremely likely.

The Blackface Traditions, originally country–wide, are the oldest form of Morris dancing. All others derive from them. 'Morris' is thought by some to have evolved from 'Moorish'. Because falsetto singing and nasal resonation entered the modern European tradition through the Moorish invasion of Spain and parts of France, Moorish, Morris and falsetto–use appear to be linked. In original ancient practice, however, the 'black face' was made with ash and soot from the magic fire, rubbed on to imbue the dancer with the potency of both sun and fire. This resulted, certainly by Shakespeare's time, in 'Moorish' being applied loosely to the existing Blackface male folk–dancing tradition.

Nevertheless, though it is little in evidence now, singing is thought to have been once much involved in Morris dancing. Possibly it occurred in certain highly significant moments of ritual and dance and was not necessarily performed by the dancers themselves. Morris is a masculine tradition. As in other such societies, groups, or traditions, singing is likely eventually to demand the full range of effects available from the male voice. In this case, the magical 'disembodied male voice', falsetto, would probably have been employed for its appropriate qualities.

In pre–Christian England, male magic was performed separately from female magic. What we have come to call 'Morris' dancing was essentially 'outward' magic. The equivalent female ritual is thought to have been more secretive.

The sun was perceived as male: the life–giving force, the father; the fecund earth was seen as female, the mother. Each gender is likely to have had simulations, or part–representations of the other in the separate rituals. In the male liturgy, the magic fire, the symbol of the sun, had to be tended. Fire–tending was women's work in daily life; therefore no male could be seen to do it, even in ritual. A disguised man–woman figure was therefore necessary for this specific task, and eventually some such figure became widely, if variably, established in English folk–ritual.

Though the dancers in Morris usually work in 'sides' [sic], a group generally numbering between six and twelve men, traditional practice seems to have a strange, perhaps accidental, affinity with another ritual: more expressive but less physical; that of formal singing in quire. In Morris dancing, the whole 'side' consists of two teams which usually begin and finish by facing each other. In the cathedral or monastic quire, two choirs face each other similarly, 'in sides'. The ritual of Six–Man's Morris (which recalls Three–Man's Song) which has three per side (or, properly, sub–side) seems to be a particularly apt analogy, for in church singing,

---

[55] Robert Stewart, *Where is St George? Pagan Imagery in English Folksong* (Blandford Press, 1988 edn), p. 100; also see G. B. Chambers, *Folksong–Plainsong* (Merlin Press, 2nd edn, 1972)

three men per side of the quire is the minimum number for antiphonal harmony: counter-tenor, tenor, and bass. We may even note the disposition of the British style of debating chamber, as represented in the Westminster parliament's two Houses: the Commons and the Lords. There is a link both visual and actual with ritual antiphony and the development of organised and balanced debate, and perhaps also with seeing both sides of an argument!

Also awaiting further research are possible links with the Elizabethan jig, and dancing and singing pastimes.[56]

Some ritual folk-songs inherently suggest strong links between secular liturgy, religious liturgy and movement. *The Cutty Wren* is a significant example: the symbolism of it bears a close relationship with various forms of mythological, religious and mystical modes of thought, and its text repays close study. Stewart describes the teams and choirs which are part of intricate performance procedures: '... The characters ... are those of a principal officer (John the Red Nose) ... and two teams of liturgists, Milder & Malder, and Festle & Fose. These two teams or *choirs* [the present author's italics] create the interrogative, question-and-negation pattern which the principal officer grandly solves at the end of each verse.'[57] *The Cutty Wren* has, significantly, three participating elements; it also proceeds by the alternate singing which is the parallel of antiphonal plainsong chant.

An almost-formal performance procedure seems to be a deeply-rooted phenomenon common to the British Isles. Ancient folk-dance and song share a ritual characteristic: 'Musical forms such as leader and response, overall choruses and inspired solo passages, and certain shapes of melodic phrasing, are naturally common to the British people. Excluding the lost inspirational element, this situation survived until quite recently in folk-music.'[58]

Ritual drama must be included in our considerations of the male high-voice in folk tradition. One example, Hoodening, is an ancient East Kent custom which can still be found to be performed there in the days just before Christmas. Best described as secular ritual drama with songs and music, it includes the Hooden Horse and his men, Molly, Waggoner and Rider. It is not a Mumming play and it is not Morris-dancing, but it is related to a number of folk customs which can all be included in a broad category known as Animal Guising. In Wales, Mari llydd is related to Kentish Hoodening, and they derive from a common ancient source. Disguising (the origins of this word are clear) involves more than mere appearance. Voices, too, must be disguised. The high voice is particularly useful for this. The Molly character is of special interest: 'First to the threshold would come the Molly or Man-Woman, dressed in women's garb and carrying a besom broom, to clear both bystanders and evil spirits out of the way...'[59] (The broom is one of the fire-tender's accoutrements.) Before and after the performance, the characters would sing songs both traditional and more contemporary, and this practice continues. Extra singers and instrumentalists would accompany the team, though numbers and instruments varied greatly.

The Molly in Hoodening, the Molly, Betsy, Queen, Daisy or Witch in Morris dancing, the 'man-woman' in Mumming Plays, Purcell's Mopsa and Sorceress, Pantomime Dame and Principal Boy, Minnie Bannister of *The Goon Show*, Dame Edna Everage, and the men-women of *Monty Python's Flying Circus* – all these, though some are serious and others

---

[56] see C. R. Baskervill, *The Elizabethan Jig* (University of Chicago Press, 1929; Dover, 1965), esp. pp. 6 and 7

[57] Stewart, op. cit., p. 21; see the whole discussion and text on pp. 15–23

[58] Stewart, op. cit., p. 102

[59] Mark Lawson, *Hoodening – the East Kent Tradition* (privately publ., Whitstable), p. 1

are comical, have an ancient joint origin. These bizarre characters, though separated by countless time, seem linked originally by falsetto vocal techniques.

Of more usual English folk-singing, it is sometimes remarked that most male performers adopt a high, sometimes quavery, semi-head-voice. The reason given by Ralph Vaughan Williams and Cecil Sharp, the most notable folk-song collectors, is that young men always learned the songs from the old. Certainly, Sharp reported that most men from whom he noted songs were elderly. Where younger, he commented: 'Young singers sang like old men' – that is, with high and thin sounds.

Did Sharp, Vaughan Williams and others fail to wonder if they might be hearing the remains of a male high-voice folk-singing tradition which once existed independently of man-woman rôles? John Jacob Niles, the American 'hill-billy' singer and a fine tenor-altino, who has recorded folk-songs from the Appalachian Mountains (originally from England), seems to be a vivid example of the traditional English male high-voiced folk-style, even if at one remove.

Often, it would seem, indications of original male high-voice use goes unnoticed. For example, there is a theory that the Commedia Del Arte characters are partly descended from a form of Guising. Punch, whose origins are connected with the Commedia, is required to have a squeaky voice. This is not necessarily connected with his puppet size, for the other male puppets speak normally.

Exclusively male gatherings, formed for whatever reason, are likely eventually to encourage use of the full male voice-range in consort singing, or in essentially informal groups of various descriptions. Possible past connections with the use of falsetto in prisons, for reasons musical, psychological, communicative (perhaps even sexual) has been suggested, when male inmates were segregated from female. To this instance might be added naval and sea-going life in general.

The work-song termed 'sea-shanty', or 'forebitter' (a song sung by the crew for entertainment and relaxation in the forecastle or on the deck above) probably included impromptu or even customary falsetto effects. High head-voice, possibly together with the mature but still unmutated voices of ships' boys would carry advantageously in the open air and brighten the tone in an enclosed environment. There may have been crude harmony, especially in the easier off-duty hours during the second dog-watch, from 4 p.m. to 6 p.m. or from 6 p.m. to 8 p.m. [sic]. Instruments were also used. We know that Joseph Emidy (or Emidee), a former African negro slave, who later became a well-known instrumentalist, teacher and composer, was impressed into serving on the frigate *Indefatigable*. 'They had long wanted for the frigate a good violin player, to furnish music for the sailors' dancing in their evening leisure, a recreation highly favourable to the preservation of their good spirits and contentment.'[60]

Of course, as in all collected folk-music, he who noted down songs for posterity heard only the version offered, probably by a single unaccompanied voice. Such simple harmony and effects as were extemporized in original performance were therefore unrepresented and unrecorded.

The original shanty singers were mostly illiterate and possibly slow to learn. Songs were not written down in musical notation, so the assimilation of tunes and words was by rote. Apparently, almost half the crew on many return voyages to Britain in the eighteenth and nineteenth centuries were negroes. Often, their presence was a result of death or desertion

---

[60] William R. Tuck, *Reminiscences of Cornwall* (Truro, n.d.), pp. 18–20. See also Richard McGrady, 'Joseph Emidy: an African in Cornwall', *The Musical Times*, Nov. 1986, pp. 619–623

amongst the original ship's company. In such cases, the two watches were divided thus: one black, one white, normally. This was not because of racialism, an automatic 'knee-jerk' assumption today, but to promote healthy rivalry throughout the ship; though, apparently, Emidy, as the only negro on board, had to eat alone and was looked down upon as inferior – except when playing to the crew, when he was in high favour.[61] No doubt competition extended to the singing of shanties and sea-songs, and encouraged the employment of the full male-voice range. This is likely to have included falsetto, an instinctive predisposition of negroes and probably common practice among European seamen.

Though shanty-singing seems to have been most popular during the nineteenth century, the earliest songs are well over two hundred years old. (One, *Lowlands*, was sung on Sir Walter Raleigh's ship at a time when the high counter-tenor was widely employed.) It is arguable, therefore, that a fresh look should be taken at shanties, with a view to their performance in simple harmony which could include falsetto.

We have seen that Sir Francis Drake (c1545-1596) is thought to have sung counter-tenor. His father, Edmund Drake, moved with his large family from the west country to live near Chatham Dockyard, near Rochester, Kent, where he was a 'reader of prayers to the navy'. At the accession of Elizabeth I to the English throne, Drake senior, an outspoken Protestant, became vicar of Upchurch, near Chatham. Francis Drake, too, was a fervent Protestant. He seems to have had many qualities which might have encouraged counter-tenor singing. He was extrovert, daring, dashing, mercurial, self-confident, artistic and humorous, with a touch of flourish and eccentricity. He was apparently 'fond of his own voice' (probably in both speaking and singing modes) and it is recorded that he loved music, engaging trumpeters and lutenists to play while he dined during voyages. On one voyage, the Norwich city waites, whom he had begged from the Mayor, played for him. While Member of Parliament for Plymouth, he even rode alongside his newly completed water supply for the city to the sound of trumpets.

Perhaps also influenced, when young, by visits to Rochester Cathedral, he insisted on daily religious services aboard his fleets. His own voice was heard with the others when the psalms were sung, and viols accompanied the hymns. He even preached on occasion. The famous song *Drake's Drum* might well have been set for counter-tenor, except that it would not have been acceptable to late-Victorian England! It therefore seems more than possible that his 'counter-tenor' label originated both from his singing in his father's church, and from his later career on board ship. There is another possibility.

The plangent carrying quality of the male high voice was useful at sea in other ways. It seems that head-voice was sometimes employed in the shouting of orders. An example of its use, dates from as late as 1911, when Captain John Ford was Master of the famous barque *Discovery*. Able Seaman (now Captain) Williamson wrote that he (Ford):

> ... was a sailor of the old school ... and when he ordered us to man the braces
> to trim the yards to a shift of wind, we were intrigued by the way in which
> he chanted his orders in an old-fashioned manner, no longer heard in modern
> windjammers – 'Well, the main yard! Be-e-lay there; Oh, be-e-lay!'[62]

---

[61] Tuck, loc. cit.
[62] Ann Savours, *The Voyage of the Discovery* (Virgin Books, 1992), p. 130

Captain Williamson, now (1993) aged over 100 years, recollected the details to Ann Savours, the Polar historian, and to Dr P. van der Merwe of the National Maritime Museum, Greenwich. Williamson remembered exactly the tonality of Captain Ford's chanted orders, and he recorded them for the Museum's collection using high head–voice.[63] There is no suggestion that this was merely the voice of a very old man who was reminiscing.

The significance of, and the *raison d'être*, for traditional, or folk–music at sea is widely acknowledged, but the unique world aboard ship had no equivalent on land. Though at first sight, Army life might seem comparable with that of the sea, any parallel is not exact. No doubt traditional music had its place, but many other musical influences were at hand. Military life always offered off–duty opportunities for meeting the opposite sex and therefore segregation was not complete. This must have affected any normal use of the male high head–voice. Nevertheless, when we remember 'Colonel Newcome's' counter–tenor solo (page 112), it seems likely that, in past centuries, the male high–voice was commonly heard in mess or barrack room during informal entertainments.

It should therefore be discerned that, like many other folk–cultures elsewhere which still use the male high voice, in British folk and traditional music and in places reached by British folk culture, there was a high likelihood of the employment of the male high voice in various ways and for differing reasons.

---

[63] Related to the author in conversation with Ann Savours, 13 May 1993

APPENDIX 9 Castrati

The castrati were some of the greatest vocal artists in human history. Nevertheless, mention of them can still give rise to smirks. Even today, it is sometimes hinted that the counter-tenor's voice has the same origin. The object of this appendix is to dispel misunderstandings of this sort and to allay the confusions that arise from the historical facts that lower-voiced castrati and higher-voiced counter-tenors sang at similar pitches, and that late-eighteenth century castrati occasionally were called 'counter-tenor' in England.

Eunuchism has existed for thousands of years. The practice of castrating young boys to preserve one or more of their boyish attributes, their voice or their looks, or to create impotence in order to provide sexually 'safe' harem guardians was, if not widespread, not uncommon. The eunuchs of India, previously the protectors of harems, invariably seem to have been different; they were castrated after puberty, so Indian eunuchs of today retain their masculine voices.

The attribute of the castrati which is relevant here is the continued development of the boy's singing voice. Castrati were also variously known as 'musici', or 'evirati'; terms which seem to be euphemistic. 'Musici' was also a term given in the late eighteenth century to women mezzo-sopranos. It was borrowed from the 'evirati', presumably to suggest a brilliant and high voice.

Eunuchs were much used in antiquity as singers. The church of Byzantium employed them long before they were employed in Europe. By A.D. 1000, they seem to have sung in the churches of most Eastern countries. The practice spread to Europe and continued into Medieval times and beyond. Other than being one of the obvious results of Eastern influence, one factor which accelerated the advent of the castrati in Europe was the development of extremely complex *a capella* singing in the middle of the fifteenth century. This demanded extremely competent and proficient treble singers. Several drawbacks of using boys for this music arose, one of which was that by the time they had become expert ensemble-singers their voices were on borrowed time, but the chief of which was connected with their vocal power.

As we have seen, in Spain, where the falsettists' art was highly developed, they began to be used to supply the power and maturity needed for the new contrapuntal music. The Spanish had developed a method of greatly increasing the upward range of the male voice – higher than the usual counter-tenor – without involving the disadvantages of castration.

However, castrati did exist in Spain, and it has been argued that Spanish falsettists may have been castrati masquerading under another name. This might have been so in a few cases. At any rate, castrato-tone was considered more pleasing than that of higher falsettists. Furthermore, it was found that the vocal folds of high falsettists did not last well – the strain of such singing wore them out. With the tacit approval of Pope Clement VIII (1592–1605), the numbers and popularity of castrati increased greatly.

Late-Renaissance and Baroque audiences in churches and eventually in opera houses wanted not *voce bianca* but *voce colorata* with fire, power, excitement and novelty. Boys could not supply these qualities; falsetti could, but only to a limited extent. Castrati possessed them all.

How were castrati produced? It is common belief that the boy's testicles were removed. This is an over-simplification.

When we consider castration from our late-twentieth-century viewpoint, we should remember that many practices of previous centuries seem to us to be brutish and callous. Civil punishment for crimes was often barbaric and commonly involved maiming and branding. The death penalty was imposed for many crimes not now regarded as serious. Surgery was performed without genuine anaesthetic and with scant regard for hygiene. Strangely enough, the Church refused to countenance maiming as a punishment, yet was still one of the first institutions to use castrati and was the last to give up the practice. However, it would not condone publicly the means by which the castrati were produced. Italy, Spain, Germany and Austria were the only European countries where castration was actually perpetrated.

There were three possible methods of attaining the required results: (a) disease, (b) accident and (c) deliberate surgery. Elsa Scammell comments:

> Excuses for castration were many and various, but the most popular was the child's having been attacked there by a wild boar – evidently prevalent in 17th, 18th, and 19th century Italy. The boar did so much, and the barber surgeons would do the rest to 'save the child's life'. Of course, all this was largely manufactured as an excuse.[64]

Some diseases, such as mumps at a certain age, cause the hormones necessary for normal sexual development to be suppressed. Apart from the obvious drawbacks of such an occurrence, secondary sexual development is also arrested, including the growth of body hair and thickening of the vocal folds. Nowadays, the problem is easily remedied by injection of the necessary hormones. Indeed, in the 1950s, before such hormone treatment was widely known, Michael Howard, then director of The Renaissance Singers [London], advertised for such natural castrati to take the soprano part. Not surprisingly – for how many such sufferers happen to be singers? – he was unsuccessful. He therefore employed high falsettists.

No doubt accidental castration happens but it is surely rare. Nonetheless, accident or surgery following accident was the accepted (and acceptable) reason used for the Church to condone castrati as ecclesiastical singers. The Hierarchy was naturally averse to encouraging publicly what was, after all, the deliberate maiming of children.

Deliberate surgical castration, at about the age of ten years, was the most widely used method of producing castrati. Disease and accidents simply could not have coped with the increasing demand for them. By today's standards, the operation must have been comparatively minor, although potentially dangerous. Following administration of a drug, such as opium, the child was placed in a hot bath. The drug and heat rendered him virtually insensible. While he was in this condition, the ducts leading to the testicles were severed, so that the testicles

---

[64] private letter to the author, citing F. Haböck, *Die Kastraten und ihre Gesanskunst* (Stuttgart, Berlin and Leipzig, 1927, and Alberto de Angelis, *Domenico Mustafà* (Nicola Zanichelli, 1926)

eventually shrivelled away. Another method was to sit the boy in the bath. Decoctions of plants were added. Warm water, and pressing and bruising of the testicles with the fingers broke down their structure and prevented further growth. Actual removal of the testicles was a third method.[65]

To preserve the boy's youthful voice, the operation would have to have been carried out before the vocal folds began to thicken. It would be no use castrating a tenor or bass, and expecting him to sing treble immediately, as is the popular humorous misunderstanding. Also, it would have been useless to castrate children at random. The boy had to show some vocal aptitude first.

Despite their many claims of noble birth, most castrati came from fairly lowly families who hoped, no doubt, that eminence in their future profession would enable their sons to provide for them. Such seldom happened: only two well–known castrati came from well–to–do families – Farinelli and Caffarelli – and these may well have been operated–on as a result of accident or disease.

Apart from the parents' wishes, it was the law that, before the operation could be carried out the child himself had to desire it. In one known case, apparently, the child did request it to preserve his voice, of which he was very proud. It is said that four thousand boys were castrated in Italy annually between the years 1600 and 1800.

Just before or just after his operation, the young castrato would have been apprenticed to a singing master or sent to one of the conservatorios or singing schools which graced many Italian cities. Though they were originally set up as charitable institutions for the education and upbringing of children, by the middle of the seventeenth century they were music schools pure and simple. To boost insufficient funds, pupils were often hired out by the conservatories for public or private musical events (in the same way as major English choirs were used in Tudor England).

The life of castrati in conservatorios was a little less spartan than that of the other pupils. They had better food, warmer living accommodation, and better practice facilities. Yet they do not seem to have had a happy life. Their physical condition would have set them apart from the other students and encouraged spiteful ragging. Their preferential treatment would have caused resentment. Though ordinary pupils may have been thrown out for idleness or misbehaviour, they seldom ran away, as castrati were prone to do. The inference is obvious.

Provided his voice came up to expectation, the young castrato would make his début in his mid–to–late teenage years at an opera house, usually in a female rôle to begin with. This suited his youthful appearance and vocal quality. It is a convincing suggestion that, in the mature, highly–developed treble or boy soprano, such as the superb, deservedly much–recorded Ernest Lough in the 1920s, Aled Jones, or the boy–alto John Hahessy (recorded almost a generation before Jones) whose effective voice range probably resembled the young castrato's chest–register, we hear the quality and voice–range of the young castrato[66] or indeed the young contralto–castrato.

From then on, if his acting ability and voice appealed to the cognoscenti, and provided he did not become too gawky, obese, or suffer from over–long legs or arms (a common problem), the young castrato would be accorded all the trappings of stardom, very much in the modern

---

[65] See Robert Sambler, *Eunuchism Display'd* (London, 1718), an English translation of Charles Ancillon, *Traité des Eunuques* (Amsterdam, 1707)

[66] Hahessy's 1961 recording of Britten's *Abraham and Isaac (Canticle II)*, is now on CD: London 425 716–2 LM

idiom. If he failed to make the grade as an actor, he could always find himself employment as a church singer. Nevertheless, the production of castrati for ecclesiastical choirs not only antedated, but continued to be largely independent of, that for the operatic stage. Not until the eighteenth century, when castrati dominated opera throughout Europe, did churches give shelter and employment to what Burney called 'the refuse of the opera houses'. It has been suggested recently that, by the beginning of the eighteenth century, nearly three-quarters of all male solo singers were castrati.

The success of the castrati depended to some extent on their stage presence. They often had extraordinary chest development. Their unique vocal organs, lung capacity and control were responsible for their amazing powers.

In the seventeenth and eighteenth centuries, though other countries had their own native traditions of musical drama, Italy led the field. She boasted the highest form of operatic art and arguably still does. A singer's chances of employment were much higher there than elsewhere.

Other than in Italy (but certainly there, in the early days of operatic development) there was a tendency for opera to be exclusively a diversion for nobility and the court. It was confined, therefore, to prominent cities. As a result, openings for singers would have been more limited. Like soloists today, distinguished Italian castrati were able to tour other countries, to give opera-lovers there the thrill of hearing unsurpassable voices and technique.

Castrati sang with extreme virtuosity but little if any emotion, according to Tosi.[67] They were the first singer-teachers of the voice. Their influence as excellent vocal pedagogues lasted well into the nineteenth century and even, in a few cases, to the twentieth.

Sending singers abroad was also a matter of national pride and rivalry. Charles II sent the English counter-tenor, John Abell, to Italy to be trained in the Italian style and, probably, to show the Italians that other nations possessed good voices, too! Abell would have been a high counter-tenor, with the ability to sing easily to the top of, and beyond, the G-clef treble stave. It has been suggested that he may have been a castrato, but there seems little evidence to support the theory. Despite the Champernowne rumour, England subscribed only late to the use of (imported) castrato celebrities, relying on the home-grown counter-tenor for high parts in opera and stage music, and first on boys, then on women, for feminine rôles, and boys for the treble in church music.

William Shakespeare appreciated the humorous possibilities of a reference to eunuchoid singing:[68]

Cleopatra:	Give me some music – music, moody food
	Of us that trade in love.
All:	The music ho!
	(Enter Mardian the Eunuch)
Cleopatra:	Let it alone; let's to billiards.

That Cleopatra preferred billiards to the singing of a castrato is not the only possible meaning here.

Despite popular misconceptions, castration did not lessen or necessarily alter their sexual urges. Stories of the amorous intrigues of castrati with their well-born female fans are legion,

---

[67] Tosi, *Opinioni de' Cantori Antichi e Moderni* (1723; modern edn, Stainer & Bell, 1987)
[68] *Antony & Cleopatra*, act II, sc. IV

and differ little from the behaviour of 'stars' through the centuries, though in the case of castrati, women no doubt found them attractive precisely because they could toy with them but not become pregnant.

On the other hand, as Elsa Scammell writes, 'Medical evidence exists to suggest that some castrati might well have had difficulty in penetration and orgasm. Castrati differed from one another as much as other men do. Some might have had 'infantile' erections and 'dry' orgasms.'[69] Of course, they were sterile; though rumours abide that mistakes were made and that castration, in rare cases, was not total, and that at least one 'castrato' fathered a child.

Castration neither shortened nor lengthened their careers, but castrati had to protect their voices, like all singers. Pacchierotti took care of his throat by wearing a scarf at all times, according to Fanny Burney, Dr Burney's daughter. Such precautions in varied climates, plus the comfort bought with money, would have given them a better than average life–span, vocally and in actuality.

A decline in the use of castrati in opera began towards the end of the eighteenth century. The Italian musical climate of the 1790s had degenerated into frivolity and the Napoleonic invasion, with its political upheavals, caused fashions to change. This is the accepted perception. Nevertheless, there were plenty of castrati available for a new opera to be per- formed at the National Theatre at Prague for the coronation of Leopold II as King of Bohemia in 1791:

> I shall be given and assigned six thousand florins, or six thousand five hundred if the castrato Marchesi be engaged.
> I obligate myself to engage a first castrato, of leading quality, such as for example Marchesini [Marchesi], or Rubinelli, or Crescentini, or Violani, or another, but always of leading quality.[70]

With the weakening of the conservatorios, a new type of composer (notably Rossini, later) had little trouble in setting new trends in which castrati played a lesser part. By the first few decades of the nineteenth century, secular castrati were mostly finished, although a few, Velluti and Pergetti for example, lingered a little longer.

Velluti had sung with many famous singers, including Maria Malibran (née Garcia). He appeared with her in Meyerbeer's *Il Crociato in Egitto* in 1825. He was the first castrato to appear in London for about twenty–five years. A reviewer wrote that his voice '... sounded like a peacock's scream or a superannuated lady scolding her servants'.[71] Though he was not popular at first, the public seems to have warmed to him, and he spent a few years there. He last appeared in London in 1829 to a mixed reception. Pergetti appeared twice in 1844, on the concert stage only. He was never asked back.

Because his was a well–established ecclesiastical voice, the castrato continued in employ- ment in some Italian churches, and notably the Capella Sistina, for much longer. The musical foundation of the Sistina is the Pope's personal choir. In the nineteenth century, it comprised thirty–two singers: eight male sopranos, eight male contraltos, eight tenors and eight basses. The alto part appears to have been populated by contralto–tenors (and castrati–contraltos?).

---

[69] Elsa Scammell, in letter to the author, July 1990

[70] H. C. Robbins Landon, *1791, Mozart's Last Year* (Thames & Hudson, 1988; Flamingo, 1990), p. 88

[71] *The Times*, 1 July 1825

As the century wore on, high falsetti seem to have been used to replace castrati, who were becoming difficult to obtain. In any case, Pope Leo XIII is said to have banned them from the Sistina in 1878, though no written record of this has been discovered. As before, Pope and Church seem to have said one thing and done another, because the castrati continued. One interpretation is that no new castrati were to be 'made' or admitted. Pope Pius X was to continue his predecessor's anti–castrato campaign.

Haböck disliked the practice of replacing castrati with falsetti. He was certainly a champion of the castrati; he conceived a plan for initiating a 'Farinelli revival' in 1914. He hoped to collect the remaining evirati so as to have them sing the arias in which the legendary Farinelli had excelled. Their ages and fading powers, and the first world war, put an end to that idea.[72] Haböck criticized falsetti because they used chest–voice for their lower notes (in which case, says Jacobs, they should be called high counter–tenors), but it is well known that castrati used their chest–voices too, so Haböck's comment is rather puzzling.

Domenico Mustafà (1829–1912), a true coloratura castrato with great vocal control, was one of the last eunuch sopranos to be appointed to the Sistina. He was made choir–director in 1860 by Pius IX. Mustafà directed the Papal Music until 1895. He was a noted composer of church music, and a teacher. He taught the celebrated operatic diva, Madame Emma Calvé (1858–1942), how to find the 'fourth voice'. Mustafà recommended that she practise every day for ten years with her mouth shut (a method which has affinity with Ernest George White's theories, methodology, writing on and teaching Sinus Tone Production from the early years of the twentieth century); this was to achieve the eerie, sexless, disembodied notes which were Mustafà's speciality. Calvé claimed to have accomplished this technique in three years.

Apparently, Mustafà was wanted by Wagner for the rôle of Klingsor, the emasculated sorcerer, in *Parsifal* but, for some reason, nothing came of the proposal.

A castrato–phobe, Perosi, succeeded Mustafà in 1895. Perosi – Don Lorenzo (later Monsignor), Maestro di Capella at St Mark's, Venice – was sent to Rome by the then Patriarch of St Mark's, Guiseppe Sarto (later Pope Pius X and, later still, Saint Pius X). Perosi was Mustafà's nominee – at first. Despite this, with the help of Leo XIII and his successor Pius X, Perosi tried to have the remaining castrati pensioned off; there were still three of them, besides the ageing Mustafà. He wished to reform the Sistina, and return to the old style. He did not succeed, but he did re–introduce boys (his 'ragazzi') to the top line. However, the castrati remained until old age forced them into retirement.

During Perosi's first, short incumbency, the soprano line consisted of ageing castrati and boys and possibly even ageing high falsetti. He would never have actually admitted falsetti, probably regarding them as too similar to the castrati he wished to banish. (Of course, there was no chance of women being allowed to replace castrati, or indeed falsetti. They were still forbidden to sing in Roman Catholic churches at that date.) Perosi was noted for his compositions, and was recalled, as an old man, to conduct the Sistine Choir in 1947!

The last of the Papal castrati was Alessandro Moreschi (1858–1922) who became director of the Sistine Choir in 1902. He followed Perosi upon his resignation, which was probably due to ill health. Moreschi himself retired in 1913. His voice may still be heard on gramophone records made from 1902 to 1904. They provide us with the only audible link with those strange artists of another age. Despite the poor quality of his recordings which were certainly made when he was past his best (as early as 1914 his highest note was only G), he seems to

---

[72] Elsa Scammell, broadcast talk on the castrati: 'Angel Voices', BBC Radio 3, 19 May 1978

have once possessed traditional castrato vocal prowess. His records also demonstrate that the unemotional style and quality associated with castrato singing had become influenced to some extent by the demands of the Romantic age.

Haböck considered that Moreschi had a voice like a crystal. He could sing – probably – to E6: a note which is the high point in the exacting rôle of the Seraph in Beethoven's oratorio *The Mount of Olives*. The Seraph's aria has an obligatory D6 above the stave but an alternative high C6 for the high E6. (Farinelli was credited with singing a high F6.) Moreschi sang this aria at the age of twenty–six, in 1884. He was destined to sing it at the funeral of two kings. It was his showpiece.

Like counter–tenors in England at that time, Moreschi and the few other surviving castrati sang in such places as university drawing rooms and select clubs, in addition to the Sistina. They did not appear on the public concert platform, or the stage, by this time.

Seventeen of Moreschi's original recordings have been re–processed, with some success, and re–issued recently on a long–playing record, and on compact disc,[73] with valuable sleeve and insert notes.

It is not always realised that several Sistine castrati were photographed. The magazine, *Opera Fanatic*,[74] published three photographs from the Robert Connolly Collection. Two are of Moreschi. In one, he is shown standing, and looks extremely short. It is unlikely that he could have enjoyed an operatic career at the height of the castrato–age. There was also a group photograph which is labelled as including no less than four castrati. One is bald, and has a moustache; these attributes seem surprising on two counts, because castrati are not normally associated with cranial hair–loss or the growth of other bodily hair. Was the original labelling of the photographs correct?

We have first–hand descriptions of some of the great castrati. These not only provide us with musical and physical aspects; there is also the sexual ambiguity noticed by Casanova in a café:

> An abbé with an attractive face walked in. At the appearance of his hips, I took him for a girl in disguise, and I said so to the abbé Gama; but the latter told me that it was Beppino della Mamana, a famous castrato. The abbé called him over, and told him, laughing, that I had taken him for a girl. The impudent creature, looked fixedly at me, told me that if I liked he would prove that I was right, or that I was wrong.[75]

As a sexual expert, Casanova was clearly fascinated by these 'feminine men'. He commented on one when visiting Rome in 1762:

> We went to the Aliberti theatre, where the castrato who took the prima donna's rôle attracted all the town. He was the complaisant favourite, the mignon, of Cardinal Borghese, and supped every evening tête–a–tête with His Eminence.

---

[73] 'The Last Castrato', Pearl Opal, LP 823 and CD 9825, with insert notes by Elsa Scammell

[74] *Opera Fanatic*, 1989, no. 3, pp. 6 & 7

[75] Giacomo Casanova, *History of my Life*, translated from French, W. R. Trask (Longman, 1967–8), vol. 1

In a well–made corset, he had the waist of a nymph, and, what was almost incredible, his breast was in no way inferior, either in form or in beauty, to any woman's; and it was above all by this means that the monster made such ravages. Though one knew the negative nature of this unfortunate, curiosity made one glance at his chest, and an inexpressible charm acted upon one, so that you were madly in love before you realised it. To resist the temptation, or not to feel it, one would have had to be cold and earthbound as a German. When he walked about the stage during the ritornello of the aria he was to sing, his step was majestic and at the same time voluptuous; and when he favoured the boxes with his glances, the tender and modest rolling of his black eyes brought a ravishment to the heart. It was obvious that he hoped to inspire the love of those who liked him as a man, and probably would not have done so as a woman.[76]

We also have some individual eye–witness descriptions of probably the greatest castrato, Farinelli (1705–1782) whose real name was Carlo Broschi. The castrati must have been among the very finest singers of all time and Farinelli was the best even of this exalted band. Mancini, the eighteenth–century singing teacher, wrote of him:

His voice was thought a marvel, because it was so perfect, so powerful, so sonorous and so rich in its extent, both in the high and low parts of the register, that its equal has never been heard in our times. He was, moreover, endowed with a creative genius which inspired him with embellishments so new and so astonishing that no one was able to imitate them. The art of taking and keeping the breath so softly and easily that no one could perceive it began and died with him. The qualities in which he excelled were the evenness of his voice, the art of swelling its sound, the portamento, the union of registers, a surprising agility, a graceful and pathetic style, and a shake as admirable as it was rare. There was no branch of the art which he did not carry to the highest pitch of perfection ...[77]

England's own ubiquitous music critic, Dr Burney, heard him when the singer was only seventeen years of age, in 1722:

During the run of an opera, there was struggle every night between him and a famous player on the trumpet, in a song accompanied by that instrument; this, at first, seemed amicable and merely sportive, till the audience began to interest themselves in the contest, and to take different sides; after severally swelling a note, in which each manifested the power of his lungs, and tried to rival the other in brilliancy and force, they had both a swell and shake together, by thirds, which was continued so long, while the audience eagerly awaited the event, that both seemed to be exhausted; and, in fact, the trumpeter, wholly spent, gave it up, thinking, however, his antagonist as much tired as himself, and that it would be a drawn battle; when Farinelli, with a

---

[76] Ibid, vol. 7
[77] G. B. Mancini, *Pensieri e Riflessioni Pratichi sopra il Canto Figurato* (Vienna, 1774)

smile on his countenance, shewing he had only been sporting with him all the time, broke out all at once in the same breath, with fresh vigour, and not only swelled and shook the note, but ran the most rapid and difficult divisions, and was at last silenced only by the acclamation of the audience. From this period may be dated that superiority which he ever maintained over all his contemporaries.[78]

Burney heard him again in England in 1734:

Every one knows who heard, or has heard of him, what an effect his surprising talents had upon the audience: it was ecstasy! rapture! enchantment! In the famous air 'Son qual Nave', which was composed by his brother, the first note he sung was taken with such delicacy, swelled by minute degrees to such an amazing volume, and afterwards diminished in the same manner, that it was applauded for full five minutes. He afterwards set off with such brilliancy and rapidity of execution, that it was difficult for the violins of those days to keep pace with him. In short, he was to all other singers as superior as the famous horse Childers was to all other running–horses; but it was not only in speed, he had now every excellence of every great singer united. In his voice, strength, sweetness, and compass; in his style, the tender, the grateful, and the rapid. He possessed such powers as never met before, or since, in any one human being; powers that were irresistible, and which must subdue every hearer; the learned and the ignorant, the friend and the foe.[79]

Burney's, and other eye–witness descriptions, help us to appreciate the reactions of their audiences to the castrato. The cry 'eviva il coltello' ('long live the knife') went up from enraptured audiences after brilliant performances by evirati.

It is not always realised that castrati used much the same singing technique as other singers, incorporating chest– and head–voices. By head–voice is meant falsetto – pure head–voice, produced properly. The difference between castrati and other singers concerned tonal quality, pitch, and power. Moreschi's optimum range seems to have been from B3 to B5. René Jacobs has suggested that it consisted of three overlapping registers, B3 to B4, D4 to D5 and D5 to B5.

Senesino and Guadagni were famous for sonorous chest–tones, which they combined with a truly ringing, brilliant falsetto. Haböck called their middle tones (upper–chest or *voix mixte*?) 'tenoral'.[80]

A contemporary of the castrati wrote:

Their timbre is as clear and piercing as that of choirboys, and much more powerful; they appear to sing an octave above the natural voice of women. Their voices have always something dry and harsh, quite different from the

---

[78] Charles Burney, *A General History of Music* (London, 1789; reprinted Dover Publications, 1957), vol. 2

[79] Ibid.

[80] Haböck, op. cit., p. 210

youthful softness of women; but they are brilliant, light, full of sparkle, very loud, and with a very wide range.[81]

We should remember that castrati varied in their vocal ranges and qualities, like other singers.

   Castration involved risks, even death, to a boy. Sometimes, the vocal results were mediocre and provided the singer with a voice no better than a very ordinary falsetto, at the price of permanent emasculation.

   Various representations of castrati have survived. William Hogarth (1697–1764) included one in his series *Marriage à la Mode*: 'The Countess's Morning Levée'.[82]

   Hogarth's biting observation depicts the castrato in the left foreground: huge, over–weight, dandified; he is half–reclining while singing from a part–book. A flautist accompanies him. A lady seems to be swooning. Hogarth, concerned to tell his story, never lost an opportunity to caricature the excesses, artificialities and crudities of his age, of which the castrato was an integral part. One was also included in Hogarth's *The Rake's Progress*; he is thought to be Farinelli.

---

[81] Quoted by Michael and Mollie Hardwick, *A Singularity of Voice* (Proteus, 1980), pp. 84–5
[82] National Gallery, London

It is hoped that this brief discussion of castrati will have explained away any lingering misunderstanding of the difference between the counter–tenor and eunuchoid voices.

Elsa Scammell has researched the castrato in absorbing detail and is preparing a major book on the subject: *Angel Voices*, to be published by Duckworth.

From time to time, novels appear which not only help understanding of a vanished historical subject but also form part of the 'entering in' approach to be discussed in another volume. The castrato has attracted a number of novelists, whose work is often vividly perceptive and excellently researched.[83]

We conclude with a witty indication of the popularity of many of the eighteenth–century castrati with the ladies:

The Ladies' Lamentation for ye Loss of Senesino

As musing I rang'd in the Meads all alone.
   A beautifull Creature was making her Moan,
Oh! the Tears they did trickle full fast from her Eyes,
   And she pierc'd both the Air and my Heart with her Cries.

I gently requested the Cause of her moan,
   She told me her sweet Senesino was flown,
And in that sad Posture she'd ever remain.
   Unless the dear Charmer would come back again.

Why who is this Mortal so cruel, said I,
   That draws such a stream from so lovely an Eye,
To beauty so blooming what <u>Man</u> can be blind,
   To passion so tender, what Monster unkind.

'Tis neither for Man, nor for Woman said she,
   That thus in Lamenting I water the Lee,
My Warbler Celestial, Sweet Darling of fame,
   Is a shadow of Something, a Sex Without Name.

Perhaps 'tis some Linnet, some Blackbird, said I,
   Perhaps 'tis your Lark, that has soar'd to the Sky;
Come dry up your Tears, and abandon your grief,
   I'll bring you another to give you relief.

No linnett, no Blackbird, no Skylark, said she,
   But one much more tunefull, by far than all three,
My sweet Senesino for whom thus I cry,
   Is sweeter than all the wing'd Songster's that fly.

---

[83] For example: Lawrence Goldman, *The Castrato* (John Day Co., New York, 1973); Anne or Annie Rice, *Cry to Heaven* (Alfred A. Knopf, New York, 1982); Kingsley Amis, *The Alteration* (Jonathan Cape Ltd., 1971)

Adieu Farinelli, Cuzzoni, Likewise,
  Whom Stars and whom Garters extol to the skies,
Adieu to the Opera, adieu to the Ball,
  My darling is gone, a Fig for them all.

From *The Musical Entertainer*, London, 1738.[84]

---

[84] Quoted from letter to present author from Susan Butt, 1987. See also Fiske, op. cit., p. 154, for a similar but less witty poem about the loss of Farinelli.

APPENDIX 10 A King's Musician for Lute and Voice, John Abell (1652/3–1724)

By Dr HENRY GEORGE FARMER

"Celebrated for his fine alto voice and skill on the lute".
—E. F. Rimbault:
The Old Cheque Book of the Chapel Royl (1872)

How it came about that Scotland was bereft of music in the Reforming days of 1560 *et seq.* has already been related at length.[1] Briefly, it was due to the Scots interpretation of Calvinistic doctrines that florid music in church praise was disturbing to Christian worship. Alas! the Reforming brethren in the "North Countrie" went further still in prohibition and took the view, as did many others, that music in secular life was inimical to Christian morality. This condemnation of secular music found rigid acceptance only for a generation, but its influence was far-reaching, for even when the Reforming zeal had spent its force, music as a profession was long suspect in Scotland, as the late Sir John McEwen experienced. As a result of this *anathema*, Scottish musicians of any eminence were rare in the seventeenth century. That being so, it seems rather desirable that when one does appear to have made his mark in that era some space ought to be accorded him, more especially when so little is known about him, and certainly when that "little" is, in itself, of an informative and an entertaining character.

Although for many a year he has been claimed as an Englishman, John Abell (1652/3-1724) is a case in point. It may be perfectly true that his name was made in England, a predicament which has been common to most of the famed Scottish musicians (from Robert Johnson in the sixteenth century to Sir John McEwen in the twentieth), but both his name and his birth must be claimed for Scotland. Sir Samuel Forbes of Foveran (1653-1717), in his *Description of Aberdeenshire* (1716-17), says:

> Music here is much in vogue, and many citizens sing charmingly. The well known Abel was a native of this place, and his kindred are known by the name of Eball; and, it is said, there are others [of the family] as good as he.

We are generally told in the biographies that Abell was educated as a chorister in the English Chapel Royal, but there is no evidence

---

[1] Farmer, *A History of Music in Scotland*, Part IV (Hinrichsen, 1947).

of this in any of the state papers nor in *The Old Cheque Book of the Chapel Royal* (1872) edited by Rimbault. On the other hand, although there is no evidence, it is very likely that Abell was educated at the Aberdeen Sang School under Thomas Davidson, who flourished there from 1640 to 1675. In any case, the first reference to Abell in England is given in *The Old Cheque Book of the Chapel Royal* which reads as follows:

> Mr John Abell sworn Gent of his Maties Chappell extraordinary the first of May 1679.

By May 31, a vacancy had occurred which gave the opportunity to promote Abell from "extraordinary" to "ordinary", as the following lines in Lafontaine's *King's Musick* (1909) indicate:

> Warrant to swear John Abell as musician for the private music of his Majesty [Charles II] in ordinary, with fee, in the place of Anthony Roberts, deceased [May 9, 1679]. Patent for a grant for £40 yearly as wages, dated 5 June, 1679.

Roberts was one of the King's musicians included under "Lutes and Voices", and Abell may have been appointed to serve in the two capacities. We know from the *Angliae Notitia* (1679), of Edward Chamberlain, exactly of what the "King's Musick" consisted:

> Musicians in Ordinary—sixty-two. . . . Trumpeters in Ordinary and Kettledrummers—in all fifteen. . . . Drummers and Fifes—Seven. . . . Twenty Gentlemen, commonly called Clerks of the Chappel . . . perform in the Chappel the office of Divine Service in . . . Singing, &c. One of these being well skilled in Musick, is chosen Master of the Children. . . . Three others of the said Clerks are chosen to be Organists, to whom they are joyned upon Sundayes, Collar-days, and other Holy-dayes, a consort of the King's Musick, to make the Chappel-Musick more full and compleat.

This, then, was the world of music into which Abell entered.

Charles II so "admired his singing", as Hawkins tells us, that he sent Abell to Italy in 1680 for further study or, as old Sir John has it, "in order to show the Italians what good voices were produced in England". The latter, however, held the opinion that the visit to Italy was merely a project which did not materialize owing to a certain "Mr Gosling" of the Chapel Royal, who was to have accompanied Abell, being "unwilling to go". There are good reasons for assuming that Hawkins may have been misinformed in that affair, because Evelyn, the famous diarist, confirms the Italian visit.

According to the *Calendar of Treasury Books*, Abell is marked down for £40 per annum in July 1681, and was also in receipt of other payments during that year, such as £62 odd from sundry funds. On December 20, 1681, there is the following entry in the Lord Chamberlain's papers:

> John Abell appointed musician for the lute and voice in the place of Alphonso March, deceased.
> John Abell appointed musician for the violin in the place of Richard Dornye, deceased.

These entries may appear confusing to the reader, more especially when one looks further into the Lord Chamberlain's papers at that time. Yet pluralities were quite common in those days, and it may have been that he held both posts, a conclusion which later entries seem to justify. Perhaps these appointments mark Abell's return to England. In any case, John Evelyn makes this remark under the date January 27, 1682:

> After the supper came in the famous treble, Mr Abel, newly returned from Italy. I never heard a more excellent voice, and would have sworn it had been a woman's, it was so high and so well and skilfully managed, being accompanied by Signor Francisco on the harpsichord.

The "siller" that was poured into Abell's lap (and into that of others for that matter) shows pretty well how much he was appreciated. In the year 1682 his salary was still £40 per annum, but there is mention of £90 being paid him out of "hearthmoney". That he held pluralities in 1683 and 1684 seems quite likely, since in the latter year he was paid £40 for one post, £40 for another, and £20 for a third. These salaries, together with other fees, such as those mentioned above, plus subsistence allowances and riding charges, placed Abell in quite a comfortable position. The Chapel Royal brought him £60 a year in 1687 and £100 in 1688. Meanwhile there were other happenings which call for notice.

It is stated that Abell received the Mus. Bac. degree from Cambridge University in 1684, although details of this are lacking. Unfortunately the University records at that date are not good, and Mr R. T. Dart, the Secretary of the Faculty Board of Music, informs me that "no trace of Abell's college can be found and no record of matriculation or other academic prowess seems to have survived. The only fact ascertainable about his University career is that he graduated Mus. Bac. in 1684".

Two years later Abell married. If data concerning his entry into the collegiate *baccalaureate* are wanting, there is ample evidence of his exit from this bachelorship, since it created no end of pother and gossip. His marriage took place, seemingly, in December 1685, and the lady of his choice (although in truth it appears to have been the reverse situation) was Lady Frances, the sister of Lord Banbury. The event scandalized the smart set of those days and was the chief feature of tittle-tattle, as letters in the Rutland manuscripts reveal. One of these, from Peregrine Bertie to the Countess of Rutland, dated January 1, 1686, reads thus:

> I suppose your Ladyship has already heard of my Lady Frances Abell's marriage, at which my Lady Banbury and my Lady Catherine are extremely disturbed, but for my Lady Anne Littleton, she was pleased that night at my Lord Berkeley's ball.

Why such an affair as this should have caused so much trouble and anxiety seems extremely odd at first sight. Yet when we view the picture a little closer we begin to understand why the colours were laid on so heavily. Banbury himself was already sufficiently harassed and vexed over the House of Lords' decision not to recognize him as a peer owing to the disputed legitimacy of his father. On the top of this came the news that his sister Frances had married a mere "singer". A letter from the Hon. Bridget Noel to her sister the Countess of Rutland is sufficiently gossipy to be extracted :

> Lord Banbury's sister, Lady Francis, is married to Abell, the singing master ; her brother is extremely concerned at it. As soon as Lord Banbury knew of it, he put her out of the house. She was married that night that the company was there, which was a Tuesday [December 29, 1685], and on Wednesday night my Lady Exeter and my Lord Exeter and my brothers and sister and Lord Banbury and Lady Frances and Sir Mortan and his Lady supped at Mr King's in the Great Room where the musick plays of public days, and I could not perceive anything of love between them [Lady Frances and Abell], for *she courted my brothers as much as ever she used to do.*

It would seem from this letter that "courting" was very much in the blood of the Banburys. Still, the newly wedded pair were happy enough together, and certainly under the new king, James II (1685-88), Abell stood high in favour, a circumstance which would have enabled him to maintain his wife in a fair degree of comfort.

At James the Second's accession, Abell, with others, was sworn as one of "his Majesty's private musicians in ordinary with fee and salary" on August 31, 1685, and on October 18, 1686, we read of him being paid £10 "for a guitar by him bought for his Majesty's service in his bedchamber". Abell was a Romanist and so came in closer contact with James than those who were not. In November 1688, with a "Mr Petley", he was one of two of the Chapel Royal who were "appointed to attend his Majesty in his progresses". The high social position and wealth attained by Abell is best illustrated by the aquatic entertainment which he arranged earlier in that year in honour of the birth of the Prince of Wales (the Old Pretender). It has been described :

> Mr Abel, the celebrated Musician, and one of the Royal Band, entertained the publick, and demonstrated his loyalty on the evening of the 18th June 1688, by the performance of an aquatic concert. The barge prepared for this purpose was richly decorated, and illuminated by numerous torches. The musick was composed expressly for the occasion by Signor Fede, Master of the Chapel Royal, and the performers, vocal and instrumental, amounted to one hundred and thirty, selected as the greatest proficients in the science. . . . The first performance took place facing Whitehall, and the second opposite Somerset House where the Queen Dowager then resided.
>
> Great numbers of barges and boats were assembled, and each having flambeaux on board, the scene was extremely brilliant and pleasing. The music being ended, all the nobility and company that were upon the water gave three shouts to express their joy and satisfaction ; and all the gentlemen of the musick went to Mr Abell's house, which was nobly illuminated and honoured with the presence of a great many of the nobility ; out of whose windows hung a fine machine full of lights which drew thither a vast concourse of people. The entertainment lasted till three of the clock the next morning, the musick playing and the trumpets sounding all the while, the whole concluding with the health of their Majesties, the Prince of Wales, and all the Royal Family.

Some idea of the salaries, fees and other emoluments of Abell has already been mooted. That there was still another source of income is to be found in John Y. Akerman's *Moneys Received and*

Paid for Secret Services of Charles II and James II (London, 1851), where we see that from December 1679 until October 1688, Abell received nine payments totalling £770 (cf. Grove, which copies Rimbault). How much of this was for "secret service" is doubtful, for although one payment was to cover his charges for a "journey to Scotland" in 1684 and another to defray expenses for a "journey to Italy" in 1684, most of the other payments are marked "Bounty".

However, Abell was soon to fall from his high estate. Six months after his splendid aquatic entertainment the tempestuous "Protestant wind" which blew William of Orange to the shores of Britain also drove James II and his favoured minstrel John Abell out of the country. For the greater part of ten years Abell lived as a wandering minstrel in France, Germany, Holland and Poland, whilst his wife, whom he had to leave in England, had later to depend to some extent on Royal charity. We know this from the *Calendar of Treasury Books* where, in 1695, a pension of £3 17s. 0d. is given "Mrs Abell" by the Queen, although by 1702 "Mrs Fran[ces] Abell" was being paid £7 14s. 0d. a year plus arrears of £15 odd.

John Abell himself, according to the *Calendar of State Papers* (*Domestic*), left for France on December 11, 1688, although the Lord Chamberlain's papers show that he received arrears of salary —£30—on March 25, 1689. Sir John Hawkins, in his useful *History of Music* (1776), tells us a little of the wanderings of this great virtuoso on the Continent:

> [Abell] distinguished himself by singing in public . . . and, . . . acquiring considerable sums of money, he lived profusely, and affected the expense of a man of quality, moving about in an equipage of his own, though at intervals he was so reduced as to be obliged to travel, with his lute slung at his back, through whole provinces. In rambling he got as far as Poland: and upon his arrival at Warsaw, the king having notice of it, sent for him to his court. Abell made some slight excuse to evade going, but upon being told that he had everything to fear from the king's resentment, he made an apology, and received a command to attend the next day. Upon his arrival at the palace, he was seated in a chair in the middle of a spacious hall, and immediately drawn up to a great height; presently the king with his attendants appeared in the gallery opposite to him, and at the same instant a number of wild bears were turned in; the king then bade him choose whether he would sing or be let down among the bears: Abell chose the former, and declared afterwards that he never sang so well in his life.

Further information concerning his life on the Continent is to be found in *Letters from the Dead to the Living* (1708) by Thomas Brown, and in some manuscript notes by James Cressett, Envoy Extraordinary to the Elector of Brunswick-Lunenburg, in the British Museum. These notes are contained in a copy of Abell's songs (1701) which once belonged to Julian Marshall, on the fly-leaf of which we read the following:

> Abell's *Songs*—1701—rare, with some [other music] added which appeared singly, and a portion of a letter (1699) from Mr Cresset, our

resident at Hanover, containing some statements regarding Abell. And another—This appears to be a fly-leaf from one of the letters of James Cresset, preserved in the Br. Museum. I offered Mr Bond, sometime ago, to restore it, but he declined my offer. He was then Keeper of the MSS. The details concerning Abell are curious. 1882.   J.M.

According to Mr F. Geoffrey Rendall of the British Museum, the date—October 17, 1699—on the letter of Cressett is, without doubt, in the handwriting of the period—1699—but the remainder of the letter, in a smaller script, would appear to be in a later hand. One of these notes, dated July 12, 1695 [sic] reads: "Abel the Musician who is very poor, and comes to sing and beg in these courts, is gone to Hanover to offer his services". Another, dated July 15, says: "Abel awaits the Princesses at Hannover". On September 3 we are informed that "Abel has been to Berlin, but is come back as far as Brunswick, . . . though he is tempted to stay the Carnival at Hanover, and is offered a considerable sum". September 6 contains this report: " Abel is now with me, and his Catholicity does not hinder him from singing Victoria for us". This latter probably refers to Abell's visit to Loo when the rejoicings at the capture of Namur were at their height. October 9 indicates that the "Harmonious Vagabond Abel is now here" and tells his friends that "he will hasten to England". Cressett writes that Abell "maintains the character of the *Vertuosa Canaglia*".

As early as 1696, Daniel Purcell, who was just beginning to make his name as a composer of stage music, offered Abell £500 a year to return to England. The latter did not, or could not, accept. Perhaps he still considered himself a political exile. In 1698, however, whilst at Aix-la-Chapelle, Abell offered to return for £400 a year if his debts were paid. Seemingly he had already made his peace with William III, since he was acting as intendant at Kassel during 1698-99, and indeed the official licence permitting his return to England is dated April 15, 1698, although his position at Kassel apparently prevented him from taking immediate advantage of it. That he had not returned by January 1699 is evident from an entry in the *Calendar of State Papers (Domestic)*. He returned to England in 1700, where, as Rimbault says, he "occupied a prominent position on the stage". Congreve (*Literary Relics*, 1792) makes reference to his public appearances. In a letter dated December 10, 1700, he says:

> Abell is here: has a cold at present, and is always whimsical, so that when he will sing or not upon the stage are things very disputable, but he certainly sings beyond all creatures upon earth, and I have heard him very often both abroad and since he came over.

That Abell was known as a composer when he was a member of the "King's Musick" in the "eighties" of the previous century is evident from two manuscript copies of his song "High states and honors" in the British Museum. During his sojourn on the Continent in the next decade he appears to have published a work entitled *Les airs d'Abell pour le concert Duole* (Etienne Roger, Amsterdam), although no exemplar of this seems to have survived. Settled again in England, he issued *A Collection of Songs in Several Languages* (London, 1701), which he dedicated in most fulsome flattery to King William III. The two pages devoted to the dedication reveal Abell in a new light. He thanks the king for "Favours Abroad", probably his political appointment or "secret services", and for the "Great Clemency" shown in permitting his return to his native land. Abell also mentions that some of the songs in the volume his Majesty had been "so Gracious as to hear . . . both in Holland and on my return Home", and Abell hoped therefore that "Royal Favour and Protection" would follow. In all this Abell was only doing what was right and proper, although the remainder of his dedication is a most flagrant piece of hypocrisy.

Abell then turned to his fellow-countrymen in another volume entitled *A Collection of Songs in English* (London, 1701). Here also he sought to gain their good opinion by addressing them in verse:

> To ALL LOVERS OF MUSIC
>
> After a twelve years' industry and toil,
> Abell, at last, has reach'd his native soil,
> And hopes so long an absence may prepare
> This audience to be kind as it is fair.
> Not that he vainly boasts of bringing home
> The spoils of France, of Italy, and Rome,
> Or thinks to please the judges of the town,
> From any other climate than his own;
> But humbly begs, since foreigners could raise
> Your admiration, and receive your praise,
> Since soft *Fideli* could your passions move,
> And fortunate *Clemente* gain your love,
> That he with some advantage may appear,
> And, being English, please an English ear.

It was indeed fortunate that the above was not addressed "To all Lovers of Poetry"!

In 1702 was published "Ye brave Boys and Tars", a ballad "for the encouragement of soldiers and seamen to the service of His Majesty". It was set to the music of "The Duke of Ormonde's March", a work probably by Abell, which was extremely popular. In the same year he composed "Aloud proclaim the cheerful sound: A Song on Queen Ann's Coronation" (London, 1702), the words being by Nahum Tate of *Psalms* fame. When Abell's *Choice Collection of Italian Ayres . . . Sung to the Nobility and Gentry in the North of England* (London, 1703) appeared, the composer's stock began to rise in the land.

Abell had become attached to the household of the Duke of Ormonde, and when the latter was appointed Viceroy of Ireland in May 1703, Abell accompanied him to Dublin as "Master of the State Musick". On February 7, 1704, at the festivities at Dublin Castle for the birthday of Queen Anne, Abell sang his Irish song "Shein sios agus suas liom" [Moore's "Down beside me"] to an enthusiastic gathering. This work, which was written on his return from the Continent, had already been successfully programmed at a Stationers Hall concert. In December 1704, Abell resigned

his post in Dublin and returned to England. After this date we
have but sparse information about him. Under the patronage of
the Duke of Argyll he gave a concert in Edinburgh in 1706. Save
for the fact that he sang "Katherine Ogie" at a Stationers Hall
concert in 1680 when he was a Gentleman of the Chapel Royal,
his visit to Scotland in 1681 presumably on "secret service", and
his dedication of some songs to "Nobility and Gentry in the North
of England", which presumably included Scotland, this is the sole
real connection of the Aberdeen-born Abell with the country of
his birth.

One feels, however, that Abell still continued to hold his own
in the world of music. That is the impression which the once-
celebrated book *Letters from the Dead to the Living* (London, 1708)
gives us of Abell. Its author was Thomas Brown, the coarse satirist
of "facetious memory", as the brilliant Addison dubs that exquisite blackguard. Indeed, it was Abell's success which riled
Brown. Obviously it must have been galling to the ex-schoolmaster
to see Abell being applauded and rewarded for his artistic gifts
whilst he was condemned to eke out a living by vulgar scurrility,
if not obscenity, so as to pander to the depraved tastes of roués.
Still, the lewd and venomous Brown had a genuine appreciation
of the abilities of Abell. He tells us in a side-splitting letter of
"Henry Purcel to Doctor B[low]" that in Hades "every cobbler
here . . . whilst he's waxing his thred, shall out-sing Mr Ab[e]l".
In the supposed letter of "Pomigny of Auberne to Mr Abel of
London, Singing-Master", here is what Pomigny, alias Brown, says:

> Who would not bring up their Children in a quire? or who wou'd
> not learn to sing? You have met, I must confess, Sir, with but small
> encouragement in the main, and made but a slender fortune in com-
> parison of what might have been reasonably expected from your talents.
> The most civiliz'd quarter of the world has been your audience and
> admirer, and you have everywhere a name that cannot die but with
> music, and that will survive even nature.

Yet Brown had his tongue in his cheek when penning that adulation.
His malevolent intent was soon to follow. He continues:

> Here [in Hades] are some devilist, ignorant, censorious, lying
> people, that will maintain that you were so impertinent as to give a
> gentleman the trouble of cudgelling you.

He then hints at the singer's loyalty and at an affair in which an
Irishman stole from Abell a valuable ring which had been gifted
him by Louis XIV. The thief, says the satiric Brown, alias Pomigny,
was in Hades, and there he

> suffer'd the discipline of the place for stealing the diamond ring
> from you that the King of France gave you at Fountainbleau: To
> mitigate the blackness of the fact, he alledg'd the necessitousness of
> his condition, and that it was a pity so many gallant men should want
> for their loyalty, while a jakanapes cou'd get an estate for a song.

Pseudo-Pomigny concludes his letter to Abell by offering him "a
lodging near Cerberus", the guardian beast at the mouth of Hell.
"Twill be convenient for you . . . to confer *notes* together, for he is
much the deepest *base* of any here", says the amusing but scurrile
Pomigny.

Nor does Brown forget Abell's "secret service" activities. These occasion a gibe, although astutely veiled, from the bitter-tongued Brown:

> There are some considerable stars that rise in Bavaria, whose influences are inauspicious to you, for, among friends, 'twas no better than robbing him to run away with his money, and especially before you had done anything for it.

This refers to a charge that the Elector of Hanover had paid Abell to undertake certain duties, probably secret service, but that the latter had decamped with the money without fulfilling his obligations.

Brown then continues these attacks under the guise of "Mr Abel's reply to Pomigny", and the Irish thief story is dealt with in this fashion:

> I [Abell] ever found an inbred aversion to Ireland, and your news gives me more convincing reasons why I shou'd not affect 'em: for to be strip'd by some, and strip'd by others, would of itself give a man an unfavourable impression of such people.

Abell had, at this time, resigned his position with the Viceroy of Ireland, and Brown wanted to make capital out of it and import his anti-Irish spleen at the same time.

Concerning the Bavarian affair, this is how Brown makes Abell defend himself:

> As for the article of Bavaria, I can only say but little to it more than I thought the time was come, when the Israelites should spoil the Egyptians. You have such continual couriers from these parts, that you cannot be long ignorant of the minutest springs by which all affairs are kept in motion. To me they seem everywhere to be much at the same rate, like a horse in a mill, 'tis no matter who drives him.

After Brown's onslaught we have little news of Abell. Hawkins writes as follows:

> About the latter end of Queen Ann's reign [d. 1714] Abell was at Cambridge with his lute, but he met there poor encouragement. How long he lived afterwards is not known, but the account of his death was communicated to the gentleman who furnished many of the above particulars by one, who, having known him in his prosperity, assisted him in his old age, and was at the expense of his funeral.

When this latter took place is not known. The *Dictionary of National Biography* says "? 1716", but this is based on the fact that Abell was on the programme of a Stationers Hall concert in 1716. J. D. Brown (*Biographical Dictionary of Musicians*, 1886) gives "1724" as the date, although in his contribution to *British Musical Biography* (1897) this is tempered down to "about 1724". Yet Grove's *Dictionary of Music* (1940) commits itself definitely to "1724".

That Abell was a superb singer and a deft performer on the lute seems to be universally admitted. Johann Mattheson, in his *Der vollkommene Capellmeister* (Hamburg, 1739), speaks of Abell's successes in Holland and Hamburg, saying that "this singer possessed the secret of being able to preserve his voice even to his old age". Yet if Mattheson (1681-1764) spoke from personal knowledge in Hamburg, Abell was only in his late "forties" in those days. That both Evelyn and Congreve should have paid such tributes as they

412 of the Counter-Tenor

did cannot be ignored, and certainly the esteem in which he was held in his day is the surest confirmation of his worth. Some of the music of Purcell's festival odes for the court of James II, which is preserved in the British Museum, contains Abell's name as one of the principal singers. When Daniel Purcell offered Abell £500 a year in 1696 to return to the London stage and concert, he was fully aware that he would be taking no risk. He had known Abell since 1679 when they entered the Chapel Royal together, although Purcell was only a "child".

As a composer, we have little upon which to assess the talents of Abell. In his *Collection of Songs in Various Languages* (1701) there is a fine setting of Matthew Prior's "Reading ends in melancholy", and a lengthy cantata, "To our Hero, to our King", which reveals interest. Since two of his songs appeared in *Wit and Mirth: or Pills to Purge Melancholy* (4th edit., vol. V: London, 1719), one may assume that his name as a composer was well established by that date. Eitner mentions *A Collection of Scotch Songs* in the British Museum (MS. 634) but this must be an error.

It is sad to contemplate that penury should have been the lot of so great a singer. Had he remained at court he might have ended his days in ease as a pensioner, if not in affluence. Instead of that, being faithful to his creed and to a king who had favoured him, he suffered a ten years' wandering in strange lands, and even when permitted to return home he only reached a temporary rehabilitation. His steadfastness in 1688 should stand to his credit, even though he did abjectly cry *peccavi* ten years later.

GENERAL INDEX

Glossary of Terms Pertaining to Voice
by Charles Cleall

Peter Giles has gone beyond the call of duty in defining his terms repeatedly in the course of the text. Why, then, have a glossary? Chiefly for the benefit of readers to whom voice is a new or relatively new study; who are not entirely at home with some of the terms used.

It can be a great help to know whence the terms came; so that we can see the point of naming organs or activities thus: for instance, the foundation of the tongue is a slender, U–shaped bone called the hyoid bone. Now, '–oid' means 'having the shape of', and 'hy–' means a U, V or Y. Once we know that, the term is self–explanatory. To cite etymology discourages at first: it feels off–puttingly informative ('This book told me more about penguins than I wanted to know'); but persevere with it, and insight into terms begins, and deepens, and eventually becomes a pleasure.

Abduction The moving apart of the vocal folds (from *ab–*, [away] from, plus *–duc*, to lead or draw), in order to breathe or whisper; see **Crico–arytenoideus**.

Adduction The moving together of the vocal folds (from *ad–*, toward, plus *–duc*, to lead or draw), in order to phonate; see **Crico–arytenoideus**.

Amplitude Amplitude has to do with the theory of sound–waves, which resemble waves in water not at all. In *The Boy's Own Paper*, advertisements for wireless operators depicted a pylon sending out what appeared to be expanding, concentric circles of electricity. In reality, sound–waves are even more remarkable, because they are expanding, concentric *spheres* of force. Sound begins with what amounts to a thunder–clap, with the *compression* of molecules of air, so that they are squashed more closely together than usual. Set free, they move further apart than usual to compensate: they become *rarefied*. From this point, molecules set into movement by a percussive instrument such as the piano swing together, and apart, turn and turn about, at a constant rate known as the *frequency*. No swing goes quite as far as the previous swing, so that the first swing is the greatest (and therefore the loudest), and the swings eventually reduce to a point where they are inaudible unless continued force keeps them swinging.

Voice is not normally percussive, and the amplitude (the maximum extent to which it displaces molecules of air) can be maintained (*legato*), or increased (*crescendo*), or reduced (*diminuendo*). The amplitude of a sound, therefore, is the maximum distance by which a molecule of air is displaced from its original position (A) to a new position of maximum compression (B) and back, so:

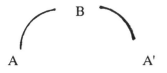 From B vertically down
to a line from A to A'
shows the displacement

From A to A' shows the distance travelled by the sound–wave. Once it has got back to A', it has reached the original point of *no–displacement* of molecular position. The name of that point of *no–displacement* is abbreviated to *node*. From the node, the molecule moves as far as B was from A, to C (the point of maximum rarefaction) and thereafter back to A'', so:

The curved line looks rather like an S which has fallen over. It has the shape of a sine–wave: the wave of purest possible sound, with no other harmonics (overtones or partials). Thus, the distance travelled by the sound–wave is shown from A to A", and, if we divide the length of the sound–wave into the speed of sound, we find the frequency, which we perceive as pitch.

A————————————————————————A"

Length of sound–wave, divided into the speed
of sound = frequency or pitch

For example, the length of the sound–wave of middle C (C4) is four feet, two (and a bit) inches. Divide that (call it 4.2044911) into the speed of sound (1100 feet per second) and we get the frequency of middle C = 261.625 Hz (**Hertz**, meaning 'vibrations per second'). We say that the maximum vertical distance from B to the horizontal line A–A' depicts the peak of the compression–phase, and the maximum vertical distance from the horizontal line A'–A" to C depicts the trough of the rarefaction–phase. Put one vertical distance above the other, and we have twice the *amplitude* (a measure of the loudness of the sound), the amplitude being represented by either A'B or A'C.

B

A'   From B vertically down to A', or
    A' vertically down to C, shows
    us the amplitude: a measure of
    loudness
C

We could think of the A–A'/A" line, therefore, as the length of the sound–wave; of B as the amplitude–peak in the compression–phase of that frequency; of A' as the node; of C as the amplitude–trough in the rarefaction–phase; and of A–A" as the length of one complete cycle of vibration. The time taken to complete one cycle is the period of vibration. In that the frequency is the number of vibrations completed each second, the period will equal the frequency divided into 1.

Antinode The amplitude–peak or the compression–trough of a sound wave, that is, the point of maximum displacement of molecules of air; see **Amplitude**, where it will be seen that the distance from a node to an antinode is one quarter of the wave–length.

Arytenoid cartilages Small, pyramidal cartilages mounted on the **Cricoid cartilage** which relate to the vocal folds rather as the hands of a rider relate to the reins of a horse: that is to say, they move to adduct or abduct them as necessary (from *–oid*, having the shape of, plus *Arytaena*, a ladle), acted on by the **Crico–arytenoid muscles**. Fibres of the **Vocalis muscle** run between the arytenoid and thyroid cartilages. Their contraction stiffens and thickens the vocal folds, and pulls the cartilages toward each other, enabling pitch to change to higher frequencies up to a point; see **Larynx**.

Atmospheric pressure Gravity pulls the molecules of air toward earth; so that air has weight, and presses on us at ground–level with a pressure of 14.7 pounds per square inch, or 760 mm of mercury. At altitudes above sea–level, the pressure becomes progressively less.

Bel canto The so–called 'lost art' of a voice so perfectly produced as to sound and feel effortless, and always under control whether loud or quiet. Literally, 'beautiful singing'. See Cornelius L. Reed, *Bel Canto: Principles and Practice* (Josef Patelson Music House Ltd, New York), or Lucie Manen, *Bel Canto: The Teaching of the Classical Italian Song–Schools, Its Decline and Restoration* (Oxford University Press, 1987), for a study in depth.

Bernoulli effect Daniel Bernoulli (1700–1782) showed why it is that, when a stream of fluid or gas is in motion, its pressure on the sides of its conduit (the passage through which it is flowing) decreases. The pressure may decrease till the sides of the conduit move toward each other, because the material on the other side of the conduit–wall is still pressing on that wall; so that the extent to which the the conduit is patent (open) may be reduced by the pressure of that matter. Without the Bernoulli efect, we could not phonate any but low pitch, because our nerve–signals and the muscles effecting adduction act too slowly to produce several hundred vibrations per second. The Bernoulli effect may be tested by suspending two ping–pong balls each on a fine thread three centimetres apart. Blow through the gap between them, and the balls will move together (as it were, be sucked together) because the pressure of air outside the gap is atmospheric, and, by blowing through the gap, you have lessened the pressure of air between them.

Breath pressure To phonate, the air in the lungs must be compressed by reducing the space within them by means of the muscles round the lungs; but it is not much more than atmospheric pressure. Interestingly, airflow on loud, high notes is less than in quieter and lower–pitched phonation, because the folds of a skilled singer stay adducted for two–thirds of the time. Professor Sundberg tells us that 70 dB is attained by a pressure equal to that of two cm. of water; 75 dB by 4.5 cm.; 85 dB by 14 cm., and 91 dB (which is ear–splitting) by 20 cm. See **Decibel**.

Chest voice The basic voice heard when most people sing; as it were, the natural voice, whether enhanced by training or not. Notes of higher pitch are obtained by increasing breath–pressure, and by tightening the muscular fibres within the vocal folds till there comes a point past which the singer is in danger of muscular cramp or even injury. Cf. **Head voice**.

Complex wave–form The entry under **Amplitude** shows us a sine wave: the simplest possible sound wave. The oscilloscope shows such a wave when only the fundamental is sounding; but it will show increasingly jagged wave–forms when more and more overtones form part of the sound.

How do overtones arise?

Let us take a vibrating string as an example. Suppose a 'cellist is bowing tenor C (C3: the C below middle C): the string as a whole vibrates 130.812 times per second, and gives us the only sound we consciously hear (the fundamental); but there is more going on than that. Halves of the string are vibrating in their own right, twice as quickly (at 261.625 times per second), and sounding middle C (C4). Thirds of the string are vibrating in their own right, three times as quickly, and sounding G4 at 391.995 Hz. Quarters of the string are vibrating four times as quickly, and sounding C5 at 523.251 Hz. Fifths are vibrating five times as quickly, and sounding E5 at 659.255 Hz. Sixths are vibrating six times as quickly, and sounding G5 at 783.991 Hz, and so on. Because these overtones (or harmonics — though note that the fundamental is the first harmonic) are sounded by parts of the string, they are also known as upper partials.

Different sound–generators achieve the same effect by different means. As we have seen, the vibrating string swings to and fro, and generates *transverse vibrations* at right angles to the wave–length. The flute generates *longitudinal vibrations* along the wave–length. The vocal folds appear to act like the lips of the bugler, causing transverse vibrations, with many upper partials which are an important part of vocal tone.

Consonant An obstruction to the flow of breath through the mouth. Whereas **Vowels** are the affective aspect of language, consonants are the cognitive aspect (show anyone a sentence with the vowels missing, and another with the consonants missing, and you will see what is meant by that). Some consonants are classified as *sonants*, because they are packed with vocal sound (or should be: poor singers fail to voice their final sonants): B, D, G, J, L, M, N, NG ('sing'), R, TH ('this'), V, W, X ('exam'), Y, Z, ZH ('leisure'). Some consonants are classified as *surds*, because they are not voiced: C, CH ('chest'), F, H, K, P, Q, S, SH ('shun'), T, X ('fix'). Eight of the surds have a sonant–equivalent (written with the same shorthand sign, but more heavily): C/G, CH/J, F/V, K/G, P/B, S/Z, SH/ZH, TH ('thick')/TH ('this'), X ('fix')/X ('exam'): which makes it the more important for their phonetic quality to be unmistakable.

Corniculate cartilages Small, conical (horn–shaped) elastic fibro–cartilages immediately above the apex of the **Arytenoid cartilages**. They are mentioned under **Larynx** for the sake of completion rather than for the work they do.

Covering A term which means different things to different people. To some, it means the distortion of sung vowels and the dulling of tone to achieve uniformity of tone throughout the range.

To Cornelius L. Reid, it means a change of resonance–adjustment by darkening vowels sung near the so–called 'register break' (E4–F♯4 in male voices: an octave higher in female voices), to avoid tone thought to be too open (that is, too raucous). Reid explains that it is the coupling of the vocal tract in such a way that the resonators control the vocal folds' conformation and, hence, vibration. Husler & Rodd–Marling agree, but add that the system of resonators depends for the quality of its functioning on optimum use of the scaffolding of muscles from which the larynx is suspended; the problem being (as they say) that the composition of the scaffolding fluctuates: now this muscle will be active; now that.

To Professor Donald F. Proctor, in *Breathing, Speech and Song* (Springer–Verlag, Wien/New York, 1980), covering is a matter of: (i) lengthening the vocal folds by means of **Crico–thyroideus**, and (ii) instituting changes in the scaffolding to supplement tension at a lower pitch than is absolutely necessary; and he quotes Dr Meribeth A. Bunch as demonstrating that enlargement of the pharynx is a major factor in covering, to be achieved by spontaneous relaxation — not by an effort to manipulate mouth, tongue or larynx.

Dr Bunch herself, in *Dynamics of the Singing Voice* (Springer–Verlag, Wien/New York, 1982) tells us that, when the Vocalis muscle contracts (see **Larynx**), there is increased thickness of the vocal folds which is directly related to increased loudness of tone. Vocalis must cease contraction, and leave higher frequencies to **Crico–thyroideus**, if there is not to be excessive muscular antagonism, making adjustment of the musculature abrupt and jerky, and causing breaks in the voice.

Crico–arytenoideus Important muscles connecting the **Cricoid** and **Arytenoid cartilages** to effect adduction and abduction of the vocal folds. The muscles between the arytenoids (*Inter– arytenoideus*) and those attaching their outer sides to the broad band of the cricoid cartilage (*Crico–arytenoideus lateralis*) adduct the folds. Professor Johan Sundberg says that it is likely that Crico–arytenoideus lateralis lowers the frequency of phonation. The muscles attaching the broad posterior surfaces of the arytenoid cartilages to the cricoid (*Crico–arytenoideus dorsalis*) abduct them. See **Larynx**.

Cricoid cartilage 'Cricoid' is the metathetic version (the swopping–round–of–letters version) of 'circoid' (circular, or ring–shaped). Imagine a signet ring incorporated in the larynx, with its broad, signet–bearing part toward the spine, and its thin part toward the front. On the broad part are placed the **Arytenoid cartilages**, which have important work to do in phonation. From the narrow part run the *Crico–thyroid muscles* connecting the cricoid and thyroid cartilages; one part of which (*Pars recta*) pulls the thyroid cartilage forward, and the other part of which (*Pars obliqua*) tilts the cricoid cartilage backward, lengthening and stretching the vocal folds to raise the pitch (note: acting on the folds from outside them). See **Head voice**.

Crico–pharyngeus An important muscle running from the broad part of the **Cricoid cartilage** to the outside of the back of the windpipe. Its antagonist, *Sterno–thyroideus*, whose point of origin is the sternum, or breast bone, and whose point of attachment is the front of the **Thyroid cartilage**, pulls the thyroid cartilage forward and down to lengthen the vocal folds by acting on them from outside. Crico–pharyngeus stabilizes that pull. It is often the weakest (because least used) of the muscles affecting phonation, but it can and should be used. It was alluded to by Caruso when he said, 'Sing from the nape of the neck'.

Crico–thyroideus An equally important muscle connecting the **Cricoid** and **Thyroid cartilages**. It has two parts: the broad, outer part (*Pars obliqua*) which pulls the thyroid cartilage forward to stretch the vocal folds by increasing the distance between the arytenoid and thyroid cartilages, and the less broad, central part (*Pars recta*), which tilts the narrow band of the cricoid cartilage upward to increase further the distance between arytenoid and thyroid cartilages, and so stretch the vocal folds.

Cuneiform cartilages Tiny wedge–shaped cartilages immediately above and slightly in front of the **Arytenoid cartilages**. They are mentioned under **Larynx** for the sake of completion rather than for the work they do.

Cycle of vibration The whole process of vibration from one peak of amplitude to the next.

Decibel The ratio of the intensity of two sounds on a logarithmic scale is shown by the number of Bels by which the sound–pressure of one exceeds the other. Note that we do not say that Bels show the *loudness* of a sound, because loudness is a subjective matter, and the same sound–pressure throughout the audible frequency–range would not sound equally loud to any of us. Sounds which seem equally loud may have different sound–pressure levels. The Bel is so large a unit that we use tenths of it, and speak of decibels (dB). The number of decibels does not tell us how loud any sound is: only how its sound–pressure level compares with that of another sound.

Every rise of 3 dB doubles the sound–pressure level; therefore, ear–muffs are legally obligatory in a factory where machines are working at 90 dB, on the ground that their sound–pressure output would cause permanent high–frequency deafness in some workers after eight hours' exposure to it. At 93 dB, it would have that effect in four hours; at 96 dB, in two hours; at 99 dB, in an hour; at 102 dB, in thirty minutes; at 105 dB, in a quarter of an hour; at 108 dB, in 7.5 minutes; at 111 dB, in 3.75 minutes; at 114 dB, in less than two minutes; and, at 117 dB, in less than a minute. Now weigh the fact that the average disco is said to operate at a level between 110 and 138 dB, and results in the hearing of teenagers subjected to such a level resembling that of most 65–year–olds.

We hear high–pitched sounds: usually between 3 and 4 kHz: more clearly than low–

pitched. Low–pitched sound at the same energy–level would seem much quieter to us because our hearing is less sensitive to it. If the F at the top of the piano keyboard (F7 = 2792.824 Hz) can be heard at a specific level of energy, C7 would need to have half again as great an energy–level to seem equally loud; C6, six times the energy–level; C5, 25 times; C4, 150 times; and C3, 3800 times.

As a rough guide, we listen to C5 (523.251 Hz) at a mean level of 60 dB above threshold–sound; this level is no less than a million times louder than the quietest sound of that pitch that most of us can discern. We tolerate an unbelievably wide range of energy–levels: at the same range of mass, when the least discernible weight were that of a human hair, the greatest would be 56,000 tons (56,898.8 tonnes).

Diaphragm The muscular floor on which the lungs rest. It used to be thought that the singer controlled the diaphragm, till it was realized that the diaphragm (i) drew breath in, but did not push it out, and, more importantly, (ii) it was an involuntary muscle. If it acts (and it acts in phonation more with some singers than it does with others), it acts without the singer's conscious control — for which reason little is now said about it.

Envelope The total picture of one cycle of sound–vibration; necessary because not all musical sounds begin as they mean to go on, or as they finish. The sound of a note on the piano, for example, begins with a bang (the *initial transient*); maintains a level of volume slightly decreasing, and eventually fades out. As a rule, of course, the next note is heard before that middle section has faded; so that, if we hear a succession of piano chords from which the initial transient has been excised electronically (as we can on the E. P. record which accompanies Professor C. A. Taylor's book *The Physics of Musical Sounds,* English Universities' Press, 1965), it sounds as if played on a harmonium. The tone of the oboe and the tone of the violin differ comparatively little once the initial transient is past. The characteristic difference between their timbres is chiefly the difference between their initial transients. The middle phase of wind and stringed instruments may be thought of as a steady state (though some musical instruments: for example, the drum and, to some extent, the piano: hardly have a steady state). Instruments such as the clavichord end each note with an equally characteristic *terminal transient*; and the envelope, on a graph or oscilloscope, would depict the wave–form of all three phases of each tone.

Epiglottis The leaf–shaped cartilage above the larynx which is its first sphincter (point of closure); the others being (i) the vestibular folds, and (ii) the vocal folds. When we swallow, all three sphincters close to prevent inundation of the airway. To some extent, the epiglottis can extend or broaden itself. When a skilled singer sings AH, the epiglottis widens; when EE, the epiglottis lengthens; when OO, it is moderately long.

Falsetto Head–voice in the original sense. *The Oxford Dictionary* tells us that 'falsetto' was first used in 1774 to mean 'a forced voice of a register above the natural'; which describes something *un*natural, and therefore bogus. Peter Giles explains to us at length that that is not at all its meaning; and he sets out with exemplary care what it actually means. The word therefore resembles the word 'sunrise' in saying something which thoughtful people perceive to be untrue, and yet in being used so widely that its use is unlikely ever to be stopped; which makes it the more important that we know what it means, and share our knowledge with those who do not.

Folds, vocal Why 'folds' and not 'cords' or 'chords'? Because the international term for them is *Plicae Vocales*, of which 'vocal folds' is an exact translation. If one buys the larynx of a sheep from the butcher, and cuts it in half with a bread–knife, it can be seen that the folds do indeed look like an undulation in the soft membranous tissue of the interior of the larynx.

Formant A formant is a region of pitch where the partials are particularly strong: one might say, disproportionately strong; and therefore characteristic. The G string of a violin, for example, sounds its fundamental (the only frequency we are conscious of hearing: G3 = 195.997 Hz) with one thousandth of the energy of the sound. The second harmonic (G4 = 391.995 Hz) has 260 times as much energy; and the third (D5 = 587.329 Hz) has no less than 450 times as much energy as the fundamental. Such partials are strengthened by the natural frequency of the cavities through which they pass. Violin tone passes into the body of the violin. Voice passes through the larynx, the pharynx, the cranial sinuses, the mouth (with its velum: the soft, mobile part of the roof: and tongue and lips); every one of which has its own resonating frequency could we but find it. By changing the shape and position (to use the technical word, by changing the *conformation*) of the velum, tongue and lips, we can change markedly the formants of vocal tone.

That is how we produce different vowels.

The most skilled singers can emit a very special group of sounds called the *singer's formant*, resulting from adjustments of the third, fourth and fifth vocal formants which move their frequencies closer, and cause them to enhance each other; and from the widening of the laryngeal tube which occurs when the larynx is lowered. In general, the singer's formant will occur at about 3000 Hz (3 kHz); though it will vary from 2.3 kHz to 3 kHz in basses, and from 3 to 3.8 kHz in tenors.

The first five vocal formants change their power and frequency to some extent with the vowels being sung (the first depending on the extent to which the jaw is lowered; the second, on tongue position; the third, on the position of the tip of the tongue; the fourth, on the conformation of the laryngeal tube; and the fourth and fifth on the length of the laryngeal tube); but the singer's formant stays relatively constant through all the vowels. The greatest advantage of the singer's formant is that, where lower frequencies are radiated equally in all directions, the singer's formant scatters much less, and is concentrated toward the front, and to some extent the sides.

The greatest power of the orchestra with all its instruments lies at about A4/B♭4 within the treble staff (about 450 Hz), so that the sound of a skilful singer can be distinguished even above the might of the orchestra without difficulty, no matter what note he or she is singing, even when (as at some moments in the operas of Wagner) he/she cannot hear his/her own voice.

Fry, vocal If low notes below the range of **Chest voice** are attempted with a raised larynx and lowered epiglottis, a rough, squeezed tone not unlike the death–rattle is heard, and named thus. It has no musical value.

Fundamental For a sound to be audible, there must be vibration at a frequency between 20 and 20,000 Hz (for some people, 30,000 Hz). The fundamental (the first harmonic) is the lowest–pitched or (as with a pure–tone generator) only frequency audible. See **Formant**.

Fundamental voice See **Chest voice**.

Glottis The edges of the vocal folds; adducted (*ad*, to/toward, plus *duc*–, led: hence, caused to meet) for phonation, and abducted (*ab*–, [away] from: hence, caused to part) for respiration. The folds do not always meet along their entire length in phonation (though they are likely to in normal tone when singing loudly), but may be partly open, as Peter Giles so cogently explains.

Harmonic See **Complex wave–form**.

Head–voice A term with more than one meaning. Head–voice is the higher–pitched (to some extent, overlapping) register which contrasts with the fundamental voice, or **Chest voice**.

There are two main forms of head–voice: upper and lower, which are initiated by slightly different laryngeal activity. The upper form is what uninformed people call **Falsetto**: the high, relaxed sound which arises when the folds are partly abducted, and only part of their edges is set into vibration. Used with too low a **Formant**, the result can seem unnatural; but, used with a high or medium formant, it is acceptable as a pleasing and highly musical timbre free from strain.

The lower head–voice must not be confused with mixed–voice, or the upper reaches of the chest voice which we shall describe below. It is a true *Voce mezzana*; or medium register employing adducted vocal folds at full length, with arytenoid cartilages firmly abducted.

Chest voice can continue upward in range by tightening the fibres of the Vocalis muscle; the muscular tissue of the vocal folds: which causes them to thicken, tense and shorten some-what, and by raising breath–pressure: but, if the approach of higher frequencies is not to damage the folds by sending its fibres into spasm, or even rupturing them (so causing a *haemorrhagic nodule*), the singer must change the register to that of the lower head–voice, which acts on the folds *from outside*, by: (i) tension of the muscles controlling the **Arytenoid cartilages**, especially Lateralis and Inter–aryenoideus; (ii) tension of the muscles controlling the position of the **Cricoid cartilage**; and (iii) tension of the muscles which cause the **Thyroid cartilage** to change position on its attachments to the **Cricoid cartilage**. This triple tension pulls the vocal folds out long, rarefying their tissue, and raising the pitch of their vibration.

Vocal pitch is never determined *solely* by tightening the fibres of the folds: (i), (ii) and (iii) always play some part in the process; but, in lower head–voice (other than changes in breath–pressure), they play the chief part, aided by changes in the musculature of the scaffolding supporting the larynx. See **Covering**.

Hertz The name of Heinrich Hertz (1857–94) is used to mean 'vibrations per second'. Middle C (C4) has a frequency of 261.625 Hz; by which we mean that an oscillator emitting Middle C is vibrating 261.625 times every second; and that, at any point in space affected by that vibration, 261.625 sound–waves will pass in any one second.

Imposto Lucie Manen is very fond of this word, which she uses as though it were a rune. It comes from the same root as our verb 'to impose', meaning (in effect) 'to put in position', and means the coupling of every resonator which ought to be affecting tone desirably.

Initial Transients See **Envelope**.

Larynx A most sensitive and subtle organ at the top of the windpipe consisting of the **Thyroid cartilage**; the **Cricoid cartilage**; two **Arytenoid cartilages**, and the **Cuneiform and corniculate cartilages**, topped by the **Epiglottis**. The whole is lined within by mucous membrane, which also covers two pairs of elastic ligaments stretching from the arytenoid cartilages behind to the thyroid cartilage in front, containing the *superior* and *inferior thyreo–arytenoideus muscles* (note how the name of those muscles describes their points of origin and attachment respectively: the point of attachment, or insertion, being what the muscle is designed to move, while the point of origin stays where it is).

The superior thyreo–arytenoideus is better known as the **Vestibular folds**, and the inferior (which merely means 'lower') thyreo–arytenoideus is better known as the **Vocal folds**. The vocal folds are composed of (i) an inner band of muscle, known as *Vocalis*; (ii) the vocal processes (as they are called; the 'sticky–out bits') of the arytenoid cartilages, and (iii) the free upper edge of a thickened membrane called *Conus elasticus*, arising from the upper surface of the Cricoid cartilage. The larynx is set within a muscular scaffolding which holds it steady, against which some of its cartilages and muscles are pulled; but that is best left for study in Johan Sundberg's text, *The Science of the Singing Voice* (Northern Illinois University Press,

1987).

The larynx has three sphincters (organs of closure): the epiglottis, the vestibular folds, and the vocal folds: whose primary office appears to be to protect the windpipe from inundation ('a wave coming in', or food going down the wrong way). Husler & Rodd–Marling's book, *Singing: The Physical Nature of the Vocal Organ* (revised edn, Hutchinson, 1976) has some excellent illustrations of these organs, but should not be taken as gospel in its explanations, which are bettered by Professor Sundberg's.

Mean pitch When a singer uses vibrato/tremolando, etc., the frequency of the note changes, say, 6–14 times per second, alternately rising above and falling below the note the singer believes him/herself to be singing. If the change from that note (the mean pitch) is by more than quarter of a tone, the result is felt not to be musical, and displeasing.

Mezzo– A prefix meaning 'middle', or, as we say colloquially, 'middling'.

Natural Frequency See **Pocket**.

Node See **Amplitude**.

Oscillation Another name for vibration, or the periodic movement (the regularly repeated movement to and fro) of a medium such as the molecules of air. An oscillator is any agent which causes such movement.

Overtones See **Complex wave–form**.

Pharynx The tube running from behind the larynx to the base of the skull, composed of fibrous tissue reinforced with muscle. The upper part is known as the naso–pharynx; it extends as far as the *posterior nares*, where the nose opens into the throat. The middle part is known as the oro–pharynx, through which food passes from the mouth to the lower part known as the laryngo–pharynx, which extends to the gullet or food–pipe. Some of the laryngo–pharynx (not least, the *pyriform* (pear–shaped) *sinuses* to right and left of the base of the laryngo–pharynx) and all the oro– and naso–pharynx are used by voice.

Pocket In the vocal tract there are cavities, such as the spaces in the throat above the larynx, within the nose, or within the mouth. Each cavity, or pocket, will sound a distinctive note if a current of air is blown through it at a certain angle, or across its entrance. That is its *natural frequency*. If a sound–wave includes that frequency, the pocket will reinforce that frequency so that its energy increases. That is how formants occur. That is resonance.

Ponticello The bridge between **Chest voice** and lower **Head–voice**: a range of pitch which could be sung in either register.

Phonation From the Greek word *Phon*, meaning sound, or voice. In the world of voice, we tend to use it as though it could only mean 'voice'; and it is salutary to remember that it can simply mean sound–making. Its usefulness as a rule is to signify the sound of speaking or singing: in other words, using voice in any mode.

Rappresentativo style A style of composition and singing, suited to the expression of agitation or anger, used notably by Monteverdi.

Reed theory The behaviour of reeds is not unlike the behaviour of the vocal folds, but subject to laws of its own, because the material from which reeds are made is different. We can talk of vegetable reeds (such as those of the oboe), or of metal reeds (such as those of certain organ–pipes), or of lip–reeds (like those of the trumpeter), or even of air–reeds (such as make the sound of a flute). Wind–pressure and reed–stiffness affect the tone of a reed–instrument. Voice is normally conceived of as a lip–reed instrument.

Regeneration condition This is a subtle idea of the self–sustaining vibration of vocal folds. The energy of sound is dissipated by friction of the movement of the vocal folds, because the soft tissues of the vocal tract absorb sound–energy; and because two–fifths of the energy of the sound–wave is reflected downward from the upper lip of the larynx. To keep vibration going, more energy must be put into the system, and is (in large measure), by that reflection downward from the lip of the larynx (see **Bernoulli effect**). Bernoulli–force (the sucking together of the vocal folds because of lessening pressure between them) reaches its maximum just after the folds have abducted furthest. Therefore the force is greater when the folds are closing than it is when the folds are opening. That is the regeneration–condition which causes vibration to draw energy from the airflow past the folds.

Register The vocal timbre resulting from the use of a particular set or team of muscles. Cf. **Chest voice** and **Head–voice**.

Resonance See **Pocket**.

Singer's Formant See **Formant**.

Sinus–tone theory Sinus–tone theory is an aspect of E. G. White's technique which holds that the contribution made to voice by the cranial sinuses is so great and so helpful that the singer is advised to concentrate on what he feels within them, as well as what he hears, while he sings. If that sounds inconclusive, think about these points: (i) voice is produced by the integral activity of the vocal tract, composed of the organs and pockets from the lungs to the cranial sinuses; (ii) in training and developing voice, attention is best directed to the cranial sinuses, leaving all the muscular organs to function freely and, for the most part, automatically. Sinus–tone theory used to be thought of as eccentric, but physicists and medical scientists are continually finding more evidence to substantiate it, and teachers of singing are finding it more and more helpful.

Siren theory The idea of voice as a kind of siren has been entertained; and there is something to be said for it, because a siren creates sound by forcing air to pass an obstacle in rapid puffs; and that is what muscles round the lungs and in the abdomen do when they force air past the vocal folds. Some conceive of a siren as 'hard', and, of course, most of the so–called sirens to which our attention is drawn *are* hard; but there seems no reason to restrict our definition to hard sirens.

Sonority Deep, full, rich, resonant sound. Charles Kennedy Scott used to say that the object of the singer was a maximum of tone with a minimum of sound; in other words, a maximum of pleasing overtones with a minimum of *noisiness*.

Sound–energy The work done in giving rise to sounds transmitted by a sound–wave. The most remarkable aspect of our perception of sound–energy is that the only part of the sound we are conscious of hearing is likely to be that of the fundamental, which may arise from but a thousandth of the total sound–energy. See **Formant**.

Sound–radiation See **Sounding–space**.

Sounding–space A sound–wave will move as far as it can in all directions (but see **Singer's formant**). As it radiates from the mouth, the energy of voice will be dissipated via absorption by the movement of molecules of air till the sound ceases to be audible. Within the vocal tract, pockets add the energy of their natural frequency to voice, so that its energy is enhanced; though it never regains the energy that it had at source. See **Pocket**.

Sound–stream The sound–wave and its successors: not a jet of air, but the motion of 'expanding, concentric spheres of force', causing the movement to and fro (by never more than a hundredth of a millimetre, even in the loudest sound down to the lowest G on the piano) of molecules of air.

Sound–system A system, composed of an air–compressor, an oscillator, and a resonator, whose activity results in sound. The lungs, vocal folds, and pharynx, sinuses and mouth compose the vocal sound–system.

Square wave The sound–wave characteristic of a clarinet, whose formants are the odd–numbered harmonics only.

Standing wave Most sound–waves travel. Their shape (their profile) moves through the medium they affect (as in the wake of a boat across a mill pond). The medium is affected, but moves so little that we are surprised to find that the fisherman's float does not follow the wake, but merely moves up and down as the wake passes. If another sound–wave of the same frequency moves in the opposite direction (usually, by reflection from a hard surface), the profiles of the two waves do not move, though the molecules of air continue to swing to and fro. The result is that the nodes stay where they are, and the antinodes stay where *they* are; which makes voice more effective, because one of its antinodes occurs just outside the lips: an important standing wave is set up at the upper lip of the larynx, where two–fifths of the energy of voice is reflected back to the glottis, thus helping to regenerate its cycle.

In the U.S.A., a standing wave is termed 'a stationary wave'; which seems more sensible than our own term.

Steady–state theory That aspect of acoustics which discusses the settled and relatively unchanging phase of sound once any initial transients are past, before any terminal transients have been initiated. It should be remembered that some musical sounds (for instance: the piano or the drum) have virtually no steady state. See **Envelope**, and **Vocal Tract**.

String–theory See **Formant**.

Substitution–theory How does a person speak if the larynx has had to be excised because the folds have become cancerous? The usual method is to swallow air, and phonate on the burp that follows; but medical scientists have put forward explanations citing more than one possible oscillator as a substitute for the vocal folds. Because more than one was cited, some have said 'A plague on all your houses'; but (patients' residual organs not being identical) there could indeed be more than one possible oscillator left.

Transients, Initial and Terminal See **Envelope**.

Timbre The characteristic sound–quality composed of a fundamental with or without over-tones. See **Formant**.

Tone Not merely sound, but *quality* of sound. See **Sonority**.

Total sound–energy Unless a sound is pure tone (in which case it has no more than the fundamental frequency, and sounds very dull), most of the energy of the sound–pressure will be used to make overtones audible. The total sound–energy comprises both the fundamental and the overtones. See **Formant**.

Transfer of energy The energy with which the vocal folds open and close comes partly from the pressure of breath, and partly from the tension by means of which they resist that pressure. Some of that energy is transferred to the sound–wave set up, but a portion will be lost in the form of a small quantity of heat generated by friction in the moving tissues.

Ventricle, Laryngeal On each side of the larynx, between the vestibular folds above, and the vocal folds below, is an expansible cavity called the *Ventricle of Morgagni* (after Giovanni Battista Morgagni, born 1682). The mucous glands lining it make it 'the oil–can of the larynx'; which is important, because the folds must be kept moist to do their work properly. When AH is sung, the ventricles virtually disappear, by being squashed flat. When EE, they partly open. When OO, they open fully, as though inflated; so that there is more to singing these primary vowels than most of us suppose.

Vestibular folds Within the larynx are two round–edged pink folds of mucous membrane which mirror the white vocal folds beneath them. The vestibular folds, adducted, present a flat surface to prevent air leaving the lungs; whereas the vocal folds, adducted, present a flat surface to prevent air *entering* the lungs. Their international name is *Plicae Ventriculares*.

Vibration–amplitude At maximum amplitude, molecules of air swing furthest from their normal position; at first, closer to each other (in compression), and, next, further apart than normal (in rarefaction). Even with the loudest sound down to the lowest G on the piano keyboard, they do not move further than a hundredth of a millimetre. See **Amplitude**.

Vocal folds Two sharp–edged white folds of mucous membrane in the larynx which mirror the pink vestibular folds above them. Adducted, they present a flat surface to prevent air entering the lungs; but air leaving the lungs can, and does, pass through them in puffs frequent enough to result in phonation when its pressure surpasses their adductive pressure. Their natural purpose seems to have been to prevent foreign matter entering the windpipe rather than to institute phonation. The folds thicken at their edges, and press firmly against each other, for the vowel AH. For EE, they hardly meet, and their edges are thin. For OO, they adopt an intermediate state in both respects.

Vocal tract The outward path of the sound–wave of voice from glottis to lips. If the path runs simply thus, with little wave–motion in the naso–pharynx, voice tends to be raucous and ill–controlled; but, if the oro– and naso–pharynx and cranial sinuses are part of the tract, voice can achieve its optimum tone with least effort. Several areas of the tract are relatively mobile, and the vocal folds, ventricle of Morgagni, vestibular folds, velum, tongue and lips can all change their conformation in ways which alter tone; and they do so during the onset of phonation before settling into a steady state.

Vocal vibration Vocal vibration is a complicated affair, because the organs within and immediately above the larynx begin by behaving in one way, and change that way in milliseconds in response to the energy which returns to them from the furthest limits of the vocal tract; and then, of course, what comes back to them changes in milliseconds in response to their changed behaviour; and so on.

Voce de finte A late term for **Head–voice**.

Voce de petto A late term for **Chest voice**.

Voce de testa A late term for **Head–voice**.

Voix de fausset Garcia's term for notes in the middle of the vocal range, whether sung in **Chest–** or **Head–voice**.

Voix de poitrine Garcia's term for **Chest voice**.

Voix de tête Garcia's term for the upper **Head–voice**.

Voix pleine Garcia's term for **Chest register**.

Vowel A recognizable tone of voice determined chiefly by the conformation of the vocal folds and the relative positions of the tongue and lips. The *point de départ* is the primary vowel AH, in which the tongue lies flat, and the lips are parted without smiling. The tongue progressively rises through the vowel–sequence *u* ('cup'), ER, *a* ('cap'), *e* ('peck'), AY, I, *i* ('pick'), EE. Returning to AH, and leaving the tongue flat, the lips progressively purse through the vowel–sequence *o* ('pot'), AW, OH, *oo* ('put'), OO. The italicized vowels here are said to be short vowels, and the capitals show long vowels. If the sequence is whispered from OO to AH and onwards, the vowel–formants will be clearly heard from lowest–pitched to highest.

Vox capitis De Moravia's term for the upper **Head–voice** used in its upper range.

Vox gutturis De Moravia's term for the upper or lower **Head–voice** used in its middle range.

Vox integra The earliest pre–Renaissance term for **Chest voice**.

Vox media Von Zabern's term for upper or lower **Head–voice** used in its middle range.

Vox plena Von Zabern's term for **Chest voice**.

Vox valida Von Zabern's term for **Chest voice**.

Vox subtiliata Von Zabern's term for upper or lower **Head–voice**, particularly in its upper range.

Wave (initial phase); Sound– The settling–down phase in the generation of sound. See **Envelope** and **Vocal vibration**.

Wave (middle phase); Sound– The steady state reached by a sound–wave in milliseconds after its onset. See **Envelope** and **Vocal vibration**.

Wave–form Different timbres have different wave–forms, as a glance at any illustrated physics textbook, such as Campbell & Greated's superb *The Musician's Guide to Acoustics* (J.M. Dent & Sons Ltd, 1988), or the classic book: James Jeans, *Science & Music* (Cambridge U.P., 1937), will show. The simplest wave–form is the sine–wave (see **Amplitude**); another simple form is the **Square wave**. Most sound–waves are more complex. See **Complex wave–form**.

Here endeth Dr. *Gyles* his firſt Service of 1.2.3.4.5.
& 6. Parts to the Organs.